Debord, Time and Spectacle

Historical Materialism Book Series

The Historical Materialism Book Series is a major publishing initiative of the radical left. The capitalist crisis of the twenty-first century has been met by a resurgence of interest in critical Marxist theory. At the same time, the publishing institutions committed to Marxism have contracted markedly since the high point of the 1970s. The Historical Materialism Book Series is dedicated to addressing this situation by making available important works of Marxist theory. The aim of the series is to publish important theoretical contributions as the basis for vigorous intellectual debate and exchange on the left.

The peer-reviewed series publishes original monographs, translated texts, and reprints of classics across the bounds of academic disciplinary agendas and across the divisions of the left. The series is particularly concerned to encourage the internationalization of Marxist debate and aims to translate significant studies from beyond the English-speaking world.

For a full list of titles in the Historical Materialism Book Series available in paperback from Haymarket Books, visit:
https://www.haymarketbooks.org/series_collections/1-historical-materialism

Debord, Time and Spectacle

Hegelian Marxism and Situationist Theory

Tom Bunyard

Haymarket Books
Chicago, IL

First published in 2017 by Brill Academic Publishers, The Netherlands
© 2017 Koninklijke Brill NV, Leiden, The Netherlands

Published in paperback in 2018 by
Haymarket Books
P.O. Box 180165
Chicago, IL 60618
773-583-7884
www.haymarketbooks.org

ISBN: 978-1-60846-079-3

Trade distribution:
In the US, Consortium Book Sales, www.cbsd.com
In Canada, Publishers Group Canada, www.pgcbooks.ca
In the UK, Turnaround Publisher Services, www.turnaround-uk.com
All other countries, Ingram Publisher Services International, ips_intlsales@ingramcontent.com

Cover design by Jamie Kerry and Ragina Johnson.

This book was published with the generous support of Lannan Foundation and the Wallace Action Fund.

Printed in the United States.

10 9 8 7 6 5 4 3 2 1

Library of Congress Cataloging-in-Publication data is available.

Contents

Acknowledgements   VII
List of Illustrations   X

Introduction: Radioactivity   1

PART 1
Subjectivity, Temporality and Spectacle

1   Interpreting the Theory of Spectacle   17

2   Five Aspects of Debord's Theoretical Work   39

PART 2
The New Beauty: 1951–62

3   'We are Artists Insofar as We are No Longer Artists'   81

4   The Everyday and the Absolute   108

5   'Avant-Gardes Have Only One Time'   141

PART 3
'Everything that had Formerly been Absolute Became Historical'

6   Debord and French Hegelianism   155

7   Subjects and Objects: Debord, Lukács and the Young Marx   191

8   Life and Non-Life   219

PART 4
In Pursuit of the Northwest Passage: 1963–73

9   Never Work!   241

10   'I am Nothing and I Should be Everything'   270

11   The 'Fetishism of Capital'   306

PART 5
The Integrated Spectacle: 1974–94

12   Moving with History's 'Bad Side'   333

13   Strategy and Tactics in the Integrated Spectacle   354

14   The Knight, Death and the Devil   390

     Bibliography   401
     Index   422

Acknowledgements

This book grew from PhD research that was conducted at Goldsmiths, University of London, under the supervision of John Hutnyk. I remain as grateful to John now as I was then. That thesis was completed in 2011, and I began trying to turn it into a book soon after that date. Doing so, however, took far longer than I first anticipated, and I must thank the editors of the Historical Materialism book series for the patience that they have shown towards this project. I am also grateful to all of the staff, students and friends at the various universities at which I worked whilst writing this book, but particular thanks are due to those at the University of Brighton, where I was eventually able to settle and concentrate on the book's completion. There are too many names involved here to mention them all, but I would like to thank Eugene Michail, Toby Lovat, Becca Searle and Zoe Sutherland in particular.

Some sections of this book draw upon and develop material that has been published elsewhere. The Introduction and some passages in Chapter 13 borrow from articles that appeared in 2014 ('Relevance in Obsolescence: Recuperation and Temporality in the Work of Guy Debord and the Situationist International', *Fungiculture*, 1) and 2011 ('Debord, Time and History', *Historical Materialism*, 20, no. 1: 3–36). Chapters 1 and 2 began life as a single article that was published in *Parrhesia* in 2014 ('"History is the Spectre Haunting Modern Society": Temporality and Praxis in Guy Debord's Hegelian Marxism', *Parrhesia*, 20: 62–86). In addition, a few of the comments made in Chapter 12 are informed by a text that I co-wrote with the Aufheben group in 2009 ('Capital and Spectacle', *Aufheben*, 19: 47–58). I am grateful to all who helped me with those earlier texts.

I would also like to thank all those who kindly read and commented on some of the draft versions of this book's chapters. Bob Brecher, Matt Charles, Andrew Chitty, Anthony Hayes, Phil Homburg, Giovanni Marmont, Meade McCloughan, Ben Noys, Chris O'Kane, Sean Sayers, Heath Schultz, and Alberto Toscano all offered very useful advice and commentary. Particular thanks are due to Alastair Hemmens and Gabriel Ferreira Zacarias for their comments on the book's opening chapters, and to Alastair for arranging a very useful work in progress session with Gabriel and myself.

I must also thank Laurence Le Bras at the Bibliothèque Nationale de France. Laurence was very helpful indeed when I visited the Debord archive in 2014, and she has helped me with a large number of enquiries since then. As discussed in this book's introduction, the archive contains a great deal of material, and it includes a vast collection of Debord's reading notes. I make a number of references to these notes in the book, and Laurence has helped me with the difficulties involved in referencing them. The notes typically take the form of small cards, onto which Debord copied sections of the texts that he was studying. These cards are often un-dated, and as Laurence is in the process of arranging a more precise classification of this archive's contents, their location within their respective folders and sub-folders is subject to change. I have, therefore, provided as much information as I can. Following Laurence's advice, I have omitted the numbers of the cards, listed the folders and sub-folders in which I found them, and added approximate dates (these dates were provided by Laurence; they are based on the publication dates of the books that we can suppose Debord was working on, and the type of cards that he was using). If anyone chooses to follow up my references, the most important information will be the names of the authors and books that Debord was studying, as these details will obviously not be subject to future archival re-organisation.

I have also had a great deal of help from John McHale, who has provided much assistance and input over the past few years. John's knowledge of Debord and the Situationists is truly formidable, and so too is his command of Debord's texts. I am very grateful indeed for all of the material that he has sent me, for his willingness to help with questions, and for checking and correcting some of my more awkward translations.

This brings me to the following point. Some of the English translations of Debord and the Situationists' texts that I have used in this book have been altered slightly. My aim in doing so has certainly not been to make existing translations any more elegant or correct – if anything, I may have made them more unwieldy – but rather to bring key words or phrases a little closer to their French originals. When making such alterations I have always taken my bearings from existing English translations. For example, when quoting from Debord's *The Society of the Spectacle*, I have consulted the Knabb and Perlman translations of that book, as well as Nicholson-Smith's. (All of my page references to *The Society of the Spectacle* have been taken from the Nicholson-Smith version. This is largely for sentimental reasons: I can still remember buying a copy of that text in Brighton, towards the end of the 1990s, and I can also recall being almost completely baffled by its contents when I tried to read it on the beach). When using material from *Internationale situationniste*, I have referred to Ken Knabb's translations, and to those available online. Likewise, when quoting from Debord's correspondence, I have often consulted the selection of letters that Bill Brown has translated at his Not Bored! website. Needless to say, this means that any translation errors are entirely my own fault.

On a more personal level, I would like to thank M. Beatrice Fazi for her support and encouragement throughout the many years that I have been working on this book. I would also like to thank my parents and grandparents, whose help and support made this entire project possible.

List of Illustrations

All of the images used in this book have been drawn from Wikimedia Commons and are in the public domain. The attribution details follow below.

Title Page to Part One

Albrecht Durer, *Knight Death and the Devil*, 1513
Albrecht Dürer [Public domain], via Wikimedia Commons
https://commons.wikimedia.org/wiki/File:Albrecht_Dürer_-_Knight,_Death_and_the_Devil.jpg

Title Page to Part Two

Claude Lorrain, *Port Scene with Villa Medici*, 1637
Claude Lorrain [Public domain], via Wikimedia Commons
https://commons.wikimedia.org/wiki/File:Claude_Lorrain_-_Port_Scene_with_the_Villa_Medici_-_WGA04978.jpg

Claude Lorrain, *Ulysses Returns Chryseis to her Father*, circa 1644
Claude Lorrain [Public domain], via Wikimedia Commons
https://commons.wikimedia.org/wiki/File:Claude_Lorrain_-_Ulysses_Returns_Chryseis_to_her_Father_-_WGA04992.jpg

Title Page to Part Three

Hans Holbein the Younger, *The Abbot*, from 'The Dance of Death', 1523–5
By Hans Holbein [Public domain], via Wikimedia Commons; Typ 515.38.456a, Houghton Library, Harvard University
https://commons.wikimedia.org/wiki/File:Houghton_Typ_515.38.456a_-_Totentanz,_14.jpg

LIST OF ILLUSTRATIONS XI

Title Page to Part Four

The 'Erebus' and 'Terror' in the Arctic Regions, from Henry Davenport Northrop's *Makers of the World's History and their Grand Achievements*, 1903
By Internet Archive Book Images [No restrictions], via Wikimedia Commons
https://commons.wikimedia.org/wiki/File:Makers_of_the_world%27s_history_and_their_grand_achievements_(1903)_(14595998708).jpg

Title Page to Part Five

Pieter Bruegel the Elder, *The Tower of Babel*, 1563
Pieter Brueghel the Elder [Public domain], via Wikimedia Commons
https://commons.wikimedia.org/wiki/File:Brueghel-tower-of-babel.jpg

INTRODUCTION

Radioactivity

'Eminently Noxious'

In 1979, and thus several years after the Situationist International's (SI) dissolution in 1972, Guy Debord remarked in a letter to a correspondent that 'the SI is like radioactivity: it's scarcely ever mentioned yet traces of it can be found almost everywhere, and it lasts a long time'.[1] Today, one could reply that the group and its practices are now spoken of a great deal, and perhaps to the detriment of their corruptive aspirations. The SI's anti-art stance has been canonised into the pantheon of art history, the group's techniques of 'psychogeography'[2] and *détournement*[3] have become established cultural tropes, and Situationist material is now a staple of both the bookshop and the lecture-hall. This contemporary endorsement does, however, stand in marked contrast to the reception that first greeted Debord and the SI's work. For example, in 1966, Strasbourg University found itself at the centre of a national scandal, as the entirety of its Student Union's funds had been used to print 10,000 copies of the Situationist tract 'On the Poverty of Student Life'. The text denounced the university as an institution, railed against the quiescence of students and their faux radicalism, and called for the total, revolutionary transformation of society as a whole. Its virulence led the judge presiding over the Union's subsequent closure to direct the following, memorably damning remarks at the students who had organised its publication:

---

1 Debord 2006a, pp. 45–6.
2 Psychogeography is a concept that originates from Debord's early, pre-SI years in the Parisian avant-garde. It was retained and employed by the SI, and it was succinctly defined in the very first issue of *Internationale Situationniste* as: 'The study of the specific effects of the geographical environment (whether consciously organized or not) on the emotions and behaviour of individuals' (SI 2006, p. 52; 1997, p. 13). For useful overviews of issues pertaining to these themes, see Sadler 1999 and Coverley 2007.
3 In brief, *détournement* was a technique employed by the SI through which they would subvert existing cultural forms into new, politically oppositional configurations. See McDonough 2007 for a discussion that places the SI's use of *détournement* within a broader historical and cultural context.

... these five students, scarcely more than adolescents, lacking all experience of real life, their minds confused by ill-digested philosophical, social, political and economic theories, and perplexed by the drab monotony of their everyday life, make the empty, arrogant, and pathetic claim to pass definitive judgements, sinking to outright abuse, on their fellow-students, their teachers, God, religion, the clergy, the governments and political systems of the whole world. Rejecting all morality and restraint, these cynics do not hesitate to commend theft, the destruction of scholarship, the abolition of work, total subversion, and a world-wide proletarian revolution with 'unlicensed pleasure' as its only goal. In view of their basically anarchist character, these theories and propaganda are eminently noxious. Their wide diffusion in both student circles and among the general public, by the local, national and foreign press, is a threat to the morality, the studies, the reputation and thus the very future of the students of the University of Strasbourg.[4]

Rather different judgements seem to be passed upon this material today. Not only have Debord and the SI been firmly embraced by the academia that they once denounced: in addition, the French Ministry for Foreign Affairs has actively supported the dissemination of Situationist texts as a means of promoting French culture overseas,[5] and in 2009, the French State bought an archive of Debord's work for the nation. This acquisition, which was conducted in order to prevent its sale to Yale University, resulted in the archive's installation in the Bibliothèque nationale de France (BnF). To predictable consternation,[6] this required the President of the Bibliothèque to dub Debord's work a 'national treasure', and it prompted Nicolas Sarkozy's minister of culture to describe Debord as a 'great French intellectual'.[7] What was once a 'threat' had thus become a 'treasure'.

This transition might lead one to ask whether any 'radioactive' or 'noxious' elements still remain within this material. Such a question bears direct relation to the familiar problematic of 'recuperation': a term that the SI used to denote the neutralisation of radical material through its incorporation into the culture

---

4   Quoted in Dark Star 2001, p. 9.
5   The English translation of *The Real Split in the International* published in 2003 was supported by the French Ministry for Foreign Affairs and the Institut Français du Royaume-Uni (SI 2003, p. v).
6   See, for example, Roussel 2009, Rérolle 2013 or Zagdanski 2013; see Antonucci 2012 for an alternative perspective.
7   Gallix 2009.

that it once challenged. Unsurprisingly, those who would defend the group's political and theoretical legacy have often made reference to the concept of recuperation; after all, one can now buy 'Situationist' t-shirts and mobile phone applications, and references to Debord and the SI pepper the contemporary discourses of art, popular culture and the press. Yet however apposite it may be, recuperation is also a potentially problematic concept. Stressing the contrast between the original, radical purity of Situationist material and its contemporary appropriations can foster a degree of protective reverence that jars with the SI's rejection of their own revolutionary fetishisation ('mythological recognition' on the part of their 'feeble admirers' was typically denounced by the SI in the harshest of terms).[8] There is, however, a further dimension of the concept of recuperation that seems pertinent here: one that can help to explain the important connections that should be drawn between Debord and the SI's dismissal of such reverence on the one hand, and their notions of 'spectacle' and 'spectatorship' on the other. This, however, requires a few initial, explanatory remarks.

Time and Spectacle

According to the interpretation that will be advanced within this book, Debord's concept of spectacle cannot be fully understood if it is treated independently from his views on time and history. To put this very briefly, as a more detailed account will be provided later: time, for Debord, exists independently of humanity; history, however is specific to human beings, as it corresponds to humanity's existence in time, and to its awareness of that existence.[9] For

---

8 Debord 2003a, p. 281. See SI 2003 for extended comments on the spectacular nature of the 'pro-Situ' phenomenon.

9 See, in particular, thesis #125 of *The Society of the Spectacle*. Debord writes there, by way of a *détournement* of the young Marx (Marx 1975, p. 208), that 'History has always existed, but not always in a historical form'. This rather cryptic remark is used in that thesis to indicate that 'natural history', which comprises non-human and pre-human events, only comes into existence with the advent of human consciousness: not because such events did not exist prior to human thought, but simply because without such thought, there can be no history. History is a human awareness of time, and of the events that occur within it. Thus, 'the unconscious movement of time', which forms a blind, unthinking part of the 'unfolding of the universe', undergoes a 'humanisation' when it is grasped by 'the only agency capable of capturing this historical whole', i.e. by human consciousness. Thus, time exists prior to human beings; history corresponds to humanity's awareness of its own existence within a temporal universe (Debord 1995, p. 92, translation altered; 2006b, p. 820).

Debord, human beings are capable of shaping and determining their own lives and circumstances. Consequently, history, in his view, is something that can be *made*: we can consciously shape our own existence in time. History, therefore, is not just a retrospective catalogue of events for Debord, and nor is it just the discipline of studying such events. Instead, it is a process through which human agents shape themselves and their world, and through which they come to know themselves through such activity. In this regard, Debord's most famous work – 1967's *The Society of the Spectacle* – is best understood as a book about history. Or, to put that more precisely: it is a book that describes a society that has become detached from its capacity to consciously shape and determine its own future.

Debord's basic claim in *The Society of the Spectacle* is that modern society has become characterised by a passive, contemplative attitude towards the conduct and results of its own activity. This is because activity within this society is conducted in tacit accordance with the requirements of an effectively autonomous economy. However distinct and opposed they may seem, practically all areas of life, and all social and political institutions, now operate as elements of a single biopolitical order, which serves, in Debord's view, to regulate and manage lived activity in a manner that allows the capitalist economy to continue operating. In his theoretical work, Debord describes this as a condition in which human subjects have become dominated by their own creations: they live within a social order that they have created, but which ultimately rules them. Society has thus become characterised by a state of separation from its own history. Life has become alienated from those who live it, and historical time now unfolds as an object of detached contemplation. Consequently, for Debord, we have become 'spectators' of our own lives: mere observers of a historical existence that we could, potentially, consciously shape and direct. Or, as he put it in 1961:

> History (the transformation of reality) cannot presently be used in everyday life because the people who live that everyday life are the product of a history over which they have no control. It is of course they themselves who make this history, but they do not make it freely or consciously.[10]

This condition of separation is conceived in terms of the subordination of human agents to their own powers and capacities, which have become alienated and localised within the various institutions and formations that compose

---

10   SI 2006, p. 93; 1997, p. 32.

the governing social order of spectacular society.[11] Because these are the very same powers that alienated individuals might use to shape their own lives, the task of the modern revolution, for Debord, was to reclaim and employ them: to take charge not just of the means of production, as in classical Marxism, but of the means of collectively producing and directing life as a whole. Such a revolution could not be content with a more equitable rearrangement of the existing social system. Instead, the Situationists' unabashedly utopian goal was to infuse lived experience with the passion, creativity and imagination that had previously only been articulated within the cultural realms of art and poetry. For the Situationists, whose political goals had developed from their early concerns with avant-garde art, the modern revolution would afford a ludic, creative relation to lived time: art would cease to function as a means of representing and commenting upon life, and would instead become one with life itself. This would be achieved through using society's previously alienated technological and creative powers to consciously create the 'situations' that compose lived time. Within modern society, they claimed, all such situations are dull, rationalised components of the spectacular social order; the all-encompassing revolution that the SI envisaged would, however, afford a social existence within which these moments of experience would take on more festive qualities. This would result, according to Debord, in a 'new historical life', wherein those currently '*estranged from history*' would be able to directly '*live* the historical time' that their own social activity creates:[12] to thus shape their own collective experience, and to thereby make their own history.

The emphasis that has been placed here on the importance of time and history within Debord and the SI's work may sound a little strange to those who have been introduced to their ideas by Anglophone academia. Within the latter context, the SI is often treated as a group of artists,[13] and Debord is frequently discussed as if he were a media theorist. Yet whilst the SI certainly emerged from the milieu of avant-garde art and culture in the 1950s, they went on to reject their status as an art movement in the strongest terms ('there is

---

11   Vaneigem expresses this theme particularly clearly in his *The Revolution of Everyday Life*, where he complains of 'hypostatised, gnarled forms: Power, God, the Pope, the Fuhrer, Other People. The fact remains that every time we refer to Society, God, or all-powerful Justice, we are referring – albeit feebly and indirectly – to our own power' (Vaneigem 2003, p. 219).

12   Debord 1995, p. 106; 2006b, p. 829.

13   For an important critique of this tendency, see T.J. Clark and Donald Nicholson-Smith's polemical essay 'Why Art Can't Kill the Situationist International' (Clark and Nicholson-Smith 2004).

no such thing as *Situationism*', they stressed, 'or a Situationist work of art');[14] and whilst Debord's spectacle does indeed pertain to the adverts, images and entertainment to which it is commonly reduced, his theoretical work has a far broader and more ambitious scope than those reductively media-centric readings would allow. Such readings are, in fact, directly undermined by statements made within the very first chapter of *The Society of the Spectacle*, where we are explicitly told that the 'mass media' is only the spectacle's 'most stultifyingly superficial manifestation'.[15] The typical reduction of Debord's thought to a diatribe about modern society's visual culture is thus quite wrong. Greater purchase on his ideas can be gained if we focus instead on the manner in which he describes the spectacle as a 'paralysed history': as an 'abandonment of any history founded in historical time', and as '*a false consciousness of time*'.[16] Rather than presenting a simple complaint as to the functional importance of the media and mass entertainment within modern capitalism, Debord's theory describes a society that has become separated from its own historical agency.

Debord's concept of spectacle is also often reductively identified with modern capitalism. This is hardly surprising, given that he clearly presents the society of the spectacle as a moment in the development of capitalist society. However, and as we will see later, Debord also indicates that the dynamic of separation described above is much older than modern capitalism. Society's complete colonisation by capital and the commodity had simply generalised that dynamic, bringing it to an extreme, and thereby rendering it the defining feature of the age. Therefore, the problematic of spectacle (the alienation of collective power and agency) can be distinguished, to some degree, from modern capitalism's complete *actualisation* of that problematic, and can also be ascribed to other forms of separated power. Hence Debord and the SI's attribution of the term 'spectacular' to religion, dogma, political leadership, etc.; hence also Debord's indications that 'all separate power has been spectacular',[17] and that 'at the root of the spectacle lies the oldest of all social specialisations, the specialisation of power'.[18] What is at stake here, therefore, is not just a rejection of capitalism and commodification *per se*, but rather a much broader concern with the alienation of historical agency. In Debord's view, such alienation could not be fully superseded, within the modern period, through the destruction of

---

14   SI 2006, p. 115, translation altered; 1997, pp. 266–7, italics in the original.
15   Debord 1995, p. 19; 2006b, p. 772.
16   Debord 1995, p. 114; 2006b, p. 834.
17   Debord 1995, p. 20; 2006b, p. 772.
18   Debord 1995, p. 18, translation altered; 2006b, p. 771.

capitalism alone, but only through the abolition of *all* forms of hierarchy, separation and representative leadership.

Contentions such as these can help to explain the Situationists' concerns that the SI itself might become a spectacular figurehead (hence their rejection of, and contempt for, their own 'pro-Situ' admirers). They can also help us to address their attendant pursuit of non-hierarchical forms of political organisation (one cannot 'combat alienation', they claimed, 'by means of alienated forms of struggle').[19] Furthermore – and to return now to the points with which we began – they also serve to cast the notion of recuperation in a slightly different light.

This is because the issues described above lend themselves to a profound concern with the separation of theory from practice. Given that the ultimate aim of revolution was a condition of self-determinate engagement with lived time – and given also that spectacle was ultimately identified with the deprivation of such a temporality – bodies of putatively radical theory that stood removed from concrete praxis were themselves considered to be instances of spectacle. This is because such theories could only function as *representations* of the praxis that they purported to facilitate; as constructs that might appear to articulate and express radical agency, but which in fact serve to arrest it, by virtue of their separation from that agency's actualisation. This is why Debord warned, in typically prescient fashion, that if his 'critical concept of spectacle' were to be removed from the 'practical movement of negation within society', then it too would become 'just another empty formula of sociologico-political rhetoric', serving only to 'buttress the spectacular system itself'.[20] Perhaps needless to say, this bears obvious relation to the SI's transition from a 'threat' to a 'national treasure'. It also implies the following points.

If recuperation means a collapse into spectacle – and if spectacle essentially means a state of separation from praxis – then recuperation occurs whenever radical potential is diverted away from its actualisation, due to its having been identified with a static construct that serves to merely transfix such potential agency. This certainly pertains to the piles of Situationist t-shirts, academic conferences and books that have accrued around Debord and the SI's work, and indeed to its contemporary cultural endorsement. Yet more importantly, it also relates to any perspective that would view this material as being possessed of some kind of timeless truth. For Debord, radical theory should be akin to *strategic* theory, insofar as both are required to intervene within chan-

---

19   Debord 1995, p. 89; 2006b, p. 819.
20   Debord 1995, p. 143; 2006b, p. 852.

ging contexts. If it is not superseded once the moment in which it sought to intervene has passed, but instead remains in place – perhaps due to its prominence and celebrity – then theory becomes dogma, and praxis gives way to spectacle. Hence the following lines, taken from Debord's 1978 film, *In Girum Imus Nocte et Consumimur Igni*:

> Theories are only made to die in the war of time. Like units of varying strength, they must be sent into battle at the right moment; and whatever their merits or insufficiencies, they can only be used if they are on hand when they are needed. But they have to be replaced because they are constantly being rendered obsolete – by their decisive victories even more than by their partial defeats.[21]

Theories are thus attempts to clarify a given moment. Their task is to afford an understanding of a political and economic landscape, to provide insight into the forces ranged upon it, and to thereby further the work of those that would hasten its passage into the past. Clearly, any such theory can only be properly valid within the context that it seeks to articulate, and cannot be arbitrarily imposed upon other contexts. Therefore, just as no general would use the same plans in each and every engagement, so too would it seem problematic, if one treats this material on its own terms, to transpose Debord and the SI's fifty-year old analyses onto our own present circumstances.

Consequently, rather than contending, with some enthusiastic commentators, that 'never before' has Debord's theoretical work 'seemed quite as relevant as it does now',[22] a sympathetic reading of this material might instead focus on the sense in which it explicitly invited its own supersession. If one did indeed set out to identify the more critical and antagonistic dimensions of this material, and to thus ascertain whether any 'noxious' and 'radioactive' elements still remain within it, then there would seem to be some virtue in attempting to address the notions of time, history and praxis that support it. This is because they drive this body of work's impetus towards opposition and intervention, and indeed towards the generation of new, more contemporary theoretical positions.

This book is intended to serve as a contribution towards the study of those foundational conceptions of temporality and praxis. It will try to draw out the conceptual mechanics and philosophical framework that support Debord's

---

21 Debord 2003b, pp. 150–1, translation altered; 2006b, p. 1354.
22 Self 2013.

work, and which motivate its demands for intervention within the 'war of time'. To that end, it will pursue the following goals.

Temporality, Hegelian Marxism, and a Philosophy of Praxis

Firstly, and primarily, this focus on time, history and spectacle will be used as a means towards developing a holistic reading of Debord's oeuvre. The contention that motivates this goal is that temporality is absolutely crucial to Debord's thought, and that many of the more seemingly disparate aspects of his work can be illuminated by attending to their shared bases in this concern. Doing so can also serve to highlight elements thereof that tend to be overlooked. As we will try to show, such an approach can provide a means of addressing the aesthetic, strategic, ethical, ontological and epistemological dimensions of his work, which exist alongside and inform its more obvious and celebrated components. Of course, it would be a mistake to develop a philosophical system from the work of a writer who rejected all such systems,[23] but treating Debord's work in this manner can nonetheless reveal it to be a far more substantial, considered and coherent body of thought than might otherwise be supposed.

Addressing Debord's work in this manner involves reconstructing, and thereby evaluating, his Hegelian Marxism. This is an aspect of his work which is also often referred to within the extant literature, but which has seldom been addressed in great detail.[24] That neglect is a serious problem: for as Debord put it in a letter to a correspondent, 'one cannot fully comprehend [*The Society of the Spectacle*] without Marx, and especially Hegel'.[25] In accordance with that statement, this book will attempt to read Debord's work through these key influences.

---

23 Debord qualifies this point in a letter of 1969, where he states that after Feuerbach and Marx, and thus after the critique of Hegel, it would be a mistake to 'build new philosophical systems' (Debord 2004a, p. 95). This point will be developed in Chapters 1 and 2, and again in Chapter 10, where we will look at this issue in connection to Debord's antipathy towards dogma and economic determinism. In brief, Debord's view would seem to be that self-legitimating conceptual systems must stand at one remove from a direct engagement in the uncertainties and contingencies of lived historical time.

24 This point will be developed in Chapter 1, but it should be pointed out here that Anselm Jappe's *Guy Debord* (Jappe 1999) remains the best available work on this topic.

25 Debord 2004a, p. 454.

If one does indeed read Debord's work in this manner, it soon becomes apparent that his theoretical writings imply a particular approach to Hegelian thought. To put it rather glibly: reading Debord through Hegel and Marx also affords a means of reconstructing Debord's Marxian reading of Hegel. As this book will attempt to demonstrate, that reading of Hegel is fundamental to the interpretation of spectacle outlined earlier. Inevitably, our attempts to reconstruct Debord's approach to Hegel will need to be somewhat speculative, because his extant statements on the topic can only take us so far. We will need, therefore, to build upon those statements by reading them in the light of the philosophical and theoretical material that Debord drew upon when developing his ideas. There will, in consequence, be a large intellectual-historical component to this book's discussions. Yet whilst such an approach may seem somewhat scholastic, it should also afford something new: for if one addresses Debord's concerns with time and history in this manner, it becomes evident that his work implies a philosophy of history that effectively equates to a philosophy of *praxis*.

This can be illustrated with an anecdote. Giorgio Agamben, who had the rare honour of being one of the few modern intellectuals whom Debord did not despise, recalls in an essay that he once told Debord that he considered him to be a philosopher. Debord responded by saying 'I'm not a philosopher, I'm a strategist.'[26] Agamben does not make this point, but Debord's response to that question was no doubt due to his view that strategy is the form taken by philosophy when it becomes actualised, following Marx's critique of Hegel, in historical praxis. To put it very crudely and reductively: Hegel, in Debord's view, had developed a mode of thought capable of thinking change, conflict and historical movement, but bound it within the confines of a philosophical system that purported to herald history's closure. The young Marx rectified that error with his call for philosophy's realisation in praxis: dialectical thought would thereby cease to be a means of contemplating a purportedly finished world, and would instead serve as a means of consciously conducting the world's transformation. Debord was a 'strategist', therefore, because his interpretation of Hegelian Marxism rendered the conduct of dialectical thought very much akin to that of strategic thought. Once actualised in praxis, dialectics would become a means of thinking and conducting change, process and conflict within lived time. Hence the references to 'dialectical, strategic thought'[27] that can be found in Debord's correspondence, and indeed hence also his contention, made in the

---

26 Agamben 2004b, p. 313.
27 Debord 2008, p. 78.

personal notes that are now stored in the BnF's archive, that 'to think dialectically and to think strategically' is 'the same thing'.[28] Through looking at Debord's debts to Hegel and Marx, and by doing so with reference to his key concerns with time and history, we can try to reconstruct the ideas that inform these views. Doing so also affords the possibility that these ideas might be drawn from Debord's work and thereby developed and considered in their own right.

Having stated these aims, we should now indicate the way in which they will be pursued.

Archaeology

The difficulty faced by a study of Debord's Hegelian Marxism is that he leaves us with very few explicit statements regarding its details. Nowhere in his public writings does Debord clearly set this out *in toto*: not even in the notes that he wrote on the hundreds of reading cards that are now stored in the Bibliothèque Nationale's archive. Nonetheless, and as was indicated earlier, the conceptual framework that supports his claims can be inferred and reconstructed from textual evidence, and through reading that evidence in relation to the material that informed it. This is rendered somewhat easier by the fact that Debord provides us with important clues. He frequently employed *détourné* passages and phrases from other writers in his texts and used numerous quotations. These references are almost always unattributed, but they can be traced, identified, and used as means of piecing together his ideas.

A necessary corollary of this approach is that Debord and the SI's work cannot be treated as a known, familiar corpus that can be placed alongside more recent and popular bodies of ideas, and then measured according to their criteria. Instead, this book will try to treat this material on its own terms. This requires placing Debord and the SI in relation to a rather different set of writers than those implied by more art-historical approaches to the Situationist International, and indeed by those that would cast Debord's account of spectacle as a work of media theory. Whilst the latter interpretations might invite appeal to figures such as McLuhan ('the most convinced imbecile of the century',[29] according to Debord), Barthes (a writer who had 'nothing to say')[30] or Baudril-

---

28   Bibliothèque nationale, NAF28603, Notes de lecture; Stratégie, histoire militaire, Box 2; dossier 5; 'strat'; January 1977. NB see the comments made in this book's acknowledgements regarding references to Debord's reading notes.
29   Debord 1998, p. 33; 2006b, p. 1612.
30   Debord 2006a, p. 406.

lard (an 'idiot',[31] a 'media clown',[32] and an example of the intellectual 'lice' that cling to the media in the hope of 'drawing a reflection from it'),[33] we will instead read Debord's oeuvre through its debts to writers such as Hegel, Marx, Korsch, Lefebvre and Lukács, and through the work of Young Hegelian writers such as Cieszkowski, Feuerbach and Stirner. His reading of Hegel will be reconstructed through reference to the French Hegel interpreters whose books Debord owned and studied (chiefly, Jean Hyppolite and Kostas Papaïoannou). Likewise, when we come to address the aesthetic dimensions of his views on time, we'll do so by making reference to Debord's favoured poets and writers, such as Khayyám, Li Po and Manrique. Similarly, his interests in strategy will be considered by pursuing his references to Castiglione, Clausewitz, Gracián, Machiavelli and Sun Tzu. We will also need to address Debord's debts to the ambience and legacy of Sartrean existentialism. This may seem questionable, particularly if one notes Debord and the SI's formidable hostility towards Sartre (a 'buffoon';[34] a 'nullity';[35] one of the 'celebrities of unintelligence';[36] a consumer and purveyor of 'Stalinist illusions';[37] less of a leftist than Khrushchev;[38] one of the 'worst enemies of all revolutionary research',[39] etc.). A theory of situations, self-constitutive action and temporal becoming that emerged in 1950s France cannot, however, be fully understood in abstract isolation from Sartre's philosophy.

The approach taken to Debord's work will therefore be archaeological in a sense (albeit not in that of Foucault, who was considered a 'dupe', and one of the 'great men of recuperation').[40] This is because by addressing it in this manner, we will try to unearth some of its primary components, and attempt their assembly. This should afford a model of some of the key ideas that underlie and inform Debord's work. As admitted above, this model will be necessarily speculative; yet provided we keep as close as possible to the letter of his texts, we can hope to arrive at a position that Debord would have been able to recognise as being at least similar to his own.

---

31 Debord 2008, p. 265.
32 Debord directed this remark at both Baudrillard and Lyotard, describing them as a pair of 'media *clowns*' (Debord 2008, p. 248, emphasis and English in the original).
33 Debord 2006a, p. 445, emphasis in the original.
34 Debord 2010, p. 128.
35 SI 2006, p. 235; 1997, p. 488.
36 SI 2006, p. 413; 1966.
37 SI 2006, p. 289; 1997, p. 572.
38 Debord 2003a, p. 105.
39 Debord 2001a, p. 21.
40 Debord 2005, p. 339.

One further caveat: although this book will draw as widely as possible on Debord's books, films, letters and notes, its focus on the existential dimensions of his Hegelian Marxism obliges a prioritisation of theoretical texts such as *The Society of the Spectacle*. Strategy and aesthetics will be discussed throughout, reference will be made to his later work's departure from his earlier positions, and an entire section of the book will be devoted to his use of Marx's mature critique of political economy. All such issues will, however, be addressed by way of a primary focus on the conceptions of temporality, subjectivity and praxis that follow from his proximity to Hegelian philosophy, Young Hegelianism, and the young Marx.

The reading of Debord's work that this affords will be presented by way of the following structure.

The Structure of the Book

This book is composed of five parts. All are arranged thematically, and three are arranged chronologically. Part One introduces and discusses the primary aspects of Debord's mature theoretical work, and sets out the themes and general arguments that will be developed in the chapters that follow. Part Two then considers the SI's art-world beginnings, concentrating on the texts and films that were produced between 1951 and 1962: the period within which Debord began to fully articulate his concept of spectacle, and within which the latter came to the fore as a means of unifying and focussing the SI's various concerns. This period begins with Debord's first contact with the Parisian avant-garde, encompasses the formation of the SI in 1957, and ends with the expulsion, in 1962, of the SI's more art-oriented German and Scandinavian contingents: a turning point that was later described by Debord as the moment from which the SI set out to 'realise philosophy'.[41] Part Three then returns to the aspects of Debord's Hegelian Marxism that were set out in Part One. Its location in the book's overall structure reflects Debord's increasing turn towards a Hegelian Marx in the late 1950s and early 1960s. Its content lays a basis for the arguments that follow in Parts Four and Five, which are concerned, in differing ways, with Debord's mature account of spectacle.

Part Four covers the period between 1963 and 1973: a period that follows the expulsion of the artists in 1962, and which encompasses the events of May 1968, the publication of *The Society of the Spectacle* in 1967, 1973's cinematic version

---

41   SI 1997, p. 703.

of that text, and the dissolution of the SI in 1972. This part of the book discusses Debord's claims in critical relation to the Marxism of the classical workers' movement, and in connection to certain contemporary readings of Marx's theory of value. Part Five then covers the period that runs from 1974 through to Debord's death in 1994, paying particular attention to 1988's *Comments on the Society of the Spectacle*. It returns to the aesthetic issues introduced in Part Two, but focuses chiefly on Debord's interest in strategy, and on the latter's connection to the analysis of modern society that he presented in the *Comments*.

Cumulatively, the various sections of the book will attempt to present two connected arguments. The first is that Debord's Hegelian Marxism involves something very much akin to a Marxian 'inversion' of the Hegelian Absolute. Debord's comments on Hegel and on Hegelian thought seem to demonstrate an interpretation of Hegel's philosophy in which the latter is cast as having afforded a flawed, contextually limited, and all-too philosophical insight into the real nature of historical praxis. This set of claims will be introduced in Chapter 2, and its implications will be pursued throughout the chapters that follow. Secondly, whilst this book will not be as critical of Debord's thought as it perhaps could be, it will, nonetheless, draw attention to some of the limitations of his engagement with capitalist social relations. This critique will be developed at length in Part Four, and it will be used to add additional impetus to the following contention.

Debord and the SI's work may have become a 'treasure' rather than a 'threat'. In addition, and as will be argued later, their account of capitalist society may involve problems. This may well be true; but as we have already indicated, their work was only intended to function as one single, contextual intervention in the 'war of time'. The Hegelian Marxian conception of praxis that informs that notion of a temporal 'war' may thus deserve more attention than it has received, because it implies the generation of new instances of thought and action. If this material does indeed possess a 'radioactive' half-life, then perhaps these ideas about time and history are one of the places in which its traces might be found.

PART 1
Subjectivity, Temporality and Spectacle

Albrecht Durer, The Knight, Death, and the Devil, *1513*

'O gentlemen, the time of life is short! ... An if we live, we live to tread on kings'
— SHAKESPEARE, *Henry IV*, Part 1 (also used as the epigraph to Chapter 5 of *The Society of the Spectacle*, 'Time and History')

CHAPTER 1

Interpreting the Theory of Spectacle

'Stultifyingly Superficial'

Before we begin to address the details of Debord and the SI's claims, it may be useful to look at some of the difficulties and trends that have characterised their reception. Perhaps the best place to start in that regard is by noting that the predominantly visual terminology employed in Debord's theory of spectacle has often been treated in a literal sense. For instance, according to one symptomatic example of such commentary, Debord's notion of 'spectacle' refers to 'the system of the mass media', to 'the social force of television', and to 'the form taken by the gaze within a consumer-capitalist society'.[1] Such interpretations, however, afford only a very partial understanding of Debord's ideas.

A reading of spectacle in which the latter is conflated with the mass media is, in fact, explicitly contradicted by Debord's own remarks. As was noted earlier, the very first chapter of *The Society of the Spectacle* states that 'The spectacle cannot be understood either as a deliberate distortion of the visual world or as a product of the technology of the mass dissemination of images'.[2] A few pages further on, he states that the 'mass media' is only the spectacle's 'most stultifyingly superficial manifestation'.[3] Nonetheless, literally visual and media-centric interpretations of Debord's theory remain far from uncommon. An emphasis on the visual and on the media can even be found within readings that acknowledge the Marxian elements of Debord's theory. Seen in these terms, the spectacle becomes a unifying ideology, maintained via media forms;[4] a literally visual reformulation of Lukács's account of contemplative detachment;[5] or simply the fads, fashions, communication and entertainment that articulate contemporary desire and opinion.[6]

All of these readings are certainly partly correct: Debord does indeed address phenomena such as this. 'News or propaganda, advertising or the actual con-

---

1 Frow 1997, p. 5.
2 Debord 1995, pp. 12–13; 2006b, p. 767.
3 Debord 1995, p. 19; 2006b, p. 772.
4 Hussey 2002, p. 217.
5 Beller 2006, p. 241.
6 Dauvé 1996, pp. 24–5.

sumption of entertainment' are described in *The Society of the Spectacle* as 'particular forms'[7] of spectacle, and the very fact that such phenomena constitute the spectacle's most 'superficial' appearances necessarily implies their connection to something deeper and more important. But what, then, is that deeper problematic?

At root, Debord's notion of spectacle denotes a condition of fetishistic separation wherein human subjects become detached from their own individual and collective powers: a condition wherein these powers become alienated and localised within seemingly independent bodies that dominate the activity of those upon whose continued compliance they ultimately depend. Perhaps the easiest initial illustration of this idea can be found in Feuerbach's critique of religion. In religion, according to Feuerbach, a community of believers worship their own collective desires, powers and capacities, which they mistakenly project onto the clouds of an imaginary heaven. Debord's ideas are very similar. Spectacular society was described as a 'material reconstruction of the religious illusion'; a social condition in which the 'cloud enshrouded entities' in which religious worshippers once 'located their own powers' have been 'brought down to earth'.[8] Debord is thus also greatly indebted to Marx's account of capitalist society, for as Marx puts it in *Capital*, 'Just as man is governed, in religion, by the products of his own brain, so, in capitalist production, is he governed by the products of his own hand.'[9] Modern society, for Debord, had become entirely characterised by such a condition of subservience. The life of society as a whole, in his view, had come to be regulated and shaped by the results of society's own alienated activity.

In keeping with the Hegelian and Marxian ideas that inform his work, Debord theorised this state of affairs in terms of a subject-object relation. The core problematic of spectacle pertains to the separation of subject and object. It corresponds to instances wherein human subjects find themselves faced with objective forms that they have themselves created, into which they have alienated their own attributes and capacities, and which, despite being expressions of their own selves, appear to be quite independent and separate from them. Such subjects thus become comparatively passive, dominated by objects that have become animated by the social powers that have been transposed onto them, and they thereby become contemplative observers of their own alienated agency. By extension, the supersession of spectacle entails a condition

---

7 Debord 1995, p. 13, translation altered; 2006b, p. 767.
8 Debord 1995, p. 18; 2006b, p. 771.
9 Marx 1990, p. 772.

of subject-object unity: a condition wherein all such separated power is overcome, and in which human subjects govern their own objective actions freely and self-consciously.

These very schematic comments may help to clarify the 'superficial' status of the mass media within Debord's account. Because spectacle denotes a relation between a passive, spellbound subject and an active, seemingly independent object, it most certainly relates to the role played by imagery and entertainment within modern society. In many respects, the consumption of such imagery exemplifies that very relation. However, for Debord, the entire structure of society now embodies that same dynamic. In his view, the profusion of such imagery within modern society reflects the sense in which contemporary capitalism had brought this problematic of contemplative separation to such an extreme that it had become expressed in full, self-evident view across the surface of a society that it had moulded to the very core.[10] Thus, the concept of spectacle does not revolve around visual media alone. Instead, the key claim made by texts such as *The Society of the Spectacle* is that contemporary society has become characterised by a contemplative relation to history itself, because it has become alienated from its capacity to shape its own future. Human subjects are now passive observers of an objective world that is composed and conducted by their own alienated activity.

We will need to develop these claims later, but if they can suffice for the time being, we ought now to address the following question. Given that a literally visual and media-centric reading of spectacle jars with Debord's own statements, how could such interpretations have become so widespread?

Interpreting the Theory of Spectacle

An initial response to that question can be found in the simple fact that Debord's texts are often very dense and compact. Much of the difficulty involved in reading *The Society of the Spectacle*'s terse formulations derives from that book's attempt to combine elegant concision with the broadest of scopes; to thereby 'unify and explain a wide range of apparently disparate phenomena'[11] by gathering them under the rubric of a single concept capable of grasping the essential characteristics, and indeed the potential negation, of

---

10 Hence Debord's contention in *The Society of the Spectacle* that the spectacle must be understood as 'the visible *negation* of life; as a negation of life that has *become visible*' (Debord 1995, p. 14; 2006b, p. 768).
11 Debord 1995, p. 14, translation altered; 2006b, p. 768.

the 'historical moment in which we are caught'.¹² Both the essential problematic of spectacle and the phenomena to which that problematic gives rise are treated as instances of that single, unifying concept. Consequently, readings that pay insufficient attention to that deeper problematic can arrive at positions wherein the concept of spectacle is only identified with 'stultifyingly superficial' phenomena such as those referred to above.

The difficulty of Debord's texts is also amplified by his attempts to make their form adequate to the nature of their content. Debord was keen to ensure that his works did not merely represent and describe the refusal of spectacle, but rather instantiated it. This ambition informs *The Society of the Spectacle*'s extensive use of *détournement*. *The Society of the Spectacle* quotes, alludes to and re-works a host of passages from Marx, Hegel, and many others. Famous and forgotten phrases are shifted into new formulations that pertain to Debord's account of the present moment. Seemingly dead, ossified concepts that once possessed critical vitality are thereby revitalised in the light of the exigencies of the present. Thus, rather than merely *describing* the negation of a stagnant culture, Debord's book endeavours to actualise that negation within its own pages.

In much the same vein, Debord's work is also characterised by an Adornian refusal to stoop, through easy exposition, to the facile and degraded level of a society that he despised. Debord explicitly refused to make concessions to his audience, and his books and films are unapologetically challenging.[13] To make matters worse, his approach to writing becomes all the more complicated in his later work. In his private letters, Debord indicates that 1989's *Panegyric* is deliberately 'crammed with traps'[14] for the unsuspecting reader; similarly, 1988's *Comments on the Society of the Spectacle* begins by warning its own readers that they should beware 'certain lures'[15] within its pages. We will address, and attempt to explain, these peculiar strategies of writing in Part Five; suffice it to say here that Debord's texts are often rather unforgiving, and frequently much more complex than they may at first appear.[16]

---

12 Debord 1995, p. 15, translation altered; 2006b, p. 768.
13 See, for example, the opening statements of Debord's 1978 film, *In Girum Imus Nocte et Consumimur Igni*: 'I will make no concessions to the public in this film. ... this particular public, which has been so totally deprived of freedom and which has tolerated every sort of abuse, deserves less than any other to be treated gently' (Debord 2003b, pp. 133–4; 2006b, pp. 1334–5).
14 Debord 2008, p. 218.
15 Debord 1998, p. 2, translation altered; 2006b, p. 1594.
16 See Debord's notes to any future translator of *Panegyric* for a particularly clear illustration

This complexity, and indeed the occasional opacity of Debord's more theoretical writings, has perhaps facilitated the adoption of a reductively literal approach to Debord's visual terminology (as one particularly frustrated writer once put it: 'when Debord pompously writes "everything that was directly lived has withdrawn into a representation", the prick is simply saying that we see posters of naked women pushing brands of cigarettes').[17] A more serious obstacle to the comprehension of Debord's work was, however, set up by the intellectual ambience that coloured its initial academic appropriation.

In a letter of 1971, in which he responded to questions from a reader of *The Society of the Spectacle*, Debord remarked that 'one cannot fully comprehend [the book] without Marx, and especially Hegel'.[18] Yet during the 1980s and 1990s – and thus during the period in which his own and the SI's works first began to be adopted by academia – both writers had fallen from intellectual fashion. Debord himself complained of the degree to which the 'German origin' of 'nearly all'[19] of *The Society of the Spectacle*'s key concepts had been 'quietly' ignored,[20] and in an intellectual climate that figured Hegel and Marx as the respectively unacceptable and obsolete epitomes of a dead modernism, the conceptual mechanics of his theory became all the more inaccessible. This no doubt furthered the temptation of simply retreating from that opacity into a primarily visual interpretation of spectacle.

This certainly seems to have informed the trajectory taken by Anglophone academia, which can be schematised as follows. Initially brought to an English audience through the radical groups of the 1960s,[21] the SI came to be adopted by a more cultural and artistic milieu from the late '70s onwards. This resulted in

---

of this point (Debord 2004b, pp. 171–8; 2006b, pp. 1686–9). Martin Jay was thus quite wrong when he claimed that whilst 'other Western Marxists ... championed modernism ... Adorno was the only one who could legitimately lay claim to have been a modernist himself' (Jay 1984, p. 17).

17 Voyer 1998.
18 Debord 2004a, p. 454.
19 Debord 2005, p. 61.
20 Ibid.
21 The Castoriadis-influenced Solidarity group, who remained critical of the SI's departure from labour issues, were important in this respect. They were, however, by no means alone: the journal *Rebel Worker*, which had expressed Situationist sentiments (such as recommending Lautréamont and Blake as 'precursors of the theory and practice of total revolution' (King Mob 2000, p. 8)), evolved into *Heatwave*, which featured Situationist material in its second issue. The editors and others would go on to form the SI's short-lived English section.

the exhibition of early Situationist artwork in the late 1980s,[22] and laid the basis for the art-historical and visual cultural readings that would later proliferate.[23] Due to their disciplinary emphasis on the visual, these readings fostered the assumption that Debord's 'images' and 'representations' could be read in a literal and primarily media-focussed manner; hence the theory's contemporary currency within the fields of visual culture, art history, cultural studies and media studies. The latter adoption, it might be added, facilitated the erroneous and still widespread tendency to conflate Debord's spectacle with Baudrillard's simulacra.[24]

This then renders it all the more important to stress that Debord is not a 'postmodern' writer, as is sometimes supposed, but rather a recalcitrant modernist; not a post-structuralist, but rather a twentieth-century Young Hegelian, whose work owes far more to figures such as Cieszkowski, Feuerbach, Stirner and Marx than to any of his despised contemporaries (particularly those whom he described as having 'taken refuge at Vincennes'[25] following the events of May 1968). However, before we begin to develop this Hegelian intellectual lineage – and before we begin to outline the reading of Debord's work that it affords – we should first take note of some of the more successful analyses of his claims.

Three Degrees of Spectacle

As noted earlier, the concept of spectacle serves to 'unify and explain a wide range of apparently disparate phenomena'. This requires it to operate on several levels at the same time. Debord indicates as much at the very outset of *The Society of the Spectacle*,[26] but a useful clarification of this point can be found in a letter of 1973. He writes there that the concrete reality of the spec-

---

22 The exhibition 'On the Passage of a Few People Through a Rather Brief Moment in Time' toured between the Centre Georges Pompidou and the London and Boston Institutes of Contemporary Art between 1989 and 1990 (see Black 1996, Clark and Nicholson Smith 2004, and McDonough 2011 for commentary).
23 See, for example, Beller 2006, Crary 2001, and Jay 1994.
24 See, for example, Best and Kellner 1999. For an early study that acknowledges the important differences between Debord and Baudrillard, see Plant 2000. We will return to this difference in Chapter 13.
25 Debord 2005, p. 349.
26 See in particular thesis #3 of *The Society of the Spectacle*; the letter discussed here is, however, primarily concerned with the explication of theses #7–10.

tacle, as opposed to its relatively superficial existence as a set of mediatic and ideological practices, 'can only be justified by reference to these three degrees: simple technico-ideological appearances / the reality of the social organisation of appearances / historical reality'.[27] Outlining these three 'degrees' can provide a useful means of positioning this book's area of focus in relation to some of the existing approaches to Debord's thought.

On the first of these three 'degrees', or levels – that of 'simple technico-ideological appearances' – the spectacle is simply an ideological and media-driven 'part of society': something very much akin to Adorno and Horkheimer's 'culture industry'. Seen in these terms, the spectacle is the sector of society 'where all attention, all consciousness, converges'.[28] This is the level of Debord's analysis upon which much of the academic work referred to earlier has tended to focus.

On the second level of this schema, however, and thus 'behind the phenomenal appearances of the spectacle', such as 'television, advertising, the discourse of the State, etc.,' we find what Debord refers to as 'the general *reality* of the spectacle itself', understood as 'a moment in the mode of production.'[29] The concept of spectacle, addressed on this second, deeper level, pertains to the social operation of capitalist value, and to the manner in which society has been ordered to suit capital's continued operation. On the first, more 'superficial' level of this schema, spectators contemplate the fads, fashions, adverts and trinkets that celebrate this social order; on this second, more profound level, they become contemplative observers of their own lives, because their social activity has become so thoroughly governed and shaped by that same order. This is the dimension of Debord's theory that has been addressed by the best studies of his work. Anselm Jappe's excellent *Guy Debord* (1993, in Italian; 1999 in English)[30] is of particular significance here, as it deals with this theme in detail. It is also highly significant, given the explicitly Hegelian-Marxian nature of his interpretation, that Debord himself referred to Jappe's book in his private correspondence as 'the best-informed book about me'.[31]

However, the subordination of lived reality to capital's dictates that takes place on that second level entails that the concept of spectacle also operates on a third level: that of 'historical reality'. In this regard, spectacle needs to be understood as *a relation to historical time*. For Debord, the articulation of

---

27 Debord 2005, p. 61.
28 Debord 1995, p. 12; 2006b, p. 766.
29 Debord 2005, p. 61.
30 Jappe 1999.
31 Debord 2008, p. 453.

all social existence via capitalist social relations involves the separation of human subjects from their own lived activity. The result is a historical moment characterised by a loss of historical agency; or, as Debord puts it in another letter: modern capitalism has produced the paradox of a 'historical society that refuses history'.[32] Thus, this third and deepest level of Debord's tripartite schema concerns a state of separation from history itself. Although we will touch on the first level of Debord's theory in later chapters, and although we will also discuss the technicalities of its second level at some length, this book will focus primarily on its third, 'historical' level.

A reading of Debord's theory that attends to this more historical and existential level of analysis necessarily entails a somewhat broader perspective than that afforded by a more restricted focus on his critique of capitalist society. For example, such an approach can help to link his Marxian critique of capitalist society to his work's more aesthetic and poetic dimensions. These aspects of Debord's thought often seem to be treated somewhat independently from one another;[33] yet as we will see later, the aesthetic dimensions of his work are closely wedded to his interest in time and temporality. In consequence, a reading of spectacle that attends to such issues can afford a rather more holistic perspective.

Furthermore, focussing on the importance of temporality and history in Debord's theoretical work also serves to foreground the following, perhaps somewhat surprising issue. The problematic of spectacle – i.e. detachment from the capacity to shape historical time – cannot be restrictively and reductively identified with capitalist social relations. Capitalist society certainly exemplifies and instantiates that problematic, because its subordination to the abstract domination of capitalist value had brought that problematic to an identifiable and purportedly resolvable extreme. Yet as Debord was well aware, previous social structures had also instantiated that same problematic in a host of differing ways. Consequently, according to the reading that will be developed in this book, the *problematic* of spectacle is older than the *society* of the spectacle (Debord in fact refers to the inception of a fully spectacular society in the early decades of the twentieth century as the spectacle's emergence in 'its completed form').[34] Textual evidence[35] to support this claim will be presented and

---

32   Debord 2004a, p. 79.
33   For example, Jappe 1999 and Kaufmann 2006 focus, respectively, on the Marxian and poetic aspects of Debord's thought, and are perhaps the best available works on these topics.
34   Debord 2008, p. 331.
35   It should be noted here that many of the interpretations of Debord's work referred to in

discussed in the following chapter. The salient point here, however, is simply that if one is to address this broader *problematic* of spectacle, then one needs to identify and clarify the philosophical positions and presuppositions upon which it rests.

Doing so necessarily involves drawing out and piecing together the tacit philosophical anthropology that subtends Debord's claims concerning agency and temporal experience. Above all – and as our earlier discussion may have served to indicate – it must also involve a consideration of the Hegelian and Marxist ideas that inform his work. In the remainder of this first chapter, therefore, we will set out an initial discussion of Debord's understanding of the Marxian critique of Hegelian philosophy, and thus of his views concerning the nature and importance of Hegel's work. In order to help orient these discussions, however, we should first briefly develop some of the comments that were made earlier, in this book's introduction, concerning the manner in which the Situationist project and the theory of spectacle pertain to the concerns with time and history that we have referred to here.

The Spectacle and the Situationists

As we have already seen, Debord and the SI characterised the modern societies of their day as being subordinate to their own economic systems. Capitalism, for Debord, involves the regulation and domination of lived social activity by the abstraction of value, and in consequence, it instantiates the problem outlined above: human subjects become subordinate to the results of their own objective activity. For Debord, this subordination had become the defining feature of an entire historical moment. In *The Society of the Spectacle*, he wrote that 'capitalism' had turned 'the whole planet' into its 'field of operation',[36] and claimed that it had thereby generated an entire social order suited to its operation: a grand '*Weltanschauung*'[37] that corresponded to the needs of an effectively autonomous economy, and which had come to operate, despite its internal divisions and political tensions, as a concrete, independent force.

Capitalism was thus viewed in a manner that encompassed its state-bureaucratic and consumer-based variants alike. In 1967's *The Society of the Spectacle*, Western consumer capitalism was described as the 'diffuse spectacle', whilst

---

this chapter were written prior to the publication of Debord's collected correspondence, and indeed prior to the BnF's acquisition of Debord's archives and personal reading notes.

36 Debord 1995, pp. 36–7; 2006b, p. 784.
37 Debord 1995, p. 13; 2006b, p. 767.

the 'bureaucratic capitalism'[38] of the so-called workers' states was described as the 'concentrated spectacle'. These two forms can be briefly characterised as follows. Within the diffuse spectacle, a panoply of images of subjective satisfaction is continually presented via society's saturation with commodities, and via the commodity's celebratory derivatives. Because practically every aspect of social activity has become colonised by the demands of commodity production and consumption, this results in a mode of life moulded to capital's requirements. The concentrated spectacle is rather different: it too regulates a mode of life in which individuals have become subservient to an autonomous social system, but here the benefits and beneficence of that system are focussed upon the figure of a ruling body, Party or dictator. In addition, social activity is ordered in keeping with this image of the general good via a deeper reliance on police techniques.

In 1988's *Comments on the Society of the Spectacle*, which responded to the social changes that had taken place since *The Society of the Spectacle*'s publication, Debord claimed that the modern society had become characterised by what he referred to as the 'integrated spectacle': a new form of spectacle, that combined both the commodification and police aspects of its diffuse and concentrated antecedents, and which had managed to integrate itself into social reality to a far greater extent than either of its predecessors. Yet despite their different characteristics, all of these differing social formations instantiate the same problematic: within each, individual subjects are held to have become detached from their own collective powers and capacities.

The SI's aim, during their more theoretical and revolutionary Marxian period in the 1960s, was to herald and foster a response to this state of affairs. This response was not a call for a more equitable mode of distribution, or for better working conditions, but rather a demand for a completely new social existence (as Vaneigem put it in 1963: 'What do we demand in backing the power of everyday life against hierarchical power? We demand *everything*').[39] Debord and the SI held that whilst the alienation of society's capacity to shape its own history had increased under capitalism, so too had the sheer scale and breadth of that capacity itself. They thus called for the supersession of all forms of separated capacity and hierarchical power; for the reclamation of society's alienated and hugely augmented ability to shape its own lived time, and for the creation of a mode of social existence in which that ability could be freely employed. The images of the good that had served to maintain a social order

---

38 Debord 1995, p. 41; 2006b, p. 787.
39 SI 2006, p. 159; 1997, p. 334.

characterised by separation would be superseded by a new social condition, wherein all that modern technological capitalism had rendered possible and yet simultaneously denied could be realised.

Importantly, the SI also held that a drive towards such an extreme, all-encompassing mode of revolt had become generalised throughout modern society. Within the Western consumer capitalism with which Debord and the SI were primarily concerned, a wealth of consumer goods had seemingly alleviated the nineteenth-century poverty that had exercised Marx. For some apologetic commentators, this had even alleviated the need and desire for social change altogether.[40] Yet for Debord and the SI, the proletariat had not been buried 'beneath an avalanche of sound systems, T.V.s, small cars and planned communities',[41] but had instead been radically expanded. Because all social life had become shaped and structured by capital, disaffection and alienation had become similarly universal. This had created a 'new' proletariat: a vast, effectively classless social 'class', composed of 'all people who have no possibility of altering the social space-time that society allots to them'.[42] The separation of Marx's proletarian from the means of independently maintaining his or her own existence had thus given way to a 'higher', more existential form of poverty, marked by a separation from the means of consciously shaping and directing that existence. This meant that the modern revolutionary class would no longer be defined in traditional economic terms. As Debord put it in 1961: 'The point is not to recognise that some people live more or less poorly than others, but that we all live in ways that are out of our control'.[43]

Initially, and particularly in the years that followed the SI's emergence from the avant-garde milieu, the radical self-determinacy that would rectify that state of affairs was to be researched and fostered through the construction of 'situations': moments of lived time that would unify art and life, through being shaped and lived according to the experiencing subjects' own wishes. Ultimately, however, this condition would be attained within a communism that amounted to a condition of collective, self-determinate praxis: a communism within which no instantiation of social power would be permitted to perpetuate itself independently from those who generate it, and in which all forms of hierarchy and representative leadership would therefore be abolished (hence Debord's remark that: 'we have a great sympathy for the principal anarchist

---

40   See Plant 2000, pp. 14–16 for a discussion of this issue.
41   Vaneigem 2003, p. 68.
42   SI 2006, p. 141; 1997, p. 309.
43   Debord 2003b, p. 31; 2006b, p. 543.

manifestations in history'; 'the goals of anarchism are those of all imaginable revolutionary movements in modern society').[44]

Having now made these rather general comments concerning the connections between the theory of spectacle and the SI's project, we can turn to the ideas that informed them. In order to do so, we will need to develop our earlier remarks concerning the separation and unity of subject and object.

A 'Contemplative' Attitude towards History

Debord and the SI's concern with the construction of situations and self-constitutive action owes an obvious debt to the legacy and intellectual ambience of French existentialism, as does Debord's interest in temporality. This is not to deny that related notions of self-determination and self-constitution can also be discerned in Debord's more obviously Marxian influences.[45] It does, however, seem to be the case that the French milieu of the 1950s and '60s fostered a tendency, on Debord and the SI's part, towards a reading of Marxian ideas that was inflected by existential themes, and by the existential and temporal issues addressed within twentieth-century French Hegelianism. As a result of this confluence of influences, Debord effectively came to found the existential view that 'one is what one does'[46] not upon phenomenology, but rather upon a model of dialectical interaction between subject and object. This informed his work's essentially Hegelian association of history and self-consciousness: for if one creates and knows oneself through what one does, then abdicating autonomy over one's actions not only involves a divorce from one's own history, but also an absence of self-consciousness. Thus, just as Hegel wrote in *The Philosophy of Right* that a 'slave', unable to dictate his own actions, 'knows not his essence ... and not to know himself is not to think himself,'[47] so

---

44 Debord 2003a, pp. 140–1.
45 For the young Marx, for example, 'Objective man ... [is] the outcome of man's own labour' (Marx 1988, p. 149); or, as he and Engels put in *The German Ideology*: 'As individuals express their life, so they are. What they are, therefore, coincides with their production' (Marx and Engels 2007, p. 42; this quotation was used by Debord in his comments of 1972 on the end of the SI (SI 2003, p. 81; Debord 2006b, p. 1134)). Similar points can be found in Marx's mature work: 'Labour is ... a process between man and nature ... Through this movement he acts upon external nature and changes it, and in this way he simultaneously changes his own nature' (Marx 1990, p. 283).
46 Heidegger 1962, p. 283.
47 Hegel 2005, p. xlii.

Debord held that 'the more [the spectator] contemplates ... his own unthinking activity ... the less he understands his own existence and his own desires.'[48]

This bears obvious relation to the SI's drive towards the conscious control of lived time. It is, however, also important to note that Debord's theoretical claims also owe a great deal to Lukács's *History and Class Consciousness* (as is evidenced by the sheer number of quotations from Hegel and Marx that Debord, in *The Society of the Spectacle*, seems to have simply lifted from the pages of Lukács's book).[49] We will consider the influence exerted by *History and Class Consciousness* in Part Three, but its relevance can be outlined here as follows.

According to Lukács, the alienation of the worker from his or her own activity entails an increasingly 'contemplative'[50] attitude towards the latter: an attitude that had, as a result of the domination of society by the commodity form, begun to spread beyond the factory walls. Debord adopts and expands this position, claiming that all social activity now takes place in accordance with the demands of the economy, and contends that the dialectical relation of mutual constitution between subject and object has, in consequence, been subverted: a passive subject is now acted upon by an alien social world, composed of that subject's own separated power and activity.

Debord and Lukács also present similar theoretical responses to this problem: both indicate that the alienated detachment that they attribute to capitalist society can only be overcome through the instantiation of a form of subject-object unity. In place of that detachment, they argue that the human subject should recognise that the objective world is in fact the product of its own formative activity; that it should thereby grasp its capacity to shape its own existence, and that in doing so, it would instantiate a condition of subject-object unity, wherein that subject consciously and continuously shapes both itself and its world as an ongoing historical process. 'Man', Lukács wrote, 'must

---

48   Debord 1995, p. 23; 2006b, p. 774.
49   Debord may have borrowed the following quotations from *History and Class Consciousness*: a remark from *The Holy Family* (Debord 1995, p. 49; 2006b, p. 793; Lukács 1971, p. 16; Marx and Engels 1936, p. 115); a statement in a letter sent by Marx to Ruge in 1843 (Debord 1995, p. 92; 2006b, p. 820; Lukács 1971, p. 18; Marx 1975, p. 208); an important line from the first volume of *Capital* (Debord 1995, p. 12, 2006, p. 767; Lukács 1971, p. 49; Marx 1990, p. 932); a quotation from *The Poverty of Philosophy* (Debord 1995, p. 110; 2006b, p. 831; Lukács 1971, p. 89; Marx 2009); a line from Hegel's *The Difference Between Fichte's and Schelling's Systems of Philosophy* (Debord 1995 p. 130; 2006b p. 843; Lukács 1971, p. 139; Hegel 1988, p. 91; this latter appropriation is also noted by Jappe 1999, p. 21).
50   Lukács 1971, p. 89.

become conscious of himself as a social being, as simultaneously the subject and object of the socio-historical process'.[51] Debord does not explicitly use the term subject-object unity,[52] but his position is ultimately much the same.

The end of spectacle, therefore, can be understood in terms of the actualisation of a condition of subject-object unity, and in keeping with Debord's quasi-existential preoccupations with temporality and temporal experience, this mode of unity was framed as a self-determinate, but no less social relation to the creation and conduct of lived time. Communism was thus envisaged as a mode of collective, historical praxis wherein those currently 'estranged from history' would be able to '*live* the historical time'[53] that they create. Or, as Debord put it via a reference to one of *The German Ideology*'s comments on communist social unity:[54] the post-revolutionary attainment of such a condition would afford 'the total realisation, within the medium of time, of the communism that abolishes [*supprime*][55] "everything that exists independently of individuals"',[56] i.e. which supersedes all bodies of separated power and agency that stand removed from those from whom they derive. Or, as Debord simply put it in a *détournement* of the *Communist Manifesto*: 'history itself is the spectre haunting modern society'.[57]

Interpreting the World and Transforming the World

This then brings us to the relevance of Hegel's philosophy. Hegel's significance, for Debord, lies in the fact that his philosophy had associated history with self-determinacy and self-consciousness. In addition, Hegel had also identified the full expression of that self-consciousness with a condition of subject-object unity. Thus, Hegel's relevance, for Debord, ultimately stems from the sense in which his work could be construed as a philosophical *image* of the condition of collective praxis that would supersede spectacular society. The following remarks may help to explain that point.

---

51 Lukács 1971, p. 19.
52 He does, however, clearly have this concept in mind. See, for example, theses #74, #116, and #117 of *The Society of the Spectacle*.
53 Debord 1995, p. 106; 2006b, p. 829.
54 See Marx and Engels 2007, p. 86.
55 *Supprimer*, along with *dépasser*, is often used as a French translation of the key Hegelian term *Aufheben*.
56 Debord 1995, pp. 116–17; 2006b, p. 836.
57 Debord 1995, p. 141; 2006b, p. 851.

Hegel's work greatly informs Debord's conception of spectacular representation. The spectacular separation of subject and object involves a condition wherein the former stands at one remove from the latter, transfixed by representations of a unity that this same state of separation serves to deny. This owes a great deal to the notion of *Vorstellung* employed in texts such as Hegel's *Phenomenology of Spirit* (and it is significant to note that this word was translated as *représentation* in the French version of the *Phenomenology* that Debord used).[58] Throughout that book, subjective consciousness is continually confronted with objects that appear to be distinct from it, but which are, in truth, its own alienated self. For example: religion, in the *Phenomenology*, is described as a *Vorstellung* (or 'picture-thought') of the subject-object unity achieved at the apex of that book.[59]

The most important point that needs to be made here, however, is that for Debord, Hegel's philosophy, despite its undoubted insights, could be seen to exemplify that very same problematic of separation. Although Hegel had inadvertently depicted some of the key aspects of the subject-object unity that Debord associated with self-determinate praxis, he had done so in a manner that remained detached from the latter's actualisation. Hegel had located his vision of subject-object unity in a purportedly final philosophical system that stood at one remove from the ongoing process of the history that it presumed to crown. Hegel had thus offered only a philosophical *image* of such unity: for in Debord's view, subject-object unity can only truly reside in concrete, future-oriented praxis.

These points can be illustrated further by way of reference to Debord's comments on Hegel in *The Society of the Spectacle*, where he writes as follows:

> For Hegel it was no longer a matter of *interpreting* the world, but rather of interpreting the world's *transformation*. Inasmuch as he did *no more* than interpret that transformation, however, Hegel was merely the *philosophical* culmination of philosophy. He sought to understand a world that *made itself*. This historical thought was still part of that consciousness that always arrives too late, and which pronounces a justification *post festum*. It thus superseded separation – but *in thought only*.[60]

---

58 Debord indicates in his correspondence that he used Hyppolite's two-volume translation of the *Phenomenology*, which appeared in 1939 and 1941 (Debord 2004a, p. 65).

59 See, for example, Hegel 1977, p. 479: 'The *content* of this [religious] picture-thinking is absolute Spirit; and all that now remains to be done is to supersede this mere form [i.e. the form of religion]' (Hegel's italics).

60 Debord 1995, p. 49, translation altered; 2006b, p. 793.

The first line of the quotation reproduced above is an allusion to Marx's famous final thesis on Feuerbach ('The philosophers have only interpreted the world, in various ways; the point is to change it').[61] Debord credits Hegel with having gone beyond the efforts of the philosophers of the past. Instead of merely interpreting the world as it currently exists, Hegel had presented the world as the product of historical change. Yet as the quotation also illustrates, Debord holds that Hegel did no more than *interpret* that change, and that he thus remained within the detached, contemplative ambit of philosophy. According to Debord's (somewhat questionable) reading of Hegel, the latter's philosophy had declared history to have come to an end. It had curtailed the future, reduced the sum truth of history to its own present moment and, by that same manoeuvre, it had also cast human history as the work of a metaphysical, supra-human Subject. In effect, Hegel's philosophy had described a world that had finished making itself: a world that philosophical consciousness would now merely *contemplate*. Debord explains this in a letter of 1969, in which he comments on a translation of the passage reproduced above. He writes as follows:

> The philosophers, [before Marx], had interpreted the world as a *given* block (even Heraclitus, who showed it as pure, permanent change). Hegel interpreted concrete change, the world constituting itself *in its own history*. So Hegel interpreted the auto-transformation of the world (reduced to the supposed project of the Spirit), and so remained a contemplative philosopher before an external history. Therefore, a *leftist critique* of Hegelianism should be led to take an active part in history; to recognise that this transformation of the world has no other motor than the activity of men.[62]

The manner in which Debord sought to go beyond Hegel can be illustrated by looking at his remark, in the passage from *The Society of the Spectacle* reproduced above, that Hegel's philosophy was 'still part of that consciousness that always arrives too late and supplies a justification *post festum*'. This is a reference to Marx and Engels's *The Holy Family* (which Debord may well have lifted from *History and Class Consciousness*).[63] It draws on the sense in which Hegelian philosophy can be understood, in keeping with Hegel's own

---

61 Marx 1975, p. 423.
62 Debord 2004a, pp. 94–5.
63 As indicated above: Debord 1995, p. 49; 2006b, p. 793; Lukács 1971, p. 16; Marx and Engels 1936, p. 115.

views,[64] as a mode of thought that announces its claims after the advent of historical events, as opposed to applying itself within their creation. The 'historical thought' that Hegel's philosophy expresses – i.e. its comprehension of human existence in historical time – thus remains removed from the actual *conduct* of historical time. For Debord, all such thought *about* history needed to be superseded by a mode of thought that would *make* history. Thus, where Hegel's owl of Minerva famously took flight *after* the event, Debord advocated a mode of historical consciousness that would operate *within* such events.

The 'Dialectical Method' and the 'Reality That Seeks It'

In Debord's view, both Hegel's insights and limitations were prompted by the nature of his historical context. Like Hyppolite,[65] Korsch[66] and Lukács[67] – writers whom Debord drew upon, and who may have informed his views in this regard – Debord presented Hegel's philosophy as symptomatic of the social conditions proper to the bourgeois revolutions.[68] Hegel's work was held to have given conceptual voice to the increased awareness of historical change that had arisen within this period: an awareness that had been fostered by the social transformations proper to the bourgeois revolutions themselves, and by the rise of capitalist industry. However, Hegel's philosophy was also held to reflect the emergence of a capitalist society within which human subjects had become fetishistically subordinate to the objects that they produced: hence his philosophy's tranquil resignation to the implacable forces of human history, and hence also its 'contemplative' and quiescent attempt to 'understand a world that made itself'.

This meant that Hegel had, in effect, exemplified the challenge posed by 'bourgeois' society: namely, that of overcoming the alienated relation to history that that society had engendered. This is why Debord places Hegel at the very beginning of *The Society of the Spectacle*'s central fourth chapter on the history of the workers' movement. Hegel is described there as having presen-

---

64 According to Hegel, 'the owl of Minerva takes its flight only when the shades of night are gathering' (Hegel 2005, p. xxi), because philosophy cannot 'teach the world what it ought to be' (Hegel 2005, p. xxi): it can only explain why the world has become (or is in the process of becoming) what it must be.
65 Hyppolite 1969, p. 73.
66 Korsch 1946.
67 Lukács 1971, p. 77; see also Lukács 1975.
68 See, for example, thesis #76 of *The Society of the Spectacle*.

ted an initial, but no less profound account of the 'thought of history':[69] a term that Debord uses to refer to the self-conscious conduct of historical time. This is also why Debord states, at the outset of that chapter: 'All the theoretical strands of the *revolutionary* workers' movement stem from critical confrontation with Hegelian thought'.[70] The essence of that 'critical confrontation' lay in overcoming the detached perspective on history that Hegel had exemplified, in order to realise the unity with history that Hegel had inadvertently intimated.

Hegel's contemplative and retrospective view of a seemingly finished history thus needed to be corrected. Subject-object unity needed to be identified not with the workings of Hegel's cosmic logic, but rather with the future-oriented process of history's conscious construction. These requirements meant that the Marxian 'inversion' of Hegel took on quite specific characteristics for Debord. It certainly entailed bringing Hegel's philosophy down to earth, as in much orthodox Marxism, but not through simply replacing his dialectically unfolding categories with a series of different modes of production. Instead, Hegelian philosophy's image of historical praxis needed to be stripped of its idealist attributes, and realised in the process of constructing an open future.

Debord credits various Young Hegelian writers with having taken steps towards identifying and illuminating this central issue; hence his sympathies for their criticisms of religion, authority and dogma. One can find direct echoes of writers such as Cieszkowski, Bakunin, Bauer, Feuerbach and Stirner in Debord's work, all of whom are referenced favourably in his writings and letters. Stirner's criticisms of humanity's 'spooks' and 'fixed ideas',[71] Feuerbach's discussion of religion,[72] Bauer's rejection of all separated instantiations of human self-consciousness;[73] all bear relation to Debord's ideas, because by calling for the reclamation of these alienated constructs, the Young Hegelians came very close to recognising the need to employ such powers in history's conscious construction. Debord was thus particularly impressed by Cieszkowski's call for

---

69   Debord 1995, p. 48, translation altered; 2006b, p. 793, emphasis in the original.
70   Debord 1995, p. 50; 2006b, p. 794.
71   For example: 'What is it, then, that is called a "fixed idea"? An idea that has subjected the man to itself' (Stirner 2005, p. 43).
72   For example: 'Man first sees his [own] nature as if out of himself [i.e. in God], before he finds it in himself' (Feuerbach 1989, p. 13).
73   For example: according to Bauer's reading of Hegel, '... all powers, which exist as substance or *Absolute Idea* are but mere appearances differentiated from self-consciousness, merely religious images objectified out of self-consciousness. ... This philosophy wants no God, nor Gods ... it wants but man and his self-consciousness' (Bauer 1997, p. 181, emphasis in the original).

a philosophy of praxis, which anticipated many of his own views.[74] Principal credit was, however, given to the young Marx. In many respects, Marx's final thesis on Feuerbach exemplifies the contribution that Debord ascribes to him in this line of development. This is because for Debord, the new orientation that Marx had identified and grasped in that famous final thesis expressed a key theme that had been implicit throughout the work of Marx's Young Hegelian predecessors, and which would be made progressively more explicit by the theory and struggles that would follow: namely, that of superseding *all* social and intellectual constructs that separate human subjects from participating in the creation of their own history. As these critical developments evolved in step with the popular revolts of the nineteenth century, Debord felt able to frame this progressive articulation of 'historical thought' as a process within which 'the dialectical method' moved ever closer to a condition of unity with 'the reality that seeks it'.[75]

The Realisation of Philosophy

These ideas can be placed in useful contrast to those of Adorno, who once famously remarked that the moment for philosophy's realisation had been 'missed'.[76] This remark is a reference to Marx's early 'Contribution to a Critique of Hegel's *Philosophy of Right*'. Marx wrote there that philosophy can only become a critical, practical force in the world if it serves to articulate the struggles of those who would actively realise its criticisms in revolutionary change. Critical, philosophical thought should therefore clarify the struggles of the proletariat, who would render its criticisms a reality: thus, 'Philosophy', as Marx put it, 'cannot realise itself without the supersession [*Aufhebung*] of the proletariat, and the proletariat cannot supersede itself without the realisation [*Verwirklichung*] of philosophy'.[77] Adorno's point was that philosophy's unification with the revolutionary proletariat, and its consequent contribution to the latter's self-abolition, had failed to occur. In place of the happy unity of thought and action that he took Marx to have predicted, Adorno saw a world in which thought had become subordinate to crude instrumental demands: cap-

---

74   As we will see in the following chapter, Cieszkowski was praised for having advanced some of the primary characteristics of the young Marx's critique of Hegel before Marx himself had done so, and indeed before Feuerbach had set out his own views.
75   Debord 2006b, p. 1536.
76   Adorno 1990, p. 3.
77   Marx 1975, p. 257, translation altered.

italism had gone from strength to strength, the communist project had given rise to new forms of statist domination, and the world had entered a new age of barbarism. Within such a context, Adorno believed, the autonomy and independence of critical, philosophical thought had become more important than ever. A headlong rush towards praxis needed to be avoided, as it seemed dangerously close to the subordination of critical thought to instrumental ends.[78]

Some of Debord's views can seem quite close to those expressed by Adorno (although it should be noted that his engagements with Adorno's ideas seem to have been very limited indeed).[79] However, their views on the issue of praxis could not be more opposed. This is because Debord's entire political and philosophical perspective hinges on the view that the exigency of philosophy's realisation remained pressing and important, and that it had, in fact, taken on a new, grander and more demanding form. The realisation of philosophy, for Debord, meant employing an otherwise merely contemplative and detached body of thought in transformative action. In the latter half of the twentieth century, this exigency had not faded away, but had instead been radically expanded. The evolution of culture and technology, and the hugely augmented capacities to shape lived experience that they afforded, had brought a new, grander demand to the fore. It was now no longer just the separation of philosophical thought that needed to be overcome: the task at hand was now that of reclaiming and employing *all* such capacities in lived praxis, and of abolishing *all* such separated power. This would afford a new, post-revolutionary era, within which objective existence could finally become the conscious creation of the experiencing subject.

---

78   In a letter of 1968 to Günter Grass, Adorno speaks of his 'mounting aversion to any kind of praxis', and of the 'objective hopelessness of praxis in this historical moment' (Adorno 1969).

79   Debord's archive notes indicate that he read a copy of *Arguments* #19, which was produced in 1960, and which contained a translation of Adorno's 'Music and Technique'. His personal library also contained a copy of the first ever French translation of *Dialectic of Enlightenment*. This edition was, however, published in 1974, and thus appeared long after 1967's *The Society of the Spectacle* (thanks are due to Laurence Le Bras at the Bibliothèque nationale de France for providing this information, and to Gabriel Ferreira Zacarias for providing further confirmation). Debord did not speak or read German with any facility, and very little of Adorno's work was translated into French prior to the 1970s. There are no direct references to Adorno in Debord's books, films or correspondence (and it should also be added that Debord would have taken an extremely dim view of Adorno's reaction to 1968).

Marxism and Young Hegelianism

We can perhaps sum up at this point by stating that Debord is perhaps best viewed as a twentieth-century Young Hegelian. The issues to which his work seeks to respond are, fundamentally, those raised, identified, and initially addressed in the nineteenth century by Hegel, the Young Hegelians, and the young Marx. This is quite explicit in Debord's writings. He in fact once remarked in a letter, whilst indicating the tasks demanded by the need to supersede spectacle, that 'we have still not resolved the principal problems' raised by the 'old comrades' of the nineteenth century:[80] problems that all essentially correspond to the realisation of philosophy in praxis.

However, Debord also goes beyond Young Hegelianism. He follows the young Marx in recognising the need to explain the material basis of all alienated constructs, and in seeing that such modes of alienation could only be superseded through practically addressing the material and economic bases from which they arise. This is an important point, because it corresponds to the sense in which Debord's spectacle is not just a set of 'false', illusory ideas that mask an otherwise 'true' social reality. Instead, Debord's claim is that lived reality has *itself* become 'false', insofar as it has been turned into a mere representation of a genuinely self-determinate existence. Lived social activity instantiates the modern spectacle's paradigms and patterns of behaviour, and the spectacle is thus made real; one cannot, therefore, combat spectacular society with theory alone. Debord's relation to Young Hegelianism is therefore close to that expressed in *The German Ideology*, where Marx and Engels contend that 'the Young Hegelians consider conceptions, thoughts, ideas ... as the real chains of men', and believe that they 'have to fight only against these illusions of consciousness'.[81] In contrast, for Marx and Engels, the alienated '"apparitions", "spectres", "fancies", etc.' that were criticised by Feuerbach, Stirner, et al. could only be superseded through 'the practical overthrow of the actual social relations' that 'give rise to this idealistic humbug'.[82] Likewise, for Debord, instances of spectacle cannot be superseded through the adoption of a merely philosophical, theoretical, or individualistically subjective stance, but can only be addressed through collective agency aimed at the concrete abolition of the social relations and structures from which they arise.

---

80 Debord 2005, p. 79.
81 Marx and Engels 2007, p. 41.
82 Marx and Engels 2007, pp. 58–9.

There are, however, problems with Debord's account of capitalist society. This is an issue that we will take up in Part Four, but in broad outline, the argument that will be advanced there can be summarised as follows. Debord's theory is certainly suited to the critical analysis of the subjective and affective symptoms of capitalist society, but it is also rather limited in terms of its ability to address the social relations that cause those same symptoms. This is because its primary concern with alienation and the impoverishment of experience means that it tends to address those social relations in terms of their subjective effects, rather than in terms of their concrete causes. However, we will also propose that the presence of these problems in Debord's work does not entirely undermine it. As we will see, these problems are by no means insurmountable. Furthermore, we will also endeavour to show that the conceptual framework in which they reside remains deserving of greater attention than it has tended to receive.

CHAPTER 2

Five Aspects of Debord's Theoretical Work

Debord and Hegel

Debord's theory of spectacle, we have argued, describes a condition of separation from history, wherein social actors become detached from their own collective abilities and agency, and thus from their ability to shape their own lived time. This means that Debord's theoretical claims must involve a set of ideas concerning temporality, history and agency, which serve to support that notion of separation. The aim of this present chapter is to draw out and discuss some of those ideas. We will focus on five themes within Debord's mature theoretical work, and will show that they can be understood as key components of the essentially Hegelian Marxist conceptual framework that supports it. The five elements addressed here are: the philosophical anthropology that supports his views on time; his work's developmental conception of history; the ethical and normative dimensions of the concept of spectacle; the aesthetic aspects of his interest in time; his peculiarly dialectical conception of strategic praxis. If, however, we are to develop a reading of that conceptual framework, and thus of Debord's views concerning the relation between Marx and Hegel, we will need to begin by characterising his interpretation of Hegel's philosophy.

The nature of Debord's reading and appropriation of Hegel will be taken up in greater detail later in the book. In Part Three, we will will try to reconstruct some of the primary features of this reading, and will discuss the work of the French commentators on Hegel's philosophy whose books Debord owned and studied. We will demonstrate there that Debord seems to have subscribed to a particularly French, *Phenomenology*-centric, and somewhat existential reading of Hegel; a reading wherein Hegel is cast as having grasped some of the key aspects of human historical existence, but in which he is also seen – in a rather Kojèveian vein – as having declared history to have come to a conclusive halt. Here, however, we only need to map out the broad outlines of his use of Hegel, and in order to facilitate this, a short overview of the relevant aspects of Hegel's mature philosophy will be provided below. (This may seem excessively didactic to some readers. However, as indicated in the previous chapter, the Anglophone reception of this material has meant that those who are familiar with Debord and the Situationists are not always equally familiar with Hegel. A brief outline of his ideas may, therefore, be of some use.) This will provide a means of introducing a new line of argument, concerning the ways in which Debord appears to have re-figured some key Hegelian concepts.

The previous chapter contended that for Debord, the self-determinate, processual, and dialectically self-conscious subject-object unity described by Hegelian philosophy constituted an inadvertent *representation* – i.e. a confusedly philosophical and idealist *depiction* – of the similarly processual, self-determinate subject-object unity that would emerge through the supersession of contemporary society's historical arrest. The unity afforded by Hegel's philosophy, therefore, is really an idealist intimation of the genuine unity of thought and world that can be found in concrete historical praxis.[1] Marx, in his early criticisms of Hegel, and in his call for the realisation of philosophy in praxis, is cast as having identified and expressed this problematic to some degree; Debord appears to have seen himself as re-framing and foregrounding that problematic within the modern era, thereby showing it to entail the supersession of *all* forms of alienated detachment from historical praxis.

The basic claim here, therefore, is that for Debord, Hegel's views on history and human self-consciousness constituted a philosophical representation of the true unity of subject and object that would be afforded by free historical praxis. If follows from this that if Hegel's philosophy could indeed be seen as just such a representation, then, presumably, some of the primary characteristics of that philosophy needed to be translated from Hegel's ideal, metaphysical terms, and re-cast as elements of historical praxis. We will therefore suggest below that the general shape and structure of Debord's use of Hegelian philosophy can be schematised as a re-figuration of three central Hegelian motifs: namely, the Absolute, the Concept, and the Idea. These three terms will be defined and explained shortly, but in brief: the subject-object unity of the Idea becomes the instantiation of the praxis that Debord and the SI advocated; the negative, dialectical movement of the Concept becomes human temporality, and thus the motive force of historical existence; the Absolute becomes the latter's self-constitutive nature, and thus both its ground and conduct.

These are, of course, speculative claims. Debord does not state explicitly that he ever adopted such a position, and when stated as baldly as this, these proposals may seem to render him rather *too* Hegelian. It is important to stress, therefore, that the argument advanced here is *not* that Debord specifically and intentionally set out to re-figure these three elements of Hegel's philosophy.

---

1 A related view can be found in *The German Ideology*, where Marx and Engels claim that 'The celebrated "unity of man with nature" has always existed in industry', and thus in the interaction of thought and world involved in concrete activity (quoted in Arthur 1986; Marx and Engels 2007, p. 63).

Instead, we will simply be using them as reference points to name and describe his use of distinct Hegelian motifs. They are thus no more than labels that can help to identify and characterise some of the specific ways in which Hegel's ideas are re-worked in Debord's theory.

These contentions may also begin to seem more cogent as this chapter progresses. This is because the reading of Debord's concept of spectacle that we introduced in the previous chapter, and which we will develop further below, entails that spectacle is not *just* an aspect of modern capitalism. Instead, on a much deeper level, Debord seems to have viewed modern capitalism as having fully instantiated a much older problematic, which appears to have been rooted within the very nature of human subjectivity and temporal existence. The notions of temporality and subjectivity upon which this conception of spectacle relies correspond to the themes that we will draw out of this re-working of Hegel's philosophy. They also relate directly to the five elements of Debord's thought that we will go on to discuss below. All form aspects of his use of Hegelian philosophy, which we will now try to introduce by setting out some of the salient aspects of Hegel's metaphysics.

Infinite Power

What follows here is not an attempt to define what Hegel 'really meant', but rather a description of Hegel's thought that accords with Debord's apparent use of his ideas. The first point to make, then, is that Debord seems to have been operating with an explicitly metaphysical interpretation of Hegel's philosophy.[2] On such an interpretation, Hegel's logic is not only an epistemology, but also an ontology at the same time.[3] To quote Jean Hyppolite, the French Hegel interpreter to whom Debord was most indebted: Hegel's logic is 'an onto-logic', because 'it reconciles being (hence its ontic character) and logos (hence its logical character); it is being as logos and logos as being'.[4] Or, in other words: being, according to Hegel, is not only *accessible* to us through reason; in addition, being *is* reason. The world is accessible to human thought, because both

---

[2] See Magee 2001, pp. 14–15 for commentary on the recent interest in a non-metaphysical reading of Hegel.

[3] See Houlgate 2006a for a reading that stresses this point particularly clearly. See also Beiser 2005 for an interpretation that emphasises the importance of Spinoza and Aristotle for this aspect of Hegel's thought, and McCarney 2000 for an excellent and admirably clear discussion of its connection to Hegel's views on history.

[4] Hyppolite 1974, p. 583.

thought and the world share the same rational structure. Through recognising this fundamental identity, and through thereby grasping the inner, rational structure of all being, Hegel's philosophy attempts to 'become cognisant of the inner unity of everything there is.'[5]

Hegel's pursuit of this fundamental unity is an attempt to comprehend the true nature of what Hegel refers to as the 'Absolute'. The latter is the entirety of being, but not just in the sense of the sum total of all that exists. Instead, Hegel's Absolute is somewhat similar to a pantheistic and rationalist God, insofar as it constitutes the fundamental truth and rationale of all being. To know the Absolute, therefore, is to understand being in terms of the rational structure that is embedded within it. Hegel's philosophy purports to be able to access and express this fundamental truth, and it is able to do so by virtue of its identification of epistemology and ontology. Because human thought, for Hegel, is an element of being, it follows that if such thought were to grasp being's inherent, rational structure (its 'logos', to use Hyppolite's term), then the Absolute would become self-conscious through us: being, via *human* beings, would become fully aware of its own rational nature. We would, in effect, become the self-consciousness of God.

The connection between these ideas and the interpretation of spectacle advanced in the previous chapter may already be apparent. What is at stake here, in Hegel's philosophy, is the need to establish a condition of unity with a fundamental, formative power that is, ultimately, our own true selves: a power that may initially seem divorced and detached from us, but which we are, in truth, one with. To retain the terms of the religious metaphor employed above: where Hegel's philosophy indicates that we are to become the self-consciousness of a God that constitutes the totality of being, Debord argues that we should become the creators of our own world. In this regard, some of the basic framework of Debord's theory can be construed as re-figuring the Hegelian Absolute as humanity's currently alienated capacity to shape its own historical time.

To continue: we have stated that Hegel is concerned with the need to understand the true nature of being, and to thereby reveal its immanent 'logos'. The next point that needs to be made here is that the nature of that 'logos' entails that for Hegel, the true nature of being is that it is in a perpetual condition of *becoming*. This is perhaps best addressed by noting the important similarities that can be identified between the Hegelian Absolute and Spinoza's God-like substance (in fact, Hegel once remarked that 'you are either a Spinozist, or you

---

5   Hegel 1991, p. 184.

are not a philosopher at all';[6] Debord made reference to this comment in his personal reading notes on Hegel, albeit whilst refiguring it in more Marxian terms).[7] Both the Hegelian Absolute and Spinoza's substance express themselves into the totality of existent reality, and both are identified with reason. Much like Spinoza, Hegel also held that *'Reason'* is *'Substance*, as well as *Infinite Power'*.[8] Yet where Spinoza emphasised the infinite positivity of being, the Hegelian Absolute is characterised by a negative process of becoming. This is because the nature of the rationale that inheres within it is such that it is characterised by constant, self-determinate movement.[9] In place of Spinoza's fundamental substance, therefore, we have a living, self-determining subject: for 'the living Substance', as Hegel puts it, 'is being which is in truth *Subject*'[10] (in 'Spinozism', on the other hand, 'God is determined only as *substance*, and not as subject and spirit').[11]

To return now to our proposal regarding Debord's apparent re-working of Hegel's ideas: the general shape and structure of Debord's theory, we have claimed, seems tantamount to re-casting the Absolute as the power and potential of historical praxis. The points made here should serve to strengthen that claim. Hegel's Absolute echoes Debord's views on praxis, insofar as it too is a condition of constant, subjective, self-determinate movement. Debord in fact made explicit reference to Hegel's indications that 'becoming is the truth of being',[12] and as we will see below, his ideas indicate that the true nature of human existence lies in its processual, self-determinate and self-constitutive character.

According to Hegel, the subjective, self-determinate movement of the Absolute is animated by the nature of its own inherent rationale. This is characterised by a developmental pattern: a pattern that typically takes the form of a pro-

---

6 Hegel 1996, p. 508.
7 Debord quoted this comment in his archived reading notes on Hegel, writing in the margin: 'here one should replace Sp[inoza] with Marx, and philo[sophy] with [historical, revolutionary] thought ...' (Bibliothèque nationale, NAF28603; Notes de lecture; Hegel, dossier 1; *Histoire de la philosophie*; the note was written before 1964). In other words, just as Spinoza, for Hegel, was a foundational moment for modern philosophy, so too was Marx for modern revolutionary thought.
8 Hegel 2004, p. 9, italics in the original.
9 As Hegel puts it in the *Phenomenology*: 'of the Absolute it must be said that it is essentially a result, that only in the end is it what it truly is; and that precisely in this consists its nature, viz. to be actual, subject, the spontaneous becoming of itself' (Hegel 1977, p. 11).
10 Hegel 1977, p. 10, italics in the original.
11 Hegel 1991, p. 8.
12 Debord 2004a, p. 45.

cess in which something becomes other to itself in order to become more fully and completely itself. This tripartite movement, which is commonly reduced to the 'thesis-antithesis-synthesis' schema of popular legend, can be illustrated by way of reference to the circular pattern of the Hegelian system as a whole. Logic, the basic structure of being (described by Hegel as 'the exposition of God as he is in his eternal essence before the creation of nature and a finite mind'),[13] is detailed in the first part of the system. Logic then externalises and expresses itself into physical reality and nature. Nature gives rise to Spirit (i.e. to collective human consciousness, agency and self-awareness), which develops, through history, until it becomes capable of grasping the reason that founds its world. Human history thus comprises the closing moments of a circular process that originates in the timeless abstractions of logic, and which ultimately renders the philosophy that grasps that logic tantamount to the self-consciousness of God;[14] albeit a quasi-pantheistic 'god', whose 'manifestations' as 'nature and as spirit', to quote one of Hegel's many religious allusions, constitute 'temples which he fills, and in which he is present'.[15]

The processual, self-determinate movement of the Absolute, and thus that of the grand, circular pattern described here, is driven by what Hegel refers to as the Concept (*Begriff*). The Concept, as McCarney aptly puts it, is the 'cosmic mainspring'[16] of Hegel's metaphysics: being's dialectical 'life pulse'.[17] Its operation, which is associated with negativity and constant change, generates the processual movement described above. Its development affords the full expression of what Hegel termed the 'Idea' (*Idee*), which can be thought of, simplistically, as being's 'developmental plan':[18] a 'plan' that the Concept progressively actualises, and which achieves full realisation when Hegel's absolute Subject returns to itself at its highest level. This is only possible once Spirit has shaped the objective world into a condition of explicit accordance with the intrinsic rationale that subtends it, and once it has also grasped its own true nature through philosophy. This resolution thus affords a fully explicit, self-conscious unity between the reason that founds existence on the one hand, and a reality that fully expresses and comprehends that reason on the other. The full

---

13 Hegel 1969, p. 50.
14 As Hyppolite puts it: 'logic', i.e. the logic grasped by Spirit, is 'the absolute's thought of itself' (Hyppolite 1974, p. 583).
15 Quoted in McCarney 2000, p. 50.
16 McCarney 2000, p. 53.
17 Hegel 1969, p. 37.
18 Wartenburg 1993, pp. 108–9.

actualisation of the Idea is thus described as the '*Subject-Object ...* the *unity of the ideal and the real, of the finite and the infinite, of the soul and the body*'.[19]

The Concept and the Idea are thus aspects of the Absolute: its self-motivating process, and its self-identical goal. How then do they relate to the refiguration of the Absolute that we have ascribed to Debord?

As we have already seen, the real unity of subject and object, in Debord's view, is to be found in historical praxis: in the mutually transformative unity of subjective thought and objective activity. Debord and the SI associated this condition with the communism that would supersede spectacular separation; a communism that would amount, in effect, to a condition of perpetual, ludic and self-determinate historical praxis. Debord's basically Hegelian theoretical model can thus be seen to re-cast the Idea, or at least the latter's full expression, as that condition of communist praxis. This would be a condition wherein the universality of society's collective powers and abilities become one with the life activity of the particular individuals from whom that power derives. Likewise, where Hegel had ultimately associated the dynamic, dialectical movement of the Hegelian Concept with the self-movement of the Absolute, Debord appears to associate that negative, processual movement with the similarly dynamic and self-determinant operation of the human subject within time (e.g. through action in time, the human subject 'realises himself while losing himself, becomes other in order to become truly himself [*pour devenir la vérité de lui-même*]').[20]

How do these ideas relate to Hegel's notorious notion of historical conclusion? In order to answer that question, it is important to note that for Hegel, the complete actualisation of the Idea would *not* entail a static conclusion. Instead, it was envisaged in a manner that seems much closer to a condition of full maturation, ripening, or flourishing. Indeed, and surprising though it may seem, the fateful phrase 'the end of history' appears in Hegel's work only once (and even then, it only functions as part of a metaphor).[21] Contrary to popular belief, Hegel did not preclude the possibility of significant future changes and events on a world-historical level,[22] and nor did he rule out the possibility that

---

19 Hegel 1991, p. 288, italics in the original.
20 Debord 1995, pp. 115–16, translation altered; 2006b, p. 835, italics in the original.
21 In *The Philosophy of History* – a work that he did not write directly, but which was instead compiled posthumously from his own and his students' lecture notes – Hegel remarks that like the movement of the sun, 'The History of the World travels from East to West, for Europe is absolutely the end of History, Asia the beginning' (Hegel 2004, p. 103).
22 The 'Spiritual principle', according to his *Lectures on the Philosophy of World History*, can 'become truly congruent with external reality' only after 'it has gained its objective (i.e.

future philosophers and societies might develop more adequate and sophisticated expressions of the principles that he purported to have grasped.[23] This is because upon reaching the apex of its ascent, Spirit does not stop, but rather comprehends and aligns itself with the reason that founds its world. This does not bring the movement of the Concept to a halt: instead, the latter's 'life-pulse' continues to drive the generation of difference and identity, just as the 'Infinite Power' of the Absolute continues to express itself into the moments of creation and destruction that form existent reality.[24]

However – and perhaps largely as a result of the enormous influence in France of Alexandre Kojève's emphasis on Hegel's supposed historical end – Debord did indeed criticise Hegel for having brought history to a close. In addition, his comments also imply a reading of Hegel wherein human history is seen as a mere moment of the operation of Hegel's grand, cosmic Subject. Seen in such terms, human history simply becomes the vehicle for the Absolute's drive towards self-comprehension and full expression. These views appear to have led Debord to the following position: if the circular movement of Hegel's great Subject is concluded – and Debord does indeed take Hegel to have declared such a conclusion[25] – then Hegel's philosophy can be read as having heralded the completion of the point and purpose of human history.

---

intellectual) form' (Hegel 1975a, p. 208). Hegel, it seems, viewed himself as being stationed at a point in history where that 'principle' could indeed be identified intellectually, but at which it still needed to be rendered fully 'congruent' with the world. *The Philosophy of Right* claims that 'the unity of the divine and the human' is a principle 'charged upon the Germanic nations to bring to completion' (Hegel 2005, p. 204), and contends that 'the future is not absolute but remains exposed to accidents' (Hegel 2005, p. 54). *The Philosophy of History* famously describes America as the 'land of the future' (Hegel 2004, p. 86). See also *The Encyclopaedia Logic* for related comments (Hegel 1991, pp. 29–30).

23 Hegel wished, for example, that he could have revised *The Science of Logic* 'seven and seventy times' (Hegel 1969, p. 42).

24 Hegel writes in *The Encyclopaedia Logic* that 'the final purpose of the world is just as much accomplished as it is eternally accomplishing itself' (Hegel 1991, p. 302), and in *The Philosophy of Nature* that 'The world is created, is now being created, and has eternally been created' (Hegel 1970, p. 15). 'Eternity', in this sense, refers to the inherence of the Absolute, both before and after the attainment of the Idea, within every moment of existence (McCarney 2000, p. 52). It might also be added that Hegel depicts the actualisation of the Concept as a task that must be continually actualised. As Fackenheim (1996, p. 49) has pointed out, the actualisation of reason in the world, once achieved, is not a permanent condition; and as Harris (1995, p. 107) puts it, 'there is nothing in [Hegel's] logical theory to warrant the belief that the motion of consciousness must always be progressive'. We can, in short, regress.

25 Hegel's 'paradox' is that his philosophy 'subordinates the meaning of all reality to its

No doubt, this does Hegel a disservice. It should also be added that the outline of Hegel's views presented above is certainly questionable: as some commentators have stressed, the Hegelian Absolute is not 'an all-powerful puppet master governing history and using human beings as the vehicle for its schemes', and the presence of such an entity in Hegel's work arguably exists 'only in the minds of [Hegel's] critics'.[26] Yet if our description of Hegel's philosophy is to assist the interpretation of Debord's views, then Hegel needs to be presented in this light, for the simple reason that Debord was just such a critic (for example, he criticises Hegel for having described the operation of a 'supreme external agent').[27] This appears to have led him to take the following views.

For Debord, Hegel had made a huge advance over the philosophy of the past, because he had seen the world not as an immediate, 'given' object, or as immutable or fixed, but rather as the product of human history. Furthermore, Hegel had developed a mode of thought capable of grasping historical movement and process (i.e. the 'living', moving flux of Hegelian dialectics). With a nod towards Marx's theses on Feuerbach, *The Society of the Spectacle* thus contends that Hegel had gone some way beyond philosophy's tendency to contemplate and interpret the world, because he had attempted to think the world's historical transformation.[28] However, Debord also believed that Hegel's thought was profoundly limited, as it ultimately did no more than *interpret* the world's transformation. Hegel had arrived at a perspective that allowed him to see the world as a historical result, but he understood it, according to Debord's apparent interpretation, as the result of a 'divine'[29] rationale, the purportedly final resolution of which effectively effaced the need to engage in the construction of the future. Consequently, Hegel's depictions of subject-object unity, processual transformative movement, and of superseded alienation, had all intimated, and had nearly grasped, some of the real aspects of concrete historical activity; yet ultimately, they had done so only within the realms of philosophy. Hegel could thus be seen to have presented a grand *Vorstellung*, to use his own terms, of that activity. His conceptual image of a concluded process of historical transformation needed to be translated into reality, and realised as a process of constructing the future. It therefore seems possible to claim, on that basis, that

historical conclusion, whilst at the same time revealing this meaning by proclaiming itself to be that culmination' (Debord 1995, p. 49; 2006b, p. 793).
26 Houlgate 2005, p. 24.
27 Debord 1995, p. 51; 2006b, p. 795.
28 Debord 1995, p. 49; 2006b, p. 793.
29 Hegel 1991, p. 147.

the general structure of Debord's Hegelian Marxism involves the re-figuration of the motifs that we described above.

In short, the Hegelian Absolute, when viewed from the perspective outlined here, could be seen as an inadvertent representation of the historical praxis that needed to be actualised through revolution, and thus as a projection of human attributes onto the clouds of absolute idealism. In a manner that echoes Feuerbach's critique of religion – and which thus also accords with the interpretation of the concept of spectacle that we will develop below – Debord's critique of Hegelian thought attempts to overcome that fetishistic separation by re-phrasing some of the key shapes and structures of that philosophy as dimensions of the historical praxis that he advocated.

(It may be useful to point out that this does not entail casting Debord as having simply adopted Hegel's peculiar metaphysical cosmology: he in fact explicitly states in a letter of 1969 that 'we do not pose the question of [revolutionary] organisation on a metaphysical terrain'.[30] Debord is only concerned with human history, and seems to view dialectical thought as applying to human history alone. He does not, in other words, seem to have subscribed to an Engelsian dialectics of nature.)[31]

The claims that have been introduced here will be developed in greater detail later, but they should suffice to set out of the basic structure of the

---

30 Debord 2004a, p. 52.
31 Debord rejected the '"ideologisation"' conducted upon Marxism by 'the bad work of old Engels' (Debord 2004a, p. 64). Engels's late work sought to validate Marxism as science by casting science itself as dialectics (see in particular his *Anti-Dühring* and *Dialectics of Nature* (Engels 1987)). From such a position, one could claim that the ascendancy of the so-called workers' states was as 'natural' and inevitable as that of the stars in the sky. Stalin endorsed 'dialectical materialism' as 'the world outlook of the Marxist-Leninist party' (Stalin 1976). The evidence to suggest that Debord subscribed to a dialectics of nature is very sparse, and is in fact largely reducible to a peculiar remark made in a letter of 1986 that was not included in Debord's published correspondence (but which has been made available online at Bill Brown's Not Bored! website). The letter describes the nineteenth-century German physician Christian Hahnemann as 'resembl[ing] a Hegelian dialectician by conceiving of homeopathy' (Debord 1986). This is, however, hardly evidence for a dialectics of nature. Somewhat stronger ground can be found in a text of 1966, in which the SI wrote that they sought to see things from 'the standpoint of the dialectical reasoning inherent in all living reality, all Praxis' (SI 1997, p. 447). The latter statement could be taken to indicate that dialectics can be found in natural reality, as well as in praxis. It could, however, also be argued that the phrase really means that praxis is *itself* 'all living reality': a point that would accord with the positions developed in this book. Either way, Debord certainly held that human history possessed a dialectical character.

essentially Hegelian conceptions of history and alienated agency that support Debord's theoretical work. Having now outlined these ideas, we can begin to look at some of the aspects of that general framework in a little more detail, by taking up the five components thereof that we listed at the start of this chapter.

These five elements (which by no means exhaust the ideas and assumptions that inform Debord's work) can all be inferred from a consideration of his views on history and spectacle. They are as follows: 1) The implicit philosophical anthropology that can be found in Debord's comments on time and history; 2) the historical narrative that informs his political claims; 3) the broadly ethical themes implied by the concept of spectacle; 4) the aesthetic dimensions of Debord's political thought; 5) his identification of dialectics with strategic praxis. We will start with his notions of temporality and subjectivity.

1) Philosophical Anthropology

Time and temporality are central to Debord's thought, and to his conception of the Situationist project. Situationist praxis was to entail a form of self-determinate control over one's own lived time; conversely, the concept of spectacle describes the denial of such an autonomous temporality, as spectacular society 'separates the subject ... from his own time'[32] by replacing a potentially free, self-determinate and thus 'directly lived' existence with the latter's alienated 'representation'.[33] This is why Debord describes modern, spectacular society as suffering from a 'paralysed history', and from an 'abandonment of any history founded in historical time'.[34]

Debord holds that humanity's experience of time, and thus its conception of history, is socially mediated. In his view, different social structures engender different temporalities. The 'historical time' referred to in the previous quotation is one such mode of temporality. Debord does not define it, but his statements indicate that he characterised it as a form of temporality marked by a distinct awareness of historical change, and thus of the transformative events, actions and experiences that take place within such time. Debord claims that a deeper awareness of historical time was spread throughout society by the rise of modern, industrial society; that 'the victory of the bourgeoisie', i.e. the emergence of the social structures that followed the bourgeois revolutions, was also 'the

---

32   Debord 1995, p. 116; 2006b, p. 835.
33   Debord 1995, p. 12; 2006b, p. 766.
34   Debord 1995, p. 114; 2006b, p. 834.

victory of a *profoundly historical* time.'³⁵ Yet whilst the emergence of capitalist society fostered an awareness of such a time, capitalism itself, via its regulation and domination of lived experience, also resulted in the increasing separation of social agents from any direct, conscious control over this newly historical world. For Debord, 'the bourgeoisie unveiled historical time and imposed it on society only to deprive society of its *use*'³⁶ (this bears direct relation to Debord's view that Hegel's philosophy encapsulated both the possibilities and limitations of that new bourgeois order: for whilst Hegel had grasped the import of historical change, he had also presented history as a mere object of detached contemplation).

Consequently, for Debord, the real stakes of the modern revolutionary project lay in taking command of historical time, and in thereby shaping and determining it freely and self-consciously. Thus, for Debord, 'historical time' is both the 'milieu and goal of the proletarian revolution'.³⁷ This is because what is ultimately required, in his view, is the supersession of this alienation, and the creation of a direct, free, self-determinate relation to lived time.

All of these claims are clearly premised on the view that human subjects can become separated from their own lived time. Following the young Marx, who greatly informed his claims in this regard, Debord holds that human agents can become alienated from their own actions. This occurs when those actions are dictated by an 'external' power (e.g. that of capital), which entails that the results of those actions become 'other' to the individual concerned. As indicated, Debord's chief contention is that modern society has become fundamentally characterised by just such a condition of separation. Highlighting the conception of temporality that this involves may go some way towards undermining the crude essentialism that is often attributed to his work.

Debord seems to have viewed the human subject as an inherently mutable, processual being: as an entity that shapes itself through shaping its world. In this regard, his work displays a peculiarly French, mid-century confluence of Hegelian Marxism with the legacy and ambience of Sartrean existentialism. His texts and films display a preoccupation with the conduct of experience and self-constitutive action in time, and the manner in which these concerns are articulated seem greatly informed by French Hegelianism's characteristically existential focus on self-determinate action, time and negativity.³⁸ For

---

35 Debord 1995, p. 104; 2006b, p. 828.
36 Debord 1995, p. 105; 2006b, p. 829, emphasis in the original.
37 Debord 2004a, p. 79.
38 For useful commentaries on French Hegelianism, see: Baugh 2003; Kelly 1992; Butler 1999.

example: he states in *The Society of the Spectacle*, by way of an unattributed[39] quotation from Hegel's *Phenomenology*, that, 'Man – that "negative being who *is* solely to the extent that he abolishes being" – is one [*identique*] with time'.[40] It seems clear that any such identification of the human subject with the flow of time, and thus with negativity and change, must preclude a politics based upon the actualisation of a fixed, essential human nature.[41] So too must it rule out any appeal to a lost, original realm of authenticity (*contra* the claims of some commentators, Debord by no means 'postulates a golden age, a humanity originally transparent to itself').[42] If the human subject is indeed 'one with time', then there can be no fixed human nature at all. Instead, and as is also the case for the young Marx, human beings are simply held to possess an intrinsic ability to create and undergo historical change (Debord in fact refers to the 'self-creation of human nature').[43] Any notion of authenticity invoked in Debord's work can therefore only pertain to the full, free actualisation of that open capacity.

We have already used the term 'subject' several times in the course of these explanations. This could be deemed questionable, given that Debord's views are certainly close, in some respects, to the contemporary Marxian contention that the only *real* subject within modern society is the 'automatic subject'[44] of capitalist value.[45] In fact, Debord rarely used the term 'subject', and although he was by no means consistent in this regard,[46] he typically reserved it for references to a post-spectacular existence (e.g. 'The subject can emerge only from society, namely from the struggle within society. The subject's possible existence depends on the outcome of the class struggle').[47] We will, however, continue to use the term throughout this book, simply because his work appears to rely upon the non-essentialist, young-Marxian and quasi-Sartrean notion

---

39 The quoted phrase is taken from Hyppolite's translation of the *Phenomenology*. Thanks are due to John McHale for this reference.
40 Debord 1995, p. 92; 2006b, p. 820.
41 'The pseudo-need imposed by modern consumption clearly cannot be opposed by any genuine need or desire which is not itself shaped by society and its history' (Debord 1995, p. 44, translation altered; 2006b, p. 789).
42 Kaufmann 2006, p. 222.
43 Debord 1995, p. 95, translation altered; 2006b, p. 822.
44 Marx 1990, p. 255.
45 For a particularly clear expression of this concern, see Jappe 2015.
46 See, for example, thesis #161 of *The Society of the Spectacle*: 'a society which radically severs the subject from the activity that it steals from him separates him in the first place from his own time' (Debord 1995, p. 116; 2006b, p. 835).
47 Debord 1995, p. 34; 2006b, p. 782.

of 'subjectivity' that we have outlined here. This conception of subjectivity presents human beings as historical, self-constitutive creatures, capable of shaping both themselves and their world through time.

This conception of the human subject also bears relation to the model of Debord's use of Hegel that we set out at the start of this chapter. Like the Hegelian Concept, this human subject is engaged in a process of constant, negative, transformative movement. Because this subject is both 'negative' and 'one with time', it follows that if Debord and the SI's mode of subject-object unity were to be attained, then it could not take the form of a fixed, immutable state of affairs. Instead – and much like the full expression of the Hegelian Idea – it would constitute a condition of constant process: a unity of thought and world wherein both are continually transformed through self-determinate historical action. What we find here, therefore, is something very close to the condition implied by the *German Ideology*'s famous description of communism as 'the real movement that abolishes [*aufhebt*] the present state of things':[48] a line that *The Society of the Spectacle* links, notably, to the movement of a self-conscious history, and indeed to the dissolution of 'all separation'.[49]

Consequently, the condition of subject-object unity implied by Debord's work should not be seen as a Kojèveian 'end of history'. Instead, it resembles and develops Marx's gestures towards the end of *pre*-history[50] (a phrase that Debord and the SI readily appropriated),[51] insofar as this condition would constitute the emergence of a new, genuinely free, self-conscious and self-determinate form of collective temporal existence.

In order to develop that contention, we need to say a little more about the notion of history that can be found in Debord's work. This then brings us to the second item on our list.

---

48 Marx and Engels 2007, pp. 56–7.
49 Debord 1995, p. 48; 2006b, p. 792; see also 2006b, p. 866.
50 In the preface to his *A Contribution to the Critique of Political Economy*, Marx wrote: 'With that social formation [capitalism] the pre-history of human society draws to a close' (Marx 2009, p. 161). See also volume 3 of *Capital*, where capitalism is described as 'that epoch of human history that directly precedes the conscious reconstruction of human society' (Marx 1991, p. 182).
51 See, for example, Debord 2004a, p. 54.

2) Philosophy of History

There are a number of points to be made here, and we will therefore break this section down into four sub-sections. We will look at: a) the narrative of historical development that can be found in Debord's work; b) Debord's indications that the modern society of the spectacle arose from earlier, similar social formations; c) the degree to which these ideas involve teleology; d) the ways in which these three issues pertain to Debord's Hegelian Marxism.

a)   *Spectacular Society as a Historical Crux*

The Society of the Spectacle contains no less than two, seldom-discussed chapters on time and temporality. These chapters describe a historical narrative which claims that humanity's power to shape its own history has grown in tandem with that power's estrangement from its producers. Humanity's capacity to shape its existence is presented as having been augmented and expanded through a succession of technical innovations and social and economic forms; yet the development of these forms is said to have led to that capacity's increased alienation. At the apex of this line of development we find modern society, the society of the spectacle: a society in which humanity's power to shape its world is greater than ever before, yet also further removed than at any other time in the past.

Debord's narrative begins with the 'cyclical time' of early agrarian societies, which were shaped by the pattern of the seasons. He then goes on to describe the slow emergence of linear, 'irreversible' time, referring to China, Egypt, the Greeks, the Middle Ages and the Renaissance, and to the rise of the bourgeoisie. With the emergence of social classes in these early agrarian societies, he claims, 'the social appropriation of time'[52] became possible. The nobility possessed the use of this society's time, and could employ it in a manner that 'stood apart' from the temporality that characterised 'the repetitive form of production' located at 'the basis of social life'.[53] Debord describes this privileged use of time as the 'squandering of *a historical time at society's surface*'.[54] This is because the history enabled by these social structures remained the sole preserve of the nobility: a history of wars, feuds and lineages.[55] However, Debord also holds

---

52   Debord 1995, p. 93; 2006b, p. 821.
53   Debord 1995, p. 94; 2006b, p. 821.
54   Debord 1995, p. 94, translation altered; 2006b, pp. 821–2, italics in the original.
55   'This was the time of adventure, of war, the time in which the lords of cyclical society pursued their personal histories'; yet for 'ordinary men', history 'sprang forth as an alien factor' (Debord 1995, p. 94; 2006b, pp. 821–2). Yet all such 'ordinary men' remained entirely

that as society developed, historical time became far more diffused throughout the fabric of society. As noted earlier, he associates the general emergence of historical time 'with the long revolutionary period ushered in by the rise of the bourgeoisie'.[56] This is because the growth of capitalist society entailed a new mode of 'economic production that continuously transforms society from top to bottom'.[57] The problem, however, is that whilst historical change was thus rendered all the more present and apparent, it also became even further removed from its producers.

This is because the time of capitalism is characterised by time as measure, and thus by time as a mode of domination (Debord is of course drawing on Marxian value theory here). In consequence, its penetration into lived experience, as engendered by capitalist social relations, entailed the latter's regulation and domination. Paradoxically, therefore, despite history's increasing proximity to everyday existence, the possibility of governing and shaping that existence became all the more distant. With the rise of capitalism, historical time had become increasingly present and prominent, and yet the possibility of a 'directly lived'[58] relation to that time had become increasingly removed from common reality.

According to Debord, this paradoxical tendency towards an increased sense of historical time on the one hand, and towards the deprivation of its use on the other, had reached a contradictory extreme within contemporary society. According to *The Society of the Spectacle*, every aspect of human life had come to be shaped and coloured by humanity's own economic constructs. The social world, and the subjective experience thereof, was now constructed by human actions to a far greater extent than at any other time in the past. Yet by the same token, society's complete subordination to the requirements of capital had meant that control over this vastly increased capacity had also become ever more distant.

Debord's narrative, therefore, presents his own society as constituting a grand, world-historical crux, insofar as the contradictory extremes that characterised it – the extreme expansion of humanity's historical agency, and the

---

       capable of governing their own destinies, even though the awareness and opportunity to do so was seldom fully formed. One might think here of the following lines from Shakespeare's *Julius Caesar*, which Debord referenced in a letter of 1974: 'Men at some time are masters of their fates: The fault, dear Brutus, is not in our stars, but in ourselves, that we are underlings' (quoted, in part, in Debord 2005, p. 195).

56   Debord 1995, p. 48; 2006b, p. 793.
57   Debord 1995, p. 104; 2006b, p. 828.
58   Debord 1995, p. 12; 2006b, p. 766.

equally extreme alienation of that agency – had forcibly imposed a demand for the reclamation and actualisation of this power. Historical time would now be not only the *site*, but also the *stakes* of political struggle.

These ideas also entail a strong sense in which Debord's historical moment had afforded the emergence of a 'higher' communist project than those of the past. A classical working class would always remain in the forefront of the SI's analyses, for reasons that we will address in Chapter 10. However, the modern proletariat, in their view, was not just composed of all those who had been separated from the means of independently *maintaining* their existence, as in Marx, but rather of all those who had been separated from the means of *directing* their existence, and thus from mastering their own lived time. As this corresponded to virtually everyone within modern society, the demand for revolution was held to have broken the class divide, and was no longer bound to industrial struggles within the workplace (indeed, this 'new proletariat' was 'tending to encompass virtually everybody [*tout le monde*]').[59] The possibility had thus arisen, within the modern period, for a transformative break with the classical workers' movement of the past, and for a new, far more total and expansive communist project, aimed at nothing less than the reclamation of life itself.

The scope and scale of this project owes much to the SI's avant-garde roots, and thereby to Surrealism's own, earlier interest in combing art with social revolution (as Breton put it: 'Marx said "Change the world", Rimbaud said "Change life": for us these two watchwords are one').[60] However, as regards our current concerns, the point that needs to be stressed here is simply this: the modern revolution, in demanding the resolution of the existential impoverishment of modern life, was held to have revealed the real core of all previous revolutionary struggles. In largely alleviating the material poverty of the past, contemporary capitalism had clarified and brought to the fore a demand for self-determinacy that had been implicit throughout the struggles of the past. As Debord put it: 'The very development of class society to the stage of the spectacular organisation of non-life leads the revolutionary project to become *visibly* what it always was *essentially*';[61] for 'In the demand to *live* the historical time that it creates, the proletariat finds the simple unforgettable core of its revolutionary project'.[62]

---

59   SI 2006, p. 111; 1997, p. 253.
60   Quoted by Trebitsch in Lefebvre 2008a, p. xx.
61   Debord 1995, pp. 89–90; 2006b, p. 819.
62   Debord 1995, p. 106; 2006b, p. 829.

To sum up: by the middle of the twentieth century, 'man', according to Debord, though 'separated from his product,' had become 'more and more, and ever more powerfully, the producer of every detail of his world'; and yet at the same time, 'the closer his life comes to being his own creation, the more drastically he is cut off from that life'.[63] This contradictory crux was seen to have engendered a revolutionary demand for nothing less than 'life' itself. The modern revolution, therefore, promised the potential flourishing of the temporal subject described above.

b) The Roots of the Society of the Spectacle

These observations bring us to a further set of issues. As we have just seen, the revolutionary demands proper to modern society were situated at the apex of a long line of historical development. The contemporary society of the spectacle had rendered explicit a problematic that had been implicit throughout the social formations and struggles of the past. Earlier insurrectionary moments were thus framed, retrospectively, as relatively unconscious gestures towards the condition of full self-determinacy that could now be realised within Debord and the SI's present,[64] insofar as that 'present moment' was seen as an instance wherein 'the revolution discovers its task in the general and direct realisation of all historical life'.[65]

This then gives rise to the following implication. The problematic expressed and foregrounded by modern society cannot be reductively identified with modern society, because it has inhered throughout the social formations of the past. By extension, it could arise again within the future. Or, to put this more explicitly: spectacle, understood as the problematic of separation described here, cannot be reductively identified with capitalism, even though the latter certainly instantiates the former. Even if capitalism were to be overthrown, some new form of spectacular separation could emerge.

---

63   Debord 1995, p. 24; 2006b, p. 775.
64   One might think here, for example, of Debord's views on the Paris Commune and medieval millenarianism. As regards the Commune, the SI wrote as follows: 'Underlying the events ... one can see the insurgents' feeling that they had become the masters of their own history ...' (SI 2006, p. 398; Debord 2006b, p. 628). As regards millenarianism, Debord wrote that 'millenarianism, the expression of a revolutionary class speaking the language of religion for the last time, was already a modern revolutionary tendency, lacking [insofar as it was still religious, and thus still posited a heavenly beyond] only the consciousness of being *historical and nothing more*' (Debord 1995, p. 102; 2006b, p. 827, italics in the original).
65   Debord 2004a, p. 44.

This may seem a rather odd claim, given Debord's explicit identification of the spectacle with capitalist society. However, it is the only explanation that can fully accommodate the textual evidence.

Debord consistently dated the spectacle's emergence to the early decades of the twentieth century. The dates and events that he employed as evidence and as illustrations for its emergence shift a little within his writings, but all are located around the 1920s (we will look at these dates in greater detail in Chapter 4). Yet when identifying such markers, Debord was not contending that the modern spectacle simply sprang into existence *ex nihilo*. Instead, its emergence was seen as the full, complete expression of a much older historical tendency. For example, in a letter of 1971, Debord writes as follows:

> [The spectacle] has its basis in Greek thought; it increased towards the Renaissance (with capitalist thought); and still more in the 18th century, when one opened museum collections to the public; it appeared under its completed form around 1914–1920 (with the propaganda [*bourrage de crâne*][66] of the war and the collapse of the workers' movement).[67]

Surprising though these statements may seem, one need not trawl through Debord's letters in order to find evidence for these views. For example, he states explicitly in *The Society of the Spectacle* that 'power draped itself in the outward garb of a mythical order from the beginning'; that 'all separate power has been spectacular';[68] and that 'at the root of the spectacle lies the oldest of all social specialisations, the specialisation of power'.[69]

The modern spectacle, therefore, was seen as the contemporary, revealed face of a much older problematic. This is why Debord's concept of spectacle subsumes older critical categories, re-casting them in the light of the new, clearly revealed revolutionary context of his present. For example, in a letter of 1969, Debord explains that the concept of spectacle denotes the 'present face' of the phenomena named by the terms 'culture', 'capital', 'ideology', etc.; for although such concepts were crucial to the analysis of older social formations, and were still important, they now needed to be re-cast under the rubric of spectacle:

---

66   This term was used by French soldiers to denote the patriotic propaganda to which they were subjected.
67   Debord 2004a, pp. 455–6.
68   Debord 1995, p. 20; 2006b, p. 772.
69   Debord 1995, p. 18; 2006b, p. 771.

> ... it seems to me that the spectacle is *currently* much 'larger' than *culture* ... Overall, the spectacle contains an essential and *dominant* part of social life: it is a *historical moment* of society. By contrast, in the totality of past historical development, culture, which is much older, occupied a greater place than the spectacle. One can also say that the commodity and capitalism are 'larger' realities and concepts that come from much further in the past, and have more fundamentally produced the current world: but it is now *the hour* of the spectacle, which is the *present* face of these realities (thus, in the same movement, one also recognises the present moment as that of the struggle against the spectacle; the moment at which the revolution discovers its task in the general and direct realisation of all historical life).[70]

Modern society was thus seen as a juncture at which human history might become fully and actively self-conscious: as a point at which the implicit content of earlier social formations could be recognised and addressed. This is underscored in the following quotation, which is taken from the same letter. Contending that ideology emerged from myth, and that differing ideologies have now come to be fused together in the dissonant homogeneity of spectacular society, Debord writes that the latter expresses the inner core of its antecedents:

> One can make an analogy with the place of *ideology*. Ideology is older than the spectacle ... Today, ideology has become essentially spectacular: which it has not always been. Ideology is itself historically quite young in comparison to the immensity of the mythic-religious past. ... Of course, one can discover the germs of the spectacle in original ideology. And, moreover, the germs of ideology in the religion of 'cyclical' myth. These discoveries are effectively true in the sense that history existed and that, where there is history, 'becoming is the truth of being.' The most developed shows the origin in another light [*sous un autre jour*], which is *finally* its true light.[71]

The modern society of the spectacle, therefore, 'finally' reveals the implicit content of those earlier social forms, because it forcibly engenders an awareness of their inherent dynamic.

---

70 Debord 2004a, p. 44.
71 Debord 2004a, pp. 44–5.

c)   *Teleology*
Clearly, the historical narrative described above seems teleological. So too does Debord's conception of his relation to his own philosophical and theoretical antecedents.

In a letter of 1962, and whilst discussing the need to recover the 'lost history' of the revolutionary past, Debord wrote as follows. Genuine 'comprehension of the highest moments attained' via the struggles of the past only really resides within 'an action of a new, more developed and more complex type': for 'in the light of this action', he continues, 'one easily recognises the "grains of truth"' that lie within the 'errors' of the past.[72] The exigencies of the present, in other words, which foster new revolutionary actions, reveal both the merits and deficiencies of those of the past (and Debord immediately adds that the term 'action' should be seen to encompass 'the theory of this action').[73] This perspective, which can be readily identified throughout Debord's mature work,[74] pertains not only to the evaluation of previous struggles, but also to his work's relation to its own conceptual predecessors.

Debord tended to position his work as a development and clarification of both that of Hegel and Marx: a development in which the real core of their thought is drawn out and foregrounded due to the nature of Debord's historical moment. The line of development that this implies can be sketched as follows. Hegel, in Debord's view, glimpsed some of the key features of human historical existence, but he confused the latter with the operation of a quasi-divine Absolute. The Young Hegelians then helped to bring Hegel's insights down to earth; the young Marx completed that task with his call for the realisation of philosophy in praxis. Yet Marx's subsequent thinking was muddied, in Debord's view, by his 'scientific' preoccupation with economic 'laws', which fostered the Second International's economic determinism. For Debord and the SI, however, contemporary capitalism had utterly invalidated any sense in which revolutionary agency could be left to the putatively self-destructive mechanics of the economy. So too had the failings of the so-called workers' states invalidated any abdication of such agency to representative leaders. Stripped of the errors of external determinism and political representation, the real core of the revolutionary project now stood revealed as a drive towards the non-alienated command of historical agency: as a demand, in other words, for a

---

72   Debord 2001a, p. 138.
73   Ibid.
74   It not only informs his comments on the history of the workers' movement in *The Society of the Spectacle*: in addition, it is also central to his numerous remarks on the evaluation of strategic theory (see, for example, Debord 1998, pp. 85–7, or Debord 2004b, pp. 3–5).

fully self-determinate life. As we have already indicated, Marx's early call for the realisation of philosophy in praxis had thus been radically expanded, so as to include the supersession of *all* forms of representative and contemplative detachment from lived historical time (e.g. art, culture, philosophy, technology, etc.; *all* of society's creative and critical capacities would now be collectively and consciously employed). Debord's historical moment had foregrounded the real stakes and content of the insights developed by his forebears. The 'grains of truth' contained within the Hegelian supersession of alienation, the Young Hegelian critique of detached abstractions and, of course, the young-Marxian drive towards praxis, now stood revealed and re-cast as the real core of the modern revolutionary project.

A similar notion of cumulative development can, of course, be found in the historical narrative described in the section above. It is, however, important to note that the teleological dimensions of Debord's work certainly do not imply any sense in which history may have been marked by an inevitable, fateful ascendance towards a pre-ordained outcome.

To treat history as an agent that stands over and above those who compose it, or to credit it with some kind of guiding force that steers the actions of those individuals, would be to replicate the problematic of spectacle. If Debord had adopted such a fatalistic view, his work would have made no real advance beyond the Second International economic determinists whom he criticised,[75] because it would still involve ascribing historical agency to an external force (i.e. to a putative historical fate). Therefore – and despite the rather grandiose phrases that Debord sometimes employs when referring to history – his position is in fact close to that of Marx and Engels in *The Holy Family*, who stressed that '*History* does *nothing*, it ... is not, as it were, a person apart, using man as a means to achieve *its own* aims; history is *nothing but* the activity of man pursuing his aims.'[76]

This is not to defend the teleological aspects of this account unreservedly. For example, elements of Debord's claims do indeed come close to echoing Hegel's own Western-centric understanding of human history (Sontag's famous ascription of a 'breath-taking provincialism'[77] to Debord's theory is unjust,[78]

---

75 See theses #96–7 of *The Society of the Spectacle*.
76 Marx and Engels 1936, p. 125.
77 Sontag 2003, p. 98.
78 One might think here, for example, of the SI's comments and essays on Algeria (e.g. 'The Class Struggles in Algeria' in *Internationale Situationniste* #10), China (e.g. 'The Explosion Point of Ideology in China' in *Internationale Situationniste* #11), the Arab-Israeli war and the Vietnam war (e.g. 'Two Local Wars' in *Internationale Situationniste* #11), and

but not entirely so).[79] It must, however, be defended from the assumption that it ascribes a supra-human agency to history. History, in Debord's work, is driven by nothing other than the interests and struggles of human agents[80] (and in this regard, his vision of history seems somewhat close to that of Kant).[81]

Czechoslovakia ('Reform and Counter-reform in the Bureaucratic Bloc' in *Internationale Situationniste* #12).

79   Although the SI were concerned with global struggles and events, one can find strong traces of the view that the 'developed' Western societies had brought the contradictions of the modern world to the fore, and that those societies would thus be decisive grounds for its contestation. In his 'Report on the Construction of Situations' of 1957, whilst discussing the negative development of art and culture towards the Situationists' concerns, Debord wrote: 'As for the productions of peoples who are still subject to cultural colonialism (often caused by economic oppression), even though they may be progressive in their own countries, they play a reactionary role in the advanced cultural centres' (SI 2006, p. 35; Debord 2006b, pp. 319–20). The 'advanced' centres, therefore, were held to stand at the forefront of world history, insofar as their contradictions revealed explicitly those that remained implicit within developing countries. The SI thus stated in 1962 that 'the revolutionary project must be realised in the industrially advanced countries' (SI 2006, p. 111; 1996, p. 253). In 1966, they wrote in their 'Address to Revolutionaries of Algeria and of All Countries' that 'The fundamental problem of underdevelopment must be resolved on a worldwide scale, beginning with the revolutionary overthrow of the irrational *overdevelopment* of productive forces in the framework of the various forms of rationalised capitalism. The revolutionary movements of the Third World can succeed only on the basis of a lucid contribution to global revolution'. Although the SI stated that 'Development must not be a race to catch up with capitalist reification', as 'The next revolutions *can find aid in the world only by attacking this world as a whole*', it remained the case that the essential nature and the stakes of that attack were held to have been brought to the fore by developments within the modern West. Consequently, 'modern Western poetry and art', together with 'the thought of the period of the supersession of philosophy (Hegel, Marx, Feuerbach)', needed to be united with 'the liberation struggles from the Mexico of 1910 to the Congo of today' (SI 2006, pp. 190–2; SI 1997, pp. 457–9, emphasis in the original). These points should, however, be tempered by noting statements such as the following: in 1963, in a letter to a correspondent, Debord acknowledged a 'central question: if the revolution is now, overall, to be reinvented, it must be admitted that the point about which we know the least, and which requires the most imagination, study, and without doubt experimentation, is surely that of the revolutionary movement in under-developed countries' (Debord 2001a, p. 256).

80   The comments presented here are indebted to Sean Sayers's forthcoming work on Marx and teleology, which was circulated and discussed at a meeting of the Marx and Philosophy Society in 2014 (Sayers 2014).

81   See Kant's 'Idea for a Universal History from a Cosmopolitan Point of View' (Kant 1963).

Debord does, however, certainly indicate that human agency has been transposed onto economic, ideological and political structures throughout the past. In previous societies, these structures have operated as if they were the real locus of historical agency. This is because the aims, interests and actions of individual actors have both responded to, and operated within, social frameworks that have been oriented towards the operation and perpetuation of such structures (religion, state, economy, crown, etc.). These particular ends and interests have, however, tended, often inadvertently, towards an increased mastery of nature, and thus towards an increased capacity to shape lived time. History can thus be seen by Debord as having developed, in the absence of any grand metaphysical Subject, towards the crux that he and the SI identified within their own historical moment: a juncture at which the power to shape history has grown to such an extent that history itself could become a conscious project, and at which that possibility could become an identifiable and potentially resolvable revolutionary demand. Debord can thus be taken to have adopted a posture close to that implied by Engels in *Anti-Dühring* (a text that Debord read and made archived notes on):

> Man's own social organisation, hitherto confronting him as a necessity imposed by nature and history, now becomes the result of his own free action. The extraneous objective forces that have hitherto governed history pass under the control of man himself. Only from that time will man himself, with full consciousness, make his own history ... [This] is humanity's leap from the kingdom of necessity to the kingdom of freedom.[82]

In Debord's account, entry into such a 'kingdom' entails achieving a condition that would accord with, and which would allow the full expression and fruition of, the historical and self-determinate nature of Debord's human subject.

d) *History and the Absolute*

The three subsections above have argued that Debord's account of history describes the emergence of a condition wherein human subjects might fully actualise their own inherently historical, self-determinate nature. He not only describes a specific *moment* of history; in addition, his understanding of that moment entails a reading of history *per se*. In this respect, as in many others, Debord echoes some of Lukács' claims in *History and Class Consciousness*.

---

82 Engels 1987, p. 270. The relevance of this quotation was indicated by Sean Sayers's forthcoming work on Marx and teleology (Sayers 2014).

For Lukács, the proletariat has been forced into a condition in which it must recognise itself as the author of its own history. This recognition affords the insight that society is mutable, that human history has been shaped by alienated human agency, and that the end of such alienation could afford the conscious construction of a better future. Debord makes much the same claim, and seems to hold that such an insight into the nature of history affords further insights into the nature of the human subjects that create history. Once human beings are seen as the authors of their world, they can be recognised as the historical, self-determinate creatures described above.

This certainly places Debord very close to Hegel. For example, the following description of Hegel's own views on history could easily apply to Debord: 'human beings have no fixed, given identity, but rather determine and produce their identity and their world in history, and ... gradually come to the recognition of this fact in history'.[83] The difference, however, is that for Hegel, this emerging awareness is driven by the progressive pursuit and actualisation of reason within the world, and reason, for Hegel, is the driving force of the Absolute. Human history is thereby seen as a mere moment of the Absolute. The actions and interactions of human subjects – the whole of history, with its contingencies, conflicts, struggles and disasters – serves as the final stage of the circular, self-determinate movement of the Hegelian Absolute on its passage towards self-consciousness and full expression. Yet where Hegel thus presents the collective human agency of Spirit as a moment of his philosophy's rationalist 'God', Debord's account describes human beings' realisation that *they are* 'God': there is no grand metaphysics, and no 'external agent'; there are only human beings and their actions.[84]

This, then, returns us to the interpretation of Debord's use of Hegel that we outlined earlier. Just as Feuerbach treated religion as the projection of human capacities onto an imaginary heaven, so Debord treats Hegelian philosophy as the projection of human characteristics onto the equally fictitious and 'divine'[85] Subject of the Absolute. The task faced by a Marxian reading of Hegel, therefore, would be to bring those qualities down to earth: to show that the only true Absolute is the collective agency of human subjects, and to demand the supersession of that agency's spectacular alienation.

---

83 Houlgate 2005, p. 17.
84 Debord does, however, indicate that Hegel came close to such a view: despite the philosophical and metaphysical trappings of his claims, Hegel, for Debord, was nonetheless 'already' able to grasp that 'what existed could only be the totality of the movement of history' (Debord 1995, p. 49; 2006b, p. 793).
85 Hegel 1991, p. 147.

3) Ethics

It seems apparent, then, that Debord understood the problematic of separated power expressed by the society of the spectacle to be much older than modern capitalism. Modern society is the fullest expression yet of a problematic that has been inherent in all previous societies, that is not reducible to modern society alone, and which could well arise in the future. After all, on the reading of Debord's work that we are developing here, that problematic would seem to be rooted in the social and historical nature of the human subject itself, because it derives from conditions wherein social individuals become separated from their own collective formative powers. Consequently, there is no guarantee that the end of capitalist society would resolve this problem, because some manifestation thereof may well arise in the future (or, as Debord put it, albeit in a slightly different context: 'wherever there is independent *representation*', the spectacle 'reconstitutes itself').[86] It seems possible to claim, therefore, that Debord's concept of spectacle not only demands the supersession of capitalist society, but that it also entails a continual opposition to *all* such forms of separation. It thus carries distinct implications as regards the modes of organisation and interaction that would be appropriate to an anti-spectacular politics.

This is why a distinction was made, in the previous chapter, between spectacle – i.e. the separation of social power, and the consequent alienation of historical agency – and the contemporary social formation held to have fully instantiated that problematic, i.e. modern capitalism. Throughout the rest of this book, the term 'spectacle' will be used to denote that problematic of separation, and the phrase 'the society of the spectacle' will be reserved for the social formation that had brought that problematic to its 'perfected [*achevée*]'[87] form. It is perhaps worth adding here that if spectacle is understood in this much more expansive manner, then not only does it become easier to make sense of Debord's indications that the roots of the spectacle reach back to antiquity: in addition, it also becomes considerably easier to accommodate all of the differing phenomena that Debord and the SI refer to as 'spectacular'. Such a reading can, for example, incorporate Debord's views on the mass media, modern culture, and his discussions of capitalist society; it can also accommodate his objections to Leninism and its apologists,[88] his numerous

---

86   Debord 1995, p. 17, translation altered; 2006b, p. 770, emphasis in the original.
87   Debord 1995, p. 11; 2006b, p. 766. '*Separation* is the alpha and the omega of the spectacle' (Debord 1995, p. 20; 2006b, p. 772).
88   Lukács, Debord writes, 'was an ideologist speaking for a power that was in the crudest way

critical descriptions of leaders and figureheads,[89] and indeed his concern, in the late 1960s, that the SI itself was growing dangerously spectacular.[90] All can be seen as instantiations of this same problematic of separated social power.[91] By extension, this reading can also help to explain Debord and the SI's view that an anti-spectacular project must embody its rejection of dogma, ideology and hierarchy within its own practical mode of organisation. As Debord put it, the modern revolutionary project cannot 'allow the conditions of division and hierarchy that obtain in the dominant society to be reproduced within itself';[92] to do otherwise would be to 'combat alienation by means of alienated forms of struggle'.[93] Spectacle, in other words, could not be allowed to arise within the revolutionary movement that would end spectacular society. Therefore – and as is no doubt already apparent – this interpretation of Debord's claims entails that the concept of spectacle must be seen to involve something akin to an *ethics*.

Such a contention invites obvious objections. Firstly, the identification of an ethics within this material could seem to contradict the SI's inherently anti-dogmatic stance. After all, the SI consistently described morality in terms of ideology, and Debord (indirectly) associated the rejection of moral norms with the communist project.[94] Furthermore, his concerns with autonomy owe a

---

    external to the proletarian movement, believing and giving his audience to believe that he himself, his entire personal being, partook of this power as if it were truly *his own*' (Debord 1995, p. 81; 2006b, p. 814).

89   See for example his description of the hierarchical structure within the *Pouvoir Ouvrier* group: 'In the P.O. spectacle there are stars [*vedettes*]' and 'spectators ...' (Debord 2001a, p. 83). One might also note Debord's observation in 1969, when announcing his desire to step down from the editorship of *Internationale Situationniste*, that he was in danger of becoming the group's figurehead to outside observers (Debord 2004a, p. 103).

90   As was noted in the introduction to this book, Debord and the SI made a host of scathing remarks about 'pro-situs', who were viewed as 'enthusiastic spectators of the S.I.' (SI 2003, p. 32; Debord 2006b, p. 1107). Debord was also concerned that the '"pro-Situ" mind-set' could be found emerging within the group itself (SI 2003, p. 87; 2006b, p. 1138).

91   Granted, a more exclusively Marxian reading of Debord's work could explain such remarks through stressing a connection between these phenomena and economic determinants. However, not only would such an interpretation require some dogged ingenuity: in addition, and as we will see in Part Four, it would also run entirely counter to Debord's critique of 'economism' (Debord's term for the dogmatic, typically Second International explanation of all cultural and political phenomena on the bases of economic factors).

92   Debord 1995, pp. 88–9; 2006b, pp. 818–19.

93   Debord 1995, p. 89; 2006b, p. 819.

94   The epigraph to the fourth chapter of *The Society of the Spectacle* is taken from a parlia-

debt to Stirner, for whom 'the dominion of morality' is also that of 'the sacred',[95] and thus an imagined, self-imposed authority that must be rejected. The SI even quoted Stirner in *Internationale situationniste*, stating that he was 'not wrong' in saying that 'moralists sleep in the bed of religion'.[96] Yet textual evidence for the presence of ethical themes can certainly be found in Debord's writings: not only for the reasons given above, but on a personal[97] and anecdotal[98] level too. After all, Debord's claims imply the pursuit of a mode of collective 'association' – to use a phrase that he borrowed from the *Communist Manifesto*[99] – 'in which the free development of each is the condition for the free development of all'.[100] If conditions of spectacle arise from flawed, detached modes of social mediation, then the liberation of 'each' from such a condition also requires the liberation of 'all'. But how, then, do these issues relate to the reading of Debord's Hegelianism that we are trying to develop?

The positions set out here should serve to ward off charges of relativism to some degree. This is because they clearly imply that spectacle cannot be overcome simply by 'making history' in the abstract, i.e. by doing just anything at all, and by pursuing any arbitrary direction. If the potential re-emergence of spectacle is a continual threat – as would seem to be indicated by the observations made above – then that collective praxis must be continually oriented towards recreating its own conditions of existence. Thus, what one finds here is a unity of means and ends, evidenced in the SI's view that 'self-

---

mentary inquest into the Paris commune of 1871: 'Equal right to all the goods and pleasures of this world, the destruction of all authority, the negation of all moral restraints; if one goes to the heart of the matter, this is the raison d'être of the March 18th insurrection and the charter of the fearsome organization that furnished it with an army' (Debord 1995, p. 47; 2006b, p. 792).

95 Stirner 2005, p. 49.
96 SI 1997, p. 553.
97 On a subjective level, Debord clearly possessed a strong sense of personal honour, albeit one that was clearly connected to the 'duty of *revolutionary distrust* towards all the values, habits and persons bound to the world that we want to change' (Debord 2001a, p. 30, italics in the original). See Stone-Richards 2001 for an interpretation that attributes a noble, almost aristocratic form of stoicism to Debord.
98 One might think here, for example, of Debord's early description of the 'Declaration on the Right to Insubordination in the Algerian War' as 'perfectly honourable ethically' (Debord 2001a, p. 23). It can also be added that as early as 1952, Debord called for the development of a 'science of situations', which would include, alongside other elements, an 'ethics' (Debord 2003a, p. 4; 2006b, p. 63).
99 Marx and Engels 1985, p. 105.
100 SI 2003, p. 83; 2006b, p. 1135.

management' must be 'both the means and the end of ... struggle', as it is 'not only what is at stake in the struggle, but also its adequate form'.[101] This then means that the collective, self-conscious historical praxis implied by Debord's work must have *itself*, or rather further instantiations of itself, as its own goal. We have already seen that 'historical time' was said to be both the 'milieu and goal of the proletarian revolution';[102] here, following our earlier comments on subjectivity, we can now add that 'the *subject* of history', according to *The Society of the Spectacle* – the full, self-conscious instantiation of historical agency – 'can only be the self-production of the living: the living becoming master and possessor of its world – that is, of history – and coming to exist as *consciousness of its own activity* [*conscience de son jeu*]'.[103] Crucially, this subject would have 'no goal [*n'a pas d'objet*] other than the effects it works upon itself'.[104] In other words, it would have no goal other than itself, and thus no aim beyond its own perpetuity. It would, therefore, be a constant process of self-determination.

Let us now place this in relation to the ideas with which we began this chapter. We have already seen that the supersession of spectacle would give rise to a processual, moving condition of subject-object unity. We can now add that this is a process that takes itself as its own goal, and which continually generates its own conditions of existence. Thus, once again, it seems possible to argue that the notion of collective praxis that one can find in Debord's work closely resembles the self-determinate and self-constitutive movement of the Hegelian Absolute.

We can take these claims further by incorporating the aesthetic aspects of Debord's views on time into this interpretation of his mature thought.

4)   Aesthetics

The identification of an aesthetics in Debord and the SI's work may appear questionable, given that Debord explicitly rejected such a view. In 1961, he wrote that 'the revolutionary project ... can in no sense produce an aesthetics because it is already entirely beyond the domain of aesthetics. The point is not to engage in some sort of revolutionary art-criticism, but to make a

---

101   SI 2006, p. 210; 1997, p. 432.
102   Debord 2004a, p. 79.
103   Debord 1995, p. 48, 2006a, p. 792.
104   Debord 1995, p. 48, translation altered; 2006a, p. 792.

revolutionary critique of all art.'[105] This statement can, however, be misleading. The 'aesthetics' that it refers to concerns artistic beauty understood in terms of the contemplated art object, and thus as an element of the spectacular society that the SI sought to supersede.[106] Such a notion of beauty is certainly absent from Debord's work. However, whilst he and the SI certainly distanced themselves from the identification of beauty with the contemplated object, their claims clearly entail an association of beauty with moments of lived experience.

The fact that Debord and the SI's work involves aesthetic themes should come as little surprise. After all, and as we will see in Part Two, the mature critical theoretical ideas addressed in this first part of the book emerged from Debord and the SI's avant-garde origins during the 1950s. The notions of beauty associated with these aesthetic themes are intimately connected to experience and action in time, and advocate a form of direct, self-conscious communion with time's passage. This entailed an aestheticisation of finitude, change and temporal process, and identified beauty with conscious, self-determinate action in time. Beauty, therefore, is accorded to the historical praxis that Debord set in antithesis to spectacle, and life itself becomes the locus of that beauty; albeit 'life' in the sense of the collective, self-determinate existence that Debord placed in contrast to the 'non-life' of spectacle.

Debord did not deny that such beauty could be *represented* within art and poetry. Indeed, he and the SI clearly held that the history of culture was replete with such depictions of creativity, imagination and passion. However, such art works were understood as static images of the creative potential that Debord and the Situationists sought to actualise within lived experience. Admired and venerated by a respectful public, and often credited with almost religious qualities, such art works constituted frozen, dead depictions of the passion, imagination and creativity that the SI wanted to bring to life. In contrast to such static arrest, poetry, for the SI, should infuse language and communication, and art should take the form of the conscious creation of moments of lived time (thus Debord: 'The point is to take effective possession of the community of dialogue, and the playful relationship to time, which the works of the poets and artists have heretofore merely *represented*').[107] Seen from such a perspective, traditional art and culture could be characterised as 'spectacular', insofar as they

---

105   SI 1997, p. 394.
106   The statement is directed towards all aspects of 'the artistic and technological apparatus that constitutes an aggregation of spectacles separated from life' (SI 1997, p. 393).
107   Debord 1995, p. 133; 2006b, p. 846, italics in the original.

constituted separated, static, and yet fetishistically revered bodies of potential. Debord and the SI thus sought to advance a 'new beauty':[108] a beauty of lived time.

This obviously relates to the SI's eponymous interest in the construction of situations: an activity that Debord originally conceived in the early 1950s, prior to the SI's formation in 1957, and which initially derived from his concern with the development of Surrealism's own earlier gestures towards the unification of art and life. Through creating situations – deliberately crafted moments of lived experience and action – the creativity, passion and imagination that had previously been employed in art's representations of lived experience could be actualised in life itself. The art of the past had represented emotion, aspiration, fear, lived experience, etc. via frozen 'images' that stood at one remove from the actual conduct of life; in contrast, and as Debord put it in an early text, written prior to the SI's formation: 'the new beauty can only be a beauty of situation'.[109]

This association of beauty with lived time is connected to a host of different issues that we will need to return to later (particularly in Parts Two and Five). We will simply signal the presence of three themes here, before relating these issues back to the Hegelian Marxian ideas outlined above. These are: Debord's interest in intense moments of experience; the identification of beauty with the temporal finitude of such moments; and the existential emphasis that Debord and the SI placed on the need to act and choose within those moments of time.

Debord was greatly interested in passionate, intense moments of experience, and remained so throughout his life. In fact, he was concerned, above all, with 'the enjoyment of the passage of time', or rather with the pursuit of a social context in which human 'life' could 'recognise itself' as such an 'enjoyment'.[110] This notion of the 'passage' of time is particularly important. Firstly, it pertains directly to the finite, fleeting nature of the moments that compose lived experience. For Debord – and this becomes particularly apparent in his later work[111] – the pathos and significance of life's moments stem from their finite, fleeting nature. In consequence, his comments on time's passage tend to possess a distinctly tragic and romantic character. Emphasis is placed on the creation of exuberant, joyful moments of experience, the beauty of which stems, in part, from their inevitable demise. As we will see in Part Five, this somewhat melan-

---

108   SI 2006, p. 11; Debord 2006b, p. 208.
109   SI 2006, p. 11; Debord 2006b, p. 208.
110   Debord 1995, p. 103; 2006b, p. 827.
111   See, for example, 1978's *In Girum Imus Nocte et Consumimur Igni*.

cholic, but no less hedonistic conception of beauty can be found in much of the poetry that Debord admired and quoted in his work (e.g. the work of François Villon, Jorge Manrique, Omar Khayyám, and Li Po; all present reflections on the inevitable flow of time, but all either accord poignancy to its passage, or advocate its enjoyment).

It is important to stress that the beauty thus accorded to time's passage was associated with *action* in time. Journeys and undertakings, possibilities and potentiality; all were associated with this 'new beauty'. Choice and decision are particularly important here. If temporal experience and action are to be deemed beautiful, then beauty must be associated with the sense in which we can never know the future. At every moment, we are obliged to choose and act on the basis of limited knowledge, and we are continually exposed to contingency. Quite consistently, and like the Surrealists before them, Debord and his friends thus became interested in incorporating chance into the production of artworks, although the 'artworks' concerned would no longer be paintings or sculptures, but rather situations, i.e. moments of life. Constructed situations, in other words, were deliberately designed so as to include chance elements, and were seen to involve 'the invention of concrete conditions determining the movement of desirable chances'.[112] This is, in part, because the chance elements of life were held to render lived experience potentially ludic. Life, as realised art, would become akin to play. As we will see below, this same concern with choice and chance also bears direct relation to Debord's interest in strategy. Here, however, having made these general comments, we now need to return to the manner in which these themes pertain to our reading of Debord's Hegelianism. This can be introduced by way of the following.

In 1960, and whilst commenting on Henri Lefebvre's closely related theory of 'moments', the SI stated that the constructed situation 'tends towards the absolute'.[113] It would be much too quick to claim that this was intended as a deliberate reference to the Hegelian Absolute. Instead, the 'absolute' invoked here is best understood as a kind of romantic sublime. One can find traces of such a notion of sublimity throughout Debord's comments on time, and on the experience of the passage of time. For example, in his autobiographical *Panegyric*, which was written towards the end of his life, Debord talks of 'a terrible and magnificent peace, the true taste of the passage of time';[114] similarly, a notion of sublimity can be found in the very early conceptions of chance

---

112 Debord 2006b, p. 296.
113 SI 1997, p. 119.
114 Debord 2004b, pp. 30–1; 2006b, p. 1669.

and *dérive* that Debord and his friends developed during the 1950s.[115] It seems, in other words, that the experience of the passage of time – i.e. lived, active experience within time – was credited with qualities that render it akin to a romantic absolute. This certainly seems to inform those comments of 1960, made in relation to Lefebvre, concerning the absolute accessed by the SI's constructed situation. The absolute that those comments described was clearly understood as a moving, shifting, temporal condition. The constructed situation, the SI claimed, 'tends towards the absolute' – i.e. it attempts to grasp this absolute – but it also tends towards its 'undoing':[116] for that moment of communion with this absolute passes away, because it is just one moment in time, and because a new situation thus needs to be constructed. The situation, therefore, was said to be both a 'proclamation of the absolute' and a 'consciousness of transitoriness [*conscience du passage*]'.[117]

This bears obvious relation to the interpretation that we are attempting to develop of Debord's Hegelian Marxism. Although the absolute referred to here seems to have been chiefly understood in romantic, aesthetic terms, it seems possible to suggest that as Debord and the SI's ideas developed – and indeed as Debord turned towards Hegelian and Marxian theory in the late 1950s and during the 1960s – this sublime, aesthetic absolute came to be re-figured in more Hegelian terms. That contention can be supported by noting that the SI's early interest in the unification of art and life was never abandoned: they simply came to view the project of art's 'realisation' more in terms of the collective, 'directly lived' history that would replace the society of the spectacle. In other words, the conception of collective historical praxis that we described earlier does not replace, but rather incorporates and develops those earlier visions of a ludic, passionate engagement with time. It therefore seems possible to claim that the sublime, romantic absolute of the SI's earlier years gradually evolved into the Hegelian Absolute that we have identified as implicit in Debord's mature conceptions of historical praxis.

This then brings us to the final item on our list: the dialectical conception of strategy that would afford the self-conscious conduct of that relation to lived time.

---

115   See Sadler 1998, pp. 69–81 for useful commentary.
116   SI 1997, p. 119.
117   Ibid.

5) Strategy

As was indicated in the introduction to this book, Debord had a deep and abiding interest in strategy and military theory. This interest even led him to devise a military board game, which was intended to simulate the principles of Napoleonic warfare. This game was referred to as the *Kriegspiel* (perhaps unintentionally, Debord dropped the additional 's' of the German term), and it first appeared in English in its complete form in 2007.[118] Since that time, Debord's interest in strategy has become increasingly widely acknowledged. It has, however, been treated only very rarely in connection to the philosophical themes and influences that subtend his work (this point will be developed in Part Five). Consequently, although this interest is now often noted, it is rarely discussed in substantial detail; at worst, it has simply provided Debord's biographers with a means of adding depth and shade to their portraits. Debord has, for example, been variously presented as a melancholy philosopher-poet, given to 'ruminate' on 'quiet, lonely summer days' over classics of military theory;[119] as a self-consciously Machiavellian figure[120] (in the moralistic sense of that term), and as a 'player of human chess'.[121] The limitations of academia's engagement with this part of Debord's work are, however, hardly surprising, for at no point in Debord's public work, correspondence or archive material does he provide us with a clear, distinct summary of his views on the topic.

However, the primary aspects of Debord's views on strategy can be reconstructed from textual evidence, and a contribution towards such a reconstruction will be set out in Part Five. It suffices for our present purposes to indicate that they cannot be understood in abstraction from his Hegelianism. Simply put, this is because strategy was to be the form taken by dialectical thought following its Marxian 'inversion' and realisation in historical praxis.

Let us briefly recapitulate the claims that have been made so far concerning the nature of that 'inversion'. Debord did not see Marx's appropriation of Hegelian ideas as a 'trivial substitution',[122] in which Hegel's unfolding categories were replaced with developing social relations. Instead, he seems to have understood

---

118 The rules of the game (without the record of a game played, which was included in the full edition of the *Kriegspiel*) were first published in English as an appendix to Len Bracken's *Guy Debord: Revolutionary* (1997, pp. 240–51).
119 Merrifield 2005, p. 11.
120 Hussey 2002.
121 Bracken 1997, p. viii.
122 Debord 1995, p. 51; 2006b, p. 794.

Marx's critical use of Hegel chiefly in terms of a change of perspective. Hegel, for Debord, had described his present as the conclusion of the past; Marx's critique renders the present the basis of an open future. The end of history thus becomes the end of *pre*-history.

Debord's views in this regard are clearly informed by Marx's comments in his afterword to the second German edition of *Capital*. Marx claims there that dialectical thought, once extracted from its 'mystical shell', is inherently critical, historical and revolutionary, because it 'includes in its positive understanding of what exists a simultaneous recognition of its negation', and thus 'regards every historically developed form as being in a fluid state'.[123] This description no doubt struck a chord with Debord (and he in fact alludes to it directly in his work),[124] as it exemplifies the sense in which dialectical thought, in his view, could afford a means of achieving a self-conscious engagement with the flow of time. Dialectics, once recast as the self-consciousness of historical praxis, would serve as a means of thinking change, movement and conflict as elements of a condition of constant, processual movement within time. Dialectical thought, in short, was to become the self-consciousness of history itself.

We can clarify that point by looking at Debord's comments on the work of a Polish Young Hegelian named August von Cieszkowski, whom we referred to earlier. Cieszkowski's *Prolegomena to Historiosophy* appeared in 1838: five years before Marx's critique of Hegel's *Philosophy of Right*, and one year before Feuerbach's critique of Christianity. Debord did not discover Cieszkowski's work until 'after 1972',[125] but he was clearly struck by it once he had done so. In his correspondence, Debord remarks that Cieszkowski presented the 'first sketch of a philosophy of praxis', that he constituted 'a decisive turning point between Hegel and the young Marx',[126] and that he was in fact '*more important than Feuerbach*'[127] in this regard.

Cieszkowski was thus placed at the outset of a long line of post-Hegelian theoretical and political development, along which dialectical thought came ever closer to its actualisation in praxis. Cieszkowski's significance, therefore, was to have lain, 'five years before the young Marx, and one hundred and twenty

---

123   Marx 1990, p. 103.
124   Debord 1979; 2006b, p. 1465; see Debord 2006a, p. 19; see also thesis #75 of *The Society of the Spectacle*.
125   Debord 2008, p. 84. The following year saw the book's publication through Champ libre, the publishing house with which Debord was affiliated.
126   Debord 2004a, p. 541.
127   Debord 2005, p. 78, italics in the original.

years before the Situationists', the 'primary basis' upon which 'the modern project of the social revolution is constituted'.[128] In a text that was to serve as a preface to a proposed 1983 reprint of Cieszkowski's book,[129] Debord explained this as follows:

> Cieszkowski surpasses Hegel in purely Hegelian terms: he negates the central aporia of the system by simply acknowledging that time has not ended. Hegel had concluded history, in the form of thought, because he ultimately accepted glorifying his present. In a single manoeuvre, Cieszkowski reverses the system, by bringing it into contact with the 'moment' of the future. This is because he recognised, in the thought of history – the supersession of philosophy – the power to transform the world.[130]

Debord often refers to 'the thought of history' and 'historical thought' in his work, although, characteristically, he does not define these terms. It seems apparent from their usage, however, that they denote the self-consciousness of the conduct of human historical existence, and that they are closely connected to the notion of 'historical time' that we described above. Debord associates the emergence of 'historical thought' with the period proper to the 'revolutionary struggles of the long historical period ushered in by the rise of the bourgeoisie',[131] and indicates that this thought was given seminal, albeit problematic, articulation by Hegel.[132] It was then subsequently developed by the writers and revolutionaries who followed, as part of the slow emergence of the self-conscious awareness of humanity's historical existence that Debord identified in the years leading up to his own era's potential 'end of *pre*-history'.

The key point here is not only that such thought was explicitly identified with dialectics[133] (insofar as dialectical thought could articulate and conceive the flux of historical circumstances). In addition, for Debord, when historical thought ceases to be contemplative – when it ceases, in other words, to be thought *about* history, and becomes the thought *of* history – it must then

---

128 Debord 2006b, p. 1536.
129 The reprint was shelved following the assassination of Gérard Lebovici.
130 Debord 2006b, p. 1536.
131 Debord 1995, p. 48; 2006b, p. 793.
132 '... [T]he "thought of history" ... the dialectic ... a truly historical thinking that is not content simply to seek the meaning of what is but aspires to understand the dissolution of all that is – and in the process to dissolve all separation' (Debord 1995, p. 48; 2006b, p. 793).
133 See thesis #75 of *The Society of the Spectacle*.

become tantamount to *strategic* thought; a self-conscious awareness of engagement and action in the changing circumstances of historical time.

If Debord's views on dialectics and Hegelian philosophy are understood in this manner, it becomes much easier to understand his otherwise enigmatic contention that both Machiavelli and Clausewitz should be seen as proponents of 'dialectical, strategic thought',[134] and that a study of both writers would be required, 'in the current era', if one was to 'complete' one's 'readings of Hegel and of other old friends of the International'.[135] A particularly explicit illustration of these views was written on one of the personal reading notes that are now housed in the Debord archive at the Bibliothèque nationale. It reads as follows:

> It is the *same thing* to think dialectically and to think strategically. When one *separates* their terrains and their terms, one specialises such operations, and one draws an ideological mantle over their methods and all their practical applications. For these terrains are evidently one single terrain, *since both denote the totality*. It is the thought of praxis, which must act; *practical theory*, in the course of its combat in time. They are the *same mode of thought*, and they are judged by the same *result*.[136]

Strategy, therefore, corresponds directly to Debord's concerns with the need for consciousness to move in step with time and history. This pertains to the existential dimensions of his thought,[137] as it connects to his Sartrean view that human subjects exist within momentary situations that they are obliged to traverse (and which, following the Situationist project, they might deliberately shape). If the human subject is an inherently 'negative' being, located in perpetual opposition to its present moment – and if it is also finite, and characterised by limited, contextual knowledge, as Debord also stresses – then that subject must continually operate and negotiate its circumstances on the basis of limited knowledge. The very conduct of life itself is thus strategic in

---

134 Debord 2008, p. 78.
135 Debord 2005, p. 42.
136 Bibliothèque nationale, NAF28603, Notes de lecture; Stratégie, histoire militaire, Box 2; dossier 5; 'strat'; January 1977.
137 Compare, for example, De Beauvoir's claim that 'we must decide upon the opportuneness of an act and attempt to measure its effectiveness without knowing all the factors that are present' (De Beauvoir 1976, p. 123) and Clausewitz's assertions that 'the only situation a commander can know is his own' (Clausewitz 1993, p. 95), and that 'war is the realm of uncertainty' (Clausewitz 1993, p. 117).

this sense, and its constant contingencies relate to Debord's interest in turning life into a game: play, like strategy, requires knowing how to act at the right time.

We will return to these issues later. Here, we now need to relate them to the reading of his Hegelian Marxism that we have been trying to develop.

The Absolute

Throughout this chapter, we have attempted to draw out some of the conceptions of temporality, subjectivity and historical activity that Debord's claims rely upon. We have also attempted to flesh out some of the previous chapter's comments regarding the nature of his Hegelian Marxism, and have indicated that the general shape and structure of the latter can be schematised as refiguring some of the primary components of Hegel's philosophy: the Idea, the Concept, and the Absolute. In order to conclude, we can now try to synthesise these claims.

Debord's theoretical work, and indeed his broader oeuvre, employs a tacit philosophical anthropology in which human subjects are cast as inherently temporal, self-constitutive and mutable creatures. His work also involves an account of historical development, an implicit ethics, an aestheticisation of temporal experience, and a view of philosophy's realisation wherein dialectics becomes tantamount to strategy. Taken together, these issues imply a very specific view of the collective history that would supersede spectacular society. Such collective praxis was seen in terms of the actualisation of a condition of subject-object unity that arises from the human subject's non-alienated identification with its own objective activity. This unity was clearly held to be possessed of an inherently dynamic, processual nature. It also appears to have itself as its own goal, because it must continually generate its own conditions of existence. In addition, it operates via a dialectical self-consciousness. Debord's broadly Hegelian conceptual framework, therefore, can be seen to accord the characteristics of the Hegelian Absolute to the collective praxis that would supersede spectacle. By extension, it associates the Concept (the Absolute's motive force) with the negative, processual and dialectical nature of temporal existence. It also appears to frame Debord's vision of fully communist praxis in terms that resemble the Idea (the subject-object unity of the Absolute's full, self-conscious expression).

It bears repeating that Debord does not state explicitly that he intended to employ or advance such a re-working of these three Hegelian motifs (he would, no doubt, have been quite sceptical about framing his ideas in such explicitly Hegelian terms). Nonetheless, they provide a means or articulating and describing a model that accords with the ideas and assumptions evidenced in his work and which, one can therefore suppose, may not be too far removed from his own position.

Having made that final qualification, we can conclude with the following remarks. In essence, Debord's adoption of the Marxian contention that philosophy must be 'realised' in concrete praxis entailed treating Hegel's philosophy in a manner that recalls Feuerbach's critique of religion. In both cases, the powers and capacities of real human beings had been associated with mythical, ethereal constructions; and in both cases, those powers and attributes needed to be recognised, reclaimed, and identified as aspects of human existence. Thus, just as Hegel's *Phenomenology* cast religion as a mere *Vorstellung* of absolute knowing, so too does Debord cast Hegel's absolute philosophy as a similarly mystified and separated depiction of a fully self-conscious history.

The subsequent chapters of this book will attempt to develop the various dimensions and implications of this approach to Hegelian Marxism. To that end, Part Two will now look at Debord and the SI's early avant-garde concerns. We will begin to do so by focusing on the connections between the classical Marxian desire to realise philosophy in lived praxis, and the SI's post-Surrealist desire to unite art and life.

PART 2
The New Beauty
1951–62

Claude Lorrain, Port Scene with Villa Medici, *1637*

Claude Lorrain, Ulysses Returns Chryseis to her Father, *circa 1644*

I scarcely know of anything but those two harbours at dusk painted by Claude Lorrain – which are in the Louvre and which juxtapose extremely dissimilar urban ambiances – that can rival in beauty the Paris Metro maps. I am not, of course, talking about mere physical beauty – the new beauty can only be a beauty of situation – but simply about the particularly moving presentation, in both cases, of a *sum of possibilities*.
 – GUY DEBORD, 'Introduction to A Critique of Urban Geography', 1955

CHAPTER 3

'We are Artists Insofar as We are No Longer Artists'

Spectacle, Art and Culture

Part One of this book sought to introduce and discuss some of the key features of Debord's mature theoretical work. Here, in Part Two, we will now trace the gradual emergence of those same ideas from Debord and the SI's early, avant-garde concerns with art and culture. To that end, we will focus here on the period that falls between 1951 and 1962: a period that begins with Debord's first engagement with the Parisian avant-garde in 1951, and which ends with the decisive splits that the SI underwent in 1962. Through these splits, Debord and those who shared his views parted ways with much of the SI's artistic past, and entered into a new phase of the SI's history: one in which Debord's concept of spectacle would orient much of the group's activity, and in which they became more explicitly focussed on the production of social and revolutionary theory.

Because our aim here is to trace the evolution of Debord's mature ideas from within this early period, we will need to look at the SI's early work through a primary focus on Debord's own output, and on his interpretation of events. This is an admittedly problematic approach to the early SI, and it has been rightly criticised for effacing the broader specificities of Situationist work through a restrictive emphasis on the group's most famous member.[1]

---

1   Debord's growing prominence has been framed as having eclipsed the more interesting and potentially radical aspects of the Situationist project. In consequence, attempts have thus been made to draw out overlooked elements of the SI from the lengthening shadow of Debord's growing academic acceptance. Because Debord's prominence within the SI is closely connected to the expulsions of the early 1960s, some of these recent studies have turned towards the chiefly Scandinavian and German artists from whom Debord's French faction broke at this time (as will be detailed later in this chapter). See, for example, Jakobsen and Rasmussen, who write in their introductory essay that 'the emphasis on Debord has overshadowed the existence of other Situationists and the different praxis they developed within the broader Situationist project' (Jakobsen and Rasmussen 2011, p. 8). Their desire to draw out 'some of the marginalised dimensions of the Situationist International' and to thus 'wrench the Situationist material from its place in anthologies from MIT Press and museums the world over' is thus set against 'the ruling Debord industry' (pp. 9–10). A stronger version of the view advanced by Jakobsen and Rasmussen can be found in the work of Stewart Home, who holds that 'In recent years far too much attention has been focused on Guy Debord as an allegedly key figure within the SI' (Home 2005). Home characterises the influence of Debord

Those complaints are certainly pertinent, but the limited scope of this book means that they cannot be fully accommodated here. What follows below will, therefore, involve a rather limited and selected take on some of this early material.[2] This is because particular attention will need to be paid to the gradual emergence of the views that informed Debord's perspective on the expulsions and splits of 1962: namely, his contention that the concept of spectacle, and his attendant vision of the SI's role, necessarily implied the supersession of all traditional art practices. Given this focus, we should begin by briefly characterising the mature views on art and spectacle that slowly emerged from this early period.

As we saw in Part One, 1967's *The Society of the Spectacle* presents a developmental narrative, according to which humanity's capacity to shape its own historical existence has grown throughout the socio-economic formations of the past, but in which that power has also become ever-more alienated from its producers. For Debord, the twinned development and estrangement of this ability to shape lived time had reached a potentially explosive extreme within his own society. Modern capitalism, in its penetration into every aspect of life, had displayed an unprecedented technical ability to shape lived experience; at the same time, the extreme existential poverty that it had engendered had also prompted a generalised demand for the appropriation of that power and potential, and for the latter's application in the conscious construction of a 'new historical life'.[3] Crucially, the actualisation of this 'historical life' required overcoming the estrangement of not only modern society's technical capacities, but also that of all other means of conceiving and conducting lived time. We saw in Chapters 1 and 2 that philosophical thought about history was to be rejec-

---

as having given rise to what he terms 'specto-Situationism' (named after Debord's concept of spectacle), and he claims that more interesting material can be found in the comparatively neglected artistic and avant-garde dimensions of the SI's work (and thus in that of its excluded artistic members). A less polemical version of this approach can also be found in the work of McKenzie Wark (2008, 2011).

2   Extended commentary on the early SI also seems superfluous here, as there is already a great deal of material available on the topic. Studies of the SI's ideas about architecture and urban planning are relatively well established (see Sadler 1998 for a seminal work in this regard), and they have been boosted by a renewed interest in the group's notion of psychogeography (see Coverley 2006 for a useful overview; see also McDonough 2009 for translations of early and pre-SI texts on these themes). In addition, Bracken 1997, Ford 2005, Gray 1998, Hussey 2002, McDonough 2009 and Sadler 1988, et al., provide useful introductions to the SI's emergence and early years. See also Kaufmann 2006, Marcus 1989, Merrifield 2005 and Wark 2008 and 2011.

3   Debord 1995, p. 106; 2006b, p. 829.

ted in favour of the realisation of such thought in history's conscious conduct; that forms of conceptually representing lived experience were to be employed in the latter's conscious creation. The same holds true for art. As Debord put it in a letter of 1959: both philosophy and art tend toward their 'disappearance in praxis'.[4] Like philosophy, art would cease to function as a mode of representing and commenting upon lived experience, and would instead be employed in the creation of such experience. The passion, romance and imagination that had previously been expressed in art and poetry would now be used to shape and invigorate the moments that compose lived time. Or, as Debord succinctly put it in *The Society of the Spectacle*: 'the point is to take effective possession of the community of dialogue and the game with time that up till now have merely been *represented* by poetic and artistic works'.[5] Art would thus undergo a Hegelian *Aufheben*, insofar as it would be negated as a means of representing life, and realised as a mode of conducting life.

These views grew directly from Debord's very early, post-Surrealist interest in uniting art and life in the creation of situations. By the early 1960s, however, this interest had come to be articulated via a broad and complex theoretical perspective that posited such activity as the next necessary step in the evolution of both avant-garde art and modern society as a whole. The impasse of the twentieth century's stagnant culture, the alienation of modern capitalism, and indeed the arrested efforts of the communist project, would all be resolved by identifying the goal of the modern revolution with the ludic, creative use of lived time; or, in other words, with the construction of situations. This perspective on the cultural and historical context of the period, which coalesced via the development of Debord's notion of spectacular society, necessarily entailed a break with the SI's artistic origins. This is because these ideas led Debord to hold the view that within such a context, any self-proclaimed avant-garde that involved itself with traditional art practices would be inherently reactionary. If the task of the modern revolution was to supersede art's extant form, then that revolution could hardly be furthered through the continued production of such art. The progressive development of these ideas greatly informed the splits of 1962, whereby the primarily French, theory-oriented members of the SI centred around Debord broke away from the group's predominantly German and Scandinavian members, who did not share this scepticism towards traditional artistic production.

---

4 Debord 2009, p. 262.
5 Debord 1995, p. 133; 2006b, p. 846.

The line of development that we need to trace, therefore, is that through which Debord and the SI's early views on art and culture developed into those outlined in the paragraphs above. We can begin by looking at Debord's earliest engagements with the Parisian avant-garde.

'Poetry Will Only Survive in Its Destruction'

In August 1951, when he was just 19 years old, Debord went to the Cannes film festival. Whilst there, he met Isidore Isou: a Romanian-born poet, artist and filmmaker. Isou was the primary theorist and figure within an avant-garde group who referred to themselves as the Letterists,[6] and was attending the festival with several other members of that group. Their aim was to promote Isou's film, *Traité de bave et d'éternité* (*Treatise on Slobber and Eternity*): a deliberately provocative work that featured scratched and bleached celluloid, a babbling soundtrack of nonsense poetry, and grand, manifesto-like pronouncements. Debord was clearly impressed: he remained in contact with the Letterists after the festival, and with the ostensible aim of studying law at the Sorbonne, he soon moved to Paris to join them.

The Letterists expressed a particular enthusiasm for negativity and destruction that owed much to Dada and Surrealism. However, they articulated this via a very distinct set of ideas, according to which contemporary art and culture could only progress through the negation of their extant forms. According to Isou, culture moves through cyclical periods of expansion and reduction, respectively termed 'amplic' and 'chiselling' phases. Once a maximum degree of development has been attained, culture begins to decompose; progress can only take place through 'chiselling' it down into its constituent elements, so as to rebuild it once more. The Letterists believed themselves to be located at a point close to the completion of that negative phase, and sought to complete it by breaking words down into single letters (hence the group's name), so as to inaugurate an entirely new mode of poetry.[7] Isou's *Treatise*, for example, declares modern cinema to have become bloated and stagnant, and calls for its destruction through the creation of anti-cinematic films that would disassemble the cinema's standardised unities of sound and image.[8]

---

6   English translations of the term *Lettrisme* vary. 'Lettrism' and 'Lettrist' are often used, but as the term stems from the French word for letter, we will refer to the movement as 'Letterism'.
7   See Black 2013 for useful commentary. See also Kaufmann 2006.
8   Wark 2011, pp. 13–14. See Cabañas 2014 for a more involved account of Letterist cinema.

This association of negativity with progression, and of creativity with destruction, bears obvious relation to Debord's later, more overtly Hegelian work, which would also contend that cultural advancement required the negation (or rather, the *Aufheben*) of culture's extant form. Likewise, the attendant aestheticisation of negativity that one can find in these early views and works would also go on to echo throughout Debord's subsequent texts and films. For example, his writings from this period contain grandiose assertions such as 'poetry will only survive in its destruction',[9] and 'Letterist poetry screams for a crushed universe'.[10] These sentiments would be given particularly explicit and provocative expression in his first film. This was 1952's *Howlings in Favour of Sade*: a work that did not simply follow Isou's attempts to break film down into its constituent elements, but which rather set itself against the very institution of the cinema as a whole.

Debord's *Howlings* is entirely devoid of images. A blank, white screen, accompanied by obscure statements and snatches of dialogue, is interspersed with periods of complete silence where the screen goes black. The film ends with one such period that lasts for no less than 24 minutes. *Howlings* is by no means without formal considerations, and the peculiar pronouncements that compose its soundtrack were obviously carefully thought out;[11] yet in keeping with the Letterist's enthusiasm for Dada-esque provocations,[12] the film was also clearly intended to aggravate its audience, and to test their capacity for boredom, confusion and acceptance (Debord, it might be noted, would later state his admiration for Brecht's own endeavours).[13] Long before the articulation of Debord's mature theory of spectacle in the 1960s, therefore – and indeed prior to the formation of the very concept of spectacle, which would not begin to appear in his writing until around 1955 – Debord was already setting out to

---

9   Debord 2006, p. 36.
10 Debord 2006, p. 46.
11 The soundtrack, and indeed the film as a whole, seems intended to express a sense of disorientation, dissociation and potential. These themes are evidenced in many of Debord's works during this period (*Mémoires* and *Critique of Separation*, for example), and they seem to have been intended to express the frustrated confusion and stifled possibility of modern life (see, for example, thesis #157 of *The Society of the Spectacle*). See Kaufmann 2006 and Cabañas 2014 for extended discussions of *Howlings*.
12 Perhaps the most famous of these events took place in 1950, when a trio of Letterists managed to make their way into Notre Dame for High Mass: dressed as a priest, one of them ascended the pulpit and proceeded to inform the gathered congregation that God was dead.
13 SI 2006, p. 35; Debord 2006b, p. 320.

subvert forms of passive, detached spectatorship. Indeed, the passive dynamic between a cinema-goer and the screen would soon be referred to as 'the best representation of an epoch'.[14] Debord and his friends were thus understandably delighted when the film's first showing, in June 1952, resulted in uproar and altercations; and he was no doubt cheered even further when the film proved to be too much even for some of the Letterists, who left the group in protest against Isou's endorsement of this deliberately antagonistic film.[15] Isou's support for the film was, however, very limited. Three days after the screening, he wrote to Debord, warning him that he had pushed things too far.[16] Debord was thus stretching the bounds of the Letterist group, and would soon break from it as a result.

However, before we move on to describe that break, a few points should be underscored. Firstly, we have seen that during this very early period, Debord's work already expressed the view that cultural advancement required the negation of culture's extant forms. This is an issue that would come to the fore in his later contentions that art needed to be both negated and realised in lived praxis. Secondly, and similarly, these early ideas also express the view that modern culture fostered the quiescent acceptance of its own redundancy. Modern culture, in other words, generated a form of spellbound, passive acceptance that was exemplified by the cinema, and which needed to be broken down and destroyed. Although these ideas pre-date Debord's mature theory of spectacle, they bear obvious and direct relation to it. We can, therefore, contend that many of the basic concepts that would come to be articulated and developed through Debord's Hegelian Marxism were formulated *prior* to his turn to Hegelian and Marxian thought towards the end of the 1950s. This is particularly true for the ideas that Debord developed following his break from Isou's Letterists.

---

14   SI 1997, p. 8. This remark recalls Lefebvre's own earlier observation that 'someone sitting in front of a cinema screen offers an example and a common model of [modern] passivity' (Lefebvre 2008a, p. 32), and may also be inspired by comments made by Isou. For example, Isou's *Treatise* contains the following assertion: 'Screens are mirrors that petrify the adventurous by returning their own image to them and halting them in their tracks. If one cannot pass through the screen of photography to something deeper then cinema holds no interest for me' (quoted in Black 2013, p. 50).
15   Marcus 1989, p. 331.
16   Isou's letter to Debord is quoted in Cabañas 2014, p. 107.

Passionate Houses

Despite his initial admiration for Isou, Debord soon came to oppose the latter's mysticism and authoritarianism. The trigger for his departure from Isou's group came in the October of 1952, when Debord was involved in sabotaging a press conference given by Charlie Chaplin.[17] Isou initially condoned the actions conducted by Debord and his friends, but he then condemned them when he realised that they were the work of a breakaway faction.[18] Isou's Letterists and those allied to Debord then engaged in a war of mutual denunciation, and in December 1952, Debord and what amounted to the Letterists' left wing left the group, declaring themselves to be an independent entity named the Letterist International (LI). The LI continued to exist until the SI's formation in 1957.

It is worth drawing attention to the nature of the LI's lifestyle during this period. The group's existence was marked by genuine excess, marginality and extremity, and it was fuelled by petty crime and by formidable quantities of alcohol[19] (it was thus also set in deliberate opposition to the more genteel Left Bank milieu of Sartre and his followers). Yet despite this lifestyle, or indeed perhaps because of it, the period in which the LI operated saw the development of some of Debord's key ideas. As we will see shortly, the concept of the constructed situation, and a nascent notion of spectacle emerged at this point; so too did the now-famous techniques of psychogeography, *dérive* and *détournement*, which would also become closely associated with the Situationists. These ideas are now so famous that they should require very little introduction: *détourne-*

---

17 Chaplin had been popular within some avant-garde circles, not least because he had been barred from the US for an alleged sympathy towards communism (Black 2013, p. 51). However, Debord and his allies selected him for attack not only on account of his celebrity and involvement in the film industry, but because he had accepted a medal from the chief of police (Mension 2002, p. 115). In a pamphlet distributed at the event (signed by Debord, Berna, Brau and Wolman), titled 'No More Flat Feet', they declared Chaplin to be a 'swindler of emotions and a master singer of suffering', whose films presented a sentimental and reactionary ideology that served to stifle revolt: 'behind your rattan cane, some have felt the truncheon of a cop ... but we who are young and beautiful, reply Revolution when we hear suffering' (Debord 2006b, p. 84).

18 Hussey 2002, p. 66. Isou distanced himself and the Letterists from the event by publishing a letter in *Combat*, in which he wrote: 'We dissociate ourselves from our friend's leaflet [distributed at the event] and we associate ourselves with the homage paid to Chaplin by all of the population' (Cabañas 2014, p. 107).

19 See Mension 2002 and Rumney 2002 for memoirs of this period; see also Debord's *In Girum Imus Nocte et Consumimur Igni* and *Panegyric* for his own memoirs.

ment entailed the subversion of existing forms in order to reveal the potential for change within the present; psychogeography studied the interconnection of urban structures and psychic states, and was researched, in part, through the *dérive*, or 'drift'. The latter entailed 'drifting' through the city, individually or in groups, following no prior plan other than the whims and desires provoked by the local ambiences.

Perhaps less famous, although of greater importance for our concerns, is the notion of 'unitary urbanism' that the LI advanced at this time. The significance of this concept can be introduced by way of analogy to *Howlings*. if the latter film can be read as anticipating aspects of Debord's mature critique of alienated detachment, then the themes associated with unitary urbanism can be seen to prefigure the conception of collective self-determinacy that would ultimately be set against spectacle. This is because unitary urbanism essentially denoted a kind of artistic and social holism: a unity within which currently isolated and fragmented techniques proper to architecture, urban planning, technology, culture and the arts would all be used to shape a collective lived experience.[20] The concept is thus closely associated with Debord's interest in the construction of situations, and like the notion of the situation, it too grew from the concern that Surrealism's gestures towards the unification of art and life remained unfulfilled.

A key figure who helped to articulate the LI's visions of such ludic, post-Surrealist collectivity was Ivan Chtcheglov, whose seminal and justly famous 'Formulary for a New Urbanism' was written in 1953. It was later published, in abridged form, in the very first issue of *Internationale situationniste* in 1958. Chtcheglov's visions are perhaps best introduced by way of their departure from those of Le Corbusier. Where the latter presented a functional, Taylorist approach to the organisation of social life,[21] Chtcheglov and the LI advocated the construction of cities and buildings that could be altered according to the desires of their inhabitants. 'We will build passionate houses',[22] the LI promised, when describing their views; or as Chtcheglov memorably put it: 'everyone

---

20 The concept of unitary urbanism was retained by the SI and was defined, in the first issue of *Internationale Situationniste*, as the 'theory of the use of the whole of arts and techniques combined in the integral construction of an environment in dynamic connection with behavioural experiments' (SI 2006, p. 52; 1997, p. 13).

21 Le Corbusier, according to Chtcheglov, had advanced an architectural style 'suitable for factories and hospitals, and no doubt eventually for prisons' (SI 2006, p. 2). Related criticisms of Le Corbusier had previously been advanced by the COBRA group (see Sadler 1998, p. 7).

22 Quoted in McDonough 2009, p. 42.

will ... live in their own personal "cathedrals" ... There will be rooms more conducive to dreams than any drug, and houses where one cannot help but fall in love'.[23] Where contemporary architecture and urbanism amounted to 'the logic of alienation and reification writ in stone',[24] to borrow McDonough's apt phrase, the LI envisaged a mode of collective, urban experience in which life would be ludic, festive, and characterised by the deliberate, artistic organisation of subjective affect and experience.

These views were, of course, obviously and unapologetically utopian, but they directly informed the SI's later concern with the liberation of *all* aspects of society from subordination to the functional requirements of capital. They thus bring us to the formation of the SI itself.

'Destroy the Bourgeois Idea of Happiness'

The SI was founded in 1957, in the Italian town of Cosio d'Arroscia, following an initial meeting in Alba the previous year. The earlier meeting – which was grandly titled The First World Congress of Free Artists – had been set up by Asger Jorn and Giuseppe Pinot-Gallizio, both of whom were members of an avant-garde group called the International Movement for an Imaginist Bauhaus (IMIB).[25] The aim of the conference was to unite a number of European groups on the grounds that all shared common cause, and it resulted in the consensus that art, culture and architecture should be employed in the conscious construction of lived experience (the LI were thus able to report in their journal, *Potlatch*, that the positions established at the meeting accorded with 'the Letterist International's programme regarding urbanism and its possible uses').[26] A subsequent meeting took place the following year, which was attended by ex-members of COBRA,[27] members of IMIB, the London Psychogeographical

---

23 SI 2006, p. 6; 1997, p. 19.
24 McDonough 2009, p. 29.
25 The International Movement for an Imaginist Bauhaus was concerned with the importance of expression in the production of art, and ran between 1954 and 1957. It emerged from the demise of COBRA in 1951, and was founded by Jorn and Enrico Baj (Sadler 1998, p. 4).
26 SI 2006, p. 21; Debord 2006b, p. 248.
27 COBRA was a group of writers and artists from Copenhagen, Brussels and Amsterdam (hence the name) that ran between 1948 and 1951. The group was characterised by an interest in spontaneity and expression, and their pursuit of a politicised, Marxian art differed from the apolitical artistic currents of their day (Sadler 1998, p. 4). Asger Jorn was

Association,[28] and by Debord and his first wife Michèle Bernstein, who together represented the Letterist International. The result was the formation of the Situationist International.

The group's name and initial orientation were greatly informed by a text that Debord had produced in preparation for the conference, titled the 'Report on the Construction of Situations', which he read to the attendees. He had been working on the 'Report' for almost a year. It represented the clearest and most complete expression of his thought that he had yet produced, and it anticipates many of his later claims. The central premise of the 'Report' echoes some of the early Letterist concerns outlined above, insofar as it too claims that culture can only progress via its destruction. For example, the 'Report' argues that contemporary art and culture had become hopelessly stagnant. Although the avant-gardes of the past had made gestures towards the abolition of bourgeois culture, and towards the application of artistic creativity in the transformation of every life, such a change had yet to be realised. This failure was attributed to the demise of the revolutionary workers' movement, which should have served as a vehicle for that social transformation, but which had since degenerated into Statist domination and orthodoxy. Western culture was thus unable to progress and to realise its own stifled potential. Its last serious artistic contributions had been made by revolutionary Surrealism, after which time it had simply degenerated into the empty repetition of familiar, faux-revolutionary gestures and forms that did little to seriously challenge the status quo.

There is much more to be said about the analysis of the contemporary context advanced in the 'Report', as it evidences the development of the perspective that would later coalesce around the concept of spectacle (it is significant in this regard that the 'Report' includes some of Debord's earliest substantial references to 'the modern spectacle').[29] We will therefore need to return to it later. For the time being, however, we can simply state that the 'Report' set out the need to 'destroy the bourgeois idea of happiness',[30] and argued for a new social condition in which art would become one with life. In doing so, the 'Report' framed Situationist activity (in the sense of experimenting with the creation of situations, and exploring the possibilities that they might afford) as being, at one and the same time, the next step in the evolution of the avant-

---

a key member of this group, as was Constant Nieuwenhuys, and both would go on to figure significantly in the SI.
28 This was an 'association' formed of just one member: Ralph Rumney (for his recollections see Rumney 2002, p. 37).
29 SI 2006, p. 43; Debord 2006b, p. 328.
30 SI 2006, p. 43; Debord 2006b, p. 328.

garde, and the next stage in the development of society as a whole. Situationist activity would pick up the baton that had been dropped by revolutionary Surrealism and Dada, and which had been subsequently ignored by the cultural productions that had followed. It would thereby complete twentieth-century art's tendency towards its own negation, and fulfil the Surrealists' promises of unifying artistic fantasy with everyday life. Through doing so, Situationist practice would also provide a means of researching the forms of socio-cultural activity that could be actualised within a future society. Debord was thus positioning the SI as heralds of a new revolution: a revolution that would afford a social condition in which art would no longer be 'a report about sensations', and in which it would instead 'become a direct organisation of more advanced sensations'.[31] As indicated at the outset of this chapter, art would no longer function solely as a mode of commentary and reflection *about* lived experience. It would no longer be located in galleries and museums, and thus at one remove from everyday life, but would instead involve creating *moments of* experience. This, then, bring us to the importance of time and temporality to Debord's early views on the construction of situations.

Time and the Situation

As noted above, references to situations, and to the need to engage in their construction, can be found in Debord's work from as early as 1952.[32] *Howlings in Favour of Sade*, which appeared that same year, makes reference to the 'totally new goal' of 'the conscious creation of situations',[33] and in 1953, Debord wrote a 'Manifesto for a Construction of Situations'. 1957's 'Report', however, presents a more developed account of the situation than those set out in his earlier writings.

The concept of the situation employed in texts such as the 'Report' not only demonstrates the import of avant-garde art and culture to Debord's thought, but also indicates the influence of the intellectual ambience surrounding Sartrean existentialism (an influence that has been noted by many commentators on Debord and the SI).[34] This requires a few words of explanation.

---

31 SI 2006, p. 53; 1997, p. 21.
32 See Debord 2006b, p. 46 for the earliest reference in his collected works.
33 Debord 2003b, p. 4; 2006b, p. 63.
34 See, for example, Jappe 1999, pp. 125–8, p. 181, Plant 2000, pp. 20–1, Wollen 1989, p. 30, and Stracey 2014, pp. 12–14.

Sartre, following Heidegger, had claimed in his *Being and Nothingness* of 1943 that we are always 'immediately "in situation"'.[35] Our lives, he held, are a succession of momentary, contextual instances of freedom and experience: situations within which we find ourselves, and within which we define ourselves through our choices and actions. Thus, for Sartre, consciousness always 'arises in situation'.[36] Sartre would then go on to develop these ideas in his subsequent work; most notably in a ten-volume series titled *Situations*, which began to appear in the late 1940s (volumes 1–3 appeared during that decade, and members of the LI read these works).[37] Debord, despite his extreme hostility towards Sartre, was unquestionably influenced by these ideas. Like Sartre, Debord acknowledges in the 'Report' that a person's life is composed of a succession of situations. Yet where Heidegger wrote of being 'thrown' into the world, and where Sartre claimed that the human condition lay in continually finding oneself cast into life's contexts and moments, Debord advocated the conscious, deliberate creation of the situations that compose lived experience. In other words, the distinction between Debord and the SI's notion of situations, and that advanced by existential philosophy, bears direct relation to the theme of philosophy's realisation in praxis (outlined in Chapter 1). One can in fact find Debord and the SI making direct allusions, in this connection, to Marx's final thesis on Feuerbach: in 1964, the SI claimed that 'philosophers and artists have only interpreted situations'; 'the point now is to transform them'.[38] Indeed, some of the remarks that Debord made in this vein anticipate his later modifications of Marx's views on commodity fetishism. For example, in 1958, and in connection to the need to produce situations rather than traditional art works, he wrote that the task now was 'to produce ourselves rather than things that enslave us'.[39]

The point that needs to be addressed here, however, is that the construction of situations required a primary concern with time. Constructing situations meant constructing moments of lived time.[40] This carries the following,

---

35   Sartre 2003, p. 63.
36   Sartre 2003, p. 115.
37   Jean-Michel Mension, a member of the LI, notes in his memoirs that he was reading Sartre's *Situations* at this time (Mension 2002, p. 9).
38   SI 2006, p. 178, translation altered; 1997, p. 388.
39   SI 2006, p. 53; 1997, p. 21.
40   Debord's interest in temporality is not, therefore, just an artefact of his later theoretical concerns, but rather runs throughout his life. This interest is perhaps encapsulated by the following quotation, taken from a letter of 1959: 'At that charming party at the end of the conference, Madame Van de Loo came over to joke with me that she was surprised to hear talk of practical actions in my regard, as she had imagined me more of a theoretician.

important corollary. If artistic creation could no longer stand at one remove from the actual conduct of such experience, it would need to become one with the passage of time. This meant that the new artistry of Situationist practice had to involve a rejection of static permanence, and that it needed to embrace the ephemerality of life's passing moments. Pretentions towards permanence were thus viewed as running entirely counter to the ethos of the lived activity that Debord and the SI were pursuing. For example, in 1958, Debord wrote that 'the goal of the Situationists is immediate participation in a passionate abundance of life by means of deliberately arranged variations of ephemeral [*périssables*] moments.'[41] The 'success of these moments', he added, 'can reside only in their fleeting effect [*leur effet passager*].'[42] Likewise, in the 'Report' of 1957, he writes:

> [O]ur entire program ... is essentially transitory. Our situations will be without a future; they will be passageways [*lieux de passage*]. The immutable character of art, or of anything else, does not enter into our considerations, which are serious. Eternity is the grossest idea a person can conceive of in connection with his acts.[43]

The 'Situationist attitude', Debord explains in the 'Report', thus entails 'going with the flow of time'.[44] These remarks, and indeed these references to the grotesque nature of any such claim to perpetuity, bear direct relation to Debord's later views concerning the 'frozen historical time'[45] described in *The Society of the Spectacle*. Likewise, so too would the more ludic, creative and self-determinate temporality envisaged in these early texts go on to inform the notion of historical praxis that would replace modern society's spectacular arrest (remembering here that the 'subject of history' described in Chapter 2 was to attain '*conscience de son jeu*').[46]

She was greatly surprised when I told her, sincerely, that "nothing has ever interested me beyond a certain practice of life". (It is precisely this that has kept me from being an artist, in the current sense of the word, and, I hope, a theoretician of aesthetics!)' (Debord 2009, p. 244).

41   SI 2006, p. 53;1997, p. 20.
42   SI 2006, p. 53; 1997, p. 20.
43   SI 2006, p. 41, translation altered; Debord 2006b, p. 326.
44   SI 2006, p. 42; Debord 2006b, p. 327.
45   Debord 1995, p. 141, translation altered; Debord 2006b, p. 851.
46   Debord 1995, p. 48; 2006b, p. 792.

The ludic dimensions of Situationist activity were closely connected to the importance of contingency in the creation and experience of situations. Every constructed situation was to involve a degree of contingency: not so much as to entail complete randomness and chaos, but rather so as to facilitate what Sadler has described as the situation's 'organised spontaneity'.[47] Just as games involve unexpected moves and events, so too would the SI's situations.

This notion of play can be found throughout much of Debord's work. *The Society of the Spectacle*, for example, describes the temporality that would replace spectacle as being 'playful in character'.[48] Almost ten years earlier, the constructed situation was described as a 'moment of life' that amounts to a 'game of events',[49] and in his correspondence, Debord refers to the 'superior cultural creation' that the SI's efforts sought to establish as 'the Situationist game'.[50]

The roots of this interest in play can be found in Debord's earliest work and influences. Surrealism is particularly important here, as the Surrealists had also been interested in employing chance in the construction of artworks. On a more theoretical level, one can find echoes of Lefebvre's work. Debord and the SI would not come into contact with him until much later, but the importance of play is addressed in the first volume of his *Critique of Everyday Life*: a book that was published in 1947, and which Debord no doubt read. However, perhaps the most important influence in this vein comes from Johan Huizinga's *Homo Ludens*, which Debord read in the early 1950s,[51] and which links play to freedom, beauty, poetry and war.

The conjunction of themes that can be found here – moving with time, play, creativity and action – all bear relation to Debord's views on the forms of temporal action and experience that could rectify the stagnation of modern society, and would ultimately go on to inform the mature conceptions of praxis that we discussed in part one. Given the relation between these themes and that later notion of praxis, the connection between temporal play and Debord's interest in strategy seems particularly important.

Because the ludic experience of time proper to the constructed situation stemmed from the presence of chance and contingency within it, the construction and negotiation of situations required acting in response to unforeseen events. It involved attempting to make advances and subjective gains through

---

47 Sadler 1998, p. 78.
48 Debord 1995, p. 116; 2006b, p. 836.
49 SI 2006, p. 51; 1997, p. 13.
50 Debord 2009, p. 164.
51 Hussey 2002, p. 73.

engaging with chance, and through making choices and decisions on the basis of limited knowledge. In consequence, it was not altogether dissimilar from gambling (it might be added here that the remark quoted above, which identifies the 'Situationist attitude' with 'going with the flow of time', reads in French as *'miser sur la fuite du temps'*). By the same token, so too was it similar to strategic thought: for strategy, as we discussed earlier, also requires action and decision in response to unknown eventualities.

To sum up: the temporality proper to the experience of constructed situations was to be creatively and passionately rich, but also ludic *qua* strategic. It was seen to stand in direct opposition to the dull, stagnant and pre-ordained patterns of behaviour proper to modern society. It therefore seems possible to contend that one can find here, within the SI's early views on constructed situations, the beginnings of the themes of time, spectacle and praxis that we sought to outline in Part One. These themes would later be re-articulated and developed through Debord's turn to Hegel and Marx, but they are no less apparent here in the SI's early years.

Cultural Decomposition and Spectacular Society

The concept of spectacle developed later than that of the constructed situation. Debord's first significant uses of the term 'spectacle' begin from around 1955,[52] and its relatively fragmentary applications in 1957's 'Report' are amongst its first substantial uses. In order to trace its emergence, therefore, we should look at the ideas that coloured its development; and in order to do that, we need to place it in relation to the concept of cultural decomposition that Debord developed from his engagements with Isou and the Letterists.

Earlier, when outlining the general argument of Debord's 'Report', we stated that Debord presents modern society as existing within a condition of stagnation, caused by the failure of the revolutionary movement to actualise the rad-

---

52 A very early reference to spectacle can be found in 1952 (Debord 2006b, p. 70), but it is not until the mid-'50s that the term starts to appear sporadically (see, for example Debord 2006b, p. 189). There is, however, little evident theoretical consistency in its use: in 1955's 'Introduction to a Critique of Urban Geography' Debord seems to use the term to refer to sensory appearances and dramatic presentations in general (SI 2006, p. 10; Debord 2006b, p. 207). Evidence of its application as a means of denoting false or impoverished appearances appears soon after – in 1956, for example, Debord talks of a 'spectacle of a unity that never existed' (Debord 2006b, p. 241) – but although the term had clearly entered Debord's vocabulary by this stage, it is not frequently invoked.

ical possibilities that had been glimpsed within modernist avant-garde culture. Before that, when discussing Debord's initial engagements with the Letterists, we also noted that Debord was indebted to Isou's contention that modern culture had grown bloated and obsolete, and that its consequent decomposition needed to be assisted through works of artistic negation. The LI, and later the SI, would adopt this view, although they abandoned Isou's cyclical view of cultural growth and collapse. Decomposition, for them, simply named the stagnation of modern culture that had been caused by the absence of a revolutionary cultural advance.

The concept of decomposition, therefore, initially served the LI and the SI as a means to denote the problematic that the construction of situations would resolve. It thus performed a very similar role to that which the concept of spectacle would later play in Debord's more developed theoretical work. However, the concept of spectacle did not simply replace that of decomposition. Instead, the notion of decomposition remained in use alongside that of spectacle throughout the 1960s, and it can even be found in Debord's writings from the 1990s.[53] This is because decomposition came to be viewed as a symptom, or indeed a specifically cultural dimension, of the broader socio-economic problematic of spectacle. In what follows below, we will therefore try to demonstrate: 1) that Debord's notion of spectacle grew from the concept of decomposition; and 2) that it ultimately came to subsume it. The best way to begin addressing this is by attempting to reconstruct Debord's views on art's tendency towards its own abolition.

The development of modernist art had inflected art's traditional preoccupation with representing moments of life, or representational comments upon it, with more formal considerations. If one follows the development of such art, one can trace a trajectory away from representation, and towards critical engagements with art *per se*: a trajectory that might thus pass from Cézanne, through cubism and abstraction, to works such as Malevich's *Black Square* and Duchamp's urinal. Dada then levelled challenges against art's separate, privileged and quasi-religious status. Indications – however nascent – were also made as to the possible forms that art might take if it were to be pushed beyond its traditional representative role. Futurism, for example, despite its fascist inclinations, gestured towards art's revolutionary combination with modern technology; Surrealism, as indicated earlier, pointed towards the unification of art, creativity and imagination within lived experience. The SI's relation to this lineage is best expressed in a formulation from *The Society of the Spectacle*,

---

53   See for example Debord 2008, p. 237.

where Debord writes that 'Dadaism sought to *abolish* [*supprimer*] *art without realising it*,' that 'Surrealism sought to *realise art without abolishing it*',[54] and that the 'critical position since worked out by the Situationists demonstrates that the abolition and the realisation of art are the inseparable aspects of the one same *supersession* [*dépassement*] of *art*'.[55] Art, in Hegelian fashion, was thus to be realised through its own negation, so as to bring the work of the avant-gardes of the past to a conclusion. For Debord, this required revolution; and this brings us to the dates accorded to the onset of cultural decomposition.

Throughout his work, Debord consistently maintained that a unification between revolutionary politics and avant-garde culture had been possible in the early decades of the twentieth century. This was attributed to the co-existence, at that time, of the near culmination of art's trajectory towards its own negation, and the ascendancy of the workers' movement. However, Debord also held that that possibility had ultimately been stifled, due to the collapse of the revolutionary project into its own static, statist representation. Thus, in 1955, and whilst still a member of the LI, he claimed that 'the movement of [cultural] discovery' had 'culminated around 1930', because it had been arrested by the 'very serious retreat of revolutionary politics', and by 'the blinding bankruptcy of the workers' aesthetic'.[56] This view is echoed in 1957's 'Report',[57] and in many other writings (a letter of 1958, for example, states that the conditions for such change 'were already ripe in the 1920s'),[58] and it was expressed particularly succinctly in a remark of 1956, in which he declared that 'the premises for revolution' within modern society were 'not only ripe', but had 'begun to rot'.[59] When commenting on Germany, Debord linked this stagnation to the rise of the Nazis;[60] in other texts, he associated it with the neutralisation of potential tools for the liberation and creation of lived experience (psychoanalysis, for example).[61] In general, his basic claim here is that the

---

54 Debord 1995, p. 136, translation altered; 2006b, p. 848, emphasis in the original.
55 Debord 1995, p. 136, translation altered; 2006b, p. 848, emphasis in the original.
56 Debord 2006b, p. 195.
57 'The ebbing of the international revolutionary movement, which became apparent within a few years after 1920 and increasingly obvious over the next three decades, was followed, with a time-lag of five or six years, by an ebbing of the movements that had tried to promote liberatory innovations in culture and everyday life' (SI 2006, p. 33; Debord 2006b, p. 317).
58 Debord 2009, p. 228.
59 SI 2006, p. 14; Debord 2006b, p. 221.
60 Debord 2001a, p. 141.
61 Debord 2010, p. 229.

cultural stagnation of the present – i.e. the vacuity and empty repetition that Debord attributed to modern culture – had resulted from the missed opportunities of the past. As the SI put it in 1964: 'artistic movements' since 'the 1910–1925 period' have 'only been imaginary repercussions from an explosion that never took place, an explosion that threatened and still threatens the structures of this society'.[62]

This periodisation of decomposition remained relatively consistent throughout Debord and the SI's work. This is significant, because it fits very neatly with the dates that Debord gave for the full emergence of spectacular society (or, following the reading of Debord's work advanced in this book: the dates concerned are those of the full expression and realisation of a much older tendency towards spectacular separation). The most prominent statement that Debord gave concerning the periodisation of the society of the spectacle can be found in 1988's *Comments on the Society of the Spectacle*, which places the spectacle's full emergence in the late 1920s.[63] There are, however, many further examples of this periodisation. As we saw in Chapter 2, Debord states in a letter of 1971 that the spectacle 'appeared under its completed form around 1914–1920 (with the brain washing [*bourrage de crâne*] of the war and the collapse of the workers' movement)'.[64] He was clearly convinced of this view, as 20 years later he made much the same claim: in a letter of 1992, he writes that 'the modern spectacle' 'commence[d] with the war of 1914', with its 'patriotic "propaganda [*bourrage de crânes*]"', with 'Kronstadt [1921]', and with 'the March on Rome [1922]'.[65] Although further examples of this periodisation can be found, and although slightly different dates and events are sometimes invoked, the society of the spectacle's full emergence is always placed – like that of decomposition – in the early decades of the twentieth century.

If spectacle is understood in the manner proposed in this book – i.e. if the real core of the problematic of spectacle is not just society's saturation with commodities, but rather the alienation and reification of social power and agency – then the connection between decomposition and spectacle can be easily explained. Debord's concept of spectacle, once it had been fully formulated and clarified, overarches and subsumes the older concept of decomposition. This is because the consumption and veneration of a dead, obsolete culture constitutes an instance of spectacle, insofar as it entails alienated subservience to the creative and transformative powers congealed within such a

---

62 SI 2006, p. 179; 1997, p. 388.
63 Debord 1995, p. 3; 2006b, p. 1595; see Crary 2002 for commentary.
64 Debord 2004a, pp. 455–6.
65 Debord 2008, p. 331.

culture. The concept of decomposition initially gave rise to that of spectacle (one might think here of Debord's early, Letterist views that a defunct culture bred passive acceptance, and of his attendant attacks on the *literal* spectacle of cinema); yet ultimately, the concept of spectacle came to subsume that of decomposition.

It might also be added that if spectacle is understood in the manner proposed in the preceding chapters, it also becomes considerably easier to make sense of the events that Debord associates with the emergence of a fully spectacular society. The full emergence of the society of the spectacle was certainly driven by the rise of consumer capitalism. For Debord, and as we will see in Part Four, the dominance of the value-form entailed the generalisation of a condition in which society became subordinate to its own alienated activity. Yet phenomena such as Kronstadt, militaristic nationalism, fascism and state-bureaucracy, all served to complete capital's domination of society by neutralising and appropriating the energies of the revolutionary workers' movement. The subsequent collapse of revolutionary agency into its own ineffectual representations, and the degeneration and stagnation of avant-garde culture, afforded the 'perfection' of modern separation, and thereby the appearance of spectacular society 'under its completed form'.

It seems possible to argue, therefore, that whilst the concept of decomposition served initially as a means of describing the cultural issues to which the LI and early SI sought to respond, the notion of frozen potential that it entailed ultimately led to the development of Debord's concept of spectacle.

The beginnings of this development can be seen in his 'Report' of 1957. Although that text is primarily concerned with decomposition, it describes capitalist society as marked by spectacle, and states that the 'principle' of the latter is 'non-intervention'.[66] However, Debord's references to spectacle in this text are chiefly concerned with the 'methods of propaganda' of an 'evolved capitalism',[67] and fall short of identifying the concept with modern life as a whole. This, however, would soon change: in 1960, the term 'spectacle' was being used to name the entirety of modern culture,[68] and by 1961, the SI were claiming that 'modern capitalism ... organises the reduction of all social life to

---

66 SI 2006, p. 40; Debord 2006b, p. 325.
67 SI 1997, p. 43, translation altered; Debord 2006b, p. 328.
68 For example, in an essay of 1960, the 'entire cultural spectacle' is denounced, albeit with a primary orientation towards the 'degraded spectacle, which is the representation of dominant society put within reach of the exploited in order to mystify them (televised sports, virtually all films and novels, advertising, the automobile as status symbol)' (SI 2006, pp. 74–5, translation altered; 1997, p. 111).

a spectacle'.⁶⁹ By 1965, which is when Debord first started writing *The Society of the Spectacle*,⁷⁰ the concept had clearly become central to the SI's analyses.

As the concept of spectacle was also largely Debord's creation, this line of development is one in which the SI gradually hardened and condensed around Debord himself. Understandably, and as was noted at the outset of this chapter, this has prompted contemporary researchers to develop alternative, non-Debordian readings of the Situationist International. For our purposes, however, the salient issue here is the manner in which this theoretical focus led to the splits of 1962.

The Expulsions of 1962

In 1968, in a text titled 'The Organisation Question for the Situationist International', Debord described the SI as having passed through two distinct stages, and as having entered into a new, third one. An initial period, encompassing the material and ideas discussed in this chapter, and focussed around 'the supersession of art', had been superseded in the early 1960s by a second period, geared towards the fermentation and articulation of revolutionary activity. This second period covered the SI's more theoretical and militant work during the 1960s. Yet in 1968, Debord held that the SI had entered a new, nascent period, within which the SI had 'emerged from silence', the group's views having gained a degree of prominence, and in which society's 'new revolutionary tendencies' had begun to 'appear in the streets'⁷¹ (these remarks were typically prescient: this text was written only two or three weeks before the events of May 1968). The splits of 1962 can thus be taken as a marker for the transition between that first, avant-garde period, and the SI's second, more overtly theoretical period. They can also be viewed as symptomatic of the emergence, within the SI, of a political position that accords with those expressed in Debord's mature theoretical work. In order to address these issues, we should, however, begin with some background.

As noted above, one of the initiators of the Alba conference of 1956 was Asger Jorn: a painter and prolific writer who had helped to found COBRA in 1948, and who had also been associated with the International Movement for an Imaginist Bauhaus. Debord met and became friends with Jorn in 1954, and

---

69 SI 2006, p. 86; 1997, p. 214.
70 Debord 2003a, p. 21.
71 SI 2006, p. 380, translation altered; 1997, p. 680.

whilst Debord's letters display an evident irritation with Jorn's punctuality and reliability, he always viewed him with a good deal of respect.[72] Jorn was thus a founding member of the SI, and he played a major role in the group's initial artistic period. So too did Constant Nieuwenhuys, another ex-COBRA figure perhaps best known for his architectural designs for a utopian city built around Situationist principles,[73] and Giuseppe Pinot-Gallizio: an artist whose rolls of machine-produced 'industrial painting' were championed by Debord in the SI's early days,[74] and who helped Jorn to set up the Alba event in 1956.

By the early 1960s, however, Jorn, Constant and Pinot-Gallizio had all left the group. Jorn began to move towards a departure in 1961, no doubt sensing the group's immanent change of orientation[75] (he would, however, remain on good terms with Debord, and continued to fund the SI through the sale of his paintings). Pinot-Gallizio had been excluded the previous year, due to the 'serious shortcoming'[76] of his readiness to operate within the traditional art world (Debord in fact described him as the SI's 'right wing');[77] Constant left the SI soon after.[78] The SI was thus drifting away from the traditional arts and towards the development of revolutionary theory. This came to a head with the expulsion of two art-oriented factions within the SI: the German members associated with a group called Spur, and the Scandinavian Situationists centred around Jorn's brother, Jørgen Nash. As we will see shortly, these expulsions bear direct relation to Debord's developing views on the realisation of philosophy.

The German Spur group became part of the Situationist International in 1959. Asger Jorn had made contact with the group the previous year, having been impressed by some of Spur's paintings. According to Dieter Kunzelmann, a member of Spur, Jorn was keen to advance the SI's reach into Germany, and to strengthen its artistic side.[79] However, Spur's affiliation with the SI would not last long. Some of the first major fractures began to appear in 1960,

---

72   This is particularly evident in the first volume of Debord's correspondence (Debord 2009).

73   This was Constant's 'New Babylon'. We will return to Constant's ideas in the following chapter, but see Sadler 1998 for commentary.

74   Pinot-Gallizio's industrial paintings were produced by machines and supplied in rolls like wallpaper (see the first volume of Debord's correspondence for his initial enthusiasm for Pinot-Gallizio's work (Debord 2009)).

75   Jorn remained a member for one year under the pseudonym George Keller. Thanks are due to Anthony Hayes for highlighting this point.

76   Debord 2009, p. 250.

77   Debord 2009, p. 299.

78   See Debord 2009, pp. 358–60 for Debord's response to Constant's departure.

79   Altindere and Boynik 2004.

at the SI's fourth conference in London. A discussion of the SI's status as a political movement, conducted during that conference, led to the question of the group's connection to revolutionary forces within society. It emerged from that debate that members of Spur did not share the view that a revolutionary proletariat, capable of throwing off the extant social order, could actually be identified within modern society. They also demonstrated the rather fanciful supposition that social change might be brought about by artists. They placed their faith, they said, in the transformative capacities of 'avant-garde artists', who have been 'placed by the present society in intolerable conditions', and who can 'count only on themselves to take over the weapons of conditioning'.[80] This view received a predictable degree of criticism, and Spur retracted their comments in response. As a result, concerns were raised regarding the need for theoretical coherence between the SI's various sections.

This accorded with Debord's growing preoccupation with the need for a distinct, theoretically defined position as a means of unifying the SI's actions and interactions. His views in this regard are intimately connected to his conceptions of history and praxis, which we will take up in Chapter 5. In brief, he held that an avant-garde group should be defined by its collective aims, and by its attempt to respond to the social and cultural context that had engendered it. If such a group could not express a clearly defined exigency that bears relation to its context, then there would simply be no point to its continued existence (hence his repeated assertions that the SI's seemingly self-immolating propensity for exclusion was actually its 'best weapon':[81] the removal of defunct elements from within the group would ensure that it remained a relevant, pertinent threat, focussed around a distinct problematic). Needless to say, these views added impetus to the divisions that were forming within the group, which were widened further at the SI's fifth conference in Gothenburg, in August 1961.

Some of the more decisive blows struck at the conference were delivered by Raoul Vaneigem. A Belgian schoolteacher of philosophy, Vaneigem had been deeply impressed by the ideas advanced in *Internationale situationniste*, and had joined the group earlier in the year. At Gothenburg, he presented an 'orientation report' to the conference that reflected the increasing importance of a clearly defined theoretical line. He made the following claims:

---

80 SI 2006, p. 82; 1997, p. 166.
81 Debord 2001a, p. 278.

The Situationist International finds itself, due both to the present historical conjuncture and to its internal evolution, at a stage of development such that the activity it considers itself capable of carrying out ... depends henceforth on its ability to maintain critical rigour, a rigour that will serve as a cohesive force.[82]

This demand for 'rigour' was rendered all the more pertinent by the admissions made by Heimrad Prem, a German member of the group, who stated that he found Situationist theory 'incomprehensible',[83] and that he held a degree of scepticism towards the importance of theory (a position that obviously jarred with Debord's emphasis on theoretical focus and coherence).

Vaneigem also expressed the view that artistic production within a period dominated by decomposition must be reactionary. Aiming his comments at elements of the German Spur group, who had been suspected of using the growing cachet of the term 'Situationist' as means of advancing artistic careers[84] – and whilst also making remarks that jarred with the Scandinavian artists associated with Jørgen Nash – Vaneigem announced the following:

> The point is not to elaborate a spectacle of refusal but to refuse the spectacle. In order for their elaboration to be artistic in the new and authentic sense defined by the SI, the elements of the destruction of the spectacle must precisely cease to be works of art. There is no such thing as *Situationism*, or a Situationist work of art, and no advantage to [being] a spectacular Situationist. Once and for all.[85]

To continue to produce art, in other words, was to perpetuate decomposition, and to thereby reduce the Situationists' revolutionary project to a mere *spectacle* of itself. Attila Kotányi (a relatively new member of the SI who would himself be excluded in 1963) then followed Vaneigem's remarks by contending that artistic works produced by members of the SI should be termed 'anti-Situationist'.[86]

This was not intended to constitute an outright ban on artistic production altogether. In fact, Debord himself had been engaged in artistic production of a sort. With Jorn, he had produced two books of collage and experimental writing

---

82 SI 2006, p. 114; 1997, p. 266.
83 SI 1997, p. 269.
84 Altindere and Boynik 2004.
85 SI 2006, p. 115, translation altered; 1997, pp. 266–7.
86 SI 2006, p. 116; 1997, p. 267.

titled *Fin de Copenhague* (1957) and *Mémoires* (1959). He had also made a series of psychogeographical maps, together with his films *Howlings in Favour of Sade* (1952), *On the Passage of a Few Persons Through a Rather Brief Moment of Time* (1959), *and Critique of Separation* (1961). It is, however, significant that he did not regard such works as specifically Situationist – they were not constructed situations – and he pointedly remarked at the conference that he had 'never made a Situationist film'[87] (*contra* the views of some commentators,[88] Debord's cinematic work is a contribution to the critique of spectacular culture, and not an instance of fully fledged Situationist activity).[89] The remarks made by Vaneigem and Kotányi were simply intended to separate truly Situationist activity from more traditional art forms,[90] and to thereby undermine those who would make use of the growing fame of 'Situationism', or simply conflate the latter with traditional art.

The Gothenburg conference thus laid the grounds for the splits that would follow. Nash's antipathy to the notion of 'anti-Situationist' art-work hastened the expulsion of the so-called 'Nashist' faction in 1962. This exclusion that was given further impetus by his subsequent publication of a tract in which he attacked the SI in the name of the Scandinavian section[91] (he would later go on to found the less well-known 'Second Situationist International'). The Germans were also excluded in 1962.

Debord's contingent would prove to be somewhat less than stringent in their rejection of traditional artistic production in the years that followed,[92] but the breaks of 1962 were nonetheless decisive in terms of securing the group's subsequent orientation. Much of that new direction was famously cemented during the French section's return from the Gothenburg conference in 1961. Whilst on a *dérive* through 'a series of randomly chosen bars in Hamburg',[93] *en*

---

87   SI 2006, p. 115; 1997, p. 267.
88   See, for example, Knabb in SI 2006, p. 482.
89   See Jappe 1999, p. 108, who also expresses the view presented here.
90   Kotányi qualified his remarks with the following statement: 'I don't mean that anyone should stop painting, writing, etc.'; 'I don't mean that we could continue to exist without doing that' (SI 2006, p. 115; 1997, p. 267).
91   See 'The Counter-Situationist Campaign in Various Countries' in *Internationale Situationniste* #8.
92   See in particular the SI's 'Destruction of RSG-6' exhibition (dubbed a 'demonstration [*manifestation*]' rather than an exhibition (SI 1997, p. 395)) of 1963, which was organised by the Danish Situationist J.V. Martin. For Debord's commentary, see his 'The Situationists and the New Forms of Action in Politics and Art' (SI 2006, pp. 402–8; Debord 2006b, pp. 647–53). See Rasmussen 2011 for commentary.
93   SI 1997, p. 703.

route back to Paris, they formulated the SI's now famous, but never published 'Hamburg Theses'.[94] This text could be encapsulated, according to Debord's recollections in 1989, in one decisive sentence: 'The SI must now realise philosophy.'[95]

We referred to Marx's own famous call for the realisation of philosophy in Chapter 1. As was indicated there, it can be found in the introduction to his 'Contribution to a Critique of Hegel's *Philosophy of Right*', where he states that 'Philosophy cannot realize itself without the supersession [*Aufhebung*] of the proletariat,' just as 'the proletariat cannot supersede itself without the realisation [*Verwirklichung*] of philosophy'.[96] That declaration is made at the end of Marx's text, but it draws upon the equally famous comments on religion presented at its beginning. When Marx claims, at the outset of that text, that religion is 'the opium of the people',[97] he is not simply dismissing religion as a dream or fantasy. Instead, his point is that, just as drugs can serve to make miserable social situations tolerable, so too does religion; thus, one cannot overcome religion simply by pointing out its fallacy, but only through combatting the social conditions that engender a demand for such illusory comfort. This directly informs the text's closing comments on the realisation of philosophy. Marx's claim is that critical, philosophical thought remains impotent and ineffective if it simply criticises society whilst remaining solely within the realm of ideas. If it is to be effective, it must unite with the practical social forces that would abolish the problems that it identifies. Critical philosophy, therefore, must unite with the revolutionary proletariat (thus, philosophy's practical realisation requires the self-abolition of the proletariat *qua* proletariat, and *vice versa*).

These views can be mapped onto the tensions within the SI prior to the splits of 1962. As noted above, the excluded parties had held that emancipation might come through art *per se* – a view that corresponds to the mistaken notion that religion could be dismissed simply through intellectual critique – and some had also expressed scepticism as to the very existence of a revolutionary proletariat. Debord, as a result of his developing conception of spectacle, had become increasingly convinced that a critique of culture's separation from everyday life could not be conducted via a separated culture. Thus, like Marx, he held that critique needed to become an active force; and just as the critique of religion, in Marx's day, needed to join forces with those suffering the material

---

94   See Hayes 2015 for a longer discussion of this text.
95   SI 1997, p. 703, translation altered.
96   Marx 1975, p. 257.
97   Marx 1975, p. 244.

deprivations that prompted the demand for religion's palliatives, so too should the critique of art join forces with those currently obliged to find subjective satisfaction in the alienated trinkets, museums and commodification of modern culture. For Debord, this meant joining with the 'new' proletariat: all those individuals within modern society who suffered from its generalised existential impoverishment.

By the early 1960s, therefore, the SI's critique of modern culture had become a critique of spectacular society, and had thereby expanded in such a manner as to incorporate and re-figure earlier, nineteenth-century criticisms of religious alienation and philosophical detachment. *All* forms of alienated separation could now be gathered under the rubric of spectacle. As the SI put it in 1964:

> The Situationists consider that they must supersede [*hériter*] art – which is dead – and separated philosophical reflection – whose corpse no one, despite all the present efforts, will succeed in 'reviving' – because the *spectacle* that is replacing this art and this thought is itself the heir of *religion*. And just as was the case with the 'critique of religion' (a critique that the present Left abandoned at the same time it abandoned all thought and action), the critique of the spectacle is today the precondition for any critique.[98]

By the 1960s, and via the development of Debord's concept of spectacle, the SI had adopted a greatly expanded critical paradigm. That concept had come to function as a defining summary of the problems and possibilities presented by an entire historical moment. Furthermore, the nature of this concept – which had grown from a utopian, avant-garde critique of modern culture's failure to actualise its own possibilities, and which was now developing into a Marxian critique of the general social form of modern society – necessarily entailed a far grander, more extreme and all-encompassing demand than those advanced by the traditional workers' movement. As Debord would later put it, when reflecting on the 'Hamburg Theses' and the splits of the early 1960s:

> This outline conclusion recalls a famous passage from Marx's 1844 *Contribution to the Critique of Hegel's Philosophy of Right*. It signalled that it was now time for the ideas espoused by those extant revolutionary groups bequeathed by the liquidated emancipatory social movements of the early twentieth century to be comprehensively dismissed and that

---

98   SI 2006, p. 175, translation altered; 1997, p. 368.

only the Situationist International could very soon be expected to kick-start a new era of dissent by giving fresh impetus to what first emerged in the 1840s.[99]

Therefore, in the early 1960s, a need was identified to revisit Hegelian, Marxian and Young Hegelian thought: to reconfigure that thought's insights in relation to the possibilities and predicaments of the present. This led to the positions described in Chapters 1 and 2, and to those that will be discussed in the subsequent parts of this book. It also meant that in 1963, at the end of the SI's 'first era – that of the search for a genuinely new artistic terrain (1957–61)'[100] – they could claim that:

> … just as in the first half of the nineteenth century revolutionary theory arose out of philosophy (out of critical reflections on philosophy and out of the crisis and death of philosophy), so now it is going to rise once again out of modern art and poetry, out of its supersession, out of what modern art has sought and *promised*, out of the clean sweep it has made of all the values and rules of everyday behaviour.[101]

Or, as they succinctly put it in 1964: 'We are artists only insofar as we are no longer artists [*plus des artistes*]: we come to fulfil [*réaliser*] art'.[102]

---

99   SI 1997, p. 703; thanks are due to John McHale for help with the translation of this passage.
100 SI 1997, p. 703.
101 SI 2006, p. 139; 1997, p. 307.
102 SI 2006, p. 179; 1997, p. 389.

CHAPTER 4

The Everyday and the Absolute

The Turn to Everyday Life

This chapter will focus on the conceptions of everyday life and constructed situations that the SI developed during the late 1950s and early 1960s. In order to do so, it will address Debord and the SI's relation to the work of Henri Lefebvre and Sartrean existentialism. Before we begin to address those topics, however, we should first map out some of the events and ideas that informed these aspects of the SI's conceptual development. To that end, we will start by taking up the narrative presented in Chapter 3, which closed with the expulsion, in the early 1960s, of the SI's artistic 'right wing',[1] and with the consolidation of the SI's remaining members around Debord's more overtly theoretical perspectives.

Debord was becoming increasingly engaged with Hegelian and Marxian thought at this time. Sections from Lukács's *History and Class Consciousness* had started to appear in French from 1957 onwards, and Debord was evidently aware of the relevance of both Lukács's ideas and those of Lucien Goldmann by the end of the 1950s.[2] In 1960, he began a short-lived and ultimately ill-fated friendship with Henri Lefebvre, which we will discuss below. In addition, between the end of 1960 and May 1961 (and in violation of the SI's prohibition of simultaneous membership of other groups)[3] Debord also engaged

---

1   SI 1997, p. 703.
2   In a letter to Jorn of July 1959, Debord enclosed an article by Lucien Goldmann on 'Reification' which had been published in *Les Temps Modernes*, and advised him to address both that text and Lukács's *History and Class Consciousness* in a pamphlet on value that Jorn was then producing. 'Lukács', Debord remarks in the letter, 'is becoming very fashionable here' (Debord 2009, p. 264). *History and Class Consciousness* would not, however, receive a full French translation until the following year.
3   Khayati, who resigned in 1969, would later be attacked for his dual membership of the SI and the Popular Democratic Front for the Liberation of Palestine (SI 2003, p. 84; Debord 2006b, p. 1136; see also Gray 1998, p. 132, and Dauvé 1996, p. 31). Debord's affiliation with S ou B also jarred with his own earlier hostile stance towards that group. In a letter of 1958, he refers to them as 'mechanistic to a frightening extent' (Debord 2009, p. 152). His views had, however, mellowed by 1959: the departure of Claude Lefort (who would later be attacked in the pages of *Internationale Situationniste*) and 'the rebel wing of the anti-organisationalists' within S ou B was said to have led to 'progress' within the group's eponymous journal (Debord 2009,

in an even briefer affiliation with Socialisme ou Barbarie (s ou b): a radical left-communist group who were engaged in an attempt to critically re-think Marxian thought by investigating the changing nature of modern capitalism and militant struggle.

The ideas advanced by both Lefebvre and s ou b certainly informed Debord and the SI's interest in everyday life. It is, however, important to note that this interest was by no means solely engendered by these influences, and that an interest in everyday life can be found in Debord's work from a much earlier date. One can find references to the everyday in Debord's writings from as early as 1953,[4] together with indications that the goal of the modern revolution would be its ludic, festive and creative transformation. For example, in 1954, he and the LI declared: 'Let us not demand the guarantee or the increase of the "minimum wage [*minimum vital*]", but rather that the masses are no longer kept at the minimum of life [*minimum de la vie*]'.[5] Such views anticipate the SI's later contention that the modern revolution would be motivated by the existential poverty of the 'new' proletariat. For example, in 1957, in his 'Report on the Construction of Situations', Debord claimed that the moments that compose contemporary life were 'so undifferentiated and so dull that they give the distinct appearance of sameness';[6] in 1961, Debord can be found arguing that the 'scandalous poverty'[7] of modern everyday life could only be rectified through a 'reinvention of revolution'.[8] By 1962, and thus by the time of the splits described at the end of the previous chapter, the SI's initial avant-garde interest in the re-figuration of a stagnant culture had become an explicit call for total, universal social transformation: for the creation of 'a society of *realised art*'.[9] These concerns thus clearly pre-date Debord's more overt turn to social theory during the early 1960s. However, they certainly became more concrete and sophisticated at that time, and this increasing sophistication brings us back to the influence of s ou b.

For Cornelius Castoriadis, s ou b's primary theorist, modern capitalism evidenced the following contradiction: it was obliged to reduce individuals to 'mere

---

p. 265). The reason that Debord would go on to provide for leaving s ou b was that he didn't 'feel up to the task': he remarked, somewhat ironically, that 'it must be very tiring organising a revolutionary organisation' (Hussey 2002, p. 163; see also Guillaume 1995).

4 Debord 2006b, p. 108.
5 Debord 2006b, p. 141.
6 SI 2006, p. 40; Debord 2006b, p. 325.
7 SI 2006, p. 92; Debord 2006b, p. 574.
8 SI 2006, p. 94; Debord 2006b, p. 577.
9 SI 2006, p. 114; 1997, p. 257.

order-takers' in production, whilst also cultivating and promising the satisfaction of their desires in consumption. It thus reduced them to the status of objects on the one hand, and yet fostered their subjective aspirations to become more than mere objects on the other.[10] This diagnosis is, of course, extremely close to Debord and the SI's own claims. So too is the conclusion that Castoriadis drew from this observation. In his view, the frustration engendered by this contradiction could foster the demand for a revolution that would not simply pursue a fairer system of production and distribution, but which would instead challenge the entire social modality of contemporary life. Thus, modern society, Castoriadis claimed, harboured the potential for 'a *total* movement, concerned with all that men do in society, and with their real daily lives.'[11]

The correspondences that can be drawn between these positions and the Situationists' views are certainly striking, but it is worth remembering that Debord had reached his own version of this conclusion long before his brief association with S ou B.[12] In this regard, an equal, if not greater significance needs to be accorded to his understanding of the legacy of Surrealism. The latter's celebration of dream and desire *vis-à-vis* the banality of the quotidian greatly informed his own and the SI's demand for the revolutionary invigoration of a stagnant social existence. Furthermore, lessons could also be drawn from Surrealism's problematic political engagements.

As Maurice Blanchot once neatly put it, 'the service that Surrealism expects from Marxism is to prepare for it a society in which everyone could be Surrealist'.[13] Yet where the Surrealists had asserted that poetry must be put at the service of revolution, Debord and the SI declared that what was really required was 'to put revolution at the service of poetry'.[14] Doing so, they maintained, would ensure that 'the revolution does not betray its own project'[15] by subordinating its romantic core to crudely instrumental ends. In this regard, the SI's desire to transform everyday life can be understood, in part, as an element of their intention to critically develop the Surrealist legacy. Indeed, the very first issue of *Internationale situationniste* contained the observation that 'for us, Surrealism has been only a beginning of a revolutionary experiment in culture, an

---

10   Castoriadis 1974.
11   Ibid.
12   For example, the very first edition of *Internationale Situationniste* stated that 'The Situationists will execute the judgement that contemporary leisure is pronouncing against itself' (SI 2006, p. 49; 1997, p. 6).
13   Quoted in Baugh 2003, p. 54.
14   SI 2006, p. 151; 1997, p. 327.
15   SI 2006, p. 151; 1997, p. 327.

experiment that almost immediately ground to a practical and theoretical halt. We have to go further'.[16]

The manner in which the SI conceived this need to 'go further' was much informed by Henri Lefebvre's contentions that everyday life had become banal and structured by preordained social patterns, and that it needed to be radically transformed. Debord had read Lefebvre prior to their brief friendship in the early 1960s, and the first volume of Lefebvre's *Critique of Everyday Life*, which was published in 1947, seems to have coloured the ideas advanced by the LI during the 1950s.[17] Furthermore, as the SI gravitated towards Hegelian and Marxian ideas, Lefebvre's significance took on a different hue: for one of Lefebvre's key concerns, and indeed one of the chief points of connection between his views and those of the SI, was that the banality of everyday life needed to be understood as a key aspect of the generalised *alienation* engendered by modern capitalist society.

In this regard, Lefebvre's influence on Debord's thought bears relation to that of Lukács. Indeed, there are strong points of resemblance between the claims presented by the two writers. Although there was no direct line of influence from Lukács to Lefebvre,[18] the latter's presentation of a society characterised by alienation certainly echoes aspects of *History and Class Consciousness*. For example, both Lukács and Lefebvre reject a crudely orthodox notion of economic 'base' and cultural 'superstructure'. *History and Class Consciousness* views society as an interrelated totality, conceived under the governing rubric of the commodity; through doing so, it addresses the presence of the economic within the cultural and the quotidian. Likewise, Lefebvre's concern with the everyday reflected a similar shift from the traditional pre-eminence of the factory towards social life as a whole.

These ideas played an important part in shaping Debord and the SI's desire to move beyond classical Marxism and the traditional workers' movement of the past. They both imparted a sense that the workplace was by no means the sole space within modern society that was dominated by the dictates of capital. Both indicated that social activity in general might be shaped and dominated by those same dictates (for example: according to Lefebvre, 'the alienation of the worker by fragmented labour and machines is only one aspect of a larger – a total – alienation which as such is inherent in capitalist society').[19] These ideas clearly informed Debord's developing conception of spectacle. They also

---

16   SI 2006, p. 48; 1997, p. 6.
17   Jappe 1999, p. 73.
18   Trebitsch in Lefebvre 2008a, pp. xvii–viii.
19   Lefebvre 2008a, p. 37.

led the SI to claim that this state of affairs could only be rectified through the destruction and transformation of all extant capitalist social relations, and through the subsequent generalisation of Situationist activity throughout society as a whole. Just as Surrealism had demanded a revolution in which everyone would become a Surrealist, so too did the SI advocate a society in which 'everyone will be a Situationist'.[20] Yet before we go on to look at that ambition in a little more detail, it may be useful to gain a clearer sense of the sheer scale of its utopian and romantic dimensions.

'All or Not at All'

Debord has often been commended for his prescience and acumen, but he was, unfortunately, a little wide of the mark when he claimed in 1959 that the use of 'one-man helicopters' would 'spread to the general public within twenty years'.[21] Likewise, Constant Nieuwenhuys was a little optimistic when he declared, also in 1959, that 'space travel, which seems likely in the near future', would further the development of Situationist architecture. This was because 'establishing bases on other planets will immediately raise the problem of sheltered cities, which may provide models for our study of future urbanism'[22] (similar views were expressed in the SI's 'Manifesto' the following year: 'unitary urbanism' was to be 'extensible to all habitable planets').[23]

These views reflect a utopianism that runs throughout the SI's oeuvre, and which often makes Marx and Engels's rhapsody about being able to 'hunt in the morning, fish in the afternoon', and 'criticise after dinner'[24] seem tame in the extreme. For example, according to the SI's short-lived English section, post-revolutionary society would be 'an endless adventure, an endless passion, an endless banquet'.[25] One might also think here of Constant's attempts to envision a city that would be worthy of such an existence. His 'New Babylon' was designed according to Situationist and psychogeographical principles, and was intended to afford a state of perpetual *dérive*: composed of endless branching corridors and interconnected environments, the new *Homo Ludens* who would inhabitant New Babylon would wander through the city at whim, rearranging its ambiances according to their wishes as they did so.

---

20   SI 1960a.
21   SI 2006, p. 70; 1997, p. 104.
22   SI 2006, p. 72; 1997, p. 107. Lefebvre also refers to 'interplanetary travel' in the second volume of his *Critique of Everyday Life* (Lefebvre 2008b, p. 3).
23   SI 1997, p. 145.
24   Marx and Engels 2007, p. 54.
25   Heatwave 1966, p. 4.

The SI's utopianism was also quite unabashed. Like Breton and the Surrealists, the SI explicitly celebrated figures like Fourier for having linked the pursuit of alternative societies to utopian demands.[26] In addition, the SI possessed a tremendous enthusiasm for the possibilities afforded by modern technology; an enthusiasm that is perhaps best expressed by Vaneigem's much later and characteristically dramatic announcement that 'our dreams will come true when the modern world's technical know-how is placed at their disposal'.[27] The visionary aspects of these dreams are, however, nowhere more apparent than in the group's earliest work, where they tend to possess a poetic quality. For example, in his pre-SI 'Formulary for a New Urbanism' of 1953, Chtcheglov wrote:

> The latest technological developments would make possible the individual's unbroken contact with cosmic reality while eliminating its disagreeable aspects. Stars and rain can be seen through glass ceilings. The mobile house turns with the sun. Its sliding walls enable vegetation to invade life. Mounted on tracks, it can go down to the sea in the morning and return to the forest in the evening.[28]

Yet regardless of their poetic dimensions – and no matter how delirious the notion of Situationist helicopters and space-bases may seem – the fact remains that the more utopian aspects of the SI's work remained wedded, throughout, to a comparatively cold evaluation of modern society. These views did not stem from an uncritically euphoric, or indeed historically deterministic view of technology, but rather from a simple disdain for the evident distance between modern society's vast technical capacities, and the meanness and banality of their current applications. This gap between 'the wealth of present technological potentials' and 'the poverty of their use'[29] needed to be overcome, and when faced with such contradictory extremes, the only rational response, according to the SI, was to demand nothing less than utopia ('Be realistic! Demand the impossible!').[30]

Consequently, the SI's desire to transform everyday life should also be seen as a marker of their distance from the 'actually existing socialism' of their day,

---

26 Debord 2004a, p. 42. See also Lefebvre (2008b, p. 288): 'Marx owes much more to Fourier than is generally admitted'.
27 Vaneigem 2003, p. 244.
28 SI 2006, p. 3; 1997, p. 16.
29 SI 2006, p. 179; 1997, p. 389.
30 SI 2006, p. 451.

and as an indication of their desire to re-think the classical workers' movement of the past. The goal of revolution, for the SI, was the full flourishing of human life, and this necessarily entailed moving beyond comparatively tame, traditional ambitions towards appropriating the means of simply *maintaining* life. To demand anything less than the passionate, creative *enrichment* of lived existence would thus be tantamount to a regression into the politics of the past; a view that can be neatly encapsulated in the following motto, employed by members of the SI's English section, prior to their brief affiliation with the Situationists: 'all or not at all'.[31]

Absolute Knowing and the Unhappy Consciousness

Having now set out some of the background to the SI's concerns with the everyday and the construction of situations, we can begin to look at their ideas in a little more detail. In order to do so, we will focus on the two key lines of influence mentioned at the outset of this chapter: namely, the work of Lefebvre, and Sartrean existentialism. Furthermore, the discussions of these influences that follow below will endeavour to show that one can find traces, within the views expressed by the SI during the late 1950s and early 1960s, of the Hegelian and Marxian concerns that were introduced in Part One. Our approach will be as follows.

1) Debord and the SI's conception of constructed situations owes a marked debt to Sartrean existentialism. Whilst looking at this connection, we will show that Debord's relatively early views on Situationist activity involve ideas that resemble, and which would seem to prefigure and anticipate, his later, Hegelian Marxian conceptions of history, agency and praxis.
2) We will then move on to Lefebvre, in order to consider his views on the everyday, and his attendant theory of 'moments'. The aim will be to show that whilst Lefebvre's theory of 'moments' was certainly close to the SI's interest in situations, it was nonetheless seen to be different in some important respects. Once again, through discussing these differences we will highlight the presence, within Debord and the SI's early views on situations, of themes that would later come to the fore in their later, more overtly Hegelian Marxian work.

The manner in which these two strands will be pursued requires a few words of explanation. This is because the difference between Debord and Lefebvre, and

---

31 Heatwave 1966, p. 2.

indeed that between the SI and Sartrean existentialism, will be presented via the relation between two famous Hegelian motifs, both of which are described in Hegel's *Phenomenology of Spirit*: namely, the 'unhappy consciousness', and 'absolute knowing'. Before we can proceed, therefore, we first need to explain them.

Hegel's *Phenomenology* is intended to provide normal, everyday consciousness with a 'ladder' to 'Science [*Wissenschaft*]',[32] i.e. to the standpoint of the speculative philosophy set out in the Hegelian system.[33] As we saw in Chapter 2, that standpoint entails that the thought set out in the Hegelian system can operate as both ontology and epistemology at the same time. The 'being, pure being'[34] with which we begin in the *Logic*, and which the latter text proceeds to unfold, is not just the being of matter, or the mere *idea* of being, but rather being *per se*: being that encompasses both thought *and* matter. This standpoint – the starting point of the Hegelian system – can only be achieved through superseding the normal, commonplace assumption that consciousness and its object are inherently distinct. Thus, the task of the *Phenomenology* – the 'ladder' to this standpoint – is to demonstrate that subject and object are one. The book shows that the truth obtained by the highest, most developed form of consciousness – i.e. absolute knowing, the apex of the book – is in fact a knowledge of consciousness' own identity with the object that confronts it.[35]

The *Phenomenology* traces the evolution of a series of 'shapes' of consciousness from the simplest forms of awareness of the objective world all the way up to absolute knowing. This evolution takes place because each shape is shown to generate its successor. Each shape of consciousness has an initial conception of the object that confronts it, but each finds that its experience of that object reveals that it is in fact facing something quite different from that which it initially supposed the object to be. This then gives rise to a new conception of the object, and thereby to a new form of consciousness, which once again finds that its object is not what it first supposed. This process continues throughout the book. Consciousness develops into self-consciousness, and eventually into Spirit (the self-consciousness of a community). The subsequent

---

32 Hegel 1977, p. 14.
33 Hegel 1969, p. 28.
34 Hegel 1969, p. 82.
35 As Hegel puts it in the *Logic*: the *Phenomenology* exhibits 'consciousness in its movement onwards from the first immediate opposition of itself and the object to absolute knowing', i.e. to the supersession of that opposition; a movement that 'goes through every form of the *relation of consciousness to the object* and has the Concept of science for its result' (Hegel 1969, p. 48, italics in the original).

iterations of Spirit then give rise to science, art, religion, and eventually to philosophy. Each stage in consciousness' evolution posits a new object, and with each step of its ascent, it moves ever closer towards realising that its object is, in fact, the Absolute. This is made possible by the 'absolute knowing' attained at the end of the book. There, a philosophical form of Spirit passes beyond religion's attempts to represent the Absolute as 'God'. Such religious 'picture-thoughts' (*Vorstellungen*) stand removed from the object that they attempt to represent. By passing beyond them, Spirit comes to realise that it is, in fact, *one* with the Absolute. It reaches this awareness because it realises, at the end of the book, that the object that it confronts is, in fact, the rational structure of all being. The Absolute, in other words, is being that possesses the same rational structure as Spirit itself. This means that subject and object share the same rational structure (i.e. that of the Concept, which we described in Chapter 2 as the dynamic, 'living' logic of the Absolute). Because they share this structure, Spirit is able to comprehend this final object, and to recognise its identity with it. Ultimately, therefore, Spirit recognises that it is, in effect, the Absolute's knowledge of itself. Upon attaining absolute knowing, Spirit grasps its own true nature, realises its fundamental identity with the Absolute, and comprehends that subject and object are one. The standpoint of speculative philosophy is thus attained.

The *Phenomenology* is famously obscure, and has been interpreted in differing ways. The short summary presented here may, therefore, differ from Debord's own reading.[36] Yet all that matters here, in terms of explaining the use to which Debord put these ideas, is the relatively uncontroversial claim that upon reaching the *Phenomenology*'s consclusion, Spirit grasps its own identity with the Absolute. This is because Debord's re-figuration of that moment of 'absolute knowing' seems very close to Lukács's own position in *History and Class Consciousness*.

36 Debord's archived reading notes on the *Phenomenology* are obviously important here, but as they consist almost entirely of quotations it is hard to draw a great deal from them. However, comments expressed in one of his letters seem close to aspects of Hyppolite's interpretation of the *Phenomenology* (Hyppolite 1974, p. 35). According to Debord, the first sections of the book set out the 'history' of the emergence of individual consciousness; following the emergence of Spirit, the book then rehearses that individual development in more collective terms, thereby detailing historical moments that echo that individual development (Debord 2004a, p. 65). Although Debord's letter was written in 1969, it seems very similar to Lukács's description of the *Phenomenology* in his *The Young Hegel* (Lukács 1975, pp. 470–1), which was not translated into French until 1981.

In *History and Class Consciousness*, Lukács basically reframes Spirit's final attainment of 'absolute knowing' – its final comprehension of its own true nature, and thus of its fundamental identity with the Absolute – as the proletariat's recognition that it is in fact the alienated author of its own world.[37] In Hegel's philosophy, as we have seen, the Absolute is the ground, source and goal of Spirit's efforts, and whilst it initially appears as something other and distinct from the consciousness that addresses it, the *Phenomenology* ultimately shows that it is, in fact, Spirit's own true self. In much the same way, Lukács's proletariat initially views its own historical and formative agency as a distinct, separate object. However, according to Lukács, the nature of the proletariat's social circumstances will oblige it to overcome this state of misrecognition and alienation, and to thereby recognise itself as the potential master of its own future (thus, in effect – and although Lukács does not state this explicitly – his claims effectively re-frame the Hegelian Absolute as the proletariat's own agency, activity and potential). The ideas that underpin *The Society of the Spectacle* seem to be very close indeed to this position.

Absolute knowing, therefore, is an important concept for the interpretation of Debord's mature theoretical work introduced in the opening chapters of this book. It thus seems pertinent that one can find, as we will see below, aspects of Debord's early views on the constructed situation that chime with this idea: aspects that rendered his views on Situationist activity amenable to the Hegelian Marxian rearticulations that they would go on to receive during the 1960s. Absolute knowing, then, is the first of the two Hegelian motifs that we will draw upon.

The second of these two motifs is the unhappy consciousness; and where absolute knowing chimes with Debord's later Hegelianism, the unhappy consciousness echoes the existential material that informed his own and the SI's work.

Like absolute knowing, the unhappy consciousness is one of the 'shapes' of consciousness that constitute the rungs of the *Phenomenology*'s 'ladder' to the Absolute. It appears at a comparatively early stage in the *Phenomenology*, at which consciousness has arrived at a position where it understands that the object that confronts it is a God-like Absolute, but at which it still believes itself to exist in total distinction from that object. Hegel seems to associate this stage of the book with medieval Catholicism, and he holds that this form of consciousness' 'unhappiness' follows from its awareness of its inherent separation from this sublime object. The latter is described as the

---

37 See Lukács 1971, pp. xxii–iii.

'Unchanging'. This is because the unhappy consciousness knows itself to be finite and contingent, and associates the infinitude and necessity that it lacks with this absolute object. It thus believes itself to be particular and transitory, and views this Unchanging object as universal and permanent. It continually strives to overcome its separation from this God-like object, but it finds that every attempt that it makes to do so simply recreates that distance anew: every time it seems to draw closer to this object, the latter recedes once more. Because it lacks the perspective of absolute knowing, it remains unaware, throughout these attempts, that this entity is, in truth, its own alienated, unrecognised self.[38]

Just as absolute knowing has served writers and commentators as a figure for the *end* of alienation (e.g. Lukács), so too has the unhappy consciousness served as a seminal figure *for* alienation and self-separation. This is certainly true within the French Hegelian tradition, largely as a result of Jean Wahl's highly influential *Le Malheur de la conscience dans la philosophie de Hegel* of 1929: a book that may well have made an impact on Sartre, given that he once stated that 'human reality' is 'by nature an unhappy consciousness with no possibility of surpassing its unhappy state'.[39] Just as the unhappy consciousness is tormented by its constant inability to reach a God-like, 'Unchanging' absolute, so too is the human individual, for Sartre, continually tormented by

---

38   A longer account of the unhappy consciousness seems out of place here, but the following remarks may help (although see Harris 1995, pp. 42–6, Houlgate 2013, pp. 113–22, and Hyppolite 1974, pp. 190–215 for useful overviews). The *Phenomenology* stresses that self-consciousness is characterised by negativity. This negativity drives the lord and bondsman's (or master and slave's) famous struggle to the death, as for each to recognise the other as a self-consciousness, each must negate the other; it later prompts a stoical consciousness to negate the world by retreating into itself, and it then causes a sceptical consciousness to declare that it alone is true, necessary and existent. This sceptical consciousness, which precedes the unhappy consciousness in the *Phenomenology*, is marked by the following contradiction: it has become sure of itself through negating an allegedly false world; yet doing so renders it contingent upon that which it declares to be secondary to its own supposed necessity. The unhappy consciousness brings that contradiction to the fore. It knows itself to be both necessary and contingent, and locates its own necessity, permanence and stability within a separate object that resides beyond itself: a universality that perpetually eludes its own finite particularity. Every attempt that it makes to grasp this 'Unchanging' absolute fails, because every attempt arises from – and thereby demonstrates – its own separation from the latter. As Hegel's commentators have pointed out (e.g. Inwood 1992, p. 218; Houlgate 2005, p. 75), he held the unhappy consciousness to be exemplified by medieval Catholic Christianity.

39   Sartre 2003, p. 114.

an unrealisable desire to become the necessary foundation of his or her own irredeemably arbitrary existence. The correspondence is readily apparent: the unhappy consciousness desires unity with its God-like, Unchanging object; for Sartre, 'the best way to conceive of the fundamental project of human reality is to say that man is the being whose project is to be God'.[40] Yet just as the unhappy consciousness constantly fails to access this divine object, so too, for Sartre, is human existence marked by the continual pursuit of an unattainable resolution.[41] For Sartre, we can never become 'God': we are continually cast into the situations that compose our lives, and can never become the author of our own existence.

We will return to Sartre's claims shortly, but the comments above should suffice to support the following explanation. As we saw in Chapter 2, Debord's

---

40 Sartre 2003, p. 587.
41 For the Sartre of *Being and Nothingness*, human existence is inherently tragic. This is because it is characterised, in his view, by a split between its concrete facticity (the 'in-itself', in Sartre's terminology), and its conscious capacity to comprehend and put that facticity in question (the 'for-itself'). The latter, for Sartre, can never be reducibly identified with the former: for where the former denotes our factical being (our body, our past, our current context, etc.), the latter corresponds to our non-being. According to Sartre, because we are conscious, temporal creatures, we are always not what we are at any given moment of time (or as De Beauvoir put it: 'between the past which no longer is and the future which is not yet, this moment when he ['man'] exists is nothing' (De Beauvoir 1976, p. 7)). We cannot be reduced to any instance of our own extant being, as we always exceed that which we currently are: we are always becoming 'other' to our own extant selves. Because we can never be reduced to a particular, extant moment of our lives, we are, for Sartre, absolutely and fundamentally free: we can always redefine ourselves and choose alternative courses of action, no matter how fixed and restricted things may appear. However, for Sartre, this absolute freedom is a source of angst, and a burden that we typically choose to hide from. We may want to identify ourselves with our present circumstances, or with our past, but we can never do so; and if we were to attempt to do so, we would simply be hiding from the fundamental freedom that follows from our own inherent 'nothingness'. Even though our lives are the results of our own actions and choices, we can never be reducibly identified with those results. As Sartre puts it in one of his typically convoluted sentences: 'the being of human reality is suffering because it rises in being as perpetually haunted by a totality which it is without being able to be it' (Sartre 2003, p. 114). Or, to put that rather more straightforwardly: my life is a totality that I construct, but I can never be reductively identified with that totality, as I am always exceeding it: I am always becoming other to whatever I have made myself. Nonetheless, for Sartre, we always desire to become 'in-itself-for-itself'; to supersede the for-itself's constant supersession of the extant being of the in-itself. In fact, for Sartre, all of the values that we posit are, at root, iterations of this desire (Sartre 2003, pp. 117–18).

views on temporality echo elements of Sartre's work. We have also noted that his notion of constructed situations owes a great deal to existential phenomenology. There are, however, crucial differences. The predicament of the Sartrean existential subject, which Sartre himself links to the angst of the unhappy consciousness, seems closely related to that of Debord's spectators, who are similarly condemned to pursue their own alienated selves within the spectacle's commodified satisfactions. In other words, when seen from Debord's Hegelian Marxian perspective, the ontology that underpins Sartrean existentialism can be seen to naturalise capitalist alienation. This is why the distinction between absolute knowing and the unhappy consciousness is important here. For Hegel, the advent of absolute knowing resolves the constant self-estrangement of the unhappy consciousness; likewise, for both Debord and Lukács, the angst of capitalist alienation could be resolved through the advent of a revolutionary condition of subject-object unity.

It is significant, therefore, that whilst Debord's early views on constructed situations owe an obvious debt to Sartre, they nonetheless contain ideas that seem far closer to the subject-object unity of absolute knowing. These ideas developed, in Debord's early work, from largely aesthetic concerns, and not from a direct engagement with Hegel; yet nonetheless, they would later take on a more explicitly Hegelian form, following Debord's turn towards Hegelian and Marxian thought at the end of the 1950s. Therefore, if we can show that elements of Debord's early views on constructed situations echo (however inadvertently) the subject-object unity of absolute knowing, we will be able to explain the evolution of Debord's later work from his early views; and if we can signal the proximities between Sartrean existentialism and the unhappy consciousness, we will also be able to explain Debord's critical relation to Sartrean philosophy.

These same themes will also prove useful when we come to look at the influence exerted by Lefebvre. This is because the same constant pursuit of an unreachable resolution that we have identified in Sartre's work can be found in Lefebvre's Hegelian Marxism. Although Lefebvre's Hegelian Marxism certainly led him to posit a condition of subject-object unity, he did so whilst framing that condition of unity as an effectively unattainable goal: a vision of unity that continually recedes into an unreachable future, and which is thus just as constantly elusive as the unhappy consciousness' divine object. This seems very different indeed from Debord's own position. In Debord's more Lukácsian model, subject-object unity is not an unreachable end-point, but rather the very grounds of an open, self-determinate history. The relation between absolute knowing and the unhappy consciousness can thus also help us to consider Debord's debts towards, and departure from, Lefebvre.

The remainder of the chapter will be split into two halves. In the first half, we will look at Debord and the SI's debts to existentialism; in the second half, we will turn to Debord's relation to Lefebvre.

1) **Existentialism and the Constructed Situation**

Debord, Sartre and Heidegger
In his *Being and Nothingness* of 1943, Sartre claimed that our lives are composed of distinct situations, and that it is within these situations that our freedom arises and operates. We define ourselves and know ourselves through the actions that we choose to undertake in response to these distinct contexts. Perhaps as a result of the general impact and ambience of Sartrean existentialism within France at the time, Debord, in the very early 1950s, seems to have adopted this general idea, and developed it as a means of resolving Surrealism's unfinished gestures towards the unification of art and life. Rather than finding oneself cast into life's situations, one should instead attempt to consciously create them.

None of Sartre's works were present in Debord's personal library as of his death in 1994 (the contents of which are catalogued in the BnF archive), but it seems extremely hard to believe that Debord never read Sartre's work.[42] Yet whilst it seems safe to say that Debord took the notion of the situation from Sartre, or at least that his ideas were much informed by Sartre's views, it remains the case that Sartre himself appropriated the concept of the situation from from Heidegger, which then raises the further question of whether Debord and the SI engaged with Heidegger directly.

There are, undoubtedly, Heideggerian themes within Debord's work. Like Heidegger, Debord offers melancholic and poetic reflections on the existential importance and experience of time, and although one needs to squint a little in order to see this, there are, perhaps, also echoes between elements of Heidegger's work and Debord's comments on spectacular society.[43] Yet there were no works by Heidegger in Debord's library either (although Debord clearly read an article by Heidegger on Nietzsche in *Arguments*),[44] and it seems reason-

---

42   Zacarias 2014, p. 17.
43   One might think here of Heidegger's comments on Das Man, and on the loss of authenticity that arises when Dasein 'lets itself be carried along by the looks of the world' (Heidegger 2008, p. 216).
44   The article is Heidegger's 'The Word of Nietzsche: "God is Dead"', and it appeared in *Arguments* 15. Thanks are due to Gabriel Zacarias for details of the passage that Debord quotes

able to contend that many of the Heideggerian echoes that can be found in his work are either coincidental or simply derive from Heidegger's own debts to Lukács's early work (principally, Lukács's *Soul and Form* and *History and Class Consciousness*).[45] We should also add that there are almost no direct references to Heidegger within the pages of *Internationale situationniste*,[46] or indeed in Debord's broader oeuvre, and that there is only one reference to Heidegger in all eight volumes of Debord's correspondence: in a letter of 1966, he attacks the editors of a journal called *Aletheia* for having 'not even managed to see Heidegger for what he really is'.[47] The latter remark is hardly surprising, given that Debord's evaluation of an author was typically tied to his assessment of that individual's life and actions (Heidegger had stated his allegiance to National Socialism). Yet however peripheral Heidegger may have been to Debord and the SI's work, he certainly had an impact upon the French Hegelian and existential thought that informed Debord's writings.

In *Being and Time* (1927), Heidegger claimed that human beings find themselves 'thrown' into 'situations' within the world. These situations, for Heidegger, are composed of the network of relations with and within the world that Dasein 'discloses', and through which it thereby gives meaning to itself and to its own present moment. Sartre's own version of the situation is very similar: in his view, human consciousness always finds itself within a given, factical situation (we always exist 'immediately "in situation"',[48] for Sartre, and our consciousness always 'arises in situation').[49] Although these situations are simply given to us, they are, nonetheless, the arena within which freedom operates. They are identified and understood through the manner in which consciousness (or rather the 'for-itself') freely interprets and makes sense of its own status and

---

      from Heidegger's text (which, incidentally, includes the following, significant remark: 'Thought metaphysically, the situation is never anything other than the stage for the action of the subject'), and to Laurence Le Bras for assistance with enquires concerning the contents of Debord's library.

45   This point was highlighted by Lucien Goldmann; see Lukács 1971, p. xxii; see also Trebitsch in Lefebvre 2008a, p. xviii.

46   One such reference can be found in the pages of the ninth issue of *Internationale situationniste*, where a 'poor Heidegger!' and a 'poor Sartre!' are grouped together with an equally 'poor' Barthes, Cardan [a pseudonym used by Cornelius Castoriadis], Lefebvre and Lukács, on the grounds that offered only 'caricatural fragments of the innovating ideas that can simultaneously comprehend and contest the totality of our era' (SI 2006, p. 176; 1997, p. 368).

47   Debord 2003a, p. 147.

48   Sartre 2003, p. 63.

49   Sartre 2003, p. 115.

factical existence, and through our ability to posit future goals and projects that lead beyond the situations that we find ourselves within.

As indicated above, the core difference between these views and Debord's own account lies in the rejection of the inevitable *givenness* of the situation. In Debord's view (and this accords with his Lukácsian ideas, which we will consider in Chapter 7), any sense in which social reality might be simply thrust upon us as an immediate 'given' needed to be rejected. In place of such a view, objective reality needed to be understood as a historical construction: a construction that had been shaped unconsciously by alienated action in the past, but which could now be created consciously.

As Debord turned to Hegel and Marx towards the end of the 1950s, and around the beginning of the 1960s, this aspect of the constructed situation became more apparent. This may have been reinforced by the degree to which Debord's later, Hegelian views on temporality echo and accord with the aspects of Sartre's philosophy outlined above.

As we will see in Chapter 6, the French Hegelianism that informed Debord's mature conception of temporality was greatly inflected by its famous early twentieth-century proponents, who tended to emphasise Hegel's association of dialectical negativity with human temporality. The manner in which they did so was, at times, coloured by Heidegger's philosophy (Koyré and Kojève are particularly significant here). In consequence, the French Hegelianism of the 1930s and 1940s was marked by an approach to Hegelian thought that involved an emphasis on existential themes. This conflux of ideas coloured the development and subsequent reception of Sartre's philosophy. Debord's work is also informed by this mixture of ideas, and in consequence, his own Hegelian views on time are, at points, remarkably close to those of Sartre. We have already referred to Debord's claim in *The Society of the Spectacle* that 'man – that "negative being who *is* solely to the extent that he abolishes being" – is one with time'.[50] The phrase that Debord quotes in that statement was drawn from Hegel's *Phenomenology*, but it bears a significant resemblance to Sartre's views on the 'nihilating structure' of human 'temporality'.[51] According to Sartre, who also seems indebted to Hegel here, we are always *not* what we are at any given moment. In Sartre's view, the 'for-itself' (the human individual's consciousness and free agency) can never be reduced to the 'in-itself' (his or her factical being: their body, past, and present circumstances). In other words: for Sartre, we are always becoming *other* to what we are, and we can never be reductively

---

50   Debord 1995, p. 92; 2006b, p. 820.
51   Sartre 2003, p. 58.

identified with a particular moment of our being. We are, therefore, inherently temporal and transitory creatures.

Thus, on the one hand, and like Debord (or, perhaps more accurately: like the aspects of French Hegelianism that inflect Debord's account), Sartre presented the human subject as perpetually engaged in a process of negation and self-realisation in time. Yet on the other hand, there is also an important difference here. With Sartre, this temporal existence is almost an *affliction*. It can only ever deliver the individual into further states of separation, ambiguity and angst. As we indicated above, when referring to the impossible desire to 'become God', the Sartrean 'for-itself' cannot establish itself as its own foundation, despite its constant compulsion to do so. According to Sartre, we can never be united with the totality of our own existence, because we are continually exceeding its extant form. Consequently, whilst Sartre's phenomenological framework would not, strictly speaking, admit the term 'subject-object unity', the latter is effectively denied within his work: the 'subject' (such as it exists within that framework) always exceeds its 'object', and can never be identified with it.

Debord, however, locates that constant, negative process *within*, and not *against*, a condition of subject-object unity. He is able to do so because in his work, such unity is not understood as a static state, but rather as a condition of constant, self-determinate process within time. This is because subject-object unity is identified with the interaction of thought and world afforded by self-determinate historical praxis. All moments that occur as instances of this condition of unity are moments of the same developing identity. The additions thus made to the totality of the subject's life do not, therefore, entail the constant 'otherness' that troubles Sartre, but rather constitute instances of self-authorship.[52]

One can, however, find something rather close to Sartre's position in Debord's views on spectatorship. In 1967's *The Society of the Spectacle*, he wrote that 'Each and every new product represents the hope for a dazzling short-cut

---

52   These points can be illustrated by returning to Debord's self-confessed proximity to August von Cieszkowski, and to the latter's views on Hegel. For Cieszkowski, thought would not be united with reality solely through comprehending it, as in Hegel's philosophy; instead, the real unity of thought and concrete reality lay in the latter's conscious construction. Because those circumstances that we plan and actualise are 'active event[s] which [are] entirely ours', they are 'no longer foreign but already conscious before being realised' (Cieszkowski 2009, p. 55). Debord's views are much the same, and pertain to his distinction from Sartre. The totality of a historical life is an open-ended construction, but conscious praxis renders this a process of self-creation, rather than one that resembles the constant flight of Sartrean nothingness.

to the long-awaited promised land of total consumption', adding that once each commodity is purchased, 'its essential poverty stands revealed', and another is 'assigned to supply the system with its justification'.[53] Hegel's unhappy consciousness, in its constant pursuit of the Absolute that eludes it, continually strives to reach an unattainable resolution to its alienation; likewise, Debord's spectators continually reach for images of satisfaction that dissolve as soon as they grasp them. Such a dynamic bears a striking resemblance to *Being and Nothingness*' account of the basic structure of human subjectivity. After having likened human existence to a donkey that continually plods towards a carrot that is dangled before it, Sartre writes that we constantly 'run towards ourselves', but always remain 'the being which can not be reunited with itself'.[54] The crucial point here, of course, is that in Debord's work, the spectator *can* be reunited with his or her own alienated self. If the situations that compose one's life are consciously created by the acting subject – or, to put that in terms of Debord's mature theory: if society supersedes its separation from its own historical agency – then the subject ceases to be 'thrown' into an alien world, but instead (to quote the young Marx) 'sees himself in a world that he has created'.[55]

We are, however, getting a little ahead of ourselves here, as these themes do not really come to the fore in Debord's work prior to his turn to Hegel and Marx in the late 1950s. Before that point, the primary impetus towards the construction of situations was the post-Surrealist, avant-garde concern with the unification of art and life that we described earlier. The discussions presented in this section of the chapter have, however, attempted to suggest a degree of continuity between those early concerns and the elaborations and developments that they would later receive. The very notion that human subjects should consciously create the situations that compose their lives necessarily invites a notion of self-authorship that would gradually develop into the conception of historical praxis that we discussed in Part One of this book.

The Existential Situation and the Realisation of Philosophy

Debord and the SI's growing engagements with Marx and Marxist theory also fostered the view that key aspects of existential thought amounted to an apology for capitalist subjectivity. They were, of course, by no means alone in holding that opinion. Lukács, when discussing Heidegger, once stated that the latter had turned 'an essentially social alienation' into 'an eternal *"condition*

---

53   Debord 1995, p. 45, translation altered; 2006b, p. 790.
54   Sartre 2003, p. 225.
55   Marx 1988, p. 77.

humaine":[56] for if the phenomenological investigation of 'being' reveals an ontology that prevents subject-object unity (as in Sartre, according to Dunayevskaya),[57] or if subject is effectively reduced to object (as Adorno claims is the case with Heidegger),[58] then angst, anguish, alienation and anxiety are grounded within the very nature of being itself, and are thereby rendered eternal characteristics of human existence. A resolvable social predicament is thus cast as an insurmountable and inescapable human condition. Yet, for Debord and the SI, the Sartrean view that 'hell' is 'other people' simply reflected the failings of an atomised society.[59] Besides, if meaning can only be accorded to such an existence through this subject's constant orientation towards a distant and unreachable absolute (e.g. Sartre's impossible 'in-itself-for-itself', Kierkegaard's God, and perhaps also Heidegger's death), then – as we have suggested above – one ultimately arrives at a model of human existence that not only echoes the unhappy consciousness' constant alienation, but which also bears a striking resemblance to Debord's notion of capitalist spectatorship.

Therefore (and despite its French exponents' loudly declared distaste for bourgeois values), existential philosophy came to be viewed by the SI as far too complacent and politically neutral. In this regard, the influence exerted by

---

56 Lukács 1971, p. xxiv.

57 'One would have thought that Sartre, who returned to a work of philosophical rigour [with his *Critique of Dialectical Reason*] after he had become, or at least was in the process of becoming, an adherent of Marx's historical materialism, would at least in theory attempt to end the bifurcation between subject and object [which characterised *Being and Nothingness*], would concretise his project of "going beyond" as the Subject appropriating objectivity, not *vice versa*' (Dunayevskaya 2002, p. 203).

58 For Adorno, Heidegger's supersession of the subject-object distinction takes 'being' as a primal object to which subjectivity is reduced. This not only removes the difference required for critique, but consecrates a world marked by commodity fetishism: 'if men no longer had to equate themselves with things, they would [not] need ... an invariant picture of themselves, after the model of things' (Adorno 1990, p. 96). Lukács makes a similar point: '*Sein und Zeit* is ... merely a document of the day showing how a class felt and thought, and not an 'ontological' disclosure of ultimate truth' (Lukács 1973).

59 Vaneigem would later put this particularly clearly in his *The Revolution of Everyday Life* of 1967: 'Suppose that a tyrant took pleasure in throwing prisoners, who had been flayed alive, in a small cell; suppose that to hear their screams and see them scramble each time they brushed against one another amused him no end, and caused him to meditate on human nature and the curious behaviour of human beings. Suppose that at the same time and in the same country there were philosophers and wise men who explained to the worlds of science and art that suffering had to do with the collective life of men, the inevitable presence of Others, society as such – wouldn't we be right to consider these men the tyrant's watchdogs?' (Vaneigem 2003, p. 48).

existential thought on Debord and the SI bears a resemblance to that exerted by Hegel on Marx: both were held to offer important resources to the modern revolutionary project, yet both were taken to have couched those resources within a perspective that remained amenable to existing social conditions. There is, in fact, a sense in which the SI's relation to Sartrean existentialism bears relation to the Marxian realisation of Hegelian philosophy in praxis. As we saw earlier, the SI made this point explicitly in 1964. Since 'individuals are defined by their situation', they wrote, such individuals 'need the power to create situations worthy of their desires';[60] and in consequence, whilst the 'philosophers and artists' of the past had 'only interpreted situations', the 'point now' was to creatively 'transform them'.[61] Thought that had previously interpreted the world, and tacitly justified its extant form, would now be employed in its conscious transformation.

We can close here by summarising the key points that have been made so far. Debord's initial relation to the Sartrean notion of the situation was simply one of appropriation. Life, as Sartrean existentialism had pointed out, was composed of situations; the post-Surrealist need to unify art and life would, therefore, involve creating situations. However, the increasing theoretical sophistication of Debord's thought entailed a critical engagement and break with the phenomenological frameworks that writers such as Sartre and Heidegger had employed. Once placed within the context of Debord's developing Hegelian Marxian ideas, the project of creating situations differs markedly from the constant, miserable flight of the Sartrean for-itself. Debord replaces Sartre's account of the human individual's impossible attempt to 'become God' with the almost Feuerbachian contention that humanity could, through revolution, effectively *be* 'God', i.e. that it could become the conscious master and author of its own existence. Thus, in place of a stance that recalls the constant alienation of the unhappy consciousness, we instead have a mode of subject-object unity that seems closer to a Lukácsian conception of absolute knowing.

In the following sections we will look at the connections between the SI's constructed situations and Lefebvre's theory of 'moments'. Through doing so, we will try to advance our attempts to indicate the roots of Debord's later, Hegelian Marxist ideas within his early views on the constructed situation.

---

60   SI 2006, p. 178; 1997, p. 388.
61   SI 2006, p. 178, translation altered; 1997, p. 388.

2) Lefebvre: The Moment and the Absolute

In Pursuit of the Total Man

A great deal of ink has been spilled over the details of Lefebvre's relationship with Debord and the SI. This is a relationship that Lefebvre would later describe as 'a love story that ended badly, very badly',[62] and which came to a close in 1962 over mutual accusations of plagiarism.[63] There is some confusion over the dates of this short-lived friendship. Lefebvre, perhaps eager to claim influence, stated that it began in 1957, the same year that the SI was founded;[64] Hussey holds that Debord and Lefebvre met in 1958;[65] Kaufmann claims that their meeting did not take place until 1960.[66] The latter claim is persuasive, and it can be backed up by evidence within Debord's correspondence.[67] Furthermore, whilst Lefebvre certainly exerted an influence, their relationship was reciprocal in that regard, and both informed each other's ideas between between 1960 and 1962.[68] Debord and the SI had, however, already formulated their own positions prior to their contact with Lefebvre. Debord had no doubt read Lefebvre's work before their meeting, but he was hardly a disciple. Instead, it seems that both writers were simply moving in similar directions.

---

62 Ross 2004, p. 268.
63 The text in question is the SI's 'Theses on the Paris Commune' (see the SI's 'Into the Trashcan of History!' for their account). Further conflict may well have been provoked by Lefebvre's lingering connections to the PCF, his association with the journal *Arguments*, and by more personal, romantic intrigues.
64 Ross 2004, p. 267.
65 Hussey 2002, p. 138 and pp. 174–6.
66 Kaufmann 2006, p. 167.
67 Lefebvre wrote to Debord in January 1960, saying that 'I've been wanting to meet you since the beginning of your journal' (Debord 2009, p. 331n). The journal first appeared in 1958, so Lefebvre's claim that they met in 1957 is immediately suspect. The following month, Debord noted in a letter to a fellow Situationist that aspects of Lefebvre's work were 'very interesting; and close to us', but added that 'I haven't seen him yet' (Debord 2009, p. 331; see also Kaufmann 2006, p. 167). Letters sent by Debord within the SI prior to 1960 indicate that he was excited by the similarities between Lefebvre's work and the Situationist project, but there is no prior reference to any personal meeting. It also seems that Raoul Vaneigem was directed towards Debord by Lefebvre, who had appreciated an essay by Vaneigem on Lautréamont (Vaneigem 1956). This was in 1960; Vaneigem joined the SI the following year.
68 For Jappe, Debord's 'Perspectives for Conscious Changes in Everyday Life' (a text that was famously delivered via a tape recorder in a suitcase to Lefebvre's Group for Research on Everyday Life) and the second volume of Lefebvre's *Critique of Everyday Life*, both of which appeared in 1961, 'correspond almost word for word' (Jappe 1999, p. 75).

These similarities also extend to their approaches to a Hegelian Marx, which can, at first sight, seem very close to one another. For example, Lefebvre placed particular stress upon the importance of alienation, and he also drew heavily, but not exclusively,[69] on the young Marx (he was in fact the initial French translator of Marx's early *Manuscripts* in 1933). Lefebvre also associated the end of alienation with a condition of subject-object unity, and he even identified the latter with a conception of the absolute (albeit not the Hegelian Absolute, as we will see below). Yet there is also a crucial difference between Debord and Lefebvre's views. This is as follows: where Debord frames such subject-object unity as the *grounds* of historical praxis, Lefebvre casts it as a constantly receding, and indeed seemingly inaccessible *goal*. Therefore, and as Bruce Baugh has pointed out,[70] Lefebvre's views – despite their overtly Hegelian Marxian nature – can, at times, echo the unhappy consciousness' continual pursuit of an unattainable absolute.

In order to begin demonstrating the presence of this dynamic within Lefebvre's work we should start with his notion of the 'total man'. Lefebvre's total man was first presented in his *Dialectical Materialism* of 1940, and he would go on to develop and employ it for the next two decades. It would in fact remain in use until the appearance of the second volume of his *Critique* in 1961. The idea grew from a line that Lefebvre found in Marx's *Manuscripts*: 'Man appropriates his integral essence in an integral way, as a total man'.[71] It essentially denoted the goal of historical praxis, which, according to Lefebvre, was to realise the 'total' or '"de-alienated" man':[72] a figure of perfect resolution, understood as a 'living subject-object'.[73]

Lefebvre, who had been expelled from the Parti Communiste Français (PCF) in 1958, was a remarkably prolific writer. He in fact wrote more than sixty books, and perhaps as a result, his writing is often a little hastier, and rather less precise, than one might desire. His conception of the total man is a perfect example of this rather frustrating tendency. At times, Lefebvre presented it as a discrete, final goal, located at the end of history; at others, it seems closer to the totality of human action conducted *en route* towards that final goal,

---

69   There are, however, also important engagements with the mature Marx's notions of social form in Lefebvre's work. See O'Kane (forthcoming) for a critical discussion of this issue.
70   Baugh 2003. See also Trebitsch (in Lefebvre 2008a, p. xvii), who points out that Lefebvre's earlier *La Conscience mystifiée* draws on Hegel's account of the unhappy consciousness.
71   Marx 1988, p. 106; the translation used here has, however, been taken from Lefebvre 2008a, p. 65.
72   Lefebvre 1968, p. 162.
73   Ibid.

albeit gathered together and united at that point of ultimate achievement.⁷⁴ In all of its instantiations, however, the concept denotes a final end-point. As it developed through the course of Lefebvre's work, it came to function as a vision of all that the present lacks: a redemptive figure of complete subject-object unity, located at the end of a fractured history (and 'redemptive' is certainly the right word to use here: Lefebvre's ideas are by no means devoid of Christian undertones).⁷⁵ Because the vision of the total man was held to emerge immanently from the privations of everyday life, it was also said to afford a goal for lived praxis. As such a goal, it was credited with providing activity oriented towards remedying the present with an 'ethic'.⁷⁶

This meant that the total man was cast as an 'absolute', i.e. an absolute value, the certainty and beneficence of which stood in contrast to the contextual perspectives and banalities of everyday existence. It is, however, important to note that Lefebvre was at pains to show that the total man was not a fixed, transcendental absolute. Instead, he announced that it was 'dialectical',⁷⁷ because it was interwoven with the everyday from which it arose. This corresponds to the utopian dimensions of the total man. Because the demand for this perfect, 'de-alienated' condition was engendered by the inadequacies of the present, each present moment would give rise to new visions of this utopian condition, insofar as each such moment would be marked by different privations. Yet although the absolute of the total man was thus continually being posited anew, Lefebvre clearly conceived it as a solid, lasting goal. It would arise gradually, he claimed, and it would become progressively clearer through the 'ongoing evolutionary process'⁷⁸ of human history.

This, then, gives rise to two observations. On the one hand, history, for Lefebvre, would seem to have an end;⁷⁹ yet on the other hand, this end is, in effect, unattainable, as it is continually being reformulated and posited anew. Lefebvre thus not only described the total man as a 'figure on a distant horizon bey-

74 For example, the total man was described as 'the subject who is broken up into partial activities and scattered determinations and who surmounts this dispersion' (Lefebvre 1968, pp. 161–2).
75 Lefebvre's early work is in fact informed by his attempts to extricate himself from Catholicism (Trebitsch in Lefebvre 2008a, pp. xxii–iii).
76 Lefebvre 2006, p. 56; see also Lefebvre 2009, p. 580; see Baugh 2003, pp. 62–9 for a discussion.
77 Lefebvre 2009, p. 580.
78 Lefebvre 2008a, p. 67.
79 Baugh makes the same point (2003, p. 68).

ond our present vision':[80] in addition, he stated that its complete actualisation was a 'mathematical limit' to which 'we are forever drawing nearer but have never reached';[81] 'a limit', moreover, which he located at the end of 'the infinity of social development.'[82] The total man, therefore, appears as an impossible, tantalising absolute, similar to that pursued by the unhappy consciousness: a utopian state of perfect subject-object unity that we can never quite reach.

This, of course, differs from the positions that we have ascribed to Debord. His own conception of historical praxis does not involve any such constant deferral of subject-object unity. Instead, we have argued that he re-casts Hegel's supposed end of history as an 'end of pre-history'.[83]

We can therefore contend that there would seem to be some rather different notions of the absolute in operation within Debord and Lefebvre's work. The 'absolute' identified with Lefebvre's total man is a chiefly aesthetic and ethical concept. It is an absolute good, posited in contrast to that which the present lacks. It does not seem to have been envisaged as a re-formulation of the Hegelian Absolute (Lefebvre in fact distances himself from the latter when discussing the Hegelian Idea *vis-à-vis* the total man).[84] In contrast (and it bears repeating here that Debord did not explicitly state his adoption of the position that we have ascribed to him), we have argued that Debord's work does indeed imply a re-figuration of the Hegelian Absolute, wherein the latter becomes the praxis that makes history. Subject-object unity is not figured here as a static end-point, but instead constitutes both the grounds and conduct of an open, self-determinate future.

Having made these distinctions, we can now consider the ways in which they inform those that can be discerned between Lefebvre's 'moments' and the SI's constructed situations.

Tragic Moments

Lefebvre's theory of moments was first introduced in 1959, in his *La Somme et le reste*. The theory was presented there as a contribution to critical sociology, the aim of which was to address the emergence of moments of passionate intensity within everyday life. Such moments, for Lefebvre, give rise to the change and disruption of everyday routines.[85] According to Lefebvre, moments tend to fall

---

80   Lefebvre 2008a, p. 66.
81   Lefebvre 1968, p. 109.
82   Lefebvre 2008a, p. 66.
83   Debord 2004a, p. 54; see also SI 2006, p. 111; 1997, p. 253.
84   Lefebvre 2008a, pp. 68–70.
85   Elden 2004, p. 170.

into distinct types (examples included 'play, love, work, rest, struggle, understanding, poetry').[86] Signigicantly, he also held, in *La Somme et le reste*, that 'it is always possible', as he put it, 'to discover or constitute a moment'.[87]

Debord developed his own theory of situations prior to the publication of this book, but he clearly read its claims with interest. He made detailed personal notes on *La Somme et le reste*'s theory of moments in February 1960, and later that year, those notes would become a short and rather opaque article in *Internationale situationniste* (the notes were sent to André Frankin, who seems to have typed them up without adding a great deal of polish or embellishment). Titled 'The Theory of Moments and the Construction of Situations', the article expressed guarded enthusiasm for Lefebvre's claims, and attempted to place them in relation to the SI's own views.

As far as Lefebvre himself was concerned, the relation between the situation and the moment was very simple. In an interview of 1983, in which he recalled his contact with the SI, Lefebvre explained that he had simply devised a means of addressing and categorising intense instances of lived experience; the SI, on the other hand, had set out to create new forms of experience. He stated this as follows:

> They [the SI] more or less said to me ... 'what you call "moments" we call "situations", but we're taking it further than you. You accept as "moments" everything that has occurred in the course of history: love, poetry, thought. We want to create new moments'.[88]

This perhaps illustrates the sense in which Lefebvre, in the SI's view, had in effect remained on the same level as Sartre's philosophical 'interpretation' of situations. They wanted to transform and create moments of life; Lefebvre seemed too ready to interpret life as it currently existed. For example, in the very first issue of *Internationale situationniste* (1958), and whilst referencing Lefebvre's 'Vers un romantisme révolutionnaire' (1957) – a text that called for a Marxism able to revitalise the cultural as well as the economic spheres of society – Debord argued that Lefebvre had indicated the need for revolutionary cultural transformation, but had failed to investigate what forms it might actually take. Or, to put that more succinctly: Lefebvre had failed to identify

---

86 Lefebvre 2009, p. 640.
87 Ibid.
88 Ross 2004, p. 271.

the importance of realising art in lived activity (it is significant that Lefebvre, in later years, effectively parroted the SI's views in this regard: 'the transformation of the world', he would later claim, 'is not only a realisation of philosophy but also a realisation of art').[89] The SI's claim, therefore, was that where they were concerned with researching and actualising a radically different future, Lefebvre had remained content to simply demonstrate the need for that future, and had kept himself focussed on the present.

This objection pertains to Lefebvre's concept of the 'possible/impossible', which the SI also alluded to when making these comments. Lefebvre's notion of the 'possible/impossible' accords with the dynamic of the total man, which we described above. It refers to the sense in which the present that declares a revolutionary future to be impossible also makes that future necessary, and to the sense in which the impossibilities of the past become the possibilities of the future. For Debord and the SI, however, this amounted to a fixation on the present that omitted the need to proactively pursue such a future. Rather than pursuing 'profound cultural modification', Lefebvre, in their view, had instead developed a 'consciousness of the possible-impossible (still too remote), which can be expressed in any sort of form within the framework of cultural decomposition.'[90] It was not enough, in other words, to demonstrate the inadequacies of the present: new forms of cultural activity and behaviour were required in order to move beyond the failings of a decomposing society.

The connection between the 'possible/impossible' and the total man is important, because it also relates to Lefebvre's theory of moments. As we saw above, the total man functioned as an emergent and continually reformulated 'absolute', capable of providing a goal, and thus an 'ethic', to lived praxis: for 'only the notion or idea of the absolute gives a sense', according to Lefebvre, 'in other words both a meaning and a direction', to 'historically acquired knowledge.'[91] The total man is thus 'possible/impossible' in the sense described above. His advent is impossible within the present, and yet his contemporary possibility engenders a drive towards facilitating his appearance within the future. This amounts to a perpetually elusive goal. Lefebvre indicated that this goal would be continually posited anew, because the differing inadequacies of every contextual instance would give rise to differing visions of utopian resolution. This accords with his notion of the 'total man', who is himself both possible

---

89   Quoted in Roberts 2006, p. 68.
90   SI 2006, p. 54, translation altered; 1997, p. 21.
91   Lefebvre 2008a, p. 67.

and impossible. Like the God-like object pursued by the unhappy consciousness, the total man would seem to be perpetually drawing away from every attempt to access and realise him.

One can find something very similar in Lefebvre's 'moments'. When introducing his theory of moments in *La Somme et le reste*, Lefebvre stated that it 'gave new meaning to the theory of "the total man"'.[92] This is because Lefebvre's moments afforded intimations of the total man: glimpses of an as-yet unrealised condition in which alienation would be superseded.

Lefebvre's moments are instances of passionate intensity that emerge from, and which temporarily supersede, the banality of the everyday. Each, according to Lefebvre, constitutes an 'absolute'. In the second volume of his *Critique*, when developing and elaborating *La Somme et le reste*'s account of moments, Lefebvre stated that 'every moment becomes an absolute'; in fact, every moment, he claimed, has a 'duty' to become such an absolute (for 'what love worthy of the name does not want to be unique and total, an impossible love?').[93] The moment thus 'becomes an absolute'[94] because it stands above the triviality of the everyday. Yet this renders each moment inherently 'tragic', because in 'proclaim[ing] itself to be an absolute, it provokes and defines a determined alienation [from the rest of lived experience]'.[95]

Furthermore, to live a moment is to 'exhaust it as well as to fulfil it'.[96] Each moment is a finite instance in time (moments are 'mortal'; they are 'born, they live and they pass away'),[97] and in consequence, the absolute accessed by the moment 'cannot endure'.[98] Therefore – and in keeping with the motif of the total man – the absolute glimpsed via the moment remains 'ever-sought and ever-inaccessible'.[99] Once again, we have a dynamic that echoes that of the unhappy consciousness.

We have already made a number of references to Lukács in this chapter, so it may be useful to point out that rather similar positions can be found in his early work. Before he turned towards Marxist theory in the early 1920s, Lukács adopted a critique of modern life that prefigured aspects of Lefebvre's claims. In his *Soul and Form* of 1910, he described lived experience as banal and impov-

---

92   Lefebvre 2009, p. 644.
93   Lefebvre 2008b, p. 346.
94   Ibid.
95   Lefebvre 2008b, p. 347.
96   Lefebvre 2008b, p. 348.
97   Lefebvre 2008b, p. 354.
98   Lefebvre 2008b, p. 345.
99   Lefebvre 2008b, p. 355.

erished, but wrote that fleeting moments of authenticity arise within it. He describes these moments as hints towards an 'absolute' (as in Lefebvre, this is a sublime, aesthetic absolute: it is not the Absolute of Hegelian philosophy). Life within present society, Lukács claimed, 'is always unreal, always impossible', until 'suddenly there is a gleam, a lightning that illuminates the banal paths of empirical life: something disturbing and seductive, dangerous and surprising; the accident, the great moment, the miracle; an enrichment and a confusion.'[100] This is strikingly similar to Lefebvre's account of the moment, and the similarity is reinforced when Lukács adds that such moments 'cannot last':[101] 'no one would be able to bear it ... One has to fall back into numbness.'[102]

The early Lukács of *Soul and Form*, therefore, would seem to prefigure Lefebvre in contending that moments of authenticity arise within everyday life, and that such moments highlight that which contemporary society lacks. In addition, Lukács's claims also correspond to the sense in which those moments, for Lefebvre, are inherently tragic: partly because of their inevitable distinction from the everyday, and partly because of their finite, fleeting nature. However, this early, tragic view of everyday life contrasts with the claims that Lukács would go on to make in 1923's *History and Class Consciousness*. In that book, the fleeting, ineffable absolute described above takes on a more overtly Hegelian form, and ceases to function as an ungraspable, tantalising beyond. Instead, it becomes the social praxis that creates history, and a lasting communion with it can be afforded through the subject-object unity of revolutionary class-consciousness.

In what follows below, we will try to show that the relation between Lefebvre's moments and Debord's situations can be viewed in somewhat similar terms. Just as Lefebvre's theory of moments chimes with aspects of Lukács's claims in *Soul and Form*, so too does Debord's conception of constructed situations come close to the views expressed in Lukács's later *History and Class Consciousness*. In order to make these claims, we will focus on Debord's notes on *La Somme et le reste*, and on the SI's article about Lefebvre's theory of moments (both texts were written in 1960). We will thereby attempt to show that whilst Debord's views on the constructed situation during this time certainly carry echoes of Lefebvre's fleeting, ephemeral absolute, they also imply something closer to the ongoing, processual subject-object unity of *History and Class Consciousness*. The latter resemblance, we will argue, rendered these early views all

---

100   Lukács 2010, p. 176.
101   Ibid.
102   Ibid.

the more amenable to the Hegelian Marxian reformulations that they would subsequently undergo within Debord's later work.

Constructing Moments and Situations

As we indicated above, Lefebvre's discussion of moments indicates the possibility that they could be consciously constructed, and need not arise purely through chance (e.g. 'the moment is constituted by a choice').[103] In order to discuss this *vis-à-vis* Debord and the SI's own interest in constructing situations, we will need to employ some of Lefebvre's excessively baroque technical terminology. This is because Debord himself uses this terminology when commenting on Lefebvre's position.

The first set of terms that need to be introduced in this regard do in fact bear a marked resemblance to Debord's own thought.[104] According to Lefebvre, the everyday is the domain of 'tactics' and 'strategies', because it is characterised by strategic 'projects, decisions, plans for action and for the future'.[105] As is also the case with Debord, this notion that life could be understood in terms of strategic action followed from Lefebvre's views concerning the inevitability of chance within human affairs. In addition – and again, like Debord – Lefebvre held that engagements with the chance aspects of lived reality should become characterised by play.[106] The strategic traversal of lived reality was thus said to be analogous to 'gambling'.

Secondly, Lefebvre also refers to the 'conjunctural' and the 'structural'. The 'structural' corresponds to stability and continuity within the everyday, i.e. to forms that repeat or last for a period of time. The 'conjunctural' denotes links and relations between the various elements that compose a structure. According to Lefebvre, these conjunctural relations force the change and rupture of structures, and thereby necessitate their 'inclusion in strategies.'[107]

Thirdly and finally, Lefebvre's moments, as we saw earlier, can be characterised and sorted into 'types', e.g. poetry, play, work, rest, etc. (ever the romantic, Lefebvre's own favourite example was love).[108] This means that moments cor-

---

103   Lefebvre 2008b, p. 344.
104   We should remember, therefore, that the second volume of Lefebvre's *Critique*, which we will be focussing on in what follows, was written during his friendship with Debord.
105   Lefebvre 2008b, p. 106.
106   If the importance of the ludic to Debord is to be taken in relation to the question of Lefebvre's influence, then it is significant to note that Debord had already established his own views on the potentially ludic dimensions of lived time in the early 1950s.
107   Lefebvre 2008b, p. 148.
108   'When we [Lefebvre and the SI] talked about [the constructed situation and the moment]

respond, by and large, to 'structure', because they are repeated types.¹⁰⁹ The contingent context in which the moment takes place, on the other hand, corresponds to the 'conjunctural'.

If we now put this rather complicated collection of terms together, we can sum up as follows: creating a moment, according to Lefebvre, entails engaging strategically with a conjuncture and gambling upon it with the aim of establishing structure in the form of a particular type of moment. As was also the case for the SI – with whom, we must remember, Lefebvre was in contact at this time – life could become play through the deliberate creation of moments of lived experience.

However, whilst Lefebvre's moments were broadly associated with 'structure', the SI's constructed situation was deliberately less pre-ordained. In his notes on *La Somme et le reste*, Debord praised Lefebvre's theory of moments as having conceived a 'path to *STRUCTURAL CONJUNCTURAL* dialectical unity'.¹¹⁰ It seems that the situation, in his view, would come somewhat closer to realising such a unity. The constructed situation, Debord stated, was an 'attempt at structure of (in) conjunction':¹¹¹ a structure that would be deliberately geared towards fostering desirable conditions of chance (i.e. ludic experience). It would thus constitute a 'structure' that 'controls (and favours) ... chance instants', and which would thus be 'particularised and unrepeatable'.¹¹² Each situation would thus be different.

This entails a further difference from Lefebvre's moments, which, as we saw earlier, were held to take the form of repeated types. Where the problem for Lefebvre, according to Debord's notes, was that of providing a list of his various types of moments ('why 10 rather than 15 or 25, etc.'),¹¹³ the only difficulty faced by the SI lay in 'marking [the situation's] precise end'¹¹⁴ (the following, much later remark, made by Raoul Vaneigem in 1967, seems apposite here: 'What do I want? Not a succession of moments but one huge instant').¹¹⁵

The difficulty involved in marking a situation's precise end is particularly important, as it pertains to the sense in which constructed situations would,

  I always gave as an example – and they would have nothing to do with my example – love' (Ross 2004, p. 271).
109 Lefebvre 2008b, p. 352.
110 Debord 2009, p. 337.
111 Ibid.
112 SI 1960b; 1997, pp. 118–19.
113 Debord 2009, p. 335.
114 SI 1960b; 1997, p. 118.
115 Vaneigem 1994, p. 93.

within a fully realised Situationist existence, flow into one another. Where the Lefebvrian moment was conceived as a discrete point in time, and would pass away within it, the constructed situation – though also finite, and 'without a future'[116] – was described as affording a 'direction or "way" [*sens*]'[117] towards new forms of action and experience. As Debord put it in a different text, which was also written in 1960: the constructed situation was not conceived as 'an indivisible, isolatable instant', but 'as a moment in the movement of time, a moment that generates its own dissolution [*contenant ses facteurs de dissolution*] and negation'.[118] A situation was thus a passage through time: a period of temporal experience that would pass away, and which would – through the creation of new situations – thereby pass into the next.

These observations allow connections to be drawn between the positions described here, and the notion of strategic, historical praxis discussed in Chapters 1 and 2.

If we accept the view that the self-determinacy of creating and traversing constructed situations amounts to a form of subject-object unity – or at least that it would later become conceived and articulated in such terms – then we can state that situations would function as 'passageways' towards further instances of subject-object unity (i.e. towards further situations). We thus have something very much akin to the processual, dynamic condition that we identified, in Chapter 2, with Debord's vision of communism *qua* collective historical praxis. We argued there that this would be a mode of subject-object unity obliged to continually recreate its own conditions of existence as it moves through time. Furthermore, and in keeping with both Lefebvre's terminology and Debord's own views, we can now also add the following.

The operation of that process must involve a degree of strategic agency, because it would need to be continually engaged in negotiating the chance contingencies of lived time in a manner that afforded new iterations of its own conditions of existence. In addition, this strategic process could be construed as ludic (in accordance with Debord's association of strategy with play, and in keeping with the SI's association of Situationist activity with play). This then leaves us with a position that anticipates some of the claims that would later be presented in *The Society of the Spectacle*: for as we saw earlier, Debord claims there that following the supersession of spectacle, 'the *subject* of history' would have 'no goal [*n'a pas d'objet*] other than the effects it works upon itself',[119] and

---

116   SI 2006, p. 41; Debord 2006b, p. 326.
117   SI 1960b; 1997, p. 118.
118   Debord 2006b, p. 507.
119   Debord 1995, p. 48, translation altered; 2006b, p. 792.

would 'exist as *consciousness of its own activity* [*conscience de son jeu*]'.[120] History would thus become an open process of self-determination.

It thus seems that one can find the beginnings of this view in Debord and the SI's early conceptions of Situationist activity. We can develop that claim by returning to Lefebvre's references to the absolute.

The Moment, the Situation, and the Absolute

The distinction that we have drawn between the moment and the situation resembles the differences between the unhappy consciousness and the subject-object unity of absolute knowing. Where the Lefebvrian moment provides access to a fleeting, ephemeral absolute that slips away as soon as it is touched, the SI's situation, we have proposed, seems much closer to a state of ongoing communion with that absolute. This can be reinforced if we return to Debord's personal notes on Lefebvre's theory of moments, as they involve an explicit endorsement of Lefebvre's references to the 'absolute'. Debord writes as follows: 'H[enri] L[efebvre] is right in this: the moment tends towards the absolute, and is undone in it [*et s'en défait*]. It [the Lefebvrian moment] is, at the same time, proclamation of the absolute and consciousness of transitoriness [*conscience du passage*].'[121] Those comments were repeated, with only very slight modifications, in the SI's subsequent article on Lefebvre's theory of moments, which states the following:

> Lefebvre ... has revealed many of the fundamental conditions of the new field of action across which a revolutionary culture may now proceed: as when he remarks that the moment tends toward the absolute and is undone in it. ... [T]he moment, like the situation, is *at the same time* proclamation of the absolute and consciousness of transitoriness.[122]

The slight differences between Debord's notes and this article are telling. As the quotation above illustrates, we are told that one of the 'fundamental conditions' that characterises the 'new field' of revolutionary cultural action entails an engagement with the 'absolute'. In addition, we are also told that it is not only the Lefebvrian moment that 'tends towards the absolute', as in Debord's notes: the constructed situation does so as well.

---

120   Debord 1995, p. 48, translation altered; 2006b, p. 792.
121   Debord 2009, p. 337.
122   SI 1960b; 1997, p. 119; Cf. Debord 2009, p. 337.

As we pointed out earlier, it would be far too quick and easy to view this 'absolute' as if it were the Hegelian Absolute. According to the arguments that we advanced in Part One of this book, it would certainly *become* the Hegelian Absolute, following Debord's turn to Hegel and Marx in the 1960s; here, however, in 1960, it appears to function as a more straightforwardly aesthetic category. Furthermore, here in 1960, Debord seems to place the situation close to the moment, insofar as both must pass away in time (both are a 'proclamation' of this absolute, and both entail a 'consciousness of transitoriness'). Yet as we have tried to show, the ongoing process of constructing situations would afford a continuous engagement with this aesthetic, temporal absolute. Given that Debord's subsequent turn to Hegel and Marx was informed by his study of Lukács's *History and Class Consciousness*, it seems possible to claim that these relatively early ideas would soon be rearticulated in a manner that echoed Lukács's re-figuration of Hegelian absolute knowing. In other words, the early, aesthetic and quasi-sublime absolute referred to here would ultimately become the temporal praxis that makes history.

We will look at those more overtly Hegelian ideas in greater detail in Part Three of this book. In the following chapter, we will try to develop a clearer sense of one of the core themes that runs throughout these concerns: namely, Debord's advocacy of a subjectivity that would be able to move in step with time's passage.

CHAPTER 5

'Avant-Gardes Have Only One Time'

Fire and Water

The primary aim of this chapter is to introduce and consider the conception of the avant-garde that Debord developed in the years that followed the splits and expulsions of 1962. Through doing so, we will try to foreground the notions of temporality and agency that this involved: themes that would come to the fore in the more overtly Hegelian and Marxian conception of historical praxis that Debord later expressed in works such as 1967's *The Society of the Spectacle*. In order to facilitate this, we will begin by departing from this book's broadly chronological structure to some degree, in order to look at Debord's 1978 film, *In Girum Imus Nocte et Consumimur Igni* (hereafter *In Girum*). This is because the comments on the avant-garde that can be found in that film bear direct relation to those that Debord set out in the early 1960s. *In Girum* is also useful for our purposes here because it foregrounds the theme of praxis, understood as activity and intervention in time, that those earlier conceptions of the avant-garde entail.

In Girum is a primarily autobiographical film, and it was made six years after the demise of the Situationist International. It begins with a set of characteristically hostile comments on the failings of modern society, and indeed on those of its own audience. This 'particular public', Debord tells us, 'which has been so totally deprived of freedom and which has tolerated every sort of abuse, deserves less than any other to be treated gently'.[1] Yet after a lengthy opening discussion in which that public is handled in a suitably robust manner, Debord soon moves on to more personal matters. 'I am going to replace the frivolous adventures typically recounted by the cinema,' he states, 'with the examination of an important subject: myself'.[2] This deliberately provocative self-aggrandisement can be seen in many of Debord's writings, and it is particularly evident in his later works. To some degree, it reflects the more Stirnerian elements of his thought, but it is principally due to his tendency to present his cherished 'bad reputation' as a symptom of the singularity of his rejection

---

1 Debord 2003b, pp. 133–4; 2006b, pp. 1334–5.
2 Debord 2003b, p. 149; 2006b, p. 1352.

of modern society.³ In *In Girum*, these 'extravagant [*démesurée*] pretensions',⁴ as he describes them, are closely wedded to the film's scornful stance towards its audience and cultural context. They are also presented within a film that embodies that contempt within its very mode of expression.

Like most of Debord's other films, *In Girum* is composed of *détourné* fragments of other films (Debord: 'I pride myself on having made a film out of whatever rubbish was at hand; and I find it amusing that people will complain about it who have allowed their entire lives to be dominated by every kind of rubbish').⁵ *In Girum* thus instantiates the very critique of modern society that it enunciates. In thereby uniting its form and content, it succeeds, like many of Debord's other works,⁶ in avoiding the contradictory status of merely describing and representing the rejection of spectacular society.⁷ Yet rather than expressing simple hostility and refusal, the film also displays a very particular and accomplished aesthetic: a mature, fully articulated version of the

---

3   For example, Debord claimed in 1985's *Considerations on the Assassination of Gérard Lebovici* that he occupied a 'singular place' in 'society and in the history of my times' (Debord 2001b, p. 2, translation altered; 2006b, p. 1539); 1993's *Cette mauvaise réputation* works through a long series of critical and condemnatory media reports about his own person and writings (Debord 1993); In *In Girum*, he talks of his 'underground and negative [*mauvaise*] celebrity' (Debord 2003b, p. 183, translation altered; 2006b, p. 1391); in 1989's autobiographical *Panegyric* he describes the life that had generated such purported intolerability as 'exemplary' (Debord 2004b, p. 6; 2006b, p. 1658).
4   Debord 2003b, p. 192; 2006b, p. 1401.
5   Debord 2003b, p. 146; Debord 2006b, p. 1349.
6   This approach is evident throughout Debord's cinematic work, but it also clearly informs his written work too: one might think here, for example, of *The Society of the Spectacle*, *Comments on the Society of the Spectacle*, and the two volumes of *Panegyric*.
7   It is perhaps worth dwelling on the connection between this unity of form and content and Debord's concerns with time. As we have seen throughout the previous chapters of this book, Debord's famous concept of spectacle is best understood as a condition of historical arrest: as a state of alienation from historical time. Conversely, and as we have also seen, the supersession of spectacle lies in moving *with* time. It is significant, therefore, that the film evidences an aestheticisation of temporal flow and movement: not only within its script, which we will turn to in a moment, but in the very fact that it is composed from *détourné* fragments of other films. *Détournement*, as the SI pointed out, had 'a historical significance' (SI 2006, p. 67; 1997, p. 78), because it involved negating and transforming elements of spectacular society in order to facilitate its passage into the historical past (see, for example, the article '*Détournement* as Negation and Prelude' in *Internationale Situationniste* #3). *In Girum*, therefore, does not just describe its opposition to spectacular society, but also instantiates it; through doing so, it also actualises the desire to move in step with time that its script expresses.

aestheticisation of temporal movement that can be found in Debord's relatively early views on the construction of situations. In fact, the script to *In Girum* is arguably one of the best and most accomplished pieces of writing that Debord ever produced. The film is marked by a peculiar and occasionally melancholic beauty which bears direct relation to the political claims made within it. This is an aesthetic in which beauty, passion, poetry and revolt – even, on occasion, traces of sublimity – are all linked to personal identification and alignment with the passage of time.

This aesthetic is perhaps best approached by way of the Latin palindrome that gives the film its title: *in girum imus nocte et consumimur igni*; 'we turn around in the night and are consumed by fire'. The film as a whole relies heavily on the imagery of water and fire. These images correspond, respectively, to the flow of time, and to the momentary brilliance of actions and experience within it.[8] Debord's autobiographical reflections are used to address the significance of distinct events within the passage of time, as such moments are always doused and swept away by time's constant, inevitable flow. The film's autobiographical elements thus introduce meditations on the flares of 'revolution', 'youth', 'love' and 'negation'[9] that arise within the flow of time, and it accords poignancy and pathos to such moments due to their finitude.

This is why the beauty accorded to temporal movement within the film is at least partly melancholic. In this regard, it recalls the tragic Lefebvrian 'moments' that we discussed in the previous chapter, and indeed the 'lightning' flashes of authenticity of Lukács's early *Soul and Form*. Such views on time certainly come to the fore in Debord's later writings, and their more melancholy dimensions have no doubt served to reinforce the widespread but mistaken contention that Debord's later works express a degree of resignation and remorse. We will argue against that reading of Debord's later work in Part Five, and should stress here that whilst the conception of time presented in *In Girum* does indeed possess a tragic dimension,[10] it is also marked by a joyful, exuberant acceptance of finitude (or, as Debord puts it, by way of a quoted battlefield remark from Frederick II: 'Dog! Were you hoping to live forever?').[11] The film's

---

8   See Debord's 'The Themes of *In Girum*' (Debord 2003b, p. 223; 2006b, pp. 1410–1).
9   Debord 2003b, p. 223; 2006b, pp. 1410–1.
10 See Kaufmann 2006 for a reading of this aestheticisation of time that dwells on its melancholic dimensions. Kaufmann's interpretation is perceptive, but it emphasises the retrospective element of Debord's views on time to the detriment of their proactive, revolutionary aspects.
11 Debord 2003b, p. 182; 2006b, p. 1390.

concern with the emergence and demise of distinct moments of passion and experience does not simply express resignation and melancholia. Instead, it conveys a desire to move in step with time, and to engage in the construction of new, equally subjectively significant moments. In this respect, it remains true to Debord's contention of 1957, expressed in his seminal 'Report on the Construction of Situations', that 'the Situationist attitude consists in going with the flow of time'.[12]

The point that the film stresses, therefore, is simply that any such identification with the movement of time entails embracing the fact that the moments that compose one's life will inevitably pass away; that all such moments should therefore be lived with as great an intensity as possible. This lies at the heart of Debord's outright contempt for a society that he viewed as 'having lived below its means'.[13] It also bears relation to the film's motif of constant, cyclical recurrence, which is exemplified by its palindromic title. As Debord indicates in his notes, this motif functions on several levels at the same time.[14] At first sight, it appears to invoke spectacular society's historical arrest; for as he puts it in the film's script:

> ... nothing expresses this restless and exitless [*sans issue*] present better than this ancient phrase that turns completely back on itself, being constructed letter by letter like an inescapable labyrinth, thus perfectly uniting the form and content of perdition: *In girum imus nocte et consumimur igni*. We turn in the night, consumed by fire.[15]

Spectacular society seems to be presented here as something akin to a fever dream: we toss and turn in the night, burning up with frustrated passions that are constantly denied outlet. Yet this same circular motif also conveys antithetical meanings. As Debord puts it in his notes to the film,[16] the real theme of *In Girum* 'is not the spectacle but rather, on the contrary, real life'.[17] In this latter regard, the film's motif of cyclical repetition seems intended to

---

12 SI 2006, p. 42; Debord 2006b, p. 327.
13 Debord 2006b, p. 1537.
14 Debord 2006b, p. 1420.
15 Debord 2003b, pp. 165–6; 2006b, p. 1371.
16 The film's closing injunction – 'To be gone through again from the beginning' (Debord 2003b, p. 193; 2006b, p. 1401) – not only means that the film itself should be repeated: in addition, it also functions as a demand 'to critique, to correct, to blame' and, above all, to redo 'the film or the life of the author' (Debord 2006b, p. 1421).
17 Debord 2006b, p. 1412.

invoke a Nietzschean notion of eternal recurrence, and to thus function as an exhortation to live every moment of one's life to its fullest possible intensity,[18] even though all such flares of passion will be washed away by time's inevitable flow.

Broadly speaking, therefore, the film's overall message is as follows. The beauty of the moments that compose lived experience follows from their tragic, finite nature. Each moment of intensity, passion and subjective significance must pass away in time. Therefore, to embrace this beauty – to 'go with the flow of time', and to thereby pursue an affinity with time's passage – must *also* entail accepting the finite, fleeting nature of those moments, and indeed ultimately one's own mortality (Debord, we might add, had nothing but contempt for spectacular society's fixation on youth and the denial of death: that 'social absence of death', he wrote, is 'one with the social absence of life').[19]

Having made these points, we can now connect them to Debord's views on the avant-garde.

'Are We an Avant-garde? If so, to be Avant-garde Means to Move in Step with Reality'[20]

As noted above, *In Girum* is largely autobiographical, and its content is phrased via the film's motifs of fire and water. Consequently, when Debord recounts his experiences with the SI in the film, he casts the group, together with the earlier, Left Bank milieu with which he was initially involved, as one such fleeting and ultimately extinguished moment of 'fire'. Through doing so, he underscores the sense in which the SI did not attempt to attain perpetuity, but rather sought to move *with* time, and to burn away the static and fixed forms of its own present context. Yet *In Girum*'s twin images of fire and water are not dichotomously opposed. Instead, they stand as a dialectical double, because the negative burning and destruction of the present is seen to be one with the flow of time that washes the negated moment away. Consequently, an alignment with the passage of time also entails a degree of subordination *to* time (hence, according to Debord: 'those who have chosen to strike with the time know that [the time

---

18   In Nietzsche's parable, a 'demon' creeps into your 'loneliest loneliness' and tells you: 'This life as you now live it and have lived it you will have to live once again and innumerable times again'. Nietzsche's question is this: would you 'curse the demon who spoke thus', or would you answer 'never have I heard anything more divine'? (Nietzsche 2005, p. 194).
19   Debord 1995, p. 115; 2006b, p. 835.
20   SI 2006, p. 159; 1997, p. 334.

that is] their weapon is also their master';[21] or, as he simply remarked in an unpublished poem: 'time is our friend and our enemy').[22]

This means that any agency that would correspond to these aspirations could only hope to function as an intervention into a specific historical context. It could not – or rather, *should* not – hope to subsist beyond the moment that defines it. Thus, when Debord discusses the SI's credentials as one such moment of 'fire' in *In Girum*, he does so whilst showing *détourné* footage of the Light Brigade charging into the cannons at Balaklava: 'Marching forward under the cannon fire of time', he states, 'our formation as a whole never swerved from its line until it plunged into the very core of destruction'.[23] This footage also relates to the film's allusions to the military roots of the term 'avant-garde', which in turn inform the following remarks:

> Avant-gardes have only one time; and the best thing that can happen to them is to *have had their day* in the fullest sense of the term [*au plein sens du terme, d'avoir fait leur temps*]. After them, operations move onto a vaster terrain. Too often have we seen such elite troops, after they have accomplished some valiant exploit, remain on hand to parade with their medals and then turn against the cause they previously supported. Nothing of this sort need be feared from those whose attack has carried them to the point of dissolution.[24]

Debord is alluding here to the SI's dissolution in 1972, following the events of 1968. However, his remarks serve to illustrate the importance of contextual specificity to his conception of the avant-garde, and indeed to revolutionary thought and activity more generally. In doing so, they also bring us back to the problematic of spectacle.

In Chapter 2, we described that problematic as a condition of separation from historical time, or rather as a condition in which individuals become alienated from their ability to shape and direct their own time. As we also saw there, Debord's works include remarks that indicate that this problematic pre-dates capitalist society, and that it could reappear in a new form following capitalism's demise. Consequently, the concept of spectacle must be seen to posses what we referred to as an 'ethical' dimension, as it involves a constant opposition to any collapse back into conditions of spectacle. These ideas bear

---

21 Debord 2003b, p. 174, translation altered; 2006b, pp. 1380–1.
22 Debord 2004a, p. 184.
23 Debord 2003b, pp. 178–9; 2006b, pp. 1386–7.
24 Debord 2003b, p. 182, translation altered; 2006b, pp. 1389–90.

direct relation to the issues under discussion here: for they entail that if a body of revolutionary or avant-garde agency resisted the flow of time with which it initially sought to move in step – if it persisted, in other words, beyond the moment that engendered its intervention – then it would, in consequence, become an instance of spectacle.

In other words, cultural or political forms (avant-gardes, radical groups, bodies of theory, etc.) that may seem to afford or embody a direct engagement with historical change, but which, by virtue of their obsolescence or quiescence, become disconnected from the latter, can afford no more than an *image* of identity with historical time. If a group, agent or set of ideas presented itself in this regard, and yet proved to be, or became, entirely commensurable with their present moment, then they would offer no more than a *representation* of the transformative potential that they purported to embody or express. Hence Debord's remark, in the passage quoted above, about 'elite troops' parading their 'medals', and thus turning 'against the cause they previously supported'.

Clearly, this pertains to the issues discussed in this book's introduction. As was noted there, to some extent, the SI has itself been forced, via the group's contemporary cultural and academic endorsement, to parade its own oppositional 'medals'. Yet it is not only cultural recuperation that serves to remove their work from the 'practical movement of negation within society',[25] but also the passage of time itself: for in Debord's view, *all* bodies of radical theory and agency are only discrete interventions within the 'war of time',[26] and need to be constantly replaced by new, contextually relevant forms of theory and action.

This then means that the conceptions of temporality and intervention that underpin Debord's conception of the avant-garde, and indeed his concept of spectacle more broadly, amount to a nascent philosophy of praxis: a philosophy of self-determinate and transformative movement in time, that views all such movement as articulated by the constant generation of new, contextually specific forms of thought and action.

As an aside, it might be remarked here that this constitutes an important dimension of the model of subject-object unity *qua* collective praxis that has been developed in the preceding chapters of this book. If the subject-object unity that would supersede spectacular separation is a condition of historical praxis, as Debord indicates; and if, as he also indicates, it would have no goal other than the effects that it works upon itself; then it must, in consequence, be

---

25   Debord 1995, p. 143; 2006b, p. 852.
26   Debord 2003b, p. 150; 2006b, p. 1354.

oriented towards its own perpetuity as a state of constant process and temporal movement. In order for this to be possible, it would need to be characterised by a distinctly *strategic* conception of theory and action, given that its conduct through time would require it to continually engage, via new forms of thought and action, with the differing contexts and circumstances that it creates and passes through.

These are, however, topics for later chapters. In what follows below, we will look at the manner in which Debord conceived the SI's own status as an avant-garde, and thereby at the group's own strategic response to its historical and cultural circumstances.

The Last Avant-garde

We saw earlier that the SI was not, and indeed could not be, an art movement in any traditional sense of the term. Instead, they sought to function as the *final* avant-garde: as an avant-garde that would abolish itself *qua* avant-garde by opening a revolutionary path towards that which lay beyond the extant forms of art, culture and society.

The rationale behind these views was essentially as follows. If art and culture were to progress, then they would need to be abolished, along with all existing social relations, so as to unite art with lived reality. Thus, a genuine avant-garde, within this historical and cultural context, would need to destroy the very conditions that had engendered its existence (i.e. the separation of art from life that this very same avant-garde would overcome). In doing so, it would destroy its own *raison d'être*, thereby necessitating its own demise. Rather like the Marxian proletariat, the modern avant-garde would thus be obliged to negate itself within the very revolution that would fulfil its project. As Debord put it in *The Society of the Spectacle*:

> As a negative movement which seeks the supersession of art in a historical society where history is not yet lived, art in the epoch of its dissolution is simultaneously an art of change and the pure expression of the impossibility of change. The grander the exigency from which it arises, the more the true realisation of that exigency is beyond it. This art is perforce *avant-garde*, and [at the same time] it *is not*. Its avant-garde is its disappearance.[27]

---

27 Debord 1995, p. 135, translation altered; 2006b, p. 847, italics in the original.

Debord's claim in this rather opaque passage is as follows. Avant-garde art needs to express the exigencies of its moment. Within the contemporary context, it can only express a stifled need for change, i.e. the need for the supersession of art's current existence as a separate sphere that stands apart from everyday lived activity. Art can thus only be avant-garde insofar as it demands the *end* of art; and yet insofar as it remains art, it contradicts itself, and falls short of true avant-garde status. Art, therefore, can only fully realise itself by destroying itself. The SI's historical task was to carry out this auto-negation of avant-garde art.

This supersession of art required revolution (thus, in a letter of 1963, Debord can be found stating that 'today, we are at the point where the cultural avant-garde can only define itself by joining (and thus *superseding* [*supprimant*] *as such*) the *real* political avant-garde').[28] The role of the avant-garde in the age of art's demise would not, therefore, be to produce art-objects. Instead, such a group or agency ought to be given over to the production and dissemination of theory capable of facilitating revolution. This can be illustrated by jumping forward to a letter of 1967, in which Debord can be found explaining the role and function of the SI in the following terms. The SI, he writes there, should be understood as 'an extreme avant-garde'. Its role was not to produce art, but rather 'to produce the most adequate critical theory', so as to 'free' the 'spontaneous movements' that would emerge within the current context.[29] In doing so, the avant-garde would not be imposing an arbitrary vision of the future upon the present moment. Instead, if it was a *true* avant-garde, in Debord's sense of the term, it would draw out and express the tensions and possibilities that defined its historical moment. It would show what this historical moment could and should achieve, whilst also reacting against that which prevented the actualisation of such possibilities.

In this regard, Debord's views can seem close to some of Marx's early positions. We saw earlier that Marx's claims concerning the realisation of philosophy in revolutionary praxis entailed using critical thought to clarify the revolutionary proletariat's demands and goals. The latter view was set out in the introduction to Marx's critique of Hegel's *Philosophy of Right*, which Marx wrote in 1843. In that same year, Marx made the following point in one of his letters to Ruge (and we should note that Debord was evidently familiar with these letters):[30]

---

28   Debord 2001a, p. 192.
29   Debord 2010, p. 329.
30   Debord evidently read Marx's letters to Ruge, as published in the *Deutsch-Französische*

> [We shall not] confront the world with new doctrinaire principles and proclaim: Here is the truth, on your knees before it! ... [W]e shall develop for the world new principles from the existing principles of the world. ... [W]e shall simply show the world why it is struggling, and consciousness of this is a thing it must acquire whether it wishes it or not.[31]

Similarly, the SI could not impose its vision upon the world 'in a doctrinaire way'. If it did so, it would fall back into the problematic of spectacle, through the dogmatic, 'external' imposition of socio-political claims. For Debord, such positions could only be derived immanently from the concerns of a given moment. Furthermore, and as is also the case with Marx's notion of philosophy's 'realisation', any theory produced in this manner was required to do rather more than simply describe, and to thus *represent* the nature of the struggles and tensions of its historical moment. The SI's desire to 'move in step with reality' was essentially a drive towards unity with the movement of history itself, and in consequence, it carried a related obligation to attain some form of identity or commonality with those who actually *make* history (hence, once again, Debord's prescient concern that his theory might become appropriated and separated from the 'practical movement of negation within society').

The peculiarity of the position described here is that the avant-garde turns into something that bears at least some resemblance to a revolutionary vanguard. This is because any agency that would correspond to these principles would need to clarify, convey and make manifest the contradictions and struggles that characterised its own moment. Through doing so, it would enable those living and engaged within that moment to recognise these concerns, and to thereby address and resolve them. However, the theory and activity that any such agency produced could never be imposed from 'without', as in the Leninism that the SI rejected.[32] It could point the way, and it could clarify the stakes of struggle; or, to use a military analogy in keeping with Debord's views: theory, *qua* strategy, could describe the terrain of struggle, and the forces employed upon it, and it could also identify potential points of attack. Yet if spectacle was to be avoided, such theory could only be presented to the actors concerned, who would either reject or adopt it, depending on the degree to which it served to clarify and articulate their circumstances. All hierarchical leadership had to

---

Jahrbücher. They provide the epigraph to the eighth chapter of *The Society of the Spectacle*, and are alluded to in thesis #51 of that book; he also quotes from them in *In Girum* (Debord 2003b, p. 192; 2006b, p. 1401).

31 Marx 1975, pp. 208–9.
32 See, for example, thesis #112 of *The Society of the Spectacle*.

be avoided. *'We will only organize the detonation',* the SI stated; 'the free explosion must escape us and any other control forever'.³³

Debord developed these ideas during the 1960s, whilst attempting to formulate a theory of the avant-garde in the wake of the expulsion of the Nashists. His attempts to do so are expressed particularly clearly in an important letter to Robert Estivals in 1963, in which he responds to Estivals's own conception of the avant-garde.³⁴ In this letter, Debord states that the merits of an avant-garde depend upon the degree to which it generates and disseminates knowledge about the present and its potential future that is not, as yet, generally understood and accepted. 'The properly avant-gardist moment', Debord writes, resides 'at the frontier between the moment of pure arbitrary prognosis as to what the future can be', and 'the moment at which this novelty is recognised', i.e. that at which it is accepted and grasped by a broad majority who are willing to act upon it.³⁵ He continues:

> The avant-garde does not have its field in the future, but in the present: it describes *and begins* a possible present, which history will confirm in the extended sequence of events that follow (by making a certain number of errors apparent). The activity of the avant-garde, in practice, struggles against the present to the extent that it characterises the present as the weight of the past, and as an inauthentic present (as a delay).³⁶

The role of the avant-garde is to make *explicit* the potential for the future that lies *implicit* within a given historical moment. Like military strategy, its validation thus depends upon the degree to which its visions and efforts are successfully realised in concrete action. As Debord remarks in the same letter: 'If it really is an avant-garde, it carries in itself the victory *of its criteria of judgment* against the era ... because the avant-garde exactly represents this era from the point of view of the history that will come.'³⁷ The *truth* of the avant-garde, therefore, can only be established through praxis. This is because in Debord's view, the avant-garde is, in essence, an attempt to judge and resolve the present moment on the basis of the future that that moment harbours within it.

---

33   SI 2006, p. 148; 1997, p. 324.
34   The letter was written partly in response to Robert Estivals's *La Philosophie de l'histoire de la culture dans l'avant-garde culturelle parisienne depuis 1945* of 1962.
35   Debord 2001a, p. 191.
36   Ibid.
37   Debord 2001a, p. 194.

The notion of the avant-garde that one can find in Debord's work at this time is thus tantamount to a conception of agency: an agency, moreover, that moves in step with historical time, and which thus stands in marked contrast to the separation from history that characterises spectacle. And, as we have already indicated, the ideas that one can find emerging here anticipate the conception of communism *qua* historical praxis that we discussed in part one. This point can be reinforced if we also note the following.

We saw above that the SI was to be the last avant-garde: both the final nail in art's coffin, and the midwife to the new social existence that would follow art's demise. We also saw that this this last avant-garde must pass away, along with the culture that it served to negate. It would be superseded by the new, post-revolutionary socio-aesthetic existence that it thus helped to inaugurate. Yet that new social modality would not be entirely dissimilar from the identification with time's passage that characterises Debord's conception of the avant-garde. Instead, that new, post-revolutionary social existence would fully instantiate, as generalised social praxis, the communion with time that the avant-garde had intimated and sought to make manifest. In the letter quoted above, Debord writes as follows:

> To surpass the avant-garde (all avant-gardes) means: to realise a praxis, a construction of society, through which at every moment *the present dominates the past*[38] (see the project of a society without classes in Marx, and the permanent creativity implied by its realisation). The creation of such *conditions of creation* will mark the end of the historical conditions that have commanded the movement of the avant-garde, which is to say, the resistance to the domination (the predominance, the authority) of the past over each moment of the present ...[39]

The end of art would thus afford the birth of a new historical existence. In order to pursue these ideas further, we will now move, in Part Three, to Debord's engagement with Hegel and the young Marx.

---

38 Cf. the *Communist Manifesto*'s notion of a present that dominates its past (Marx and Engels 1985, pp. 97–8. See also Debord 1995, p. 85; 2006b, p. 816).
39 Debord 2001c, pp. 193–4.

PART 3
'Everything That Had Formerly been Absolute Became Historical'

Hans Holbein the Younger, The Abbot, *from 'The Dance of Death',* 1523–5

[Both Marx and Feuerbach] show that speculative philosophy, Hegel's absolute knowledge, is itself also a form of alienation, a substitute for religion. Man believes in another world in order to escape from the hostility of the one in which he lives; he projects into the 'beyond' his own essence because his own essence is not realised in this world.

– JEAN HYPPOLITE, *Logic and Existence*

CHAPTER 6

Debord and French Hegelianism

The Context of Debord's Hegelianism

In Part One, we looked at some of the primary characteristics of the ideas that support Debord's mature theoretical writings, and tried to map out the key features of his Marxian use of Hegelian philosophy. Part Two then sought to highlight the roots of those same ideas within the SI's early avant-garde concerns. Here, in Part Three, we will now look at the themes and influences that informed the further evolution of these ideas into the positions that were expressed in works such as 1967's *The Society of the Spectacle*. In terms of this book's chronological structure, this third part of the book thus corresponds to Debord's more explicit turn towards Hegelian and Marxian thought at the end of the 1950s and at the beginning of the 1960s. By setting out some of the key features of Debord's reading of Hegel, and of his use of Lukács and the young Marx, Part Three will lay a basis for Part Four's discussions, which will address the account of capitalist society expressed in Debord and the SI's mature work during the mid to late 1960s.

This chapter will attempt to place Debord in relation to the tradition of French Hegelianism. It will discuss his distinction from, and connections to, some of the key figures within that tradition. It will also look at the influence exerted by the work of the French Hegel commentators to whom he seems most indebted. These discussions will provide a means towards developing the model of Debord's use of Hegelian thought that we proposed in Chapter 2. However, before setting out this chapter's aims and argument in any more detail, it may prove useful to begin with some general comments concerning the intellectual context that informed Debord and the SI's turn to Hegel.

Perhaps the best place to start in that regard is with Marx's early *Economic and Philosophical Manuscripts* of 1844: a text that first became available in 1927,[1] and which did much to shape Debord and the SI's approach to a Hegelian Marx. The importance of the *Manuscripts*, particularly at the time of their release,

---

1 The *Manuscripts* were made available in 1927, and were published in German in 1932. Sections of the text began to appear in French from 1929 onwards (some of which were translated by Lefebvre). A French edition that omitted the first manuscript was published in 1935; a more complete and accurate French translation was published in 1962. Thanks are due to Anthony Hayes for his help with these details (see also Baugh 2003, p. 64, n. 59).

was that they offered insight into the genesis of Marx's thought. Their explicitly Hegelian emphasis on alienation garnered particular interest in this regard, not least because the *Manuscripts*' romantic humanism seemed to present an early, heartfelt expression of the sentiment that motivated the later, more sober and technical analyses advanced in texts such as *Capital*. The *Manuscripts* were, however, treated with considerable scepticism by the Communist Party (as Lefebvre later indicated, this was perhaps partly due to the fact that the text's critique of alienation need not pertain solely to self-confessedly capitalist societies).[2] The Party line was that Marx had not simply developed, but had instead vanquished Hegel's bourgeois and idealist philosophy; a focus on the Hegelian aspects of Marx's early work could thus be seen as dangerously reactionary, and the *Manuscripts* themselves safely viewed as an item of Marx's juvenilia. Such official condemnation, however, gifted Marx's early Hegelianism with potentially subversive credentials, adding further credence to the supposition that such texts might afford a more authentically radical reading of Marx's ideas.

In the years that followed Stalin's death, the Party's antipathy to Hegel relaxed somewhat. As the apparent humanism evidenced in Marx's early writings offered an alternative to the crudely mechanical Marxism of Communist orthodoxy, interest grew in a Hegelian Marx and in Hegelian Marxism. In France, Lukács and Korsch came to be translated and discussed, although both had been roundly criticised by the Party for the deliberately anti-dogmatic forms of Hegelian Marxism that they had developed in the 1920s. A full French translation of Lukács's *History and Class Consciousness* first appeared 1960, and received a reprint in 1974; a French translation of Korsch's *Marxism and Philosophy* appeared in 1964. Lefebvre's early Hegelian works, such as his *Dialectical Materialism* of 1940, were also republished. However, this surge of interest prompted a reaction. In France, this took the form of Althusser's avowedly anti-Hegelian and anti-humanist structuralist Marxism, which had achieved a degree of prominence when Debord and the SI were formulating their later, more overtly theoretical ideas (*For Marx* appeared in 1965; *Reading Capital* was published in 1968). In consequence, during the period in which Debord turned towards Hegelian and Marxian thought, Hegelian philosophy was not only very much present within the intellectual milieu: in addition, the potentially subversive character that had been ascribed to a Hegelian Marx in the 1920s and '30s could be given further credence by virtue of its distinction from the aca-

---

2 Lefebvre (1968, p. 16): 'We cannot confine the use of the concept of alienation to the study of bourgeois societies.'

demic fashions of the day (Debord would later recall that the 'large dose of Hegel' that he added to his own use of Marx was intended to be 'completely contrary' to Althusser's 'sombre dementia').[3] This then brings us to the reading of Hegel that informed Debord's own approach to a Hegelian Marx.

This chapter will try to approach and reconstruct that reading by presenting a series of discussions of some of the key figures that helped to shape the intellectual climate of French Hegelianism: namely, Jean Wahl, Alexandre Koyré, Alexandre Kojève, Jean Hyppolite and Kostas Papaïoannou. We will discuss their claims, so as to foreground the themes that their work served to highlight. Through doing so, we will also identify the connections and lines of influence that can be drawn to Debord's own ideas and theoretical claims. Not all of these connections are direct. Some certainly are: Debord owned several works by Hyppolite and Papaïoannou, and he attended Hyppolite's lecture course on Hegel. Other influences, however, such as that of Kojève, may have operated via the general intellectual ambiance of the time. All, however, are important, and addressing them can help us to develop our interpretation of Debord's Hegelian Marxism. Before we start, therefore, we should briefly recapitulate some of the claims that we have made concerning Debord's apparent use of Hegelian philosophy.

Unity and History

We have argued that the 'perfected [*achevée*]'[4] separation that Debord associated with spectacular society needs to be understood as a condition of extreme separation between subject (*qua* human consciousness and agency) and object (*qua* the concrete actualisation of that agency, and the powers and capacities that its actualisation affords). We have also seen that Debord located this condition of separation at the end of a long line of historical development. Debord and the SI cast their own historical moment as a context in which the separation of subject and object could be overcome: as a context in which human agents (*qua* subject) could take conscious command of their own historical activity (*qua* object). Modern society was therefore held to harbour the potential for the revolutionary actualisation of a condition of subject-object unity.

Crucially – and we have tried to underscore this point throughout the preceding chapters – the actualisation of that unity was not understood as some

---

3   Debord 2008, p. 212.
4   Debord 1995, p. 11; 2006b, p. 766.

kind of static, final historical conclusion. It was not seen as an end-point; or, as Debord put it in a letter of 1969: 'the revolution is not the end of history'.[5] Instead, it was seen as the beginning of an entirely open, free and self-determinate future. Rather than signalling an end of history, the emergence of this condition of subject-object unity would afford the end of *pre*-history, i.e. the end of an unconscious, alienated relation to historical time. Of course, one could argue that this is, in truth, really not so very far removed from Hegel's own views. Debord, however, certainly seems to have viewed it as a significant departure from Hegel's philosophy. His appropriation and development of Hegelian ideas seems to have been envisaged as a re-figuration of Hegel's claims, in which subject-object unity ceases to be a state of final resolution, and instead becomes the ground of a self-determinate future.

We will try to unpack the details of Debord's views in a moment, but we can already begin to place the views outlined here in relation to French Hegelianism. On the one hand, the re-figuration described above seems greatly informed by the fact that the Hegel that Debord criticises is a rather Kojèveian figure. During the 1930s, Kojève presented a series of hugely influential seminars on Hegel, in which he presented Hegel's philosophy as having heralded the end of history. These seminars were attended by some of the most significant figures in twentieth-century French thought, and greatly informed the French and continental tradition's subsequent conceptions of Hegel. There is no evidence to show that Debord read Kojève directly, but his criticisms of Hegel seem coloured by this line of influence: after all, he explicitly presents Hegel as having declared human history to be over.[6] Yet, at the same time, Debord's emphasis on constant, self-determinate process reflects a rather more nuanced reading of Hegel. Despite his Kojèveian characterisations of Hegel's project, Debord clearly recognised that Hegel's philosophy also constituted an attempt to grasp life, movement, and constant, negative change, and to thereby conceive human existence as an ongoing, self-constitutive process. For Debord, this conception of 'living', processual movement needed to be drawn out of the shell of Hegel's supposedly conclusive system, and identified as the movement of historical life. We will therefore argue that, whilst the Hegel that Debord *criticises* certainly seems Kojèveian, the Hegel that Debord actually *uses* in his work is a rather more subtle and interesting figure. In fact, the Hegelian themes employed in Debord's work appear to owe a great deal to Jean Hyppolite, who placed particular stress on the retention of constant, negative movement

---

5 Debord 2004a, p. 52.
6 See, for example, thesis #74 and thesis #76 of *The Society of the Spectacle*.

within the unity of Hegelian philosophy's purportedly final resolution. Indeed, there is direct evidence to suggest that Hyppolite was the Hegel commentator whom Debord studied most closely of all. To sum up, then: although Debord objects to Hegel's supposedly final historical conclusion, he does not reject Hegelian resolution *per se*. Instead, he rejects the manner in which Hegel conceived it, and re-casts its self-determinate, self-constitutive movement as the open process of a genuinely self-determinate history.

It may be useful to underscore the fact that Debord's antipathy to historical conclusion is *not* a rejection of subject-object unity, not least because such unity is often identified, within the Continental tradition, with just such a conclusion. Certainly, Debord holds that negative, dialectical movement ought really to be operative *within* history, and he complains that Hegel bound that same movement within a system that merely contemplated the world as if it were a finished object. In this regard, Debord can seem close to writers like Breton, Bataille, Adorno, and others, who sought, in differing ways, to break dialectical negativity free from the confines of the Hegelian system. The crucial difference, however, is that where such writers have often treated subject-object unity as the imposition of an arrest upon such dialectical movement, Debord does not: instead, such unity is viewed as the very grounds and condition of an open future. Indeed, as we saw earlier, *The Society of the Spectacle* explicitly commends Hegel for having 'superseded separation'; it criticises him, however, for having done so '*in thought only*'.⁷ This is because the essence of Debord's critique of Hegel is that the latter's philosophy affords only an *image* of the real, processual and dynamic unity of concrete praxis. In Hegel, subject-object unity brings the world into conjunction with the logic that founds it, but it does so (in Debord's view) by effectively declaring history to be over. Yet for Debord, following his reading of Lukács and the young Marx, subject-object unity need not be identified with any such grand metaphysics, because the real identity of thought and world lies in *praxis*. In praxis, the human subject shapes and determines its objective actions and world in accordance with its own conscious designs. Seen in these terms, subject-object unity, *qua* praxis, can be construed as an open process. Hegel's philosophy can then be viewed as a confusedly idealist and philosophical *representation* of what Marx and Engels once referred to as the 'real movement that abolishes [*aufhebt*] the existing state of things'.⁸

---

7 Debord 1995, p. 49, translation altered; 2006b, p. 793.
8 Marx and Engels 2007, pp. 56–7.

Inverting the Absolute

This then returns us to the model of Debord's use of Hegel that we proposed in Chapter 2. If we are right in interpreting him as having viewed Hegel's philosophy in this manner – i.e. if Hegel's account of dynamic, negative movement was indeed seen as an inadvertent and idealist *depiction* of such historical praxis – then it follows that Debord's use of Hegel must re-figure some of the key elements and motifs of Hegel's philosophy as dimensions of that praxis. The secondary aim of this chapter, therefore, which we will endeavour to pursue via a discussion of Debord's relation to French Hegelianism, is to flesh out and develop our earlier contentions regarding the nature of that re-figuration.

In Chapter 2, we suggested that the basic architecture of Debord's use of Hegelian thought could be characterised as involving a reformulation of three primary aspects of Hegel's mature philosophy. These are: 1) the Concept; 2) the Idea; and 3) the Absolute (definitions of these three terms were provided in Chapter 2). The Concept becomes human temporality; the Idea becomes communism, or rather Debord's somewhat idiosyncratic conception thereof; the Absolute becomes the praxis that creates and shapes historical time. We will try to demonstrate that these reformulations accord with the currents in French Hegelianism to which Debord would seem to be closest, and to aspects of the claims made by the writers whom we will consider below. This can be outlined in brief here, before we begin.

1) Koyré, Kojève, Hyppolite and Papaïoannou all highlight the connections between the Concept and human experience and action in time. Debord's work appears to follow them in this regard, as he describes human temporality in terms that echo the Concept's perpetual negative, dialectical movement (for example, and as we saw earlier: 'time', according to *The Society of the Spectacle*, is 'the milieu in which the subject realises himself whilst losing himself, becomes other in order to become truly himself').[9]

2) Debord also seems to re-frame the Idea as communism *qua* a condition of historical self-determinacy. He follows Hyppolite here, who argued that Marx refigured the Hegelian Idea as 'the divinisation of man, *authentic man,*' i.e. as revolutionary, communist 'man', become 'fully aware that he is the one who *makes his own history'*.[10] Debord may also follow Lefebvre in

---

9   Debord 1995, pp. 115–16; 2006b, p. 835.
10 Hyppolite 1969, p. 104, italics in the original.

this regard, who also linked the Idea to communism, albeit via his notion of the 'total man'. The latter, Lefebvre claimed, 'is the Idea';[11] or, rather, 'the Idea but without Idealism'.[12] We will see later, in Chapter 8, that if communism is indeed associated with the organic unity in difference of the Idea, then rather more sense can be made of Debord's references to the dialectical 'life' that would supersede the frozen, fragmented 'non-life' of spectacular society.

3) In Hegel, the actualisation of the Idea affords the fruition of the Absolute. If, in our model, the Idea becomes communism *qua* historical praxis, then the Absolute can be understood as the grounds and conduct of that praxis: as the human historical activity that would attain full fruition with the actualisation of the Idea's condition of subject-object unity. This figuration of the Absolute bears relation to Marx's early notions of 'human essence' and 'species-being'. When seen in this light, the Absolute becomes humanity's historical existence, and thus humanity, to quote Marx, understood as 'the totality of human manifestations of life'.[13]

Therefore, according to this model: 1) the self-determinate operation of the Concept (i.e. human action and experience in time) leads to 2) the actualisation of the Idea (i.e. to the full expression of human self-determinacy in a condition of subject-object unity), and thereby to 3) the full, self-conscious flourishing of the Absolute (i.e. to the flourishing of the self-constitutive historical action that comprises human existence).

It bears repeating that Debord does *not* explicitly state his adoption of the positions outlined here. Instead, this is only a model that has been inferred from his claims. Yet whilst it is an entirely speculative construction, it nonetheless accords with the available textual evidence; and whilst it may seem rather baroque, and perhaps also excessively Hegelian, it ultimately amounts to no more than an elaboration of Lukács's contention that Hegel's 'absolute knowing' should be viewed as the revolutionary proletariat's self-identification as the subject-object of history.

This, then, is the interpretation and use of Hegel that we will go on to attribute to Debord, and we will do so through a discussion of the themes and writers within the French Hegelian tradition that appear to have informed his

---

11 Lefebvre 1969, p. 165.
12 Lefebvre 2006, p. 56; quoted in Baugh 2003, pp. 63–4 (Baugh adds the capitalisation of the letter 'I', which is absent from Lefebvre's French).
13 Marx 1988, p. 111.

work. The writers discussed here will be treated in broadly chronological order, starting with Jean Wahl's seminal reading of the *Phenomenology*'s 'unhappy consciousness'.

Jean Wahl and the 'Unhappy Consciousness'

French Hegelianism is most obviously associated with the *Phenomenology*-centric readings of the 1920s and 1930s. However, Hegel's work was translated and discussed in France from the 1850s onwards, and those early twentieth-century readings need to be understood as responses to that older set of interpretations.[14] In fact, and in contrast to twentieth-century French Hegelianism's familiar orientation towards the *Phenomenology*, French commentary was initially focussed on Hegel's *Encyclopaedia*, and thus upon the grand arc of his philosophical system.[15] Twentieth-century French Hegelianism grew from a reaction to those earlier nineteenth-century readings. It is, therefore, somewhat ironic that the post-structuralist criticisms of Hegel that eventually emerged as a reaction to twentieth-century Hegelianism actually echo some of the earlier, nineteenth-century concerns that those twentieth-century readings initially responded to. This is because those earlier concerns involved seeing Hegel's all-encompassing 'pan-logicism' as troubling and implicitly imperialist.[16] That concern gave rise to two opposed responses: firstly, that of rejecting Hegel's philosophy of history and its account of ascending developmental stages, whilst retaining his epistemology; and secondly – once it was recognised that Hegel's epistemology was in fact the real source of the problem – that of attempting to salvage his conception of history from his epistemology, by problematising the degree to which the latter ensured the former's completion and finality.[17] Focus thus shifted towards Hegel's views on history and historical action, and an interest developed in extracting negative dialectical movement from the positivity of a completed system. The latter concern is one of the key themes in twentieth-century French Hegelianism that pertains to

---

14   Baugh 2003, pp. 10–12.
15   The three key components of the system were translated and published much earlier than the *Phenomenology*, which would not receive a full French translation until 1939. Hegel's *Logic* appeared in French in two volumes in 1859; the *Philosophy of Nature* appeared in three volumes between 1863–6; the *Philosophy of Spirit* appeared in two volumes between 1867–9 (Kelly 1992, p. 71).
16   Baugh 2003, pp. 10–12.
17   Baugh 2003, pp. 10–17.

Debord's work, and one of the primary figures who helped to shape this field is Jean Wahl: a highly influential writer, whose important *Le Malheur de la conscience dans la philosophie de Hegel* appeared in 1929.

Just as Kojève would later place the *Phenomenology*'s lord and bondsman (or 'master and slave') relation at the centre of Hegel's work, Wahl indicated, much more persuasively,[18] that the *Phenomenology*'s account of the 'unhappy consciousness' expressed the real core of Hegel's concerns. On his reading, the constant, 'restless' movement of this 'shape of consciousness' exemplified the dynamism and constant drive towards unity that characterises Hegelian thought. As we saw in Chapter 5, the section of the *Phenomenology* that discusses the unhappy consciousness describes its constantly thwarted attempts to supersede its separation from the seemingly divine object that confronts it. All such attempts simply recreate that separation anew, as every time that it seems to grasp this object, the latter recedes once again. In consequence, this section of the *Phenomenology* describes a constant movement from separation to unstable unity, and from such unity to separation once again. For Wahl, it therefore provided an emblematic example of the characteristic dynamism of Hegel's philosophy.[19]

In placing such stress on the importance of separation and diremption within Hegelian thought, Wahl's reading located a constant, 'restless' negativity within the very heart of Hegelian resolution. It thus served to foreground the sense in which Hegel could be seen as a philosopher of difference, negativity and movement, rather than as a thinker who had one-sidedly celebrated unity and resolution. Of course, Wahl understood that in the course of the *Phenomenology*, the unhappiness of this form of consciousness ultimately gives rise to the happiness of absolute knowing: 'the unhappy consciousness', he wrote, 'is but the darkened image of the happy consciousness.'[20] Yet crucially, Wahl placed great emphasis on the importance of this negative, dynamic movement towards Hegelian resolution, thereby implying that Spirit's final happiness entails a rather stoic acceptance of sadness and tragedy. His theologically informed reading (which was embraced by French Catholic approaches

---

18   Harris (1995, p. 42) points out that Wahl is much closer to the mark than Kojève in this regard.
19   This 'perpetual transfer of contrary to contrary', he wrote, is 'one of the most profound traits of Hegelian thought' (Wahl 1951, p. 1). Hyppolite would later reiterate Wahl's claim that the unhappy consciousness could be seen as a defining motif of Hegel's *Phenomenology* (Hyppolite 1974, p. 190).
20   Quoted by Heckman in Hyppolite 1974, p. xxx.

to Hegel)²¹ thus situated human loss and suffering within the 'divine' rationale of Hegelian metaphysics, and thereby identified the purported inevitability of the former with the metaphysical necessity of the latter. His reading thus also helped to shape the long-standing interest in viewing Hegel's philosophy as presenting an inherently tragic vision²² (as evidenced in Hyppolite's later contention that Hegel's 'panlogicism' is in truth a form of 'pantragedism'),²³ and it also greatly informed French existentialism's subsequent debts to aspects of Hegel's thought.²⁴ In many respects, Debord's work reflects the confluence of Hegelian and existential themes that Wahl helped to foster. However, the most important aspect of Wahl's reading, as regards our current concerns, is the emphasis that he placed on constant, restless, negative movement.

Wahl's approach informs two themes within French Hegelianism that feed directly into Debord's own account. Firstly, in indicating that Hegelian resolution is not a state of static repose, but rather a condition of movement and rupture, he laid a basis for Hyppolite's later interpretation: for as we will see below, Hyppolite presents the Hegelian Absolute as constant movement and process. Our argument will be that these aspects of Hyppolite's reading colour Debord's own use of Hegel. Secondly, in foregrounding the retention of negative, dialectical movement within Hegel's seemingly conclusive resolution, Wahl's reading also informed the subsequent interest in contending that Hegelian negativity might somehow exceed or resist its enclosure within Hegel's purportedly final, finished and conclusive system (a point that Baugh has discussed at length in his own account of twentieth-century French Hegelianism).²⁵ Indeed, as Wahl

---

21 Kelly 1992, pp. 32–3; Heckman in Hyppolite pp. xxix–xxx.
22 In some respects, Hegelian philosophy can be viewed as analogous to tragic art: it offers, to use Nietzsche's (1992a) terms, an 'Apollonian' image that placates its observers through neutralising the 'Dionysian' negativity that it rationalises. Theodor George's (2006) discussion of Hegel and tragedy explicitly highlights these conservative themes. George's reading ultimately argues for the virtues of viewing tragedy as a trope of resignation to a world that one cannot control: Hegel's 'deep concern for tragedy', George writes, may point towards the 'joy' that can be found by 'those who learn to accept that they belong to a world they cannot master' (George 2006, p. 133). Such resignation is of course antithetical to Debord's own use of Hegel.
23 Hyppolite 1975, pp. 30–1, see also p. 194. Indeed, 'negativity', for Wahl, 'is the unhappy consciousness of God' (Wahl 1951, p. 107; Wahl 2004, p. 12).
24 Kelly 1992, p. 33.
25 Baugh 2003. Emphasising the theme of the unhappy consciousness, Baugh presents an alternative account of twentieth-century French Hegelianism that does not take its primary bearings from Kojève, but rather from Wahl. Some of the claims presented in this chapter are indebted to Baugh's book.

himself put it at the outset of his book, Hegelian negativity – when understood as just such a constant, restless movement – could be seen to 'even risk breaking the bounds of the [Hegelian] system' itself.[26]

The Hegelianism that we have ascribed to Debord seems influenced by both of these themes. On the one hand, he too wants to liberate dialectical movement from the Hegelian system; on the other, the manner in which he does so seems informed by the sense in which Hegelian resolution is *itself* a condition of perpetual process. The two positions combine in Debord's Hegelianism, in which the 'rational kernel' of constant, dialectical movement is extracted from the system's 'mystical shell'[27] not by simply rejecting subject-object unity, but rather by re-figuring the latter as a condition of continual historical praxis.

As this chapter progresses, we will try to develop this reading of Debord's Hegelianism. We will show that Debord's scepticism towards Hegel's purported historical closure echoes, and indeed seems informed by, the work of Koyré and Kojève. Having done so, we will then place his work close to that of Hyppolite and Papaïoannou, both of whom gestured towards viewing Hegelian resolution as a constant, collective, historical process.

Alexandre Koyré: *'Geist ist Zeit'*

According to Jean Wahl, the *Phenomenology*'s section on the unhappy consciousness echoed aspects of Hegel's earlier work. The pathos and angst of the unhappy consciousness, he held, showed that the embers of Hegel's earlier, more passionate and romantic philosophy could still be found within the comparatively cold logic of his later writings.[28] Wahl's reading of Hegel thus accords with a further aspect of French Hegelianism that also informs Debord's own use of Hegelian ideas: namely, the notion (prompted by the publication of Hegel's early theological writings in 1907, and by his Jena manuscripts in 1923, 1931 and 1932) that Hegel's early writings might stand in a degree of tension with his mature philosophical system. Early twentieth-century French Hegelianism was thereby marked by a similar stance to that provoked by the appearance of Marx's early *Manuscripts*, insofar as Hegel's early writings, like those of the young Marx, could be seen to foreground the vitality, change and movement that his later, more sober systematic logic sought to grasp, but nonetheless froze

---

26 Wahl 1951, p. 194.
27 Cf. Marx 1990, p. 103.
28 Wahl 1951 p. vi.

into a finished philosophical system. Such was this interest that by 1934, Alexandre Koyré was able to claim that modern Hegel interpretation had become characterised by an attempt to find the 'hot passion' of Hegel's youth beneath the 'frozen steel' of his later 'dialectical formulas'.[29]

Koyré was careful to acknowledge that addressing Hegel's mature work through his early writings invited misinterpretation and misrepresentation. Hegel's work had changed during the course of its development, and it would be an error to use the earlier writings as a key to his later texts. Consequently, Koyré sought to locate and address a point of transition between the early and late writings; to thereby draw out a key problematic, evident within that point of transition, that marked both the virtues of his earlier work, and the limitations of his later thought. Importantly for our concerns, he did so by advancing an almost existential reading of time in Hegel. In his highly influential 'Hegel à Iéna' of 1934, Koyré translated and compared the conceptions of time expressed in the *Jenenser Logik* of 1804–5 with that set out in the *Jenenser Realphilosophie* of 1805–6.[30] Through doing so, he attempted to highlight a distinction between the vitality of Hegel's early views on time, and the comparatively 'dead'[31] time described in Hegel's mature system.

Once again, there is no evidence to show that Koyré exerted a direct influence on Debord's thought. Debord may well have read him, and there are undoubted echoes of Koyré's views in his work, but Koyré, like Wahl, was absent from Debord's personal library when he died in 1994.[32] Koyré's reading of Hegel is, however, relevant, as it too helped to shape the currents within French Hegelianism that inform Debord's work. For example, Koyré presented Hegel's philosophy as an anthropology,[33] and contended that it is, 'in its deepest intuitions, a philosophy of time'.[34] Koyré associated Hegelian negativity with both human subjectivity and with the flow of time, and his reading presented such negative, temporal subjectivity as inherently resistant to any final, systematic resolution.

Koyré was particularly drawn to the 'phenomenological' conception of time that he found in Hegel's earlier Jena manuscripts.[35] This conception of time is focussed upon the human experience of temporality, and it involves an

---

29 Koyré 2006, p. 149.
30 See Jeffs 2012, who focuses on this distinction.
31 Koyré 2006, p. 153.
32 Thanks are due to Laurence le Bras at the Bibliothèque nationale for assistance with these enquiries.
33 Baugh 2003, p. 26.
34 Koyré 2006, p. 163; also quoted in Baugh 2003, p. 25.
35 Koyré 2006, p. 152n.

intimate association between Spirit and time. Time is in fact held to constitute the very fabric of Spirit's historical consciousness, and as Koyré points out, Hegel even went so far as to remark in a marginal note from this period that '*Geist ist Zeit*', i.e. that Spirit *is* time.[36] He seem to have held the view that for Hegel, the passage of time moves by way of a dialectical process, and that this process is the moving, animating force that drives the life of Spirit. Time, in other words, is viewed in very similar terms to the role played by the Concept in Hegel's mature philosophy. However, Koyré also held that these ideas raise an important problem for Hegel's work.

For Hegel, Spirit becomes conscious of itself and of its world through its actions in time, because it is continually engaged in defining and constituting itself through those actions and experiences. Koyré observed that if Spirit continually constitutes itself through temporal action, then it must always be engaged in a condition of *becoming*. The implication that Koyré drew from this observation reflects his debts to Heidegger, and indeed his subsequent legacy to French existentialism: for if Spirit is continually creating and defining itself in time, then it is, in effect, continually engaged in constructing itself from out of its own future.[37] Hegel's philosophy famously presents becoming as the truth of being. If that is the case, then the truth of the present (being) is its future (i.e. its becoming), and the past from which the present has emerged is itself defined by the future (for the future must also be the truth of the past). Or, to use the notorious 'thesis-antithesis-synthesis' shorthand: if the synthesis is the truth of the thesis and the antithesis, then the synthesis, as outcome, must somehow precede itself.[38] According to Koyré, this precludes any conclusion to the dialectic of history, because at every moment, the present must be deriving itself from out of its own future. His position can perhaps be summarised as follows: if one accepts that human consciousness of time exists (and one must if one holds that *Geist ist Zeit*); and if one also arrives at the view that the future is always anterior to the past; then history can never come to an end, for in order for there to be a past and a present, there must always be a future.[39]

Koyré's reading is of course questionable, not least because there would seem to be a degree of slippage here between the end of history (i.e. the end

---

36 The marginal note is taken from Hegel's lectures of 1803–4. Koyré acknowledges that Hoffmeister, the editor of the manuscript, proposed that this could be read as Spirit is *in* time; Koyré, however, maintains that Spirit *is* time (see Jeffs 2012; Koyré 1971, p. 179).

37 Koyré helped to introduce Heidegger to a French audience, and his claims accorded, like those of Wahl, with nascent elements of Sartrean existentialism (see Sartre 2003, p. 164).

38 Baugh 2003, pp. 24–5.

39 Grier 1996, p. 187.

of the developmental process that Spirit needs to conduct within history) and the end of time. Nonetheless, the key issue is that this interpretation implied the following, rather existential themes: a) human consciousness is wedded to the conduct and awareness of historical change; b) this is a perpetual and inescapable condition; c) if consciousness is thereby identified with the negation of the present moment, it then follows that consciousness must cease to exist if that temporal process of negation came to an end.[40]

In addition to foregrounding these themes, which of course bear direct relation to Debord's views, Koyré's reading of the early Jena manuscripts served to further Wahl's indications that Spirit's existence must be viewed as an intrinsically tragic affair. The issues that Koyré identified indicate that Spirit can never reach a state of repose and final satisfaction without abandoning the temporal structure that defines it.[41] If a consciousness of history is to exist, history itself cannot have an end, and a continual temporal restlessness, or *inquiétude*, to use Koyré's term, must therefore be located at the very heart of Spirit.

However, Koyré also contended that in his later Jena manuscripts, Hegel presented a rather different view of time to that set out in his earlier Jena texts. This later view was much closer to that expressed in his mature philosophy, insofar as it reflects a desire to unite the finite with the infinite. In this later text, according to Koyré, Hegel's quasi-religious concerns led him to attempt the unification of the discrete, finite moments of Spirit's lived time with the infinitude of eternity, *qua* the timeless logic that Hegel's mature work holds to be intrinsic to all being. In this slightly later account of temporality, Koyré claims, the human experience of time is no longer derived from a perpetually 'open' future, as in the earlier manuscript. Instead, it is derived from the eternal 'now' of that ontologically fundamental logic. This later position indicates that both time and Spiritual experience can only be fully comprehended once Spirit has grasped the true nature of that fundamental 'now', i.e. once it has completed its historical tasks, and has attained absolute knowing (thereby grasping the true nature of the logic that underpins and founds its existence). For Koyré – who held that Hegel's mature system, in contrast to his earlier work, is 'dead, very dead'[42] – this new conception of time stills Spirit's *inquiétude*. This later conception of time, he writes, is 'paralysed': it is 'no longer time', but 'in effect, is *space*'.[43]

---

40 Koyré 1971, p. 178.
41 Jeffs 2012.
42 Koyré 2006, p. 153.
43 Koyré 2006, p. 178; also quoted in Jeffs 2012.

Koyré's contention that Hegel had imposed an unwarranted arrest upon an otherwise dynamic existence bears direct relation to Debord's conception of spectacle (it also echoes Lukács's contention that within modern capitalism, 'time sheds its qualitative, variable, flowing nature', and is thereby 'transformed into abstract, exactly measurable ... space').[44] Koyré's reading of Hegel's Jena texts chimes with Debord's view that Hegelian thought possesses an inherent dynamism, and that this negative, dialectical movement cannot be held within the bounds of a completed philosophical system, or indeed arrested by the imposition of an historical end point. As we saw in Chapter 2, Debord made the following remark in his 1983 preface to Champ Libre's edition of Cieszkowski's *Prolegomena to Historiosophy*:

> ... the central aporia of the [Hegelian] system [is] ... that time has not ended. Hegel had concluded history, in the form of thought, because he ultimately accepted glorifying his present.[45]

Similarly, when describing Hegel's early model of temporality in 'Hegel à Iéna', Koyré writes as follows:

> It is because man says 'no' to his present – or to himself – that he has a future. It is because he negates himself that he has a past. It is because he is time – and not simply temporal – that he has a present ... [Yet] if time is dialectical and constructed *from out of the future*, it is – whatever Hegel says – eternally unfinished.[46]

Statements such as these should serve to illustrate the sense in which Debord's views on time and subjectivity are not simply drawn from Bergson or Sartre, as is sometimes assumed. Instead, they are primarily informed by French Hegelianism's identification of dialectical movement with both temporality and subjectivity. This may help to reinforce our earlier contention that Debord's Hegelianism effectively re-casts the movement of the Concept in terms of human existence in time. In addition, Debord's attendant desire to remove that movement from the seeming fixity of the Hegelian system can be seen to accord with Koyré's own scepticism towards Hegel's systematic closure.

---

44   Lukács 1971, p. 90.
45   Debord 2006b, p. 1536.
46   Koyré 2006, pp. 188–9; also quoted in Baugh 2003, p. 27.

The key difference, however, is that Koyré's concerns entail an objection to Hegelian resolution, whereas Debord's does not. The 'open' temporality that Koyré identifies in the early Jena manuscript echoes the unhappy consciousness' pursuit of a resolution that forever exceeds it. The openness of Debord's own vision of historical movement, on the other hand, does not rely upon the continual deferral of a condition of unity, but is instead grounded upon the identification of the latter with a condition of praxis. As we tried to explain above, Debord's antipathy to Hegel's attempt to compose a philosophical system does not entail a rejection of Hegelian unity *per se*.

Alexandre Kojève and the End of History

In 1933, Koyré left Paris, and passed his lectures on Hegel at the École Pratique des Hautes Études to Alexandre Kojève. Yet Kojève inherited more from Koyré than his lecture series. He also adopted an apparent paradox, which Koyré had highlighted in his 'Hegel à Iéna' essay (he would in fact later describe Koyré's reading of Hegelian time as the 'source and basis'[47] of his own interpretation of Hegel). The paradox was as follows: if humanity and human consciousness are inherently historical, then history cannot stop insofar as humanity exists; and yet if human consciousness is to attain its fullest manifestation, and if it is to understand itself completely, then history must come to a close.[48] Kojève's response was to cut this knot very simply and abruptly. History, he claimed, had indeed come to a close, and in consequence both 'Man' and historical time had simply ceased to exist.

Kojève's views on the end of history need to be approached via his central concerns with the *Phenomenology*'s lord and bondsman relation (known more popularly as the 'master and slave' relation). Kojève is in fact not only responsible for the prominence of an almost eschatological reading of Hegel's views on history: so too is he responsible for the venerable but no less erroneous myth that the lord and bondsman are the key to understanding both Hegel and Marx.[49] The long-standing prominence of these two idiosyncratic contentions can be at least partly explained by two simple facts. Firstly, there was no

---

47 Kojève 1980, p. 134.
48 Grier 1996, p. 188.
49 See Arthur 1983 for a useful discussion of these issues. This view remains widespread to this day, and it was certainly current within the French milieu at the time: Sartre and Hyppolite, for example, would later claim, respectively, that 'the ... master-slave relation ... profoundly influenced Marx' (Sartre 2003, p. 61, also quoted in Arthur 1983), and that

complete French version of the *Phenomenology* available at this time, as Hyppolite's translation would not appear until 1939.[50] Secondly, Kojève's lectures were attended by some of the most significant figures within early twentieth-century French thought (Aron, Breton, Bataille, Lacan and Merleau-Ponty all attended: Sartre, contrary to popular belief, did not).[51] Kojève must have been an extremely impressive and persuasive speaker, because his vision of Hegel became a primary influence and point of reference within much of the French thought that followed. Kojève's influence was, in fact, enormous, and however indirect Debord's relation to Kojève may have been, the latter's reading of Hegel remains relevant to our concerns.

We should begin with the relation between the lord and the bondsman. Like the unhappy consciousness, it is one of the 'shapes' of consciousness that emerge during the course of the *Phenomenology*'s path towards absolute knowing. Whilst Kojève's treatment of this relation is perhaps questionable, its importance for the book as a whole is not. This relationship, which arises from a struggle for recognition, lies at the very basis of Spirit.[52] The salient point for our concerns, however, is that one of the lessons that consciousness learns upon this 'rung' of the *Phenomenology*'s 'ladder'[53] towards absolute knowing is that consciousness (and, by extension, Spirit) is able to recognise itself in the objective and transformative actions that it performs upon the world. That lesson is imparted via the experience of the bondsman, who, through his 'formative activity', 'posits *himself* as a negative in the permanent order of things, and thereby becomes *for himself*, someone existing on his own account'.[54] This section of the *Phenomenology* is thus resonant with the existential themes of self-constitutive activity that inform Kojève's rather Heideggerian reading of Hegel, and it also accords with the aspects of Marx's early, and then recently-

---

'the master and slave ... became the inspiration of Marxian philosophy' (Hyppolite 1969, p. 29, also quoted in Arthur 1983).

50   Heckman in Hyppolite 1974, p. xxiii.
51   Arthur 1983.
52   This is because Spirit is basically the active self-consciousness of a community. In order for consciousness to develop into Spirit, mutual recognition must occur. As self-consciousness has been shown, by this stage in the book, to affirm itself through negation, the collective self-consciousness of mutual recognition requires each instance of self-consciousness to demonstrate that it is just such a negative process. This means that each sets out to negate the other, giving rise to a struggle for recognition. The loser in the struggle becomes the bondsman, and the winner becomes the lord.
53   Hegel 1977, p. 14.
54   Hegel 1977, p. 118.

translated, *Manuscripts*, which Kojève also drew upon. After all, the bondsman *is* what he *does*, and he knows himself as a result of his actions; his activity brings him to self-consciousness. The lord, by contrast, does not partake in any such formative activity. In consequence, he stagnates (a point that is somewhat reminiscent of the a-historical spectatorship that Debord identified with the commodified wealth of modern society).

This theme of self-consciousness through self-constitutive, transformative, and thus *historical* activity is central to Kojève's reading of Hegel's views on history. In fact, one of the key motifs of Kojève's account is that it transposes the relation between lord and bondsman onto history as a whole. Reading Hegel with one eye on Marx's famous remark that 'The history of all hitherto existing society is the history of class struggle',[55] Kojève presents the engine of human history as a fundamental struggle between masters and slaves. History thus becomes a progression towards a condition of final reconciliation and recognition that will still that state of unrest.

The manner in which Kojève conceives this accords with our earlier observation that many of the writers in this French tradition emphasise the connection between the Concept and human temporality; a connection that can also be found, we have proposed, in the Hegelianism that we have ascribed to Debord. This is explicit in Kojève, and it perhaps follows, to some degree, from Koyré's own indications in this regard.[56] Yet where Koyré was concerned with the phenomenological *experience* of time, Kojève's emphasis falls on human *action* in time. With his characteristic predilection for capitalised nouns, and again with an obvious nod to Marx, Kojève refers to such action as 'Work'. 'Work' is understood as the negative, transformative actions that 'Man' conducts upon the world in his historical pursuit of harmony, recognition and resolution. 'Work', therefore, is understood as the operation of the Concept as it plays out in the lived time of human history. This leads Kojève to hold that 'Man is the Concept', that 'the Concept is Work', and that 'Man and the Concept are also *Time*'.[57]

The odd synthesis of Hegel, Marx and Heidegger that informs these ideas resulted in a philosophical anthropology that resembles some of Debord's own views. As we've seen, Debord contends in *The Society of the Spectacle*, by way of a quotation from the *Phenomenology* (which was drawn, it would seem, from Papaïoannou),[58] that 'Man – that 'negative being who *is* solely to the extent

---

55 Marx and Engels 1985, p. 79.
56 Koyré 2006, p. 175.
57 See, for example, Kojève 1980, p. 145.
58 Papaïoannou in Hegel 2009, p. 14.

that he abolishes being' – is one [*identique*] with time'.⁵⁹ Kojève's comments are very similar. He writes as follows:

> ... if Man *is* Time, he himself is Nothingness or annihilation of spatial Being. And we know that for Hegel it is precisely in this annihilation of Being that consists the Negativity which is Man, that Action of Fighting and Work by which Man preserves himself in spatial Being while *destroying* it ... And this Negativity – that is, this Nothingness nihilating as Time in Space – is what forms the very foundation of the specifically human existence ...⁶⁰

Humanity, for Kojève, is thus a negating, temporal process: an entity that does not coincide with the world that it works upon, but which is instead different from it, opposed to it, and which affects changes upon it. Kojève then goes on to associate this distinction between 'Man' and 'Being' with 'Error', and he identifies its supersession with 'Truth'. He thereby arrives at the following conclusion:

> Man opposed to single and homogeneous spatial Being ... is necessarily Error and not Truth. For a Thought that does not coincide with Being is false. Thus, when specifically human error is finally transformed into the truth of absolute Science [i.e. *Wissenschaft*, Hegelian philosophy], Man ceases to exist as Man and history comes to an end. The overcoming of Man (that is, of Time, that is, of Action) in favour of static Being (that is, Space, that is, Nature), therefore, is the overcoming of Error in favour of Truth.⁶¹

To summarise: Kojève associates the operation of the Concept with 'Man', 'Time' and 'Work', i.e. with human history, and he identifies its result with a condition of 'Truth' that supersedes the distinction of 'Man' from 'Being', or rather of 'Man' from the true nature of being, i.e. from the Absolute. The resultant identity of subject and object is thus held to resolve the condition of 'Error' that defines 'Man' as a historical creature. Kojève contends that Hegel heralds this 'Truth', and holds, quite consistently, albeit somewhat bizarrely, that the achievement of this 'Truth' entails the end of both history and 'Man'.

---

59 Debord 1995, p. 92; 2006b, p. 820.
60 Kojève 1980, p. 155.
61 Kojève 1980, p. 156.

There is a strong sense in which Debord's criticisms of Hegel seem informed by the influence exerted by Kojève's account. Debord appears to have avoided the error of reading Hegel and Marx through a primary focus on the lord and bondsman (Vaneigem, it would seem, did not),[62] but his work employs themes that are clearly foregrounded within the *Phenomenology*'s section on the lord and bondsman, and which Kojève underscored. His criticisms of Hegel also seem informed by Kojève's concerns. For example, in *The Society of the Spectacle*, he describes Hegel as having been driven to conclude history as a result of his adoption of a 'paradoxical posture'.[63] This 'posture' echoes the problem that Kojève drew from Koyré (i.e. the view that for a complete knowledge of history to be possible, history must be concluded): for 'in order to express itself', Debord writes, Hegelian philosophy 'must assume that the total history in which it has vested everything has come to an end'.[64] Yet whilst Debord no doubt read Kojève at some point,[65] it seems unlikely that he would have been particularly impressed. Despite his debts to Marx – and indeed despite his protestations that Fukuyama later misrepresented him[66] – Kojève ultimately presented modern capitalism as a condition proper to the conclusion of history's struggle for mutual recognition and freedom. Indeed, Kojève would later comment that 'the "American way of life"' is 'the type of life specific to the post-historical period'.[67] Kojève appears to have been quite serious in his claims: he actually worked for the French Ministry of Economic Affairs following the war, and helped to shape the EEC and GATT.

---

62   See Vaneigem's 'Basic Banalities', which was published in two parts in *Internationale situationniste* #7 (SI 2006, pp. 117–31; 1997, pp. 272–81) and #8 (SI 2006, pp. 154–73; 1997, pp. 330–43). See also Vaneigem 2003.
63   Debord 1995, pp. 49–50; 2006b, p. 793.
64   Debord 1995, pp. 49–50; 2006b, p. 793.
65   It should be added, however, that Kojève's writings were absent from Debord's library as of his death in 1994. He is not mentioned in Debord's writings or personal correspondence.
66   Although Kojève's account differs from Fukuyama's own, the latter can serve to illustrate the spectacle's status as an illusory end of history. This point was not lost on Debord himself (Debord 2001a, p. 31). Fukuyama's views on the events of May 1968 are also pertinent, because they are as ironically close to Debord and the SI's own contentions. In *The End of History and the Last Man*, Fukuyama claims that once the 'just' cause of liberal democracy has been realised, there is no longer anything significant and substantial to rebel against; there can only be empty, directionless revolts against that cause itself. For Fukuyama, those who took part in the uprisings fought 'out of a certain boredom', and the 'substance of their protest ... was a matter of indifference; what they rejected was life in a society in which ideals had somehow become impossible' (Fukuyama 1992, p. 330).
67   Kojève 1980, p. 161n.

In short, there is a strong sense in which Kojève's reading of Hegel served to shape Debord's views on the latter's shortcomings. In this regard, he was by no means alone. Kojève's great emphasis on historical conclusion helped to further an interest in rejecting or problematising the apparent finality of Hegelian unity. Given our concerns with Debord and the Situationists, the manner in which this interest informed the Hegelianism of the Surrealists seems particularly significant. Breton, for example, attended Kojève's lectures, but even before he did so, he was already adamant that Hegelian closure needed to be opposed. In 1929, and whilst pledging Surrealism's allegiance to both dialectical materialism and to Communism,[68] he claimed that the Hegelian dialectic's 'negation of the negation' entailed the supersession of any fixed limitations, including those set by Hegel himself.[69] In a similar vein, Bataille, who also attended Kojève's lectures, and whose work Debord owned and read,[70] would advocate a deliberately 'open' dialectical negativity: a negativity that opposed any final closure, which he identified with excessive, festive destruction, and which he even placed in connection to a notion of 'spectacle' (albeit one that differs from Debord's own).[71] However, the positions adopted by both Bre-

---

68 Both 'Surrealism' and 'historical materialism', Breton claimed, took 'the "colossal abortion" of the Hegelian system' as their 'point of departure' (Breton 1996, p. 447).

69 According to Breton, it is 'impossible to assign any limitations ... to the exercise of a thought finally made tractable to negation, and to the negation of the negation' (Breton 1996, p. 447).

70 As of his death in 1994, Debord owned Bataille's *Le Procès de Gilles de Rais* and *The Accursed Share*, and he also owned a copy of De Sade's *Justine* that included a preface by Bataille. Thanks are due to Laurence Le Bras for assistance with these details.

71 For Bataille, the rejection of the imposition of 'limitations' upon dialectical negativity entailed the impossibility of imposing utility, purpose and function upon it. Consequently, the negativity articulated within the Hegelian system, according to Bataille, ought properly to be free from any rationalisation. This is expressed particularly clearly in an essay of 1955 entitled 'Hegel, Death and Sacrifice', in which he built upon ideas advanced in such earlier works as 'The Notion of Expenditure' (1933) and *The Accursed Share* (1946–9). The essay focuses on Hegel's famous assertion that Spirit neither 'shrinks from death' nor 'keeps itself untouched by devastation', but rather 'wins its truth' upon finding itself 'in utter dismemberment' (Hegel 1977, p. 19). Strongly influenced by Kojève, albeit located in steadfast opposition to the latter's notion of historical conclusion (see the discussion in Agamben 2004a, pp. 4–5) – and perhaps also exhibiting the influence of Heidegger, whom he'd read as early as the 1930s – Bataille advanced the claim that Hegel's true profundity lay in the degree to which he'd understood the human subject as a fundamentally *negative* creature: as a 'living death', driven towards negation and towards its own ultimate demise. Yet Hegel, according to Bataille, had overlooked the fact that if death constituted the subject's true identity, then self-consciousness could only be attained at the point of

ton and Bataille still rely upon the association of dialectical 'openness' with the constant deferral of final unity, and they thus echo, as indicated earlier, the unhappy consciousness' constant flight towards an unreachable absolute. Debord's position is somewhat different. Whilst the Hegel that Debord criticised was certainly a rather Kojèveian figure, the Hegelian ideas that Debord adopts and employs seem much closer to the account presented by Jean Hyppolite. This is because Hyppolite presented the Hegelian absolute not as a final end state, but rather as a condition of perpetual, negative process.

Jean Hyppolite: Pantragedism

Debord's proximity to Hyppolite's interpretation is by no means coincidental. Hyppolite's *Genesis and Structure of Hegel's Philosophy of Spirit* of 1946, his

---

death itself; such self-consciousness was thus unattainable, and the human subject was thus denied full, final resolution. Like the unhappy consciousness, Bataille's human subject was thus constantly opposed to its own self: a self that it perpetually strives towards, but which it can never reach. In Bataille's view, this drive towards unity underlies Hegel's own philosophical ambitions, insofar as his desire to tame negativity by binding it within the positive unity and rationality of his system reflected a fundamental human characteristic. We are driven towards death, for Bataille (we are fascinated by our own and that of others); we take pleasure in death (it lies, for Bataille, at the base of eroticism); but insofar as we are alive, we remain forever separated from it. As a result of this constant separation we are compelled, he claims, to construct 'spectacles' and 'representations' of death (Bataille 1990, p. 20). Tragic art, for Bataille, is an example of this compulsion: for 'In tragedy', he writes, 'it is a question of identifying with some character who dies, and of believing that we die, although we are alive' (Bataille 1990, p. 20). His claims are thus close to those of Nietzsche, as tragedy is viewed as affording a safe, neutered communion with the negative, and he holds Hegel's system to present just such a 'representation of the Negative' (Bataille 1990, p. 21). It would be wrong to claim a strong line of influence between these aspects of Bataille's thought and Debord's own notion of spectacle (although see Brown 1986), but Bataille's account of tragic 'representations' in Hegel is nonetheless analogous to the spectacle's representation of historical agency. Given that Debord read Bataille, it may have informed his ideas. Furthermore, and as is also the case with Lefebvre, Debord and the SI shared Bataille's view that negativity might involve festival and excess (e.g. for the SI, 'proletarian revolutions will be festivals or nothing' (SI 2006, p. 429; 1966)). Bataille argued that a truly 'sovereign' negativity must be completely exempt from utility or constructive purpose (Bataille 1990, p. 25), and although he seems to indicate that the 'representation' of death and negativity can never be entirely overcome, he does allude to the need for glorious, purposeless negation and destruction; for 'a luxurious squandering of energy in every form!' (Bataille 1991, p. 33).

Introduction to Hegel's Philosophy of History of 1948, and his *Studies on Marx and Hegel* of 1955 were all present in Debord's personal library as of his death in 1994. The Debord archive at the Bibliothèque nationale de France now contains his notes on Hyppolite's work, together with notes from Hyppolite's lectures (and whilst there are no letters in Debord's published correspondence to confirm this, it seems that he may even have been in direct contact with Hyppolite for a time).[72] These connections are significant, because Hyppolite's account accords with the re-figuration of Hegelian philosophy that we have attributed to Debord's work.

The first point to make here is that Hyppolite's Hegel is the author of a deeply tragic philosophy. In this sense, Hyppolite's approach is informed by the work of Jean Wahl. Indeed, like Wahl, Hyppolite claimed that the unhappy consciousness could be seen as a defining figure in Hegel's *Phenomenology*.[73] Yet rather than associating the tragic with the *experience* of consciousness, Hyppolite emphasised the retention and importance of negativity, process and rupture within Hegelian unity, and thereby cast tragedy – *qua* the perpetuity of negativity and opposition – as a fundamental ontological feature of reality itself. In fact, Hyppolite went so far as to describe Hegel's tacitly pantheistic 'panlogicism' as a form of 'pantragedism'.[74] In his account, the attainment of Spirit's full maturity arises, in part, from a sober recognition of the constancy and permanence of this condition.[75]

This acknowledgement of the inevitability of death, destruction and change carries both existential and conservative implications. It stresses Hegel's attendance to mortality and human finitude, and it is also connected to the association of Hegelian negativity with 'death', 'dismemberment' and 'devast-

---

72   Clark and Nicholson-Smith (2004, p. 479) recall visiting one of Hyppolite's lectures with Debord. Debord owned and made notes on Hyppolite's *Introduction to Hegel's Philosophy of History* of 1948 and his *Studies on Marx and Hegel* of 1955; the reading notes are now stored in the BNF's Debord archive. According to Merrifield, just prior to the publication of *The Society of the Spectacle*, Debord was in fact 'all set to help [Hyppolite] out' with a lecture (perhaps this was to be one of the papers commented upon in the previous quotation) 'until Hyppolite had a change of heart and asked someone else' (Merrifield 2005, p. 50). Hussey (2002, p. 115) writes that 'Debord first encountered Hegel via the work of Jean Hyppolite, then a professor at the Collège de France'. This is incorrect: Hyppolite took up that position in 1963, and Debord was clearly involved in Hegelian ideas from a much earlier date.
73   Hyppolite 1974, p. 190.
74   Hyppolite 1974, pp. 30–1; see also p. 194.
75   Hyppolite 1997, p. 165n.

ation'[76] and the horrors of human history (after all, the latter is described in *The Philosophy of History* as the 'slaughter-bench'[77] upon which reason works). However, on the other hand, Hyppolite's emphasis on the tragic bears direct relation to the aspects of Hegel's work that seem particularly important to Debord.

Hegel's preface to the *Phenomenology* contains the following, often quoted remark: Spirit 'wins its truth only when, in utter dismemberment, it finds itself'.[78] Like the more recent reading advanced by Jean-Luc Nancy,[79] Hyppolite's account ultimately comes close to indicating that Spirit 'wins its truth' not simply by identifying an implicit wholeness *within* such a condition of disunity, but rather by recognising itself *as* a condition of perpetual 'dismemberment'. Spirit, we remember, is an expression of the Absolute: it is the means by which the latter comes to self-awareness of its own fundamental nature. For Hyppolite, the Absolute continually 'divides and tears itself apart in order to be absolute'.[80] Thus, Spirit's full self-consciousness entails not only a recognition of, but also an identification with, that process of constant change and rupture.

Hyppolite presents the Absolute as a fundamental and essentially unitary power that generates, unites and inheres within all negative, particular difference. It is the fundamental ground and source of all being: the ultimate unity of all existence, albeit a unity that constantly expresses itself into the distinct moments that compose that existence. It is, as Hyppolite puts it, 'an inexhaustively creative activity' that lies 'at the source of reality', and which 'ceaselessly creates and engulfs various incarnations of absolute life'.[81] This entails that on Hyppolite's reading, Hegelian logic's grand unification of universality and particularity is not a static structure. It is not, as Hyppolite puts it, 'an immobile synthesis',[82] but rather a dynamic condition: a fundamental unity that continually generates negative difference and particularity within itself, but which ultimately remains one with itself within that very difference. Because Hyppolite understands the Absolute to be a condition of restless, perpetual process, Spirit's self-identification with it cannot bring human history

---

76 Hegel 1977, p. 19.
77 Hegel 2004, p. 21.
78 Hegel 1977, p. 19.
79 Nancy 2002.
80 Hyppolite 1969, p. 7.
81 Hyppolite 1996, p. 37. This phrase is taken from Hyppolite's comments on Hegel's early romantic views concerning 'the creative energy of God' (Hyppolite 1996, p. 37).
82 Hyppolite 1997, p. 183.

to an 'end' in any crude sense of the term. In fact, in his *Genesis and Structure of Hegel's Phenomenology of Spirit*, Hyppolite explicitly (and correctly) dismissed the view that 'Hegel naively thought that history came to an end with his system'.[83] Instead, Hyppolite's interpretation presents us with something that seems much closer to a notion of *fruition* than a state of total conclusion.[84] In marked distinction from Kojève's eschatological end of history, Hyppolite indicates that Spirit simply attains a condition that allows it to recognise and fully express the fundamental logic that founds both itself and its world. History does not end, and 'Man' does not disappear along with his condition of 'Error'. Instead, Spirit comes to understand the dynamic, processual nature of its own historical life, and finds forms of social organisation that allow that life to flourish.

To some degree, these views follow from the way in which Hyppolite understands Spirit. In his *Studies on Marx and Hegel*, he made a remark that seems similar to, but which nonetheless differs from, Koyré's own account of Spirit. Quoting both the *Phenomenology* and Hegel's early Jena texts (the same texts that Koyré had addressed), Hyppolite refers to the whole that 'develops itself, resolves its own development, and in the movement simply preserves itself'. This 'whole', he writes, can only become 'present to itself' in 'the temporality of a consciousness'.[85] If it is an infinite process of continual self-separation and reunification; and if, as Hegel also indicates, that process is to become present to itself within human historical consciousness; then human consciousness must itself continue to exist in time, as a temporal continuum within which that process can continue to operate. Thus, 'Spirit', for Hyppolite, is 'always oriented towards the future'.[86] It cannot come to a stop, but instead arrives at a stage of development at which it can comprehend and fully express its own negative, historical nature.[87] This is, of course, rather similar to the position that we have attributed to Debord.

Consequently, and whilst it does so rather tacitly, Hyppolite's reading gives us a view of the actualisation of Hegelian logic in human praxis that goes beyond the conservative political visions of *The Philosophy of Right*. From Hyp-

---

83   Hyppolite 1974, p. 45.
84   Hyppolite 1969, p. 13.
85   Ibid.
86   Ibid.
87   Hyppolite 1974, pp. 596–7. Hyppolite remarks that Marx's famous eleventh thesis on Feuerbach 'was not too unfaithful to Hegelian thought' (Hyppolite 1974, p. 598). This is because within Hegel's own work, according to Hyppolite's interpretation, we already have a notion of realising philosophy in lived activity.

polite – and this, we will propose, is crucial to Debord – one can draw a sense in which Spirit needs to comprehend, master and fully actualise the living process of its own historical, collective existence. As Hyppolite emphasises in his excellent work on Hegel's philosophy of history,[88] the processual and organic unity in difference that comprises the 'living' collectivity of Spirit (i.e. the continuum and unity of Spirit *vis-à-vis* the finite, particular lives that compose it) reflects Hegelian thought's defining attempt to think the interrelation of universality and particularity. Indeed, 'man', as Hyppolite would later put it, 'is the house of the Logos';[89] and the 'Logos', for Hegel, as Hyppolite clearly understood, is a living, dynamic force that finds actualisation in human historical existence. Hence, once again, we have a sense of historical fruition rather than a Kojèveian conclusion. Spirit simply comes to comprehend and self-consciously direct its own dynamic, historical existence.

We will look at Debord's connection to these aspects of Hyppolite's account in Chapter 8. Here we can simply make some general remarks concerning his apparent debts to Hyppolite's interpretation of Hegel.

Hyppolite provides us with a particularly strong impression of the sense in which the Hegelian unification of the universal and the particular, of the finite and the infinite, cannot be understood as a static arrest, but should instead be seen as a condition of perpetual, self-determinate movement. Hyppolite's reading of Hegel, therefore, may well have provided Debord with the crucial insight that Hegel must be understood as a philosopher of process, change and movement. If this insight is placed in conjunction with Debord's somewhat Kojèveian characterisations of Hegel, according to which the latter's philosophy purports to bring history to a close, we can contend that it perhaps furthered the sense in which that philosophy amounted, for Debord, to a blurred, philosophical *depiction* of the genuine process and flux of praxis. Most importantly of all, Hyppolite's interpretation also indicates that this perpetual movement is not something that is ultimately stifled and arrested by Hegelian unity, but is instead intrinsic to that unity. This differs from the view that an open process relies upon the constant *deferral* of such unity. It also accords with Debord's own indications that such unity should be seen not as the end, but rather as the basis of a self-determinate history. Furthermore: we proposed earlier that the collective historical agency implied by Debord's work must be marked by the need to continually recreate its own conditions of existence. It seems significant, therefore, that in one of the books that Debord owned and studied,

---

88 Hyppolite 1996, p. 43 and *passim*.
89 Hyppolite 1997, p. 74.

Hyppolite linked similar themes to Marx: communism, he claimed, for Marx, is a self-constitutive process, engaged in 'forever re-creating its own foundations'.[90]

In his *Logic and Existence* of 1953 (a book that was not in Debord's library, but which he may nonetheless have consulted), Hyppolite remarked as follows:

> [Both Marx and Feuerbach] show that speculative philosophy, Hegel's absolute knowledge, is itself also a form of alienation, a substitute for religion. Man believes in another world in order to escape from the hostility of the one in which he lives; he projects into the 'beyond' his own essence because his own essence is not realised in this world.[91]

In the same text, Hyppolite also contends that Hegel's absolute Idea ultimately became, for Marx, 'the idea of concrete and social man',[92] and thereby a conception of communism. His work thus accords with, and perhaps directly informed, Debord's view that Hegelian philosophy could be construed as a philosophical *image* of real historical freedom.

Kostas Papaïoannou: The Absolute as *'l'oeuvre commune'*

Although Hyppolite appears to have played a particularly important role in the formation of Debord's approach to Hegel, we should also acknowledge the influence of Kostas Papaïoannou. Debord owned several works by Papaïoannou, on Marx, Hegel, history and ideology, and some of the quotations from Hegel that Debord employs in *The Society of the Spectacle* seem to have been taken from Papaïoannou's work.[93] In fact, if we can contend that Hyppolite helped to shape the general architecture of Debord's interpretation of Hegel, then we can also propose that Papaïoannou informed its political dimensions. This is because Papaïoannou's reading not only accords with Hyppolite's emphasis on negativity and dynamism: in addition, it also stresses the rejection of separated abstractions, and it gestures towards viewing the Absolute

---

90   Hyppolite 1969, p. 13.
91   Hyppolite 1997, p. 178.
92   Hyppolite 1997, p. 180.
93   The quotations in theses #125 and #180 of *The Society of the Spectacle* may have been taken from Papaïoannou (the quotations can be found in Papaïoannou's preface to Hegel 2009, p. 14, and in Papaïoannou 2012, p. 28; the latter quotation could, however, have been found in Lukács 1971, p. 139).

as a condition of collective historical praxis. We can begin to approach these aspects of Papaïoannou's work by turning, albeit briefly, to the early origins of Hegel's mature philosophy.

Hegel's Absolute does not subsist beneath existent reality, as if it were some kind of distinct, primal substance. Nor does it stand above it as a similarly distinct, transcendental entity. Neither a separated substance nor a Platonic form, it is instead intrinsic to the existence to which it gives rise, for it is, in effect, both the rationale and the life of that existence. Hegel's views in this regard are certainly informed by his undeniable debts to Spinoza's rationalist pantheism, and indeed by Aristotelian thought and traces of Schellingian romanticism. According to Papaïoannou, however, it is also coloured by Hegel's early and implicitly revolutionary rejection of all separated, transcendent abstractions. The template for this rejection of separation can be found in Hegel's early theological writings. In order to address it, therefore, we should first make some brief comments concerning the views expressed in those early texts.

Hegel's early work is very much oriented towards religion. In fact, Hegel initially studied as a theologian: whilst at the Tübingen academy, he took philosophy for two years, before transferring to theology for a further three. Yet perhaps somewhat surprisingly, Hegel's early work on religion contains something rather similar to a Feuerbachian *critique* of religion: a critique that addresses religious forms within which human agents become detached from their own fundamental essence.[94] In brief, Hegel argues here for the benefits of 'subjective' forms of religion over their 'objective' counterparts. The former, as defined in 1793's 'On the Prospects for a Folk Religion', are linked to sentiment, feeling and lived experience; the latter are associated with dogma, ritual and the imposition of scripture as positive 'fact'.[95] Hegel's argument here is a broadly romantic claim that religion should be lived and felt rather than submitted to as if it were an external doctrine. He reiterated this point in his 'The Positivity of the Christian Religion' of 1795: a text in which he described objective religion as an 'external' truth, separated from the particularities upon which it is imposed. Against such separation, Hegel would argue for the Christian model of a congregation, composed of mutually loving and forgiving believers

---

94   Feuerbach, it should be added, was unaware of this. Hegel's early texts were not available when he was working on *The Essence of Christianity*.

95   'Subjective religion is something individual, objective religion a matter of abstraction. The former is the living book of nature, of plants, insects, birds and beasts living with and surviving off each other ... The latter is the cabinet of the naturalist, full of insects he has killed, plants that are desiccated, animals stuffed or preserved in alcohol ...' (Hegel 1984; see also Hegel 1977, p. 31 for the continuity between this view and Hegel's later work).

who actualise their faith within their lived social activity. This is, in effect, an argument for the realisation of philosophy in praxis,[96] as divine love becomes actualised, within the operation of the Christian congregation, as an operative, concrete force within the world. Religion ceases to be oriented towards an entirely separate absolute. Instead, the latter becomes intrinsic to the life and interaction of the community of believers, who actualise it via their love and mutual forgiveness. These early views on love and religion would go on to form the basis for Hegel's later account of Spirit: for just as God's will becomes concrete and manifest through the activity of the congregation, so too does Spirit function, in Hegel's mature philosophy, as the means through which the Absolute attains full, self-conscious expression within the world. Likewise, just as Hegel's early work opposes God's detachment from his creation, so too does his mature philosophy reject any separation between the Idea and the world that the latter articulates.

The connection between these themes and Debord's own views should be readily apparent – he too rejected all 'external' forms of power and separated essence, and argued for their unification in the life of a community – but let us return here to Papaïoannou, who drew upon these aspects of Hegel's thought when advancing his claims. Through emphasising these themes, Papaïoannou presented Hegel's philosophy as having emerged from an attempt to supersede separated conceptual abstractions. Hegel's early work, in his view, sought to move beyond a vision of God that cast the latter as a separated, dogmatic abstraction, and argued, in a decidedly romantic vein, that the divine should instead be identified and expressed within the lived actions of a community. For Papaïoannou, Hegel's mature work should be read in much the same way: it too argues that the fundamental logic grasped by the final philosophy must be actualised in historical praxis.

By drawing upon and highlighting these themes, Papaïoannou is able to present Hegel's philosophy as a body of work that sets itself against all forms of alienation and separation. Papaïoannou casts Spirit's historical efforts as a project oriented towards the full expression of a rationale that necessarily opposes alienation, and which must be expressed and actualised within the living praxis of a community. This obviously accords with Debord's views. Just as Hyppolite presented 'man' as 'the house of the Logos', Papaïoannou

---

96 In his 'On the Prospects for a Folk Religion' Hegel writes: 'my concern is with what needs to be done so that religion with all the force of its teaching might be blended into the fabric of human feelings, bonded with what moves us to act, and shown to be efficacious' (Hegel 1984).

claimed – in a book that Debord owned, and which he recommends in his correspondence[97] – that the 'vehicle of the Absolute' is 'the people'.[98]

That reference to 'the people' reflects the fact that Papaïoannou viewed the Absolute as an explicitly *political* project. The full realisation of that project entails the supersession of society's separation from its own powers and constructs, and indeed the overcoming of the alienation of individuals from one another. In fact, some of Papaïoannou's quotations and statements would not seem at all out of place within the pages of *The Society of the Spectacle*. For example, he presents the following quotation from Hegel's *Early Theological Writings*, which Debord must have greatly appreciated:

> Thus the despotism of the Roman princes had chased the Spirit from the surface of the earth; the abduction of Spirit's freedom forced the projection of its absolute nature, its eternality, into the divinity. The misery that this despotism spread forced it to pursue and expect its happiness in heaven.[99]

In addition, and like Debord, Papaïoannou also claims that within modern society, 'the isolated individual confronts social powers that he has himself created, but which present themselves as independent powers: these are the powers of the state and wealth'.[100] Against such separation, Papaïoannou posits 'the communal work [*l'oeuvre commune*]' of 'the Absolute'.[101]

Papaïoannou's emphasis on the political derives from Hegel's claims that Spirit's final goal is freedom, and that this freedom is to be afforded through the establishment of the rational political state. However, rather than taking his bearings from *The Philosophy of Right*, Papaïoannou attends to Hegel's early celebrations of the purported harmony of ancient Greece. He thereby links the Absolute's self-realisation to a modern rebirth of the 'democratic city'.[102] Within such a 'city', alienation and the separation of social powers are to be superseded. The realisation of this political condition would afford the

---

97 The book in question is Papaïoannou's excellent *Hegel* of 1962. This book was present in Debord's library as of his death in 1994, and it is referenced favourably in Debord 2004a, p. 541.
98 Papaïoannou 2012, p. 77.
99 This passage has been translated from Papaïoannou 2012, p. 35; a slightly different translation can be found in Hegel 1975b, pp. 162–3.
100 Papaïoannou 2012, p. 84.
101 Papaïoannou 2012, p. 88.
102 Papaïoannou 2012, p. 80.

actualisation of the Absolute within the collective praxis of a social totality. The 'reality of the Logos' could then be understood as 'the action of one and all within the organic life of the free city':[103] for in Papaïoannou's view, it is 'only active participation in the life of the terrestrial city' that 'can give man the idea of an Absolute that renders impossible and superfluous all flight [*fuite*] into the beyond'[104] (i.e. all retreat into alienation and spectacle).

Papaïoannou also connects these political themes to Hegel's early enthusiasm for the French revolution. In doing so, he stresses that Hegel was not always the conservative apologist of *The Philosophy of Right*,[105] and he addresses this in a manner that serves to frame Hegel's contemporary status and relevance in a very clever and effective manner.

In his 'Theses on Hegel and Revolution' of 1931 (a text that Debord references in *The Society of the Spectacle*)[106] Karl Korsch contended that 'Hegelian philosophy and its dialectical method cannot be understood without taking into account its relationship to revolution'.[107] Korsch adds, however, that Hegel's work does not ultimately amount to 'a philosophy ... of the [French] revolution', but is instead best seen as a philosophy 'of the restoration'[108] that followed the revolution. In his *Hegel* of 1962 – a text that Debord owned – Papaïoannou presents a very similar view, but does so in a rather more nuanced manner. For Papaïoannou, Hegel's conservatism in *The Philosophy of Right* demonstrates a morose, resigned reaction to the revolution's failure:[109] an acceptance of history's apparent conclusion in the bourgeois state. This differs, for Papaïoannou, from the more romantic exuberance of his early writings. Furthermore, Papaïoannou deliberately alludes to the failures of Russian communism when making these claims. He thereby plays on the (rather Debordian) idea that the revolt and vitality of the early part of the twentieth century may still haunt the present, whilst also contending that the romantic, revolutionary spirit of Hegel's early writings remains similarly latent within his mature philosophy.

In his preface to *The Philosophy of Right*, and whilst commenting on the historical appearance of philosophy within the world, Hegel famously remarks

---

103 Ibid.
104 Papaïoannou 2012, p. 35.
105 Legend has it that on the 14th of July 1793, together with Schelling and Hölderlin, he planted a 'freedom tree' around which the three of them danced whilst singing the *Marseillaise* in German.
106 Debord 1995, p. 49; 2006b, p. 793.
107 Korsch 1946.
108 Ibid.
109 Papaïoannou 2012, p. 88.

that 'the owl of Minerva takes its flight only when the shades of night are gathering', i.e. when a 'form of life has become old'.[110] Hegel meant to indicate that philosophy only appears at a point of conclusion. Papaïoannou, however, describes the post-revolutionary period of Hegel's maturity as a 'twilight world':[111] as an era that could be interpreted, with equal justice, both as the end of the day and as a new dawn. His metaphor thus indicates that philosophy need not contemplate a purportedly completed world, but could instead herald its transformation; that whilst the mature Hegel may well have identified bourgeois society with the setting of the 'sun' of human history,[112] that same society could also be viewed as harbouring a new beginning. Once again, the correspondences between these views and Debord's own are readily apparent. Against any Kojèveian (or indeed Fukuyama-esque) notion of historical conclusion, Papaïoannou indicates that our present historical 'arrest' might contain the potential for a new future. 'The crest of a wave is not the ocean', he writes; Marx's 'old mole' has 'not finished its work',[113] and 'a time of [historical] arrest is not the end of time'.[114]

Hegel is framed here as an implicitly revolutionary figure, despite his ostensible conservatism, and the content of his philosophy is presented in a manner that casts it as both revolutionary and relevant to our modern circumstances. Crucially, this is connected to the view that Hegel's work advocates the supersession of social separation, and indeed that of all detached abstractions. In Papaïoannou's account, the earthly actualisation of the Absolute becomes an explicitly political project, and emphasis is thereby placed on the sense in which that ultimate realisation would constitute a condition of human flourishing. This places Papaïoannou close to Hyppolite, as does his indication that the Absolute cannot be construed as a static condition.[115] In addition, he also associates the human subject with time, the Concept, and thus with constant, negative, dialectical process. For example: 'because he *is* the Concept,' Papaïoannou writes, 'man must, by his own same essence, negate nature and abolish (*aufheben*) matter, fixity and finitude, until they cease to res-

---

110   Hegel 2005, p. xxi.
111   Papaïoannou 2012, p. 91.
112   See Hegel 2004, p. 103, where Hegel describes the history of the world as the rising of the sun in the East, and its setting in the West.
113   Papaïoannou 2012, p. 91.
114   Papaïoannou 2012, p. 97.
115   Like Hyppolite, he emphasises the 'tragic' presence of negativity and finitude within the infinitude of the absolute (e.g. 'History is tragic, but tragedy, said the young Hegel, "expresses the absolute condition"' (Papaïoannou in Hegel 2009, pp. 17–18)).

ist Spirit; until they enter into the tumult of his moving life [*le tourbillon de sa vie mobile*].'¹¹⁶ In fact, Papaïoannou implicitly associates the Concept with a drive towards such temporal self-determinacy, and he also links this to the struggles of the revolutionary proletariat. Having stated that 'man' is initially 'ignorant, enslaved, bounded',¹¹⁷ Papaïoannou goes on to describe 'the meaning of history' as 'the complete realisation of the infinite force that lives in the inmost depths of a being who originally is nothing and must become everything';¹¹⁸ a remark that can only have been intended as a direct allusion to the words that Marx famously ascribed to the revolutionary proletarian: *'I am nothing and I should be everything'*.¹¹⁹ In short, Papaïoannou's reading sets out a very similar position to that which we attributed to Debord, wherein the Absolute is identified with human historical existence, and in which historical experience and action drive human actors towards a condition in which that existence might flourish. This then returns us to the model of Debord's Hegelianism with which we began this chapter.

Philosophy as Representation

Our proposition was that Debord's use of Hegelian thought could be characterised as involving the re-figuration of three key elements of Hegel's philosophy: 1) the Concept; 2) the Idea; and 3) the Absolute. The discussions advanced in the main body of this chapter should now allow us to develop those suggestions.

1) In previous chapters, we saw that Debord associated human subjectivity with a dynamic, dialectical relation between subject and object, understood in terms of activity and experience in time. In Chapter 4, we saw that these ideas owe much to the general ambience of French existentialism. We can now add that it also owes a great deal to French Hegelianism. Koyré, Kojève, Hyppolite and Papaïoannou all associate the Concept with human action and experience in time. In our proposed model, Debord follows suit: the Concept becomes human temporality, understood in terms of the processual, transformative interaction of the human subject with the objective world.

---

116   Papaïoannou in Hegel 2009, p. 12, italics in the original.
117   Papaïoannou in Hegel 2009, p. 14.
118   Papaïoannou in Hegel 2009, pp. 14–15.
119   Marx 1975, p. 254, emphasis in the original.

2) In Hegel's mature philosophy, the Concept is the driving force of the Absolute. It works towards the realisation of the subject-object unity of the Idea, which can be understood as the Absolute's immanent goal. The Idea is a condition of harmony between existence and the logic that founds it, and it is thus the condition of full self-expression in which the Absolute flourishes and attains complete realisation. In our model, the Concept becomes human temporal action and experience. The Absolute becomes human historical existence, and the Idea becomes the conditions wherein that existence might attain full self-conscious realisation. It is, therefore, a condition in which subject and object unite via self-determinate praxis. The Idea, in other words, becomes communism *qua* collective praxis: a communism that would allow human historical existence to flourish ('history', we remember, was directly identified with 'the spectre haunting modern society').[120] These proposals correspond to claims made by some of the writers whom Debord drew upon. As noted earlier, Lefebvre associates the full actualisation of the 'total man' with the Idea, and Hyppolite also identifies the Idea with communism. The latter, for Marx, Hyppolite claims, 'is the Idea in actuality, the divinisation of man'; man who 'makes his own history'.[121]

3) In his influential *Logic and Existence* of 1953, Hyppolite presented another version of this claim. 'It is clear', he wrote, 'that Marx replaces the Hegelian absolute Idea with ... species-being'.[122] This statement can be used to illustrate our contentions regarding the status of the Absolute in the model that we have ascribed to Debord. However, this requires a few words of explanation.

Firstly, 'the absolute Idea' is not quite the same thing as the Absolute. Instead, Hegel uses this term to signify the highest, most sophisticated expression of the Idea. It arises from the unity of 'the theoretical Idea' (the self-consciousness of the Concept, as afforded by Spirit) with 'the practical Idea' (the concrete actualisation of the Concept, as actualised via the activity of Spirit). It is, therefore, a condition in which Spirit fully comprehends its own nature, and in which it fully and adequately expresses that nature within its concrete activity; a condition in which Spirit understands itself intellectually, and realises itself practically, as a manifestation of the logic of the Absolute.

---

120 Debord 1995, p. 141; 2006b, p. 851.
121 Hyppolite 1969, p. 104.
122 Hyppolite 1997, p. 180.

Hyppolite's claim is that Marx replaces the absolute Idea with 'species-being'. Species-being is a concept that Marx developed from Feuerbach, who used the term in his *The Essence of Christianity* to denote the 'infinite' characteristics, powers and capacities of human beings that religion had erroneously transposed onto fictitious deities.[123] For Feuerbach, this capacity is 'infinite' insofar as it comprises all that the human species is capable of: a totality of possibilities that can only be actualised collectively, during the course of historical time[124] (significantly, Feuerbach viewed this as a materialist correction of the Hegelian Absolute). Marx's own version of species-being is somewhat different to Feuerbach's, but it too denotes an open field of potential; and like Feuerbach, Marx also presents history as the arena within which such capacity is to be actualised and comprehended. Consequently, when Hyppolite claims that Marx replaced the absolute Idea with humanity's species-being, his claim is that Marx replaces Spirit's comprehension of its own true nature with humanity's recognition and actualisation of its own species-being; and just as Spirit's self-awareness involves recognising itself to be one with the 'Infinite Power' of the Absolute, so too is humanity to recognise that it is one with its own collective, formative agency and potential.

Hyppolite's remark, therefore, presents a very similar view to that which we have ascribed to Debord: namely, that the Absolute becomes the collective activity and capacities of human agents. The 'living Substance'[125] of the Absolute thus becomes akin to Marx's 'species-life'.[126]

This point can be reinforced if we also bear in mind that species-being, for Marx, is an inherently *historical* affair. It is not only a collective capacity, but also the active conduct and application of that capacity.[127] Species-being is thus actualised in historical time. Indeed, 'the *real*, active orientation of

---

123 'The mystery of the inexhaustible fullness of the divine predicates is ... nothing else than the mystery of human nature considered as an infinitely varied, infinitely modifiable, but, consequently, phenomenal being' (Feuerbach 1989, p. 23). It is 'a ludicrous and even culpable error to define as finite and limited what constitutes the essence of man, the nature of the species, which is the absolute nature of the individual' (Feuerbach 1989, p. 7).

124 The 'realities or perfections' of God are the collective attributes of the human species, 'dispersed among men and realizing themselves in the course of world history'; for 'what the individual man does not know and cannot do all of mankind knows and can do' (Feuerbach 1986, p. 17).

125 Hegel 1977, p. 10.

126 Marx 1988, p. 105.

127 As Marx puts it: 'it is ... in his work upon the objective world ... that man really proves himself to be a species-being. This production is his active species-life' (Marx 1988, p. 77).

man to himself as a species being', Marx writes, 'is only possible by his really bringing out of himself all the *powers* that are his as the *species* man'; and this, Marx claims, 'is only possible through the totality of man's actions, as the result of history'.[128] The term 'species-being', therefore, does not designate some kind of immutable essence, as is sometimes supposed, but rather an open capacity for collective action, change and experience. It denotes, in other words, an inherently historical existence: an existence in which human beings define and shape themselves through their actions in time. This point was clearly recognised by Hyppolite. Having made the remark quoted above, he immediately adds that 'History is therefore the realisation of Man'.[129]

To sum up: in the model that has been proposed here, according to which Hegelian philosophy could be construed as a representation of historical praxis, the Absolute becomes human historical existence. The latter is driven, via the Concept – i.e. via its own dynamic, temporal nature and experience – towards the realisation of the Idea, which becomes Debord's vision of communism: a socio-political and temporal condition capable of affording the full, self-conscious expression of human existence's historical and self-constitutive nature. This then means that the *problematic* of spectacle (as opposed to the modern *society* of the spectacle, which brings that problematic to its full expression) can be understood as a misrecognition of this 'Absolute': as a misrecognition, in other words, of the historical and existential nature of the human subject, caused by the attribution of society's collective powers to specific instantiations or concentrations of those powers.

The following two chapters will try to build on these claims. Having outlined Debord's connection to French Hegelianism, and having now also advanced a model of his use of Hegelian philosophy, we will turn, in Chapter 7, to his use of ideas drawn from Lukács and the young Marx. Having done so, we will then move, in Chapter 8, to the notion of historical 'life' that can be found in his work.

---

128 Marx 1988, pp. 149–50, italics in the original.
129 Hyppolite 1997, p. 180.

CHAPTER 7

Subjects and Objects: Debord, Lukács and the Young Marx

The Relevance of the Young Marx

Serious contemporary engagements with Debord's theoretical work tend to take their bearings from the proximity that can be established between the theory of spectacle and the new readings of Marxian value-theory. This is an issue that will be discussed at length in Part Four, where we will have cause to look at those readings of Marx in rather more detail. Suffice it to say here, however, that because these readings of Marx tend to focus upon his mature critique of political economy, and not upon his earlier writings, their increasing prominence has fostered a turn towards addressing the Marxian elements of Debord's and the sı's thought by way of a primary orientation towards the Marx of the *Grundrisse* and *Capital*. It remains the case, however, that one needs to consider Debord's use of the young Marx before one begins to address his debt to Marx's mature writings. This is not only because Debord clearly read and drew upon Marx's early work (indeed, he explicitly stated that almost all of *The Society of the Spectacle*'s references, *détournements* and allusions to Marx come from texts that Marx produced between 1843 and 1846).[1] In addition, Debord read later works such as *Capital* through the themes of alienation, activity and history that are foregrounded in Marx's early writings. Consequently, if we are to understand his use of Marx's later texts, we first need to consider his engagement with these young-Marxian themes. For these reasons, this chapter will focus on the decidedly young-Marxian ontology that supports Debord's theoretical work.

It matters little whether Debord did, or did not, deliberately and consciously set out to construct the philosophical anthropology that we will attribute to him.[2] This is because Debord's claims certainly *imply*, and indeed *presuppose*, just such an ontology. After all, any attempt to make political claims concerning the temporality, agency and experience of human beings must involve at least

---

1 Debord 2004a, p. 140.
2 In this regard, Anselm Jappe may well be entirely correct when he writes that 'Debord nowhere considers constructing an "ontology"' (Jappe 1999, p. 31).

some ideas about what human beings are. This is not to deny that philosophical anthropologies are problematic. Undoubtedly, they run the risk of naturalising the norms of their era and culture. Nor is to deny that such problems have been identified in Marx's early writings. Moishe Postone, for example, has contended that the ontology of formative activity employed in Marx's early writings seems uncomfortably close to a naturalisation and affirmation of labour.[3] Others have viewed Marx's early account of human subjectivity as an expression of an antiquated humanism, and as deserving of trenchant feminist and postcolonial critique.[4] These are not, however, views that Debord shared, and nor are they entirely justified. Neither Debord nor the young Marx essentialise capitalist labour, and neither of them posit a fixed human nature. As we have already seen, the only fixity in Debord's view of the human subject is the potential for constant change. If we can gain a clearer sense of his views in that regard, we should also be able to develop a fuller account of his work as a whole. With these aims in mind, this chapter will try to piece together Debord's ideas concerning the ontology of human subjectivity by considering his position *vis-à-vis* the differing views adopted by Georg Lukács in *History and Class Consciousness*, and by the young Marx in the *Economic and Philosophical Manuscripts of 1844*.

The Limitations of *History and Class Consciousness*

As the preceding chapters of this book have sought to demonstrate, the general argument advanced by Debord's theoretical work resembles Lukács's argument for an identical subject-object of history in *History and Class Consciousness*. One of our tasks here will be to elucidate the nature of this connection between Lukács and Debord. However, this connection raises an important question of its own. In drawing on *History and Class Consciousness*, did Debord also replicate that book's errors?

As we will see in greater detail below, Lukács eventually came to reject his own most famous work. *History and Class Consciousness*' argument for a con-

---

3 Postone, for example, expresses the concern that Marx's early use of Hegel essentialises labour, and indicates that the young Marx was thus, in some respects, a victim of capitalist ideology (Postone 1996, pp. 74–8; Jappe comes close to making a similar point, albeit in connection to Lukács (Jappe 1999, p. 151)). Postone's concern is greatly informed by his view that Hegel's philosophy is really an inadvertent expression of the inner workings of capitalist value ('the social relations that characterise capitalism ... possess the attributes that Hegel accorded to the *Geist*' (Postone 1996, p. 75; see Arthur 2004a p. 7 and *passim* for similar contentions)).
4 See, for example, Wendling 2009, p. 6.

dition of subject-object identity, he would later claim, involved a form of tacit idealism that rendered it inadequate as a contribution to a genuinely materialist Marxian philosophy. This problem, according to Lukács, arose from the fact that his book had conflated two important and distinct concepts: *alienation* (*Entfremdung*), understood as the human subject's estrangement from its own concrete activity, and *objectification* (*Vergegenständlichung*), understood as the necessary and inevitable externalisation of subjective will and agency in such activity. Simply put, Lukács felt that he had fallen short of the following view, which broadly corresponds to the position adopted by the young Marx.

All forms of activity necessarily involve *objectification*. Whether through speech, action, work, play, we externalise our will and agency, making it concrete and objective within the physical world. In capitalist society, however, the conduct of objectification can involve *alienation*. The objectification of agency takes place, as is always the case, but the acting subject becomes estranged from its results, and from the activity itself (as in wage labour). For such alienation to be superseded, therefore, the acting subject needs to overcome the estranged nature of its own objective activity. Or, to put that in more overtly Hegelian terms: it needs to establish a condition in which it is one with itself in its own externalisation. It is very important to note that this does *not* involve the overcoming of all objective otherness: the world is not to be collapsed into the perfect self-identity of a solipsistic subject. Instead, the results of objectification remain external to, and independent from, the acting subject; yet insofar as they accord with the direct aims and desires of that subject, the latter is no longer alienated from them. Objectification is thus conducted in a non-alienated manner.

According to Lukács's later critique of *History and Class Consciousness*, the young Marxian perspective that we have just outlined lay beyond the scope of his book. This is because its claims amounted, inadvertently, to an impossible demand for the supersession of *both* alienation and objectification at the same time. In *History and Class Consciousness*, the attainment of a condition of subject-object unity becomes, according to Lukács's own critique, an idealist construct, in which all objective, material otherness is collapsed into a perfected identity. This is, in fact, a step towards idealism that goes beyond Hegel's own position. Hegel's work certainly advocates a condition of identity, but it by no means proposes that all difference should become effaced within that identity. Consequently, *History and Class Consciousness*, as Lukács later put it, suffers from an inadvertent attempt to 'out-Hegel Hegel'.[5]

---

5 Lukács 1971, p. xxiii.

Nonetheless, and despite that important distinction, Lukács's book ends up with a very similar problem to that which the young Marx identified in Hegel's work. This shared problem was the primary motivation for his own criticisms of *History and Class Consciousness*, and it became apparent to him after he had read Marx's *Economic and Philosophical Manuscripts*: a text that only became available after *History and Class Consciousness* had been published. In the *Manuscripts*, Marx criticises Hegel for having similarly conflated alienation and objectification. In Hegel, to borrow Lukács's own terms, 'the object, the thing, exists only as an alienation from self-consciousness'.[6] All objective existence is an alienated expression of the logic that founds it, and every instantiation of Spirit's activity and will within the world is also an instance of alienation. That alienation can be overcome, for Hegel, through philosophical thought, which recognises that all objective reality is ultimately one with the consciousness that confronts it. In the *Manuscripts*, Marx criticises this view as a conservative metaphysics, according to which alienation can be overcome through simply grasping thought's identity with the extant world: alienation is superseded through an act of philosophical thinking, and the world is left effectively unchanged.[7]

According to Lukács's own critique, just as Hegel's philosophy resolves alienation through an act of thought that leaves the world untouched, so too, in effect, would *History and Class Consciousness*, for the simple reason that the book suffers from an inability to think objective activity. For Lukács, *History and Class Consciousness*' argument for an identical subject-object had implied an unworkable holism that came uncomfortably close to (and indeed even exceeded) Hegelian idealism. It had done so because its ontology could not conceive the necessary externalisation of agency through objective activity; and because its philosophical framework could not conceive objective activity adequately, the book could not really conceive the objective transformation of social conditions either. Thus, like Hegel, *History and Class Consciousness* had, in effect, posited a beautiful condition of non-alienated identity that subsisted only in conceptual abstraction from the historical reality that it purported to articulate.

---

6 Ibid.

7 As Marx puts it, whilst characterising Hegel's position: '... this act of superseding is a transcending of the thought entity; ... because thought imagines itself to be directly the other of itself, to be *sensuous reality* – and therefore takes its own action for *sensuous, real action* – this superseding in thought, which leaves its object standing in the real world, believes that it has really overcome [the alienated nature of that object]' (Marx 1988 p. 160).

In contrast – and this point will become important below – the stance adopted by Marx in the *Manuscripts* involves no such tacit holism. Instead of a Hegelian and idealist condition of subject-object *identity*, Marx's claims imply a condition of subject-object *unity*,[8] wherein the externality of objective activity is retained, but in which the acting subject overcomes its alienation from such activity. Such a position affords a far more adequate ontology. The aim of this chapter will be to show that Debord is in fact much closer to this young Marxian position than he is to Lukács's own.

The first half of the chapter will be primarily descriptive. Its aim will be to set out Lukács's claims in *History and Class Consciousness*, whilst also demonstrating their pertinence to Debord's theory. We will then discuss the problems that Lukács later identified in that book in a little more detail, with a view towards considering whether or not Debord can be charged with repeating those same problems. We will argue that he does *not* do so. Certainly, his theory's general argument echoes the overall shape and structure of Lukács's views. Like Lukács, Debord holds that history must become a collective, self-conscious project. Yet as we will try to show, by way of a further discussion of Debord's conception of time, the ontology that underlies Debord's argument is actually much closer to that which Marx employed in the *Manuscripts*.

We begin, then, with an overview of Lukács primary contentions in *History and Class Consciousness*.

The Subject-Object of History

One of the primary lessons of Hegel's philosophy is that subject and object are one. The Hegelian Absolute is not just a fundamental substance, as in Spinoza, but rather a moving, self-acting subject that shapes and determines itself to a point at which it can know itself as its own object. Within the sphere of human history, this is afforded by the efforts of Spirit, which, *qua* subject, comes to know itself in and through its own objective actions. For the Lukács of *History and Class Consciousness*, this meant that Hegelian thought afforded a means of responding to what he regarded as one of the most problematic characteristics of modern capitalist culture: namely, its tendency towards a passive, contemplative and essentially accepting attitude towards a world that was shaped by humanity's own alienated social activity. We will need to characterise and dis-

---

8 This distinction is drawn from Arthur 1989.

cuss further the nature of that 'contemplative'[9] attitude, but the salient point here is simply this: for Lukács, Hegelian philosophy – or rather, a Marxian reworking thereof – could help to highlight the sense in which human beings are both subject and object at the same time; both the producer and the product of their world. If human beings shape both themselves and their world through their own actions, then they could, potentially, do so freely and self-consciously. In order to do so, they would need to become aware of the real nature of the social practices that occlude their capacity for such self-determinacy, and which thus alienate them from their own objective activity. In order to articulate this possibility, Lukács turned to Hegel's *Phenomenology of Spirit*.

As we saw earlier, Hegel's *Phenomenology* describes the ascension of Spirit, and thus human consciousness, to a condition of 'absolute knowing': a condition in which subjective consciousness grasps its identity with objective being, and in which it thereby comes to understand the rational structure that it shares with the totality of being *per se*. In understanding both itself and its efforts as expressions of the fundamental logic that inheres within all being – and through comprehending the dialectical interrelation of universality and particularity that characterises that logic's operation – consciousness (to quote one of Lukács's later works) 'comes to perceive that the real character of society and history is something created by men together', and thus ultimately attains 'an understanding of the laws governing the movement of history, in short of the dialectics of reality'.[10] Spirit grasps itself as its own object, and thereby comprehends its history and its world as its own creation.

In *History and Class Consciousness*, Lukács adopted and re-framed Spirit's path towards this moment of apotheosis in terms of the proletariat's developing awareness of its own historically formative agency. Spirit's ascension was thereby re-cast as a 'socio-historical' process that 'culminates when the proletariat ... becom[es] the identical subject-object of history',[11] i.e. when the revolutionary proletariat understands that it has made its world, and that it has the capacity to shape its own future. It is important to note that within this re-formulation, the self-consciousness that is thus attained by the proletariat is not afforded by philosophy, as in Hegel, but rather via the self-consciousness proper to a revolutionary praxis that sets out to alter its world. Thus, like Debord, Lukács used Hegel to present history as a process that had previously been *un*conscious, but which could now become *self*-conscious.

---

9   Lukács 1971, p. 89.
10   Lukács 1975, pp. 470–1.
11   Lukács 1971, pp. xxii–iii.

There are, of course, important differences between Lukács's claims and Debord's own views. The most obvious example of these differences can be found in Lukács's assertion that 'the party is the historical embodiment and active incarnation'[12] of this new self-consciousness, which differs markedly from Debord's own antipathy to such forms of political representation.[13] We will need to return to this issue later, but the important echoes between their respective uses of Hegelian thought should, nonetheless, be apparent.

One such point of correspondence can be found in the sense in which *History and Class Consciousness* comes close to echoing Debord's view that a Marxian re-figuration of Hegelian philosophy would not just afford a convenient way of theorising revolutionary politics, but would instead amount to a correction and clarification of an important truth about human history that Hegel, due to his historical and social context, had been unable to fully grasp.[14] Lukács acknowledges that for Hegel, both human agents and the world that confronts them need to be understood as the outcome of humanity's historical efforts and actions. This led Hegel to theorise an identical subject-object of history: a subject that knows itself as its own object, and which constitutes the objective outcome of its own subjective activity. For Lukács, Hegel's insights in this regard constituted a significant advance over the dualistic and formalist rationalisms of other bourgeois philosophers (e.g. Kant's abstractly universal categories and unknowable noumena). Yet Lukács *also* contends that Hegel was ultimately unable to identify this entity within real history: for whilst, according to Lukács, it ought really to have been identified with the revolutionary proletariat, Hegel's contextual perspective led him to situate it within the clouds of absolute idealism.[15] As a result, human history was thereby cast as part of the workings of a 'divine',[16] idealist reason: as a part of the process

---

12 Lukács 1971, p. 42.
13 In fact, Lukács's steadfast allegiance to the Hungarian Communist Party led him to adopt some truly absurd positions. Adorno, in his lectures on negative dialectics, recounts the following: 'Lukács ... had just quarrelled with his party. ... [He] explained to me that the party was in the right, even though his ideas and arguments were better than the party's. The party was in the right because it embodied the objective state of history, while his own position, which was more advanced both in his view and in terms of the sheer logic of the ideas involved, lagged behind that objective state of affairs' (Adorno 2008, pp. 16–17). As Parkinson (1977, p. 54) puts it: 'Lukács' Party members may seem to resemble the Guardians in Plato's *Republic*'.
14 Lukács 1971, p. 17.
15 Lukács 1971, p. 147.
16 Hegel 2004, p. 13.

by which the Absolute achieves full, self-conscious expression via Spirit's historical labours. According to Hegel, the subject-object of human history could only arise within a world that had been brought into final alignment with the reason that founds it. In consequence, the actualisation of this grand subject-object brought the central *telos* of human history to resolution. For Lukács, however, the *real* subject-object of history was to be found in the modern revolutionary proletariat: a revolutionary subject that recognises itself as the author of its own world, and which thereby grasps its ability to shape its own future.[17]

Reaching for the Absolute

Having described the general shape of Lukács's claims in *History and Class Consciousness*, and having also indicated their pertinence to Debord's own thought, we can now begin to look at his views in a little more detail. This requires acknowledging the central importance of praxis to Lukács's conception of subject-object identity. This can be introduced by noting that Lukács cast such praxis *qua* subject-object identity as lying beyond the perspective proper to 'bourgeois thought'.

History and Class Consciousness distinguishes the perspective on society proper to 'bourgeois thought' from the perspective attained by the revolutionary proletariat. Simply put, bourgeois thought is characterised as being unable to fully penetrate the reified social relations of capitalist society. In this regard, and like Debord, Lukács describes the modes of thought and culture proper to capitalist society as being possessed of an inherently passive, contemplative attitude towards the extant social world. Seen from such a perspective, that world appears largely immutable, and plans and strategies for operating within it tend to entail negotiating its given structures, rationalising chance occurrences, and selecting optimum paths for advancement according to pre-existing templates and patterns for behaviour.

Lukács also holds that the attributes of such a mode of thought can be found in the philosophical works that bourgeois culture produced during the rise of capitalist society. Speaking very generally – and whilst clearly keeping Kant as his primary point of reference – Lukács characterises such philosophies as rationalistic and dualistic systems that apply fixed, conceptual categories

---

17   See Connerton 1974 for a useful and very clear overview of *History and Class Consciousness*' central arguments.

to a noumenal, irrational, or merely 'given' world. Just as everyday 'bourgeois thought' attempts to negotiate and make sense of an objective world that stands at one remove from the subjects that confront it, so too does 'bourgeois philosophy' attempt to rationalise and make sense of a world that seems other to it.

Lukács then proceeds to outline what he takes to be the contradictions and shortcomings of such philosophies. His arguments are complex, but his central complaint is that these philosophical systems run into trouble when they are: a) called upon to justify the rational coherence and interrelation of the concepts through which they interpret the given world; and b) required to justify the correspondence between those concepts and the objects to which they are applied. Lukács takes this to be a major problem: in the absence of such justifications, these philosophies would be no more than arbitrary frameworks, containing assorted, jumbled content.

Acknowledging that the philosophers with whom he is concerned were well aware of this problem, Lukács contends that their various attempts to resolve it led them, in differing ways, to posit a subject that creates the object that it confronts, and to thus advance 'a conception of the subject which can be thought of as the creator of the totality of content.'[18] His arguments in this regard serve to advance his contention that the limitations and 'antinomies' of bourgeois philosophy led towards the generation of a notion of an identical subject-object.

Of course, and as we noted above, Lukács holds that such an identical subject-object can only be found in the praxis of the revolutionary proletariat. The philosophers whom he addresses, however, could not attain this perspective. The nature of the social classes, struggles and economic context of their day meant that they could not find this self-identical entity in empirical reality, as the modern revolutionary proletariat simply did not exist at that point. This led them to the construction of an identical subject-object that subsisted *beyond* the immediate empirical appearances of human existence: a perfect entity that could thus function as a 'fundamental nodal point'[19] from which the empirically existing separation of thought and world could be deduced, and from which 'every duality' could be seen as 'a special case' derived from that fundamental and 'pristine unity'.[20] A resolution to the antinomies described above – i.e. the need for correspondence between the given object and the subjective

---

18   Lukács 1971, pp. 122–3.
19   Lukács 1971, p. 123.
20   Ibid.

categories that render it intelligible, and the rational coherence of the categories themselves – could thus be derived from this absolute 'nodal point'.

Lukács's comments in this regard might appear to be targeted most obviously at the notions of God invoked by early modern philosophers, such as Descartes and Spinoza, or indeed Schelling's absolute. However, Lukács's discussion quickly moves to Kant and Fichte. This is because in his view – and this is crucial – the real 'unity' that such dualistic philosophical frameworks struggled to grasp is to be found in '*activity*'.[21] Lukács therefore praises the steps that were taken towards such a view: Kant's *Critique of Practical Reason* is commended for gesturing towards the supersession of the contemplative 'barriers' that were erected by Kant's first critique; Fichte is then credited with having taken these gestures further. Lukács also presents a long quotation from the *Wissenschaftslehre* in which Fichte argues that if philosophy were to begin with '*action*' rather than with given 'fact', it would then be able to 'stand at the point where the two worlds [i.e. subject and object] meet and from which they can both be seen at a glance.'[22]

The core idea that Lukács is advancing here is that the true unity of subject and object is not to be found in any God-like and transcendental 'pristine unity', but rather in *praxis*, i.e. the practical interaction of subjective thought and objective reality afforded by historical action. This insight, however, is held to lie beyond the reach of the philosophies that he discusses. Despite their advances towards focussing on practical action, the philosophical frameworks employed by figures such as Kant and Fichte cannot really conceive the subject-object that such practical action entails. This is because they are only able to view the interrelation of subjective reason and the objective world in terms of the imposition of formal, rational structures upon given, contingent contents (e.g. Kant's categorical framework). This falls short of the subject-object of Lukács's self-conscious historical praxis, wherein the generation and development of subjective thought is interwoven with the transformations that such thought works upon its object.

This leads Lukács to praise Hegel's dialectical philosophy for having taken a crucial step towards this perspective. Hegel is credited with having set out a mode of thought that not only emerges immanently from a process of change, but which constitutes that process of change's self-conscious form. This, in Lukács's view, is what one finds in 'the logic of the [Hegelian] *concrete Concept*, the logic of totality'.[23]

---

21 Ibid.
22 Ibid, italics in the original.
23 Lukács 1971, p. 142, italics in the original (the 'c' of 'concept' has been capitalised for continuity).

Lukács thus embraces Hegel's account of a fundamental condition of subject-object identity that does not subsist *beyond* the conduct of existent being, but which is instead immanent *within* the latter's processual operation. Of course, he also indicates that Hegel's insights in this regard were fundamentally flawed. The self-constitutive, self-comprehending dynamism that Hegel had grasped had, in effect, been attributed to the actions of a rationalist and pantheistic God. If the real identity of subject and object is to be found in human praxis, then Hegel's account of the Absolute's self-determinate movement can constitute no more than a conceptual *representation* of such identity (a point that obviously places Lukács close to the critique of Hegel that we have ascribed to Debord). The task of a Marxian philosophy, therefore, was to strip away the metaphysical dimensions of Hegel's Absolute, and to thereby locate its moving centre within the real conduct of human historical praxis. As Lukács put it: 'man himself' would then be 'the objective foundation of the historical dialectic, and the subject-object lying at its roots'.[24]

The connection between these views and Debord's claims can be reinforced if we underscore the following points. Lukács's argument involves rejecting any fixed, transcendental systems of thought that stand removed from the ongoing conduct of lived existence. It also rejects the projection, above and beyond lived history and experience, of any 'pristine' centres of absolute truth and surety. Indeed, for Lukács, any contention that the meaning and truth of lived activity might be derived from or measured against such a transcendental point could be 'nothing but the fixation of thought', and a 'projection into myth of the intellectual failure to understand reality concretely as a historical process.'[25] These ideas bear obvious relation to the aspects of Debord's concept of spectacle that we described in the first part of this book. Like Debord, Lukács rejects the fetishistic association of characteristics proper to collective praxis with detached constructs. Furthermore, and like Debord, Lukács also held that by rendering that problematic a defining concern, modern capitalism had foregrounded the pertinence of Hegel's insight that *becoming* is the truth of *being* (a statement that both Debord and Lukács quote in their work).[26] For

---

24 Lukács 1971, p. 189.
25 Lukács 1971, p. 187.
26 Debord quotes this phrase several times (e.g. Debord 2004a, p. 45), but in characteristic fashion, he neglects to provide references. It is possible that he simply took it from Lukács (Lukács 1971, p. 181). This is rendered all the more likely by the difficulty involved in locating the precise origin of the phrase in Hegel's own work. The differences in translations between French, German and English make it hard to pin down, but it seems that the most likely candidate is paragraph 88 of *The Encyclopaedia Logic* ('the truth of being and

both Debord and Lukács, that insight could be used to articulate the sense in which the truth of human existence does not reside in a transcendental point that lies beyond or outside lived praxis, or indeed in any constructs that such praxis might generate, but rather in humanity's own historical, dynamic and self-constitutive nature.[27] Consequently – and whilst Lukács himself does not state this explicitly – *History and Class Consciousness* would seem to imply a Marxian anthropomorphisation of the Hegelian Absolute. In this regard, it seems very close to the views that we have attributed to Debord, and no doubt helped to form them.

However – and to return now to the argument that we outlined in the introduction to this chapter – Lukács, as we've seen, would go on to claim that *History and Class Consciousness* was marked by important conceptual errors. If it is indeed the case that Debord's thought is indebted to the aspects of Lukács's thought that we have outlined here – and if these aspects of Lukács's work are in fact connected, as we will show below, to the problems that Lukács found in his book – then might it not also be the case that Debord adopted Lukács's mistakes, together with his insights?

In order to begin to address that question we first need to gain a clearer sense of the problems that Lukács diagnosed in *History and Class Consciousness*. It is to these problems that we will now turn. To that end, we will look at the comments that Lukács presented in the long and self-critical preface that he added to the 1967 re-edition of *History and Class Consciousness*.

---

nothing alike is the *unity* of both of them; this unity is *becoming*' (Hegel 1991, p. 141, italics in the original)). Similar statements are made in *The Science of Logic* (see for example Hegel 1969, p. 105 and p. 254). Thanks are due to Tim Carter for his assistance in finding these passages.

27   As an aside, it might be added that this rejection of external absolutes does not entail relativism, and that in fact carries normative implications. Because the motive core of historical becoming is human praxis, a comprehension of the latter's true nature entails recognising that human beings are the creators of an essentially mutable, historical world. By extension, acting in accordance with that truth is therefore tantamount to pursuing and maintaining a condition wherein human subjects possess a free, self-conscious and self-determinate mastery over their own historical activity. This normative claim is relatively weak and tacit in Lukács, but it is much stronger in Debord (provided, that is, one follows the 'ethical' interpretation of spectacle that we outlined in Chapter 2).

Alienation and Objectification

History and Class Consciousness was first published in 1923. Korsch's *Marxism and Philosophy* (which Debord also drew upon) was published in that same year, and both works received heavy criticism for their deviations from established dogma. Korsch was largely unapologetic,[28] and was expelled from the German Communist Party in 1926; Lukács, however, despite initially defending his work,[29] proved rather more willing to recant. To some degree, this was no doubt partly due to strategic reasons: Lukács was keen to remain within the Party. However, his willingness to criticise his book was chiefly due to a newfound awareness, prompted by a reading of Marx's *Manuscripts* in 1930, of its inadvertent conflation of alienation and objectification.

In his *The Young Hegel* of 1938, Lukács explicitly discussed the problems posed by such a conflation. By the time that *History and Class Consciousness* appeared in French in 1960, Lukács had grown thoroughly detached from his own book, and when it received a reprint in 1967, due to the influence that it had exerted (much to its author's alarm) upon 'French existentialism and its intellectual ambience',[30] it came with a long, self-repudiating preface in which Lukács detailed its mistakes.

In this preface, Lukács complains that *History and Class Consciousness* tends towards the view that 'only a knowledge of society and the men who live in it is of relevance to philosophy'.[31] In fact, in the book itself, Lukács goes so far as to present the somewhat counter-intuitive claim that 'society is reality'[32] (or rather: society frames reality for those within it).[33] As a result, Lukács now

---

28 See Korsch's 1930 text 'The Present State of the Problem of *Marxism and Philosophy*' (Korsch 1970, pp. 89–126).
29 Lukács 2000.
30 Lukács 1971, p. xvi.
31 Lukács 1971, p. xvi.
32 Lukács 1971, p. 19.
33 This issue, which bears direct relation to the status of nature in *History and Class Consciousness*, is connected to the rather confusing and difficult question of whether the book advocates a dialectical conception of nature. The general position of *History and Class Consciousness* seems to be that nature itself is not dialectical, and that Engels was mistaken when he indicated otherwise (see Parkinson 1977, pp. 47–8 for a discussion of this point; see also Jay 1984b, pp. 115–16). Dialectics, it seems, should thus be restricted to society and culture (e.g. Lukács 1971, p. 24n). However, elsewhere in the same book, Lukács indicates that *both* nature and society are dialectical, albeit whilst noting that nature, though dialectical, is devoid of the active human consciousness that characterises society (Lukács 1971, p. 207; for helpful comments see Rees in Lukács 2000, p. 21; see also Vogel

argued, the book struggles to address the world that exists *beyond* society. This means that whilst it certainly talks of human agents and of their conduct, it is obliged to do so in abstraction from the material reality upon which those social agents act. Therefore – and somewhat ironically for a work of Marxian philosophy – *History and Class Consciousness* struggles to think labour, and indeed human activity in general, as action upon a material world. As Lukács himself put it in the 1967 preface: the 'basic Marxist category, labour as the mediation of the metabolic interaction between society and nature, is missing'.[34] This issue is linked to the problems that we described at the outset of this chapter.

History and Class Consciousness argues for a fundamental identity between subject and object. But what is this subject, and what is the object? Broadly speaking, the subject, for Lukács, is associated with consciousness and agency, and the object comprises the concrete actualisations of that agency. To talk of proletarian subject-object identity, therefore, is to contend that the proletariat can become self-consciously active. In attaining a non-alienated identity between subject and object, the proletariat, as conscious subjectivity, becomes capable of mastering and directing its own objective manifestations. When this occurs, the objective social reality created by this subject ceases to appear as an immutable, given 'other' to that subject, because both become one.[35]

When seen from this perspective, instances wherein social activity becomes 'other' to the subjects that conduct it amount to instances of alienation: for if such separation takes place, then those subjects have lost control over their own affairs. This is connected to what Lukács terms 'reification': capitalism's fetishistic hypostatisation of historical movement, wherein social processes appear as static, seemingly immutable things. For Lukács, that hypostatisation can be corrected through recognising that all such reified phenomena are generated by human agents, and through thereby superseding the apparent

---

1996 for a useful overview of the problems). This seems contradictory, but the initial claim that nature is not dialectical can be read as the contention that whilst *both* nature and human history are dialectical, the former cannot be addressed via the dialectics proper to the latter, because they emerge and develop in a different manner to those of the natural world. Lukács's subsequent *In Defence of History and Class Consciousness* goes some way towards clarifying his position (e.g. Lukács 2000, pp. 102–3), but it ultimately remains very unclear.

34 Lukács 1971, p. xvii.
35 As Lukács puts it: 'since consciousness here is not the knowledge of an opposed object but the self-consciousness of the object *the act of consciousness overthrows the objective form of its object*' (Lukács 1971, p. 178).

independence of such phenomena from the agents that create them. Therefore, and much like Debord, *History and Class Consciousness* argues against instances wherein the objective results of social activity stand at one remove from the human subjects that conduct such activity. Yet because *History and Class Consciousness* is so driven towards the need for *identity* between subject and object – and because this drive leads to a rejection of *all* forms of separation between the two – the book struggles to accommodate the sense in which at least *some* forms of independent objective otherness are both an inevitable and necessary part of human existence.

As noted above, Lukács was led to recognise this when reading Marx's *Economic and Philosophical Manuscripts* at the Marx-Engels institute in 1930 (he was able to consult the text prior to the *Manuscripts*' publication in 1932). In his 1967 preface, he states that this experience 'swept to one side all the idealist prejudices'[36] that he had inadvertently expressed in *History and Class Consciousness*. This is because the *Manuscripts* demonstrate the conceptual distinction between alienation and objectification that we described earlier. We should now recapitulate and develop that distinction here.

In the *Manuscripts*, Marx uses the term *Entfremdung* to refer to estrangement and disaffection, and *Vergegenständlichung* to denote the objective process of making one's will, desire and intentions concrete and actual through their practical externalisation in activity.[37] It should be added here that objectification (*Vergegenständlichung*) should not be confused with reification (*Verdinglichung*). This is because objectification is simply the actualisation of subjective will and agency in real, practical activity. It is an inevitable, universal aspect of human existence[38] (as Lukács puts it in his 1967 preface: 'every human expression including speech objectifies human thoughts and feelings').[39] Yet where objectification is an inevitable aspect of every social formation, alienation – *Entfremdung* – is not. Alienation arises when the social relations that articulate and mediate objective activity (i.e. which articulate the social operation of *Vergegenständlichung*) operate in a manner that escapes the conscious control of the actors concerned. Marx's position thus indicates that alienation could be resolved through the creation of alternative social relations, and through thereby conducting objectification in a less problematic manner. One

---

36   Lukács 1971, p. xxxvi.
37   See the appendix to Arthur 1986 for a helpful discussion of this terminology; for an alternative view, see Sayers 2011, p. ix.
38   'Objectification comprises all human manifestations, expressions and creations. Marx does not ascribe to it any negative judgement or class determination' (Kovaly 1973, p. 33).
39   Lukács 1971, p. xxiv.

need not abolish objectification in order to end alienation: instead, objectification simply needs to be conducted in a more adequate, self-determinate manner.

Lukács's concern was that *History and Class Consciousness* could not accommodate this view. His book's association of alienation with all forms of objective otherness prevented it from doing so. Consequently, and as we noted above: although *History and Class Consciousness* certainly spoke about labour, it had no real conceptual tools with which to think labour, because the book had effectively omitted objectification from its conceptual framework.[40] This gives rise to a number of difficulties.

Firstly, it becomes difficult to fully address alienation as the product of a particular socio-economic structure. This is because it renders it hard to view alienation as the result of a society arranging and conducting its objective activity in a particular manner. Secondly, and by extension: because *History and Class Consciousness* effectively equates all instances of objectification to alienation, it comes close to rendering alienation a timeless, transhistorical condition, rather than a result of the particular social formation of capitalist society (hence the book's connection to existential themes, and hence also Lukács and Goldmann's later suggestions that it informed Heidegger's *Being and Time*).[41] Thirdly, and most importantly: the book's occlusion of the necessary retention of objectification within any post-revolutionary future leads to a position that casts the end of alienation as an idealist moment of redemption, wherein all objective otherness would be recovered and united as moments of a self-identical whole. In this regard, the book's identical subject-object echoes the Hegelian sublation of external reality into the completed workings of an absolute Subject. At best a purely subjective perspective, and at worst a merely philosophical entity, posited outside and beyond real historical praxis, the book's identical subject-object was thus later described by its author as an 'edifice boldly erected above every possible reality'.[42]

---

40   As a result, the book had come close to the position that the Marx of the *Manuscripts* had identified in Hegel: 'The only labour which Hegel knows and recognises is *abstractly mental* labour' (Marx 1988, p. 150, italics in the original).

41   Lukacs 1971, p. xxii.

42   Lukács 1971, p. xxiii.

The 'Necessary Alienation' of Time

Having now outlined the nature of the problem that Lukács identified in *History and Class Consciousness*, and having also indicated Debord's debts to that book, we need to consider whether Debord incorporated its errors into his own work. The first point that we will need to address in order to answer that question is this: could Debord have been aware of Lukács's change of views, and of the details of his critique of *History and Class Consciousness*?

Lukács's self-critical preface was first published in 1967, and it was not translated into French until 1974. *The Society of the Spectacle* appeared in 1967, and Debord, who had begun work on his book in 1965,[43] would not have been aware of the details of Lukács's auto-critique. However, he was certainly aware that Lukács had distanced himself from the book. This could be due to a short statement from Lukács that appeared in *Arguments*, following *History and Class Consciousness*' French publication, in which Lukács warned of the book's errors.[44] The rather curt brevity of that published statement, when coupled to the unavailability of a more detailed explanation for Lukács's changed views, may well have informed Debord's contention that Lukács had only criticised his book in order to remain within the Party.

In fact, and despite its evident debts to *History and Class Consciousness*, *The Society of the Spectacle*'s sole reference to Lukács is a critique of his repudiation of his earlier views. Debord seems to have held that Lukács only rejected *History and Class Consciousness* in order to toe the line, and this sole reference to Lukács is consequently damning and dismissive.[45] Thus, whilst Debord was clearly aware that Lukács had criticised *History and Class Consciousness*, he does not seem to have been fully cognisant of the philosophical concerns that had motivated that critique. There is, however, a good deal of evidence to suggest that Debord was nonetheless aware of the general substance of those concerns.

Firstly, we can develop that claim on a purely bibliographical level, as the problems involved in Hegel's own conflation of alienation and objectification are explicitly addressed in books that Debord owned and studied. Most obvi-

---

43   Debord 2003a, p. 21.
44   Thanks are due here to Anthony Hayes for highlighting this point.
45   Despite his 'profound theoretical work', Debord writes, Lukács's 'endless self-repudiations' revealed 'with caricatural clarity' the sheer poverty of an intelligentsia that would align itself with the Party, insofar as it demonstrated Lukács's own personal readiness to identify himself 'with the opposite of what he had supported in *History and Class Consciousness*' (Debord 1995, pp. 81–2; 2006b, p. 814).

ously and importantly, the point is addressed in Marx's *Manuscripts*, which Debord drew upon when developing his ideas. The first volume of Lefebvre's *Critique of Everyday Life* also addresses this issue,[46] and so too does Hyppolite's *Studies on Marx and Hegel* of 1955.[47]

One can also find textual evidence to support the view that Debord avoided the conflation of alienation and objectification. In his own study of Debord, Anselm Jappe places a great deal of emphasis on the connection between the theory of spectacle and the Lukács of *History and Class Consciousness* (albeit chiefly via Marxian value theory rather than via Debord's Hegelianism). In doing so, he too considers whether Debord replicated Lukács's mistakes, and answers that Debord was in fact 'at pains to avoid' what Lukács himself had referred to as the 'fundamental and crude error'[48] of blurring alienation with objectification. When making this claim, Jappe refers to Debord's contention in *The Society of the Spectacle* that 'time ... is a *necessary* alienation, the milieu in which the subject realises himself while losing himself, becomes other in order to become truly himself'.[49]

Jappe reads this statement as indicating that human action entails the generation of some kind of objective 'otherness', i.e. the objectification (*Vergegenständlichung*) that we discussed above. This seems entirely valid. Granted, the primary burden of the statement is not to indicate a notion of objectification; instead, Debord's concern here is with the importance of subjective change and development in time, i.e. with the sense in which we constantly become 'other' to who we once were as time passes, due to the qualitative experiences that we undergo. However, the sentences that follow the quoted statement link such experience to activity,[50] and it therefore seems possible to follow Jappe in contending that Debord *does* distinguish alienation from objectification; to thus hold that becoming 'other' to oneself in time involves the necessary 'otherness' of objectification. After all, Debord clearly held that human beings are self-constitutive creatures, and that this self-creation occurs through historical action.

---

46 Lefebvre 2008a, pp. 68–71 (NB Lefebvre addresses the issue obliquely here, but it clearly informs his claims).

47 Hyppolite 1969, pp. 81–2. Debord also owned a copy of Lukács's *The Young Hegel*, in which Lukács himself addresses the problem, but this text was not published in French until long after *The Society of the Spectacle* was written.

48 Jappe 1999, p. 26.

49 Debord 1995, pp. 115–16, translation altered; 2006b, p. 835, italics in the original.

50 Debord writes that: 'a society that radically severs the subject from the activity that it steals from him separates him ... from his own time' (Debord 1995, p. 116; 2006b p. 835).

However, textual evidence such as this can only take us so far. Debord may well have been aware of the issues involved in conflating alienation and objectification, but according to our interpretation, his account employs a decidedly Lukácsian notion of subject-object unity; and as we saw above, *History and Class Consciousness*' problems are intimately connected to its arguments for an identical subject-object of history. So, could it be the case that *any* argument for subject-object unity is bound to result in an attempt to 'out-Hegel Hegel', regardless of whether a distinction is made between objectification and alienation? Or is it in fact the case that Lukács's problems follow from the *manner* in which he conceives that subject-object relation? If so, might it then be the case that an alternative formulation could avoid those difficulties?

Let us briefly revisit the core of the issue. As we saw above, the object with which Lukács's subject was to unite was its own concrete, objective actualisation, i.e. the social activity that it conducts.[51] This is reinforced by Lukács's claim that 'society' is 'reality'.[52] Because reality is effectively reduced to society ('society', Lukács claims, 'is *the* reality for man'),[53] a perfect condition of subject-object identity can be attained, wherein the author of this reality identifies with its creation. Subject-object identity can be attained, in other words, because anything that is *not* produced by human activity is effectively bracketed out of the picture. The problem, however, is that having bracketed out that which lies beyond society, Lukács cannot really think labour as activity conducted upon an independent physical, natural world. There is, in short, no room for the necessary otherness involved in the objectification of conscious agency in transformative action upon and within the physical world. As a result, Lukács's identical subject-object is really a perfect, idealist entity: a metaphysical fiction, posited in abstraction from the practical activity that composes real social and historical existence.

It therefore seems possible to contend that *History and Class Consciousness*' problems follow from the manner in which it conceives the object in its subject-object relation. This then raises the possibility that a *different* conception of the object could avoid these difficulties. We will now go on to argue that this is precisely what one finds in Marx's *Manuscripts*. The object pole in the subject-object relation that can be inferred from the young Marx's work is not 'society', but rather human existence, understood as a process of interaction with an independent physical reality. The subject's unification with this object would

---

51   Lukács 1971, p. 21.
52   Lukács 1971, p. 19.
53   Ibid.

thus not omit, but would instead *include* the objectification that Lukács missed. Having made these claims, we will then propose that one can find something very similar in Debord's work.

A Mediated Existence

In his introduction to his 'Contribution to the Critique of Hegel's *Philosophy of Right*' of 1843, Marx stated that 'man is no abstract being squatting outside the world', but is instead 'the world of man – state, society'.[54] The human subject, in other words, cannot be understood as a timeless, abstract entity. Instead, such subjects are the products and producers of their own socio-historical contexts. In his *Economic and Philosophical Manuscripts*, which were written the following year, Marx developed this idea, and did so by stressing the sense in which human existence needs to be conceived as a historical, transformative and social process. The *Manuscripts* express a nuanced position, wherein the human subject is not seen to exist in immediate unity with nature, and yet is not seen to stand in a dualistic state of immediate separation from it either.[55] Instead, the human subject exists in a relation to the physical world that is mediated by its own activity.

Human beings are thus not utterly distinct from nature, or immediately one with it, but are instead *interwoven* with it. This interconnection with the natural world is seen as a dynamic, transformative process, in which both sides of the relation change through their mutual interaction. Human productive activity effects changes upon the world, and aspects thereof (e.g. natural resources) become integral to the conduct of human existence. Reciprocally, this engenders change within the acting subject. For Marx, therefore, human beings exist in a state of 'continuous interchange'[56] with the physical world, and this interchange is mediated by their own activity. The young Marx thus saw human existence as an inherently *historical* affair: as a constant, transformative process.[57] He did not, however, view this existence solely in terms of society, i.e. society considered in isolation from the natural world (as in *History and Class Consciousness*). Instead, human existence is seen in terms of the conduct of objective activity upon an otherwise independent world that lies *beyond* society.

---

54 Marx 1975, p. 244.
55 Arthur 1986; see also Mészáros 2006, p. 164.
56 Marx 1988, p. 76.
57 Marx 1988, p. 156.

Marx's position is rendered more complicated by his contention that the conduct of this 'continuous interchange' between human agents and the natural world is shaped by social structures. This can be clarified if we follow Arthur[58] and Shortall[59] in adopting Mészáros's useful identification of two orders of mediation in the young Marx's ontology. The simple conduct of formative, objective activity upon the world constitutes a 'first order' of mediation; the social relations that articulate that activity within any given moment of history constitute a 'second order' of mediation. This 'second order mediation', according to Mészáros, 'can only arise on the basis of the ontologically necessary "first order mediation"',[60] but it shapes the conduct of the activity proper to that first order. The second order of mediation, therefore, concerns the social arrangement and conduct of the primary interaction with nature that takes place in the first order of mediation. It is, therefore, a historically specific mode of arranging and conducting that primary interaction with nature. Or, as Mészáros puts it: society's social relations (the second order of mediation) always form 'a *historically specific* mediation of the *ontologically fundamental* self-mediation of man with nature'[61] (i.e. of the objective activity proper to the first order of mediation).

Marx's views entail that alienation is seen to arise from failings within the second order of mediation, and thus from problematic modes of conducting the inevitable, fundamental interaction with the objective world that takes place within the first order of mediation. This is important, as it means that Marx cannot be said to have conflated objectification with alienation. The former can take place without the latter, so long as the second order of mediation operates in a non-alienating manner. If, however, such problems occur, human subjects become estranged from the activity that defines and shapes their own objective existence. Overcoming alienation, therefore, requires the creation of alternative, non-alienated means of conducting objective activity.

For the young Marx, therefore, overcoming alienation is tantamount to establishing a condition of unity between conscious human agents (subject) and their own objective, historical existence (object). Yet whilst this obviously resembles Lukács's claims, it lies beyond the perspective of *History and Class Consciousness*, simply because it relies upon the distinction between alienation and objectification that Lukács's book omits. We will propose below that despite Debord's obvious debts to *History and Class Consciousness*, it is in fact

---

58 Arthur 1986.
59 Shortall 1994.
60 Mészáros 2006, p. 79.
61 Ibid.

the young Marx's ontology, and not that of Lukács's most famous book, that informs his work. In order to begin to develop that point, we need to look at the conception of alienation employed in Marx's *Manuscripts*.

Alienation, Identity, and Unity

We have already referred to the distinction between objectification (*Vergegenständlichung*) and alienation. We should now add that Marx also uses two distinct terms when referring to 'alienation' in the *Manuscripts*. These are *Entfremdung*, which we employed above when first outlining the young Marx's ideas, and *Entäusserung*. *Entfremdung*, which is sometimes translated as 'estrangement', refers to the sense in which the conduct and results of objective activity become alien and antagonistic to those who conduct it. *Entäusserung*, however, is tied rather more closely to the practical realities and conduct of alienation. Marx uses it to denote the renunciation, loss or relinquishment of objective property, or indeed of waged activity. Although some have questioned the importance of this terminological distinction,[62] it seems significant that Marx indicates, when describing alienated labour in the *Manuscripts*, that the more subjective and interpersonal dimensions of *Entfremdung* arise from forms of *Entäusserung*.

This can be illustrated by looking at the four different modes of alienation that Marx describes in the *Manuscripts* (and given Debord's debts to Marx's *Manuscripts*, it is perhaps unsurprising that analogues of these four modes of alienation can be found within the pages of *The Society of the Spectacle*).[63]

---

62 See, for example, Sayers 2011, p. ix.

63 Debord's descriptions of spectacular separation echo the four issues listed above (i.e. alienation from (a) the product of activity, (b) activity itself, (c) species-being, and (d) others). For example: within spectacular society, (a) 'all the time and space' of the acting individual's 'world become foreign to him' (Debord 1995, p. 23, translation altered; 2006b, p. 774), because (b) 'the individual's gestures', i.e. the activity that shapes that world, 'are no longer his own' (Debord 1995, p. 23; 2006b, p. 774). This is caused by the subordination of all such activity to the dictates of an autonomous economy, which results in (c) 'the exile of human powers' into a spectacular 'beyond', and (d) a society composed of 'atomised and manipulated masses' (Debord 1995, p. 154; 2006b, p. 859). The 'new historical life' (Debord 1995, p. 106; 2006b, p. 829) that the book calls for thus requires a condition wherein (a) collective human agency can '*recognise itself* in its world' (Debord 1995, p. 127; 2006b, p. 842, italics in the original; cf. Marx 1988, p. 77) through having attained (b) a 'directly lived' (Debord 1995, p. 12; 2006b, p. 766) relation to the practical activity that shapes that world. Such a relation would entail (c) 'society reassuming the powers that

Firstly, (a) wage labour entails that workers becomes detached and separated from the results of their activity. 'The *alienation* [*Entäusserung*] of the worker in his product', Marx writes, 'means ... that his labour becomes an object, an *external* existence', and 'something alien to him'.[64] This entails that (b) the act of production also becomes separate and detached. Sold for a wage, it becomes 'external labour, labour in which man alienates [*entäussert*] himself'.[65] Through wage labour, collective, social activity becomes a means to an individual end. In consequence, (c) the collectivity of species-being is undermined: such labour 'estranges [*entfremdet*] the *species* from man'.[66] This gives rise to (d) '*the estrangement* [*Entfremdung*] *of man* from *man*', because 'what applies to a man's relation to his work, to the product of his labour and to himself, also holds of a man's relation to the other man, and to the other man's labour and object of labour.'[67] The *Entäusserung* of (a) and (b) thus give rise to the *Entfremdung* of (c) and (d).

If *Entfremdung* (feelings of estrangement) can indeed be seen to arise from modes of *Entäusserung* (social forms of relinquishment and separation), then it seems possible to view the relation between *Entfremdung*, *Entäusserung* and *Vergegenständlichung* (concrete, objective activity) in terms of the first and second orders of mediation discussed above. Seen in these terms, *Vergegenständlichung*, i.e. the objective activity proper to the first order of mediation, is governed and shaped by the *Entäusserung* of wage labour and commodity exchange, i.e. by the second order of mediation, thus causing *Entfremdung*. This may seem overly technical, but it may also be important: for if this holds true, Marx's views would then indicate that the *Entfremdung* addressed by Lukács does not simply arise from the *Entäusserung* of social activity, as in *History and Class Consciousness*, but is instead engendered by the manner in which the social structures of *Entäusserung* shape the *Vergegenständlichung* of objective action upon and within the physical world.

It also entails that Marx's account implies a rather different approach to the resolution of the separation of subject from object. Lukács argues for a condition of subject-object *identity*. He can posit such an identity because the object with which his subject is to unite is social activity; social subjects need

---

were detached from it' (Debord 1995, p. 125, translation altered; 2006b, p. 841), and would thereby afford (d) a condition in which 'individuals' become '"directly bound to universal history"' (Debord 1995, p. 154; 2006b, p. 859; cf. Marx and Engels 2007, p. 56).

64 Marx 1988, p. 72.
65 Marx 1988, p. 74.
66 Marx 1988, p. 76.
67 Marx 1988, p. 78.

to become one with their own activity. Marx's views, however, are perhaps best seen as implying not a condition of subject-object *identity*, but rather a condition of subject-object *unity*.[68]

As stated earlier, the human subject, for Marx, is neither distinct from, nor identical to, the physical world, but rather always exists in a state of dynamic interaction with the latter. Consequently, if the object pole of the subject-object relation is the practical, material conduct of human existence, as is the case in Marx's work, then that object cannot be seen as social activity alone (as in Lukács). Instead, that object must be the interaction between human agents and the portion of physical reality with which they engage, and which they thereby transform. As Arthur puts it: 'man', for Marx, takes both 'himself and nature as his object';[69] for whilst engaging with nature, 'man' is increasingly led to address 'himself', and to understand the manner in which society mediates the dialectical relation that comprises and generates his own existence. Ultimately, therefore, it is humanity's own physical existence within the world that constitutes the object pole within Marx's conception of the subject-object relation (e.g. 'Man makes his life-activity itself the object of his will and of his consciousness. ... his own life is an object for him').[70] The object, in other words, is not just human society or action, as in Lukács, but rather the world combined with such social action.

Because this object involves the physical world, or at least a portion thereof, there can be no claims here to a condition of *identity* between subject and object (or at least there cannot be such a claim in the absence of idealism). Instead, and in place of such an identity, the supersession of alienation gives rise to a condition of mutually transformative *unity*: a unity wherein 'thinking and being', as Marx puts it, would be brought into '*unity* with each other', but in which they would still remain '*distinct*'.[71] In other words, this would be a unity of subject and object wherein 'man', despite being in many ways distinct from physical nature, nonetheless 'sees himself in a world that he has created',[72] and in which human subjects thereby exist in a non-alienated relationship with the results and conduct of their own objective actions.

We will return to this distinction between subject-object identity and subject-object unity towards the end of this chapter. Here, we should summarise

---

68 Arthur 1986.
69 Ibid.
70 Marx 1988, p. 76.
71 Marx 1988, pp. 105–6.
72 Marx 1988, p. 77.

our primary claims regarding Marx's work, before moving on to consider the latter's similarities to Debord's own views.

The young Marx's ontology provides an argument for the supersession of the alienation of subject from object that seems close to that advanced in *History and Class Consciousness*. However, it avoids the problems that Lukács later identified in his book. This is because the object in Marx's account is not reducible to human society (or rather to Lukács's 'social activity'), but is instead the concrete actuality of human existence. This existence is understood as a constant, dialectical interaction between human agents and the physical world, and thus necessarily involves the objectification that Lukács neglected. If we can now show that Debord's position echoes that of the young Marx, we should be able to demonstrate that whilst Debord certainly presents a broadly Lukácsian argument, the ontology that underpins his call for subject-object unity nonetheless avoids *History and Class Consciousness*' problems.

In order to begin making that case, we will now turn to the technicalities of Debord's views on time and history.

The 'Humanisation' of Time

Many of Debord's contentions regarding time and temporality are evidenced in the remarkably rich (and remarkably dense) thesis with which he begins the fifth chapter of *The Society of the Spectacle*. It starts with a quotation from Hegel's *Phenomenology* that we discussed earlier, and it employs a further quotation and a *détournement* from the young Marx. The thesis reads as follows:

> Man – that 'negative being who is solely to the extent that he abolishes being' – is one [*identique*] with time. Man's appropriation of his own nature is at the same time his apprehension of the unfolding of the universe. 'History is itself a *real* part of *natural history* – of nature's coming to be man [*la transformation de la nature en homme*]' (Marx).[73] Conversely,

---

73   This is a quotation from Marx's *Manuscripts*. It is drawn from a passage in which Marx argues that because human beings shape themselves and their world, 'human nature', despite emerging from nature, is really a product of human history and agency: a product, in other words, of the human fraction of nature that is made historical and distinctly human through humanity's own actions. Marx writes: 'All history is the preparation for '*man*' to become the object of *sensuous consciousness*, and for the needs of 'man as man' to become [natural, sensuous] needs. History itself is a *real* part of *natural history* – of nature's coming to be man' (Marx 1988, p. 111, italics in the original).

> this 'natural history' has no effective existence other than through the process of human history, the only agency [*la seule partie*] capable of recapturing this historical whole; like the modern telescope whose scope captures, *in time*, the flight of nebulae to the periphery of the universe. History has always existed, but not always in a historical form.[74] The temporalisation of man, as effected through the mediation of a society, is equivalent to a humanisation of time. The unconscious movement of time manifests itself and *becomes true* within historical consciousness.[75]

The rather enigmatic reference to truth in the thesis' final sentence can be put to one side for now. It requires a good deal of explanation, and we will look at Debord's notion of truth in some detail in Chapter 12. The rest of the thesis can be addressed by noting, first of all, that the claims presented here indicate that time exists independently of humanity, but that history – humanity's awareness of its existence within a temporal reality – only arises with the emergence of human beings. The thesis indicates that this awareness can reach back in time, prior to the advent of the human mind (hence the reference to nebulae and telescopes). Human beings, therefore, are a conscious element of an otherwise independent, pre-existing reality. This point is underscored by the thesis' *détournement* of a letter sent by Marx to Ruge in 1843. Marx writes there that 'reason has always existed, but not always in a rational form'.[76] Debord's *détournement*, which replaces 'reason' with 'history', indicates that with the advent of human agents, blind, natural history becomes conscious, *human* history. This is because human agents are credited, due to that conscious awareness, with the capacity to determine their own actions in time. Consequently, following the emergence of human beings within the universe, some small part of its 'unfolding' temporal reality – i.e. the sphere proper to human agency – ceases to be a blind, unthinking process, and instead becomes shaped by conscious action. Again, Debord draws on the young Marx to make this point. The quotation employed in the thesis' third sentence comes from a section of the *Manuscripts* in which Marx argues that whilst 'human nature' emerges from the natural world, it is shaped by, and is thus a product of, human history and agency. A fraction of nature is thus made distinctly human through humanity's own actions.

---

74   Cf. Marx 1975, p. 208.
75   Debord 1995, p. 92, translation altered; 2006b, p. 820, italics in the original.
76   Marx 1975, p. 208.

Debord's claims thus seem somewhat close to the ontology employed in the *Manuscripts*. Human existence is seen here not just in terms of society and social relations, but rather as a transformative, historical interaction with a preexisting natural world. In contrast, when Lukács talks of 'reality' and 'existence' in *History and Class Consciousness*, he is really talking about society,[77] because he takes 'society' to be '*the* reality for man'[78] (indeed, in his 1967 preface, he complained that *History and Class Consciousness* exhibits a 'tendency to view Marxism solely as a theory of society').[79] Debord, however, would seem to be thinking on a grander scale. Social activity is framed, in the thesis quoted above, as a facet of temporal reality.

It therefore seems possible to contend that Debord's account must involve something akin to the first and second orders of mediation outlined above. The ontology that informs his work appears to involve a primary engagement with the physical world, which is then articulated via differing social relations at different periods in history. We have already seen that these social relations give rise to differing conceptions of temporality, and can engender the alienation from history that characterises spectacle; an alienation that appears here as a state of detachment from the processual, transformative objective activity that generates and shapes human existence. In the *Manuscripts*, Marx refers to the 'self-estrangement [*Selbstentfremdung*]'[80] of the worker: to the separation of the human subject from his or her own self, and thus to a condition of detachment from the activity that shapes and defines collective existence. One can find something rather similar in Debord. As in Marx, 'life activity'[81] is seen as a historical, transformative interaction with the physical world. For Debord, the object that the subject addresses should ultimately be nothing 'other than the effects it works upon itself'.[82] Consequently – and as is also the case in Marx – the supersession of alienation entails taking conscious control of the historical, transformative activity that constitutes human existence. Because that existence comprises an engagement with an independent physical reality, the non-alienated condition that Debord advocates must differ from Lukács's tacitly idealist subject-object *identity* (an identity that is, in effect, solely between the subject and its own social activity), and must instead be

---

77 As Kovaly remarks, Lukács 'relates [the concept of] totality entirely to society, rather than to reality as a whole' (Kovaly 1973, p. 31).
78 Lukács 1971, p. 19.
79 Lukács 1971, p. xvi.
80 Marx 1988, p. 80.
81 Marx 1988, p. 76.
82 Debord 1995, p. 48, translation altered; 2006a, p. 792.

closer to a young Marxian condition of subject-object *unity* (a unity between the subject and its own concrete interactions with an external reality).

Therefore, and to summarise this chapter's central argument: although the claims presented by Debord's theoretical work are certainly Lukácsian, an ontology of formative action akin to that of the young Marx appears to be present – or at least implicit – within his theory's broadly Lukácsian framework. Debord can thus be said to avoid the problems that follow from Lukács's own conception of the relation between subject and object.

Having made these claims, we will now move to a discussion of the ways in which Debord seems to have developed the young Marx's notion of 'life activity'.

CHAPTER 8

Life and Non-life

'Real Wealth'

Despite his numerous references to 'life', Debord never fully explains quite what he means by that word. He does not present us with a particularly developed account of the more passionate, intense life that would supersede spectacle, and nor does he fully explain its spectacular denial. Giorgio Agamben has made much the same point. 'What this "more intense" life was', he notes, and 'what was inverted and falsified in the spectacle, or even what one should understand by "life of society" is nowhere clarified'.[1] Debord seldom deigned to define his terms. It is, however, possible to reconstruct his views on this topic. The aim of this chapter is to do just that: to develop an interpretation of Debord's conception of life, and to thereby provide a basis for addressing what he refers to as the 'non-life'[2] of spectacle.

The claims that follow below will draw heavily on the philosophical anthropology that we have attributed to Debord. This anthropology is much informed by Hegelian, existential and young Marxian themes, and it views the human subject as a processual, self-constitutive entity, characterised by a continual, dialectical interaction with the objective world. Human subjects shape themselves and their world through time, and are, in consequence, inherently historical creatures. It is, therefore, an anthropology that views 'human nature' as characterised by 'self-creation' and 'plasticity'.[3]

It follows that if the human subject is seen in these terms, then there cannot be any fixed, essential and stable human essence in Debord's work. 'Human nature', such as it is, can only be an open capacity for self-constitutive change. Therefore, Debord's numerous references to 'life' cannot denote a pristine, originally authentic humanity, as is often assumed; nor can the end of spectacular society afford the restitution of such a condition. Instead, the end of spectacle would afford the full flourishing of the human subject's open capacity for action and experience in time.

---

1 Agamben 2015, p. xix.
2 Debord 1995, p. 89; 2006b, p. 819.
3 Debord 1995, p. 95; 2006b, p. 822.

It would seem, therefore, that the 'life' that spectacular society denies was understood in terms of such action and experience. The spectacular denial of life involves the suppression and alienation of its self-constitutive characteristics. Within spectacular society, according to Debord, all activity has become channeled into the perpetuation of the spectacle's frozen moment. The supersession of spectacular society, on the other hand, would afford life's ludic, creative flourishing. Thus, spectacle can be understood as an *impoverishment* of life, and the end of the spectacle as affording the latter's *enrichment*.

We can develop that point by noting the following. The very first line of *The Society of the Spectacle* is a *détournement* of Marx's own opening statement in *Capital*. 'The whole life of those societies in which modern conditions of production prevail', Debord writes, 'presents itself as an immense accumulation of spectacles.'[4] In *Capital*, Marx writes: 'The wealth of societies in which the capitalist mode of production prevails presents itself as an "immense accumulation of commodities".'[5] Debord's *détournement* replaces the commodity with spectacle. It thereby foregrounds the spectacle's connection to the commodity, whilst also positioning the book as a descendent and development of Marx's own work. This much is obvious. It is, however, also important to note the further substitution that Debord makes in that same opening *détournement*: 'wealth' is replaced with the word 'life'.

Capital's first sentence indicates that within capitalist society, wealth takes the form of commodities. By implication, it also indicates that wealth need not be expressed in such a form within *other* societies.[6] It can be argued that Debord's opening *détournement* displays a degree of sensitivity to this point. By replacing social 'wealth' with 'the whole life' of society, Debord indicates that real wealth – real social plenitude – may not just be the material goods that a society creates, but may instead be the *life* of that society: its capacity for activity, interaction, and enriched experience. Real wealth, in other words, may be a society's 'use of time'[7] (we might also think here of the epigraph to the sixth chapter of *The Society of the Spectacle*, which Debord took from Baltasar Gracián's *The Art of Worldly Wisdom*: 'We have nothing that is ours except time, which even those without a roof can enjoy').[8]

---

4 Debord 1995, p. 12; 2006b, p. 766.
5 Marx 1990, p. 125, translation altered for continuity. In the second part of the sentence Marx is quoting his own *A Contribution to a Critique of Political Economy* of 1859.
6 See Postone for a related discussion of this point (Postone 1995, p. 26).
7 Debord 1995, p. 15, translation altered; 2006b, p. 768.
8 Debord 1995, p. 109; 2006b, p. 831.

Although *The Society of the Spectacle* was written prior to the French publication of Marx's *Grundrisse*, this interpretation would place Debord very close to some of the views expressed in that text.[9] Marx claims there that whilst wealth in capitalism takes the form of money and commodities, 'real wealth' is in fact 'the developed productive power of all individuals', and that within communism, the 'measure of wealth' would not be 'in any way, labour time, but rather disposable time'.[10] Within communism, in other words, wealth would not take the abstractly quantitative form of capitalist value: instead, it would be a collective potential to actualise qualitatively differentiated moments of lived experience. It would seem that Debord held much the same view. The 'real wealth' of any given society is its capacity to live its own time as fully and completely as possible.[11]

These ideas bear direct relation to the sense in which Debord's notion of spectacle corresponds to instances of separated social power. This wealth *qua* capacity can become confusedly identified with the objective results of that capacity's actualisation. In spectacular conditions, society fetishistically attributes its own powers and abilities to its own products, and views those same products as if *they* were the real wealth and worth of its existence. Whilst society's real wealth lies in its ability to mould and shape its own temporal experience, that same ability has been transposed onto the social relations, structures and economic entities that this same society has created. In capitalist society, for example, the real worth of human existence has become confusedly identified with an 'immense accumulation of commodities'.

The Society of the Spectacle's claims are, however, somewhat stronger than this. As we have already seen, spectacle *per se* needs to be understood as a general, transhistorical problematic that can arise within any social formation. Capitalist society, i.e. the *society* of the spectacle, is only one such instantiation of that problematic. Debord viewed modern consumer capitalism as having brought that older, more general problematic to an identifiable extreme, and to have thereby rendered it the defining revolutionary problematic of the age.

---

9   The *Grundrisse* appeared in France in two volumes in 1967 and 1968. Marx's comments on time as wealth appear towards its end, so would presumably have become available after *The Society of the Spectacle*'s publication in 1967 (Debord had begun work on *The Society of the Spectacle* in 1965 (Debord 2003a, p. 21)).

10 Marx 1973b, p. 708.

11 One might also think here of Marx's remark in 'Wages, Price and Profit': 'Time is the room of human development. A man who has no free time to dispose of, whose whole lifetime, apart from the mere physical interruptions of sleep, meals, and so forth, is absorbed by his labour for the capitalist, is less than a beast of burden' (Marx 2004, pp. 126–7).

This is because life, within modern capitalist society, was not only mystified and impoverished, as had been the case in previous social formations: instead, it had gone one step further, and had collapsed into the condition that Debord refers to as '*non*-life'.

Life, for Debord, is the temporal process through which human subjects shape and determine their world, actions and own selves. Yet within modern spectacular society, that existence has suffered a fundamental distortion, as the self-determinacy that Debord associates with a fully flourishing life has been replaced by the complete *antithesis* of such self-determinacy. All lived activity is now shaped and regulated by the spectacular order's patterns and templates for behaviour, interaction and experience. The result is 'the spectacular negation of life':[12] the subordination of human self-determinacy to the autonomous, self-perpetuating movement of an independent economic system.

Debord's views in this regard are much informed by Marx's presentation of capital as the rule of 'dead labour' over 'living labour'.[13] His descriptions of modern society as 'a concrete inversion of life', and as 'the autonomous movement of the non-living',[14] are thus premised upon the view that all lived social activity has become subordinated to the operation of capitalist value. In Part Four, we will try to address that vision of capitalist society, and to thereby consider the ways in which Debord drew upon Marx's mature work. Here, however, we will be primarily concerned with his links to Marx's earlier writings.

In the previous chapter, we saw that for the young Marx, social relations shape the ways in which a collectivity conducts its activity and interaction, and thus its collective life. Our initial goal will be to develop the sense in which spectacular non-life arises from flawed modes of social mediation. If that point can be developed here, we will then be in a stronger position, in Part Four, when we come to connect Debord's notion of non-life to Marx's crucial claim that capital must be understood as a 'social relation':[15] a mode of mediating the actions and interactions, and thus the 'life activity',[16] of those who inhabit capitalist society.

---

12   Debord 1995, p. 87; 2006b, p. 818.
13   Marx 1990, p. 342.
14   Debord 1995, p. 12, translation altered; 2006b, p. 766.
15   Marx 1990, p. 932.
16   Marx 1988, p. 76, italics in the original.

'Life-Activity'

Although the SI explicitly indicated, in 1960, that they were not 'vitalists',[17] it remains the case that an emphasis on life and its potential flourishing runs throughout their work. In terms of Debord's thought, this seems greatly informed by the Left-Hegelian, nineteenth-century material that he drew upon, which often associates vitality with a collective capacity for self-constitutive activity. One might think here of Feuerbach's emphasis on the actualisation of human 'life',[18] and indeed of Cieszkowski's call for an 'organic union of vitality'.[19] It remains the case, however, that the young Marx's conceptions of 'life activity',[20] and of the 'vital expression' of 'species-life',[21] seem to be of key importance to these aspects of Debord's work: not least because they incorporate a notion of alienation, and imply a version of subject-object unity.

In Chapter 7, we argued that whilst the conception of subject-object unity presented in *The Society of the Spectacle* owes much to Lukács, the ontology that supports it seems informed by the young Marx. The conception of subject-object unity that can be inferred from it must involve a self-conscious awareness of the social relations that compose a 'living' social totality. In order to clarify that point, we should briefly recapitulate the following claims.

For the young Marx, the object with which the subject is to unite is human society's *'life-activity'*.[22] This object – 'life-activity' – is the concrete, active existence of the human subject itself. This object involves the interactions through which human agents create and reproduce their own conditions of existence. This interaction is mediated by the activity that they conduct upon the physical world (Mészáros's 'first order of mediation', as discussed in Chapter 7), but that activity is itself mediated by the social relations through which they organise that activity's conduct (Mészáros's 'second order of mediation'). Alienation arises from the problematic arrangement of those same social relations: for if those mediating structures take on a degree of relative autonomy from

---

17 SI 2006, p. 80; 1997, p. 150.
18 Feuerbach refers to 'life', and to its illusory appearance as the divine, throughout *The Essence of Christianity*. In addition, his *Principles of the Philosophy of the Future* contains the rather Debordian claim that 'Truth is only the totality of man's life and being' (Feuerbach 1986, p. 71): that there is no external value beyond the conduct of life activity (Debord read and made archived notes on this text).
19 Cieszkowski 2009, p. 101.
20 Marx 1988, p. 76.
21 Marx 1988, p. 105, translation altered.
22 Marx 1988, p. 76, italics in the original.

the human agents whose activity they articulate, then the human agents concerned will become estranged from their own objective activity. Therefore, if alienation is to be overcome, and if subject and object are to be united – if human agents, in other words, are to take self-conscious control of their own objective existence – then the social relations that articulate their conduct must be understood and corrected. 'Life-activity', therefore, needs to be conducted freely and self-consciously.

This 'life-activity' needs to be understood in relation to the young Marx's conception of 'species-life', and thus to the 'species-being' that is expressed through such life. As we have already seen, Marx adopted the concept of species-being from Feuerbach, who used it to denote the characteristics and capacities of human beings: characteristics that religion, in his view, had projected onto imaginary deities. Marx's own version of the concept is similar, because it too denotes the abilities and potential of collective human existence. Species-being, for Marx, is a capacity that is actualised through social activity, and which is thus expressed in different forms via different social formations. This is, of course, very similar to the notion of life that we have attributed to Debord. It is significant, therefore, that like Debord, Marx holds that individuals can become alienated from this 'species-life'.

According to the young Marx, capitalist labour entails that a workers' relation to society's collective powers is reduced to the self-interested pursuit of means towards satisfying his or her own atomistic ends. All that society can do collectively is of significance only in terms of what he or she can gain individually. At the same time, as far as society as a whole is concerned, the activity of that same individual becomes abstract and inconsequential, as its distinctive characteristics are largely redundant. Thus, capitalist labour, according to Marx, 'tears' the alienated worker 'from his *species-life*',[23] and thereby 'makes individual life in its abstract form the purpose of the life of the species'.[24] Only fragmentary, individualised access to society's collective 'life-activity'[25] is afforded to such individuals. In consequence, the operation of social life takes on a degree of independence from those who conduct it.

Marx is describing a condition wherein the particular human individuals that compose capitalist society become alienated from the universality of the social whole. This is a point that we will return to very shortly. First, however, we should note that Debord's position is in fact very close indeed to the views out-

---

23   Marx 1988, p. 77.
24   Marx 1988, p. 76.
25   Ibid.

lined above (as is perhaps unsurprising, given his evident study of Marx's early writings). He seems particularly indebted to Marx's indications that a community could become separated from its own powers and agency, and indeed to the implication that it can only flourish by overcoming these alienating social relations. Characteristically, this is expressed in Debord's work through a concern with temporality. As we indicated above, the life of a collectivity, for Debord, is expressed in its 'use of time', and that use of time is always 'effected through the mediation of a society'.[26] The mediation effected by contemporary society amounts to a 'time of human non-development':[27] a time in which all use of time has become subordinated to the self-development of an autonomous economy. In consequence, if those individuals within modern society who are currently '*estranged from history*' are to truly '*live* the historical time' that their social activity creates,[28] then their doing so would require them to correct those same mediating social relations.

Alien Mediations

When theorising the problematic nature of these social relations, Debord seems to focus on the sense in which they involve a flawed interrelation between forms of social *universality* (collective power, agency, social relations, the abstraction of value, etc.) and *particularity* (the qualitatively differentiated reality governed by these forms of universality, and above all the individual agents that create and submit to them). A concern with the unification of the universal and the particular, and with conceptual and social forms that fall short of such a unification is, of course, a central theme within Hegel's philosophy. In this regard, Debord's vision of spectacular society – and, indeed, Marx's account of capitalism – can be viewed as analogous to the 'lifeless' categories of what Hegel referred to as the everyday 'understanding' (*Verstand*): for 'The abstract universal of the [everyday] understanding', Hegel writes, 'relates itself to the particular only by *subsuming* this particular which it does not have in itself'.[29] As against this 'lifeless' separation, Hegel argues for a more organic unity of the particular and the universal: a condition wherein 'the universal', to quote *The Science of Logic*, 'takes its other within its embrace, but without *doing*

---

26 Debord 1995, p. 92; 2006b, p. 820.
27 Debord 1995, p. 110; 2006b, p. 831.
28 Debord 1995, p. 106; 2006b, p. 829.
29 Hegel 1991, p. 280, italics in the original.

violence to it'.[30] This is because in such a unity, it is, 'in its other, in peaceful communion with itself', and should thus be thought of as '*free love* and *boundless blessedness*, for it bears itself towards its other as towards *its own self*'.[31]

Debord's use of these Hegelian notions of organic unity and atomisation is greatly informed by the young Marx, who adopted and employed them when discussing social formations such as capital, ideology and the state. Marx's early writings often described problematic modes of social mediation as false, illusory forms of universality, which occlude or mystify the real social divisions that they arise from and perpetuate. Such detached, independent forms of universality give rise to alienation, mystification, and to a loss of social cohesion. For example, Marx's early criticisms of Hegel's political philosophy and of the bourgeois state present the latter as an illusory mode of unification that masks opposition and inequality: as an abstract universality that binds together, and which effaces the atomisation of, the particular individuals whom it purports to unite. Hegel's celebration of that state in *The Philosophy of Right* is thus said to entail treating 'the people ... as *idea* [*Vorstellung*], fantasy, illusion, *representation*,' and to thereby occlude 'the real opposition between people and government'.[32] Similarly, in *On the Jewish Question*, Marx claims that within the bourgeois state, the individual is rendered 'the imaginary member of a fictitious sovereignty', and 'is divested of his real individual life and filled with an unreal universality'.[33] Likewise, in *The German Ideology*, Marx and Engels write that 'social power' appears to such individuals 'not as their own united power, but as an alien force existing outside them ... the origin and goal of which they are ignorant, [and] which they thus cannot control'.[34] Remarks such as these present bourgeois society as being marked by a fundamental rupture between the universal and the particular: by a social condition in which particular individuals are merely bound and aggregated together (as in a 'sack of potatoes', to borrow one of Marx's own images),[35] rather than being united by their collective, conscious will. In the absence of such unity, they are held together by an effectively independent form of universality that arises from their own alienated activity.

---

30 Hegel 1969, p. 603, italics in the original.
31 Ibid, italics in the original.
32 Marx 1975, p. 134, italics in the original.
33 Marx 1975, p. 220.
34 Marx and Engels 2007, p. 54.
35 Referring to the French peasantry, Marx writes that 'the great bulk of the French nation is formed by simple accretion, much as potatoes in a sack form a sack of potatoes' (Marx 2009, p. 117).

Debord seems to have been particularly sensitive to the following point. Marx's claims can be taken to imply that the life that these forms of separated social power regulate must become separated from those who live it. Following the young Marxian ontology that we described earlier, human life is shaped by forms of social mediation. If those mediating structures take on a degree of autonomy, and thereby become relatively independent from those whose conduct they articulate, the life of the social whole must then come to be shaped not in accordance with the aims and will of the individuals concerned, but rather in accordance with the dictates of those autonomous mediating structures. Admittedly, these themes are not always explicit in Marx's early writings, but they can certainly be inferred from his texts. For example, in a notebook of quotations from Marx, which is now stored in the Bibliothèque nationale, Debord copied a series of passages from Marx's 'Comments on James Mill': a text in which Marx describes money as an *'alien mediator'*, and as 'the *alienated* species-activity of man',[36] through which 'man gazes at his will, his activity, his relation to others as at a power independent of them and of himself'.[37] Money, in this sense, is an independent form of social universality that serves to mediate collective activity. Its separated independence gives rise to a condition in which human agents become detached from their own collective powers and capacities (or rather from their 'species-being').

These themes are by no means restricted to Marx's early writings. Similar issues can also be found in his mature work, where they inform his account of capitalist value. In *Capital*, Marx holds that the quantitative abstraction of socially average labour-time homogenises the qualitatively distinct labours from which it derives, and that it thus functions as an abstract, independent form of universality that relates and directs those particular labours via the vagaries and contingencies of the market. Because those interactions are driven by capital's continual impulse towards quantitative growth, capitalist value is described as a self-perpetuating 'automatic subject':[38] as an abstract, intangible, but no less profoundly real force, driven by the 'dead', alienated labour of the objectified human subjects whose actions it both directs and mediates. The life of society thus becomes dominated by the autonomous, independent 'life' of capital.

The issues that have been outlined here are readily apparent in Debord's work. In *The Society of the Spectacle*, he describes capitalist society as a false

---

36   Marx 1975, pp. 260–1, italics in the original.
37   Ibid, italics in the original.
38   Marx 1990, p. 255.

and fragmented form of unity, in which 'spectators are linked only by a one-way relationship to the very centre that maintains their isolation from one another'.[39] Indeed, just as Marx described capital as a 'social relation'[40] in which 'men are ... related in a purely atomistic way',[41] so too does Debord describe the society of his day as a 'unity ... of generalised separation'.[42] In contrast to such separation, both Debord and Marx imply a more organic unity of the universal and the particular, in which the fragmented atomisation of modern society could be overcome.

Let us now put this in more overt connection with this chapter's concerns with Debord's notion of life. We claimed earlier that Debord associates the life of a society with its collective self-actualisation. We also indicated that the flourishing or denigration of that social life depends upon the nature of the mediating social relations that articulate its conduct. We can now add, in light of the above, that the degeneration of life into spectacular non-life arises from flawed modes of social mediation, in which particular individuals become divorced from their collective capacities and agency.

This then brings us to the following point. Identifying and rectifying such a condition – and, indeed, continuing to avoid its resurgence in the future – requires a comprehension of these flawed social relations, and of the shifting iterations of universality and particularity that characterise them. We will now try to show that for Debord, such a comprehension required dialectical thought. This is not just because dialectical thought would be capable, in Debord's view, of comprehending a social totality (dialectical thought is, after all, able to grasp the interrelation of universal and particular forms that characterises any such totality): in addition, it also bears relation to Debord's view that philosophy needed to be actualised in lived praxis. The key point here is that, for Debord, dialectical thought needed to be used not just as a means of comprehending and *interpreting* the social relations and living interrelations of a society's 'life-activity': in addition, it also needed to be employed as a means of consciously *conducting* such activity. Dialectical thought, in other words, needed to become the *self-consciousness* of a collective 'historical life'.[43]

As is perhaps already apparent, addressing this point can help to advance our earlier remarks concerning Debord's conception of strategy (insofar as strategy, for Debord, was to be the form taken by dialectical thought when

---

39 Debord 1995, p. 22; 2006b, p. 774.
40 Marx 1990, p. 932.
41 Marx 1990, p. 187.
42 Debord 1995, p. 12; 2006b, p. 767.
43 Debord 1995, p. 106; 2006b, p. 829.

actualised in historical praxis). In order to do so, however, we first need to look at his interest in Hegel's early, romantic conceptions of 'love' and 'life'.

Love of Life

As we saw in Chapter 6, Hegel's early philosophy involved an almost Feuerbachian antipathy to religious views that presented God as standing at one remove from his creation. In such presentations of the divine (and Hegel takes Judaism as his prime example), God becomes an abstract universal, removed from the particularities of his creation, despite also functioning as the absolute truth of that same creation. These early religious concerns thus anticipate the *Phenomenology*'s account of the unhappy consciousness' removal from its own seemingly divine absolute: for as is also the case in Hegel's mature philosophy, his early writings indicate that this state of removal can be rectified by actualising the universality of a divine truth in collective activity and interaction. In Hegel's early work, Christianity's great virtue is to have resolved God's Judaic distance from creation by actualising his will and divine love in the lived activity of the congregation. The 'rending of life' that resulted from a 'lifeless connection between God and the world' was thereby resolved, for Hegel, by the 'living connection'[44] of the Christian congregation. Rather than worshipping a detached deity through dead, formal ritual, the congregation would actualise God's will and rationale by instantiating mutual forgiveness and love within their own interactions with one another. God, in effect, would be brought down to earth, and made one with the living activity of his worshippers. In a manner that anticipates the position that we have ascribed to Debord, the absolute, formative power of the world would cease to a detached, awe-inspiring other, and would instead become identified with the life of a community.

At this stage in his intellectual development, Hegel employed rather idiosyncratic notions of 'life' and 'love'. 'Life' was understood as the inner, essential unity of existence;[45] 'love' was understood as a similarly fundamental yearning for the wholeness of that 'life', and thus as a drive towards grasping and expressing that fundamental unity. This can be illustrated by placing it in relation to the Christian congregation described above. The 'love' expressed in the congregation's mutual forgiveness and interaction serves as a concrete, human and self-consciously expressed instantiation of the divine 'life' that underpins

---

44 Hegel 1975b, p. 259; quoted in Sembou 2006, p. 84.
45 Sembou 2006, p. 82.

their existence. Thus, like Debord and the young Marx (although unbeknownst to Marx, as Hegel's early writings were not published until the early twentieth century), Hegel's early philosophy associates the full expression of 'life' with the actions and interactions of a social collectivity. Furthermore, it also indicates that the actualisation of that 'life' is denigrated or undermined by forms of alienated universality that purport to contain the truth and meaning of the particularities to which they pertain.

It seems that Debord was well aware of these resonances and connections. He clearly read Hegel's early writings in some detail, as they feature in his archived reading notes. In fact, he seems to have been particularly struck by Hegel's early 'Fragment on Love', which he quotes more than once in these notes, and which he also used as the dedication to his wife, Alice, that he placed at the start of 1973's film version of *The Society of the Spectacle*. The dedication reads as follows:

> Since each particular feeling is only a part of life and not life in its entirety, life yearns to spread into the full diversity of feelings so as to rediscover itself in the whole of this diversity ... In love, the separate still exists, but it exists as unified, no longer separate: the living meets the living ... THIS FILM IS DEDICATED TO ALICE BECKER-HO.[46]

This is obviously a very personal message. However, its location at the outset of a film that describes a condition of generalised separation does indicates that it was also intended to evoke the inter-personal unity that Debord placed in opposition to spectacle. This is not to suggest that Debord was naïve enough to cast love alone as an adequate response to a set of extant socio-economic structures. Instead, as in the young Marxian and Young Hegelian texts referred to above, 'love' becomes a marker for 'living', authentically self-determinate social relations (the actualisation of which, it might be added, would be a necessarily complex, agonistic and even antagonistic affair).[47]

---

46 This translation has been taken from Knabb's *Guy Debord: Complete Cinematic Works* (Debord 2003, p. 43; 2006b, p. 1196), and is a direct translation of the French text. The rendering of Hegel's original German that can be found in Knox's translation, included in *Early Theological Writings*, is slightly different (Hegel 1975b, pp. 304–5). All subsequent translations will be taken from Knox.

47 One might think here of Debord's outright contempt for Vaneigem's tendencies in this regard. Debord complained that Vaneigem tended towards presenting revolution as redemption, and held that he thus did not fully grasp or accommodate the conflicts and practicalities involved in its realisation. Vaneigem, according to Debord, sought to make

Dialectical Life

The dynamic unity of distinct elements that can be found in Hegel's early conceptions of life gradually developed into the dialectical logic of his mature philosophy. This is a logic that 'deviates', as Kroner puts it, 'from all former conceptions and schemes of logic'.[48] It does not attempt to represent and describe existent reality. Instead, it attempts to give voice to the mobile, dynamic nature of reality itself. In Hegel's philosophy, 'thought is made mobile' and 'moves',[49] so as to express, through this 'living, fluid logic',[50] the 'life pulse'[51] of reality itself. It was, therefore, explicitly intended to differ from more traditional ways of thinking, which rely upon the separation of discrete concepts, categories and propositions. Hegel viewed such modes of thought as inadequate means of conceptualising the inherent dynamism of reality. Such ways of thinking were only capable of separating and categorising static contents, and thus presented the world like 'a skeleton with scraps of paper stuck all over it', or like 'the rows of closed and labelled boxes in a grocer's stall'.[52] In contrast, Hegel's philosophy endeavours to think life as process and movement, and as unity in difference. This is why it has often been held to be so suited to attempts to conceive the shifting interconnections of a social totality.

Debord was entirely convinced of the need to conceive society, and indeed history, as a totality. In a letter of 1959, he wrote that the SI's 'necessary activity' was 'dominated by the question of the *totality*'.[53] In another letter from 1964, he stated that 'methodologically, the centre of revolutionary dialectical thought is the concept of the *totality*';[54] in 1967's *The Society of the Spectacle*, he stresses the need to conceive society as a totality, makes reference to 'the totality of human existence',[55] and talks of the 'totality of the movement of history'.[56]

---

the SI an organisation of 'sublime and perhaps even absolute excellence' (SI 2003, pp. 148–9; Debord 2004a, p. 310), and supposed that 'the French or Russian worker, the black miner in South Africa or the peasant in the Andes is able to go, without considering anything else, from pleasure to pleasure, and that the revolution will thus be quickly made. ... *Priests have always been defined by the promise of paradise*' (Debord 2006a, p. 41, Debord's italics).

48   Kroner in Hegel 1975b, p. 30.
49   Ibid.
50   Kroner in Hegel 1975b, p. 30.
51   Hegel 1969, p. 37.
52   Hegel 1977, p. 31.
53   Debord 2009, p. 235, italics in the original.
54   Debord 2001a, p. 304.
55   Debord 1995, p. 30; 2006b, p. 779.
56   Debord 1995, p. 49; 2006b, p. 793.

His views in this regard seem much informed by Lukács's own attempt to give 'the category of totality' a 'central position' within Marxian thought,[57] and by Lukács's contention, in *History and Class Consciousness*, that 'history' is the 'uniquely possible life-element of the dialectical method'.[58] To think a moving totality, in other words, would be to think the living movement of a social collectivity.

Debord was also convinced that dialectics could afford a means of thinking a historical totality. This can be illustrated by way of reference to his reading notes. An archived note on Karl Korsch connects Hegel's account of Spirit to the 'theory of the social revolution comprehended and put in practice as a living totality';[59] likewise, a note on Jean Hyppolite states that 'the fundamental experience of Hegelianism' is 'the experience of relations and of their becoming'.[60] A letter from 1969 goes so far as to state that 'history is dialectic',[61] and in another letter from 1972, he writes that 'a dialectician' possesses 'the intelligence of the real'.[62] Thus, dialectical thought, for Debord, provided a means of thinking history, i.e. of grasping the shifting interrelations of historical social existence.

These comments should go some way towards explaining Debord's identification of dialectics with strategy. Because 'a dialectician possesses the intelligence of the real', he or she is also able to intervene effectively. Furthermore, because lived historical reality was held to be dialectically mobile, dialectical thought can also afford the self-conscious conduct of a historical life (this is why 'workers', for Debord and the SI, needed to 'become dialecticians').[63] In addition: because thinking strategically necessarily entails grasping the interrelated factors at work within a given situation, strategic thought, for Debord, necessarily involves an attempt to conceive a conflictual, developing totality. This then returns us to another archived reading note, which we discussed in Chapter 2. In one of his many notes on strategic theory, Debord writes as follows:

---

57 Lukács 1971, p. xx.
58 Lukács 1971, p. 147.
59 Bibliothèque nationale, NAF28603; Notes de lecture; Marxisme; dossier 2; Korsch; the note was written after 1964.
60 Bibliothèque nationale, NAF28603; Notes de lecture; Marxisme; dossier 2; Hyppolite, *Etudes sur Marx et Hegel*; the note was written after 1964.
61 Debord 2004a, p. 60.
62 Debord 2004a, p. 609.
63 Debord 1995, p. 89; 2006b, p. 819.

It is the same thing to think dialectically and to think strategically ... *since both denote the totality*. It is the thought of praxis, which must act; practical theory, in the course of its combat in time.[64]

It would seem, therefore, that dialectics, in Debord's view, could afford a means of thinking historical life. This is because it constituted a mode of thought suited to conceiving the actions and interactions of a 'living' totality, and indeed to diagnosing and addressing the failings of a social totality that had become marked by the impoverished 'non-life' of spectacle.

We can now take these views further by returning to the important influence of Jean Hyppolite's interpretation of Hegelian philosophy. In order to do so, we should briefly recapitulate some of the observations made in Part One, as they may help us to address some of the ideas that Hyppolite's work brings to light.

'To Think Life, That is the Task'

Debord's archived reading notes on Hegel's early writings include the following quotation: 'The totality, in its highest vitality, is only possible through a reconstitution from the most profound separation'.[65] This remark no doubt resonated with Debord's contention that spectacular society amounted to a condition of 'perfected [*achevée*]'[66] separation; a state of separation, moreover, that harboured the potential for an entirely new mode of life. This is because never before, in Debord's view, had humanity's power to shape its own lived experience been so great. Yet never before had this power been so removed from its producers. On the one hand, society, through its collective social ability and agency, was engaged in transforming the world, and effecting changes to everyday life that penetrated ever more deeply into every aspect of lived experience. On the other hand, because these abilities were being conducted according to the dictates of an effectively autonomous economic system, the ability to master this new potential for historical change seemed entirely removed from its producers. For Debord and the SI, this deepening contradiction was fostering a new awareness of historical time, and above all, a new demand to shape its lived conduct. If this demand could be satisfied, there would emerge,

---

64 Bibliothèque nationale, NAF28603, Notes de lecture; Stratégie, histoire militaire, Box 2; dossier 5; 'strat'; January 1977.
65 Bibliothèque nationale, NAF28603, Notes de lecture; Hegel; dossier 2; *Écrits théologiques de jeunesse*; the note was written after 1964.
66 Debord 1995, p. 11; 2006b, p. 766.

from the non-life of spectacular society, a social condition in which the historical, self-constitutive nature of the human subject could flourish. Thus, in short: historical change had become infused throughout the fabric of society, due to the constant innovations and invasions perpetrated by capitalism; this had prompted a new-found awareness of historical time amongst the populace, and a consequent demand to 'live' that time. We can now add, on the basis of the observations made in this chapter, that in order to do so, those who would pursue such a life needed to understand the nature of the social relations that had engendered this situation. Or, as Debord put it by way of one of his many *détournements* of the *Communist Manifesto*: because human beings have been 'thrust into history', they 'find themselves obliged to view their relationships in a clear-eyed manner'.[67]

It seems possible to contend, therefore, that Debord would have been struck by the following passage from Hyppolite's *Studies on Marx and Hegel*, which he copied into his reading notes. It reads as follows:

> Since history pervades the entire realm of thought and human action, one must penetrate to the root of history, to the human existence that makes this same history possible, and ask, as Hegel did in the *Phenomenology*, what are the conditions of self-consciousness or of the very existence of man.[68]

For Debord, the very nature of spectacular society had fostered just such a need to 'go to the root' of history. Debord also seems to have been impressed by Hyppolite's indications that such a self-consciousness of historical existence required a comprehension of the 'life' and vitality of Hegelian dialectics. On more than one occasion, his reading notes on Hyppolite quote the latter's characterisations of Hegel's work as an attempt to conceive the life of history. 'To think life, that is the task',[69] states one; another reads as follows:

> In the *Logic* of Jena, Hegel thinks of infinity as a dialectical relation of the one and the many, but we can recognise in this logical dialectic the very

---

67 Debord 1995, p. 48; 2006b, p. 792; cf. Marx and Engels 1985, p. 83.
68 Bibliothèque nationale, NAF28603; Notes de lecture; Marxisme; dossier 2; Hyppolite, *Études sur Marx et Hegel*; the note was written after 1964. The quotation can be traced to Hyppolite 1969, p. 155.
69 Bibliothèque nationale, NAF28603; Notes de lecture; Hegel; dossier 2; Hyppolite, *Introduction à la philosophie de l'histoire de Hegel*; the note was written after 1964. This line is also quoted in Hyppolite 1974, p. 30.

idea of life. Reciprocally, life is this dialectic itself, and life forces the Spirit to think dialectically.[70]

To one side of this quotation, in the margins of the card onto which it was copied, Debord wrote '*a contrario* la non-vie'. The life spoken of in this passage was thus evidently viewed as opposed to the 'non-life' of spectacle. In consequence, it deserves to be addressed in some detail.

Debord copied this quotation from Hyppolite's *Studies on Marx and Hegel*, but it can also be found repeated in Hyppolite's *Introduction to Hegel's Philosophy of History*: a text that Debord also owned and studied. In both texts, Hyppolite uses the same phrase to make much the same point. Whilst referring to Hegel's early dialectical logic, and to the themes of life that Hegel was engaged with at that time, he contends that dialectical thought provides Spirit with a means of conceiving its own historical existence. The text that surrounds the quotation in Hyppolite's *Introduction* affords the clearest explanation of this claim.

The quotation can be found in a section of that book in which Hyppolite draws connections between Hegel's early dialectical logic and the historical life of Spirit. Sketched in very broad brushstrokes, these connections are as follows. Spirit is the self-consciousness and lived activity of a community. It is thus a collective identity, and for that reason, Hegel refers to it as an 'I that is we', and as a 'we that is I'.[71] In addition, because this universal, collective identity arises from the interaction of the particular lives that compose it, Hyppolite highlights the dialectical character of its existence (this is why it is also associated with 'infinity': Hegel's peculiar conception of infinity is intimately connected to his notion of identity in difference).[72] The quotation thus associates the collective life of Spirit with dialectical movement: 'life is this dialectic itself, and life forces the Spirit to think dialectically'.

If we now bear in mind the '*a contrario*' remark that Debord wrote in the margin of this note, we can contend that spectacular 'non-life' is: a) characterised by the *absence* of an awareness of the living, dialectical interactions of a

---

70 Bibliothèque nationale, NAF28603; Notes de lecture; Marxisme; dossier 2; Hyppolite, *Études sur Marx et Hegel*; the note was written after 1964. The phrase can be traced to Hyppolite 1969, p. 6 (see also Hyppolite 1996, p. 43; the translation used here has been taken from the latter text).
71 Hegel 1977, p. 110.
72 True infinity, for Hegel, as opposed to bad (*Schlecht*) infinity, 'consists ... in remaining at home with itself in its other' or, 'when it is expressed as a process', in 'coming to itself in its other' (Hegel 1991, p. 149).

historical totality; and b) that in place of those 'living' interactions, spectacular society involves fragmentation and atomisation.

We can also add the following. Debord's note evidently places spectacular non-life in direct contrast to the historical life that Hyppolite identified with the activity of Spirit. This means that Hyppolite's views on the life of Spirit must be able to tell us something about the life that Debord opposed to that spectacular non-life. It therefore seems possible to contend, given the importance that Hyppolite ascribes to Spirit's awareness of its own living, dynamic interrelations, that Debord's notion of life must involve the active, self-conscious conduct of a collectivity. Spectacular non-life involves the denigration of such self-consciousness, and the subordination of the particular to the abstractly universal; in contrast, the life of Debord's imagined collectivity would be marked by a more organic interrelation of the universal and the particular.

Despite his general reticence concerning the precise nature of this notion of life, the ideas that we have reconstructed so far can be illustrated, to some degree, by quoting a passage from Debord's preface to the fourth Italian edition of *The Society of the Spectacle*. Towards the end of that text, and having acknowledged the 'difficulty' and the 'immensity of the tasks' faced by any attempt at modern revolution, he adds that such a project:

> ... can quite easily begin anywhere that autonomous proletarian assemblies, not recognising any independent authority or proprietorship beyond themselves, and placing their will above all laws and specialisations, abolish the separation of individuals, the commodity economy, and the state. But it will not triumph unless it imposes itself universally, and unless it ensures that it does not allow a single piece of the territory of alienated society to remain in place. There, we will see again an Athens or a Florence from which no one is rejected, and which extends to the ends of the earth; and which, having defeated all of its enemies, will finally be able to surrender itself joyously to the true divisions and endless confrontations of historical life.[73]

This notion of a new Athens or Florence recalls Papaïoannou's Hegelian call for the modern rebirth of the 'democratic city',[74] which we discussed in Chapter 6. The key point here, however, is that this vision of a condition in which difference and confrontation do not involve the abstract separation of social parts,

---

73 Debord 1979, translation altered; 2006b, p. 1473.
74 Papaïoannou 2012, p. 80.

but rather arise from their organic interrelation, bears direct relation to the Hegelian themes that we have drawn on above. In *The Encyclopaedia Logic*, and whilst discussing the relation of parts to whole, Hegel writes that 'the members and organs of a living body should not be considered merely as parts of it, for they are what they are only in that unity and are not indifferent to that unity at all. ... [They] become mere "parts" only under the hands of the anatomist; but for that reason he is dealing with corpses rather than living bodies'.[75] Atomised and deprived of qualitative singularity, and yet rendered quantitatively homogenous by that same abstract universality, the life of modern society takes on similar attributes: it becomes a form of *non*-life. In contrast, the organic community that would resolve this 'lifeless' condition was envisaged as a cohesive, dynamic interrelation of social universality and particularity.

Having made these claims, we can now close by connecting them to our proposed model of Debord's use of Hegelian philosophy.

An 'Inexhaustively Creative Activity'

We have argued, in previous chapters, that Debord's use of Hegel entails refiguring some of the key aspects of the latter's philosophy as aspects of collective historical praxis. In this regard, his general approach to Hegelian Marxism owes much to Lukács's argument that 'man must become conscious of himself as ... the subject and object of the socio-historical process'.[76] In Hegel's mature philosophy, Spirit ultimately identifies itself with the Absolute, and thus with the force and rationale that has shaped its world, and which has driven its ascent towards this moment of self-awareness. In *History and Class Consciousness*, this becomes the revolutionary proletariat's emergence as the identical subject-object of history: an entity that recognises itself as the author of its own world, and as the potential master of its own future. Similarly, Debord holds that through superseding spectacular separation, revolutionary subjects would become one with their own historical agency, thereby attaining a condition of free self-determinacy. The Hegelian Absolute – the object with which the subject of history is to unite – thus becomes the practical, formative activity that generates and shapes historical existence.

We also saw, in Chapter 6, that Debord's reading of Hegel owes much to Hyppolite's presentation of the Absolute as a state of constant, restless process

---

75 Hegel 1991, p. 204.
76 Lukács 1971, p. 19.

('negativity', according to Hyppolite, 'is at the very heart of the absolute', which cannot 'be conceived independently of it').[77] The re-formulation of Hegelian philosophy that we have attributed to Debord views the Absolute in similar terms, albeit re-cast as human historical existence. The latter is thus seen as both a fundamental ground and as 'an inexhaustively creative activity'[78] (to borrow an apposite phrase from Hyppolite). Furthermore: just as the Absolute, for Hegel, is to be comprehended via a mode of thought (i.e. Hegelian logic) that grasps and expresses the Absolute's own dialectical 'life', so too, for Debord, is the dialectical movement of historical life to be comprehended and directed via dialectical-strategic praxis.

This is to be afforded by the emergence of the collective historical life that the society of the spectacle suppresses: a collective condition of subject-object unity, in which the alienated nature of the social relations that mediate social praxis would be resolved. Consequently, not only does this model echo Hegel's account of the recognition and comprehension of the dialectical self-movement of the Absolute: in addition, it also echoes the full realisation of the unity of universality and particularity proper to the actualisation of the Idea. The latter thus becomes analogous to the actualisation of social relations capable of affording the supersession of spectacular capitalism's abstract universality and isolated, atomised particularity. It becomes tantamount, therefore, to what Debord describes as 'the end of all specialisation, all hierarchy, and all separation'[79] through the realisation of a 'generalised historical life';[80] a form of life that would be enabled by, and which would flourish within, 'a harmonious society that was capable of controlling all its forces'.[81]

To sum up: the attainment of the historical life that Debord advocates requires an organic, self-determinate relation between the particular and the universal. Conversely, the deprivation of such a life arises from their separation. In Part Four, we will consider the ways in which these themes pertain to Debord's use of Marx's mature critique of political economy. We will begin, however, by looking at some of the criticisms that have been levelled at Debord's account of capitalist society.

---

77   Hyppolite 1996, p. 59.
78   Hyppolite 1996, p. 37. NB This phrase is taken from Hyppolite's comments on Hegel's early romantic views concerning 'the creative energy of God' (Hyppolite 1996, p. 37).
79   Debord 1995, p. 87; 2006b, p. 817.
80   Debord 1995, p. 116; 2006b, p. 836.
81   Debord 2003b, p. 169; 2006b, p. 1375.

PART 4
In Pursuit of the Northwest Passage 1963–73

'The 'Erebus' and 'Terror' in the Arctic Regions', *from Henry Davenport Northrop's* Makers of the World's History and their Grand Achievements, *1903*

'We need to discover and open up the "Northwest Passage" toward a new revolution that cannot tolerate masses of followers, a revolution that must surge over that central terrain which has until now been sheltered from revolutionary upheavals: the conquest of everyday life. *We will only organize the detonation:* the free explosion must escape us and any other control forever.'

– Situationist International, 'The Counter-Situationist Campaign in Various Countries'

CHAPTER 9

Never Work!

Assessing the Situationist International

The first part of this book sought to introduce some of the key aspects of Debord's mature theoretical work. Part Two then focussed on the theory of spectacle's emergence from Debord and the SI's early avant-garde concerns during the 1950s. In Part Three, we considered the further elaborations that those ideas received, towards the end of that decade, following Debord's increasingly overt turn to Hegel and Marx. Having traced the emergence of the theory of spectacle from its initial roots, and having also discussed the ideas that informed its development, we can now address the theoretical work that Debord and the SI advanced during the 1960s. The chapters that follow will concentrate on the Marxian dimensions of works such as 1967's *The Society of the Spectacle*, and will try to develop: 1) an analysis of Debord's relation to Marx's mature critique of political economy; and thereby 2) a critical approach to Debord and the SI's theoretical legacy. This present chapter is intended to lay an initial basis upon which those two aims can be pursued. It will do so by looking at some recent critical discussions of the Situationists' theory and activity.

The critical analyses that we will consider in this chapter are chiefly concerned with the SI's somewhat vexed allegiance to the workers' movement of the past. Seen from these critical perspectives, that allegiance is often assumed to involve an endorsement of the classical workers' movement's *affirmation* of labour, and thus of its pursuit of better working conditions, its celebration of a putative working class identity, and indeed of traditional Marxism's desire to liberate labour from its capitalist exploitation. Such an apparent affirmation of labour can seem to jar with the SI's calls for labour's outright *rejection*.

(This requires a word of clarification. The term 'labour', as used here, is not intended to indicate work in general. It is not, therefore, synonymous with the more general conception of formative activity that we discussed in Chapter 7. Instead, it denotes social activity conducted under the rule of value. 'Labour', understood in this sense, denotes specifically *capitalist* labour, and is specific to social conditions wherein qualitatively distinct forms of concrete human activity are obliged to function as moments of abstract, quantitatively homogenous and socially average labour time.[1] This definition will be developed below, and we will return to it in subsequent chapters).

---

1 It should be added that Marx himself is not as clear on this point as he could be. The opening

This tension – that between SI's allegiance to the classical workers' movement on the one hand, and their drive towards an entirely new, post-labour form of social existence on the other – has often been phrased by way of reference to their similarly vexed enthusiasm for workers' councils. For example, as the Anglo-American Endnotes group put it: 'the potential and all the limits of the SI were contained in the tension between their call to "abolish work" and their central slogan, "all power to the workers' councils"'.[2]

The analyses of the SI that we will discuss below are often informed by aspects of contemporary readings of Marxian value theory, which tend to indicate, or to at least imply, that communism cannot be achieved through liberating labour. On such a view, labour cannot be viewed as a neutral, unproblematic, and perhaps also transhistorical social form that needs to be freed from its capitalist fetters, but must instead be seen as entirely integral and proper to social relations governed and composed by capitalist value. To affirm labour, therefore, would be to treat a symptom as it if were a cure.

The critics with whom we will be concerned tend to hold that the SI should be praised for coming close to such a position. The Situationists advocated the end of labour, and called, as we saw in Chapter 4, for the total transformation of all existing social relations. On the other hand, however, these critics can also fault the Situationists for having failed to completely break away from the traditional Marxism of the past; for having remained too tied to a traditional framework of class struggle, and for having mistakenly viewed the *emancipation* of labour as a route towards labour's *negation*. In short, Debord and the SI are thus positioned on the cusp of a break with the radical politics of the past: a break that they did not quite manage to make.

This chapter will try to outline the common concerns that characterise these critical positions. It will also propose that some of these criticisms are, in fact, rather misplaced. This should serve to clear a ground for our own criticisms of Debord and the SI's work, which will be advanced in Chapters 10 and 12.

---

sections of *Capital* come very close to indicating a transhistorical notion of labour. Marx's aim here is perhaps to evoke something closer to the rather more neutral conception of 'activity' that we discussed in Chapter 7: 'Labour', he writes, 'as the creator of use-values, as useful labour, is a condition of human existence which is independent of all forms of society; it is an eternal natural necessity which mediates the metabolism between man and nature, and therefore human life itself' (Marx 1990, p. 133). Yet labour, in the sense in which we are using the term, is by no means a transhistorical inevitability, but is instead specific to a particular social formation (i.e. capitalism). See Trenkle 1998 for a discussion of this point.

2 Endnotes 2008, p. 7.

We will start by characterising the perspective that the SI came to adopt, during the 1960s, towards the radical politics of the past.

A Frozen History

In 1963, and thus shortly after the splits of the previous year, the SI stated that their aim was to chart a 'Northwest Passage' towards 'a new revolution' that would involve 'the conquest of everyday life.'[3] This new path would afford a route out of the 'frozen'[4] history of the capitalist present, past the latter's similarly gelid bureaucratic opposition, and through the dangerous pitfalls and crevasses of political representation. The SI's aim, in other words, was to rethink both communism and the route by which it might be attained. Yet whilst this new path was intended to differ from those that had been attempted in the past, it is also important to note that it was understood, by Debord and the SI, as a *continuation* of a much older political enterprise. Indeed, in Debord's view, the Situationists' ambitions constituted a contribution to a project that had been pursued for 'more than a century':[5] namely, that of the revolutionary proletariat's attempt to extricate itself from capitalist society.

In Part One, we saw that Debord associated Hegel's philosophy with the perspective afforded by the bourgeois revolutions. This bears repeating here, as it can help us to develop the sense in which the SI's new enterprise constituted a continuation of the past.

For Debord, the emergence of bourgeois, capitalist society ushered in a new awareness of historical time, together with a growing sense of that time's alienation from its producers. This was a society which had become marked by historical change, and which had thereby developed a new, more profound sense of historical time. This new awareness of historical time was, however, marked by alienation, insofar as the time engendered by these new social relations was governed by capital, and was thus removed from the direct control of its producers:[6] the rise of capitalism ushered in 'the time of things',[7] not the time of human subjects. It thus afforded a conception of historical change wherein the latter follows an independent rationale that overarches and exceeds the aims

---

3 SI 2006, p. 148; 1997, pp. 323–4; see also Debord 1979; 2006b, p. 1465.
4 Debord 1995, p. 141; 2006b, p. 851.
5 Debord 1979; 2006b, p. 1465.
6 As Debord puts it: 'the bourgeoisie unveiled historical time and imposed it on society only to deprive society of its use' (Debord 1995, pp. 104–5; 2006b, pp. 828–9).
7 Debord 1995, p. 105; 2006b, p. 829.

of individual human agents. Society had gained a sense of history, but history remained a detached object of contemplation. For Debord, Hegel exemplified this perspective: his philosophy reflected this new sense of humanity's ability to shape its own world, because it presented history as a process of free, self-constitutive and self-determinate activity; yet it also reflected the contemplative detachment proper to this new, bourgeois, 'time of things', because his work, in Debord's view, had also adopted a detached, resigned attitude towards a history that had 'made itself'[8] and run its course.

Nonetheless, for Debord, Hegel's work remained a crucial resource. Although Hegel had adopted a detached, philosophical view of history's creation, he had nonetheless come a long way towards thinking its conscious construction. In Debord's view, this insight was progressively developed, and its removal from real history corrected, by the critical engagements with Hegel's work that followed. Young Hegelian engagements with notions of alienation and praxis, and above all the young Marx's own efforts in that regard, were all construed as attempts towards remedying this fault. These efforts reflected a growing awareness of the need to supersede bourgeois society's contemplative detachment from history. They thus amounted to progressive steps towards actualising a *real* condition of subject-object unity: a unity that would not exist as a philosophical representation, as in the imaginary clouds of Hegel's absolute idealism, but which would instead take the form of a self-creating, proactive and future-oriented historical praxis.

As we have seen, Debord associated such a condition of subject-object unity with the supersession of spectacular separation, and thus with the end of the spectacle's illusory end of history. In this regard, he and the SI located themselves within a line of theoretical development that descended from Hegel, and which sought to remedy the contradictions of capitalist temporality. Yet Debord did not locate this line of development solely within the realms of theory. In addition – and this brings us back to the concerns of this present chapter – that gradual move towards recognising the importance of praxis was also held to have been afforded by the struggles of the revolutionary workers' movement (as we saw earlier: according to Debord, 'All the theoretical strands of the *revolutionary* workers' movement stem from critical confrontation with Hegelian thought').[9] In *The Society of the Spectacle*, he writes as follows:

---

8 Debord 1995, p. 49; 2006b, p. 793.
9 Debord 1995, p. 50; 2006b, p. 794.

> The class struggles of the long *revolutionary epoch* inaugurated by the rise of the bourgeoisie have developed in tandem with the *thought of history*, the dialectic, the thought which no longer stops to look for the meaning of what is, but rises to a knowledge of the dissolution of all that is, and in its movement dissolves all separation.[10]

The struggle to supersede capitalist society's flawed relation to its own time was thus understood as having taken place within both theory and practice. Within the realms of theory, Marx, the Young Hegelians and their successors had sought to identify dialectical thought not with the world's contemplative interpretation, but rather with the conscious conduct of its transformation; within practice, concrete, if flawed, efforts had been made to break down capitalism's social structures. These two lines of development were seen to have been moving towards unification, as 'the dialectical method' was brought progressively closer to 'the reality that seeks it'.[11]

Debord positioned his own and the SI's work at a point of conjunction between these lines of theoretical and practical development. The SI were seen to be stationed at a point at which it had become evident, in the light of past events, that the dialectical thought of history needed to *make* history through revolutionary change, and that genuinely revolutionary practice could only be conducted by agents who would master their own affairs rather than following representatives and figureheads (hence, 'workers', for Debord and the SI, needed to 'become dialecticians').[12]

It follows from the remarks set out here that the SI's attempts to find a new path towards the future were *not* envisaged as an abrupt break with the struggles of the past. The SI certainly sought to differ from classical, orthodox Marxism, and from the traditional modes of politics that had been employed by the workers' movement. However, their search for a new 'Northwest Passage' that would lead through and beyond such theoretical and political impasses was not seen as a break with the efforts of the past, but rather as a *return* to a classical project that had long since lost its way, and which had become stranded amongst the ice floes of political representation and bureaucratic state-capitalism.

---

10   Debord 1995, p. 49, translation altered; 2006b, p. 793, italics in the original. Cf. Marx 1990, p. 103.
11   Debord 2006b, p. 1536.
12   Debord 1995, p. 89; 2006b, p. 819.

The latter point is obviously crucial, given the nature of the criticisms of the SI that we will go on to consider in this chapter. We therefore need to develop it further.

'... We Remain Relentlessly "Nineteenth Century"'

As we saw in Chapters 2 and 3, Debord located the emergence of spectacular society in its full, 'completed'[13] form in the early decades of the twentieth century. This is because those early decades were seen to be pregnant with a new potential for the abolition of capitalist society, and for the inauguration of a genuinely different social order. Throughout the late nineteenth and early twentieth centuries, art had been moving towards its own negation as a means of representing life, and of depicting life's possibilities; the workers' movement had also been developing towards a point at which it could, through revolution, realise art's promises and passions within life itself. In the early decades of the twentieth century, art's auto-negation and an ascendant workers' movement had come close to combining with one another, and had thereby reached a point at which they had offered the potential for a new, radically expanded and enriched historical existence. Yet this newfound potential for a free history collapsed into its own antithesis: the commodity triumphed, culture stagnated, and the workers' movement fell prey to its own state-bureaucratic representation.

The key point here, therefore, is that the emergence of the spectacle's 'completed' form in the early twentieth century resulted from a failure to actualise the very same historical agency that spectacular society denied. For Debord and the SI, however, the circumstances of the mid to late twentieth century had caused that lost set of possibilities to return. The increasing banality of consumer capitalism; the evident dead-end of the so-called workers' states; the increasing tension between capitalism's inflated promises of happiness, and its enforced deferral of that fulfilment; the stagnation of modern art and culture; taken together, all of these factors were seen to have engendered a revolutionary demand for an entirely new social revolution that would fulfil the possibilities that had been intimated in the past.

The SI's political project was thus an attempt to actualise those lost possibilities. They wanted to break with traditional Marxism, certainly; but in doing so, they sought to *return* to the potential that Marxism and the revolu-

---

13   Debord 2004a, pp. 455–6.

tionary attempts of the past had harboured. This is quite explicit: in 1967, the SI stated that 'we flatter ourselves on ... the fact that we remain relentlessly "nineteenth century"'.[14] According to the SI, the 'proletarian project of a classless society ... began badly.'[15] Yet, they also stated that despite our 'avant-gardism', or rather *thanks to it*, it was 'this movement alone to which we wish to return.'[16]

This was by no means seen as a simple, straightforward return to those older ambitions and struggles. Instead, it would constitute a re-vitalisation, a re-figuration, and a development of those older concerns. In practical terms, the disasters suffered by the revolutionary efforts of the past had imposed an awareness of the limitations and dangers of Leninist leadership. Furthermore, given that the stakes of struggle now stood revealed as the demand for a free, autonomous history, the illusions of economic determinism that had plagued traditional Marxism could also be dismissed. In addition, for the SI, the bloated, facile nature of modern art and culture, and the tension between the paltry nature of capital's gilded trinkets and its huge technical abilities, had forcibly imposed, upon an existentially immiserated population, a nascent awareness of the need to conjoin 'the supersession of art' with 'social revolution'.[17] For Debord and the Situationists, therefore, the conjunction of these factors within their own period had provided a clearer perspective on the needs and nature of revolution than had been possible within the past.

The latter point is important, because one might be led to ask, given that their aims were so different, quite what the SI's project had in common with the older struggles with which they aligned themselves. The answer lies in the new sense of historical time that Debord associated with the advent of bourgeois capitalist society, and which we referred to above. Simply put: for Debord, *all* of those past struggles against capitalist society had *implicitly* been attempts to lay claim to that time, and to overcome its alienation from its producers; the SI had simply made that previously implicit demand *explicit*. We will return to this point later in the chapter.

The issues that have been outlined so far can be summarised as follows. Whilst the SI certainly saw themselves as picking up the baton that had been dropped by the classical workers' movement, they also held that the modern revolutionary project needed to go far beyond those older visions and ambi-

---

14   SI 1967; 1997, p. 562.
15   Ibid.
16   SI 1967; 1997, p. 66.
17   Debord 1979; 2006b, p. 1465.

tions. Although they saw themselves as continuing the efforts of the past, they also held that such a continuation necessarily entailed rejecting the past's illusions and errors. It could now see that the modern revolution could not be reduced to a demand for a more equitable, centralised version of the current system of industrialised production and distribution. Communism, in other words, could not amount to a society of bureaucratically managed labour. Instead, the goal of charting a path out of capitalist society had evolved into the pursuit of an entirely new, ludic mode of social existence.

Breaking Away from the Classical Workers' Movement

Having now mapped out the manner in which Debord and the SI conceived their relation to the classical workers' movement, we should be in a position to address the criticisms that we referred to in the introduction to this chapter. As we indicated there, these criticisms tend to identify a tension between the SI's allegiance to the workers' movement, and their desire to move beyond the latter's traditional demands and struggles. The identification of this tension owes a great deal to the nature and status of labour within contemporary Marxian theory, and to the degree to which Debord and the SI's ideas echo that theoretical material.

The SI's new, expanded vision of revolutionary communism required the complete *rejection* of labour, as social activity and interaction were to be liberated from the dominating abstractions of value. The classical workers' movement, however, had pushed towards the reform and eventual abolition of capitalist society via the pursuit of better, more equitable working conditions. In consequence, the workers' movement's struggles for a better society could be construed as efforts towards the emancipation and *affirmation* of labour. This is why the SI have been located in a potentially contradictory position that stands between these two perspectives: for whilst the Situationists clearly advocated the end of labour, their desire to remain 'relentlessly nineteenth century', and their attendant sympathies for the workers' movement, could be construed as involving a continuing and problematic allegiance to labour's affirmation. As Gilles Dauvé puts it: the 'SI stand at the crux of a contradiction between two contradictory slogans: "Down with Work!" and "Power to the Workers!"'[18] (the remarks made in the sections above, concerning the sense in which the SI saw themselves as developing and clarifying that older project, rather than merely

---

18   Dauvé 2000.

continuing it, should already serve to indicate that these criticisms need to be viewed with some degree of scepticism).

Much of this commentary has grown from studies of Marxian value theory that indicate that the labour proper to capitalism cannot be understood as a transhistorical constant (as in some strains of traditional Marxism). The rationale here is relatively simple: if labour is integral to capitalism, then its affirmation and liberation can only lead to new arrangements and modifications of existing social relations. Therefore, the end of capitalism cannot involve the emancipation of labour, but rather requires its complete destruction.

It may be helpful to briefly contextualise the emergence of these views. As we saw in Chapter 1, Anglophone academia has often viewed Debord and the SI's account of spectacular society as a body of art theory, or as an inexplicably angry critique of the mass media. Today, this situation is gradually improving. Serious contemporary discussions of Debord's work now tend to focus on the links between capitalism and spectacle, and on the details and genealogy of Debord's Marxian ideas. Yet progress remains slow: Anselm Jappe's *Guy Debord*, which presented a seminal study of Debord's links to Marx and Lukács, first appeared over twenty years ago,[19] and yet it still remains a relatively solitary text within a very small field of work. Jappe's influence on serious engagements with Debord's thought is thus justly great, and this influence extends to studies that would critically address Debord and the SI's theoretical legacy. This is important, because Jappe's reading of Debord laid a basis for assessing the latter's work in terms of its relative proximity to Marxian value-theory. Informed by the work of writers such as Moishe Postone[20] and Robert Kurz,[21] who criticised 'traditional Marxism' for its insufficiently critical account of labour and class struggle, Jappe's book praised Debord for describing a society dominated by value, whilst criticising him for failing to fully break away from a classical politics. According to Jappe, the 'relevance' of Debord's work stems from its connection to 'the Marxian theory of value' – i.e. to Marx's account of society's subordination to the abstractions of value – whilst his thought's weaker points follow from the degree to which he remained 'under the influence of the Marxism of the workers' movement'.[22]

Jappe's chief concern is that Debord and the SI remained in thrall to the purportedly outdated assumption that class struggle might afford something

---

19   The book was published in Italian in 1993; it appeared in English in 1999.
20   Jappe 1999, p. 163n.
21   Jappe 1999, p. 148n.
22   Jappe 1999, p. 18.

more than a mere modification in the distribution of the booty produced by the existing system of production. For Jappe, capitalism is a system that tends towards subsuming the totality of society, including the social and political entities that were once held to oppose it. In his view, the existence of a 'powerful proletariat' in the past was merely a 'precapitalist relic'[23] that had not yet been integrated into the capitalist whole. Today, however, 'the proletariat and the bourgeoisie cannot be anything but the living instruments of variable capital and fixed capital', and their struggles are 'merely struggles over distribution within a system that nobody now seriously challenges'.[24] Seen from such a perspective, the SI's allegiance to the classical workers' movement stands as a serious defect in their thought.

Some of the sharpest criticisms that have been levelled at the SI in recent years have adopted a similar perspective. Debord and the Situationists' theoretical work is now often praised for its resemblance to readings of Marx which stress the rule of value, and which imply a critique of any politics that would place its faith in a traditional conception of class struggle. At the same time, their work is also criticised for its relative proximity to classical Marxism.

The Critique of Political Economy and Critical Political Economy

The approaches to Marx that have informed these criticisms are, primarily, the value-form theory[25] of the so-called *Neue Marx-Lektüre* – a predominantly German field of study concerned with reconstructing and reconsidering Marx's account of capitalist value[26] – and the somewhat less prominent, but also

---

23 Jappe 1999, p. 37.
24 Ibid.
25 'Value-form theory' is the term that is now commonly applied to a field of Marxian scholarship that emerged in Germany in the later 1960s, partly in response to Adorno's teaching and the publication of Marx's *Grundrisse*. It consists of an attempt to reinterpret Marx's theory of value in the light of his early drafts of *Capital*, and it lends itself to the view that the primary problem with capitalist society is not just the exploitation of one class by another, but rather the subordination of the entirety of lived activity to the rule of value (and thus to the import of socially abstract labour). To study the 'form' of value is to study the forms that value takes and engenders as it manifests itself in relations between social actors and their products.
26 The work of figures such as Arthur, Backhaus, Bonefeld, Heinrich, Postone and Reichelt are particularly significant here. For relevant overviews, see the opening chapter of Arthur 2004a, and that of Heinrich 2012; see also Bellofiore and Ridolfi Riva 2015; Bonefeld 2014; Elbe 2013; Endnotes 2010.

primarily German field of 'value-critique' (or '*Wertkritik*').[27] There are important differences between these bodies of thought,[28] but there are also a number of common themes that we will attempt to outline below. These themes have gained a degree of prominence within Anglophone discussions of Marx. This has been assisted by the recent surge of interest in 'communisation' theory (a primarily French strand of Marxian radical thought that emerged from the post-SI ultra-left).[29] Cumulatively, this has led to a growing familiarity with the

---

27   See Jappe 2014 for a useful introduction to this school of theory, which is closely associated with the work of Robert Kurz and the German Krisis group. Some of the texts produced by Kurz and other members of Krisis have been made available in English in pamphlet form by Chronos Publications (see Krisis 2002a, Krisis 2002b, and Kurz 2012; Robin Halpin has also translated Kurz's *The Substance of Capital* (Kurz 2016)). See also Trenkle 1998 and Larsen, Nilges, Robinson and Brown 2014. Engster 2016 presents a critical response, together with useful comments on the difference between *Wertkritik* and *Neue Marx-Lektüre*.

28   Value-critique (also sometimes referred to as the Critique of Value) is characterised by a more vocal opposition to labour and classical Marxist politics than *Neue Marx-Lektüre* (for a symptomatic critical discussion, see Bonefeld 2004), and where the latter largely arose from academic study, value-critique emerged from a largely extra-academic radical milieu. Furthermore, where *Neue Marx-Lektüre* tends to theorise the operation of capitalist value as an abstract system, value-critique has attempted to address the forms of subjectivity that capitalist society both engenders and naturalises (the notion of human subjectivity that we have identified in Debord's work would no doubt seem problematic when viewed from such a perspective). There are also important differences between the conceptions of value employed by these two bodies of thought. Where writers associated with *Neue Marx-Lektüre* tend to argue for a monetary theory of value focussed on exchange, those associated with value-critique tend to highlight the importance of value within the sphere of production. The distinction between these two differing understandings of value concerns the degree to which Marx can be said to have employed a 'substantialist' conception of value, wherein value is actually embodied within commodities prior to exchange. The non-substantialist monetary theory of value presented by *Neue Marx-Lektüre* writers such as Heinrich indicates that value is established via exchange, whereas the quasi-substantialist approach associated with *Wertkritik* runs counter to this view (thus, for Engster, the writers associated with the Krisis group 'did not really break with the left-Ricardian understanding of value' (Engster 2016, p. 50)). This difference has allowed proponents of *Wertkritik* to argue that the very existence and operation of capitalist value is in a condition of immanent crisis, insofar as modern technological capitalism is marked by a progressive fall in the total mass of value produced by society, due to the diminishing role played by living labour in production ('capitalism', as Jappe puts it whilst outlining this position, 'is sawing off the branch on which it sits' (Jappe 2014)). Thanks are due to Alastair Hemmens and Robin Halpin for their comments on these issues.

29   The term 'communisation' refers to a set of often conflicting concerns within the French

issues that characterise these approaches to Marx, and thereby to a growing impetus towards the adoption of the critical approach to the SI that we saw Jappe exemplify above. We should, therefore, briefly outline these common themes (albeit whilst noting that some very broad generalisations will need to be made in the interests of brevity and synthesis).[30]

We can begin by highlighting the important distinction that needs to be made between a *critique of political economy* and a *critical political economy*. Political economy, for Marx, constituted bourgeois society's attempt to understand itself. A *critique of political economy* would therefore identify and examine the categories that that self-understanding uncritically presupposes (e.g. money, labour, wage, circulation, etc.). Such a critique would not just explain *how* these categories operate within modern society: instead, it would explain *why* they take the form that they do, and it would thereby indicate how and why capitalist society might foster a tendency towards their uncritical naturalisation.[31] A *critical political economy*, on the other hand, is less ambitious. Rather than identifying political economy's presuppositions, it instead sets out to indicate more equitable or more efficient ways of arranging that which is presupposed (so as to achieve less exploitation and fairer wages, for example). Marx can certainly be said to have presented both to some degree.[32] The key issue, however, is that he partially effaced the import and scope of his *critique of* political economy by embedding it within a *critical* political economy.

---

ultra-left that broadly share the view that communism should be viewed as a historical process oriented towards the eradication, as opposed to the affirmation, of labour and a working-class identity. Communism is not viewed as a discrete state of affairs, or as a specific social modality that might be attained at the end of a programmatic struggle against capitalist society, but rather as the very process of struggle. Communism thus becomes something that needs to be made both in and against the capitalist present (see Endnotes 2008 and 2010 for useful overviews that pertain to our concerns here; see also Noys 2011). The work produced by the French Théorie Communiste group also forms part of this current (see Simon 2009 for a related critique of the SI), as do the somewhat Vaneigem-esque claims presented by the now-defunct Tiqqun group and the associated Invisible Committee (Invisible Committee 2009; see McDonough 2011 for commentary pertaining to the SI).

30   For a useful overview that manages to avoid some of these difficulties, see Elbe 2013.
31   Political economy, for Marx, thus 'takes for granted what it is supposed to explain' (quoted in Reichelt 2005, p. 37; see also p. 41).
32   See, for example, Bellofiore and Ridolfi Riva, who highlight the *Neue Marx-Lektüre*'s tendency to insist 'on the critique of political economy, as if Marx's critique was not also, as surely he intended it to be, a critical political economy' (Bellofiore and Ridolfi Riva 2015).

Again, this is a point that we will need to return to later, but suffice it to say here that the approaches to Marxian theory with which we are concerned are informed not only by the fact that Marx failed to complete his own work (*Capital* is, famously, an unfinished project), but also by the view that Marx failed to fully grasp the nature and implications of his own insights. His desire for greater accessibility and intelligibility led him to occlude the nuances of his conception of value, and to abandon the more overtly Hegelian exposition of its workings presented in the initial drafts of *Capital*'s opening sections. These elements of Marx's work were further obscured after his death. The efforts made by figures such as Engels and Kautsky to edit, promote and disseminate Marx's work led to the emergence of 'Marxism': a discrete system of thought that afforded, at its worst, an entire scientific, political and philosophical worldview, and which revolved around a critical political economy that effectively turned Marx into a left-wing Ricardo. Marx's critique of political economy and its concerns regarding capitalist society's fetishistic naturalisation of its own oppressive economic system were thus occluded to some degree. It is this occlusion that the new readings of Marx referred to above endeavour to resolve: for just as Marx identified an implicit, 'esoteric' content within the published, 'exoteric' writings of Adam Smith, so too is it possible, according to this rationale, to identify an esoteric and an exoteric Marx, and to attempt the extraction of the former from the latter: to draw out, in other words, Marx's critique of political economy from his critical political economy.

If Marx's *Capital* is read as a *critical* political economy, one could take it as an account of how social production might be conducted more equitably. On such a reading, once the extraction of surplus-value is understood, a more palatable system could be devised, and the capitalist class rendered obsolete. The proletariat would simply need to appropriate the existing means of production, rectify the flaws of the existing system, and thereby inaugurate a fairer organisation of labour.[33] Labour, in effect, would then be something that needed to

---

33   The Endnotes group put this particularly clearly. If the chief problem with capitalism is exploitation, and if exploitation is 'a matter of the deduction of a portion of the social product by a parasitic ruling class then socialism does not have to substantially alter the form of commodity production; but may simply take it over, eliminate the parasitic class, and distribute the product equitably' (Endnotes 2010, p. 72). Elbe presents a similar characterisation of this traditional approach to Marxian theory. Seen from such a traditional perspective, the advent of communism will entail that 'social necessity (above all the law of value), which operates anarchically and uncontrolled in capitalism, will be, by means of Marxism as a science of the objective laws of nature and society, managed and applied according to a plan'; this, Elbe points out, is not 'the *disappearance* of capitalist

be redeemed, or saved, as its emancipation from the fetters of the capitalist class would render it a means towards establishing a better world. However, a *critique* of political economy would identify and address the presuppositions that political economy takes for granted. 'Labour' is one such presupposition: for according to the views with which we are concerned, it is not a transhistorical constant (i.e. it is not reducible to formative human activity *per se*), but is instead a very specific socio-historical phenomenon, proper to capitalist society alone. This is because labour is peculiar to a mode of production in which qualitatively distinct instances of concrete human activity only 'count' as instances of socially productive activity when they can be validated as particular units of the general universality of abstract labour, and thus as quantities of socially average labour-time. Like the commodity, capitalist labour possesses a dual aspect. It must be concrete and qualitatively particular on the one hand (this aspect of labour is analogous to the use-value dimension of the commodity); on the other, it must also be abstract and quantitatively equivalent with all other instances of labour (analogous to the commodity's exchange-value dimension). Its existence is therefore restricted to a social context in which concrete, qualitative human activity is only socially valid (i.e. treated as a unit of the general productive activity of society) when it can be recognised as a portion of a quantitatively homogenous abstraction that arises from, and which relies upon, commodity production and exchange. Labour, in consequence, is inseparable from a system that lends itself to the regulation and rationalisation of qualitatively particular activity; a system in which such activity must always be validated, in exchange, as a portion of a quantitative abstraction. It is, therefore, wedded to a system in which human subjects are reduced to the level of mere objects, insofar as their actions and interactions are dictated by the economic objects that they create, and in which those objects shape social activity as if they were themselves subjects. It follows that this inversion of subject and object cannot be rectified through the *emancipation* of labour. Instead,

---

form-determinations,' but rather 'their *alternative use*' (Elbe 2013, italics in the original). Postone makes much the same observation. In his view, a planned economy based on the value of abstract labour will retain the problems of capitalist society: for if 'value remains the form of [social] wealth', he writes, then 'public planning does not, in and of itself, suffice to overcome the system of abstract domination ... Public planning should not be abstractly opposed to the market, as the principle of socialism to that of capitalism' (Postone 1996, p. 127). See also Trenkle, who claims that 'Marx ... never attempted to propose a positive theory that could be in any way used as an instrument of economic policy. His concern, rather, was to demonstrate the irrationality, the inner contradictions, and hence the ultimate untenability of a society based on value' (Trenkle 1998).

that inversion results from the very nature of labour itself, which cannot be redeemed through simply shrugging off the parasite of the capitalist manager, and by instating a bureaucratic overseer in the latter's place.

Needless to say, once seen through this lens, orthodox Marxism's celebration of the dignity of labour becomes inherently problematic. So too does any political project that would set out to supersede capitalism through the programmatic liberation of labour. Workers' self-management of the workplace becomes deeply questionable, as do socialist reforms; indeed, at its cruellest, this perspective also invites a harsh judgement on the long, bitter struggles of the workers' movement.[34] Dauvé and Nesic of Troploin put this particularly clearly. In their view, 'former social movements ... failed because the labourers ... tried to liberate themselves by using the very medium of their enslavement'; in contrast, 'true emancipation would be based on the refusal of work, seen as the only effective subversion of bourgeois and bureaucratic domination alike.'[35] Therefore, whilst the various writers whose ideas we are drawing upon take different positions concerning what should replace a traditional Marxist politics, the views outlined here tend towards the following position: the proletariat cannot resolve its situation by affirming itself *qua* labour; instead, it must negate itself *qua* proletariat, together with the conditions that define it.

Broadly speaking, this is the view that has informed much of the criticism that has been directed towards the SI's allegiance to the classical workers' movement. By extension, it also informs the criticisms that have been placed against the SI's interest in workers' councils. Yet as we indicated earlier, the SI has also been praised for coming close to some of these views. Before looking further at those criticisms, we should, therefore, address their points of correspondence with the SI's own contentions. It will become apparent through doing so that the Situationists were by no means as enthusiastically affirmative about labour as some of these criticisms might lead one to assume.

---

34 Marx himself once remarked that 'instead of the *conservative* motto, "*A fair day's wage for a fair days work!*"', workers 'ought to inscribe on their banner the revolutionary watchword, "*Abolition of the wages system!*"' (Marx 2004, p. 137). In contrast, the struggle for safer working conditions, shorter hours, rights, weekends, etc., has ultimately served to make an intolerable economic system progressively more tolerable (see Jappe 1999, pp. 37–8, for comments in this vein).

35 Dauvé and Nesic 2008, p. 105.

Never Work!

The first point to make here is that Debord's theory of spectacle bears obvious and direct relation to these Marxian concerns regarding society's subordination to economic abstractions. Debord clearly saw that the domination of social life could not be resolved through simply changing the system's managers, and in this regard, his views constitute an extension of some of Marx's own. Throughout *Capital*, Marx indicates, very clearly, that both the worker and the capitalist play out social roles that suit the requirements of capital. The capitalist, he writes, acts as the representative of capital, and is thus 'just as enslaved by the relationships of capitalism as is his opposite pole, the worker, albeit in a quite different manner'.[36] For Debord, this same dynamic was at play within the so-called workers' states. *The Society of the Spectacle* contends that in such societies, the continued operation of capital simply engendered different social actors, who were required to play analogous roles to the worker and the capitalist within Western societies. As he put it in a letter of 1963: 'Russian "socialism" fundamentally reproduces the modes of being and the interests' of capitalist society 'under a rival variant.'[37] In fostering the emergence of capitalism, 'the bourgeoisie created a power so autonomous that it is capable of maintaining itself even without a bourgeoisie'.[38] Thus, 'behind the bureaucracy', one finds 'the continuation of the power of the economy and the salvaging of the essence of the market society commodity labour'.[39]

It is important to note that Debord's views in this regard owe a great deal to his brief association with Socialisme ou Barbarie, and not to any direct engagement with the readings of Marx described above. Such an engagement was certainly possible: the *Neue Marx-Lektüre* began to emerge in Germany in the mid-1960s, when Debord was developing his mature thought. However, he does not seem to have read this material, and in fact struggled to read German. Instead, he seems to have arrived at these views simply through the evolution of his concept of spectacle. This is because the latter concept entails, as we have stressed, the critical rejection of *any* instance wherein human subjects become subordinated to their own social power.

This is why the theory of spectacle chimes so neatly with contemporary scepticism towards the classical project of attaining communism via the eman-

---

36 Marx 1990, p. 990.
37 Debord 2001a, p. 226.
38 Debord 1995, pp. 72–3, translation altered; 2006b, p. 808.
39 Debord 1995, p. 72, translation altered; 2006b, p. 808.

cipation and affirmation of labour. The concept of spectacle was viewed as encapsulating the revolutionary problematic of Debord and the SI's historical juncture, and amounted to a new, corrected perspective on the possibilities that had been glimpsed in the past. From this new perspective, which had been engendered by the *failings* of the past, it could now be seen that it was 'no longer' possible to 'combat alienation by means of alienated forms of struggle';[40] and because, following this logic, alienated labour could hardly provide a path towards a non-alienated future, firmer ground was sought in the *refusal* of work. In 1966, the SI thus indicated that in order to transform the totality of society, labour must be destroyed:

> Since the struggle between the system and the new proletariat can only be in terms of the totality, the future revolutionary movement must abolish anything within itself that tends to reproduce the alienation produced by the commodity system – i.e. the system dominated by commodified labour. It must be a living critique of that system, a negation embodying all the elements necessary for its supersession.[41]

The SI, therefore, were by no means as close to traditional Marxism as some might lead us to believe.

The manner in which Debord lived his own life is also relevant here (after all, he declared his life to be 'exemplary').[42] In 1953, he painted the motto 'NEVER WORK' on the walls of the Rue de Seine. This slogan, which he had adapted from Rimbaud,[43] was clearly a significant statement: in 1963, a photograph of this graffito appeared in the eighth issue of *Internationale situationniste*,[44] and the image was also used in the second edition of his autobiographical *Panegyric*. It was also a motto that Debord endeavoured to live by.

Debord never had a job. Granted, and as he acknowledged, 'never to have given more than very slight attention to questions of money, and absolutely none to the ambition of holding down some brilliant post in society, is a trait so rare to my contemporaries that some will no doubt consider it incredible',[45] but

---

40   Debord 1995, p. 89; 2006b, p. 819.
41   SI 2006, pp. 425–6; 1966.
42   See for example Debord 2004b, p. 6; 2006, p. 1658.
43   In 'A Season in Hell', Rimbaud writes: 'Never show me jewels, for I'd grovel and writhe on the floor. I want my wealth to be covered in blood. Never shall I work ...' (Rimbaud 2004, pp. 158–9).
44   See Debord 2001a, pp. 244–7.
45   Debord 2004b, pp. 12–13; 2006b, p. 1662.

it does, nonetheless, appear to be true. Having felt 'neither the obligation nor the desire' to devote himself 'to any kind of work, neither salaried nor any other kind of lucrative activity',[46] he managed to avoid work for an entire lifetime. He appears to have been quite penniless at times,[47] but he was able to survive on patronage,[48] royalties,[49] a small inheritance,[50] his abilities at poker,[51] his 'wits',[52] and, presumably, unemployment benefit on occasion. Debord also advocated the refusal of work as a means of political revolt.[53] So too did the SI in the pages of *Internationale situationniste*. For example, as early as 1963, they stated that the 'very core of the revolutionary project' is 'nothing less than the suppression of work in the usual present-day sense'.[54]

This rejection of work is certainly in keeping with the implications of the views that we outlined above. So too is Debord and the SI's reformulation of the proletariat. According to the Situationists, the 'new' revolutionary faction that had arisen within the modern era differed from the proletariat of the past. This 'new' proletariat was not an economic class in any traditional sense of that

---

46 Debord 2005, p. 142.
47 In 1964, Debord wrote to Chtcheglov stating: 'I believe that the world of money is a load of nonsense [*intégralement une connerie*]. I will never recognise in it more *value* than the truncheon of a cop ... The sad conclusion of all this: I am absolutely penniless at the moment. ... [On] many days the simple purchase of wine and cigarettes has posed dramatic problems' (Debord 2001a, pp. 297–8, italics in the original).
48 Sponsors included Gérard Lebovici, Gianfranco Sanguinetti and Michèle Bernstein (Sanguinetti 2015), and no doubt others too.
49 Debord's late work, *Des Contrats*, details the contracts for his cinematic work.
50 In *Panegyric*, Debord claims that he was 'born virtually ruined', that he did 'not expect an inheritance, and in the end ... did not receive one' (Debord 2004b, pp. 11–12; 2006b, p. 1661).
51 Debord 2006b, pp. 1790–1.
52 In an interview, Lefebvre recalled the following when asked about the SI's finances during the time of his friendship with the group (i.e. between 1960 and 1962): 'No one could figure out how they got by. One day one of my friends (someone to whom I had introduced Debord) asked him, "What do you live on?" And Guy Debord answered very proudly, "I live off my wits." [*Laughter.*] Actually, he must have had some money; I think that his family wasn't poor. His parents lived on the Côte d'Azur. I don't really think I know the answer. And also Michèle Bernstein had come up with a clever way to make money, or at least a bit of money. Or at least this is what she told me. She said she did horoscopes for horses, which were published in racing magazines. It was extremely funny' (Ross 2004, p. 268).
53 For example, in his 1979 preface to the fourth Italian edition of *The Society of the Spectacle*, Debord listed, amongst the reasons why 'the workers of Italy' constituted 'an example to their comrades in all countries', their 'absenteeism' and 'their lucid refusal of work' (Debord 1979; 2006b, p. 1463).
54 SI 2006, p. 132; 1997, p. 300.

term. Marx had described the proletariat as all those individuals who had been separated from the means of independently maintaining their own existence, and who were thus forced to work for a wage;[55] the SI, recognising that this condition now pertained to practically everyone within modern society, devised a conception of the proletariat that transcended classical class boundaries. Within a world in which the needs of survival could be met through automation, the 'new' proletariat were all those who had been separated from the means of independently shaping their own lives. This new proletariat encompassed all those who, 'regardless of variations in their degree of affluence',[56] had become obliged to live a life moulded by the distractions and behavioural tropes fostered by an increasingly obsolete economic system. The modern proletariat, therefore, was said to be composed of 'all people who have no possibility of altering the social space-time that society allots to them'.[57] Quite obviously, the latter view cannot be reduced to a traditional conception of social class. Nor could it entail an uncritical affirmation of labour. Instead, this new, effectively class-less revolutionary class would pursue nothing other than the destruction of the social relations that compose class society.

In sum, Debord and the SI placed themselves in opposition to the rule of the economy, rather than to that of its managers, and it is quite undeniable that they sought to step away from a traditional class-based analysis. Yet even so – and this has been the major bone of contention for many critics – their ideas remained intimately linked to a much more traditional view.

When describing the newly expanded proletariat, Debord and the SI, often qualified it as an aggregation of *workers* (e.g. Debord described the proletariat as 'the vast mass of workers who have lost all power over the use of their own lives').[58] The SI also stressed that workers – understood in the traditional sense of the term – would play the decisive role in the coming revolution. In consequence, there would seem to be good grounds for identifying at least some degree of tension, and perhaps even an outright contradiction, between these aspects of the SI's claims and their views concerning the rejection of labour. Inevitably, the SI's interest in workers' councils has provided a focal point for these criticisms.

---

55   Marx 1990, p. 272 and p. 874.
56   SI 2006, p. 141; 1997, p. 309.
57   SI 2006, p. 141; 1997, p. 309.
58   Debord 1995, p. 84; 2006b, p. 816.

Contradictions in the SI's Councilism?

As we saw earlier, the Endnotes group have claimed that 'the potential and all the limits of the SI were contained in the tension between their call to "abolish work" and their central slogan, "all power to the workers' councils"'.[59] According to Endnotes, this amounts to a contradiction between the form and content of revolution. They describe this as follows: 'On the one hand, the content of the revolution [for the SI] was to involve a radical questioning of work itself (and not merely its organisation)'; and yet 'on the other hand the form of this revolution was to be workers taking over their work places and running them democratically.'[60]

Endnotes' views are at least partially informed by their debts to the French Théorie Communiste group, who have also advanced related criticisms of the Situationist International. Théorie Communiste employ a historical periodisation of communist struggle which Endnotes have, in part, adopted, according to which the conditions of struggle prior to the 1970s are different from those proper to our contemporary period. According to this view, the working class of the past was not fully integrated into the operation of capital, and stood outside the latter to some degree. Within that past context, the negation of capital could indeed be appropriately linked to the affirmation of the proletariat's own identity within that class relation. Today, however, any such affirmation has become inherently problematic. Since the 1970s, capitalist society has been marked by the 'real subsumption'[61] of all social life under the dictates of capital. The inadequacy of all forms of 'workerist' politics, therefore, has been forcibly revealed, and attempts at workers' self-management – as exemplified by the SI's call for workers' councils – could be seen to have become an entirely untenable means of destroying the capital-labour relation.[62] For Théorie Communiste, it has become crucial to move beyond what they refer to as 'programmatism': the view that communism can be made through a 'programme' of progressively liberating labour from its current integument within the extant class relation. The SI have thus been described as having pushed programmatism to its very limits by articulating decidedly *anti*-programmatist demands (the abolition of labour and the transformation of everyday life) whilst also adopting a programmatist

---

59 Endnotes 2008, p. 7.
60 Ibid.
61 See Marx 1990, pp. 1019–25.
62 This is held to be true for both 'factory councils on the one hand and central planning by the workers' state on the other' (Endnotes 2008, p. 213).

politics (the advocacy of workers' councils).[63] The SI are therefore praised for having led programmatisim to 'its point of explosion',[64] and yet also criticised for having been unable to fully extricate themselves from that approach.

Gilles Dauvé, whom we quoted earlier, has also criticised the SI's interest in workers' councils. His views are motivated by his contention that Debord and the SI did not fully understand the nature of capitalism. For Dauvé, Debord's theory of spectacle can only grasp the symptoms of capital's operation, and not the latter's concrete causes.[65] He recognises that Debord's theory describes a society that has lost control of its own economy, and that it also stresses that the functioning of that economy engenders isolation and alienation; yet he contends that Debord had little purchase on the reasons why this takes place. We will adopt a rather similar line of critique in the following chapter, although we will do so by somewhat different means. This is because Dauvé's critique stems from what appears to be a rather narrower conception of spectacle than that which we have sought to develop in this book. Dauvé seems to associate spectacle with the fads, fashions, ideologies and roles to which capitalist society gives rise. He thus understands spectacle chiefly as an effect, rather than as a cause, and is thereby able to contend that Debord's attempt to define society under the rubric of spectacle involved addressing a *part* of society (capital's ideological and affective repercussions) as if it were the *whole* of society (the totality of capitalist social relations).[66] This informs his critique of the SI's councilism. He recognises, quite correctly, that the SI saw the councils as a means of resolving spectacular separation through fostering direct interaction and participation. Yet, for Dauvé, the SI did not fully understand that labour forms the basis of social atomisation. Their assumption that workers' councils could afford a site for the resolution of that problem therefore reflects their limited grasp on the problem itself.

---

63   This accords with their critique of the ultra-left. According to Théorie Communiste's Roland Simon: 'We can call the ultra-left all practice, organisation and theory which poses the revolution as the affirmation of the proletariat', and which considers this affirmation 'as a critique and negation of everything which define the proletariat in its implication with capital and the state' (Riff Raff 2006). For Théorie Communiste, the ultra-left is thus the extreme point of programmatism: a point that opens onto the contemporary problematic of communisation (the creation of communism through the negation of existing class relations, rather than through the affirmation of one pole within that relation). The SI, for Simon, exemplify this tension.
64   Riff Raff 2006.
65   See, in particular, Dauvé 1979.
66   Dauvé 2000.

As these examples may serve to show, a general trend has emerged, within contemporary critical engagements with the SI, towards locating the Situationists upon the cusp of a break with an old, defunct conception of political contestation. Seen in this manner, the SI stand with one foot planted in the politics of the traditional workers' movement, and with another in the new theoretical concerns proper to capital's contemporary subsumption of all social life. The Situationists can then be celebrated for having had the foresight to grasp some of the issues proper to contemporary contestation, and criticised for having failed to fully break away from the politics of the past. Yet as indicated above, it is possible to offer a rebuttal to some aspects of these criticisms.

Making the Implicit Explicit

We saw at the start of this chapter that the SI's pursuit of a new path towards communism was not envisaged as a radical break with the struggles of the past, but rather as a further development of a much older project. This development, moreover, was cast as revealing the hidden core of prior revolutionary demands. This informs the following contention, which is absolutely central to Debord's theory of spectacle. In his view, every effort to break away from capitalist society has had, at its core, an implicit drive – however inarticulate and misrecognised it may have been – towards the supersession of that condition of alienation, and thus towards the conscious command of lived historical time. This is why he claims, in *The Society of the Spectacle*, that 'in the demand to *live* the historical time that it creates, the proletariat finds the simple unforgettable core of its revolutionary project'.[67] Contemporary insurrection would reveal and fulfil the implicit demands of the past.

This means that the classical nineteenth-century proletariat's demand for control over the means of social production must have contained, as its implicit, buried and only partially recognised content, the modern proletariat's demand for control over the means of shaping social life. To some extent, this follows from Marx's own classical definition of the proletariat:[68] after all, the separation of individuals from the capacity to autonomously provide their own means of subsistence (Marx) must entail their separation from the means of autonomously shaping and directing that existence (Debord). If one cannot

---

67 Debord 1995, p. 106; 2006b, p. 829.
68 As Fredy Perlman puts it, via a discussion of Marx: 'It is precisely the power to shape his circumstances that the labourer sells to the capitalist' (Perlman in Rubin 1972, p. xxiv).

freely maintain one's own existence, then one is hardly in a position to self-determinately shape and determine it. In effect, Debord and the SI held that the changing nature of modern society had brought that implicit content to the fore. The growth of capitalism had rectified the *material* poverty of the past to some degree, but through doing so, it had also caused the *existential* poverty that was implicit within the poverty of the past to stand clearly revealed (as Vaneigem put it in 1967, whilst quoting a Ford worker: 'Since 1936 I have been fighting for better wages. My father before me fought for better wages. I've got a TV, a fridge and a Cortina. If you ask me it's been a dog's life from start to finish').[69] In other words, that which had been *implicit* had become increasingly *explicit*.

This should serve to clarify the SI's ability to posit new, modern demands whilst remaining aligned to the classical workers' movement. However, it does not entirely resolve the apparent contradiction that we discussed earlier. If the new conditions of struggle had engendered new demands, concerns and revolutionary actors, and if the 'new' proletariat had broken the barriers of the classical class divide, why were the SI so preoccupied with workers? There are two answers to that question, the first of which is as follows.

We saw earlier that for Marx, both the worker and the capitalist are obliged, within capitalist society, to play out roles that suit the continued accumulation of capital. Both, according to Marx, are 'just as enslaved by the relationships of capitalism' as each other. However, Marx also states in *Capital* that 'the worker stands on a higher plane than the capitalist', because 'the latter has his roots in the process of alienation and finds absolute satisfaction in it', whereas 'the worker is a victim who confronts it as a rebel'.[70] Therefore, whilst both perform social roles that suit the requirements of capital, the former is a proponent of the latter, whereas the latter is led to become its opponent. Once again, the SI's ideas are very similar. In their view, everyone is as dominated by capital as everyone else: all social actors within modern society are as alienated as each other, but their experience of this alienation and their relation to it differs. Thus, whilst a generalised awareness of society's total subordination to the economy was held to be spreading throughout the fabric of society, and to be crossing traditional class divides, the SI still recognised that the workers' conditions of existence were worse than those of other members of society, and that workers may, therefore, be at the forefront of a demand for social change.

---

69 Vaneigem 2003, p. 69.
70 Marx 1990, p. 990.

The second answer to the question is much more simple and pragmatic, as it concerns basic logistics. Without workers taking control of society's means of production, transportation, communication, etc., any fledgling revolutionary society would simply fall apart. Debord phrased this explicitly in a letter from 1969, in which he provided notes for an article on workers' councils in *Internationale situationniste*. 'Why the decisive importance of the workers?' he asks in the letter. His answer is simple: 'the workers are the *central* force that can stop the functioning of society', and 'the *indispensable* force to replace it on other bases'.[71]

The reference to replacing the current operation of society on 'other bases' is, of course, crucial, because it indicates that the SI had absolutely *no* desire to institute a society of self-managed labour. This point does, however, seem to be missed by the SI's critics. Dauvé, for example, complains that the Situationists 'failed to see that autonomous self-management of factory struggles can only be a means, never a goal in itself'.[72] Yet the SI explained very clearly that their aim was *not* to replace the capitalist with the council, thereby leaving the existing system relatively untouched. Instead, their intention was to allow the councils to operate as a starting point for the destruction of *all* capitalist social relations.

Form and Content

This then means that the SI's vision of council communism was quite different from that of councilism's 1920s heyday. That said, they certainly saw the latter as one of the high-points of the struggles of the past. In fact, Debord seems to have viewed the councilism of the 1920s as part of the great, lost revolutionary potential of that era, and indeed as an aspect of that potential which had re-emerged, in clarified form, within the SI's own period. From this purportedly higher historical perspective, the Situationists could look back on the councils of the past and acknowledge both their significance and their limits. In *The Society of the Spectacle*, Debord thus praises the councils of the past in the following manner:

> The appearance of workers' councils during the first quarter of this century was the highest reality of the proletarian movement, but this reality has gone unnoticed, or else been presented in travestied form, because it

---

71 Debord 2004a, p. 105, emphasis in the original.
72 Dauvé 2000.

disappeared along with the rest of the movement that the whole historical experience of the time belied and eliminated. From the [new, contemporary] standpoint of the renewal of the proletariat's critical enterprise, however, the councils may be seen in their true light [*ce résultat revient*] as the only undefeated point of the defeated movement. Historical consciousness, which knows that this is its only milieu of existence, can now see that the councils are no longer at the periphery of a movement that is subsiding, but rather at the centre of a movement that is rising.[73]

This did not mean an outright, uncritical return to the councilism of the 1920s. The councils of the past were seen to provide no more than a 'clear outline'[74] of the organisational modes required to supersede capitalist society. Indeed, in Debord's view, the 'actual existence' of revolutionary councils 'has as yet been no more than a brief sketch'[75] of those organisational forms. The SI's councils would not provide a new, more equitable platform for commodity exchange.[76] In a letter of 1972, Debord explicitly states that the 'self-management' afforded by councilist organisation 'obviously must not be a question of the self-management of the existing productive process'.[77] Noting 'the necessity of abolishing work', he adds that the councils of the past should not be seen as a template for those of the present, because they constitute only 'a weak and primitive image' of 'the route of necessary methods for rebuilding the world'.[78] The SI cannot, therefore, be charged with uncritically championing the autonomous self-management of the existing system of production. Their interest in workers' councils was not due to a desire for a syndicalist federation of workplaces that would exchange commodities with one another. Instead, they were interested in councilist forms of social organisation *per se*, because such modes of organisation offered a means of reducing representation and hierarchy to a bare minimum. Such forms of organisation, therefore, afforded a way of uniting the form and content of struggle: of thus finding an organisational *form* for the rejection of spectacle that would be adequate to the *content* of that same rejection.

---

73 Debord 1995, pp. 87–8, translation altered; 2006b, p. 818.
74 Debord 1995, p. 86; 2006b, p. 817.
75 Debord 1995, p. 86, translation altered; 2006b, p. 817.
76 This pertains to Debord's rejection of syndicalism, which he described as a 'false solution' (Debord 2004a, p. 105). In his view, 'today, syndicalism has as its principal function the integration of workers into society' (Debord 2001a, p. 226).
77 Debord 2004a, p. 617.
78 Ibid.

As we saw in Part One, the problematic of spectacle pertains to all instances of separated social power, and thereby to all forms of separation between social actors and their own collective agency. It thus pre-dates modern capitalism, although the latter, through its generalisation of alienation, was held to have brought that problematic to a recognisable and resolvable extreme.[79] As we also argued in Part One, it follows from this that whilst the demise of capitalist society might well afford the end of the *society* of the spectacle, it would not erase the *problematic* of spectacle, which is liable to recur in any instance of separated social power. This is why Debord states, as we saw above, that it was 'no longer' possible, following the recognition of this problematic, to 'combat alienation by means of alienated forms of struggle'.[80] The nature of modern society, in other words, and indeed the failures of the past, demanded that if spectacle was to be avoided, *all* forms of separated power needed to be abolished, including those that purported to promise a way out of capitalist society.[81] As the Situationists put it in 1966: 'self-management must be both the means and the end of ... struggle. It is not only what is at stake in the struggle, but also its adequate form'.[82]

This then brings us back to the Hegelian notion of subject-object unity discussed towards the outset of this chapter. Because councilist forms of organisation could afford a means of overcoming instances of spectacle, they were also seen as a social condition in which subject could be united with object. This point can be illustrated by noting the SI's distance from Lukács's own, somewhat similar views. For the Lukács of *History and Class Consciousness*, the locus of subject-object unity is the Party. The 'Party', he claimed, 'is assigned the sublime role of *bearer of the class consciousness of the proletariat*'.[83] The Situationists, on the other hand, saw any such deification of representative political power as dangerous in the extreme, and rejected 'any conception of the party

---

79 Hence Debord's claim, also discussed in Chapter 2, that whilst the modern spectacle's 'basis' lay in antiquity, it 'appeared under its completed form around 1914–1920' (Debord 2004a, pp. 455–6). Vaneigem held similar views (Vaneigem 1994, p. 146).
80 Debord 1995, p. 89; 2006b, p. 819.
81 As Clark and Nicholson-Smith put it: 'We shall never begin to understand Debord's hostility to the concept "representation," for instance, unless we realise that for him the word always carried a Leninist aftertaste. The spectacle is repugnant because it threatens to generalise, as it were, the Party's claim to be the representative of the working class' (Clark and Nicholson Smith 2004, p. 479).
82 SI 2006, p. 210; 1997, p. 432.
83 Lukács 1971, p. 41.

insofar as it would represent the working class'.[84] Thus, whilst they praised Lukács for recognising that the supersession of separation required specific social conditions, they utterly rejected his prescriptions:

> As Lukács correctly showed, revolutionary organisation is this necessary mediation between theory and practice, between man and history, between the mass of workers and the proletariat constituted as a class. (Lukács' mistake was to believe that the Bolshevik Party fulfilled this role.)[85]

For Debord and the SI, councilist organisation would afford a far more adequate means of uniting subject and object, as it entailed that the spectacular separation of subject from object could be reduced to a minimum. Individuals would be able to interact directly, without the mediation of a separated body of power, and could, in consequence, shape and determine their collective affairs directly. It is certainly apparent that Debord had a notion of subject-object unity in mind when discussing the councils in *The Society of the Spectacle*. For example, he writes as follows:

> In the power of the councils, which must internationally supplant all other power, the proletarian movement is its own product, and this product is the producer himself. He is to himself his own goal. Only in this context is the spectacular negation of life negated in its turn.[86]

In short, the real core of the SI's councilism lies in their view that the councils would offer a form of organisation in which separated power and political representation could be reduced to an absolute minimum. The councils would not be an end in themselves, but they would certainly afford a means of ensuring that a fledgling revolutionary society did not betray its own principles.

The latter point can be placed in useful tension with Endnotes' claim, quoted earlier in this chapter, that the SI's politics involved a contradiction between the form and content of revolution. For the SI, such a contradiction between form and content was precisely what councilist organisation could *avoid*. Rather than perpetuating alienation, the councils would instead offer a basis for opposition to 'the whole *ensemble* of alienations',[87] whilst also serving as a start-

---

84 Debord 2003a, p. 173.
85 SI 2006, p. 426; 1966.
86 Debord 1995, p. 87; 2006b, p. 818.
87 SI 2006, p. 364; 1997, p. 643.

ing point for 'the liquidation of the world of the commodity'.[88] The SI's councils, therefore, would not simply involve workers managing the existing system of production, as some of the criticisms referred to above seem to imply. Instead, they would serve as a fundamental, initial step in the process of destroying capitalist social relations. As the SI put it in 1967:

> [A councilist] organisation sees the beginning and end of its program in the complete decolonisation of everyday life. It thus aims not at the masses' self-management of the *existing* world, but at its uninterrupted transformation. It embodies the radical critique of *political economy*, the supersession of the commodity and of wage labour [*et du salariat*]. Such an organisation refuses to reproduce within itself any of the hierarchical conditions of the dominant world.[89]

Bridging the Past and the Present

Broadly speaking, the criticisms that we have addressed contend that Debord and the SI can be praised for their proximity to readings of Marx that cast labour as a central problem within capitalist society, rather than as a potential solution to the latter's ills. This has afforded readings of the SI's legacy that cast the group as bridging a position between the politics of the past, and those of the present. For these critics, the SI's sympathies for the classical workers' movement, and their enthusiasm for councils, entail that Debord and the SI remain too close to the Marxism of the past. Seen in this light, the SI have been figured as an important historical marker, signifying the boundary between an older, outdated politics, and the emergence of a new approach, more suited to present concerns.

The arguments that we have advanced in this chapter have, however, attempted to show that the SI may not be quite as close to the politics of the past as sometimes seems to be assumed. The SI's somewhat intuitive, but nonetheless pertinent conception of the value-form; their conception of the new, class-less proletariat; their nuanced views on workers' councils: all of these issues should inflect any such criticisms, and indeed undermine them to some degree, insofar as they entail that their views may in fact be rather closer to more current Marxian concerns than might be imagined.

---

88 SI 2006 p. 365; 1997, p. 643.
89 SI 2006, p. 285; 1997, p. 551, emphasis in the original.

However, Debord and the SI's theoretical work cannot be absolved from criticism altogether. In the remaining chapters of Part Four, we will go on to introduce and develop a rather different line of critique: one that also bears upon the status of labour in their work, but which does so in a rather different manner.

CHAPTER 10

'I am Nothing and I Should be Everything'

Moving beyond the Surface

In the previous chapter, we considered some of the contemporary criticisms that have been levelled against Debord and the SI. These criticisms tend to involve evaluating their work in terms of the degree to which it accords with, or departs from, aspects of contemporary Marxian thought. We will begin here by advancing a rather different line of critique: one that certainly bears an important relation to those described in Chapter 9, but which also differs in substance. Having contended in that chapter that the SI were not as tied to the classical affirmation of labour as some might think, we will now argue that they were not, in fact, quite as close to Marx as one might wish. This is because their desire to reject labour fostered a degree of inattention towards its importance.

That claim requires clarification. Simply put, there is an obvious distinction between a *political rejection* of labour, and a *theoretical neglect* of labour. There is a difference, in other words, between the view that labour might be the fundamental problem with capitalist society (insofar as it lies at the basis of the capitalist subordination of lived activity to the dictates of value), and the idea that labour is actually of little importance to a theoretical study of capitalist society. If labour is fundamentally problematic, one can hardly disregard it. Debord and the SI's theoretical work, however, tends to blur the two positions together, sliding from the conviction that labour must be abolished, to a perspective from which it is relatively neglected. Yet if one operates within a broadly Marxian framework, according to which capital stems from social labour – and despite their idiosyncrasies, Debord and the SI were operating within just such a framework – then a theoretical neglect of capital's roots in labour is likely to result in a critique of capital that pays insufficient attention to the latter's social bases.

This is not a particularly new claim. In fact, there is a long history of similar complaints being levelled against the SI, some of which were expressed during their own era, and some of which received replies. For example, in 1966, and whilst responding to the charge that they had neglected the importance of labour, the SI wrote as follows:

> [According to] *Le Monde Libertaire* of December 1964: 'The SI are incontestably on point concerning the revolutionary critique of everyday life.

One domain, however, which is far from having lost its importance, escapes them: labour.' However, we believe that we have scarcely treated any other problem than that of labour in our epoch: its conditions, its contradictions, and its results.[1]

Accused of having neglected labour, the SI responded by stating that they had hardly looked at anything else. This response was informed by the following views.

Capitalism, for Debord and the SI, had become obsolete, and so too had the labour that supported it, due to the technical possibilities afforded by modern automation. Labour was thus no longer central to a revolutionary politics, and had instead become an aspect of the old world that needed to be sloughed off. At the same time, society was viewed as having become ruled by capital: so much so that it was now no longer just the activity that was conducted in the work place that served to support capitalism, but rather the conduct of social life as a whole. This view afforded a position from which Debord and the SI could contend that *all* social activity had become a kind of 'labour', or at least now operated in accordance with the latter's logic, insofar as all social activity now served to support and serve this economic system.[2] At the same time, the SI argued that this condition had foregrounded the real stakes of the new, modern revolution, which would demand not the emancipation of work from capitalist exploitation, but rather the conscious command of lived experience.

The difficulty, of course, is that if 'labour' becomes tantamount to activity in general, then the concept of labour loses its specificity, because it becomes equivalent to a very broad notion of biopolitically regulated social activity. This is a problem, because such a position sits very uncomfortably alongside Debord and the SI's apparent retention of the classical view that capitalist value stems from labour. If capital derives from labour – and if Debord and the SI's theoretical work does not really address labour, or blurs it with life as a whole – then their account of modern capitalist society can seem somewhat ill-equipped to deal with capitalism's social bases. Needless to say, this poses obvious difficulties for their work's anti-capitalist ambitions.

It would be a mistake to say that labour was completely ignored in their work. In fact, they indicated throughout that labour is a foundational and formative part of modern society. For example, in an article published in 1964,

---

[1] SI 1997, p. 479.
[2] See also Jappe 1999, pp. 98–9.

they stated that 'labour shapes the totality of products and of social life in its own image.'[3] The fact remains, however, that Debord's theoretical focus, and indeed that of the SI as a whole, remained fixed primarily upon the subjective, affective, everyday effects of capital's operation, rather than upon the latter's objective causes.

This focus differs from Marx's own. Marx's method in *Capital* is to treat society as an interrelated social totality, and to thereby derive its surface effects from its internal relations.[4] His analysis breaks society down into its most fundamental component concepts; his mode of exposition then reassembles those concepts, moving from the abstract and the simple, to the progressively more complex. He thus begins with the basic structure of the commodity in chapter one of *Capital*'s first volume, and then gradually moves ever closer to what he refers to in volume three as the manner in which 'the configurations of capital ... appear on the surface of society'.[5] There is, however, a sense in which Debord's analysis, in texts such as *The Society of the Spectacle*, comes close to taking the opposite route. Instead of arriving at a position that shows how capital's surface appearances derive from their objective bases, Debord's theory borders on blurring those bases with the appearances to which they give rise, and thereby comes close to reducing the concrete to the abstract. Without doubt, this is closely connected to one of the chief virtues of Debord's work: as we have indicated, he was clearly sensitive to the sense in which concrete reality, within capitalism, becomes dominated by the abstractions of value. The problem remains, however, that his analysis is somewhat hampered in terms of its ability to show how and why these abstractions operate in this manner, and in what way they bind upon social reality. This is because in defining society under the rubric of spectacle, Debord treats capitalist society primarily in terms of its subjective effects, rather than in terms of its objective operation.

As we have argued throughout this book, Debord's account of modern society is best understood as a description of a society that has become separated from its own history. It certainly discusses the concrete realities of capitalist society, and it also makes reference to the mass media and visual-cultural forms that Debord is commonly assumed to be fixated upon: issues that correspond, respectively, to the second and first 'levels' of spectacle that we discussed in Chapter 1. Yet when outlining those dimensions of Debord's concept in that chapter, we also pointed out that at its core, there lies a fundamental concern

---

3 SI 2006, p. 182; 1997, p. 391.
4 Marx 1973b, p. 100.
5 Marx 1991, p. 117.

with the historical and existential predicament posed by modern capitalism. In this deepest and most important sense, the concept of spectacle is chiefly oriented towards the subjective and affective *results* of capitalism's domination of lived experience – alienation and the denigration of lived time – rather than capitalism's root *causes*.

These contentions will be discussed at greater length in Chapter 11, where we will also make some proposals towards their possible resolution. The aim of the discussions that follow is simply to demonstrate the grounds for this line of critique, and to thereby lay a basis for its further development. To that end, we will attempt to evidence and illustrate the somewhat problematic relation to Marxian labour theory that has been outlined here. These discussions will be presented in two parts.

The first part of the chapter will focus on Debord's understanding of his relationship to Marx. It will look at the faults that Debord found in Marx's work, and at the manner in which he and the SI sought to go beyond them. These issues centre round Debord's contention that Marx's mature work inadvertently laid the ground for the Marxist tradition's tendency towards economic determinism. Our primary claim here will be that Debord's antipathy towards economic determinism led him to adopt a somewhat sceptical attitude towards a theoretical focus on the mechanics of the capitalist economy, and that this informed his departure from classical Marxism's focus on labour.

The second part of the chapter will then look at the connections that can be drawn between Debord and the SI's 'new' proletariat and their views concerning spectacular alienation. As we will see, these views hinge upon Debord's use of Marx's account of the commodity-form. The point that we will try to introduce here is that this use of Marx's conception of the commodity involves taking a degree of liberty with Marx's claims, and thereby engenders some of the difficulties that we have just described.

We begin, then, with a discussion of Debord's relation to Marx.

1) 'The First Act of the End of Pre-history'

Debord and Marx's Capital

On the 21st of March 1968, *The Times Literary Supplement* reviewed Debord's *The Society of the Spectacle* and Vaneigem's *The Revolution of Everyday Life*. Admitting that 'under the dense Hegelian wrappings with which they muffle their pages several interesting ideas are lurking', the reviewer made the following analogy: 'M. Debord and M. Vaneigem have brought out their long-awaited major texts: the *Capital* and *What Is to Be Done?*, as it were, of the new movement.'[6] Comparisons such as these remain common to this day, and were cheerfully endorsed by the SI themselves. In 1964, and on the centenary of the formation of the International Workingmen's Association (the First International), the SI presented themselves as the latter's direct successors.[7] In 1969, they made the following, explicit allusion:

> It is known that Eisenstein wanted to make a film of *Capital*. Considering his formal conceptions and political submissiveness, it can be doubted if his film would have been faithful to Marx's text. But for our part, we are confident that we can do better. For example, as soon as it becomes possible Guy Debord will himself make a cinematic adaptation of *The Society of the Spectacle* that will certainly not fall short of that book.[8]

That film was eventually made in 1973, and it was followed in 1975 by another: Debord's *Refutation of All the Judgements, Laudatory as Well as Hostile, Passed up to Now on the Film 'The Society of the Spectacle'*. In the script to that film, Debord claimed that 'there have not been three books of social critique of such importance [as *The Society of the Spectacle*] in the last hundred years'.[9] The intended implication, of course, is that the only two truly important books were his own, and Marx's *Capital*. It would be a mistake to push this point too far, given that many of these allusions were humorous, but behind the irony there is, nonetheless, a sense in which Debord really did see his own and the SI's efforts as a direct continuation of those of his predecessors. Indeed, and as we saw earlier, the SI were quite explicit in their desire to return to and re-conceive the revolutionary demands of the previous century. They sought to reconsider and re-formulate those demands on the basis of the new, 'higher' historical perspective that had been afforded by the SI's twentieth-century context.[10]

---

6   Quoted by Knabb in SI 2006, p. 501.
7   A tract produced in celebration of that centenary featured a photograph of Marx with an added speech bubble: 'On 28th September 1964 it will be exactly one hundred years since we started the Situationist International. It's really going to get going now!' (Gray 1998, p. 118).
8   SI 2006, p. 379; 1997, p. 673.
9   Debord 2003, p. 127; 2006b, p. 1310.
10 This should be tempered by noting that Debord and the SI recognised their own inevitable historical location and limitation. In his 'Theses on the Situationist International and its Time', Debord wrote: 'Whoever helps the present age to discover its potential is [not] ... shielded from this age's defects' (SI 2003, p. 72; Debord 2006b, p. 1133).

Such ambitions are, of course, predicated upon the view that Marx was right in some fundamental sense, but that his ideas, like those of Hegel before him, were both limited and flawed as a result of the historical context in which he operated. This can be illustrated by way of an analogy. When concluding the preface to the first edition of *Capital*, Marx wrote as follows.

> I welcome every opinion based on scientific criticism. As to the prejudices of so-called public opinion, to which I have never made concessions, now, as ever, my maxim is that of the great Florentine: '*Segui il tuo corso, e lascia dir le genti.* [Follow your own course, and let the people talk]'[11]

Marx is quoting Dante's *Divine Comedy*. At this point in Dante's narrative, he and Virgil are about to begin their climb up Mount Purgatory. At the base of the mountain, they encounter the souls of the 'late repentant': individuals who only recanted their sins at the end of their lives, and who are punished for this indolence with a delay in their own ascent. When Dante pauses to listen to them, Virgil scolds him, and reminds him of the need to strive ever upwards.[12] Marx's 'maxim' is thus intended to signal the need to ignore the distracting chatter of those who would delay one's efforts. If, however, we read this whilst also noting one of the primary themes of the *Divine Comedy*, we can find a further point of significance: one that concerns Debord's conception of his own position, relative to that of Marx, on a path that would lead up and out of capitalist purgation.

At each stage of the *Divine Comedy*, Dante, as the poem's protagonist, reacts to the scenes and individuals with which he is confronted in a manner that mirrors the nature of the circle that he passes through. Each soul in the afterlife is only able to experience that which God has appointed for them, and in consequence, Dante, when he encounters these souls, reacts with anger, passion, and so on, according to their sins and station within the divine hierarchy.[13] At this stage in his journey, Dante's dawdling at the foot of the mountain reflects the idle souls' preoccupation with the worldly and the trivial. If we bear this in mind, we could read Marx's further literary flourishes in this preface – flourishes that are largely given over to the 'iron necessity' of the 'natural laws of cap-

---

11 Marx 1990, p. 93.
12 Alighieri, 1985, p. 49.
13 '... the soul [in the afterlife] is fixed eternally in that which it has chosen ... Therefore the reaction it calls forth in Dante can be no more than the reflection of what it has in itself' (Sayers in Alighieri 2001, p. 50).

italist production'[14] – with a certain degree of irony: for just as Dante reflects the indolence of the idle souls, so too, according to Debord, does Marx's emphasis on economic 'law' reflect the limitations of his own historical moment.

Debord's antipathy to any such focus on the 'iron necessity' of economic law is one with his rejection of 'economism' (the reduction of all social and historical phenomena to economic determinants). This antipathy is hardly surprising, given that economic determinism, in his view, amounts to the fetishistic transposition of human agency onto the mechanics of the economy. Within modern society, human subjects may indeed be ruled by their own estranged economy, and history may thus be shaped 'by the products of men's hands'[15] rather than by 'men' themselves. An economic determinist perspective, however, effectively naturalises that state of affairs, as it treats the economy's mastery over human history as an inevitable, natural condition. According to *The Society of the Spectacle*, Marx himself can be charged with having provided 'intellectual foundations for the illusions of economism',[16] and with having thus laid the ground for the Marxist tradition's subsequent proximity to, and occasional immersion within, those same economic-determinist 'illusions'.

This is not to say that Debord went so far as to reduce Marx's work to economism. Indeed, he stressed that for Marx, 'it is the *struggle* – and by no means [economic] *law* – that has to be understood.'[17] Yet Debord also seems to have held that Marx's early, existential-humanist insights into the nature and significance of history and struggle ultimately came to be distorted by a later, misguided attempt to validate revolutionary theory as 'science' (or at least as *Wissenschaft*). In this regard – and to keep with the illustration above – Marx's 'upward' progress was hampered by his adoption of a perspective that reflected the nature of his era.

Once again, this bears relation to the limitations and insights that Debord accorded to Hegelian philosophy. As we have seen already, Debord credited Hegel with having glimpsed the need for subject-object unity, but criticised him for having fallen short of realising that unity in praxis. Hegel had situated it within what Marx and Engels described as the 'misty realm of philosophical fantasy',[18] for rather than identifying thought with action in the direct construction of the future, Hegel, according to Debord, had adopted a contemplative, philosophical perspective, oriented towards a supposedly completed past.

---

14   Marx 1990, p. 91.
15   Marx 1990, p. 165.
16   Debord 1995, p. 58, translation altered; 2006b, p. 799.
17   Debord 1995, p. 52; 2006b, p. 795.
18   Marx and Engels 1985, p. 111.

Marx's critique of Hegel was praised for having shown the way towards remedying Hegel's mistake. For Debord, however, Marx mystified his own insights in this regard. Although Marx's early writings had called for the realisation of philosophy in revolutionary action, his mature work came dangerously close to confusing historical agency with economic law. For Debord, therefore, some degree of contemplative separation from praxis could still be discerned in Marx.

Debord's comments in *The Society of the Spectacle* indicate that Marx's shortcomings in this regard can be attributed to two factors. Like the limitations that Debord accorded to Hegel, Marx's own limits were said to stem from the nature of the historical context in which he was working. Firstly, 'the weakness of the revolutionary proletariat of his time'[19] is said to have reduced Marx to 'defending and clarifying' revolution through 'cloistered, scholarly work in the British Museum'.[20] The inability to realise social change in *practice*, in other words, led Marx to postulate that change's inevitability in *theory*. As had been the case with Hegel (albeit, of course, to a far lesser extent), thought thus remained somewhat removed from action. Secondly, for Debord, Marx's attempts to validate revolution through theory rather than through practice were coloured by the influence exerted by the emphasis that 'the bourgeois epoch'[21] had placed on reason and science. Marx, in short, was a little too close to the rationalist, enlightenment thought that had accompanied the bourgeoisie's rise to power.

It needs to be stressed here that Debord's concerns with such modes of thought do not derive from any naïve irrationalism or primitivism on his part (indeed, in his *Comments on the Society of the Spectacle*, he explicitly warns against the irrationalism fostered by the culture of late capitalist society).[22] Instead, they evidence his view that the static laws and systems of a rationalist science cannot hope to grasp the unpredictability and qualitative change that characterises historical existence. Such regularity may well be essential to more technical and natural-scientific fields of enquiry, but for Debord, the 'harmony' of a rationalist system, or indeed the rigidity of any set of fully predictable scientific laws, was 'hostile to history'.[23] His position here would appear to be that if history's propensity towards qualitative change becomes occluded by the uniformity of an abstract system, then historical agency can become

---

19 Debord 1995, p. 55; 2006b, p. 797.
20 Debord 1995, p. 55; 2006b, p. 797.
21 Debord 1995, p. 55; 2006b, p. 795.
22 Debord 1998, pp. 30–1; 2006b, p. 1611.
23 Debord 1995, p. 54; 2006b, p. 797.

mistakenly attributed to the putative structures that govern and maintain that uniformity (for example: to explain history on the basis of a uniform theory of economic determination would involve naturalising the attribution of human agency to the economy). Debord was thus particularly concerned with political economy, which had emerged as a relatively new discipline following the rise of bourgeois society; a discipline that he defined, rather neatly, as both 'the dominant science and the science of domination'.[24]

The Critique of Political Economy

According to Debord, 'Marx's project' was, at its heart, 'the project of a conscious history':[25] an attempt to put human agents in control of their own existence through overcoming their subordination to their own economic creations. Yet as we have just seen, Debord *also* held that Marx's ability to fully articulate this project was marred by his proximity to the bourgeois political economy that he had sought to criticise. This proximity, for Debord, left Marx's work susceptible to its later collapse, in the hands of Marx's followers, into the economistic advocacy of social change *via* the economy, rather than *from* the economy. In consequence, Debord can be understood as having adopted an analogous, but also somewhat different, interpretation of the Marxian critique of political economy to that which we described in the previous chapter. It was pointed out there that for some contemporary writers, a *critique of political economy* can be usefully distinguished from a *critical political economy*. The latter addresses the current mode of production, but it does so whilst operating within the framework of political economy's naturalised presuppositions, typically advancing suggestions as to how that mode of production might be improved. A critique of political economy, on the other hand, is far closer to critical theory *per se*. It addresses those very presuppositions, indicates their historical contingency, and highlights the manner in which they become naturalised. Seen from this perspective, Marx's work straddles both positions. On the one hand, the 'exoteric' content of his mature writings, and indeed much of his legacy within the Marxist tradition, functions as a critical political economy. Buried within it, however, and in somewhat nascent form, one finds the more 'esoteric' content of a critique of political economy. Today, attempts are made to extract the latter from the former.

To some extent, Debord's own approach to Marx is similar: he too was engaged in an attempt to highlight and extract what he took to be the real

---

24   Debord 1995, p. 29; 2006b, p. 778.
25   Debord 1995, p. 53; 2006b, p. 795.

content of Marx's critique of political economy. The material that he sought to draw out, however, was rather different. This is because the real core of Marx's project, in Debord's view, lay in Marx's insights into the nature and importance of historical praxis.

This means that Debord's position does in fact chime, in some regards, with the idea that to conduct a critique of political economy is to identify and criticise bourgeois society's naturalised presuppositions. The difference, however, is that Debord's own approach to this issue cannot be reduced to a largely academic attempt to extract a more adequate account of capitalist value from within the 'exoteric' elements of Marx's work. Instead, Debord's version of the break that needed to be made with those naturalised assumptions lay in superseding capitalist society's suppression of history, and thereby political economy's tendency to ossify historical agency. The buried heart of Marx's critique of political economy, in Debord's view, is thus a rupture with *all* attempts to scientifically systematise historical agency, and with *all* fetishised attributions of such agency to economic determinants. This is why Debord describes Marx's critique of political economy as 'the first act' of the 'end of prehistory':[26] a 'first act', moreover, that needed to be pursued, developed and fulfilled.

The 'Breach' in Marx's Thought

We can summarise the primary issues that have been outlined so far with the following remarks. The essence of Debord's position here is that despite recognising and rejecting modern history's subservience to the capitalist economy, Marx – due to the nature of his context and times – came much too close to the perspective that he himself had criticised. In attempting to bolster and reinforce proletarian struggle by providing that struggle with a scientific knowledge of economic laws, Marx allowed himself to be 'drawn onto the ground of the dominant forms of thought'.[27] This gave rise to the 'scientific-determinist side' of Marx's thought, which in turn opened a 'breach' through which the process of '"ideologisation"' was able to 'penetrate'.[28] It was 'in this mutilated form', according to Debord, which was subsequently 'taken as definitive', that 'Marx's theory became "Marxism"':[29] a body of thought that engendered a dogma (economism) that effectively naturalised the very same subservience to the economy that Marx had identified and rejected.[30]

---

26   Debord 1995, p. 52; 2006b, p. 795.
27   Debord 1995, p. 55; 2006b, p. 797.
28   Debord 1995, pp. 54–5; 2006b, p. 797.
29   Debord 1995, pp. 54–5; 2006b, p. 797.
30   Hence the SI's dismissal of Ernest Mandel as a 'Trotskyist' whose *'Treatise on Marxist*

Let us now return to the argument introduced at the beginning of this chapter. Marx's work, for Debord, attempts to address historical life's subordination to the economy. Debord sought to continue and deepen this line of thought. Yet because the pursuit of free historical agency entailed rejecting the errors of economism, the manner in which Debord sought to develop this Marxian project took on a degree of scepticism concerning any primary orientation towards the study of economics. This resulted in a somewhat contradictory position. On the one hand, Debord's account stresses the importance of capitalism's domination of the everyday. On the other hand, however, his rejection of economism lent itself to a rather limited engagement with the structural operation of that same mode of domination. As was proposed above, there is, therefore, a sense in which Debord's diagnosis of society's capitalist ills lent itself to a focus on the latter's symptoms, and entailed a relative neglect of their concrete causes.

Montesquieu's Defeat

This is exacerbated by the fact that spectacle, as was indicated in Part One of this book, cannot be reductively identified with capitalism. We argued there, on the basis of textual evidence, that Debord saw what we have referred to as the *problematic* of spectacle as having existed prior to the instantiation of the *society* of the spectacle in the early decades of the twentieth century. Modern capitalism had simply brought to full expression a problematic that had inhered in all previous forms of separated social power. Spectacle, therefore, *qua* the separation of social power from its producers, and the consequent separation of those individuals from their own collective agency, is not strictly the same thing as capitalism. Capitalism is certainly an instance of spectacle, but the latter exceeds the former. Indeed, *The Society of the Spectacle* is not just a description of capitalism, but rather of the historical and existential predicament posed by a world that has been shaped to suit capitalism. In fact – and as we will now attempt to demonstrate – Debord actually objected to a reading of society that focussed myopically upon the economy alone, as he held that the modern spectacle was composed from the unitary operation of a host of different forms of separated power, all of which operate cumulatively and collectively to ensure the smooth running of the capitalist economy.

Economics by its title alone contradicts the whole revolutionary method of Marx' (SI 2006, p. 217; 1997, p. 442).

In *The Society of the Spectacle*, and whilst discussing Marx's concerns with economic 'science', Debord also criticises Marx for having paid insufficient attention to the role of the state. However, when doing so, he acknowledges that Marx went some way towards rectifying that omission with his analyses of 'Bonapartism' (the co-opting of revolutionary sentiment and power in the service of a militarily reinforced ruling class). With his 'concept of Bonapartism', Debord writes, Marx was 'able to describe the shape of the modern statist bureaucracy', understood as the 'fusion of capital and State', and as the formation – Debord quotes here from Marx's *The Civil War in France* – 'of a "national power of capital over labour, a public force organised for social enslavement."'[31]

Debord's interest in *The Civil War in France* was no doubt informed by that text's negative implications regarding the supposed need for revolutionaries to appropriate state power. These implications were explicitly indicated in the 1872 preface to *The Communist Manifesto*, where Marx quotes from *The Civil War in France* as follows: 'One thing especially was proved by the [Paris] Commune, viz., that "the working class cannot simply lay hold of the ready-made state machinery, and wield it for its own purposes"'.[32] Those observations were clearly lost on many of Marx's subsequent followers, who held that the state could indeed be used to resolve the failings of the economy. The view that all things follow from the economy led to the assumption that economic changes made via the machinery of the state would ultimately remove the need for the state altogether, and that the latter would therefore conveniently wither away of its own accord. For Debord, the naivety of such a view had been made readily apparent by the pitfalls into which the revolutionary project had fallen throughout his century. The state, for Debord, is by no means a neutral tool. Instead, it is an integral component of the capitalist social order: a component that more traditional and reductively economistic perspectives had all too readily overlooked.

This is why Marx's notion of Bonapartism seemed so important to Debord. In it, he found a glimpse of the ways in which state, ideology, culture and manipulation might all be combined in order to ensure the dominance and perpetuity of a particular socio-economic order. Debord in fact held that in Marx's account of the Bonapartist fusion of these instruments of governance, one could find, 'in discernible outline', the 'sociopolitical bases'[33] of the modern spectacle. Indeed, in a letter of 1992, Debord wrote that 'the society of the

---

31 Debord 1995, p. 57, translation altered; 2006b, p. 799.
32 Marx and Engels 1985, p. 54.
33 Debord 1995, p. 57; 2006b, p. 799.

Twentieth Century' arose from 'the modernism that was already present in the reign of Napoleon III; the defeat of Montesquieu'.[34] That 'defeat' signifies the ultimate failure of any attempt towards the *division* of political powers, all of which, for Debord, had now come to operate in a fundamentally unitary manner in the service of the reigning economic order.

It is this unitary operation of separated forms of power that constitutes the 'unity in division' of Debord's modern spectacle. Capitalism is without doubt the primary, decisive factor within that totality, but it remains the case that for Debord, a host of further, extra-economic forms of biopolitical regulation had come to be employed as aspects of a relatively unified whole. Thus, as indicated above, the modern spectacle should not be reduced to capitalism alone, but rather corresponds to the general nature of a world that has been shaped to suit capitalism. Or, to put that otherwise: Debord's chief concern was not just capitalism *per se*, but rather *the historical and existential predicament posed by the general management of life in the service of capitalism*. The task of revolution was to resolve that predicament through the creation of a social context in which human subjects could take self-conscious and self-determinate control of their own lived time.

Consequently, for Debord, to focus reductively on the economy (and to thereby miss the importance of the state, the police, ideology, manipulation, and so on, and all of the other myriad factors that regulate the conduct of lived time) would be to miss the real nature and stakes of the contemporary revolutionary problematic, which could only be grasped by gathering all social phenomena under the single, unifying rubric of spectacle. And because all such phenomena are addressed by way of a chief concern with the experience and conduct of lived time, the concept of spectacle is chiefly oriented, on its most fundamental level, towards capitalism's subjective and existential *effects* rather than its objective *causes*.

This then gives rise to a reversal of priority. Rather than following Marxian tradition, and thereby casting the subjective as secondary to the objective, Debord and the SI effectively cast the generalised subjective alienation and disaffection engendered by modern society as more important than the concrete causes of that same alienation. This shift in priority invited a rather limited conception of capital: for as we indicated earlier, although Debord certainly draws heavily on Marx's account of value and the commodity, he does not really address capital's roots in social labour.

---

34   Debord 2008, p. 331.

The implications of this position will be considered at greater length in Chapter 11. Here, our focus will remain on the ideas that informed Debord and the SI's adoption of this perspective, and on the ways in which it informed their analyses. In what follows below, we will try to demonstrate that the manner in which Debord attempted to depart from classical Marxism entailed that his conceptions of spectacular society, and of the 'new' proletariat that confronted it, ended up suffering from the problems described at the outset of this chapter.

2)   The New Proletariat and the 'Total Commodity'

Life and Its Suppression
We will begin by returning to the SI's conception of the modern revolutionary class: the 'new' proletariat, which exceeded the class boundaries of a traditional, economically defined proletariat, insofar as it was composed of all those who demanded more from life than modern society could provide. The universality of this 'class' – i.e. the degree to which it encompassed individuals throughout society, regardless of their social station – was held to stem from the ubiquity of alienation within modern society. For Debord and the SI, the workplace had lost its privileged status as the primary locus of capitalist alienation, because within spectacular society, *all* aspects of social life were seen to be as alienated as all others.

Debord and the SI may well have advanced a central insight into the failings of contemporary capitalism when they indicated that labour had become effectively synonymous with life in general. Work time and leisure time were seen as complementary aspects of a single, monolithic temporal order, wherein all life serves the needs of a sovereign economy. Yet whilst this may capture some of the central features of a Post-Fordist existence, it also returns us to the difficulties that we introduced earlier. Debord's theory is reliant upon a Marxian conceptual framework, according to which capital derives from labour. If labour becomes blurred with life in general, then it becomes rather hard to identify the actual roots and bases of capital, and indeed to address the specificity of the social relations that allow it to function.

The claims set out below are arranged as follows. 1) Firstly, we will look at some of the theoretical influences that informed Debord and the SI's views concerning the nature of contestation within capitalist society. In doing so, we will highlight the significance of Cornelius Castoriadis's views concerning society's increasing division into the two opposing camps of social 'order-givers' and 'order-takers': factions of society that did not bear strict relation to classical Marxian economic analysis, and which were held to harbour, within their opposition, the potential for a greatly expanded set of revolutionary demands. 2) Having noted the obvious connections between these views and the SI's vision of the 'new' proletariat, we will then address the latter by way of reference to the Hegelian and young-Marxian notion of the 'universal class': a section of society whose particular interests involve the universal emancipation of society as a whole. We will then move towards considering these issues in relation to Debord's somewhat idiosyncratic use of Marx's account of the commodity-form. 3) As was indicated above, the universality of the SI's new proletariat stemmed from the ubiquity of alienation. Debord's views concerning that purported ubiquity, as set out in texts such as *The Society of the Spectacle*, are much informed by his use of a Marxian conception of the commodity's structure; a use thereof that leads to a further blurring of life with labour. 4) Ultimately, this results in a critique of capitalist society that loses sight of Marx's emphasis on the sense in which capital is not a thing, or an independent, 'non-living' force, but rather a set of social relations that have been imbued with a degree of autonomy.

We will begin, then, by looking at some of the theoretical influences that informed Debord and the SI's views concerning the nature of the modern revolutionary class, and of the social struggle that that class would endeavour to overcome. All of these influences fostered or involved a degree of departure from classical Marxian economics, principally in terms of a rejection of economism, and an increased sensitivity to more subjective, historical and existential issues.

'Order-Givers' and 'Order-Takers'

The scepticism towards economic determinism that we described above, and Debord's attendant distaste for classical Marxism's fixation on economic 'law', were no doubt at least partly informed by Lukács. As we saw in Chapter Seven, Lukács's *History and Class Consciousness* is greatly concerned with the ways in which 'bourgeois thought' attempts to rationalise its social order whilst effectively naturalising the latter through doing so. For Lukács, the essential error of 'bourgeois thought' lay in its consequent tendency to treat the historical moment of capitalist society as a transhistorical truth. Similarly, for Debord, classical Marxism (or at least its Second and Third International iterations) had treated Marxian economics in much the same way. The fact that capitalist society was ruled by its economy had been addressed via a theory of history wherein economic law *always* remains the primary determinant.

These views were also informed by Debord's reading of Karl Korsch, whose *Marxism and Philosophy* had been published at the same time as *History and*

Class Consciousness. For Korsch, whose work Debord clearly read and studied,[35] Marxism should not just serve as a 'science' of the present: instead, it had to be thought of as a revolutionary engagement in the construction of the future.[36] Henri Lefebvre, whose relevance we discussed in Part Two, was also an obvious and important influence in the late 1950s and early 1960s. Lefebvre helped to steer the SI's burgeoning Marxian theories away from a fixation on the workplace and towards the everyday as a whole. Yet whilst Lefebvre was obviously crucial in this regard, it is also worth noting that Sartre may well have exerted a further and similar line of influence at that time, however indirect that influence may have been. In his 'Search for a Method' – an essay that first appeared in 1957, and which would later form part of the introduction to his *Critique of Dialectical Reason* – Sartre objected to what he took to be Marxism's tendency to collapse the particularity of specific individuals and circumstances into *a priori* universal categories. 'For the majority of Marxists', Sartre wrote, 'to think is to claim to totalise and, under this pretext, to replace particularity by a universal'.[37] Such a method, he claimed, 'has already formed its concepts; it is already certain of their truth; it will assign to them the role of constitutive schemata. Its sole purpose is to force the events, the persons, or the acts considered into prefabricated moulds.'[38] Classical Marxism's willingness to understand society via preordained economistic categories was thus viewed as dogma, and as an approach to social existence that suppressed the real nature of subjective life. In this regard, Sartre's objections to classical Marxism are

---

35 The 'Marxisme' section of the BnF's Debord archive contains notes on Korsch's *Marxism and Philosophy*.

36 Korsch's *Marxism and Philosophy* (1923) set out to combat the Second International's tendency towards social democracy and static ideology. In a sense, it prefigures the Situationists' attempts to retrieve the communist project from its own representation. Like Debord, Korsch claims that Marxism should be an ongoing historical movement rather than a theoretical depiction of a particular historical moment. For Korsch, reducing Marxism to a set of economic laws entailed undermining its relation to the construction of history, and thus invited reformism: for if Marxist thought remains 'within the limits of bourgeois society and the bourgeois state', its criticisms will 'no longer necessarily develop by their very nature into revolutionary practice' (Korsch 1970, p. 57). The official denunciations that Korsch received (see Korsch 1970, pp. 89–129) furthered his subsequent drift towards the ultra-left (see Giles-Peters 1973 for a useful overview), and by 1950, he was arguing that 'all attempts to re-establish the Marxist doctrine as a whole in its original function' were 'reactionary utopias' (Korsch 1975). Revolutionary practice and theory, he held, needed to look to sources beyond Marx (a view that accords with the SI's views on art and poetry).

37 Sartre 1963, p. 48.

38 Sartre 1963, p. 37.

similar, in some regards, to the SI's antipathy to economism. Marxian theory, Sartre claimed, should attend to the particular desires, circumstances and dilemmas of particular human subjects, as opposed to treating them abstractly as elements of an economic class: 'Marxism', he wrote, 'ought to study real men in depth, not dissolve them in a bath of sulphuric acid'.[39] There are further theoretical influences that could be noted here, not least amongst which is Debord's engagement with Bakunin, and with elements of anarchism;[40] but taken together, all encouraged, in differing ways, a shift away from the primacy of economic structure towards a concern with personal desire and subjective frustration.

The work of Cornelius Castoriadis may well have been particularly significant in this regard. This can be illustrated by way of reference to Castoriadis's 'Modern Capitalism and Revolution': a text that was drafted in 1959, but which coincided, in terms of its publication in *Socialisme ou Barbarie*, with Debord's brief membership of S ou B.[41] Whilst stressing the importance of individual autonomy in this text, Castoriadis contended, like Debord, that classical Marxism tends to replace the actions of individual human subjects with those of 'an objective dynamic and "natural" law'.[42] He also argued that classical notions of class and exploitation needed to be re-thought, and began to move, quite explicitly, away from a traditional Marxian theory of value.

According to Castoriadis, the working class could no longer be construed as 'what Marx called "a class for itself" (i.e. a class consciously, explicitly and collectively concerned with its own fate in society)'.[43] The unions, in his view,

---

39   Sartre 1963, pp. 43–4.
40   Bakunin, a Hegelian anarchist, objected to the 'disciples of the *doctrinaire* school of German Communism' (Bakunin 1970, p. 55) in a similar vein to Debord's objections to economic dogmatism, complaining of the subjugation of life and the individual to abstract scientific law: 'What I preach', he wrote, 'is the *revolt of life against science*' (Bakunin 1970, p. 59). Debord certainly criticised anarchism (see theses 91–5 of *The Society of the Spectacle*), and showed particular disregard for its individualist variants, but his sympathy for collectivist anarchism can be illustrated by the fact that he described the Spanish anarchists of 1936 as having instituted 'the most advanced model of proletarian power ever realised' (Debord 1995, p. 64; Debord 2006b, p. 803).
41   The text appeared in *Socialisme ou Barbarie* #31–3 between 1960–1; Debord was a member of S ou B from the end of 1960 to May 1961. See his letter to the participants of the national conference of *Pouvoir Ouvrier* (a publication that grew from S ou B, and which became a group in its own right in 1963) of 5th May 1961, in which Debord expresses his concerns regarding the split between 'stars' and followers within its ranks (Debord 2001a, pp. 82–8).
42   Castoriadis 1974.
43   Ibid.

had become fully integrated into the existing system. Rather than driving for genuine change, Castoriadis claimed, they 'negotiate the docility of the workers in production in return for wage increases'.[44] The rise of consumer society had also made it increasingly possible to provide individuals with palliative remedies for their dissatisfactions. Furthermore, not only were the incentives and means towards a classically envisaged revolution becoming co-opted: on the basis of sociological and economic evidence, Castoriadis also contended that traditional Marxist analysis was becoming relatively obsolete, insofar as it had begun to struggle when called upon to identify and articulate revolutionary potential within modern society. The rationale behind that claim can perhaps be summarised as follows.

The development of capitalism had entailed that its periodic crises could now be managed within acceptable limits, and that workers' demands for higher wages could be met. Unemployment had dropped, and wages and the standard of living had risen. According to Castoriadis, capitalism's ability to support this rise in wages jarred with the theory of surplus-value. This led him to consider the following question: if the revolutionary potential within modern capitalism could no longer be understood in terms of surplus-value extraction, then how else might it be conceived?

Castoriadis's answer was that the diminishing political importance of the traditional locus of contestation within capitalist society (i.e. the wage-relation) had given rise to a new, potentially revolutionary social contradiction. Capitalism, he claimed, was obliged to both include and exclude workers at the same time: to reduce them to mere order-takers and automatons in the sphere of production, but also to foster, within the sphere of consumption, the subjectivity and desire that this alienated production denied and repressed. Neither requirement could be fully satisfied. The result, according to Castoriadis, was a disaffected workforce, and the consequent division of society into 'order-givers and order-takers':[45] into one section of society composed of those who were relatively satisfied with this state of affairs, and into another composed of those who would demand more. The latter section was still identified with the working class, as in traditional Marxism, but the motivation that would drive that class' insurrection was no longer viewed in terms of classical Marxian economics.

This obviously chimes with Debord and the SI's own views. Like the SI, Castoriadis held that this new social tension had emerged from within the

44 Ibid.
45 Ibid.

social context that traditional Marxism had addressed. It had done so due to the evolution of that older social context, and it had superseded the conceptual frameworks proper to that classical era, because it had revealed a new revolutionary potential that might prove far more radical than that of the past. For example, in lines that could almost have been written by the SI, Castoriadis made the following claim:

> The philosophy of consumption penetrates the proletariat. But this apathy also has potentially positive aspects. Working-class experience of the new phase of capitalism could lead it to a criticism of *all* aspects of contemporary life, a criticism far more profound than anything attempted in the past.[46]

Castoriadis is thus one of the principal examples of a number of writers who informed Debord and the SI's departure from classical Marxism. The ideas expressed by these writers led to a drift away from economically driven working class revolution, towards a more passionate, subjective revolt, motivated by the frustrated desires and dissatisfaction of everyday existence. This necessarily fostered a shift away from the details of Marx's critical economic work: 'narrow "economic" and "political" issues', Castoriadis claimed, were tending to become 'less and less relevant'.[47] Debord's theoretical work, we will argue, suffers somewhat due to its proximity to that view. In order to develop that claim, we will now return to the SI's 'new' proletariat, and to the connections that need to be drawn between the effectively class-less nature of that revolutionary class, and the ubiquity of alienation within modern society.

The Universal Class

In order to draw those connections, it can be useful to refer here to Hegel's concept of the 'universal class', as set out in his *Philosophy of Right*. Hegel's universal class is a segment of his envisaged society that is composed of bureaucrats: individuals whose own particular, personal interests lie in the mediation and reconciliation of other elements of society. More specifically, the task of these individuals would be to unify the particular demands of the sphere of civil society with the more universal concerns of the sphere of political society.[48] The fully rational state, for Hegel, is the pinnacle of Spirit's concrete actualisa-

---

46   Ibid.
47   Ibid.
48   'The universal class, the class devoted to the service of the government, has directly in its

tion. The role of the universal class, therefore, was to effect, through its own particular interests and actions, the full flourishing of human freedom.

Marx took a rather different view in his early 'Critique of Hegel's *Philosophy of Right*': a text in which he treated Hegel's philosophy of the state as a flawed endorsement of bourgeois society. According to Marx, the true 'universal class' within bourgeois society was not Hegel's class of civil servants, but rather the proletariat. This is because for Marx, the proletariat was the only social class whose particular interests truly coincided with the instantiation of universal freedom. In order to emancipate itself, the proletariat would need to overthrow bourgeois society as a whole, thus liberating 'all the other spheres of society', and thereby affording what Marx referred to as the 'total redemption of humanity'.[49] The proletariat, for the young Marx, was therefore the particular vehicle through which the universality of humanity as a whole might flourish. For example, Marx described the proletariat as:

> ... a class with *radical chains*, a class of civil society which is not a class of civil society, a class [*Stand*] which is the dissolution of all classes, a sphere which has a universal character because of its universal suffering and which lays claim to no *particular right* because the wrong it suffers is not a *particular wrong*, but *wrong in general* ...[50]

The famously defiant words that Marx attributed to his universal proletarian – '*I am nothing and I should be everything*'[51] – bear direct relation to the 'scandalous poverty'[52] of subjective experience that characterised the SI's own existential reformulation of revolution. This can be illustrated by noting Debord's *détournement* of Marx's words in *The Society of the Spectacle*:[53]

> The proletariat is the bearer of *the revolution that cannot leave anything outside itself*, the exigency of the permanent domination of the present over the past,[54] and the total critique of separation ... No quantitative relief of its poverty, no illusory hierarchical incorporation, can supply a

---

      structure the universal as the end of its essential activity. ... Only [through this class] is the actual particular in the state securely attached to the universal' (Hegel 2005, p. 181).

49   Marx 1975, p. 256.
50   Ibid.
51   Marx 1975, p. 254, emphasis in the original.
52   SI 2006, p. 92; 1997, p. 220.
53   Debord 2006b, p. 868.
54   This is a reference to *The Communist Manifesto*: 'In bourgeois society ... the past dominates

lasting cure for its dissatisfaction, for the proletariat cannot truly recognise itself in any particular wrong it has suffered, nor therefore *in the righting of any particular wrong*, nor even in the righting of a great many of these wrongs, but only in the *absolute wrong* of being rejected [and cast] to the margins of life.[55]

There is an important difference here. Marx's universal class was essentially an economically defined social category, situated in opposition to another such category (i.e. the bourgeoisie). Debord and the SI's proletariat, however, could not be reduced to any such economic categorisation. Yet despite that difference, there is also a conceptual continuity. Like Marx's and Hegel's own versions of the universal class, the SI's 'new' proletariat was a particular element within society that would act on behalf of the universality of humanity as a whole. In fact, the new proletariat would be rather more overt in that regard. Because, according to Debord, the demand for revolution was now rooted in a generalised existential *ennui* rather than in the working class' material poverty, opposition to capital had broken the bounds of the class divide. In consequence, the new universal class was quite *literally* universal, as it could now encompass *all* members of society (hence, for Debord, the 'new proletariat' was 'tending to encompass everybody [*tout le monde*]').[56] Thus, just as Marx had clarified and developed Hegel's views, so too were the SI developing Marx's own, by showing that the development of capitalism had brought the universal *qua* humanistic characteristics of revolutionary agency to the fore.

In order to address that point, we now need to turn to the important links between Debord's conception of spectacular society, and Marx's views on the commodity. This is because the universality of the alienation that Debord identified within capitalist society derived from the total colonisation and restructuration of social life by the commodity-form.

The Structure of the Commodity

The Society of the Spectacle contends that social life, in all of its diverse aspects, has become compressed into a single, unified whole: a homogenised, regulated object, from which all human subjects are similarly alienated, due to their equal inability to take any meaningful steps towards directing their own lives. As we will now try to show, Debord holds that this follows from the fact that within

---

the present; in Communist society the present dominates the past' (Marx and Engels 1985, pp. 97–8).

55   Debord 1995, p. 85, translation altered; 2006b, p. 816, emphasis in the original.
56   Debord 1995, p. 21; 2006b, p. 773.

spectacular society, the commodity has completed its 'colonisation of social life.'[57] In order to discuss that point, we need to look at Marx's own views concerning the nature and structure of the commodity-form.

For Marx, an entity can only be a commodity if it is to be sold on the market. In order for it to be sold, it must be desirable to someone other than its immediate possessor. It must, therefore, be useful, in some sense, to potential buyers. Consequently, Marx holds that every commodity has what he refers to as a *use-value*. This corresponds to the particular, qualitative characteristics of the commodity (for example: the use-value of a spade is that one can dig holes with it). Crucially, however, the commodity also possesses a second dimension: that of *exchange-value*. This arises from the commodity's location within a system of market exchange, and it expresses the commodity's value in relation to that of other commodities (e.g. the exchange-value of X amount of spades corresponds to its equivalence to Y amount of tea, or to Z amount of iron, and so on). For Marx, the value that is expressed in the exchange-value of commodities stems from the labour involved in their production. It does not represent the quantity of real, physical labour expended in producing the item in question, but rather the amount of socially necessary labour time that this act of production represents, i.e. the quantitative sum of the abstract, socially average labour that would need to be expended, on average, in order to produce that item given the current means of production. At issue here, therefore, is not the quantity of real, physical labour expended in producing that item, but rather the amount of socially necessary labour time that this act of production *represents*. The value of the commodity, therefore – the value that is expressed in its exchange-value – is premised upon the abstract equivalence of all social labour.[58] This abstract equivalence can only arise through the generalised exchange of different kinds of labour. The commodity-form is thus specific to a social system in which individual, particular need is met through generalised exchange, and in which every qualitatively distinct form of use-value producing concrete labour can be treated as an instance of abstract, universal, social labour. Qualitative particularity is subsumed and articulated by an abstract, quantitative generality (a point that bears direct relation to the themes of universality and particularity that we discussed in connection to spectacular 'non-life' in Chapter 8).

---

57   Debord 1995, p. 29; 2006b, p. 778.
58   'The total labour-power of society, which is manifested in the values of the world of commodities, counts here as one homogeneous mass of human labour-power, although composed of innumerable units of labour-power' (Marx 1990, p. 129).

Marx placed his account of the structure of the commodity at the very beginning of *Capital* because he viewed the basic structure of the commodity as the 'cell-form'[59] of capitalist society. It is therefore significant that one can already find, within the distinction between use-value and exchange-value, a sense in which concrete particularity has become subordinated to an abstract universality. The very structure of the commodity presupposes a society in which qualitatively distinct human activity (i.e. concrete, use-value producing labour) is required to function as abstract, quantitatively homogeneous labour (i.e. as the abstract labour of exchange-value). The subordination of the concrete to the abstract is thus inherent within the very structure of the commodity.

The significance of that point lies in the fact that Debord presents the entirety of modern society as a grand extrapolation of the commodity's structure. The commodity's complete colonisation of the everyday, he argues, has brought its implicit content to the fore, rendering the domination of the concrete by the abstract a defining feature of the modern world.

The 'Absolute Realisation' of the Commodity-Form

The epigraph to the second chapter of *The Society of the Spectacle* is a quotation from Lukács's *History and Class Consciousness*. It reads as follows: 'The commodity can only be understood in its undistorted essence when it becomes the universal category of society as a whole.'[60] For Debord, this is precisely what has happened within modern society. The commodity's 'undistorted essence' – its core principle of regulating the qualitatively distinct via the quantitatively abstract – has become the central paradigm for society as a whole.

There is, however, an important nuance that should be foregrounded here. As was signalled earlier in this chapter, spectacle cannot be reductively identified with capitalism. Spectacle, as a general problematic, is much older than the society that had brought it to full expression. Therefore, it is not so much the case that spectacle is an extension or derivative of the commodity-form. Rather, it would be more appropriate to state that the commodity-form, by virtue of its structure, lends itself to a particularly acute instantiation of spectacle. In other words, the commodity-form constitutes an exemplary distillation of the essential problematic of spectacle: namely, the separation of collective agency from a community, and the consequent deprivation of that community's capacity for a collective and self-determinate life, due to the ossification of that potential within constructs that reify and freeze collective power in forms of fixed com-

---

59   Marx 1990, p. 90.
60   Debord 1995, p. 25; 2006b, p. 776; Lukács 1971, p. 86.

mand over its producers. Or, as Debord puts it in *The Society of the Spectacle*, by way of a *détournement* of Marx:

> In the essential movement of the spectacle, which consists of taking up all that existed in human activity in a fluid state so as to possess it in a congealed state as things which have become the exclusive value by their formulation in negative of lived value, we recognise our old enemy, the commodity ...[61]

Like many of Debord's claims, that statement is rather more complex and subtle than it may first appear. At first sight, it might lead one to think that Debord is simply identifying the spectacle with the commodity. However, and as we will now try to explain, Debord is really identifying spectacle with historical arrest, and casting the commodity as one instance of that broader problematic. His claim is that modern society's colonisation by the commodity has brought the problematic of spectacle to the fore, thereby casting 'our old enemy, the commodity' in a new light.

This interpretation may become more convincing if we note the *détournement* involved in this passage. Debord's list of the *détournements* in *The Society of the Spectacle* indicates that this passage draws on Marx's 'Speech at the Anniversary of the *People's Paper*' of 1856.[62] The opening lines of that speech read as follows:

> The so-called revolutions of 1848 were but poor incidents – small fractures in the dry crust of European society. However, they denounced the abyss. Beneath the apparently solid surface they proclaimed they betrayed oceans of liquid matter, only needing expansion to rend into fragments continents of hard rock.[63]

The passage from *The Society of the Spectacle* describes the ossification of the fluidity and flux of living activity. Debord must have read Marx's speech as indicating that that same fluidity subsists beneath the seemingly fixed and frozen structures of capitalist society. The meaning of the *détournement*, therefore, is as follows. Where revolution and historical agency constitute the flowing force that underlies fixed social forms, the 'essential movement of the

---

61   Debord 1995, p. 26, translation altered; 2006b, p. 776.
62   Debord 2006b, p. 864.
63   Marx 1973a, p. 299.

spectacle' is the *opposite* of that force. Where the latter's destructive and creative vitality works against all such frozen forms, spectacle corresponds to that energy's arrest.[64] The 'essential movement of the spectacle', therefore, is the non-living antithesis of the dynamism and flux that Debord associates with 'life'. Consequently, when Debord claims that we can recognise, in the spectacle's 'essential movement', the nature of our 'old enemy, the commodity', he is really indicating that the commodity now stands revealed, in modern society, as a primary instance of spectacle. This then means that the modern revolution needs to re-figure its old, familiar struggle against capital and the commodity, and to thereby see the latter as a key component of the new, broader fight against spectacle.

This also means that it was not enough to *only* recognise the commodity in these terms. In addition, religion, bureaucracy, representative power, and indeed all of the other phenomena that Debord and the SI associated with spectacle, *also* needed to be seen as facets of this wider problem: as constructs that dictate the parameters of socially valid action and interaction, and which thereby channel social activity into their continued reproduction. Seen in these terms, the commodity becomes just one instance of the broader *problematic* of spectacle, albeit an obviously central and crucial component of the modern *society* of the spectacle.

We argued earlier that for Debord, practically all of the forms of separated power to be found within modern society operated as elements of a single, unified world system. The state, the police, religion, ideology, the miasma of consumption, seemingly opposed nation states and power blocks; however disparate they may seem, all served to maintain and manage a world suited to the smooth running of capitalism. Or, as Debord puts it in *The Society of the Spectacle*: 'it is clear that the specificity of each is subsumed under a universal system as functions of a single tendency that has taken the planet for its field of operations. That tendency is capitalism'.[65] This is why the commodity is so important: for whilst the commodity is certainly not the sole instance

---

64   We might also remember here that the transformative dissolution of fixed forms is precisely what Debord associates with dialectics *qua* the 'thought of history'. As Marx put it: 'In its rational form', the dialectic 'includes in its positive understanding of all that exists a simultaneous recognition of its negation, its inevitable destruction', and 'regards every historically developed form as being in a fluid state, in motion, and therefore grasps its transient aspect as well …' (cf. Marx 1990, p. 103).

65   Debord 1995, pp. 36–7; 2006b, p. 784. NB This statement is taken from a section of the book in which Debord is discussing the interrelation of different international blocks of power, principally *vis-à-vis* the Communist East and the more overtly capitalist West.

of spectacle within modern society, the simple fact that spectacular power perpetuates capitalism renders the commodity the lynchpin of the social order that constitutes the modern spectacle.

It may be useful to place this in relation to Lukács's own endeavours. In *History and Class Consciousness*, Lukács attempted to view society as an interrelated totality, and to analyse bourgeois culture and modes of thought in a manner that did not rely upon crude economic reductionism. By viewing society as a totality, an analyst could relate the whole to its parts, and identify the universal, shared nature of each aspect of society. 'Bourgeois thought' would not need to be stripped away in order to concentrate on the economic processes that underlie it: rather, those economic processes could be found within ideological and cultural phenomena, as all could be seen as elements of a whole.[66] For Lukács, the unifying concept that would afford this vision of totality was, of course, the commodity. *The Society of the Spectacle* attempts something very similar, but it does so whilst using a different unifying concept. Rather than opting for the commodity, Debord employs what he takes to be the 'undistorted essence' of the commodity: namely, spectacle.

As was described above, the structure of the commodity necessarily entails the separation of the abstract from the concrete, and of the universal from the particular. Such separation is certainly intrinsic to the distinction between use-value and exchange-value, but it is *also* intrinsic to the basic dynamic of spectacle, and thus to all forms of separated social power (insofar as all such forms entail the separation of concrete, particular individuals and forms of activity from the abstraction of their socially universal powers and capacities). Due to this shared nature, Debord is able to describe the totality of spectacular society in terms that bear direct relation to the commodity-form, even though many of the elements that he incorporates into this totality cannot be reduced to the commodity. He thus presents a vision of society in which a host of both economic and extra-economic factors are treated under one governing rubric: namely, spectacle, understood as the generalised separation that characterises this social order.

This combination of the economic and the extra-economic supports the extreme nature of Debord and the SI's ambitions, as it necessitates a break with the current social order in its entirety. However, it also underscores the

---

66   As a result, '"ideological" and "economic" problems lose their exclusiveness and merge into one another' (Lukács 1971, p. 34). For Lukács, the possibility of this mode of enquiry is historically specific. 'Not until the rise of capitalism was a unified economic structure, and hence a – formally – unified structure of consciousness that embraced the whole of society, brought into being' (Lukács 1971, p. 100).

problems that we outlined at the start of this chapter. Because all forms of social activity are blurred together in this manner, it becomes rather hard to prioritise the forms of activity that underpin capitalism itself. This entails that Debord comes close to advancing a body of anti-capitalist theory that suffers from a rather limited account of what capitalism actually is, and of how it might be combatted.

That contention may become more cogent if we turn to Debord's use of the Marxian notion of fetishism.

'A Weltanschauung *That Has been Actualised*'

In keeping with the view that the 'undistorted essence' of the commodity corresponds to the broader problematic of spectacle, Debord appears to have understood fetishism in a similarly broad sense: as the confused identification of particular objects or entities with the attributes that are accorded to them as a result of the social relations in which they are located (e.g. the identification of gold with value). Fetishism, understood in this broad sense, is thus one with the general problem of spectacle, because it involves the attribution of powers and attributes that derive from social relations to particular constructs within those relations. And just as the rise of consumer capitalism had brought the commodity's essential, spectacular nature to the fore, so too had the resultant social order turned this general 'principle' of fetishism into the defining feature of an entire socio-historical moment. As Debord puts it:

> [T]he principle of commodity fetishism ... is absolutely fulfilled in the spectacle, where the perceptible world is replaced by a set of images that are superior to that world [*qui existe au-dessus de lui*] yet at the same time impose themselves as eminently perceptible.[67]

As we described above, the modern spectacle is generated from the unitary operation of instances of separated power. The representations of life that they present to individuals within society thus form a common whole. Because these representations guide social activity, they become *real*.[68] The 'principle' of fetishism – i.e. the identification of concrete aspects of society with their socially derived attributes – is thus viewed as having reached its complete

---

67   Debord 1995, p. 26; 2006b, p. 776.

68   '... the spectacle, though it turns reality on its head, is itself a product of real activity. Likewise, lived reality suffers the material assaults of the spectacle's mechanisms of contemplation, incorporating the spectacular order and lending that order positive support' (Debord 1995, p. 14; 2006b, p. 768).

fulfilment in an era wherein the world itself has become subordinated to, and shaped in accordance with, a socially and historically contingent *vision of the world*. In other words, a socially derived model of life's conduct has become thoroughly actualised within the life of society, and as a result, all social conduct now accords with that same model. This is why Debord describes the spectacle 'as a *Weltanschauung* that has been actualised, translated into the material realm', and thus as 'a world view that has become an objective reality.'[69]

Having noted the rather loose manner in which Debord employs the Marxian notion of fetishism, we can now return to the sense in which he described society as a whole in terms that echo the structure of the commodity-form. Like the concrete body of the commodity, social reality functions as the bearer of a general, abstract rationale, i.e. that of the unquestioned virtues of the existing system; and just as particular use-values are equated with one another under the rubric of exchange-value, so too is every particular instance of social reality rendered effectively homogeneous with all others, because each operates as an element of a single, unified system. Inevitably, this involves a rather idiosyncratic approach to the Marxian concepts of use-value and exchange-value.

Augmented Survival

One of Debord's key claims in *The Society of the Spectacle* is that exchange-value has taken precedence over use-value. He states that although exchange-value originally functioned as a means of articulating the production and distribution of use-values, the growth of commodity production and exchange has entailed that use-value has become a mere excuse for the continued operation of exchange-value. In other words, genuine utility and need are no longer the primary issue: instead, the continued growth and circulation of value are of central importance. Or, as Debord puts it:

> Exchange-value could arise only as an agent of use-value, but its victory by means of its own weapons created the conditions for its autonomous domination. Mobilising all human use and establishing a monopoly over its satisfaction, exchange-value has ended up by *directing use*. The process of exchange became identified with all possible use and reduced use to the mercy of exchange. Starting out like a condottiere of use-value, exchange-value has ended up waging the war for its own sake.[70]

---

69   Debord 1995, p. 13, translation altered; 2006b, p. 767.
70   Debord 1995, pp. 31–2, translation altered; 2006b, p. 780.

These claims are very closely connected to Debord's view that spectacular society had arisen as a result of 'the economic realm developing for itself'[71] beyond the point of its own obsolescence. In his view, society had outgrown its capitalist economy, and had in fact been ready to move beyond it for some time. In order to mask its obsolescence, capitalism had become reliant upon continually manufacturing new consumer demand for an ever-increasing quantity of ever more trivial and pointless goods.

Debord's claims here imply a notion of authentic 'human need', which contrasts with the false needs generated by an autonomous economy. He claims, for example, that within modern society, the 'satisfaction of primary human needs' has been replaced by the 'ceaseless manufacture of pseudo-needs'.[72] This is predicated upon the view that the primary *raison d'être* of the capitalist economy had been the maintenance of human survival. Because the needs of survival could now be met without relying upon capitalism, the capitalist economy was obliged to continually re-fashion the basic requirements of social existence. The abundance of commodities within modern society had resolved the 'basic problem of survival' – food, shelter, clothing, etc. were now far more accessible than in the past – but in the midst of that abundance, humanity was still required to labour for what Debord and the SI referred to as a form of 'augmented survival',[73] because the requirements of survival were 'continually being regenerated at a higher level'.[74] Capitalism, in other words, had become reliant upon convincing its subjects that their lives would be incomplete in the absence of its latest glittering promise of commodified satisfaction. The constant pursuit of the short-lived satisfactions proper to this 'air-conditioned vale of tears'[75] was thus seen as a mode of 'consumable survival'.[76]

In this regard, Debord comes extremely close to presenting the primacy of exchange-value over use-value as entailing the *perversion* of use-value. This would be highly problematic if Debord was only talking about commodities. Strictly speaking, there is nothing natural, authentic or non-alienated about use-value, as it is simply a dimension of the commodity-form. Yet when Debord describes spectacular society as 'monopolising' the 'fulfilment' of 'all human

---

71 Debord 1995, p. 16; 2006b, p. 769.
72 Debord 1995, p. 34, translation altered; 2006b, p. 782.
73 Debord 1995, p. 28; 2006b, p. 778.
74 Debord 1995, p. 28; 2006b, p. 778.
75 SI 2006, p. 103; 1997, p. 246. This is an allusion to Marx: 'The criticism of religion is therefore in *embryo* the *criticism of that vale of tears* of which religion is the *halo*' (Marx 1975, p. 244, emphasis in the original).
76 Debord 1995, p. 30; 2006b, pp. 779–80.

use-value',[77] it seems readily apparent that he is not just thinking about the use-value of commodities. Instead, 'human use-value' seems intended in a much broader sense, and would appear to denote not some putatively authentic dimension of the commodity-form, but rather human need, desire, utility and collective activity. This point, however, also underscores the sense in which Debord's formulations come extremely close to presenting all social reality in terms of the structure of the commodity-form: as a concrete realm of real activity and interaction (use-value) that has become shaped and managed by a phantasmagoria of spectacular imagery (exchange-value) that it both bears and serves.

Spectacular Time and the Total Commodity

This then brings us to Debord's notion of the 'total commodity': the idea that society as a whole can be understood as one vast instance of the commodity-form. In order to address this, we should look at the differing ways in which that idea relates to the two distinct modes of spectacular society that Debord identified in the 1960s. These two modes are the 'concentrated' and 'diffuse' forms of spectacle, which correspond, respectively, to bureaucratic state capitalism (i.e. to examples of so-called 'actually existing communism'), and to the consumer capitalism of the West.

In the diffuse spectacle, life is reduced to the condition of 'augmented survival' that we described earlier. This is because life is characterised by the constant, desperate pursuit of the trinkets that have become the supposed essentials of existence. Social activity is thereby channelled into the creation of a panoply of commodities, adverts, shop-fronts, fashions and entertainment, through which 'the total justification of the existing system's conditions and goals' are trumpeted throughout both the 'form and content'[78] of social praxis. Life as a whole becomes regulated and managed in accordance with the needs of the reigning economic system, because every instance of life becomes an element of a unitary whole. In the concentrated spectacle, however, the management of lived existence operates in a rather different manner. All social activity is regulated in keeping with a much more narrowly defined and heavily policed vision of the good life. This vision of the good is not disseminated and diffused via a host of commodified 'image-objects',[79] but is instead promoted through propaganda and displays of power, and is centred around a

---

77 Debord 1995, p. 31; 2006b, p. 780.
78 Debord 1995, p. 13, translation altered; 2006b, p. 767.
79 Debord 1995, p. 16; 2006b, p. 769.

ruling Party or leader: a focal point that operates as both condition and validation for an officially sanctioned version of human well-being. Anything that falls outside the bounds of that vision cannot be tolerated. The ruling bureaucracy can leave no notable margin of choice to its subjects: all valid decision must be located within the bureaucracy, insofar as the latter's validity relies on its supposed status and necessity as an expression of the agency and will of the whole (Debord: 'if every Chinese has to study Mao, and in effect be Mao, this is because there is *nothing else to be*').[80] In consequence, 'any independent choice [*choix extérieur*], even the most trivial – concerning food, say, or music – is therefore the choice for [the bureaucracy's] complete destruction'.[81] The concentrated spectacle does not, therefore, involve the glittering 'augmented survival' of the diffuse spectacle's abundance of commodities, but life is still reduced here to a kind of survival. This is because all social activity is directed into the preservation of what is, in effect, the only form of life possible: that which the reigning system approves and ensures.

Both systems were seen in terms of the 'total commodity': as a social whole that is, in effect, one *giant* commodity, composed of innumerable consumable fragments, all of which are meted out, piece by mystifying piece, to the inhabitants of these societies. For Debord, within such societies, all life – and thus all of the activity, creativity, potential and social power that Debord associates with life – becomes one great, alienated bloc. The power and unity of the whole (the absolute, if we were to put this in terms of our model of Debord's Hegelianism) thus becomes separated and detached. This alienated life is then returned in fragmentary, rationalised units to the atomised subjects that compose this society, each fragment purporting to offer the subject-object unity and access to fulfilment that this very condition of removal denies. The promised whole thus remains a perpetually receding lure, prompting further efforts towards yet more moments of survival.[82] In the diffuse spectacle, the promise of this absent subject-object unity is conveyed by a profusion of commodities, and by their derivative phenomena; in the concentrated spectacle, it is presented via depictions of the beneficence and power of the state, which cast the latter as emancipator and liberator of humanity. In both cases, individual life follows

---

80 Debord 1995, p. 42; 2006b, p. 788.
81 Debord 1995, p. 42, translation altered; 2006b, p. 788.
82 '[T]he already questionable satisfaction allegedly derived from *the consumption of the whole* is adulterated from the outset because the real consumer can only get his hands on a succession of fragments of this commodity heaven, fragments from which the quality ascribed to the whole is evidently absent each time' (Debord 1995, p. 43, translation altered; 2006b, p. 788, emphasis in the original).

the pattern of the Hegelian 'unhappy consciousness': the constant pursuit of a perpetually receding absolute that is, in truth, that consciousness' own alienated self.

In *The Society of the Spectacle*, Debord describes this whilst making explicit reference to alienated labour. He writes as follows:

> The *entirety of labour sold* is transformed overall into the *total commodity*. A cycle is then set in train that must be maintained at all costs: the total commodity must be returned in fragmentary form to a fragmented individual completely cut off from the concerted action of the forces of production.[83]

Later in the book, the same dynamic is identified in the concentrated spectacle. There, according to Debord, 'the production of commodities ... takes on a concentrated form': for 'the commodity that the bureaucracy appropriates is the totality of social labour, and what it sells back is survival *en bloc*',[84] i.e. an entire mode of life composed of moments of existence and experience that accord with the dominant social paradigm.

Debord was thus not only willing to adopt a rather creative and loose approach to the Marxian categories of use-value and exchange-value. In addition, 'labour' was also invoked in a very general sense: for it follows from Debord's account of spectacle, and indeed from the SI's broader project, that what is at stake here is not just labour *per se*, but rather *social activity in general*. In other words, it is not just the time spent in the workplace that produces the 'total commodity': in addition, *all* social activity that accords with the spectacle's ruling paradigms operates in the same manner. This claim can be supported by referring to Debord's conception of 'spectacular time'.[85]

The time of capitalist production, he claims, is characterised by abstract quantitative equivalence. Due to the rationalisation of work, and following the need for concrete labour to operate as the source of abstract value, the time of the workplace (to borrow Lukács's phrasing) 'sheds its qualitative, variable, flowing nature', and is thereby 'transformed into abstract, exactly measurable'[86] space. For Debord, however, 'alienated consumption' has been 'added to alien-

---

83   Debord 1995, p. 29; 2006b, p. 779, emphasis in the original.
84   Debord 1995, p. 41, translation altered; 2006b, p. 787.
85   Debord also describes spectacular time as 'consumable pseudo-cyclical time' (Debord 1995, p. 112; 2006b, p. 833): as the recurrence, within a social framework capable of supporting linear, historical time, of the repetitive cyclical time of earlier societies.
86   Lukács 1971, p. 90.

ated production as an inescapable duty of the masses',[87] and in consequence, this rationale of abstract equivalence has extended beyond the factory and office walls. The temporality of society as a whole has thus become characterised by that same rationale: the 'time founded on commodity production', according to Debord, 'is itself a consumable commodity', and it combines, as one great mass, 'private life, economic life, political life.'[88] Practically every element of life has become marked by the abstract quantitative equivalence that characterises the commodity-form, giving rise to a total social existence in which lived time has become composed of 'homogenous and exchangeable units', and which has thus become characterised by 'the suppression of any qualitative dimension'.[89]

Towards the beginning of this chapter, we noted that when charged with having neglected labour, the SI replied, in a statement of 1966, that: 'we believe that we have scarcely treated any other problem than that of labour in our epoch'. Having now discussed the issues outlined in the sections above, one can perhaps see why they felt able to make such a claim. In their view, labour had become tantamount to social activity in general. Yet if labour loses its specificity, then we are simply left with a rather loose and amorphous notion of biopolitics: a vision of life, understood as abstract potential, that has become shaped and managed by a dominant power structure. Furthermore: if, as Debord and the SI seem to consistently assume, capital arises from social labour, then how, if the concept of labour loses its specificity, can capital be adequately addressed and combatted? The rejection of Marxist economism that we described in the first half of this chapter; the SI's view that labour could no longer stand as the focal point of an anti-capitalist politics; the blurring of labour with life, and of capital with control; taken together, these issues would seem to amount to a body of Marxian anti-capitalist theory that struggles to address capital itself.

The implications of this position will be discussed further in the following chapter. Here, we can move towards a conclusion by looking at the ways in which these ideas informed the SI's conception of revolt.

Watts

As was indicated above, Debord's analyses tend to associate use-value with the real (concrete social reality and the human activity that composes it), and

---

87 Debord 1995, p. 29; 2006b, p. 779.
88 Debord 1995, p. 111; 2006b, p. 832.
89 Debord 1995, p. 110; 2006b, p. 831.

exchange-value with the general rationale of the spectacular order. In consequence, use-value becomes associated with real, human life, and exchange-value with the latter's denial. This then provides an important focal point for Debord and the SI's understanding of revolt and revolution. Rather than opting for a politics based around subverting the growth of capital by breaking down the wage-relation, Debord and the SI opted for a politics that involved stripping the real of the mystifications that surround and pervert it, and wresting use-value away from exchange-value. This can be illustrated by way of the following.

In 1965, the Watts district of Los Angeles erupted in a riot that lasted six days, and which resulted in 34 deaths and over 3,400 arrests. The SI responded with an essay titled 'The Decline and Fall of the Spectacle-Commodity Economy', which they quickly translated and circulated in England and America. The text links racial and working class unrest to the 'new poverty'[90] of the SI's new proletariat ('the Los Angeles rebellion', they wrote, 'is the first in history to justify itself with the argument that there was no air-conditioning during a heatwave'),[91] and it explicitly casts the riot as 'a rebellion against the commodity, against the world of the commodity'.[92] The Situationists claimed that the rioters took modern capitalist propaganda '*literally*', and that they thus demanded 'to possess *now* all the objects shown and abstractly accessible, because they wanted to *use* them'.[93] Through doing so, they contended, the rioters were 'challenging [the] *exchange-value* [of these objects], the *commodity reality* which moulds them and marshals them to its own ends'.[94] Because the spectacle locates all 'human use-value' within its framework, the riot constituted a direct challenge to the spectacular order, and thus amounted to an attempt to reclaim life itself. For the SI, therefore, the Watts rioters were engaged in an attempt to claim *all* use-value, here and now:

> A revolt against the spectacle – even if limited to a single district such as Watts – calls *everything* into question because it is a human protest against a dehumanised life, a protest of *real individuals* against their separation from a community that could fulfil their *true human and social nature* and transcend the spectacle.[95]

---

90 SI 2006 p. 141; 1997, p. 309.
91 SI 2006 p. 200; 1997, pp. 419–20.
92 SI 2006, p. 197; 1997, p. 416.
93 SI 2006, p. 197; 1997, p. 416, emphasis in the original.
94 SI 2006, p. 197; 1997, p. 416, emphasis in the original.
95 SI 2006, p. 203; 1997, p. 423, emphasis in the original.

The riot could thus be seen as a demand for unification, opposed to spectacular separation, and thus as an attempt to put an end to the unhappy consciousness' continual pursuit of its own alienated self. The problem, however, is that this attempt to affirm 'true human and social nature' in the face of the latter's spectacular suppression amounts to an opposition between life on the one hand, and its denial on the other.

Debord's scepticism towards any 'scientific' approach to the study of society and history was not only informed by a deep distaste for economism and Althusserian structuralism, but also by a good degree of romanticism. Like the romantics, Debord viewed human life, passion, struggle and creativity – tropes that he associated with a genuinely historical existence – as exceeding any scientific pretensions towards the identification and mastery of overarching structures, or towards unchanging economic laws.[96] This is not necessarily a problem; in many respects, it is perhaps one of the virtues of Debord's work. Yet if the roots of capitalist domination are left largely unexamined (as we have proposed is the case in Debord and the SI's work); and if the potential for revolution comes to be located in existential malaise, and thus in the stifled potential and dynamism of human life (as is, in effect, the case with the SI's 'new', reformulated conception of the proletariat); then it seems hard to deny that the SI ended up in a position that came very close to placing a romantic and quasi-vitalist human essence in opposition to its cold, mechanistic denial. In place of the Marxian contention that capital is not a thing, but rather a complex social relation, we instead have something very close to a confrontation between life *qua* potential, and a reified conception of capital *qua* life's suppression. In consequence, this perspective comes close to replacing Marx's emphases on the intrinsic contradictions *within* capitalist society with opposition *to* capitalist society: a perspective that is eminently suited to an aesthetic, subjective conception of revolt, but one that would seem somewhat limited in terms of identifying the nature of the object of that revolt.

---

96 Indeed, *The Society of the Spectacle* warns against economic determinism and structuralism by stating that if a revolutionary project endeavoured to 'master present history with scientific knowledge', it would remain inherently 'bourgeois' (Debord 1995, p. 53, translation altered; 2006b, p. 796), because it would replicate bourgeois society's attempts to validate and maintain its social order through the identification of supposedly immutable structures and systems. To view history as driven by such structures, rather than by human subjects, would be to naturalise the loss of historical subjectivity engendered by the capitalist present ('structures', to quote a May 1968 slogan that was chalked onto a Sorbonne blackboard, 'do not march in the street' (Noys 2010)).

We will try to show later that these problems are by no means insurmountable. We will also go on to argue that even if they were, they would not undermine the broader relevance and merits of the concept of spectacle. Before developing those claims, however, we need to develop further the line of critique that has been introduced here.

CHAPTER 11

The 'Fetishism of Capital'

Rejecting the Primacy of Labour

Capital, for Marx, is not a thing. It is not money, a lump of gold, means of production, etc., but rather a *social relation*:[1] a social relation that is marked by the subordination of lived activity to the dictates of capitalist value, and which is thus predicated upon the existence of wage-labour. Therefore, Marx's account of capitalist value: a) describes the totality of society as a social structure shaped by the operation of value; and b) indicates that the operation of value relies upon the social relations that support the wage-relation.

This means that for those operating within a broadly Marxian conceptual framework, labour is obviously crucial. This remains the case even if one arrives at the view that labour cannot be viewed in the terms of traditional Marxism. One might well hold, with some of the writers discussed in Chapter 9, that labour is inseparably wedded to the subordination of concrete, particular social activity to the dictates of abstract value; that it cannot be affirmed as a vehicle towards communism, as in traditional Marxism, but must instead be negated along with the social structure that it subtends. Yet even if one does take such a position, one can hardly neglect labour's importance to capitalist society. In fact, by framing it as a defining problem, such a stance makes labour all the more important.

These observations may seem rather obvious, but they should serve to indicate that it would be a mistake to slip from a *political rejection* of labour (i.e. from a refusal to endorse a classical Marxist affirmation of labour) to a *theoretical neglect* of labour's contemporary importance (i.e. to a lack of theoretical engagement with the centrality of labour to capitalist society). The previous chapter sought to indicate that Debord and the SI's theoretical work comes uncomfortably close to such a position. They held that capitalist labour had become redundant, that the wage-relation was no longer the primary point of contestation in modern society, and that Marxist economism needed to be rejected in favour of a more holistic vision of society. On these grounds, they opted for a political rejection of labour. The problem, however, is that

---

1 '[C]apital is a social relation of production. It is a historical [i.e. contextually specific] relation of production' (Marx 1990, p. 932n).

their desire to differentiate themselves from classical Marxism fostered a drift towards a theoretical neglect of labour's nature and centrality within capitalist society. The problem, of course, is that if one adopts a Marxian conceptual framework, as Debord and the SI surely did – a framework according to which value and capital derive from social labour – and if one also pays scant regard to the social relations that define and constitute labour – then one would arrive at a position that amounts to addressing a symptom without paying due attention to its causes.

This is by no means to suggest that the SI should be attacked for having the temerity to depart from classical Marxism's fixation on labour.[2] Indeed, it may well be important, when faced with the nature of modern capitalism, to move beyond Marx's nineteenth-century analyses. The fact remains, however, that Debord and the SI departed from classical Marxism's political emphasis on labour whilst still relying upon a broadly Marxian theory of value, according to which capitalist value *arises* from social labour. There is, therefore, a degree to which their account of capitalist society relies upon Marxian terms and concepts whilst simultaneously undermining their foundations. We will propose below that this this gave rise to what Dauvé has aptly described as a fetishised conception of capital: a view of capitalist value in which the latter appears to operate as if it were a separate force, removed from the social realities from which it arises.

Life and Its Denial

One of the primary claims made in the previous chapter was that Debord's analyses effectively blur labour with social activity in general. In his view, all action and experience had become composed of 'exchangeable homogenous units',[3] because life as a whole within modern society had become dominated and regulated by an autonomous social system. This blurring undermines the Marxian identification of capital with a specific set of social relations, relying

---

2 Criticising Debord and the SI in this manner need not entail faulting them for failing to adhere to some kind of Marxist orthodoxy. After all, Marx himself was engaged in continually re-writing and re-formulating his ideas until his death, and his claim to have 'never promulgated a "socialist system"' (Marx 2009, p. 230) stands in obvious contrast to the dogmatism that later surrounded his work (one might think here of Lenin's alarming contention that: 'The teaching of Marx is all-powerful because it is true. It is complete and harmonious, providing men with a consistent view of the universe' (Lenin, quoted in Heinrich 2012, p. 25)).

3 Debord 1995, p. 110; 2006b, p. 831.

instead, however tacitly, upon a much more amorphous notion of biopolitics. In a manner that bears some resemblance to Negri's own, similarly problematic views,[4] the potential of life *qua* socially constitutive activity is placed in opposition to the repressive framework of its current integument (indeed, at times, Debord and the SI credited this oppositional vitality with a degree of excessive, transgressive and passionate energy that recalls both Nietzsche and Bataille).[5] This is compounded by Debord's views on the quasi-subjective 'life' of capitalist value. In Marx's mature work, capitalist value is described as an 'automatic subject'.[6] Debord is indebted to these aspects of Marx's work, and he places the vitality of human social life in opposition to the inhuman 'life' of capital. Yet because the latter is treated as a separate force (its roots in social labour having been neglected in favour of a more abstract notion of biopolitical activity), this opposition risks degenerating into a romantic and decidedly un-dialectical dichotomy between human life on the one hand, and a hostile, independent entity that would deny that life on the other (i.e. capital).

This opposition between life and its denial bears direct and obvious relation to the concepts of historical 'life' and spectacular 'non-life' that we developed and discussed in Chapter 8. Yet rather than reinforcing the romantic dichotomy described here (i.e. that between capital and the nascent collective human subject that would oppose it), the notions of life and non-life that we developed in Chapter 8 may actually serve to mitigate that problematic dichotomy. This is because they do not denote the humanistic essentialism that they might seem to imply. Instead, and as we sought to demonstrate in that chapter, they pertain to specific forms of social mediation, and thus to the conceptions of universality and particularity that inform Debord's theory of spectacle. 'Non-life', we argued, corresponds to modes of social existence wherein forms of social universality become alienated from the particular individuals whom they mediate and interrelate (e.g. capitalist value, which derives from their collective labour, or the rule of a Party that professes to actualise their collective will). Historical 'life', on the other hand, pertains to the organic interrelation of the universal and the particular, and was thus associated with forms of collective existence wherein particular individuals are not bound together as atomised elements, united by an alienated, autonomous universality, but in which they relate to one another directly and collectively. Debord's notions

---

[4] Negri's own Spinozist account of biopolitics collapses society into a form of monism that renders capital largely indeterminate (See Noys 2010, pp. 106–25; see also Aufheben 2006).

[5] See Hemmens 2013 for a discussion of Vaneigem's work that highlights issues such as his proximity to Nietzsche.

[6] Marx 1990, p. 255.

of life and non-life, therefore, refer to the arrangement and conduct of social relations. In consequence, they could provide a bulwark of sorts against the romantic and dichotomous essentialism outlined above.

In this sense, we will argue that Debord's references to life and its denial both reflect a weak point in his theory and offer resources towards remedying that same weakness. At times, they imply the suppression of a kind of vital essence, and the subordination of society to the latter's peculiarly animate denial; at others, they imply a much greater sensitivity to the social relations that compose a society marked by alienation.

These issues centre around the manner in which Debord used Marx's remarks concerning the pseudo-subjective operation of capitalist value. On the one hand, Debord comes extremely close to casting the spectral self-movement of capitalist value as a hostile force in its own right. The primary burden of this chapter will be to demonstrate this point, which follows directly from the theoretical neglect of labour described earlier. Yet nonetheless, it remains the case that there remain elements within Debord's work that provide the grounds for a more sophisticated view. This more satisfactory side of Debord's account of capitalist society highlights the social atomisation proper to non-life, and it foregrounds the separation of the universal from the particular which that atomisation entails. In doing so, it treats that separation as both the condition and the cause of capital's seemingly autonomous movement. To put this more explicitly: Debord's tendency to place a romanticised life, *qua* vital, excessive potential, in immediate opposition to its denial, is tempered by his indications that this denial emerges from the conduct and arrangement of a set of social relations. When seen in these terms, capital, and the spectacular nexus of separated social power that it engenders, ceases to be a mysteriously and independently animate counter-subject, and comes one step closer to being viewed as the result of a particular social framework.

This then means that it may well be possible to develop a more adequate account of capitalist social relations from Debord's theory of spectacle, or indeed to develop the latter's compatibility with those elements of contemporary Marxian theory which could support that possibility. We will close by making some comments concerning the manner in which this might be pursued. The primary focus of what follows below will, however, rest upon the more problematic side of Debord's thought: on the dimensions of his theory that come too close to locating a positive, abstract notion of human life in simple, dichotomous opposition to its suppression.

We will begin with some introductory comments that should serve to offer a response to the following question. We have repeatedly indicated that capital needs to be understood as a social relation, but what, exactly, does that mean?

The Unhappiness of Mr. Peel

The first volume of *Capital* begins by announcing that 'the wealth of societies in which the capitalist mode of production prevails presents itself as an immense accumulation of commodities'.[7] It ends by stating that 'the capitalist mode of production and accumulation, and therefore capitalist private property as well, have for their fundamental condition the annihilation of that private property which rests on the labour of the individual himself; in other words, the expropriation of the worker.'[8] Marx begins, therefore, by noting that the wealth proper to capitalist production *presents itself* as a mass of commodities; he closes, however, with the contention that this wealth relies upon impoverishment. Although we begin the book with an immense accumulation of private property (i.e. commodities), we learn, during the course of the book's analyses, that the production of these commodities entails the expropriation and exploitation of their producers. In other words: capital is not just wealth, as opposed to poverty. Instead, capital is a form of wealth that engenders, and which in fact relies upon, poverty.

Marx's presentation in *Capital* moves from the simple and abstract to the concrete and complex, and at each stage of his exposition he introduces a new set of ideas that serve to refine and develop those that have already been discussed. The book does not, therefore, begin with a discussion of capital: instead, it starts by discussing commodities, value and money. This is because capital, simply put, is value that has the capacity to become *more* value, and its ability to do so is dependent upon commodity production and exchange.

Capital is first introduced into the book's narrative when Marx begins to talk about the possibility of buying commodities cheap, and of then selling them dear. In such circumstances, 'value ... increases its magnitude' by passing through the successive forms of money, commodity and then money once more, and this 'movement', Marx writes, 'converts it into capital'.[9] It soon transpires, however, that mercantile exchange is not the true source of capital. For Marx – and this is, of course, crucial to his claims – it stems from the exploitation of labour (or rather, from the generation of surplus-value).[10] Capital, there-

---

7   Marx 1990, p. 125; translation altered for continuity with Debord 1995, p. 12.
8   Marx 1990, p. 940.
9   Marx 1990, p. 252.
10 To sketch this very briefly: workers do not sell the labour that they perform for a wage. Instead, they sell their labour-power, i.e. their capacity to labour. Once the buyer of labour-power has purchased this commodity, he or she can dispose of it as they wish: for once it

fore, is not just the accumulation of greater sums of value through exchange. Instead, that accumulation relies upon a condition of 'command over unpaid labour'.[11] Marx thus shows that the very existence of capital requires the maintenance, perpetuity, and indeed the expansion, of that condition of command.

This means that capital's existence must rely upon the ready availability of a class of individuals who have no choice but to be exploited in this fashion: individuals who cannot provide for their own means of subsistence independently, and who must, in consequence, work for a wage in order to buy the things that they require as commodities.[12] Ultimately, therefore, Marx's analyses show that capital is a social relation marked by class antagonism.[13] The peculiarity of this social relation, however, is that it masks its own contingency. Capital is value that has the capacity to grow, but value must always be attached to commodities, money and means of production. Consequently, it tends to become identified with the commodities that serve as its bearers, and as a result, the social relations of capital become reified as things. This can be illustrated with one of Marx's own examples. At the end of *Capital*'s first volume, Marx discusses the difficulty involved in transplanting capitalism to the colonies. Whilst quoting Wakefield, a 'bourgeois economist' concerned with the tendency of colonial workers to abandon their employment, Marx writes of an unfortunate Mr. Peel, who:

> ... took with him from England to the Swan River district of Western Australia means of subsistence and of production to the amount of £50,000. This Mr. Peel even had the foresight to bring besides 3,000 persons of

---

has been purchased, the buyer can use as much or as little of it as he or she wishes. There is, therefore, no reason why the price of a day's labour needs to correspond to the quantity of labour performed during that day. Consequently, whilst the wage may appear to be a fair exchange, the worker may well produce a far greater quantity of value than that which the wage represents. This is the 'trick' by which the money laid out by the capitalist can be 'transformed into capital' (Marx 1990, p. 301).

11 Marx 1990, p. 672.
12 'The capitalist class is constantly giving to the working class drafts, in the form of money, on a portion of the product produced by the latter and appropriated by the former. The workers give these drafts back just as constantly to the capitalists, and thereby withdraw from the latter their allotted share of their own product' (Marx 1990, p. 713).
13 'The capitalist process of production, therefore, seen as a total, connected process, i.e. a process of reproduction, produces not only commodities, not only surplus-value, but it also produces and reproduces the capital-relation itself; on the one hand the capitalist, on the other the wage-labourer' (Marx 1990, p. 724).

the working class, men, women and children. Once he arrived at his destination, 'Mr. Peel was left without a servant to make his bed or fetch him water from the river'. Unhappy Mr. Peel, who provided for everything except the export of English relations of production to Swan River![14]

In the new colonies, where the workers were able to abscond, and could meet their needs of subsistence independently, the capital relation broke down. The resources that Mr. Peel shipped to Australia ceased to function as capital. Mr. Peel was, however, seemingly oblivious to the fact that the social attributes accorded to these resources would dissolve once they were removed from their capitalist context. 'A mule', Marx writes, 'is a machine for spinning cotton. Only in certain relations does it become capital. Outside these circumstances it is no more capital than gold is intrinsically money, or sugar is the price of sugar.'[15] Nonetheless, he adds, the 'capitalist soul' of such items is 'so intimately wedded, in the mind of the political economist, to their material substance, that he christens them capital under all circumstances'.[16]

Mr. Peel's unhappiness was caused by his ignorance of the fact that the capitalist attributes of his goods depended entirely upon the social relations within which they were located. We will go on to argue below that in some respects, Debord can be seen to adopt a somewhat similar stance. This is because he comes uncomfortably close to neglecting the fact that within a Marxian conceptual framework, capital's seemingly autonomous and quasi-subjective attributes depend upon the social relations proper to capitalist labour.

In order to develop that claim, we will need to say a little more about the nature of capitalist value, Marx's notion of fetishism, and the apparently independent operation of capital itself.

Appearance and Essence

In 1858, when working on what would become the first draft of *Capital*, Marx wrote to Engels that he had returned to Hegel's *Science of Logic*, and noted that the latter book had greatly assisted his work. 'The fact that by mere accident I again glanced through Hegel's *Logik*', Marx writes, 'has been of great service to

---

14   Marx 1990, p. 933.
15   Marx 1990, p. 932.
16   Marx 1990, p. 933.

me as regards the method of dealing with the material'.[17] Of particular interest here is the manner in which that 'method' was informed by Hegel's conception of 'essence'. The latter's relevance can be introduced by way of the following remark, which comes from Isaak Illich Rubin's seminal study of Marx's value theory of 1924; a work that was initially forgotten, following Rubin's execution in 1930,[18] but which has since become a primary reference point for value-form approaches to Marx's theory. Rubin writes as follows:

> One cannot forget that, on the question of the relation between content and form, Marx took the *standpoint of Hegel*, and not of Kant. Kant treated form as something *external* in relation to the content, and as something that adheres to the content *from the outside*. From the standpoint of Hegel's philosophy, the content is not in itself something to which form adheres from the outside. ... [in Marx's work] the form of value necessarily grows out of the substance of value.[19]

In Kant's work, the categories of thought operate as a stable, independent structure that is brought to bear upon a content (sense-data) that is simply given to it. In Kant, therefore, the relation between form (the categories) and the content articulated by that form (sense-data) is that of an imposed structure. In Hegel's philosophy, however, form is not something that is simply imposed upon the content that it shapes and relates, but is instead intrinsic to that content, in much the same way that the physical structure of a living being is by no means arbitrarily related to its life-process. The relevance of these issues to Marx's work is simply this: value, as content, is not arbitrarily related to the forms in which it is expressed (money, commodities, etc.). Instead, value *cannot exist* independently of the forms in which it is expressed and instantiated.

This point is closely connected to the *Logic*'s discussion of the categories of 'essence' and 'appearance'. When discussing these categories of thought, Hegel rejects any sense in which an essence might lie behind or beyond the appearances to which it gives rise. Instead, he holds that that which appears

---

17 Quoted in Moseley and Smith 2014, p. 2.
18 Following Rubin's arrest in 1930, an official Soviet philosopher wrote: 'The followers of Rubin and the Menshevizing Idealists ... treated Marx's revolutionary method in the spirit of Hegelianism. ... The Communist Party has smashed these trends alien to Marxism' (quoted by Perlman in Rubin 1972, p. 277). Rubin was imprisoned, forced to confess and finally executed.
19 Rubin 1972, p. 117; also quoted and discussed in Bellofiore 2009, p. 191.

needs to be understood as a necessary expression of an essence that can only function *as* essence through manifesting itself in its appearances.[20] Something very similar can be found in Marx's account of value.

It bears repeating here that Marx's labour theory of value is quite distinct from a classical, substantialist labour theory of value (this despite the prevalence of views to the contrary: Schumpeter, for example, once described Marx as a rude Ricardo).[21] Value is not a measure of the time that an individual takes to complete a task, but rather of the socially average labour time required to perform that task.[22] Consequently, qualitatively distinct labour only 'counts', as far as capitalist value is concerned, as a portion of abstract labour, i.e. as a quantity of an entirely abstract social average, and it can only be validated as such through commodity exchange. This means that whilst value, for Marx, certainly emerges from productive labour, it cannot exist independently of commodity exchange. It does not subsist within the products of labour, but is instead associated with them by virtue of their status as commodities. Value, therefore, is an intangible abstraction, but it is an abstraction that is also profoundly *real*: it only exists insofar as it is instantiated in the labour, commodities, money, means of production, and so on, that it articulates. The debates and nuances involved here are complex,[23] but as regards our current concerns, the salient point here is simply that value, as abstract essence, cannot exist independently of the forms in which it appears.

This means that the illusory identification of value with commodities is not just an ideological confusion, but is instead fundamental to their operation *as* commodities. That is not to deny that there is an issue of mystification involved here. Marx is often at pains to indicate that the peculiar nature of capitalist social relations is such that this state of affairs becomes naturalised: abstract value becomes fetishistically identified with the concrete objects that it 'haunts',[24] and to which it accords its pseudo-life. Gold, to pick an obvious

---

20 'Essence therefore is not *behind* or *beyond* appearance, but since it is the essence that exists, existence is appearance' (Hegel 1991, p. 199, emphasis in the original).
21 Backhaus quotes Schumpeter as follows: '[Marx's] value theory is the Ricardian one … [his] arguments are merely less polite, more longwinded and more "philosophical" in the worst sense of the word' (Backhaus 1980, p. 99).
22 'Socially necessary labour-time is the labour-time required to produce any use-value under the conditions of production normal for a given society and with the average degree of skill and intensity of labour prevalent in that society' (Marx 1990, p. 129).
23 See Bellofiore and Redolfi Riva 2015, and Elbe 2013, for useful overviews.
24 Marx 1990, p. 213 (Marx uses this term to refer to money, which 'haunts the sphere of circulation and constantly moves around in it', but the principle remains the same).

example, is only yellow metal; only in certain circumstances does it function as capital. Yet whilst it may well be a socially contingent mystification to believe that a lump of gold is equivalent to a certain amount of tea, or to a certain amount of iron, such equivalence is, for Marx, a real, concrete fact of capitalist exchange; and whilst 'no chemist has ever discovered exchange-value either in a pearl or a diamond',[25] pearls and diamonds *really are* exchangeable with one another in capitalist society, because once they become commodities, they function as instantiations of value.

There is, therefore, much more at stake in Marx's notion of fetishism than is sometimes assumed. When describing and referring to fetishism, Marx is not just addressing a purely mental inability to find the 'truth' of social labour lurking behind the false veil of commodity prices. Fetishism is not just a form of purely intellectual confusion, or a kind of collective hallucination. Instead, the 'magic and necromancy'[26] that surrounds the products of labour within capitalist society stem from the fact that such objects *really do* operate as the bearers of a socially animating abstraction.

In the very first chapter of *Capital* – a chapter that sets out the abstract, basic principles that will be developed and elaborated during the course of *Capital*'s three volumes – Marx shows that capitalist value relies upon the existence of a society that has no direct control over its own economic activity. This is a society in which socially productive activity and interaction are dictated by the arbitrary, fluctuating relations between commodities. Those relations may well arise from the activity of the producers and sellers of these commodities, but in a sense, the actions and interactions of these individuals are not really their own. Their activity follows the dictates of value, which must appear as commodities and money, and which, as capital, must grow through the exploitation of labour in production. Thus, according to Marx, within the 'bewitched, distorted and upside-down world'[27] of capitalist society, the 'social action' of human producers takes on 'the form of a movement made by things, and these things, far from being under their control, in fact control them.'[28] For Marx, then, the operation of capitalist value entails the denigration of human subjectivity, and the attendant actualisation of the inhuman, ghostly subjectivity of capitalist value: a 'phantom-like'[29] subjectivity, in which 'Monsieur le Cap-

---

25   Marx 1990, p. 177.
26   Marx 1990, p. 169.
27   Marx 1991, p. 969.
28   Marx 1990, pp. 167–8.
29   Marx 1990, p. 128.

ital and Madame la Terre do their ghost-walking as social characters and at the same time directly as mere things'.[30]

A 'Self-Moving Substance'

The notion of subjectivity that Marx employs here owes a great deal to Hegel. To speak very generally: in his early work, Marx often uses the characteristic movement of Hegelian thought (i.e. the movement of the Concept, through which something becomes other to itself in order to become more fully itself) in order to think the self-constitutive activity of human subjects.[31] Seen in such terms, human subjectivity is characterised by a processual condition, in which the subject continually externalises itself through its actions upon the world, and thereby shapes both itself and its environment. If it is conceived in this manner, the human subject becomes a historically differentiated and processual entity, characterised by a constant condition of negative, transformative becoming. As we sought to show in Chapter 7, such a vision of the human subject bears direct relation to the philosophical anthropology that underlies Debord's claims.

In his later work, however, Marx tends to use that same Hegelian movement to conceive the operation of capital. Although value is abstract and intangible, it operates by taking on a succession of differing concrete forms (money, commodities, more money), growing and functioning as capital through doing so. Capitalist value is thus marked by a kind of subjective movement of its own: rather than the human agent externalising and determining itself through action, as in Marx's early ontology of human subjectivity, we instead have a process in which value operates as a 'self-moving substance',[32] and as an 'automatic subject'.[33] Because value shapes the actions and interactions of individuals within capitalist society, and because such social activity takes place according to its needs, there is a strong sense, in Marx's later work, in which human

---

30   Marx 1991, p. 969.
31   In the 1844 *Manuscripts*, Marx explicitly praises Hegel's philosophy for the conception of self-determinate activity that it presents: the 'outstanding thing in Hegel's *Phenomenology* and its final outcome', he wrote, 'that is, the dialectic of negativity as the moving and generating principle', is that 'Hegel conceives the self-genesis of man as a process' (Marx 1988, p. 149).
32   Marx 1990, p. 256.
33   Marx 1990, p. 255.

agents have become confronted and dominated by an antagonistic counter-subject that now governs society in their stead.

How, then, do these two uses of Hegelian notions of subjectivity relate to one another?

For some commentators, Marx's later view replaces that expressed in his earlier writings. Moishe Postone, for example, treats this somewhat similarly to Althusser's supposed break between the young and mature Marx, whereby the latter distanced himself from the former's ideological and unscientific errors. Postone's claims appear to rest on the view that Hegelian logic is not simply a convenient tool with which to think the operation of capitalist value, but in fact corresponds to capitalist value's real nature. Thus, for Postone, Hegel inadvertently and ideologically mirrored the real nature of capitalism in his philosophy, thereby transfiguring and mystifying capital's operation by casting it as the very framework of reality itself. Marx's early use of this philosophy as a means of conceiving the activity of the human subject is, therefore, deeply problematic for Postone, and can be criticised as an ideological error; an error, moreover, that Marx's mature work rectifies, by correctly identifying this Hegelian movement with capital.[34] Although others may not go quite as far as Postone in this regard, a similar scepticism towards conceptions of the human subject can be found in much contemporary Marxian thought. Capital is viewed as the only real subject in modern society. Focussing on human subjectivity is therefore deemed to run the risk of naturalising the modes of thought and patterns of behaviour that capitalism engenders.[35]

Debord, however, takes a rather different line. Although *The Society of the Spectacle* is greatly indebted to the Marx of *Capital*, practically all of its references and allusions to Marx are taken from the latter's early writings.[36] In fact, Debord seems to have read Marx's later work through the lens of those

---

34 For Postone, 'Marx's critique of Hegel ... is quite different from Lukács' materialist appropriation of Hegel, for it does not identify a concrete, conscious, social Subject (for example, the Proletariat) that unfolds historically ... [Such a historical Subject] would be a collective version of the bourgeois subject, constituting itself and the world through "labour"' (Postone 1996, p. 78).

35 One can find traces of this view in Jappe's study of Debord. For Jappe, Debord was too close to the 'aspect of Marx's thought that assigns a central role to the concepts of "classes" and "class struggles" – concepts that were also primary for the workers' movement' (Jappe 1999, p. 37). For Jappe, 'The workers' movement ... partook ... of the typical illusion of the bourgeois subject, which believes that it is making decisions when in reality the fetishistic system is the agent' (Jappe 1999, p. 38). Similar concerns are stressed in Jappe's more recent work (see Jappe 2015 for an overview).

36 As we noted in Chapter 7, Debord explicitly states in his correspondence that almost all

earlier texts, as his claims indicate that the seemingly subjective self-movement of value described in *Capital* is in fact an alienated perversion of the human subjectivity described in Marx's early work. The human, in other words, has become dominated by the inhuman.

This then returns us to Debord's notions of life and non-life. Sensitive to Marx's indications that the abstract pseudo-subject of capitalist value now governs society, Debord, like Marx, claimed that capitalist society has become possessed by a quasi-subjective, self-constitutive animating force. This is a force that runs counter to, and which suppresses and re-fashions, the subjective agency of human individuals. Capitalist value operates as if it were an antithetical form of self-determinacy to that of these individuals, because it parasitises their activity and interactions, rendering them a vehicle for its own pseudo-'life'. Social life has thus suffered what Debord refers to as a 'concrete inversion',[37] for within 'a world that *really has* been turned on its head, the true is a moment of the false'.[38] The latter, much-quoted aphorism is more complex than it may first appear,[39] but its basic meaning is very simple: the 'truth' of human historical life, for Debord, has become reduced to the 'falsehood' of non-life, as human subjectivity has become subordinate to that of capital.

---

of *The Society of the Spectacle*'s references to Marx are drawn from texts that were written between 1843 and 1846 (Debord 2004a, p. 140).

37   Debord 1995, p. 12; 2006b, p. 766.
38   Debord 1995, p. 14, translation altered; 2006b, p. 768, emphasis in the original.
39   Debord's claim is an oblique reference to a passage in Hegel's preface to the *Phenomenology*. For Hegel, the genuinely true subsumes the false, revealing the latter to be a necessary element within the operation and development of the true. However, Hegel also explains that this does not mean that the false can be considered to be a moment of the true. Because the terms 'true' and 'false' rely on their distinction from one another, they lose their meaning within a unity that sublates that difference. The terms no longer apply. This leads Hegel to write that within such a unity, 'the false is no longer, *qua* false, a moment of truth' (Hegel 1977, p. 23). Debord's own formulation (which he was sufficiently fond of to reference again in his *Comments on the Society of the Spectacle* (Debord 1998, p. 50; 2006b, p. 1622)) reverses Hegel's claim in two senses. Firstly, he switches the position of the 'true' and the 'false', thereby indicating that the false subsumes the true rather than *vice versa*. Secondly, he indicates that the one *really can* be considered to be a moment of the other (Hegel said that the false *cannot* be understood as a moment of the true; Debord states that the true *is* a moment of the false). The first of these two moves reflects his view that life has been rendered 'false' as a result of its capitalist subsumption. The second move is particularly important, as it keeps open the possibility for political change. This is because it implies that this subsumption does not sublate the distinction between the two terms: the terms true and false continue to apply, because life remains opposed to its capitalist falsification; the true subsists within the generalised falsehood of the spectacle (Debord

The problem, however, is that whilst these elements of Debord's theory certainly draw upon and accord with Marx's own views, Debord's relative lack of engagement with value's basis in social labour entails that value's seemingly subjective movement appears as if it were that of a separate, hostile entity. Rather than a flawed set of social relations that immanently generates its own condition of domination, we instead have a view in which the authentic vitality of human life is simply set in opposition to its outright antithesis.

This is not to deny that Debord employs the Marxian view that value arises from labour. Nor is it to deny that he explicitly links the modern spectacle to abstract labour. For example, in *The Society of the Spectacle*, he writes that the 'abstraction of all particular [i.e. qualitatively distinct and concrete] labour', and 'the generalised abstraction of the entirety of production', are 'perfectly rendered in the spectacle, whose mode of being concrete is precisely abstraction.'[40] Yet nonetheless, value's roots in labour, and above all the wage-relation that articulate the latter, are not really addressed.

This leaves Debord's work susceptible to a line of critique that Marx advanced in the *Grundrisse*. Marx indicates there that it is not enough to present capital as alienated social power, as Debord certainly does. In addition, one must view capital as fundamentally interwoven with the very genesis and operation of such alienation. Or, as Marx puts it: 'those who demonstrate that all the productive force ascribed to capital is a *displacement*, a *transposition of the productive force* of labour, forget precisely that capital itself is essentially this *displacement*, this *transposition*'.[41] Capital is a *social relation*. If this is neglected, one runs the risk of losing sight of its objective bases, and thereby of the means by which it might be addressed and attacked. Given that Debord's theoretical work was written 'with the deliberate intention of doing harm to spectacular society',[42] the problems noted here and in the previous chapter would seem to limit its anti-capitalist ambitions.

Debord's rejection of economism, the SI's focus on everyday life, their effectively class-less 'new' proletariat; all of these issues appear to have fostered a degree of slippage, in Debord's theoretical work, between a coherent and valid *political* rejection of labour's primacy within traditional Marxian politics, and a rather more questionable neglect of labour's importance to *theory*. As a res-

---

may have picked up on this statement from the *Phenomenology* via Lukács, who also discusses and re-works it in the first preface to his *History and Class Consciousness* (Lukács 1971, p. xlvii)).

40 Debord 1995, p. 22, translation altered; 2006b, p. 774.
41 Marx 1973b, pp. 308–9, emphasis in the original; quoted in Arthur 2004a, p. 48.
42 Debord 1995, p. 10; 2006b, p. 1794.

ult of that slippage, Debord ends up with a view of capitalist society wherein capital becomes tantamount to an independent, hostile force that is certainly described as being animated by alienated social power, but which is treated in a manner whereby the technicalities and causes of that alienation become somewhat difficult to discern.

We can try to clarify and develop the latter contention by noting two somewhat similar criticisms of Situationist theory.

Claude Lefort: The Production of the Phantasmagoria

The Society of the Spectacle was published in 1967, as was Vaneigem's *The Revolution of Everyday Life*. In the February of the following year, a critical review of both books appeared in *La Quinzaine littéraire*. The review was written by Claude Lefort, an ex-member of s ou B who had left that group prior to Debord's affiliation with it,[43] and it was almost entirely directed towards Debord's book.

The review begins by congratulating Debord and the SI for making an 'appeal to Marx against Stalin', and for attempting to develop radical theory whilst avoiding the 'traps' of Maoism, Trotskyism, and so on. Lefort also praises Debord for focussing on spectacle, and writes as follows:

> [Debord] is right to seek, beyond the commonly denounced triviality of advertising, an ethos of advertising; to link political power to that of representation; to show that the partitioning of sectors of activity, the isolation of individuals, and their withdrawal into private life, all accompany the increased pre-eminence of universally available imagery, and the consolidation of one or more powers fostering the mirage of a collective identity at a time when such an identity has never been so fragmented.[44]

---

43 In a letter of 1958, Debord referred to s ou B as 'mechanistic to a frightening extent' (Debord 2009, p. 152). His views had, however, mellowed by 1959, as Lefort's departure from the group, together with its 'rebel wing' of 'anti-organisationalists' was said to have led to 'progress' within its eponymous journal (Debord 2009, p. 265). Debord's antipathy towards Lefort was evidenced again in the response to Lefort's review that was published in *Internationale situationniste*. In addition to correcting Lefort's reading of his book, Debord charged Lefort with the conservatism of having cast all revolutionary organisation as doomed to collapse into bureaucracy.

44 Lefort 1968; thanks are due to John McHale for his advice regarding the translation of this passage.

Lefort's understanding of spectacle is, however, somewhat questionable. He appears to have understood spectacle as a 'phantasmagoria' that smothers and validates modern society, and which thereby justifies its mode of production. Lefort, in other words, seems to view spectacle as the ideological illusions, beliefs and mystifications that articulate contemporary culture, and which preserve its capitalist foundations. He also seems to have viewed these mystifications through a rather traditional notion of commodity fetishism, as his review treats them as though they were false conceptual and cultural illusions that mask the true reality of capitalist production. This approach to Debord's concept is highly questionable. As we have tried to show, spectacle is not just an ideological mystification, but rather the concrete reality of an entire sociohistorical moment. To put that otherwise: Debord does not simply use the Marxian notion of fetishism to address false ideas *about* the dominant mode of production, but rather to highlight the falsity and perversion *of* that mode of production; a falsehood that follows from the sense in which the collective powers of human agents really have been transposed onto an effectively independent economic system. The main thrust of Lefort's argument is, however, close to the line of critique that we have advanced here and in the previous chapter. This is because in Lefort's view, Debord does not pay sufficient attention to the nature of the social relations that give rise to this generalised mystification.

According to Lefort, Debord is 'intoxicated [*grisé*]'[45] by Marx's account of the fetish. Drunk on fetishism – or rather, following Lefort's reading, drunk on a version of fetishism that treats the latter as ideological confusion, rather than as a real inversion – Debord leads us to understand 'that it is not the system of commodity production to which we owe the phantasmagoric movement that animates things'; instead, according to Lefort, Debord effectively contends that 'the production of this phantasmagoria commands that of commodities.'[46] In other words, for Lefort, Debord was so thoroughly intoxicated by the idea of a confused representation of the reality of capitalist production that he himself confusedly ignored that very reality. For Lefort, therefore, Debord had indicated that society is driven by the illusions that celebrate commodity production, and not by commodity production *per se*.

The SI replied to Lefort's review in a text titled 'How Not to Understand Situationist Books'. In their response, they highlighted Lefort's primary error. Where Lefort contends that for Debord, the production of illusions that surround com-

---

45 Lefort 1968.
46 Ibid.

modities takes precedence over the actual production of commodities, the SI pointed out that Debord had, in fact, stated 'the exact opposite': *The Society of the Spectacle* explicitly describes the spectacle as 'simply a moment of the development of commodity production'.[47] Nonetheless, the core of Lefort's view – i.e. the contention that Debord focuses on capitalism's mystifying and alienating *effects*, rather than on the latter's objective *causes* – remains relevant.

In Debord's book, according to Lefort, '"the society of the spectacle" is laid out before a gaze that is never troubled, and which wants to know nothing of the place in which it is made.'[48] This is because alienation, in Debord's work, is said to be 'distributed according to a panoramic perspective',[49] as all aspects of society have become as alienated as all others. The SI were quite right to mock the placid vision that Lefort thus identifies ('Lefort is ... able to reach the pleasing conclusion that "according to Debord, all history is futile"!'),[50] but despite their flaws, Lefort's remarks in this regard remain pertinent. This is because they serve to illustrate the sense in which a disregard for the antagonistic relations that drive value production can render history's supposedly imminent reappearance somewhat mysterious. Indeed, whilst mocking Debord's Hegelianism (the frequency with which Hegelian sentence reversals occur in *The Society of the Spectacle* is described as 'obsessional'), Lefort characterises this re-appearance as bordering on idealism.[51]

Gilles Dauvé: Capital as a 'Living Being'

Rather similar claims to those advanced by Lefort were set out by Gilles Dauvé in his 'Critique of the Situationist International' of 1979. This text was originally written as part of a longer work that was never published, but has since gained a degree of prominence in its own right.[52] Although his understanding

---

47 SI 2006, p. 341; 1997, p. 616.
48 Lefort 1968.
49 Ibid.
50 SI 2006, p. 341; 1997, p. 616.
51 Referencing Hegel's 'cunning of reason', Lefort writes that 'unreason would also seem to be cunning', as 'the spectacle of society is accomplished in the spirit of Debord' (Lefort 1968).
52 It has been published in English three times. The text first appeared in the American journal *Red-Eye* in 1979; it was re-published as a pamphlet titled 'What is Situationism?' in 1987, and was then published once again in Stewart Home's *What is Situationism? A Reader* in 1996 (Dauvé 1979).

of spectacle differs from that presented in this book (and although Debord condemned him as a 'Bordigist-revisionist'),[53] Dauvé's critique sets out a number of points to which our own argument is indebted.

The critique draws on Marx's indications in *Capital* that we need to move beyond the sphere of circulation in order to address that of production. Marx concludes the second part of Volume 1 by stating that the reader needs to be taken beyond 'the noisy sphere' of 'circulation', where 'everything takes place on the surface and in full view of everyone', in order to enter 'the hidden abode of production', wherein one can discover 'not only how capital produces, but how capital itself is produced'.[54] One needs, in other words, to move past the surface appearances of capitalist society, in order to address their bases. For Dauvé, however, Debord 'remains at the stage of circulation, lacking the necessary moment of production, of productive labour'.[55]

This is why Dauvé claims that Debord 'made a study of the profound, through and by means of the superficial appearance'.[56] This does not mean that he is describing *The Society of the Spectacle* itself as superficial. Instead, his argument is that the book's ability to grasp the roots of the representations that it addresses is hampered by its lack of engagement with their economic bases. Debord is cast as criticising capital in its entirety, but he is faulted for having done so from a perspective that remains within the ambit of its surface appearances. Or, as Dauvé puts it: the Situationists 'had no analysis of capital: [they] understood it, but through its effects:'[57] for what 'nourishes capital', Dauvé writes, 'is not consumption, as [Debord] leads one to understand, but [rather] the formation of value by labour.'[58]

Dauvé's claims are based on the view that Debord's focus fell on the exchange of commodities, and on the fashions, adverts and mystifications that surround their exchange, rather than on capital's source in production. Debord and the SI 'criticised capital as commodity', he claims, 'and not as a system of valuation which includes production as well as exchange.'[59] To some degree, this renders his critique a little questionable, as his remarks seem informed by the view that 'spectacle' simply signifies the marketing and ideology that support the current economic system. Debord is charged with having focussed on such

---

53   Debord 2004a, p. 603.
54   Marx 1990, pp. 279–80.
55   Dauvé 1979.
56   Ibid.
57   Ibid.
58   Ibid.
59   Ibid.

phenomena, and with having neglected the mode of production that such phenomena reflect.[60] Yet nonetheless – and as was also the case with Lefort's own rather limited account of spectacle – this does not prevent Dauvé from highlighting a real problem.

Dauvé seems to think that Debord's spectacle corresponds to the images, adverts and entertainment that surround commodities. In contrast, we have stressed that the modern spectacle should be understood as the existential problematic engendered by, and instantiated within, a social formation based around the production and exchange of commodities. These views are obviously distinct, but they share a common theme. This is because both views leave Debord open to the charge that his analysis was marked by an emphasis on the appearances and effects of this mode of production (adverts and entertainment on the one hand; subjective malaise on the other). This emphasis came at the cost of a more involved engagement with capitalism's socio-economic roots. Consequently, the further charges that Dauvé develops from his rather suspect reading of spectacle remain pertinent, not least because they accord with our contention that in Debord's work, capital's seemingly 'self-moving' qualities can appear as the attributes of an independent entity.

In *The Society of the Spectacle*, and whilst quoting Hegel's *Jena Realphilosophie*, Debord refers to money as 'the life of what is dead, moving within itself'.[61] Debord's choice of this quotation was obviously due to its proximity to Marx's own description of value as an 'automatic subject'.[62] Yet where Marx shows that this movement derives from the relation between concrete and abstract labour – and thus ultimately from the social relations that subtend the wage-relation – Debord comes very close to treating this as if it were the movement of an independent force. In this regard, Dauvé's remarks seem particularly apposite. Although the theory of spectacle is obviously indebted to the Marxian notion of commodity fetishism, it employs what Dauvé describes as a fetishised conception of capital:

---

60   Because capital 'tends to ... parcelize everything so as to recompose it with the help of market relations', he writes, it also 'makes of representation a specialised sector of production', and as a result, 'wage-workers are ... stripped of the means of producing their ideas, which are produced by [this] specialised sector' (Dauvé 1979). Dauvé seems to view spectacle as this 'specialised sector', and he thus contends that Debord 'reduces capitalism to its spectacular dimension alone' (Dauvé 1979). In contrast, on the reading that has been advanced in this book, capitalism does not possess a spectacular dimension: it is an instantiation of spectacle, because it involves a generalised separation from history.
61   Debord 1995, p. 151; 2006b, p. 857.
62   Marx 1990, p. 255.

In the fetishism of commodities, the commodity appears as its own movement. By the fetishism of capital, capital takes on an autonomy which it does not possess, presenting itself as a living being ... one does not know where it comes from, who produces it, by what process the proletarian engenders it, by what contradiction it lives and may die.[63]

In consequence, Debord's focus on capital's effects results in a limited account of their causes.

The Community of Money

The problems that have been described here are not, however, insurmountable, and we can conclude by noting that it might be possible to resolve them. Doing so would require developing and reinforcing Debord's notions of life and non-life by strengthening their connection to specific modes of social mediation and interaction. If this could be made to succeed, then the subjectivism of the theory of spectacle could be corrected, because its contentions could be tied rather more tightly to an analysis of capitalist social relations. Such an attempted resolution falls beyond the scope of this book. If, however, it could be made to succeed, then Debord could be read as having produced a body of work that accords with some of the insights of contemporary Marxian value theory, but which also weds those insights to a concern with history, praxis and agency.

This possibility can be introduced by looking at the manner in which Debord associates the spectacle with money. In *The Society of the Spectacle*, he writes as follows:

> The spectacle is another facet of money: the abstract general equivalent of all commodities. But whereas money has dominated society as the representation of universal equivalence [*l'équivalence centrale*], that is, of the exchangeability of diverse goods whose uses are not otherwise compatible, the spectacle is its developed modern complement, in which the totality of the commodity world appears *en bloc*, as the general equivalent [*l'équivalence générale*] of whatever society as a whole can be and do. The spectacle is money for *contemplation only*, for in it the totality of use has already been bartered for the totality of abstract representation.[64]

---

63   Dauvé 1979.
64   Debord 1995, pp. 32–3, translation altered; 2006b, p. 781, emphases in the original.

The modern spectacle is the overall rationale and logic of a redundant economic system. It is the 'essentially tautological'[65] and 'laudatory monologue'[66] that modern society pronounces about itself, and which it actualises in its lived social activity that it engenders. And just as money, for Marx, constitutes the abstract, general equivalence that mediates the exchange of commodities, so too, for Debord, the overall rationale of the spectacle is the general equivalence that unifies the interchangeable fragments of an atomised society.

It seems possible, therefore, to read this passage as a marker for the degree to which Debord managed to break away from traditional Marxism, and for the extent to which he came close to more contemporary readings of Marxian value theory. To speak very generally and reductively: traditional Marxism has often employed a Left-Ricardian view, according to which value is embodied in the commodity by labour. On this view, money is simply a reflection of that value. This implies that value could operate in the absence of money: one could strip away money's obfuscating mask in order to reveal the 'truth' of the labour-value that lurks behind it. Through doing so, one could organise a fairer society in which the workforce would not be exploited. Contemporary value-form theory tends to argue that money is inextricable from value. It is not an inert substance that inheres within the commodity. Instead, it is an intangible, abstract form, the 'actuality' of which, as Chris Arthur puts it, is 'posited only in the *relations* commodities bear to one another'.[67] Those relations ascribe quantities of value to the commodity-objects involved. Value, to borrow Riccardo Bellofiore's apposite phrase, thus operates like a 'ghost' that must always possess and animate a 'body'.[68] Money is a lynchpin of this operation. This is because money embodies the abstract universality that binds and mediates those 'bodies'. It thereby serves to realise, through commodity exchange, the generalised connection between buyers and sellers, and between employers and employees, that capitalist value relies upon. This makes for an important distinction from traditional Marxism. Because value is understood here as an abstract social form, and not as an embodied essence, there can be no sense in which money simply reflects that pre-existing essence. This means that 'money', as Postone puts it, 'does not render commodities commensurable': instead, money functions as a necessary 'expression' of 'their commensurability'.[69] Money, in other

---

65 Debord 1995, p. 15; 2006b, p. 769.
66 Debord 1995, p. 19, translation altered; 2006b, p. 771.
67 Arthur 2004, p. 95, emphasis in the original.
68 Bellofiore 2009, p. 185.
69 Postone 1996, p. 264.

words, is a vital, unifying aspect of a set of social relations that treat incommensurable objects *as if* they were commensurable with one another.[70] Money, therefore, is fundamental to the social. Hans-Georg Backhaus thus describes it as 'the objectified social connection of isolated individuals'.[71] Money is a concretisation of the abstract connection between disparate objects and individuals that value interrelates, and a vital means of ensuring their commensurability. In order to underscore that point, Backhaus quotes Marx's indication in the *Grundrisse* that money 'is the *community*': a 'community', moreover, that can 'can suffer no other standing above it'.[72] This is because the 'community' that it establishes is not united by common consent, design or free, direct association, but rather by the abstract, quantitative equivalence of value. Such a 'community', therefore, amounts only to a unity of separated elements.

These ideas bear obvious relation to the interpretation of spectacle presented in this book. It seems possible, therefore, to suggest that Debord's contention that the spectacle is the modern form of money may, in fact, be somewhat similar to modern Marxian conceptions of money. As was indicated above, Debord presents the spectacle as a grand extension of the abstract unification that money affords: as the general rubric that binds and aggregates the separated elements that it forcibly unifies and orders under its governing rationale. Furthermore, Debord stresses that within modern society, qualitative human becoming in time has become subordinated to the quantitative accumulation of capital. This view fits very neatly with contemporary Marxian emphases on the manner in which capitalist value organises particular, individual temporalities as moments of abstract social time.[73]

---

70 Backhaus quotes the following remark from Marx's *Grundrisse*: whilst money might seem to function as 'the representant of all values', in actual fact, 'all real products', i.e. the objects animated by value, 'become the representants of money' (quoted in Backhaus 1980, p. 113). Money, therefore, allows the concrete to operate as a bearer for the abstract. It does so because it objectifies and instantiates the abstract social connection between the isolated individuals that compose capitalist society.

71 Backhaus 1980, p. 113.

72 Quoted in Backhaus 1980, p. 113.

73 Perhaps having found the quotation in Lukács's *History and Class Consciousness*, Debord, in *The Society of the Spectacle*, quotes Marx's famous remark in *The Poverty of Philosophy* that within capitalist society, 'time is everything, man is nothing; he is at most time's carcass. ... [T]he pendulum of the clock has become as accurate a measure of the relative activity of two workers as it is of the speed of two locomotives' (Lukács 1971, p. 89; Debord 1995, p. 110; 2006b, p. 831). See Postone 1996 for a more involved discussion of this theme. As Postone points out, capitalist time is tyrannical. Struggles take place over the length of the working day, as capital pursues the extraction of absolute and relative surplus-value,

Such readings of Marx certainly say very similar things to Debord. Their focus on the technicalities of the social relations that characterise capitalist value and labour, however, prevent them from degenerating into the rather vague biopolitics that one can find, at times, in Debord's theoretical work. The similarities between Debord's theory and these readings of Marx do, however, indicate that it may be possible to draw upon them in order to augment and develop Debord's account. One could thereby remedy the relative absence from his theory of a detailed engagement with the social relations that found the alienation and social atomisation that his theory diagnosed, and counter its over-emphasis on the subjective experience of such phenomena. Somewhat ironically, a means towards doing so can be found in what may, at first sight, appear to be the most romantic and naively essentialist aspect of his theory: namely, his conceptions of historical 'life', and of spectacular 'non-life'.

To recapitulate: we have argued that social life, for Debord, essentially concerns a collectivity's use of its own time. The potential to control and direct that lived time is the real wealth of any such collectivity. This life can, however, flourish, or suffer perversion. The former condition corresponds to the historical life that would supersede spectacle. Debord seems to have associated this with an organic and decidedly Hegelian interrelation of social universality and particularity: with forms of organisation, in other words, in which the universality of a collectivity's power and abilities (i.e. its ability to shape its own time) is not alienated from the particular individuals who compose that collectivity, but instead falls under their common control. In contrast, spectacular non-life entails the localisation of collective power in seemingly independent bodies (God, kings, the state, representative leadership, etc.) that govern the actions and interactions of the particular individuals within that collectivity. Because individuals are oriented towards these alienated, common centres, rather than towards each other, the social unity of such collectivities really amounts to a 'unity of generalised separation';[74] and because collective agency is effectively abdicated to these same mediating centres, the life of these communities becomes marked by the separation from history that Debord associated with spectacle. Non-life, in other words, denotes a separation of the universal from the particular, and a consequent perversion of a collectivity's ability to master and shape its own lived time.

---

and time, *qua* measure, dictates the movements, actions and expectations of those subject to it. Capitalism is thus marked by a form of temporal domination: a mode of biopolitical control over lived time.

74   Debord 1995, p. 12; 2006b, p. 767.

Admittedly, these themes are undermined by the difficulties that we have identified. Debord's rather problematic engagement with capital's status as a social relation leaves these aspects of his work susceptible to collapsing into the romantic and vitalistic essentialism that they may seem to imply. However, the more Hegelian understanding of life and non-life that we have tried to draw out of Debord's work is rather more sophisticated than that. This is because it does not rely upon a vital human essence, but rather pertains to specific forms of social mediation. In addition, it also accords with the aspects of Marxian value-theory outlined above. Value is a form of social mediation that equates and binds disparate elements by treating them as instantiations of abstract, homogenised social activity. It is, therefore, a form of universality, and indeed one that operates independently of the direct control of the social agents from whose activity it derives. Furthermore, the community that capitalist value engenders is a unity of separated, atomised elements. Seen in these terms, it exemplifies the conception of non-life that we have attributed to Debord. It may, therefore, be possible to integrate, into Debord's theoretical framework, some of the insights afforded by the new readings of Marx: to develop and shore up the notions of social mediation that can be identified in these aspects of Debord's work, and to thereby ward off some of the problems to which we have drawn attention.

PART 5
The Integrated Spectacle
1974–94

Pieter Bruegel the Elder, The Tower of Babel, *1563*

I am about to be fifty years old, and I have spent thirty of these fifty years in these eternally uneasy times of fear and hope. I had hoped for once that we might be done with it. Now I see that things are continuing forward as ever, indeed, in one's darkest hours, it seems they are getting ever worse.
 – HEGEL, letter to Creuzer, 30 October 1819 (also referenced in *Internationale Situationniste* #9)

CHAPTER 12

Moving with History's 'Bad Side'

May 1968 and the End of the Situationist International

In 1967, and whilst perhaps still smarting from their acrimonious split, Lefebvre wrote that the SI 'propose not a concrete utopia, but an abstract one. Do they really imagine that one fine day or some decisive evening people will look at each other and say, "Enough! We are fed up with working and being bored. Let's put an end to this!" And that they will thereupon proceed into endless Festival and start creating situations? Maybe it happened once, at dawn on 18 March 1871, but that particular set of circumstances can never recur.'[1] The SI quoted this statement in the 1967 edition of *Internationale situationniste*, and they reproduced it again in 1969,[2] with what Jappe aptly describes as 'considerable – and quite understandable – satisfaction.'[3]

Debord and the SI viewed May 1968 as a validation of their theories, and even went so far as to claim a degree of responsibility for the insurrection.[4] However, ever sensitive to their purported historical role, they recognised that the May events not only signalled 'the reappearance of history',[5] but also the beginning of their own demise. The scandal at the University of Strasbourg in 1966, which centred round the dissemination of the SI's 'On the Poverty of Student Life', had afforded a degree of fame and notoriety. Although this assisted the publication of Debord and Vaneigem's books in 1967, it also brought admirers and imitators.

---

1 SI 1997, p. 548; also quoted in Jappe 1999, pp. 100–1.
2 SI 1997, p. 574.
3 Jappe 1999, p. 101.
4 'In May there were only ten or twelve Situationists and Enragés in Paris and none in the rest of France. But the fortunate conjunction of spontaneous revolutionary improvisation with a sort of aura of sympathy that existed around the SI made possible the coordination of a rather widespread action, not only in Paris but in several large cities, as if there had been a pre-existing nationwide organization. ... a sort of vague, mysterious situationist menace was felt and denounced in many places; those who embodied this menace were some hundreds or even thousands of individuals whom the bureaucrats and moderates called Situationists or, more often, referred to by the popular abbreviation that appeared during this period, *situs*. We consider it an honour that this term ... served not only to designate the most extremist participants in the occupations movement, but also tended to evoke an image of vandals, thieves or hoodlums' (SI 2006, p. 317; 1997, p. 594).
5 SI 2006, p. 292; 1997, p. 575.

This tendency was furthered by the May events, and it heightened the number of groups and individuals that the SI could haughtily refer to as 'pro-situs': spectators of the SI, who constituted 'a significant product of modern history', but who in no sense 'produce it in return'.[6] The Situationist International, in other words, was starting to become a spectacle.

This caused Debord and the SI to withdraw, becoming even harder and clearer in focus (like a 'crystal', as Lefebvre would later put it),[7] which in turn meant even more of the expulsions and vituperative denunciations that had characterised the group's existence. There are a number of texts and internal documents in which Debord can be found discussing the rationale behind the SI's expulsions, and letters in which he justifies his own part in them,[8] but the result was that by 1972, the group possessed only three members (Debord, Gianfranco Sanguinetti, and J.V. Martin). Seventy individuals had passed through the SI between 1957 and 1972; of the remaining 66, 45 had been excluded. Nineteen had resigned, and two had split.[9]

In the years following the SI's dissolution, Debord produced a number of important works, principal amongst which are his cinematic version of *The Society of the Spectacle* (1973), *In Girum Imus Nocte et Consumimur Igni* (1978), and the preface to the fourth Italian edition of *The Society of the Spectacle* (1979). The latter text reflects his interest in the tumult of Italian politics, and the growing concern with manipulation, intrigue and conspiracy that would shape 1988's *Comments on the Society of the Spectacle*. Debord had also begun to withdraw from Paris by the late 1970s, but he was drawn out of this retreat in 1984 by the assassination of his friend and patron Gérard Lebovici. Speculation in the press as to whether Lebovici's death stemmed from his entry into Debord's purportedly nefarious circles led to 1985's *Considerations on the Assassination of Gérard Lebovici*, which addressed these charges. The increasing disgust with modern society that these events prompted, together with a growing concern with its tangle of conflicting interests, conspiracy and intrigue, would all inform 1988's *Comments*. Yet the latter text was only the first of a small flurry of publications that appeared towards the end of Debord's life: *Panegyric Volume 1* in 1989, *Cette mauvaise réputation* in 1993, and the posthumous *Des Contrats* of 1995 (a collection of Debord's contracts that revealed the true

---

6 SI 2003, p. 35; Debord 2006b, p. 1107.
7 Ross 2004, p. 275.
8 For an example of the SI's publicly stated positions on the exclusions see SI 2006, pp. 79–80; 1997, p. 149; for a more personal letter, see Debord 2001a, pp. 155–8.
9 See Gray 1998 pp. 132–3 for a list of the SI's exclusions, splits and resignations.

nature of his self-confessedly 'scandalous'[10] machinations), which appeared after his death in 1994. The latter book was followed by *Panegyric Volume 2* in 1997.

The growing focus on intrigue and manoeuvre that can be found in these later texts will be addressed in Chapter 14, where we will return to Debord's interest in strategy in order to consider it in connection to the vision of spectacular society that Debord presented in 1988's *Comments*. Here, however, our focus falls on the manner in which Debord held that history had proved him right.

Great Villains

Debord was particularly fond of describing the SI as belonging to the 'bad side of history'.[11] This is a reference to one of Marx's polemical flourishes in *The Poverty of Philosophy*. Ridiculing Proudhon's alleged desire to eradicate the 'bad' aspects of economic categories in order to retain their 'good' dimensions, Marx remarks there that 'it is always the bad side [of history] that in the end triumphs over the good side', because it 'produces the movement which makes history, by providing a struggle'. If one was to set about erasing that 'bad side', Marx adds, as he claims Proudhon advocated, then one 'would have set oneself the absurd problem of eliminating history.'[12]

To describe the SI as an instance of history's 'bad side' was thus to lay claim to an identity with the creation of history. It meant identifying the SI as a direct expression of the forces at work within modern society that would hasten the latter's demise. Seen in these terms, the group was not pictured as standing 'outside' the struggles of their era, imposing arbitrary perspectives and demands upon it, but rather as giving explicit voice to concerns that were held to be implicit within that historical moment. Indeed, according to Debord, the Situationists were 'merely the concentrated expression of a historical subversion which is everywhere'.[13]

This desire for identity with the historical negative bears direct relation to the conception of time's passage that we discussed in Chapter 5, and it also led Debord to pride himself on having gained a more personal air of negation and

---

10 Debord 2008, p. 458.
11 See, for example, SI 2003, p. 8; Debord 2006b, p. 1089, and Debord 2003b, p. 173; 2006b, p. 1379.
12 Marx 2009.
13 SI 2003, p. 7; Debord 2006b, p. 1088.

opposition.[14] This can be evidenced by his claim to have possessed a 'negative [*mauvaise*] and underground notoriety',[15] to have 'merited the universal hatred of the society of my time',[16] and to have been an individual who 'strove to be ... intolerable'.[17] These claims often contain interesting poetic and literary allusions. For example, whilst borrowing from Mallarmé, Debord remarks in *Panegyric* that 'Destruction was my Beatrice';[18] in *In Girum*, he states that he and the SI had enlisted in the 'Devil's Party'[19] (an unattributed reference to Blake),[20] and also casts himself and his comrades as 'emissaries of the Prince of Division.'[21] It seems possible to consider this emphasis on notoriety in connection to the following issue.

One of the peculiarities of Hegel's philosophy of history is that the 'great men' discussed within it – Socrates, Caesar, and so on – can be justifiably

---

14 As early as 1953, and whilst commenting on the 'revolutionary spirit' of the avant-garde, he remarked that 'So long as I live, I do not want to *place myself* [*me ranger*] outside of this scandalous faction, wherever it finds itself' (Debord 2010, p. 27).
15 Debord 2003a, p. 183; 2006b, p. 1391.
16 Debord 2003a, p. 146; 2006b, p. 1349.
17 Debord 2003a, p. 159; 2006b, p. 1364.
18 Debord 2004a, p. 15; 2006b, p. 1663.
19 Debord 2003a, p. 173; 2006b, p. 1379.
20 The source of the 'Devil's Party' allusion is not signalled in Debord's list of the *détournements* used in *In Girum*, but it could be a reference to Blake's *The Marriage of Heaven and Hell* (Debord was clearly familiar to some degree with English romantic poetry; in *In Girum*, whilst playing with the theme of time as water, he draws directly on Keats's epitaph (albeit whilst attributing it to Shelley): 'Here lies one whose name was writ in water' (Debord 2003b, p. 171; 2006b, p. 1377)). In the *Marriage*, Blake links the artistic, the passionate and the potentially transgressive to the 'diabolical', and contends that 'the reason Milton wrote in fetters when he wrote of angels and God, and at liberty when of devils and Hell, is because he was a true poet and of the Devil's party without knowing it' (Blake 2008, p. 129).
21 Debord 2003a, p. 174, 2006b, p. 1381. Although this is not noted in Debord's list of the *détournements* in *Panegyric*, the phrase may in fact come from the Bible, where Jesus is described as stating: 'I am come to send fire on the earth ... Suppose ye that I am come to give peace on earth? I tell you, nay, but rather division' (Luke chapter 12, verses 49–56). In the film's script, he describes himself as one of this figure's 'emissaries'. The phrase that follows could be taken to indicate that the figure in question is really the historical proletariat, as this 'Prince' is described as 'he who has been wronged' (Debord 2003, p. 174; 2006b, p. 1383; Debord notes that this phrase was used as a password by 'Italian millenarists', and that it was linked to Bakunin (Debord 2006b, p. 1418)). In his biography of Debord, Hussey mentions that Debord's wife, Alice, referred to him as the 'Prince of Division' (Hussey 2002, p. 368).

regarded as transgressors and villains rather than as heroes. Such individuals, according to Hegel, are pivotal historical figures, whose 'own particular aims involve those large issues which are the will of the World-Spirit',[22] and whose actions thereby serve, however unwittingly, to further its advance. Yet because their goals must therefore run counter to the norms of their historical periods, Hegel concedes that they can be regarded as unethical and criminal from a perspective rooted within those same periods[23] (the Athenians, for example, are said to have acted with 'unimpeachable rectitude'[24] when condemning Socrates to death for having stirred up the youth of the city against their social order).

One can imagine that Debord may have enjoyed picturing his own cherished infamy in a similar light. After all, he was by no means averse to ironic personal associations. In his letters, he employs pseudonyms such as Hegel and Feuerbach,[25] casts himself jokingly as Marx,[26] and refers to himself as Glaucos, Gondi and Colin de Cayeux.[27] He also describes himself as a member of a 'respectable series of old rogues' that included 'Bakunin, Cloots, Marx, Orwell and Rizzi', whose ideas had been 'largely confirmed by history'.[28] According to one anecdote, having been born in the evening, and thus 'when the shades of night are gathering', Debord would even joke about being the owl of Minerva.[29] An association between his own proudly declared 'bad reputation'[30] and the contextual notoriety of Hegel's 'great men' may thus have appealed. This then serves to raise the following question: could any such purported connection to the judgement of history be maintained today?

---

22   Hegel 2004, p. 30.
23   'They who on moral grounds, and consequently with noble intention, have resisted that which the advance of the Spiritual Idea makes necessary, stand higher in moral worth than those whose crimes have been turned into the means – under the direction of a superior principle – of realising the purposes of that principle' (Hegel 2004, p. 67; see also McCarney 2000, pp. 113–14).
24   Hegel 2004, p. 270.
25   Debord 2003a, p. 106.
26   Debord 2005, p. 206.
27   Glaucos is a combatant in the *Iliad* who attacks the defenders of Troy and offers poetic observations on change and the passage of time; Jean-François-Paul de Gondi, otherwise known as the Cardinal de Retz, helped instigate the Fronde; Colin de Cayeux was an accomplice of the poet-brigand François Villon (Debord 2005, pp. 157–8).
28   Debord 2006a, p. 68.
29   Hussey 2002, p. 13.
30   Debord 1993.

This returns us to some of the issues that we touched upon in this book's introduction. As we saw there, the infamy that was once attached to Debord and the SI's work has now largely dissipated, having been replaced by academic and cultural endorsement. In 1967 (and thus three years before his own departure from the group) Raoul Vaneigem wrote, in connection to the SI's enthusiasm for excluding its own members, that 'In organisations prefiguring in their essential features the type of social organisation to come, the least of requirements consists in not tolerating those people whom the established powers are able to tolerate quite well'.[31] By that same rationale, what should we make of the current acceptance of Debord and the SI's work? This question leads to a further issue. Despite the obvious significance of events such as May 1968, the great revolution that the SI confidently predicted has stubbornly failed to transpire. Today, therefore, this material not only seems to lack the notoriety that Debord was once able to boast of, but its prescience can also seem somewhat open to question. So how, then, should we relate to it?

In order to respond to those questions, we should consider the following issues. Debord consistently indicates, throughout much of his work, that the truth of a body of radical theory can only be ascertained through the degree to which it engenders and facilitates effective revolutionary action: 'it is the unfolding of an event', he claimed, 'that may or may not verify a theory'.[32] His views in this regard follow directly from his identification of radical theory with strategy, for in much the same manner, the merits of strategic plans and analyses can only be established through their application in practice. If we can reconstruct this notion of validity, we may be able to arrive at a position from which one could try to evaluate Debord and the SI's legacy on its own terms.

Truth and Falsehood

Somewhat typically, Debord's conception of truth and falsity is another aspect of his thought that he does not fully explain or define. Although references to truth and falsity occur throughout his work, and although they often carry a great deal of rhetorical and theoretical weight, nowhere does he provide us with a detailed explanation of quite what he means by these terms. It is, however, possible to construct a model of his views that seems capable of supporting and clarifying the available textual evidence.

---

31   SI 2006, pp. 277–8; 1997, p. 533.
32   Debord 2003a, p. 181; 2006b, p. 1388.

Firstly, and most obviously, Debord refers to truth and falsity in the simple, everyday sense of describing lies and distorted facts. Yet beyond this rather common-sense understanding of truth and falsehood, he appears to employ two further notions of truth, both of which are associated with history. The first concerns what we will refer to as the truth *of* history. This is the true nature of human existence in time, and a goal that historical activity should work towards. The second concerns the actualisation of that truth *in* history, in the sense of variously successful attempts to instantiate that grander truth within the moments and situations that compose historical time.

We will begin with the first of these two ideas (the truth *of* history), which follows from the ontology that we have identified in Debord's theory of spectacle. To recapitulate: 1) Human existence is inherently historical, because it takes place in time, and because the activity that characterises it changes not only the world, but also those who effect such change. 2) If human subjects could attain conscious control over their ability to effect such change, they could become the authors of their own history, and the masters of their own existence. 3) Spectacle, we have argued, arises from the denial and deprivation of that possibility, and needs to be overcome. If this is achieved, human existence could become freely self-constitutive. This conception of human existence leads Debord, as we saw in Chapter 7, to the view that the true nature of human *being* lies in its continual *becoming*. The truth of human existence in time, therefore, is its self-constitutive and transformative character. Consequently, beyond the strictures and practicalities of scientific, mathematical or logical truth (formal systems, in Debord's view, are 'hostile to history',[33] and incapable of 'taking possession'[34] of its changing, processual character), the only *true* absolute is historical praxis.[35]

This might seem to cast every single moment of human existence as 'true', insofar as all such moments can be construed as instances of such praxis. For Debord, however, this is not the case. Indeed, the entire notion of spectacle rests on the idea that human subjects can become divorced from, or fail to fully instantiate, their own historical nature. Consequently, this conception of truth

---

33   Debord 1995, p. 54; 2006b, p. 797.
34   Debord 1995, p. 53; 2006b, p. 796.
35   This truth must be entirely specific to human existence. This may serve to explain Debord's enigmatic indication that following the emergence of human beings within the natural world, the otherwise 'unconscious movement of time becomes manifest and *true* within historical consciousness', because the actions that unfold within time start to become directed and remembered by human beings (Debord 1995, p. 92, 2006b, p. 820, italics in the original).

gives rise to normative implications that correspond to the 'ethical' dimensions of Debord's theoretical work. If the truth *of* human existence is the self-constitutive, self-determinate action that creates and shapes that existence, then acting in accordance with that truth entails pursuing and maintaining a condition wherein human subjects possess a free, self-conscious and self-determinate mastery over their own historical activity. In other words, it entails attempting to actualise that truth *in* history. As we will see shortly, Debord envisaged the revolutionary tradition of the past, and indeed its possible continuation beyond his own time, as a succession of variously successful attempts to manifest and express that implicit truth.[36]

These views also give rise to a conception of falsity. If truth lies in establishing and pursuing conditions of free self-determinacy, then it follows that falsehood must lie in the deprivation or failed instantiation of such self-determinacy, and indeed in instances wherein human subjects become alienated from their capacity to govern their own time. This conception of falsehood thus accords with the 'general falsification of society'[37] that Debord associates with the modern spectacle. However, it also fits with many of his other references to falsehood. For example, it corresponds to his deep concern with the distortion of historical knowledge. If knowledge of historical events is denied or suppressed, as Debord believed was increasingly the case within modern society, then human subjects become both unmoored and unable to direct their affairs effectively (hence his observation in the *Comments* that a 'great deficit of historical knowledge' entails that actions cannot be conducted 'strategically').[38] By the same token, it does not jar with, but rather adds additional gravity to, his later works' numerous objections to misinformation, fakes, and incorrect facts. The key point here, however, is that this notion of truth and falsity can help to explain Debord's indications that the truth of a body of radical theory can only be ascertained through the degree to which it engenders concrete, revolutionary action. In other words, theory can never be true independently of action, and it can only be validated through action. If thought and theory fail to find accurate, practical purchase within the world, then they must fall short of the condition of praxis that Debord associates with truth. If thought and theory

---

36 A concern with the validation of theoretical positions through historical events can also be found in Debord's comments on the SI's own internal disputes and schisms. In a letter of 1970, he wrote: 'If opposed tendencies *clearly* expose theoretical or practical incompatibilities, the normal result is a split. Then each autonomous group will have to make historical proof of its truth' (Debord 2004a, p. 218).

37 Debord 1995, p. 101; 2006b, p. 806.

38 Debord 1998, p. 20, translation altered; 2006b, p. 1605.

are instantiated in praxis, then their validity can only be established through the degree to which they afford the pursuit of what we have termed the truth *of* history.

There are two important qualifications that need to be discussed here. The first concerns the manner in which theory might attain such practical purchase on the world, and the second concerns the nature of the events to which it gives rise.

The first point is symptomatic of Debord's departure from traditional Leninist and hierarchical politics. If the goal (or indeed the truth) of the revolutionary project is its pursuit of a condition of generalised self-determinacy, then it would be contradictory to simply *impose* revolutionary theory upon its intended adherents. Nor can they be led towards the Promised Land by the rhetoric of paternalistic leaders. Instead, theory must articulate the concerns of a given context in such a manner that it can be recognised and employed by those within that context who seek to change it.[39] The truth of such theory, therefore, is not only established on the basis of whether or not it gives rise to action: in addition, such action must follow from the degree to which that theory is *recognised* and employed by those whose predicament it purports to clarify and assist. This, incidentally, is why the SI were so fond of making seemingly presumptuous statements such as 'our ideas are in everybody's heads',[40] that 'Situationist theory is in the people like fish are in the sea',[41] or indeed that 'the workers, driven by their own problems, will find us'.[42] By making such assertions, they were contending that their work had a profoundly *historical* validity, in that it served to express a widespread and burgeoning awareness of their era's revolutionary potential.

The second point concerns the kind of actions to which theory gives rise. This notion of recognition does not mean that just any doctrine that happened to be accepted by the populace would be valid. If that was the case, the spectacle's images would themselves be true. Indeed, the German proletariat of the 1930s clearly 'recognised' National Socialism in some sense. Instead, the conception of truth outlined above means that National Socialism must be *false*, because it fosters domination, hierarchy and control.

---

39 As we noted in Chapter 5, Debord is in fact very close to some of the ideas expressed by the young Marx in the letters to Ruge that were published in the *Deutsch-Französische Jahrbücher*.
40 SI 2006, p. 275; 1997, p. 529.
41 SI 1997, p. 257.
42 Debord 2004a, p. 187.

Thus, theory is true if it is 1) recognised, and 2) if it serves to foster a condition of generalised self-determinacy. It is required, therefore, to pursue the truth *of* historical existence by attempting to actualise that truth *in* history in a manner that does not contradict, but which instead accords with the freedom and self-determinacy identified with the truth *of* history.

With these issues in mind, we can now see why Debord describes Marx's *Capital*, in a letter of 1971, as being 'obviously true and false'[43] at the same time: 'essentially', he writes, 'it is true, because the proletariat *recognised* it, although quite badly (and thus also let its errors pass)'.[44] Marx's *Capital* is *relatively* false, according to Debord, for the reasons that we discussed in Chapter 10. In Debord's view, the nature of Marx's historical circumstances led him to produce an account that was far too close to economism, and which laid a basis for the Marxist tradition's subsequent tendency towards economic determinism. *Capital*, therefore, like all other theoretical works, is a flawed and contextually limited attempt to instantiate the truth *of* history *within* history. It was an attempt to explain the workings of an economy that prevented human freedom, and to thereby afford a 'conscious history'[45] (the truth *of* history), but it drew too close to the political-economic 'science' that it criticised (due to the nature of its contextual attempt to instantiate such truth *in* history).

It is important to note here that Debord viewed his own work in the same terms. In that same letter from 1971, He writes as follows:

> If this concept [of spectacle] is *radically false* (since it could indeed just be relatively 'false', and thus currently 'true' for historical thought, in the sense that it is merely the 'maximum of possible consciousness' presently to be had concerning the society we are in and for which a far better explanation will be forthcoming once this society is consigned to the past and the process embarked upon in order to consign it is more fully underway) then in the course of this book [*The Society of the Spectacle*] I may well have said a host of *other* things that are correct (the vast majority of which come from comrades down the ages), but because I have understood and assembled them solely on the basis of this concept, they would all be *in some way flawed* ... [because] ... if the very concept of spectacle is mistaken, then the whole bloody book is scuppered. However, as far as I am aware, there is *no better* [book] on the subject that concerns

---

43   Debord 2004a, p. 457.
44   Ibid.
45   Debord 1995, p. 53; 2006b, p. 795.

us here – a point that takes us back to the fundamental question of consciousness in history, and of what it does in it.[46]

That 'fundamental question' concerns what we have termed the truth *of* history. Debord's book is intended to function as a contribution towards actualising that truth *in* history. In consequence, and like *Capital*, it too could be 'relatively' true or false. Because Debord is situated within a given historical moment, and because he is restricted to the perspective that that moment affords, the best that his book can hope to achieve is to constitute 'the maximum possible consciousness' available at that juncture. It can only hope to express, as fully as possible, that moment's capacity to instantiate the condition of praxis that Debord treats as history's goal.

This gives rise to an obvious, but rather difficult issue. If Debord's views are contextually limited, then it follows that his perspective on that 'fundamental question', and thus his view of what we have referred to as the truth *of* history, must *also* be similarly limited. Given that the latter is the lynchpin of this entire model of Debord's notion of truth, this would seem to put these views in danger of collapsing into relativism.

It is, however, possible to respond to that problem. Debord is clearly making transhistorical claims. The problem described here follows from the fact that these claims do not seem to be premised on the possession of some kind of external, God's-eye view of human history, but are instead rooted within a historically contextual perspective. One can thus propose, on the basis of Debord's account of historical development (discussed in Chapter 2), that in his view, history had unfolded in such a manner as to afford, within his own era, a perspective from which such transhistorical claims could be made (albeit cautiously). His historical moment had afforded a set of insights into aspects of the nature of human existence that had been implicit, throughout the past, and which could now be clearly recognised and explicitly stated. We have already seen that *The Society of the Spectacle* presents the social structures of the past as having engendered a growing awareness of historical time, which had come to the fore with the rise of bourgeois society,[47] and which had since evolved, by the mid-twentieth century, into a revolutionary demand for the autonomous control of such time. When coupled to the theoretical and philosophical contributions that had been made by 'comrades down the ages',

---

46 Debord 2004a, pp. 456–7. Thanks are due to John McHale for his assistance with this translation.
47 See in particular thesis #73 of *The Society of the Spectacle*.

it would seem that this had afforded a vantage-point from which one could gain a fairly confident view of the 'fundamental question' of human historical existence.

This then renders it possible to suggest – in keeping with Debord's own apparent views – that even if his attempts to theorise the instantiation of truth *in* history were flawed, his conception *of* history may be somewhat more secure. Therefore, whilst Debord's critique of his own present moment would need to be superseded, and whilst new theories and actions would need to be created in order to respond to future circumstances, he could be relatively certain about the overall direction of these efforts, and indeed about the need to keep creating such interventions.

This point can be illustrated by returning to the 'war of time' that Debord refers to in 1978's *In Girum Imus Nocte et Consumimur Igni*. As we noted in the introduction to this book, Debord states there that: 'Theories are only made to die in the war of time. Like units of varying strength, they must be sent into battle at the right moment … they have to be replaced because they are constantly being rendered obsolete'.[48] On the reading outlined here, Debord's critique of capitalist society is only one such theory *in* that 'war'. His notion *of* that 'war', however, may be more lasting. Therefore, Debord's work seems to contain what is, in effect, a philosophy of praxis. It involves a set of ideas about time, history, agency and intervention that can be distinguished from the theory that they support. This seems particularly significant in the light of the criticisms that we presented in Chapters 10 and 11: for it follows from the above that whilst Debord's critique of modern society may be limited in some regards, the ideas upon which it rests may still be of value.

By the same token, – and to return now to some of the questions with which we began this chapter – it matters little if Debord and the SI's work has lost some of its radical credentials, and has become an accepted part of the cultural establishment. The ideas that underpin it entail an acknowledgement of its inevitable obsolescence, and indeed a drive towards its critical and practical supersession. One might think here of Debord's statement in 1968 that 'we have never considered the SI to be a goal in itself,' but rather 'a moment of historical activity';[49] or, as Debord put it in 1969, whilst reflecting on the events of the previous May: 'From now on we are sure of a satisfactory consummation of our activities: the SI will be superseded'.[50]

---

48   Debord 2003b, pp. 150–1, translation altered; 2006b, p. 1354.
49   Debord 2003a, p. 280.
50   SI 2006, p. 325; 1997, p. 34; Debord 2006b, p. 963.

Those quotations bring us back to the questions with which we began this chapter, regarding the degree to which the SI's theories really did receive the practical validation to which the group laid claim. Having advanced an interpretation of that notion of validation, and having also foregrounded its implications, we should now be in a position to address this issue.

The Beginning of an Era

For Debord, the SI's status as an embodiment of history's 'bad side' was given explicit confirmation by the events of May 1968. In the April of that same year, he had written a series of theses on 'The Organisation Question for the SI', in which he stated that, having now developed its theory, the group needed to focus on the dissemination and application of that theory in practice. 'The SI must now prove its effectiveness in a new stage of revolutionary activity', he wrote, 'or else disappear'.[51] A few weeks later, that proof was seen to have been provided.

Debord had little doubt in this regard that the SI's efforts had contributed to the uprisings. 'Situationist theory', he claimed, 'had a significant role in the origins of the generalised critique that gave rise to the first incidents of the May crisis'.[52] The May events were also seen as positive proof that modern society really did contain, behind the mask of its seemingly placid surface, a mass of tensions and potential demands for a radically different form of social existence. 'Naturally we had prophesied nothing', Debord wrote; 'We had simply pointed out what was *already present*'.[53]

In addition to viewing May 1968 as a confirmation of their theories, Debord and the SI also felt able to describe the events as a victory, even though the uprising was ultimately defeated and dispersed. In an essay of 1969, significantly titled 'The Beginning of an Era', Debord wrote as follows:

> We knew that this objectively possible and necessary revolutionary movement had begun from a subjectively very low level: spontaneous and fragmented, unaware of its own past and of its overall goals, it was re-emerging after a half-century of repression and in the face of its still firmly entrenched bureaucratic and bourgeois vanquishers. A lasting victory was

---

51   SI 2006, p. 380; 1997, p. 112.
52   SI 2006, p. 307; 1997, p. 586.
53   SI 2006, p. 290; 1997, p. 572, emphasis in the original.

in our eyes only a slim possibility between May 17 and May 30. But the moment this chance existed, we showed it to be the *maximum* in play as soon as the crisis reached a certain point, and as certainly something worth risking. Already, to our eyes, the movement was then a historic victory, regardless of what could have happened, and we thought that *only half* of that which had already occurred had been a very significant result.[54]

This quotation illustrates the sense in which the SI's new revolution would not constitute an absolute break with the workers' movement of the past. Instead, it would re-figure and reinvigorate the classical revolutionary project's demands, thereby bringing it back from the spectacular stagnation and suppression that it had suffered following the rise of the commodity and the Party in the early decades of the twentieth century. Because the possibility and agency of revolution was only just beginning to emerge into the light of day, its expression, during the May events, was still 'spontaneous and fragmented', and remained, in part, 'unaware of its past', and of its essential 'goals'. Yet for that very same reason, May 1968 is described in the quoted passage as a *historic* victory. This corresponds to the notion of truth outlined in the section above. Debord described Marx's *Capital* (and, implicitly, *The Society of the Spectacle* as well) as having expressed the 'maximum of possible consciousness' available within its historical moment; in just the same way, the events of May 1968 were seen to have instantiated the 'maximum' possible revolutionary potential available within the SI's own context.

May 1968 was therefore viewed as having demonstrated the existence of the revolutionary potential that the Situationists had been diagnosing and debating for over a decade. Yet as we indicated at the outset of this chapter, although May 1968 was certainly seen as 'the beginning of an era', it nonetheless signalled the end of the Situationist International.

Debord was certainly keen to maintain the group's existence after 1968, and the SI would not dissolve until 1972. Its energy was, however dissipating, just as its prominence was rising. Debord had grown weary of editing the group's journal, believing himself to be carrying too much weight and acting as too great a focal point. In addition, the dangers of the 'pro-Situ mind set' had been identified not only amongst the SI's admirers, but also amongst the Situationists themselves. From April of 1968 onwards, and despite the interruption of the May events, the SI entered into what would become known

---

54 SI 2006, p. 317, translation altered; 1997, p. 594; Debord 2006b, p. 951.

as its 'Orientation Debate'. This was a series of meetings and circulated texts that led to a number of exclusions, and which would continue for the next few years. Eventually, what remained of the SI decided to disband.

In terms of Debord's own understanding of these events, all was as it should be. In Chapter 5, when discussing Debord's views on the avant-garde, we made reference to his claim in *In Girum* that 'avant-gardes have only one time; and the best thing that can happen to them is to have *had their day* in the fullest sense of the term' [*au plein sens du terme, d'avoir fait leur temps*].[55] In Debord's view, the role of an avant-garde, and indeed of any revolutionary organisation, is to draw out and facilitate the possibilities and potential of a given historical moment, in order to assist and hasten its passage into the future. Its role, in other words, is to move *with* time. Because any such group or agency must be entirely specific to the context that engenders it, and which it serves to negate, it must, therefore, pass away, together with the problematic that it seeks to resolve.

The May events could thus be interpreted, from Debord's perspective, as having validated the degree to which the SI had fulfilled its function. By extension, the group's subsequent lack of momentum can be seen as symptomatic of its consequent need for dissolution. Seen in these terms, the SI could be cast as leaving the stage on a note of triumph. In his 'Theses on the Situationist International and its Time' – a text that was written in 1972, and which announced the group's dissolution – Debord presents the group in just such a manner. The text begins by stating that 'The Situationist International imposed itself in a moment of world history as the thought *of the collapse of a world*, a collapse which has now begun before our eyes.'[56] For Debord, the SI had thus served as midwife to a new era of contestation. They had identified the revolutionary problematic that defined their historical moment (i.e. that of spectacle); they had brought that problematic to the fore, and had dispersed it amongst the protagonists involved ('our ideas are in everybody's heads'); perhaps most importantly of all, they had also ensured, through the group's termination, that subsequent efforts to resolve this problematic – a problematic that entailed the rejection of *all* separated power and leadership – would not be burdened and contradicted by any reliance upon the SI as some kind of spectacular figurehead. In his private correspondence Debord was more circumspect with his claims,[57] but nonetheless, the message remained much the same: the SI

---

55 Debord 2003b, p. 182; 2006b, pp. 1389–90 translation altered.
56 SI 2003, p. 6; Debord 2006b, p. 1088.
57 Debord 2004a, pp. 458–9.

had succeeded in helping to identify a 'new Northwest Passage'; future efforts now needed to enlarge and clear the path towards the future that they had uncovered.

The problem, of course, is that the grand 'reappearance of history'[58] failed to transpire. So what does this mean for the critical evaluation of their work? And how did Debord himself understand the absence of the predicted revolution in the years that followed the SI's demise?

The Continuity and Development of Debord's Theory

Perhaps predictably, Debord held that history continued to prove him right. Like Marx, he and the SI had not guaranteed that revolution *would* come; they had merely stated that it *could*, and indeed *should* come. May 1968 was viewed as having provided sufficient proof that the SI had been right in claiming that revolutionary potential lay simmering beneath the surface of society. In addition, Debord also felt able to claim that capitalism's development in the years that followed had proved the veracity of his account of spectacular society. For example, in 1979's 'Preface to the Fourth Italian Edition of *The Society of the Spectacle*', he wrote as follows:

> I flatter myself to be a very rare contemporary example of someone who has written without immediately being contradicted by the event, and I do not mean contradicted a hundred or a thousand times like the others, but not once. I have no doubt that the confirmation all my theses encounter ought not to last right until the end of the century and even beyond. The reason for this is simple: I have understood the constituent factors of the spectacle 'in the process of movement and consequently by their transient aspect as well,'[59] that is to say, by envisaging the whole of

---

58   SI 2006, p. 292; 1997, p. 575.
59   Debord's letter to Paolo Salvadori of the 7th February 1979 indicates that Marx's afterword to the second German edition of *Capital* is the source of this quotation (Debord 2006a, p. 19). Debord's words here have been altered very slightly ('ephemeral aspect' has been replaced with 'transient aspect') in order to make them fit a little more easily with Ben Fowkes's English translation of Marx's afterword: in its 'rational form', according to Marx, the dialectic 'regards every historically developed form as being in a fluid state, in motion, and therefore grasps its transient aspects as well' (Marx 1990, p. 103). Debord is quoting from Joseph Roy's nineteenth-century French translation, which was subsequently used

the historical movement that has been able to edify this order, and which is now beginning to dissolve it.[60]

The absence of the spectacle's revolutionary supersession, for Debord, had not disproved his theory at all. Indeed, whilst he would go on to modify his account of spectacular society somewhat in the years that followed, those modifications were presented as further elaborations and confirmations of his earlier claims. They describe the manner in which the spectacle's development had caused it to 'meet more exactly its concept',[61] and to thereby actualise its principle of separation all the more fully and completely throughout society.

This is most clearly evidenced in 1988's *Comments on the Society of the Spectacle*.[62] In the *Comments*, the growth and continuing successes of commodity-capitalism during the 1970s and 1980s is read in terms of the steady encroachment of its spectacular *Weltanschauung* into every aspect of everyday life. Debord claims here that this development has deepened the revolutionary potential that inheres within spectacular society, but that it has also provided the state and its allies with an increased ability to co-opt and manage that potential, thereby further reinforcing spectacular society's ability to prevent its own demise.

This concern with the management of revolt both informs and stems from Debord's interest in the intrigue and terrorism of Italian politics during the 1970s and 1980s. The *Comments* describes a society dominated by secrecy, conspiracy and espionage. With supposedly revolutionary groups co-opted and managed by the powers that they oppose, and with the vast majority of society now increasingly moulded to fit the spectacle's images, the potential for historical change, though greater than ever before, had been silenced far more effectively than in the past. An important part of this silencing, he claims, is spectacular society's tendency to 'eradicate' the 'historical knowledge'[63] that might make such change possible. He thus claims in the *Comments* that noth-

---

by Maximilien Rubel and others as the basis for Gallimard's 1965 edition of Marx's *Oeuvres*. Thanks are due to John McHale for the latter information.
60   Debord 1979; 2006b, p. 1465.
61   Debord 1979; 2006b, p. 1465.
62   The lower case 'the' in the title is important. Debord, in a letter regarding a Spanish translation of the book, wrote: 'If I had wanted to write comments on *The Society of the Spectacle*, that would have meant comments on my preceding book on the subject; and I have wanted to deal with what this same society has become, twenty-one years later' (Debord 2008, p. 93).
63   Debord 1998, p. 13; 2006b, p. 1601.

ing 'in the last twenty years has been so coated in obedient lies as the history of May 1968. Some useful lessons have indeed been learned from certain demystifying studies of those days; these, however, remain state secrets'.[64] By entrenching itself ever further into lived reality, and by undermining and occluding such exemplars of historical praxis, the spectacle described in the *Comments* had fostered a culture replete with 'unverifiable stories, uncheckable statistics, unlikely explanations and untenable reasoning.'[65] It would therefore seem that by the late 1980s, Debord had come to the view that Marx's 'old mole'[66] had not only been driven back underground following the events of May 1968: in addition, it had also been thoroughly disoriented. Crucially, however, he maintained that it remained capable of resurgence. Although many commentators have identified defeatist sentiments within Debord's later work,[67] the spectacle's development, as outlined in the *Comments*, was not presented as a cause for despair.

Debord's Hegelianism is certainly much less immediately apparent in the *Comments* than it is in *The Society of the Spectacle*. However, and as Debord points out in *Cette mauvaise réputation*, 'the dialectic' is by no means absent from this later text.[68] Although the *Comments* describes a host of problems, it also indicates, albeit rather less obviously, that these difficulties may be fostering their own resolution. The book's subtext is this: as the spectacle actualised itself ever more fully, so too had it heightened its own contradictory and self-destructive nature. Debord's *Comments* thus contends that the potential for revolutionary change had in fact grown in tandem with the spectacle's own development, but that so too had the difficulties entailed in actualising that revolutionary potential. Thus, whilst the *Comments* is certainly bleaker, or at least markedly more sober in tone than *The Society of the Spectacle*'s icy euphoria, it is by no means an admission of defeat. In fact, and as we will see in the following chapter, it indicates that the revolutionary crux that Debord

---

64 Debord 1998, p. 14; 2006b, p. 1601.
65 Debord 1998, p. 16; 2006b, p. 1602.
66 Marx 1973a, p. 237.
67 Hussey, for example, writes that by 1988 – the year in which the *Comments* appeared – 'there was clearly a sense of defeat in Debord's thought and demeanour' (Hussey 2002, p. 353); Merrifield notes the *Comments*' 'dark undertow' (Merrifield 2005, p. 123), and Crary describes it as 'deeply pessimistic' (Crary in McDonough 2004, p. 462) – 'as pessimistic', according to Plant, 'as the age in which it arises' (Plant 1992, p. 153; Plant, however, adds that 'the picture [the book] paints is by no means closed and hopeless').
68 Debord 1993, pp. 33–4; see also p. 46.

and the SI had identified in the 1960s had in fact been heightened, despite the degree to which the conscious awareness of that potential had been diminished.

A World That Had 'Hardly Changed'

Debord's general position in his later work, therefore, is that just as the events of May 1968 had proved the presence of the spectacle's potential overthrow, so too had capitalism's development in the years that followed provided further confirmation of the theory of spectacle itself. That development had simultaneously heightened and obscured the tensions that had led to the uprisings of 1968. In consequence, Debord's basic claim, in texts such as the *Comments*, is that the grand revolutionary crux that had been identified and revealed in the 1960s was still very much present, even though its actualisation had become rather more difficult. He was therefore able to claim, in a letter of 1992, that he had 'had no need to change' *The Society of the Spectacle*, 'twenty five years later, in a world that itself has hardly changed'.[69] A similar claim is made in the third French preface to *The Society of the Spectacle*, which was also written in 1992. He states there that there would be no need 'to change a single word' of that earlier book, so long as 'the general conditions of the long historical period that it was the first to accurately describe were still intact [*n'auront pas été détruites*]'.[70]

If we return now to the issue of validation discussed earlier, it seems possible to contend that as far as Debord was concerned, his work had passed history's test. If, as Debord believed, the proof of theory lies in the degree to which it is able to function as strategy, and thus in the extent to which it can facilitate praxis and predict coming eventualities, his work could certainly be deemed to have been successful (a more strictly historical or sociological approach to this question may, of course, produce rather different answers). Yet is there, perhaps, a sense in which the apparent longevity of his work's validity stands in tension with its emphasis on constant temporal movement? As was indicated earlier, Debord stated, in 1979, that he had 'no doubt that the confirmation all my theses encounter ought not to last right until the end of the century and even beyond.' In fact, according to one anecdote from the early 1980s, he was so sure of the veracity of his work that he felt able to contend that it would

---

69 Debord 2008, p. 347.
70 Debord 1995, p. 7, translation altered; 2006b, p. 1792.

remain valid until around 2030.⁷¹ But does this not jar with his work's emphasis on continual intervention, theoretical reformulation, and change?

One could contend that Debord's statements concerning the lasting merits of his work seem to contradict the emphasis on strategic praxis that underpins it. That tension does, however, reinforce the point that we made above, regarding the sense in which this notion of praxis points beyond his extant writings, towards the creation of new theoretical and practical interventions. This seems pertinent in relation to the critique that we advanced in Chapters 10 and 11: for even if Debord's theory of capitalist society does suffer from the problems that we identified in those chapters, the presence of those problems would not necessarily undermine the relevance of his work altogether. The ideas that support it still deserve attention and interest, not least because they actively demand the generation of new, more contemporary and satisfactory theoretical positions.

These observations imply that Debord's work contains a model of history and praxis that could be extracted from his published writings, and considered and developed in its own right. They imply, in other words, that despite his own reluctance to be labelled a philosopher, his texts in fact contain an implicit philosophy of praxis. But if the latter does indeed lead beyond Debord's extant writings, towards new theoretical formulations, where would this leave the concept of spectacle? Would it have a place within this philosophy of praxis?

Earlier in this book, we introduced a distinction between what we have termed the *problematic* of spectacle and the *society* of the spectacle. In order to make sense of Debord's indications that forms of spectacle can be identified in earlier social structures (and could, potentially, occur after the demise of capitalism), we distinguished a transhistorical *problematic* of separated social power from the *society* that has brought that problematic to a defining extreme. We have also sought to show that this problematic is rooted within the same philosophical anthropology that founds the conception of praxis that we have discussed here. Consequently, whilst it might well be necessary to supersede Debord's account of the *society* of the spectacle, i.e. his account of modern capitalism, doing so need not entail jettisoning the *problematic* that was taken to define that society. On the reading advanced here, the concept of spectacle need not be associated with just one particular theory within the 'war of time' (i.e. with Debord's own contextually situated account of a fully spectacular

---

71 'Around 1982, [Debord] told me that his 1967 *La Société du Spectacle* would be valid for the next fifty years. I told him: "Are you sure?" His answer was categorical, his book would last for that period of time' (Prigent 2009).

society), as it would instead denote the primary antagonist within that 'war'. To use the terms employed earlier in this chapter: theory and action need to be oriented towards the truth *of* history, and are validated according to the degree to which they facilitate the instantiation of that truth *in* history. Spectacle, as a transhistorical problematic, is essentially the falsity that such efforts work against. It is a suppression or perversion of the self-constitutive, self-determinate attributes of human historical existence that Debord associated with both truth and 'historical life'. Thus, spectacle, understood in this sense, is precisely what activity within that 'war' needs to combat: for it designates the continual possibility of degenerating into separation, hierarchy and arrest that necessitates the production of new theories and interventions. Consequently, and as was indicated above, if Debord's work is viewed in this manner, it can be seen to afford the beginnings of a philosophy of praxis. The following chapters will attempt to say a little more about this possibility.

CHAPTER 13

Strategy and Tactics in the Integrated Spectacle

The 'Theory of Historical Action'

In his complex autobiographical book *Panegyric*, Debord makes the following remark: 'I have been very interested in war', he writes, 'in the theoreticians of its strategy, but also in reminiscences of battles and in the countless other disruptions history mentions, surface eddies on the river of time.'[1] Strategy and military theory were in fact sources of great interest for Debord throughout his life. This enthusiasm even led to the creation of a military board game, which Debord named the *Kriegspiel* (he seems to have mistakenly dropped the additional 's' of the German term). This game was intended to illustrate the essential principles of Clausewitzian warfare, and its long period of gestation perhaps serves to illustrate the depth and longevity of Debord's interest in war. He had conceived a version of this game by 1956,[2] and had devised it by 1958.[3] It was then patented in 1965, developed in 1976, and it appeared in French in 1987. The game's publication in English in 2007 has since done a great deal to foster Anglophone recognition of this previously neglected side of Debord's thought.

That recognition, however, is not without limitations. Although there is now far more commentary on Debord's interest in strategy, much of it is hampered by the fact that he never presented his views on the topic as a discrete, coherent doctrine or set of ideas. The man who once declared 'I will never give explanations'[4] thus remains true to form. There are good reasons for Debord's reticence in this regard, as we will see below, but the fact remains that because Debord's understanding of strategy is not fully described, and is instead only evidenced through its application in his works and actions, the actual nature of his views on the topic can become somewhat mysterious. In

---

1   Debord 2004b, p. 55; 2006b, p. 1679.
2   Debord 2006b, p. 285.
3   Debord's archived reading notes include a quotation from General Jean-Lambert-Alphonse Colin, which reads: 'Finally, from 1848 on, the game of war, the *"Kriegsspiel"*, manoeuvres between two sides on the map, began to develop'. Debord wrote in the margin: 'and mine, from 1958' (Bibliothèque nationale, NAF28603; Notes de lecture; Stratégie, histoire militaire; box 1; dossier 2; Colin, *Les grandes batailles de l'histoire*. The note was written after 1964).
4   Debord 2006b, p. 70. The line is taken from a 'clarification' of his *Hurlements en faveur de Sade*, directed at the French Federation of Film Clubs.

consequence, Debord's interest in strategy has sometimes been viewed as if it were somehow removed from the rest of his theoretical work, or even reduced to a mere personal quirk or character flaw.[5] We should therefore note, first of all, that it was not a mere personal idiosyncrasy, but was instead treated very seriously indeed, particularly after 1968 and the dissolution of the SI in 1972. For example, in a letter of 1974, Debord wrote as follows:

> The principal work that it appears to me should be envisaged now – as the complementary contrary to *The Society of the Spectacle*, which described frozen alienation (and the negation that was implicit within it) – is *the theory of historical action*. This means to bring forth, in its moment, which has come, *strategic* theory. At this stage – and to speak schematically here – the foundational theoreticians to retrieve and develop are not so much Hegel, Marx and Lautréamont, but Thucydides – Machiavelli – Clausewitz.[6]

This did not mean that Hegel, Marx and Lautréamont were to be simply *replaced* by Thucydides, Machiavelli and Clausewitz. Instead, Debord's point is that the ideas that he and the SI had drawn from the former trio of writers now needed to be expanded via the lessons that might be learned from the latter three. As Debord indicates in his personal notes, he viewed Thucydides, Machiavelli and Clausewitz as theoreticians of historical action;[7] and as we have indicated in the previous chapters of this book, such action, for Debord, is precisely what the 'frozen alienation' of spectacle denies. Therefore, the 'strategic theory' that Debord speaks of here must not be seen as a replacement of the Hegelian Marxism that he and the SI had developed in the 1960s, but rather as its extension and augmentation.

We are, however, still left with the problem of understanding quite what Debord's 'theory of historical action' actually was. This seems pertinent, because academia's increased awareness of Debord's interest in strategy, when

---

5   This is by no means an entirely new phenomenon. In *Panegyric*, Debord recalls an article from 1972 that described him as 'a kind of cool chess player' engaged in 'manoeuvring his acolytes like naïve pawns' (Debord 2004b, p. 48; 2006b, p. 1677).

6   Debord 2005, p. 127.

7   'Thucydides is not a philosopher or a historian, but a theoretician of action; a theoretician of general strategy. It is effectively the same with Machiavelli. Clausewitz is not a historian of war, but a *theoretician of strategy* considered in its pure domain: war' (Bibliothèque nationale, NAF28603; Notes de lecture; Stratégie, histoire militaire; box 2; dossier 5; 'Strat'; the note was written after 1964).

coupled to the paucity of detailed information concerning the subject, has resulted in something of an impasse. Assertions are now often made regarding the possibility of reading Debord's works as field manuals for strategy within the modern world, but very little is typically said about what it might mean to do so.[8] However – and as is the case with almost all other aspects of Debord's work – the actual nature of his 'theory of historical action' need not remain a total mystery. One can use textual evidence and references to the writers that Debord drew upon to develop a more substantial view of this topic. By reading his work in the light of the material that influenced him, one can attempt to reconstruct a model of his views that can fit the available evidence. In this regard, it can be hoped that this book might provide some of the groundwork for such a project. It is important to note, however, that it cannot do a great deal more than that. The reasons for this can be illustrated by way of reference to the content of Debord's archive.

As we discussed earlier, the Bibliothèque nationale de France now contains an archive of Debord's personal notes. When reading – and Debord clearly read an extraordinary amount – he would write, in tiny, meticulous handwriting, quotations, notes and ideas on small cards and pieces of paper. He built up an enormous collection of these *fiches de lecture* throughout his life, all of which are now carefully catalogued and stored in the archive's boxes, folders and sub-folders. There is an entire box of material on Hegel, and a slightly larger box on Marx and Marxism. Both, however, are dwarfed by two whole boxes of notes on strategy and military history. Strategy and war thus appear to be the major concern; but this renders it all the more important to recognise that for Debord, strategic theory was in fact a form of Hegelian Marxism. As we saw earlier, he states explicitly in one of his archived notes that 'It is the same thing to think dialectically and to think strategically'.[9] Strategy, for Debord, is the form taken by dialectical thought following its Marxian actualisation in praxis. Rather than functioning as a mode of *describing* an ostensibly finished history, dialectical thought would become a means of consciously *making* history. For Debord,

---

8 For example, in a short essay on Debord's *Comments on the Society of the Spectacle*, Giorgio Agamben states that Debord's books 'should be used ... as manuals, as instruments of resistance or exodus' (Agamben 2000, p. 73). Yet whilst Agamben makes a number of excellent points (and Debord in fact wrote to him and praised him for doing so (Debord 2008, pp. 211–12)), he does not say a great deal about what it might mean to read these books in this manner. This posture has since become quite common.

9 Bibliothèque nationale, NAF28603; Notes de lecture; Stratégie, histoire militaire; Box 2; dossier 5; 'strat'; January 1977.

dialectical thought should thus become *strategic* thought: a mode of thinking suited to shaping and guiding an open-ended process of praxis within lived time.

One of the aims of this book has been to reconstruct some of the key features of this view of Hegelian Marxism, and to piece together a model of the conceptual framework that subtends it. In this regard, it can be hoped that the observations that have been set out in the book's preceding chapters may be of some use to a serious study of Debord's views on strategy. Such a study obviously exceeds the scope of this book, as it would require a similar approach to that which we have attempted here: one would need to read the many military theorists and historians whom Debord engaged with, and one would then need to study his books, letters and personal notes in the light of their work. Through doing so, one could try to reconstruct a more detailed and adequate model of his views on strategy. Yet whilst we cannot offer any such model here, it is possible, nonetheless, to set out some provisional comments on the topic. To that end, the first part of this chapter will connect Debord's interest in strategy to his views on dialectics by relating both to the importance of temporality within his work. The second part of the chapter will then look at the social terrain upon which Debord's 'theory of historical action' was to be employed, and will discuss the relevance of this notion of strategy to the vision of modern society that he set out in 1988's *Comments on the Society of the Spectacle*.

1) **Dialectical Strategy**

Cookbooks

The connection between Debord's interests in temporality and strategy has been noted by a number of writers and commentators.[10] The manner in which that connection stems from his work's tacit philosophical anthropology does, however, remain largely neglected, so we should briefly recapitulate the following points.

---

10 Wark, for example, has claimed that Debord's *Kriegspiel* is 'really a diagram of the strategic possibilities of spectacular time', but unfortunately he does not take this observation further (Wark 2008, p. 28). Jappe has also highlighted this connection, but in his seminal *Guy Debord* he presents Debord's interest in strategy as nostalgia for the certainties of a pre-spectacular past ('this interest of his could be interpreted as a desire to remain moored to a world still essentially *intelligible*' (Jappe 1999, p. 114, emphasis in the original)). This is different from the reading advanced in this book, according to which strategy, for

As we noted in Chapter 2, Debord writes in *The Society of the Spectacle*, by way of a quotation from Hegel's *Phenomenology*, that 'Man – that "negative being who *is* solely to the extent that he abolishes being" – is one with time'.[11] We are, in other words, temporal creatures, characterised by the changes that we undergo and effect within time. As has also been indicated, Debord's views here seem somewhat similar to Sartre's account of the 'for-itself': the human subject is seen to be perpetually opposed to its own present moment, and indeed to its own extant self, because the actions and experiences that it effects and undergoes within time create change within both itself and its world. It would seem, therefore, that for Debord, the human subject can be understood as a transformative force, and thus as a profoundly historical creature: as an

---

Debord, is an attempt to think and act *with* chance and uncertainty, not against it; to thus accept and engage with the contingencies of temporal existence. Kaufmann (2006, *passim*) picks up on the sense of pathos and occasional touches of sublimity attributed to the experience of time in Debord's later works, and makes note of its relation to strategy. However, he reads Debord's interest in time in terms of poetic melancholy, and therefore seems to miss the importance of *creating* the future, as opposed to reflecting on the past. In this regard, Kaufmann's view is close to that of Stone-Richards (2001), who has claimed that Debord's work can be seen to express a form of noble, aristocratic stoicism. Stone-Richards thus makes links between Debord and thinkers such as the Roman Emperor Marcus Aurelius. It is certainly the case that if one consults the *Meditations*, one can certainly find statements that echo the tone of Debord's own remarks on temporality (e.g. 'remember ... that each of us lives only in the present, this fleeting moment of time' (Marcus Aurelius 1997, p. 20); 'The art of living ... must stand ready and firm to meet whatever besets it, even when unforeseen' (Marcus Aurelius 1997, p. 65)). However, Hegel's objections to stoicism are pertinent here. Hegel points out in the *Phenomenology* – by way of oblique reference to Marcus Aurelius's status as a Roman Emperor – that the stoical consciousness is 'indifferent' as to whether it is 'on the throne or in chains' (Hegel 1977, p. 121). This seems markedly different from Debord's own views. Debord is certainly *not* a stoic. One could read him as such if one followed Kaufmann in seeing his comments on time as a melancholic acceptance of temporal events that simply happen to us. However, this jars with Debord's central emphasis on the need to shape and direct lived time: to create situations, and to take command of one's own existence. In contrast, Bracken is much closer to the views presented in this book, particularly when he acknowledges that 'for Debord [the] apprehension of time was coloured with the Hegelian preoccupation with the self-conscious creation of history with acts of negation' (Bracken 1997, p. 105). However, Bracken's book leaves these assertions undeveloped, and he ultimately seems to view Debord's interest in strategy in terms of Machiavellian (in the crude sense of the term) manoeuvring: as a means of achieving ends on 'the battlefield of everyday life' (Bracken 1997, p. 217).

11 Debord 1995, p. 92; 2006b, p. 820.

entity that makes itself, and which knows itself, through the actions that it conducts in time. However, Debord also holds that human subjects can become divorced from their ability to direct and shape this temporal movement, and thereby from their capacity to make and know their own history. According to the interpretation of Debord's theory that we have tried to develop, that separation gives rise to spectacle. The supersession of spectacle, therefore, would require the self-determinate creation and control of temporal experience. This then means that an anti-spectacular existence would need to be a fundamentally *strategic* affair, because it would involve continually negotiating, creating and responding to the shifting contexts and situations that compose lived time.

Debord's interest in strategy is thus intimately connected to the existential dimensions of the Hegelian Marxism that underpins the concept of spectacle. It corresponds to a need for self-constitutive and self-determinate choice and action in time, and therefore relates to the concerns with temporal action and experience that run throughout his oeuvre. Yet if this is so – if Debord's interest in strategy is not a peculiar supplement to the rest of his work, but rather a fundamental component of the whole – then one might very well wonder why Debord says so little about the technicalities of his views on the topic. The answer to that question lies in his antipathy to conceptual systems, which we have already seen evidenced, in Chapter 10, in his hostility towards the 'illusions of economism'.[12]

In brief, Debord's position here seems to have been as follows. If one claims that a conceptual system expresses or mirrors the true nature of the world, then one must also assume that the world itself is somehow static, or at least that what occurs within the world will accord with that system. Such thought must, perforce, be 'contemplative': for rather than engaging directly with subsequent eventualities, it effaces their significance in favour of the truth that it purports to express. Dialectics, for Debord, is different, and he seems to have viewed dialectical thinking as inherently opposed to systematisation. This, presumably, is why he claims in *The Society of the Spectacle* that Hegel's 'attempt to create a circular system' was '*undialectical*':[13] for against such circular closure, Debord viewed dialectical thought as a constant, open-ended process.[14]

---

12   Debord 1995, p. 58, translation altered; 2006b, p. 799.
13   Debord 1995, p. 51; 2006b, p. 795, emphasis in the original.
14   For example, in 1972, he wrote that a 'definitively coherent and finished system', was 'the last thing' that 'historical thought' 'claims to supply' (SI 2003, p. 30; Debord 2006b, p. 1105); or, as he put it in a letter of 1962: 'I only want to work on a "moving order"', thus 'never constructing a doctrine or institution' (Debord 2001a, p. 156). Hence the SI's announcement, in the very first issue of *Internationale Situationniste*, that 'there is no such

Dialectics, therefore, needed to be applied and used, and could not just be described. Hence Debord's approval of Clausewitz's claim that the true home of strategic knowledge is the actual *conduct* of war, and not a book *about* war. Indeed, Clausewitz clearly indicates that it would be quite impossible to concoct a *system* of strategic thought: 'the conduct of war', he claims, 'branches out in all directions and has no definitive limit', whereas 'any system, any model' has a 'finite nature'. An 'irreconcilable conflict', Clausewitz claims, exists between such a system 'and actual practice.'[15] Debord clearly recognised and embraced this view. His archived reading notes on Clausewitz's *On War* include the following quotation: 'in truth, knowledge [*savoir-faire*] cannot be set forth in a book, and no book should, therefore, use the term "art" in its title',[16] because no book could hope to encapsulate what could only be conducted in action.[17] In the margin of the card onto which Debord coped this quotation, he wrote 'cf. cookbooks!'. This must be a reference to Marx's refusal, in the afterword to the second German edition of *Capital*, to write recipes 'for the cook-shops of the future'[18] (Marx intended this statement as a dismissal of the charge that his critique of capitalist society should be supplemented by detailed prescriptions for a better future; Debord appears to have understood it as a refusal to impose pre-conceived visions and systems onto unfolding historical events). Shortly after his remark about these 'cook-shops', Marx goes on to describe 'the dialectic' as regarding 'every historically developed form as being in a fluid state, in motion'.[19] For Debord, 'dialectical, strategic thought'[20] should operate in much the same way: it should move and think in step with changing circumstances. This, then, is why he does not systematise his understanding of dialectical strategy. Rather than presenting it as a static doctrine, he sought to employ it in both his works and actions.

---

    thing as situationism, which would mean a doctrine for interpreting existing conditions' (SI 2006, p. 51; 1997, p. 13). We might also note here that the SI said that they were Marxists 'only as much as Marx was when he said, "I am not a Marxist"' (SI 2006, p. 181; 2006b, p. 1105).

15   Clausewitz 1993, p. 155.

16   Bibliothèque nationale, NAF28603; Notes de lecture; Stratégie, histoire militaire; box 2; Clausewitz, De la guerre; the note was written after 1964.

17   Clausewitz had aimed this statement against the view that the 'art of war' could be learned from a book. It was no doubt doubly significant for Debord, given his own interest in actualising art in lived praxis.

18   Marx 1990, p. 99.

19   Marx 1990, p. 103.

20   Debord 2008, p. 78.

It follows from this that a full reconstruction of Debord's views on this topic would also need to engage, to a far greater extent than can be attempted here, with his own political actions and interests. His fascination with the Italian *anni di piombo*, for example, greatly informed his *Comments on the Society of the Spectacle*, and indeed his views on the contemporary importance of strategic theory. We will touch on these issues below. Given the nature of this book's focus, however, we will concentrate, in the remaining sections of this chapter's first half, on the existential and aesthetic aspects of his views on strategy.

Life as War

Having noted that strategy, for Debord, involved engaging with changing processes and circumstances, we can now add that it also necessarily involved engaging with chance and contingency. As we have seen in earlier chapters, Debord places particular stress on the finitude of human life, the fleeting nature of temporal moments, and the limited, contextually specific nature of human knowledge. For Debord, consciousness is always bound to particular moments and contexts. Consequently, the nature of human subjectivity entails that actions must always be undertaken with a limited knowledge of the factors and forces involved. War takes this to an extreme: it is, as Clausewitz puts it, 'the realm of uncertainty'.[21] Debord was certainly sensitive to that point, and many of the quotations that he copied down in his archived reading notes reflect this theme (for example, one such note quotes Marshal Ferdinand Foch's remark that 'all armies have lived and marched in the unknown').[22] For Debord, therefore, a study of the conduct and theory of war could be instructive for the conduct of life in general,[23] as strategic skill allows one to negotiate the contingencies and unexpected eventualities of a finite, temporal existence.

Crucially, strategic ability involves doing so not by stifling or removing chance, in favour of predetermined patterns, but rather by turning chance into a source of controlled creativity and potential.[24] This bears direct relation to Debord and the SI's desire to turn life into a game, for in play as in war,

---

21 Clausewitz 1993, p. 117.
22 Bibliothèque nationale, NAF28603; Notes de lecture; Stratégie, histoire militaire; box 1; dossier 1; Foch, *Des Principes de la guerre*; the note was written after 1964.
23 Referring to his *Kriegspiel* in *Panegyric*, Debord writes: 'I have played this game and, in the often difficult conduct of my life, I have drawn a few lessons from it' (Debord 2004b, pp. 55–6; 2006b, p. 1679).
24 As Debord put it in a set of unpublished notes on chance, 'all progress, all creation, is the organisation of *new conditions of chance*' (Debord 2006b, p. 296, emphasis in the original).

one must know how and when to act. To quote Clausewitz once again: 'In the whole range of human activities, war most closely resembles a game of cards'.[25] Thus, if 'workers' can indeed 'become dialecticians', so as to take strategic, self-determinate control of their own circumstances, then they can also create their own ludic situations.

Debord's basic contention, then, is that understanding the conduct of war offers a means of understanding the conduct of life. He seems to have held that war presented, in a highly concentrated and exaggerated form, some of the essential features of human existence. War foregrounds the finite nature of human life, and underscores the need to consciously shape and respond to uncertain, changing circumstances. It requires doing so in full knowledge of the risks involved, and of the constant proximity of death. This can perhaps be illustrated with the following quotation from *Panegyric*:

> Xerxes, as his great army was crossing the Hellespont, formulated in just one sentence the first axiom at the base of all strategic thought, when he explained his tears by saying: 'It came into my mind how pitifully short human life is – for all of these thousands of men not one will be alive in a hundred years' time.'[26]

For Debord, the 'first axiom' that lies at the basis of 'all strategic thought' is simply that 'time does not wait'.[27] One must act *with* time and at the *right* time, and in full awareness of the fact that time is always passing away. Or, as another of Debord's archived quotations puts it: '"Time is always our enemy"; there is a truth which strategic studies that merit the name will reveal'.[28] We can suppose, therefore, that for Debord, war foregrounded the human condition of having been cast into a set of shifting, uncertain circumstances, within which one is obliged to act and ultimately die. Strategic thought, therefore, is not just a means of thinking the conduct of warfare, but rather a means of thinking the conduct of lived time.

Perhaps needless to say, this association of life with warfare is by no means unproblematic. Debord's acknowledgement that 'war is the domain of danger and disappointment'[29] does little to rectify the normalisation of violence and

---

25   Clausewitz 1993, p. 97.
26   Debord 2004b, p. 62; 2006b, p. 1683.
27   Debord 2004b, p. 62; 2006b, p. 1683.
28   Bibliothèque nationale, NAF28603; Notes de lecture; Stratégie, histoire militaire; box 1; dossier 2; Laurent, *Introduction aux études de stratégie*; the note was written after 1964.
29   Debord 2004b, p. 55; 2006b, p. 1679.

conflict that it invites. Furthermore, and despite his evident awareness of the grim realities of war, his comments sometimes come close to romanticising conflict.[30]

Debord's desire to realise art and poetry in lived time is perhaps one of the primary causes of this romanticisation. This is because that desire led to an aestheticisation of time and temporal experience: to an aestheticisation, in other words, of what Debord took to be the primary terrain upon which strategic thought must act. Before we attempt to reconstruct some of the details of Debord's views on strategy, we should, therefore, address these aesthetic themes.

'The True Taste of the Passage of Time'

Debord's interest in the aestheticisation of time is perhaps best approached through the writers and poets whom he admired. As Debord's wife, Alice, once pointed out, 'All Guy's favourite poets dealt with the finite aspect of time' and thus 'with its slipping away, with the fragility of life'.[31] As we indicated in Part Two, Debord clearly accorded beauty to the experience of time's passage, and in some statements, he appears to credit it with a degree of sublimity. Yet whilst an emphasis on finitude and the fragility of life may seem overly melancholic, a discussion of Debord's favoured writers – Alice mentions 'Li Po, Omar Khayyám, and Jorge Manrique'[32] – can serve to show that there is nothing passive and quiescent about Debord's views on time. Instead, what one finds here is an existential concern with the need to act, decide and pursue projects within time. Such concerns, of course, bear direct relation to the strategic themes discussed above.

We will begin with Li Po, whose Eighth Century poetry can help to illuminate the following statement from Debord's *Panegyric*: 'At first, like everyone, I

---

30   The sixth chapter of *Panegyric* is a case in point, and one might also think here of Debord's use of the King's Agincourt speech from *Henry V* in the film version of *The Society of the Spectacle*. Debord's reading notes on strategy also contain quotations such as the following, which was taken from Marshal Auguste de Marmont, and which also evidences the themes of temporality and the intensity of lived moments which Debord held so dear: 'men of war' are 'like a veritable family: for this variety in our occupations and in our pleasures, this successive employment of our faculties of body and mind, gave life an interest and an extraordinary rapidity' (Bibliothèque nationale, NAF28603; Notes de lecture; Stratégie, histoire militaire; box 1; dossier 1; Marmont, *Mémoires*; the note was written after 1964).

31   Quoted in Merrifield 2005, p. 143.

32   Ibid.

appreciated the effect of mild drunkenness; then very soon I grew to like what lies beyond violent drunkenness, once that stage is past: a terrible and magnificent peace, the true taste of the passage of time.'[33]

Li Po's poetry is much given to reflections on time, because the Taoist principles that inform it entail an emphasis on moving in step with the world.[34] In keeping with other classical Chinese poets, Li Po held that alcohol offered greater spontaneity, and a deeper unity with time's passage[35] (in fact, Li Po must surely be the hero of all romantic poets: legend has it that he died falling from a boat whilst drunkenly attempting to embrace the moon's reflection). It would seem that Debord shared these sentiments. In 1957, he wrote that the 'main emotional drama of life ... seems to be the sensation of the passage of time'.[36] Twenty years later, in 1978's *In Girum*, he stated that the 'sensation of the passing of time has always been vivid for me, and I have been attracted by it just as others are allured by dizzying heights or by water'.[37] It would seem that alcohol served to heighten this sensation, easing the transition between distinct moments, emphasising and releasing passions, and thereby bringing greater affective and aesthetic qualities to lived experience.

Time and alcohol also feature heavily in *The Rubáiyát of Omar Khayyám*, which Debord references in several of his later works. Khayyám presents the flow of time as life, and links it to alcohol that is to be consumed and enjoyed. There is an existential current to the *Rubáiyát*, and indeed a degree of hedonism ('Ah, fill the Cup – what boots it to repeat/ How Time is slipping underneath our Feet'),[38] but there is also a touch of melancholia: for example, in his *Comments on the Society of the Spectacle*, Debord quotes Khayyám as having described human agents as 'puppets' of the 'firmament', destined to be put back into the 'box of oblivion'.[39] Remarks such as these bear obvious relation to what we saw Debord refer to above as 'the first axiom' of 'all strategic

---

33   Debord 2004b, pp. 30–1; 2006b, p. 1669.
34   See Hinton in Li Po 2006, pp. xi–xxiv.
35   'Three cups and I've plumbed the great Way [the Tao],/ a jarful and I've merged with occurrence/ appearing of itself. Wine's view is lived:/ you can't preach doctrine to the sober' (Li Po 2006, p. 44).
36   SI 2006, p. 42; Debord 2006b, p. 327.
37   Debord 2003b, p. 189; 2006b, p. 1398.
38   Khayyám 1993, p. 51.
39   Debord 1998, p. 85; 2006b, p. 1644. In his translation of Debord's *Comments*, Malcolm Imrie used Avery and Heath-Stubb's 1979 translation of the *Rubáiyát* when rendering the French translation that Debord used. The lines that Debord quotes correspond to the 49th quatrain of the 1859 Fitzgerald translation (Khayyám 1993, p. 63).

thought': the view that the time in which we are obliged to act will not wait, and must be seized. This certainly seems to have been what Debord had in mind in the *Comments*, as in that text he places those lines from Khayyám alongside another quotation from Baltasar Gracián. The quotation from Gracián comes from the latter's *Oráculo manual y arte de prudencia* (translated in French as *L'Homme de cour*, and as *The Art of Worldly Wisdom* in English), and it can be traced to a section of that text titled 'Live for the Moment'. The quotation advises: 'Act when you may, for time and tide wait for no one'.[40] Debord is, of course, as opaque as ever here, but in placing those two quotations side by side he was perhaps proposing a choice between two different approaches to life: acting in and with time (Gracián), or being acted on *by* time (Khayyám). The former is, of course, the right approach to take. After all, Debord described Gracián as 'a great connoisseur of historical time'.[41] Debord was also particularly fond of Renaissance-era works, like that of Gracián, which advise how best to comport oneself with dignity and skill. He was, for example, also very interested in Baldassare Castiglione's *The Book of the Courtier*.[42] These books teach skilful action and behaviour, and thus the *artistry* of conducting lived time.

Mention must also be made here of Shakespeare. According to Debord, who quotes Prospero's remark that 'we are such stuff as dreams are made on' towards the end of *Panegyric*'s first volume, 'no one knew better than Shakespeare how life passes'.[43] Debord was also fond of the work of François Villon, no doubt partly because of his impeccable romantic credentials: Villon was both a poet and an outlaw, and his *ubi sunt* poetry concerning the finitude of human joys no doubt greatly appealed. In this respect, Villon's work shares some themes with that of the fifteenth-century Spanish poet Jorge Manrique, which Debord translated into French in 1980. In his published notes to this

---

40 Debord 1998, p. 85; 2006b, p. 1644; Gracián 2000, p. 116.
41 Debord 1998, p. 85, translation altered; 2006b, p. 1644.
42 Hussey has suggested, quite persuasively, that Debord was interested in these Renaissance visions of cultured behaviour because they evidence attempts to establish appropriate modes of conduct within a social context that predates both the modern state and the fragmentation of spectacular society (Hussey 2002, p. 293). See also Debord's comments on the Renaissance in thesis #139 of *The Society of the Spectacle*. If one were to pursue the notion of ethics that we have identified in Debord's concept of spectacle, perhaps the most appropriate means of doing so would be to use Debord's Hegelianism to establish something akin to an Aristotelian virtue ethics, informed by his interest in, and comments upon, these Renaissance writers.
43 Debord 2004b, p. 68; 2006b, p. 1685.

translation, Debord praises Manrique's emphasis on the flow of time,[44] stating that his poetry expresses life's 'brevity, the triumph of death, the dissolution and loss of all that exists in a moment of the world.'[45] Yet once again, whilst this might seem to indicate melancholia, it certainly does not involve passive resignation. Debord claims here that the 'most beautiful lesson' that we can learn from Manrique's poems is that one must fight for one's own '"true king"': the 'king' that 'one has made oneself',[46] presumably through mastering one's own existence in time.

The aestheticisation of time that one finds in Debord's work thus accords beauty to possibility, action, choice and risk: to the intensity of lived moments, and to the poignancy that follows from their finitude. This, then, is why he romanticises war. War appears to have been viewed as a particularly intense, concentrated distillation of these issues.

It is worth adding here that this aestheticisation of temporality could not be expressed or experienced in any form other than lived activity. There is no way in which instantiations of this aesthetic could be placed on a gallery wall, for example, as language and the traditional arts can only intimate and represent it. It can only be found within lived conduct; and as skill in the exercise of this conduct requires knowing how and when to act at the right time, it follows that the realisation of art in lived time needed to be a strategic affair. We can thus take some comfort from the fact that whilst Debord certainly comes close to casting war as fundamental to the human condition, the features of life exemplified by war could also be expressed in the artistic, ludic conduct of lived activity.

The Art of War

Having spoken about the existential and aesthetic aspects of Debord's views on strategy, we should now try to say a little more about their technical content. As noted above, a detailed reconstruction of these views falls beyond the scope of this book. However, in what follows below, we will make some very brief comments about three of the key strategic theorists whom Debord referenced and drew upon: Clausewitz, Sun Tzu, and Machiavelli. Debord described all three as having employed a form of 'dialectical thought'[47] in their strategic theory. By highlighting the common themes shared between them, we can try

---

44 For example: 'These are rivers, our lives,/ That descend towards the sea/ Of death' (Manrique 1996, p. 9).
45 Debord in Manrique 1996, p. 71.
46 Debord in Manrique 1996, p. 73.
47 Debord 2008, p. 204.

to draw out some of the key aspects of Debord's own version of dialectical strategy. We will begin with Clausewitz, and with his notion of resistance.

According to Clausewitz, the essence of war can be distilled down to the view that it is 'an act of force to compel our enemy to do our will'.[48] This means that the opponents within a combat are obliged to make their enemy 'incapable of further resistance.'[49] War, therefore, entails maximising and employing effectively one's own ability to resist one's opponent, whilst simultaneously seeking to destroy their ability to resist your own efforts. Clausewitz is famous for having described this relation of forces in terms that are, at times, reminiscent of Hegelian dialectics. Yet Clausewitz almost certainly never read Hegel, and Debord was well aware of this. In a letter of 1986, he wrote: 'I know that Clausewitz was not directly Hegelian, [and] no doubt did not read Hegel'.[50] Yet to deny the dialectical characteristics of Clausewitz's work on that basis would amount, Debord claims, to 'a schoolmaster's critique',[51] insofar as it would effectively assume that dialectics exists solely within philosophical books. For Debord, dialectics is fundamental to the conflicts and interactions that compose human historical existence ('contradiction', he claims, 'is the source of all movement, all life'),[52] and Clausewitz's engagements on the battlefield, together with his attempts to theorise such engagements, had forced him to become familiar with an area of life that foregrounds such movement and interaction. This, according to Debord, allowed him to become 'something truly close to a Hegelian dialectician.'[53]

This is perhaps evidenced most clearly in Clausewitz's concept of the 'culminating point', to which we will have cause to return later. The culminating point is the moment at which an attack that was initially successful exhausts itself, and thus a point at which a position of strength becomes a position of weakness[54] (for example: Napoleon's initially triumphant but ultimately catastrophic advance into Russia). One must be able to identify such moments, or at least predict their arrival. An attacking force must attain its goals before this reversal of strength occurs, just as a defender must try to hasten this moment, so as to ensure that it arrives before those goals are achieved. A similar notion

---

48   Clausewitz 1993, p. 83.
49   Ibid.
50   Debord 1986.
51   Ibid.
52   Debord 2004a, p. 317.
53   Debord 1986.
54   Clausewitz 1993, p. 639.

of dialectical reversal can be found in Clausewitz's comments on guerrilla war, and on the need to preserve an ability to resist within situations of apparent defeat. Once an enemy army has invaded one's territory, the relatively rigid and static structures of that army need to be combatted by fluid, unpredictable attacks. As Howard Caygill has pointed out, such a resistant force must be able to 'appear and disappear unpredictably'.[55] According to Clausewitz, an army in such a situation must 'pursue defence through unexpected attacks', and should avoid 'concentrating itself and risking confinement'.[56] A position of weakness and defence, therefore, can become a position of strength and attack.

The dialectical transformation of strength into weakness, and *vice versa*, is not only important to the Napoleonic conflict that Clausewitz described.[57] It is also very much present in Sun Tzu's *The Art of War*, which is now over 2,000 years old. One of Sun Tzu's central principles is that a good general should strive for 'formlessness'. In essence, this is an ability to continually adapt and mould oneself to new contexts, and to become inscrutable to the enemy. A 'military force' should have 'no constant formation', just as 'water has no constant shape'.[58] It must move with time and changing events, and should never allow the enemy to identify, fix or control it in a static form. Consequently, a successful general must be adept at misleading the enemy about the true nature of his or her forces and intentions. Because 'military operation' thus 'involves deception',[59] a general must also possess the ability to see through the enemy's own deceptions. In Sun Tzu, therefore, we find the same emphasis on constant movement and open-ended process, and on the interaction of strategic necessity and contingency, that Debord appears to have associated with dialectics. In addition, there is also a further emphasis on the need to

---

55 Caygill 2013, p. 62. It might be added here that Debord's archived notes on strategy acknowledge the merits of not being confined to a strong defensive position, and of being able to move freely (Bibliothèque nationale, NAF28603; Notes de lecture; Stratégie, histoire militaire; box 1; dossier 1; Rochambeau, *Mémoires*; the note was written after 1964).

56 Clausewitz, quoted in Caygill 2013, p. 62.

57 Another one of Debord's reading cards quotes Napoleon himself as having indicated that the real artistry of war consists in having greater *force* than one's opponent whilst nonetheless having a weaker *army* at the point where one attacks, or when one is attacked (Bibliothèque nationale, NAF28603; Notes de lecture; Stratégie, histoire militaire; box 1; dossier 1; Foch, *Des Principes de la guerre*; the note was written after 1964). Clearly, this is only possible through effective strategy.

58 Sun Tzu 1988, p. 113.

59 Sun Tzu 1988, p. 49.

be able to use and see through appearances. That emphasis is, of course, of particular significance in relation to Debord's views on spectacular society. So too are Machiavelli's analyses.

It may seem somewhat strange that Debord describes Machiavelli as having employed a form of dialectical thinking. Yet just as Sun Tzu stresses the need to mislead and delude one's enemy, so too does Machiavelli; and like that of both Sun Tzu and Clausewitz, Machiavelli's own strategic advice hints towards instances of dialectical reversal. An effective prince, Machiavelli claims, needs to be feared, but he must also avoid being hated. If such hatred occurs, the prince may have cause to fear a populace who should, ideally, fear him. Consequently, in order to be successful, a prince must be 'a great pretender and dissembler'.[60] He should, for example, 'keep the populace occupied with festivals and spectacles',[61] and 'must cunningly foster some hostile action, whenever he has the opportunity, so that in repressing it his greatness will emerge all the more'.[62] He must, therefore, turn his position of potential weakness into a position of strength by continually ensuring that those who have reason to despise and attack him are led to love and support him. Machiavelli's prescriptions, therefore, imply that the real art of governance lies in leading the subjected to accept, and indeed even to love, their own domination. One can thus see why Debord describes Machiavelli, in *The Society of the Spectacle*, as having presented an account of 'desanctified power', through which he sought 'to say the unsayable about the state'.[63]

What, then, can we infer from the commonalities between Clausewitz, Sun Tzu and Machiavelli? The points of similarity between them can be summarised as follows. All respond to the sense in which strategy requires recognising and understanding the changing relations between opposing forces. Good strategy involves using an awareness of these shifting relations to effect reversals whereby positions of strength become positions of weakness, and *vice versa*. In order to achieve this, one must be able to act at the right time; and because one's opponent will be attempting to do the same, one must also be attentive to feints and illusions. Above all, in order to act at the right time, one must also be capable of responding to unpredictable events, and of changing one's plans and ideas in keeping with changing circumstances. Thus, in sum: dialectical strategy – insofar as it can be inferred from these points of correspondence – would seem to involve an understanding of the interplay

---

60   Machiavelli 2004, p. 61.
61   Machiavelli 2004, p. 79.
62   Machiavelli 2004, p. 74.
63   Debord 1995, p. 103, translation altered; 2006b, p. 827.

between opposing forces that allows one to understand when to strike, adapt and withdraw so as to turn advantage into disadvantage, and disadvantage into advantage. Such a mode of thought would be able to think in step with the unfolding processes through which conflicts play out, and would thus think not only *in*, or *about*, but above all *with* the movement of time.

To some extent, these principles can be illustrated by a set of unpublished notes on poker that Debord wrote in 1990. These notes were written for Debord's wife, Alice, and they provide instruction as to how one can succeed at the game. The secret to poker, Debord writes, 'is conducting oneself, initially, and as much as possible, according to the *real forces* that one finds oneself to have.'[64] One should not, in other words, fixate on illusion. The bad player, he writes, 'sees bluffing everywhere, and focuses on it'; but a good player 'considers it to be negligible and follows, from the start, his knowledge of the means that are at his disposal at each moment'.[65] If one understands that bluffing may or may not be taking place, then the wisest course of action is to conduct oneself purely on the basis of one's own cards, and according to the reactions of the other players; for if someone is bluffing, then they may well believe that you are doing so too, and will act accordingly. In consequence, Debord advises, one must act according to one's own real situation: 'one must know how to employ the *kairos*[66] of one's forces at the right moment.'[67]

It seems apparent that these notes were not just intended as a guide to poker, as they bear direct relation to the context of the modern spectacle. In a spectacular world full of illusions and lies, in which history is both distorted and denied, one should attempt to see past those illusions in order to understand the reality of one's own historical context. Through doing so, one can begin to consider how best to act and respond at the opportune time. In the second half of this chapter, we will consider the ways in which these issues pertain to the account of modern society that Debord presented in his *Comments on the Society of the Spectacle* of 1988.

Debord's *Comments* describe the 'practical consequences'[68] of the manner in which spectacular society had continued to develop and evolve after

---

64 Debord 2006b, p. 1790.
65 Ibid.
66 *Kairos* is a classical Greek term referring to the opportune moment: the right time to act, but a time that cannot be measured. *Kairos* is inherently qualitative, as opposed to the quantitative sequence of *kronos*, or 'clock-time', and not only does it transcend the latter, but it also impinges upon it and disrupts it with its demands for apposite action.
67 Debord 2006b, p. 1790.
68 Debord 1998, pp. 3–4; 2006b, p. 1595.

the publication of 1967's *The Society of the Spectacle*, and in response to the uprisings of May 1968. From the outset, the book presents these consequences through military metaphors. The spectacle is 'an active force'; Debord will analyse its '*lines of advance*'; it is an 'invasion' with which some 'collaborate'.[69] We will propose below that the book can also be taken to contain some very guarded recommendations as to how a resistant force might respond to these circumstances.

2) **The Integrated Spectacle**

The Map and the Territory
Debord's *Comments* describe the advent of a new form of spectacular domination. This is referred to as the 'integrated' spectacle, because it has arisen from the fusion of the older 'concentrated' and 'diffuse' forms of spectacle described in *The Society of the Spectacle*. We should begin here, therefore, by briefly revisiting those older formations.

The diffuse spectacle was associated with the consumer capitalism of the developed West. It relies upon the commodity's colonisation of social life, and is thereby able to celebrate the benefits and bounty of its social order through its adverts, shop-fronts, fashions and entertainment. Fragmentary and often seemingly conflictual images that support the modes of life required by this social order are dispersed throughout society, engendering forms of activity that conform to its requirements. The concentrated spectacle, on the other hand, was associated with the state-capitalism of the bureaucratically managed 'Communist' countries. As in the diffuse spectacle, life is regulated and managed in accordance with the needs of an effectively sovereign economy. However, where the diffuse spectacle presents the merits of its mode of life through the constant promise of commodified satisfaction, the concentrated spectacle operates rather differently. Productive activity is not oriented towards the creation of a great mass of commodities, but is instead concentrated into the creation and conduct of an officially approved version of life. The validity, purpose and *raison d'être* of that life is also concentrated and focussed into the figure of the ruling Party or leader. An 'image of the good which is a résumé of everything that exists officially'[70] is thereby identified with the state, or even a

---

69 Debord 1998, p. 4; 2006b, p. 1595, emphasis in the original. Bracken points out that Debord's view of modern society may be inflected by the occupied France of his childhood (Bracken 1997, pp. 5–6).

70 Debord 1995, p. 42; 2006b, p. 788.

'single man', and stands as a 'catch-all of socially recognised qualities'.[71] Life is thus moulded and governed not through the illusion of consumer choice, but rather through a managed economy and greater police control.

Debord's *Comments* was written just prior to the fall of the Berlin Wall, and it constituted an attempt to theorise the unification of the two different modes of governance that had faced each other during the Cold War. The integrated spectacle thus results from the triumph of consumer capitalism over its old counterpart, because it incorporates, into the diffuse spectacle's wealth of consumer goods, the concentrated spectacle's unification of state and economy, its police power and surveillance, and its management of revolutionary potential. The circumstances that the book describes seem almost universal today, but Debord claimed in 1988 that this new form of spectacular society had been pioneered by France and Italy, partly in response to the French uprisings of 1968, and the Italian *anni di piombo* of the 1970s and early 1980s. Both France and Italy, he wrote, were marked by 'the important role of the Stalinist party and unions in political and intellectual life, a weak democratic tradition, the long monopoly of power enjoyed by a single party of government, and the need to be finished with a revolutionary contestation that had appeared by surprise'.[72] Or, to put that in more contemporary terms: the integrated spectacle involves the co-option of the left, an increasingly elitist and detached political system, and the need to manage potential opposition.

Although the integrated spectacle draws on the techniques of governance employed by both its concentrated and diffuse antecedents, it uses those techniques in a rather different manner. The centralised power structures and modes of police control previously employed by the concentrated spectacle have now become increasingly hidden, obscure and secretive. In addition, the diffuse spectacle's mechanisms of fragmentation and commodification have been taken to a new extreme. The *Comments* thus contends that the integrated spectacle merits its name not only because it arises from the integration of previously distinct forms of social control, but because it has also quite literally integrated itself into reality to a far greater extent than ever before. Debord writes as follows:

> For the final sense of the integrated spectacle is that it has integrated itself into reality to the same extent as it spoke of it, and that it was reconstructing as it spoke it. So this reality now no longer confronts it as

---

71   Debord 2006b, p. 685.
72   Debord 1998, p. 9, translation altered; 2006b, p. 1598.

something alien. When the spectacle was concentrated, the greater part of surrounding society escaped it; when diffuse, a small part; today, no part. The spectacle is mixed into all reality, and irradiates it.[73]

We will look at the nature of this new terrain in a moment, and at the manner in which Debord thought revolt might operate upon it. Before doing so, however, we should first address the fact that this statement might seem to put Debord very close to Baudrillard's notion of simulation. Given that Debord's ideas are often erroneously conflated with those of Baudrillard,[74] it may be helpful to briefly explain why this is not the case.

As we saw in Part One, the 'reality' that underlies the spectacle's representations is not a material, physical world that has become hidden by ideological confusion, but rather an alienated capacity and potential for self-determinate agency. Likewise, and as we tried to demonstrate in the previous chapter, the 'truth' that Debord opposes to the spectacle's 'falsity' is not a fixed, natural essence, but rather the process of historical praxis. Spectacular society can be understood as a kind of frame that has been imposed upon the conduct of human historical agency, through which the latter is channelled and co-opted.[75] Life conducted in accordance with the spectacle's templates and

---

73 Debord 1998, p. 9, translation altered; 2006, p. 1598.
74 As we noted earlier, Debord viewed Baudrillard as a 'media clown' (Debord 2008, p. 248). He was, however, aware of the emergent tendency towards conflating his own work with that of Baudrillard. In a letter of 1991, he remarks as follows: 'These American journalists are strangely misinformed. I do not really see how a *mutual* influence could possibly exist between this absurd [*extravagant*] Baudrillard and myself. Only once have I ever had occasion to set eyes on him for a few minutes, during which time I never said a single word to him. Neither have I ever read him. Only in recent years has he been telling journalists that he used to be a Situationist. This is obviously a deceitful pretention: the idiot was a Maoist back then' (Debord 2008, p. 265, italics in the original). Similarly, in 1989, Debord wrote to his publisher, stating that 'A cretin has written to me from the University of Montana ... informing me that Baudrillard is due to be let loose within its walls [*va y sévir*] and that I would do well to appear there in such good company ...' (Debord 2008, p. 74). In his letter, Debord thanks his publisher for refusing the invitation on his behalf, and for thus 'making this cretin grasp this truth that he finds so hard to conceive [*stupéfiante*]' (ibid.): namely the truth that Debord had absolutely no interest in presenting his work within an academic context, or indeed in appearing alongside academia's celebrities.
75 'There can be no freedom outside of activity, and in the context [*cadre*] of the spectacle all activity is negated – all real activity having been captured in its entirety and channelled into the global construction of the spectacle' (Debord 1995, pp. 21–2, translation altered; 2006b, p. 772).

paradigms thus becomes a mere alienated representation of its own potential self-determinacy. Because the conduct of life follows those same patterns, it creates a social territory than corresponds to the spectacle's genetic map.[76]

It would seem that the portion of social life encompassed by the diffuse spectacle is broader than that commanded by its concentrated counterpart, which is obliged to make greater recourse to ideology, propaganda and police methods in order to channel activity into its framing paradigms. In both cases, however, there remain aspects of life that do not fall within the spectacle's bounds.[77] With the advent of the integrated spectacle, however, all areas of life have become as 'polluted'[78] as everything else. Yet whilst this may seem to resemble Baudrillard's claim that reality no longer exists,[79] this is not, in fact, the case: for as we have tried to indicate, the 'real', for Debord, is historical time, which will *always* exist so long as human consciousness exists within time. Certainly, this 'real' can become corrupted and alienated, but it can never be erased. Spectacular society is located within history, however much it may try to deny that fact, and despite its confused sense of perpetuity, it is merely 'a period swept along by the movement of historical time'.[80] Consequently, there can be no collapse into an exitless 'hyperreality', because so long as human beings exist within time, so too does the 'real' and the 'true', if only as a dormant potential. There is, however, a strong sense in which the integrated spectacle poses serious problems for the emergence and actualisation of that potential.

A Society That 'Can no Longer be Led Strategically'

In the *Comments*, Debord states that the integrated spectacle is characterised by five primary features: 'incessant technological renewal; integration of state and economy; generalised secrecy; unanswerable lies; an eternal present.'[81] The

---

76 The spectacle is a 'map of this new world, a map which exactly covers its territory' (Debord 1995, p. 23, translation altered; 2006b, p. 774). This can be compared with Baudrillard's later use of a similar image from Borges (Baudrillard 1994, p. 1).

77 In 1966, Debord remarked that: 'in the alienation of everyday life, the opportunities for passion and playfulness are still very real, and it seems to me that the SI would be seriously in error were it to suggest that all life outside Situationist activity was completely reified' (SI 2003, p. 138; Debord 2006b, p. 1167).

78 Debord 1998, p. 10; 2006b, p. 1598.

79 For Baudrillard, 'the real is no longer real' (Baudrillard 1994, p. 13), and 'We are no longer in the society of the spectacle, of which the situationists spoke' (Baudrillard 1994, p. 30) because spectacle has given way to simulation: the real has gone, and we are lost within a 'hyperreality' devoid of any external referent.

80 SI 2003, p. 22; Debord 2006b, p. 1100.

81 Debord 1998, pp. 11–12; 2006b, p. 1599.

first two correspond to the rationalisation and instrumental logic of the spectacular societies that he described in 1967, albeit taken to a higher level: 'technological renewal' furthers spectacular domination through the refinement of modes of 'cybernetic' control and increased specialisation; the 'integration of state and economy' aids the construction and enforcement of a mode of life tailored to commodity production and consumption. The three further features of the integrated spectacle are effects of this new level of spectacular domination, which has deepened the older problematic posed by the spectacular denial of history.

Debord's debts to Machiavelli are apparent throughout the *Comments*, and they are particularly evident when he stresses that 'people who lack all historical sense can readily be manipulated'.[82] As Debord noted in *The Society of the Spectacle*, Machiavelli warned that:

> ... he who becomes master of a city used to being free and does not destroy her can expect to be destroyed by her, because always she has as pretext in rebellion the name of liberty and her old customs ... unless citizens are disunited or dispersed, they do not forget that name and those institutions ...[83]

The suppression and management of historical knowledge thus facilitates the integrated spectacle's constant moulding of society and its inhabitants to suit its requirements. Within the integrated spectacle, Debord claims, we are now continually confronted with 'unverifiable stories, uncheckable statistics, unlikely explanations and untenable reasoning';[84] hence the profusion of the 'unanswerable lies' that Debord identifies as the third key feature of this new social order.

The fourth, 'generalised secrecy', is similarly linked to this deprivation of 'historical sense', because it pertains to the spectacle's capacity to manage knowledge. It also arises because the controlling centre that the concentrated spectacle once relied upon has since become 'occult'.[85] Control and observation have become dispersed and cannot be localised, whilst society has fragmented into a conflictual web of competing political, financial, economic and criminal

---

82 Debord 1998, p. 25, translation altered; 2006b, p. 1607.
83 Debord 1995, p. 119; 2006b, p. 837; Machiavelli 2004, pp. 19–20.
84 Debord 1998, p. 16; 2006b, p. 1602.
85 Debord 1998, p. 9; 2006b, p. 1598.

interests. Within this context, it is hard to know 'who is observing whom', and 'on whose behalf'.[86] Secrecy and suspicion have become ubiquitous.

The fifth feature of the integrated spectacle, that of an 'eternal present', is more obviously connected to the condition of historical arrest that we discussed in Part One. The 'end of history', Debord writes in the *Comments*, 'gives power a welcome break.'[87] This remark, which was written prior to Fukuyama's laudatory celebration of modern capitalism, was obviously intended in an ironic manner: history, for Debord, *cannot* end. His point is simply that the integrated spectacle has progressively denigrated the means by which one might independently verify or respond to the 'facts' that it presents to its spectators. This is exacerbated by the degree to which its depictions of the past and the future are determined by the exigencies of its present: for 'when the spectacle stops talking about something for three days', Debord writes, 'it is as if it did not exist'.[88]

In sum, the central point that Debord is making here when outlining these five factors is that the loss of history leads to the loss of critical thought. History's suppression, in other words, entails the removal of a common basis and reference point. This may seem to be cause for despair, but there is also a sense in which the *Comments*' analyses of modern society echo the notion of dialectical reversal that we noted above, when trying to draw out the key aspects of Debord's views on strategy. There is a sense, in other words, in which this position of extreme disadvantage may in fact contain an implicit advantage.

According to Debord, the integrated spectacle's triumphant suppression of history has left it unable to operate coherently. 'To the list of the triumphs of power', he writes, we should 'add one result that has proved negative: a state, in the management of which is lastingly installed a great deficit of historical knowledge, can no longer be led strategically.'[89] Those who manage the spectacle are tasked with directing an entity that is antithetical to historical direction.

It is, therefore, entirely wrong to read the *Comments* as an admission of defeat. As we saw in the previous chapter, the book has often been described as exemplifying the more resigned and melancholic perspective that Debord is seen to have adopted in his later years. Without doubt, its grim description of

---

86   Debord 1998, p. 83; 2006b, p. 1642.
87   Debord 1998, p. 14; 2006b, p. 1601,.
88   Debord 1998, p. 20; 2006b, p. 1604.
89   Debord 1998, p. 20, translation altered; 2006b, p. 1605.

the 'practical consequences' of the spectacle's 'advances' lacks the coldly exultant tone of *The Society of the Spectacle*. However, the book does *not* indicate that all is lost, and that the situation has become hopeless. After all, and as Debord remarked in a letter concerning the *Comments*, 'the work of revolutionary critique is assuredly not to lead people to believe that the revolution has become impossible!'[90]

This point can be approached by considering the book's epigraph, which is taken from Sun Tzu's *The Art of War*:

> However desperate the situation and circumstances, do not despair. When there is everything to fear, be unafraid. When surrounded by dangers, fear none of them. When without resources, depend on resourcefulness. When surprised, take the enemy itself by surprise.[91]

This passage evidences Sun Tzu's emphasis on the reversal of opposites. It pertains to his indications that artistry in war involves turning one's weakness into a strength, and the strength of one's enemy into a weakness. The specific manner in which it does so is, however, perhaps significant.

The passage used for this epigraph is not included in the English translation of *The Art of War*, but it closely echoes those presented in that book's discussion of 'dying ground', or 'deadly ground': terrain upon which an army must fight or perish, and which thus provokes the fiercest fighting. Sun Tzu counsels that a victorious army should not pursue a defeated enemy onto dying ground, for fear of the desperate retaliation that will ensue. Conversely, a losing commander can rely on great efforts from his troops if they are forced into such a situation.[92] So why did Debord use this as the epigraph to the *Comments*?

We can speculate that the reasons for doing so are perhaps twofold. On the one hand, the very emergence of the integrated spectacle was provoked by the fact that spectacular society, for Debord, had been forced onto 'dying ground'. May 1968 and its attendant events; the Italian *anni di piombo*; the growing obsolescence of capitalism, and the increasing precarity of a society obliged to generate and thwart desire in equal measure; all of these factors had caused the spectacular social order to retaliate, and to become all the more virulent in

---

90   Debord 2006a, p. 450.
91   Debord 1998, p. vii; 2006b, p. 1593.
92   'Put them in a spot where they have no place to go and they will die before fleeing ... When warriors are in great danger, they have no fear. When there is nowhere to go they are firm, when they are deeply involved they stick to it. If they have no choice, they will fight' (Sun Tzu 1988, p. 154).

shoring up its defences. Conversely, the epigraph can also be taken to pertain to the possibility of revolutionary change, which has itself been driven onto its own 'dying ground'. The spectacle's retaliation had led it to strengthen its grip to an even greater extent, and to push ever further into every aspect of life. Through doing so, it had created an increasingly intolerable situation, thereby deepening the potentially revolutionary crisis that Debord had identified in *The Society of the Spectacle*. Thus, although the nature of the integrated spectacle posed serious problems for the articulation and operation of revolutionary agency, it had also greatly strengthened the latter's possibility. Or, as Debord succinctly puts it in the *Comments*: 'conditions have never been so seriously revolutionary, but it is only governments who think so'.[93]

The book is *not*, therefore, an admission of defeat. Instead, it is a cold, strategic analysis of the difficulties and possibilities of insurrectionary change. We will try to substantiate these claims in the following sections. Before doing so, however, we should first look at the manner in which Debord's views on strategy inform the peculiar mode of writing that he employed in the *Comments*.

'I Must Take Care not to Give Too Much Information to Just Anybody'
In Chapter 1, we noted that Debord often attempted to unify the form and content of his work. Such attempts were intended to respond to the problem of articulating a critique of the spectacle within the spectacle's own discourse.[94] They allowed his books and films to function not only as descriptions of the negation of spectacle, but also as instantiations of that negation. *The Society of the Spectacle*, for example, makes extensive use of *détournement* and thus actualises its critique through its enunciation. Many similar examples can be found throughout Debord's work.[95] However, this technique becomes much

---

93 Debord 1998, p. 84; 2006b, p. 1643.
94 As Debord himself acknowledged, 'to analyse the spectacle means talking its language to some degree – to the degree, in fact, that we are obliged to engage the methodology [*en ceci que l'on passe sur le terrain méthodologique*] of the society to which the spectacle gives expression' (Debord 1995, p. 15; 2006b, p. 768).
95 To pick a few: Debord's cinematic works are similarly composed of *détourné* elements; *Considerations on the Assassination of Gérard Lebovici* refuses to treat the media's 'jumbled pile of nonsense' in 'an orderly fashion' (Debord 2001b, p. 3; 2006b, p. 1540); Debord would later remark that his self-eulogising autobiography, *Panegyric*, had sought to show through its 'subjective extravagance', the 'non-value of current society' (Debord 2008, p. 228).*Panegyric* is, in fact, particularly interesting in this regard. This is because the book was deliberately written in a manner intended to evoke the *dérive* (Debord 2008,

more complicated in the *Comments* as a result of that book's account of the spectacle's 'integration' into society. Where *The Society of the Spectacle*'s unity of form and content expressed the negation of spectacular society, that which Debord employs in the *Comments* responds to and expresses the emergence of spectacle within the forces that would enact spectacular society's own negation.

In 'Theses on the Situationist International and its Time' – a text in which Debord announces and reflects upon the dissolution of the SI – Debord remarks that 'When subversion invades society and spreads its shadow in the spectacle, present-day spectacular forces also emerge within our party'.[96] By 1988, having experienced the assassination of his friend and publisher Gérard Lebovici,[97] and having become captivated by the violent intrigue of Italian politics, Debord had reached the conclusion that 'the highest ambition of the integrated spectacle is ... that secret agents become revolutionaries, and revolutionaries become secret agents'.[98] Thus, in order to truly express the spectacle's immanent negation, he was obliged to highlight the spectacle at work within that negation. He also needed to do so without denigrating his work's anti-spectacular characteristics.

This issue is very closely connected to Debord's apparently presumptuous (but in fact surprisingly prescient)[99] concern that his work could be studied and used by those 'who devote themselves to maintaining the spectacular system of domination'.[100] Despite the scale of the *Comments*' print run, he wrote that he expected his book to be welcomed by an elite readership of 'fifty or sixty people',[101] half of whom would be dedicated to maintaining the spectacular order, whilst the other half would be composed of those seeking its destruction. As a result, he explained, he 'must take care not to give too much

---

p. 218). Thus, the book is not only 'crammed with traps' (ibid.) for the unsuspecting reader, but also exhibits a 'continual *shift* of meaning' (Debord 2004b, p. 173; 2006b, p. 1687) between sentences and themes. Rather than simply describing and recounting a life lived in opposition to spectacle, the book instantiates the movement of that life within the very text of the book, thereby exemplifying the movement that opposes the fixity of the spectacle's historical arrest.

96   Debord 2003a, p. 31; 2006b, p. 1106.
97   Gérard Lebovici was assassinated in 1984. The persons responsible are still unknown (see Debord 2001b).
98   Debord 1998, p. 11; 2006b, p. 1599.
99   See Eyal Weizman's work on the Israeli Defence Force's use of Debord, Deleuze and other such writers as means of re-conceiving urban combat (Weizman 2006).
100 Debord 1998, p. 1; 2006b, p. 1593.
101 Debord 1998, p. 1; 2006b, p. 1593.

information to just anybody'.[102] This statement is followed by an even more peculiar passage, which deserves to be quoted in full:

> Our unfortunate times thus compel me, once again, to write in a new way. Some elements will be intentionally omitted; and the plan will have to remain rather unclear. Readers will be able to encounter certain lures, like the very hallmark of the era. As long as certain pages are interpolated here and there, the overall meaning may appear: just as secret clauses have very often been added to what treatises may openly stipulate; just as some chemical agents only reveal their hidden properties when they are combined with others. However, in this brief work there will be only too many things which are, alas, easy to understand.[103]

The book is thus presented as a kind of puzzle,[104] and although this is often noted in the literature on Debord, it remains unsolved.[105] One can, however, find a clue in Debord's indication that the book's 'lures' are part of its 'plan' or structure, and that the 'hallmark of the era' might be an 'encounter' with them:[106] a 'hallmark' that would then reflect the reader's own susceptibility to such deceit. This can be supported by referring to a letter of 1989, in which Debord responds to a reader of the *Comments*. This reader had proposed that a particular phrase within the book may have been one of these 'lures'. Debord's response is illuminating, and gives some insight into the peculiar complexity of his later texts:

---

102   Debord 1998, p. 1; 2006b, p. 1593.
103   Debord 1998, p. 2, translation altered; 2006b, p. 1594.
104   This is perhaps an appropriate unification of form and content in its own right: when commenting on his explanatory diagrams to the *Kriegspiel*, Debord remarked that 'the figures looked like a truly daunting puzzle awaiting solution, just like the times in which we live' (Becker-Ho and Debord 2007, p. 9).
105   Plant, for example, observes that 'there is a great deal more to the *Comments* than sits on the page' (Plant 2000, pp. 152–3), but writes that 'it is evidently up to the twenty-five or thirty revolutionary readers to put the text together for themselves' (Plant 2000, p. 153). 'The secret clauses must be made to manifest themselves somehow', writes Brown; but 'what', he asks, 'is the missing ingredient?' (Brown 1991). Kaufmann goes so far as to claim that, in order to traverse a society in thrall to a multiplicity of secret services, Debord became 'a kind of ironic Hercule Poirot' (Kaufmann 2006, p. 264), but gives little indication as to quite what the great detective has hidden.
106   *On pourra y rencontrer, comme la signature même de l'époque, quelques leurres* (Debord 2006b, p. 1594).

One can call 'lure' anything that misleads rapid reading or computers. In any case, there isn't a single inexact or deceptive piece of information [in my book]. I suggest another hypothesis to you: what if, in this book – for a reader capable of understanding dialectical, strategic thought (Machiavelli or Clausewitz) – there are in fact no lures? What if the only lure is the very evocation of the possibility of there being lures?[107]

A very similar point is made in *Cette Mauvaise Réputation*,[108] and again in a letter to a Spanish translator of the *Comments*.[109] What is perhaps most important here is the relation between the 'dialectical, strategic thought' that Debord requires of his readers and the lack of strategic capability that he attributed to the integrated spectacle itself. This has two implications: firstly, that a failure to decipher the *Comments* exemplifies the symptoms of the spectacle's eradication of history; and secondly, that the skills required to thread one's way through the book must be connected to those needed to traverse the integrated spectacle itself.

There is, therefore, a sense in which the *Comments* tries to use the spectacle's own nature against it. The book's critique presents itself as containing 'lures' and hidden meanings, thus evoking the confused and illusory nature of the spectacle. It thereby expresses the spectacle's integration into its own opposition. Through doing so, it guards its own content with the same means by which it mirrors the true nature of its object.

This interpretation may seem forced, but it can be substantiated by remarks made elsewhere. In several letters, Debord states that his aim was to create a book 'intended to paralyse a computer'[110] (elsewhere he writes that computers 'cannot understand dialectics';[111] the rigid opposition of binary language is presumably not suited to the identity of opposites).[112] Such a book would

---

107 Debord 2008, p. 78.
108 'Perhaps [the suggestion of lures] is a lure? Perhaps the only one?' (Debord 1993, p. 33).
109 'I do not believe', Debord writes, 'that one must translate "lures [*leurres*]" – originally a term used by hunters, which evokes a lost trail – by the brutal *trampa* [trap] (there is no false information in my book that might make its reader "fall into error")' (Debord 2008, p. 93).
110 Debord 2008, p. 218.
111 Debord 2001a, p. 102.
112 Debord seems to have had a distinct antipathy to computers, and for the 'unreserved acceptance' that they breed for 'what has been programmed according to the wishes of someone else' (Debord 1998, pp. 28–9; 2006b, p. 1609).

thwart any superficial reading,[113] and would be 'deliberately confused'.[114] It would thereby express the true nature of a world in which 'surveillance spies on itself, and plots against itself',[115] by 'evok[ing its] ... disorder' through a 'disordered style'.[116]

There are any number of objections that one might want to make here, not least because such an approach runs entirely counter to any notion of popular appeal or intelligibility (although Debord was never one to make concessions to his audience).[117] Yet however problematic it may be, it is perhaps of broader interest than its status as a hermeneutic peculiarity: for if the means of interpreting the book are also those of negotiating the spectacle, then we perhaps have an illustration of the sense in which Debord really did believe that his peculiarly Hegelian association of dialectics, history and strategy might afford some kind of critical purchase on modern capitalism.

This then returns us to Debord's claim that the modern spectacle's denial of history has meant that it can 'no longer be led strategically'.

The Culminating Point

Debord claims that because there is now 'no room for any reply'[118] to the spectacle's 'laudatory monologue',[119] spectacular society has suffered a 'dissolution of logic'.[120] Society's loss of logic, 'that is to say loss of the ability to perceive what is significant and what is ... irrelevant', turns theorists and philosophers into ideologues. Such individuals, he writes (and Debord would seem to be referring here to the writers associated with French post-structuralism, insofar

---

113 It is perhaps also relevant to remember Debord's interest in Johan Huizinga's *Homo Ludens* (1938). Huizinga not only links play to war and strategy, but also to poetry, which he in turn connects to riddles and puzzles. 'Only he who can speak the art-language [of poetic riddles] wins the title of poet. This art-language differs from ordinary speech in that it employs special terms, images, figures, etc., which not everybody will understand' (Huizinga 1955, p. 133).

114 'I will summarize the chapter in question, deliberately confused' (Debord 2008, p. 126).

115 Debord 1998, p. 84; 2006b, p. 1643.

116 This remark was made as a compliment to a correspondent who had demonstrated 'talent' in the 'use of détournement' by 'evok[ing] a long era of disorder by writing in its disordered style' (Debord 2008, p. 339).

117 See Kaufmann 2006, pp. 232–8 and *passim* for comments on this tendency. See also the opening lines of *In Girum*: 'I will make no concessions to the public in this film ...' (Debord 2003a, pp. 134–43; 2006b, p. 1334).

118 Debord 1998, p. 29; 2006b, p. 1610.

119 Debord 1995, p. 19, translation altered; 2006b, p. 771.

120 Debord 1998, p. 27; 2006b, p. 1609.

as these problems are rooted in the loss of universal history), have 'committed themselves to overcoming logic [*dominer la logique*], even at the level of strategy, which is the entire operational field of the dialectical logic of conflicts'.[121] In other words, and as was indicated above, the loss of history results in the denigration of critical thought and agency, insofar as it undermines the solid basis for opposition and critique constituted by historical knowledge. The loss of history thus also involves that of the capacity for strategic thought.

This was seen as a double-edged sword. The spectacle's expansion and the increasing redundancy of its economic basis had engendered increased antipathy, boredom and disaffection, and had thus furthered the purportedly explosive potential of the 'new proletariat'. However, it had also resulted in a situation in which those individuals had become less and less able to act upon and articulate this disaffection. The result is a set of circumstances in which 'no one really believes the spectacle'[122] (Debord quotes *Le Monde* as having announced 'That modern society is a society of the spectacle now goes without saying'),[123] but in which any alternative seems increasingly impossible.

This message comes with a warning, which Debord sets out in the *Comments*' final sections. These sections are, however, almost as cryptic as the book's opening passages. Debord begins these last passages by quoting Clausewitz's classical definition of strategy and tactics, according to which 'tactics teaches the use of armed forces in the engagement; strategy, the use of engagements for the object of the war'.[124] He also discusses the 'changes in the art of war'[125] that were brought about by new weaponry in the Napoleonic era. New weapons obliged the introduction of different approaches to military operations, which had to accommodate the advantages and disadvantages of these new technical advances. Musketry, Debord explains, quickly proved to be more effective

---

121 Debord 1998, pp. 30–1; 2006b, p. 1611. Despite, or rather because of, their ambition to supersede such antiquated ways of thinking, these would-be 'rebels', according to Debord, have left themselves in the same position as 'everyone else', insofar as they have willingly lost even 'the basic ability to orient themselves by the old imperfect tools of formal logic': they have divested themselves of the 'ability immediately to perceive what is significant and what is insignificant or irrelevant; what is incompatible or what could well be complementary; all that a particular consequence implies and at the same time all that it excludes' (Debord 1998, pp. 30–1; 2006b, p. 1611). In other words, such thinking involves a confused, relativist inability to identify truth, and to conceive opposition and difference.
122 Debord 1998, p. 60; 2006b, p. 1629.
123 Debord 1998, p. 5; 2006b, p. 1596.
124 Debord 1998, p. 85; 2006b, p. 1644; Clausewitz 1993, p. 146.
125 Debord 1998, p. 85; 2006b, p. 1644.

in skirmish formations, even though military thought continued to insist on its use in massed volleys from fixed lines; until, that is, the exigencies of warfare necessitated the acceptance of the relative inefficiency of such fixed lines. Debord then goes on to indicate that the new features of the integrated spectacle will engender similar revelations on the part of the rulers of spectacular society, who will inevitably come to realise the advantages offered to them by the spectacle's new nature. Those 'who serve the interests of domination', he writes, will be obliged to 'see what obstacles they have overcome, and of what they are capable.'[126]

This might seem to contradict Debord's indication that spectacular society can no longer be led strategically. However, it seems possible to propose the following interpretation. Debord's point here is that whilst these new circumstances might foster a degree of *tactical* awareness amongst the spectacle's managers, it does not give rise to *strategic* thought. In this regard, the warning set out in the closing sections of the *Comments* also contains an indication of an immanent dialectical reversal.

These closing sections are preceded by a long discussion of the importance of conspiracy, surveillance and manipulation within the integrated spectacle. Countries and companies alike now spy on one another, extracting information and presenting falsehoods. As a result, 'thousands of plots in favour of the established order tangle and clash almost everywhere, as the overlap of secret networks and secret issues or attitudes grows ever more dense'.[127] Political opposition, meanwhile – the nominal subject of surveillance and restricted information – has largely disappeared, or is at least subject to manipulation (Debord casts the construction and management of terrorism as a key issue here).[128] Surveillance and intervention now 'operate on the very terrain of this threat in order to combat it *in advance*'.[129] The latter remark is alluded to again, a few paragraphs later, during the discussion of Napoleonic innovations described above. There, Debord draws attention to Napoleon's 'strategy ... of

---

126 Debord 1998, p. 88; 2006b, p. 1646.
127 Debord 1998, pp. 82–3; 2006b, p. 1642.
128 'Such a perfect democracy constructs its own inconceivable foe, terrorism. Its wish is *to be judged by its enemies rather than by its reults*. The story of terrorism is written by the state and it is therefore highly instructive. The spectators must never know everything about terrorism, but they must always know enough to convince them that, compared with terrorism, everything else must be acceptable, or in any case more rational and democratic' (Debord 1998, p. 24; 2006b, p. 1607, emphasis in the original).
129 Debord 1998, p. 84; 2006b, p. 1643, emphasis in the original.

using victories *in advance*'.¹³⁰ Napoleon's victories, he writes, were used 'as if acquired on credit', insofar as Napoleon was able to 'understand manoeuvres ... from the start as consequences of a victory which while not yet attained could certainly be at the first onslaught'.¹³¹ Debord would thus seem to be indicating a link between the spectacle's manipulation of its own opposition and Napoleon's ability to dictate the actions of his enemies.¹³²

Debord's comments on Napoleon's skills in this regard would seem to derive from Clausewitz, who claims in *On War* that 'Bonaparte could ruthlessly cut through all his enemies' strategic plans in search of battle, because he seldom doubted the battle's outcome'.¹³³ Because military strategy is influenced by events on the tactical level, tactical superiority in warfare can sabotage the enemy's strategy. Napoleon's success stemmed from allowing tactical events to shape his own unfolding strategy, and to confound that of his opponents.

Debord's guarded message here may well be that the spectacle's 'integration' into society involves a related success in terms of tactics, and an attendant ability to sabotage strategy (hence Debord's connection of Napoleonic 'changes in the art of war'¹³⁴ to spectacular 'changes in the art of government').¹³⁵ After all, the integrated spectacle eradicates historical knowledge, and thus strategic thought, thereby disempowering its subjects. Yet as we have also seen, history's eradication has resulted in a lack of coherent organisation and continuity, which also undermines the spectacle's *own* strategic operation. Thus, although the spectacle is able to organise its own opposition 'in advance', its 'strategy' is dictated purely by the momentum of its own tactical victories. This same momentum has been described by military historians as both the strength and the weakness of Napoleon's own approach. According to Handel, its danger is that 'instead of becoming the driving force in war, strategy

---

130   Debord 1998, p. 86; 2006b, p. 1644, emphasis in the original.
131   Debord 1998, p. 86; 2006b, p. 1644, emphasis in the original.
132   Rejecting fixed, geometric formations in favour of skirmish lines, smaller divisions and mobile artillery, Napoleon adopted a far more fluid approach to combat. The *Grande Armée* was able to live off the lands that it conquered, and its flexibility entailed that large manoeuvres could be used as an element of battlefield strategy rather than as its prelude. For example, Napoleon's *manoeuvre de derrière* involved crossing the enemy army's supply lines, and thereby forcing a situation in which it was forced to either run away or fight whilst weakened and demoralised. The enemy's total annihilation was not only pursued through decisive action that dictated the nature of the battle, but also through economic and political means.
133   Clausewitz 1993, p. 462.
134   Debord 1998, p. 85; 2006b, p. 1644.
135   Debord 1998, p. 87; 2006b, p. 1645.

becomes a mere by-product or afterthought'[136] (notably, Lukács makes similar points in *History and Class Consciousness* regarding the limits of bourgeois thought).[137]

For Debord, '*precisely what defines these spectacular times*' is that 'an all-powerful economy' has become 'mad'[138] and now ploughs on towards increasingly self-destructive predicaments. Whilst discussing ecological issues,[139] he remarks that it 'has now come to declare open war against humans; not only against their possibilities for life, but against their chances of survival'.[140] Even 'science', which Debord claimed in 1972 to be 'in thrall to the mode of production', cannot 'imagine a real overthrow of the present scheme of things', and is thus 'quite unable *to think strategically*'.[141]

Clausewitz's comments on Napoleon's approach to strategy are made during a discussion of the art of defending against enemy invasion. Referencing Napoleon's Russian débâcle of 1812,[142] Clausewitz stresses that the further an attack progresses, the weaker it becomes, leading to the 'culminating point' described in the first part of this chapter. It would seem that for Debord, the spectacle's absence of strategic guidance entails that it too will advance beyond its culminating point. In fact, the SI made almost precisely the same point in 1969. In a

---

136   Handel 2006, p. 354.
137   '... capitalism is the first system of production able to achieve a total economic penetration of society, and this implies that in theory the bourgeoisie should be able to [attain] ... an (imputed) class consciousness of the whole system of production. On the other hand, the position held by the capitalist class [entails] ... that it will be unable to control its own system of production even in theory' (Lukács 1971, p. 62).
138   Debord 1998, p. 39, emphasis in the original; 2006b, p. 1616.
139   In 1971, Debord devoted an entire essay to pollution and ecological damage ('La Planète malade'), and further remarks on the subject can be found throughout his late work. In this text he writes that the slogan '"Revolution or death"' is 'no longer the lyrical expression of the consciousness that revolts, it is *the last word of the scientific thought* of our century' (Debord 2007, p. 93; 2006b, p. 1069).
140   Debord 1998, p. 39, translation altered; 2006b, p. 1616.
141   SI 2003, p. 22; Debord 2006b, p. 1100.
142   In 1812 the *Grande Armée* advanced into Russia. Alexander's forces retreated, and employed a scorched earth policy as they did so. When the exhausted and starving French finally reached Moscow Napoleon was able to claim the city. However, as three quarters of it had been burned, and as the Tsar would not come to terms, Napoleon had no choice but to abandon Moscow and retreat back to Poland. During the course of this retreat he was forced to fight again at Beresina. When the returning army finally entered Poland its original force of 420,000 had been cut down to 10,000 (Handel 2006, p. 194; see also Fuller 1970, pp. 117–18).

short paragraph titled 'The Culminating Point of the Spectacle's Offensive', they cast the events of the preceding May as inaugurating a movement that would confirm 'the dialectical thought of Clausewitz'.[143]

It would seem, therefore, that the subtext of the *Comments* is that the spectacle's development into the integrated stage has caused its veneer to wear increasingly thin. This, no doubt, is why Debord wrote in 1992 that 'the same question is about to be posed again everywhere: how can the poor be made to work once their illusions have been shattered, and once force has been defeated?'[144]

Good Taste

The problem, however, lies in the manner in which this opposition was to arise. In Part Four of this book, we argued that Debord's account of spectacular capitalism involves a problematic over-emphasis on the subjective and the affective, and that this undermines his theory's engagement with capitalism's bases in the social relations of production. There is a sense in which Debord's description of the integrated spectacle underscores these difficulties. The integrated spectacle's weakening illusions had fostered an alleged increase in the quasi-existential poverty of the new proletariat, and his analysis of this situation brings that earlier, questionable emphasis on the subjective and affective to the fore.

This can be illustrated by making reference to his views on the 'adulteration' of food, as set out in his 1985 essay 'Abat-Faim'. Once, Debord tells us, an *abat-faim* was a dish served to one's dinner-guests prior to the main meal. Today, however, the totality of the food consumed by modern society is no more than a mere 'hunger abater'. We thus have a further image of the unhappy consciousness' links to spectatorship. In this essay, food is viewed in the same terms as the spectator's hopeless pursuit of the 'augmented survival' described in 1967's *The Society of the Spectacle*. Here, Debord links the absence of history to the absence of taste,[145] and in a related writing from the same period, he states that 'taste and knowledge have both disappeared'[146] from modern society. Yet following the pattern of reversal described above, he seems to hold that the deprivation of taste, knowledge and history will engender their return. As in *The Society of the Spectacle*, he indicates that this return will emerge from

---

143 SI 1997, p. 618.
144 Debord 1995, p. 10; 2006b, p. 1794.
145 Debord 1985; 2006b, p. 1583.
146 Debord 2006b, p. 419.

the effectively classless *ennui* of spectacular consumption, insofar as the latter will drive the pursuit of individual 'taste'. In fact, in a letter of 1991, in which he dismisses 'the immense efforts that have been made by the "practical men" of our era to manage to not understand what is most important', Debord simply concludes that 'it is only necessary to know how to love'.[147] It would thus seem that one can build a route out of the integrated spectacle's confusion simply by discovering what, who and how one loves.[148]

It remains the case, however, that to 'consider everything from the standpoint of oneself, taken as the centre of the world'[149] (the approach promoted by Debord in his autobiographical *Panegyric*, and thus in his own personal history) entails a somewhat solipsistic approach to the return of history, insofar as the latter becomes so closely tied to individual subjectivity. It entails that individual subjectivity becomes not only the basis of strategic engagement, but also its defining content. A strategically motivated analysis of modern capitalism, therefore, if conducted in the manner that Debord seems to have conceived it, is likely to be given over to an account of capital's subjective effects. This focus on the subjective is not only detrimental to an engagement with the economically objective, as we discussed in Chapters 9 and 10; in addition, it is perhaps even antithetical to it. For example, in November 1985 (and thus after that summer's Live Aid event) Debord makes the following, rather disturbing comment:

> [T]he planet produces enough cereal that no one should suffer hunger, but what troubles this idyll is that the 'rich countries' abusively consume half the world's cereals in feeding their cattle. But when one has known the disastrous taste of butchered meat that was thus fattened on cereal, can one speak of 'rich countries'? It's not to make us live like Sybarites that part of the planet is dying of famine; it's to make us live in the mud.[150]

Although this remark is certainly in keeping with the concerns of the 'new proletariat', it perhaps shows the somewhat tenuous relation the latter may bear to the actual mechanics of capital.

Limitations such as this bring us back to the suggestion, advanced in previous chapters, that whilst Debord's account of modern capitalism may be flawed

---

147 Debord 2008, p. 284.
148 This claim can be traced all the way back to 1958: 'Each person', wrote the SI in the first issue of *Internationale Situationniste*, 'must seek what he loves, what attracts him' (SI 2006, p. 49; 1997, p. 11).
149 Debord 2004b, p. 7; 2006b, p. 1659.
150 Debord 1985; 2006b, p. 1585.

STRATEGY AND TACTICS IN THE INTEGRATED SPECTACLE   389

in some regards, the ideas that underpin and support it – ideas about time, history and praxis that accommodate the strategic issues outlined here – may, in fact, deserve greater attention. In the following, final chapter we will try to develop the implications of that suggestion.

CHAPTER 14

The Knight, Death and the Devil

The Bad Days Will End

The introduction to this book referred to Debord's claim, in a letter of 1979, that 'the SI is like radioactivity: it's scarcely ever mentioned yet traces of it can be found almost everywhere, and it lasts a long time.'[1] The proposition advanced there was that the 'half-life' of Debord and the SI's work might subsist not just in their extant texts, but rather in the conceptions of time, history and subjectivity that support those writings. We then tried to show, throughout the chapters of this book, that those ideas ultimately amount to a relatively coherent and substantial philosophy of praxis; to a body of ideas that actively invite the critical supersession of the work that they inform and support. This entails that those same ideas could be drawn out of this material and considered and developed in their own right. To do so in full would be to go beyond the scope of this book's project, but we can nonetheless make some closing remarks here, concerning the nature of this model of praxis. Doing so should also afford an opportunity to summarise and synthesise some of the primary issues that have been addressed in previous chapters.

We can begin by looking at the following passage, which appeared in *Internationale situationniste* in 1962. In a text titled 'The Bad Days Will End', the SI wrote as follows:

> There is no other way to be faithful to, or even simply to understand, the actions of our comrades of the past than to profoundly reconceive the problem of revolution, which has been increasingly deprived of thought as it has become posed more intensely in concrete reality. ... And to feel it with enough urgency enables one to rediscover *lost history*, to salvage and rejudge it. It is not difficult for thought that concerns itself with questioning everything that exists. It is only necessary not to have *abandoned* philosophy (as have virtually all the philosophers), not to have abandoned art (as have virtually all the artists), and not to have abandoned contestation of *present reality* (as have virtually all the militants). When they are not abandoned, these questions all converge toward the same superses-

---

[1] Debord 2006a, pp. 45–6.

sion. The specialists, whose power is geared to a society of specialization, have abandoned the *critical* truth of their disciplines in order to preserve the personal advantages of their *function*. But all real researches are converging toward a totality, just as real people are going to come together in order to try once again to escape from their prehistory.[2]

This passage encapsulates a number of the issues that we have tried to address. Firstly, and most obviously, it underscores Debord and the SI's view that art, philosophy and theory must cease operating as means of merely describing lived reality, and must now unite as means of guiding and shaping its conscious construction. In addition, it also reflects the SI's desire to radically transform the classical workers' movement: to find a new 'Northwest Passage' through the stalled and gelid politics of the past, in pursuit of 'a new revolution' that would afford 'the conquest of everyday life.'[3] Above all, however, the passage's emphasis on the need to 'rediscover lost history', and to 'escape from prehistory', serves to show that the supersession of the spectacular contemplation of lived reality would afford the communal creation of history: a communism, in other words, that would amount to a mode of collective praxis. As Debord puts it in *The Society of the Spectacle*:

> The revolutionary project of a classless society, of a generalised historical life, is also the project of a withering away of the social measurement of time in favour of a playful model of the irreversible time of individuals and groups, a model in which *independent* [but] *federated times* are simultaneously present. It is the programme of the total realisation, within the medium [*milieu*] of time, of the communism that abolishes 'anything that exists independently of individuals'.[4,5]

But what form would this collective praxis take?

A rather schematic response to that question can be found if we return now to the five different aspects of Debord's thought that we introduced and discussed in Chapter 2. They were as follows: 1) a philosophical anthropology; 2) a speculative philosophy of history; 3) an ethics, which we drew from the normative aspects of the concept of spectacle; 4) an aesthetics, based on Debord's views on time; 5) a conception of strategic praxis. Having looked

---

2 SI 2006, pp. 110–11; 1997, p. 253.
3 SI 2006 p. 148; 1997, pp. 323–4 (see also Debord 1979; 2006b, p. 1465).
4 See Marx and Engels 2007, p. 86.
5 Debord 1995, pp. 116–17, translation altered; 2006b, p. 836, emphasis in the original.

at these issues at some length throughout the rest of the book, we can now contend that these five elements operate in concert in the following manner.

We have seen that Debord's conception of the human subject 1) entails viewing human beings as temporal, self-determining creatures. His account of historical development presents these human agents as 2) having developed through history to a point at which they have become capable of comprehending and fully actualising their own self-determinate nature. When making these claims, we saw that the concept of spectacle must be rooted within this same conception of the human subject. Spectacle, we argued, cannot be reductively identified with modern capitalism, but instead denotes the alienation and deprivation of the human subject's capacity for historical self-determinacy. Yet Debord is no individualist:[6] he clearly conceived the articulation of that capacity for historical action to be a social, and thus interpersonal concern. Consequently, the concept of spectacle can be taken to contain 3) an ethical dimension. The latter concerns the constant possibility for collective social power to become alienated and independent, and would thus pertain to any future social formation that might replace capitalist society (as we saw earlier, 'wherever there is independent *representation*, the spectacle reconstitutes itself').[7] Viewed in these terms, spectacle becomes a problematic that will *always* haunt instantiations of collective agency, even after the abolition of the society that brought that problematic to full, identifiable expression: for if hierarchy, dogma and separated social power were to reappear, then so too would spectacle. Conversely, 4) the aesthetic dimensions of Debord's conception of temporality entail the pursuit of an on-going identification with the passage of time. They reflect a desire for a mode of existence that would be marked not by contemplative detachment towards the flow of historical time, but which would instead be an active, conscious determinant within it. The mode of thought proper to that engagement with time, we argued, is 5) Debord's explicitly Hegelian and dialectical conception of strategy.

These aspects of Debord's thought constitute the basis of the model of praxis that subtends works such as *The Society of the Spectacle*. They are also facets of Debord's Hegelian Marxism, which we tried to reconstruct and characterise in the first three parts of this book. We argued there that the general architecture of Debord's Marxian use of Hegelian thought can be understood as a

---

6 Although Debord's thought is certainly close in spirit to anarchism, it should be remembered that *The Society of the Spectacle* dismisses anarchism 'in its individualist variants' as 'laughable' (Debord 1995, p. 62; 2006b, p. 802).
7 Debord 1995, p. 17; 2006b, p. 770, emphasis in the original.

re-figuration of the Hegelian Absolute, whereby the latter is re-cast as a collective capacity for historical praxis. As in Lukács, to whom Debord was greatly indebted, the subject-object unity of Hegelian 'absolute knowing' becomes a revolutionary supersession of alienation, through which human subjectivity unites with this fundamental 'object', thereby giving rise to the advent of a self-conscious, self-determinate history. We can now set out some concluding comments concerning the nature of this apparent re-figuration of Hegelian philosophy. In order to do so, we should look, very briefly, at Hegel's views on religion.

Communing with the Divine

It is hard to deny that Hegel was a decidedly religious philosopher. He presented himself as a Christian, and religion remained a key concern from his early, romantic and polemical criticisms of dogmatic religious belief, through to his later, explicit claim in the *Lectures on the Philosophy of Religion* that 'the object of religion, like that of philosophy, is the eternal truth in its very objectivity, God and nothing but God and the explication of God'.[8] The 'God' with which Hegel was concerned in his mature philosophy was, however, the Absolute. Hegel's mature work presents religion as a representation, or *Vorstellung*, of the deeper and more fundamental truth accessed by philosophy.[9] This has led some writers to contend that Hegel was really a closet atheist.[10] Somewhat

---

8 Quoted in Houlgate 2005, p. 245.
9 Although Hegel certainly held that philosophy should pass beyond the *Vorstellungen* of religious allegory, he did not contend that philosophy's success in that regard would render religion obsolete. This is because religion, in his view, provided a *feeling* for the divine: a sense of the absolute that philosophy's comparatively dispassionate and analytical lens could not provide. Religion might well be a mere *image* of the absolute, but it remained a necessary one, and an important place was reserved for religious faith in Hegel's vision of the fully rational state. He recognised that not everyone was going to read the *Phenomenology*, and felt strongly that the masses were entitled to an approximation of the communion with the divine that the latter text purported to offer. Through religious worship – and above all, through the Christian religion that Hegel favoured – a community of believers could engage, in however intuitive, affective and allegorical a form, with the absolute centre of the truth and rationale of their existence.
10 Solomon, for example, contends that the 'secret, abruptly stated, is that *Hegel was an atheist*. His "Christianity" is nothing but nominal, an elaborate subterfuge to protect his personal ambitions in the most religiously conservative country in northern Europe' (Solomon 1989, p. 57, italics in the original).

similarly to Feuerbach, whose work he would inspire, Hegel indicates that the Christian God is no more than an alienated image of humanity's own true identity. Yet whilst that atheistic implication was by no means lost on Hegel's successors, it remains the case that his philosophy is, in a sense, quite fundamentally religious in spirit. His work's central aim is to reveal the immanent presence and purpose of the Absolute within the world. It does so by advancing a mode of thought capable of establishing a unity between the particular, the finite and the contingent on the one hand, and the universality, infinitude and necessity of the Absolute on the other. His philosophy, therefore, is ultimately an attempt to unite the human and the divine.

We have tried to show that this corresponds to a central theme in Debord's theoretical work: namely, that of the unification of a collectivity of particular individuals with their own socially derived powers and capacities. This unification can only be fully achieved, for Debord, through the application of those powers in collective praxis.

That theme is anticipated, to some degree, by aspects of Hegel's early religious writings, which argue against religious doctrines that present the divine as separate and removed from humanity. Hegel praised Christianity for emphasising a unity between God and humanity, and for fostering a community of believers who actualise their God's will through mutual love and forgiveness. In the congregation, he held, the divine ceases to stand at one remove from the faithful, and instead becomes the driving force of their lived social practice. The God who is the locus of the sum truth of their existence, and indeed the formative power that generates that existence, is thereby brought down to earth and rendered part of their collective activity.

Hegel's early writings were not published until long after his death, but the themes that they foreground are still readily identifiable in his mature work. In his later philosophy, the mutual love and forgiveness of the congregation becomes the mutual recognition of Spirit, and the motif of the union of the universal and the particular becomes a defining feature of a metaphysical logic that constitutes the very fabric of reality. Because these themes are readily apparent in Hegel's mature work,[11] his many critical followers, despite their

---

11 For example, the *Phenomenology* of 1807 argues that each particular, individual consciousness contains its own 'ladder' to the absolute within itself (Hegel 1977, p. 14); Hegel's mature system presents a logic that encodes the interrelation of universality and particularity into the every fabric of being; Hegel's last major text, *The Philosophy of Right* of 1820, describes the full actualisation of that logic's 'divine Concept' (Hegel 1991, p. 147) within a rational state: a society that comprises an organic totality, the universality of which emerges from the shared identity of the elements that compose it.

lack of access to his then unpublished early writings, were able to draw this problematic of unity out of his mature texts, and could thereby turn it against Hegel himself.

Hegel's early work criticised religious views in which God is posited as standing apart from his creation. In much the same vein, the state that Hegel had consecrated, the religion that he had celebrated, and indeed his philosophy itself, could all be viewed by his Young Hegelian successors as alienated expressions of human potential. Feuerbach contended that religion is an illusory, alienated expression of humanity's species-being; the young Marx described the bourgeois state as a 'fictitious sovereignty ... filled with an unreal universality';[12] both Cieszkowski and Marx, albeit in differing ways, argued against a philosophy that stood at one remove from the construction of the future. For Debord, who read this material through writers such as Lukács, Korsch and Lefebvre, this could be construed as trajectory that led towards a critique of *all* forms of separated power.

In Debord's view, all such power is ultimately a capacity to shape and determine lived existence. Thus, just as God, for Hegel, needed to be rendered part of the life of the congregation, so too, for Debord, was the true absolute of humanity's collective agency to be actualised in a communism wherein the universality of that power would become one with the life of the particular agents from whom it derived. The absolute, in other words, would cease to be something that stood over and above a community, but would instead become part of its life practice. This required a revolution that would demand the reclamation and actualisation of all separated social power: a revolution that would abolish the dominating distractions of the commodity, along with the false promises of Party bureaucracy, and which would pursue nothing less than the complete transformation of everyday life. It also meant that the subject-object unity through which the Absolute would be brought down to earth needed to take the form of a condition of perpetual historical praxis.

Self-Conscious Praxis

In his *Studies on Marx and Hegel* of 1955 – a book that Debord owned and studied – Hyppolite remarks that Hegel's '*Phenomenology* is only a caricature of what is offered by *communism*'.[13] Both the *Phenomenology* and communism, he

12   Marx 1975, p. 220.
13   Hyppolite 1969, pp. 84–5.

writes, confront 'the same task': that of 'overcoming the alienation that is the misfortune of man'.[14] Indeed, according to Hyppolite:

> [Marx's *Capital*] cannot be thoroughly understood by anyone ignorant of Hegel's *Phenomenology*, for it is the living image of it. Whereas, in the *Phenomenology*, it is the absolute Spirit, once it has become its own object, that raises itself to self-consciousness, in *Capital*, it is man's alienated social being, the gross product, or rather, the *communal labour of men*, namely capital, which, so to speak, *objectifies itself* and confronts the consciousness of the proletariat.[15]

In both cases, a subject confronts an alienated object that is, in truth, that subject in a state of estrangement from itself. In both cases, that separation is to be superseded by a condition of unity. Just as Spirit ascends to subject-object unity in the *Phenomenology*, so too would communism create a similar condition of unity. Yet for Marx, according to Hyppolite, Hegel's work can afford only a 'caricature' of the true unity that would be afforded by communism. This is because 'Hegel merely offers the prescription of philosophy – a poor remedy, in Marx's opinion.'[16] Hyppolite's point here is very simple, but it bears direct relation to the reading of Hegel that we attributed to Debord in the first part of this book. Hegel is seen to have inadvertently presented a philosophical depiction, or indeed a *Vorstellung*, of the real unity of subject and object that would be afforded by communism.

For Debord, however, who draws on Lukács when articulating a very similar claim, such unity could not take the form of a static state of affairs. It could not, in other words, be instantiated within a discrete, fixed economic system. Instead, it could only be found in a condition of open praxis; and in this crucial sense, both Hegel and traditional Marxism alike remained bound to an impoverished version of 'historical thought' that remained all too *philosophical*.

Hegel, for Debord, had recognised an important identity between human thought and self-constitutive, transformative historical activity. Yet for Hegel, a true conscious awareness of historical circumstances always arrives *after* the events that shape those circumstances ('the owl of Minerva takes its flight only when the shades of night are gathering'),[17] and the philosophy that expresses

---

14 Ibid.
15 Hyppolite 1969, p. 103; also quoted by Heckman (with a slightly different translation) in Hyppolite 1974, p. xxxvii (the capital 'C' of 'capital' has been removed for clarity).
16 Hyppolite 1969, p. 82.
17 Hegel 2005, p. xxi.

that consciousness should not, therefore, attempt 'to teach the world what it ought to be'.[18] Instead, it should simply explain how and why the world is the way it is. Hegel's 'historical thought', according to Debord, thus 'always arrives too late'.[19] For Debord, the young Marx's emphasis on praxis had corrected this contemplative detachment. However, and as we saw in Part Four, Debord also held that Marx later marred his contributions in this regard as a result of his thought's proximity to economism. If such a stance is coupled to Leninist paternalism, as was the case throughout much twentieth-century Marxism, then one arrives at a perspective according to which consciousness does not 'come to late', but rather 'always comes too soon'.[20] The proletariat's spontaneous revolts need to be curbed, because the revolutionary class needs to be 'taught'[21] to wait for the purportedly right crisis in capitalism *before* action can take place. For Debord, however, the separated power of an elite cadre of revolutionary managers cannot be tolerated. Thus, rather than arriving *after* the event, as a Hegelian reflection upon it, and indeed rather than coming *before* the event, as Leninist educative preparation for it, 'historical thought', in Debord's view, should function as the self-consciousness *of* that event.

This bears direct relation to the status of dialectical thinking within Debord's Hegelian Marxism. The unification of subject and object outlined here would render historical time a self-conscious process. Dialectical thought, having become *strategic* thought, would constitute the self-consciousness of that process. Having been drawn out of idealist philosophy, dialectical thinking would become the self-consciousness of a communism that amounted to a condition of collective historical praxis.

The nature of that condition can be fleshed out somewhat further if we connect this notion of strategy to the ethical dimensions of the concept of spectacle.

The War of Time

In Chapter 4, we tried to draw a distinction between Debord and Lefebvre's conceptions of subject-object unity. We claimed there that where Lefebvre's 'total man' constitutes an infinitely receding goal, Debord's own views seem to cast such unity not as a final outcome, but rather as the grounds and process

---

18 Hegel 2005, p. xxi.
19 Debord 1995, p. 49; 2006b, p. 793.
20 Debord 1995, p. 55; 2006b, p. 797.
21 Debord 1995, p. 55; 2006b, p. 797.

of historical praxis. This accords with our model of Debord's Hegelianism, wherein subject-object unity does not function as a final end-point, but rather constitutes the basis of an open future.

In this model, subject-object unity is conceived as a process of temporal self-determinacy. This is a process wherein human subjects identify themselves as the source of their own history, and take conscious charge of its ongoing, future-oriented conduct. It follows that if subject-object unity is thus conceived as process and movement in time, then every moment of that process must, presumably, be oriented towards re-establishing its conditions of existence. It must be characterised, in other words, by a structure that re-creates its own grounds, and which has itself as its own goal ('the proletarian movement' thus 'becomes its own product', with the result that 'the producer has himself as his own proper goal').[22]

This accords with the ethical issues that we have drawn from Debord's work. If the problematic of spectacle cannot be reductively identified with capitalist society, and if it can be seen as a problematic that always threatens to reappear, then the operation of this processual subject-object unity must be marked by the anti-spectacular ethics described above. In other words, if such an instantiation of collective, direct, non-hierarchical agency is to perpetuate itself, and if it is to recreate its own conditions of existence without collapsing back into spectacle, then it must remain continually opposed to the forms of separation from which spectacle arises ('self-management' was thus said to be 'not only what is at stake in the struggle,' but also the 'adequate form' of that struggle).[23]

There must also be a strategic dimension to this operation, as its ongoing actualisation would require thought and action within time. Strategy, in Debord's work, is a mode of thought suited to the traversal of the contingencies and eventualities that the passage of time brings. In order for this collective agency to operate and reproduce itself, it would need to be able to think strategically. This pertains to Debord's claim in *The Society of the Spectacle* that 'workers' must 'become dialecticians';[24] or rather – given that dialectics and strategy are one for Debord – 'workers' must become *strategists*, actively engaged in the conduct of the 'historical thought' that would afford the actualisation and perpetuity of the condition of praxis called for by the SI's politics. Difficult though that task may be, Debord made clear in his correspondence

---

22 Debord 1995, p. 87, translation altered; 2006b, p. 818.
23 SI 2006, p. 210; 1997, p. 432.
24 Debord 1995, p. 89; 2006b, p. 819.

that 'there is absolutely no other way to leave our sad prehistoric period'.[25] This is because if 'workers' did *not* attain such a strategic ability, there would be no way to achieve a revolutionary condition of collective self-determinacy *through* such self-determinacy, and revolution would thus collapse back into the representational and hierarchical forms of political organisation that it sought to supersede.

To now bring these observations together: the points made here concerning strategy and ethics essentially describe a process that continually generates its own conditions of existence. This bears direct relation to our claims regarding Debord's use of Hegel: for the Hegelian Absolute is, of course, just such a self-founding, processual unity. According to the reading of Debord's work that we have advanced in this book, the dynamic, self-constitutive movement of the Hegelian Absolute is re-cast as the operation and conduct of Debord's collective praxis. That operation is marked by an ethics that shapes its instantiations, and by a strategic self-consciousness that affords a direct engagement with history's construction.

As was also discussed in this book's introduction, Debord remarks, in his 1978 film *In Girum Imus Nocte et Consumimur Igni*, that 'theories' are only 'made to die in the war of time', and that they 'have to be replaced because they are constantly being rendered obsolete'.[26] Debord's critical account of modern society can only be one such finite, contextually limited intervention within that temporal 'war'. The model outlined in this chapter can be understood as the general framework that supports Debord's conception of that same 'war'. It accommodates a notion of continual, practical intervention in time, and due to its emphasis on strategy, it also implies the constant creation of new theoretical positions: for even after the full, self-conscious flourishing of this condition of praxis, and thus after the advent of Debord's 'end of pre-history', any instantiation of collective agency would be required to continually assess, address and negotiate the contexts within which it was situated. It would need to do so whilst continually combatting its potential collapse into spectacle, and would therefore need to be continually engaged in that same temporal 'war'.

The propositions outlined here rely, in part, upon the distinction that we have made between Debord's theory of the *society* of the spectacle, and his concept of the *problematic* of spectacle. Our argument was that where the former functioned as a critique of modern capitalism, the latter denoted the problematic that modern society had brought to full expression. That distinc-

---

25 Debord 2003a, p. 231.
26 Debord 2003b, pp. 150–1; 2006b, p. 1354.

tion affords the following contention. Although Debord and the SI's critique of the *society* of the spectacle can be no more than a particular contextual intervention in the 'war of time', the *problematic* of spectacle remains a constant concern throughout that temporal 'war'. In fact, spectacle, in the latter sense, constitutes the primary motivation to create new theoretical interventions, as it continually haunts the operation of this model of collective agency. An illustration can be found in Dürer's *The Knight, Death and the Devil*: with death riding in step alongside him, holding an hourglass that represents time, and with the devil, or spectacle, following closely behind, Dürer's knight continually presses onwards towards new engagements.

In conclusion, Debord's work, or at least the aspects thereof that we have considered here, can afford a philosophy of praxis. Identifying the ideas that compose it can help to clarify the theory that they support, but they could, perhaps, be considered and developed in their own right. We can therefore close with the following remarks.

Debord's theory of spectacle is often framed as a remarkably prescient description of modern society's ills. According to Giorgio Agamben, for example, Debord possessed a 'prophetic clairvoyance',[27] as 'the contemporary phase of capitalism' is without doubt 'the society of the spectacle';[28] likewise, Hardt and Negri have described his theoretical work as 'perhaps the best articulation, in its own delirious way, of the contemporary consciousness of the triumph of capital'.[29] In much the same vein, many others have stressed the contemporary pertinence of Debord's work, claiming that it is now 'more relevant than ever as a diagnostic tool in political analysis',[30] and that it possesses more 'explanatory power ... than ever'.[31] This may well be true; after all, the views set out in Debord's *Comments on the Society of the Spectacle* seem remarkably pertinent today. Yet even so, it remains the case that simply transposing Debord and the SI's work onto our contemporary conditions would jar with the conceptions of time and history that support it. In consequence, those more foundational concerns with temporality and agency may deserve rather more attention than they have, as yet, received.

---

27   Agamben 2000, p. 73.
28   Agamben 2000, p. 11.
29   Hardt and Negri 2001, p. 427.
30   Critchley 2007, p. 135.
31   Retort 2006, p. 17.

Bibliography

Adorno, Theodor W. 1969, 'A Conversation with Theodor W. Adorno', *Der Spiegel*, 5 May 1969, translated by Gerhard Richter, available at: https://cominsitu.wordpress.com/2015/09/01/a-conversation-with-theodor-w-adorno-spiegel-1969/

Adorno, Theodor W. 1990 [1966], *Negative Dialectics*, translated by E.B. Ashton, London: Routledge.

Adorno, Theodor W. 2002 [1991], *The Culture Industry*, edited by J.M. Bernstein, translated by Wes Blomster, Gordon Finlayson, Thomas Levin, Anson Rabinach and Nicholas Walker, London: Routledge.

Adorno, Theodor W. 2008 [2003], *Lectures on Negative Dialectics*, translated by Rodney Livingstone, Cambridge: Polity.

Adorno, Theodor and Horkheimer, Max 1997 [1944], *Dialectic of Enlightenment*, translated by John Cumming, London: Verso.

Agamben, Giorgio 2000 [1995], *Means Without Ends: Notes on Politics*, translated by Vincenzo Binetti and Cesare Casarino, Minneapolis: University of Minnesota Press.

Agamben, Giorgio 2004a [2002], *The Open*, translated by Kevin Attell, Stanford: Stanford University Press.

Agamben, Giorgio 2004b [1995], 'Difference and Repetition: On Guy Debord's Films', translated by Brian Holmes, in *Guy Debord and the Situationist International: Texts and Documents*, edited by Tom McDonough, London: October.

Agamben, Giorgio 2015 [2014], *The Use of Bodies*, translated by Adam Kotsko, Stanford: Stanford University Press.

Alighieri, Dante 1985 [1320], *The Divine Comedy Volume 2: Purgatory*, translated by Mark Musa, London: Penguin.

Alighieri, Dante 2001 [1472], *Hell*, translated by Dorothy Sayers, London: Penguin.

Althusser, Louis 2005 [1965], *For Marx*, translated by Ben Brewster, London: Verso.

Altindere, Halil and Boynik, Sezgin 2004, 'Nothing to Talk About', *Art-Ist*, 1, no. 1, available at: http://www.kurr.org/texte/article/nothing-to-talk-about?lang=de

Anderson, Thomas 1993, *Sartre's Two Ethics: From Authenticity to Integral Humanity*, Chicago: Open Court.

Antonucci, Ricardo 2012, 'Che cosa rimane de Guy Debord: Intervista ad Anselm Jappe', *Il Rasoio di Occam*, 9 September, available at: http://ilrasoiodioccam-micromega.blogautore.espresso.repubblica.it/2012/09/09/che-cosa-rimane-di-guy-debord-intervista-ad-anselm-jappe/?refresh_ce

Aristotle 1996 [c. 350 BC], *The Nicomachean Ethics*, translated by Harris Rackham, Ware: Wordsworth Editions.

Arthur, Christopher 1983, 'Hegel's Master-Slave Dialectic and a Myth of Marxology', *New Left Review*, 1/145: 65–75.

Arthur, Christopher 1986, *The Dialectics of Labour: Marx and his Relation to Hegel*, Oxford: Basil Blackwell, available at: http://chrisarthur.net/dialectics-of-labour/marx-and-his-relation-to-hegel/

Arthur, Christopher 1994, 'Moishe Postone: Time, Labour and Social Domination', *Capital and Class*, 54: 150–5.

Arthur, Christopher 2004a, *The New Dialectic and Marx's Capital*, Boston: Brill.

Arthur, Christopher 2004b, 'Subject and Counter-Subject', *Historical Materialism*, 12, no. 3: 93–102.

Aufheben 1997, 'Whatever Happened to the Situationists?', *Aufheben*, 6: 43–8.

Aufheben 2006, 'Keep on Smiling: Questions on Immaterial Labour', *Aufheben*, 14: 23–44.

Aufheben 2007, 'Moishe Postone's *Time Labour and Social Domination*: Capital Beyond Class Struggle?', *Aufheben*, 15: 30–51.

Aufheben 2009, 'Capitalism and Spectacle: The Retort Collective's *Afflicted Powers*', *Aufheben*, 17: 47–58.

Backhaus, Hans-Georg 1980 [1969], 'On the Dialectics of the Value-Form', *Thesis Eleven*, 1, no. 1: 99–120.

Bakunin, Mikhail 1992 [1985], *The Basic Bakunin: Writings: 1869–1871*, translated and edited by Robert Cutler, New York: Prometheus Books.

Bakunin, Mikhail 1970 [1882], *God and the State*, translated by Benjamin Tucker, New York: Dover.

Balakian, Anna 1972, *Surrealism: The Road to the Absolute*, London: Unwin Books.

Bataille, Georges 1979 [1928], *Story of the Eye*, translated by Joachim Neugroschal, London: Penguin.

Bataille, Georges 1990 [1955], 'Hegel, Death and Sacrifice', *Yale French Studies*, 78: 9–28.

Bataille, Georges 1991 [1949], *The Accursed Share*, Volume 1, translated by Robert Hurley, New York: Zone Books.

Bataille, Georges 1997 [1933], 'The Notion of Expenditure', translated by Donald Leslie, Carl Lovitt and Allan Stoeckl, in *The Bataille Reader*, edited by Fred Botting and Scott Wilson, Oxford: Blackwell.

Baudrillard, Jean 1993 [1976], *Symbolic Exchange and Death*, translated by Iain Hamilton Grant, London: Sage.

Baudrillard, Jean 1994 [1981], *Simulacra and Simulation*, translated by Sheila Faria Glasier, Michigan: University of Michigan Press.

Bauer, Bruno 1997 [1841], 'The Trumpet of the Last Judgement over Hegel', in *The Young Hegelians: An Anthology*, edited by Lawrence Stepelevich, New Jersey: Humanities Press.

Baugh, Bruce 2003, *French Hegel: From Surrealism to Postmodernism*, New York: Routledge.

de Beauvoir, Simone 1976 [1947], *The Ethics of Ambiguity*, translated by Bernard Frechtman, New York: Citadel Press.
Becker-Ho, Alice and Debord, Guy 2007, *A Game of War*, translated by Donald Nicholson-Smith, London: Atlas Press.
Beiser, Frederick 2005, *Hegel*, New York: Routledge.
Beller, Jonathan 2006, *The Cinematic Mode of Production: Attention Economy and the Society of the Spectacle*, Lebanon, NH: University Press of New England.
Bellofiore, Riccardo 2009, 'A Ghost Turning into a Vampire: The Concept of Capital and Living Labour', in *Re-reading Marx: New Perspectives after the Critical Edition*, edited by Riccardo Bellofiore and Roberto Fineschi, Basingstoke: Palgrave Macmillan.
Bellofiore, Riccardo and Redolfi Riva, Tommaso 2015, 'The Neue Marx-Lektüre: Putting the Critique of Political Economy Back into the Critique of Society', *Radical Philosophy*, 189: 24–36.
Benjamin, Walter 2005 [1955], *Illuminations: Essays and Reflections*, New York: Schocken Books.
Berardi, Franco ('Bifo') 2004, 'The Premonition of Guy Debord', translated by Arianna Bove, available at: www.generation-online.org/t/tbifodebord.htm
Bergson, Henri 2007 [1903], *An Introduction to Metaphysics*, Basingstoke: Palgrave Macmillan.
Bernstein, Richard J. 1999 [1971], *Praxis and Action: Contemporary Philosophies of Human Activity*, Philadelphia: University of Pennsylvania Press.
Best, Steven and Kellner, Douglas 1999, 'Debord and the Postmodern Turn: New Stages of the Spectacle', *Substance*, 90: 129–56.
Beyerchen, Alan 1992, 'Clausewitz, Nonlinearity and the Unpredictability of War', *International Security*, 17, no. 3: 59–90, available at: http://www.clausewitz.com/readings/Beyerchen/CWZandNonlinearity.htm
Black, Bob 1996 [1990], 'The Realization and Suppression of Situationism', in *What is Situationism? A Reader*, edited by Stewart Home, Edinburgh: AK Press.
Black, David 2013, *The Philosophical Roots of Anti-Capitalism: Essays on History, Culture and Dialectical Thought*, Plymouth: Lexington Books.
Blake, William 2008 [1790], 'The Marriage of Heaven and Hell', in *William Blake: Selected Poetry and Prose*, edited by David Fuller, Pearson, Edinburgh.
Blazwick, Iwona 1989, *An Endless Adventure ... An Endless Passion ... An Endless Banquet: A Situationist Scrapbook*, London: Verso.
Bracken, Len 1997, *Guy Debord: Revolutionary*, Venice, CA: Feral House.
Breton, Andre 1960 [1928], *Nadja*, translated by Richard Howard, New York: Grove Press.
Breton, Andre 1990 [1932], *Communicating Vessels*, translated by Mary Ann Caws and Geoffrey T. Harris, Lincoln: University of Nebraska Press.
Breton, Andre 1996 [1929], 'The Second Manifesto of Surrealism', translated by Richard

Seaver and Helen Lane, in *Art in Theory: 1900–1990*, edited by Charles Harrison and Paul Wood, Oxford: Blackwell.

Brown, Bill 1986, 'Manet in Situ: T.J. Clark's *The Painting of Modern Life*', available at: http://www.notbored.org/manet.html

Brown, Bill 1991, 'Guy Debord's *Comments on the Society of the Spectacle*', available at: http://www.notbored.org/comments.html

Bonefeld, Werner 2001, 'Social Form, Critique and Human Dignity', *Zeitschrift fur kritische Theorie*, 13: 97–112, available at http://libcom.org/library/social-form-critique-and-human-dignity

Bonefeld, Werner 2004, 'On Postone's Courageous but Unsuccessful Attempt to Banish the Class Struggle from the Critique of Political Economy', *Historical Materialism*, 12, no. 3: 103–24.

Bonefeld, Werner 2014, *Critical Theory and the Critique of Political Economy: On Subversion and Negative Reason*, New York: Bloomsbury.

Buck-Morss, Susan 1977, *The Origin of Negative Dialectics*, New York: The Free Press.

Buck-Morss, Susan 2009, *Hegel, Haiti, and Universal History*, Pittsburgh: University of Pittsburgh Press.

Burger, Peter 1984, *Theory of the Avant-Garde*, Minneapolis: University of Minnesota Press.

Butler, Judith 1999 [1987], *Subjects of Desire: Hegelian Reflections in Twentieth Century France*, New York: Columbia University Press.

Cabañas, Kaira M. 2014, *Off-Screen Cinema: Isidore Isou and the Letterist Avant-Garde*, Chicago: University of Chicago Press.

Campbell, Allan and Niel, Tim (eds.) 1997, *A Life in Pieces: Reflections on Alexander Trocchi*, Edinburgh: Rebel Inc.

Carlson, David Gray (ed.) 2005, *Hegel's Theory of the Subject*, Basingstoke: Palgrave Macmillan.

Carver, Terrel 1983, *Marx and Engels*, Brighton: Wheatsheaf Books.

Castiglione, Baldessare 1978 [1528], *The Book of the Courtier*, translated by George Bull, London: Penguin.

Castoriadis, Cornelius 1974 [1961], *Modern Capitalism and Revolution*, translated by Maurice Brinton (Christopher Pallis), London: Solidarity London, available at: http://libcom.org/library/modern-capitalism-revolution-paul-cardan

Castoriadis, Cornelius 1978 [1975], 'History as Creation', pamphlet, excerpted from *L'Institution imaginaire de la société*, Editions du Seuil, Paris, translated and published by Solidarity London, London: Solidarity London.

Castoriadis, Cornelius 1992, 'The Crisis of Marxism, The Crisis of Politics', *Dissent*, (Spring): 221–5.

Catalano, Joseph 1974, *A Commentary on Jean-Paul Sartre's 'Being and Nothingness'*, Chicago: University of Chicago Press.

Caygill, Howard 2013, *On Resistance: A Philosophy of Defiance*, London: Bloomsbury.
Chambers, Samuel 2011, 'Untimely Politics *Avant la Lettre*: The Temporality of Social Formations', *Time and Society*, 20, no. 2: 197–223.
Cieszkowski, August von 2009 [1838], 'Prolegomena to Historiosophy', in *Selected Writings of August Cieszkowski*, edited and translated by André Liebich, London: Cambridge University Press.
Clark, Simon 1991, *Marx, Marginalism and Modern Sociology: From Adam Smith to Max Weber*, London: Macmillan.
Clark, T.J. and Nicholson-Smith, Donald 2004 [1997], 'Why Art Can't Kill the Situationist International', in *Guy Debord and the Situationist International: Texts and Documents*, edited by Tom McDonough, London: October.
Clausewitz, Carl von 1993 [1832], *On War*, translated by Michael Howard and Peter Paret, New York: Princeton University Press.
Colletti, Lucio 1972, 'From Hegel to Marcuse', in *From Rousseau to Lenin: Studies in Ideology and Society* (originally titled *Ideologia e società*, 1969), translated by John Merrington and Judith White, New York: Monthly Review Press, available at: http://www.autodidactproject.org/other/colletti1.html
Connerton, Paul 1974, 'The Collective Historical Subject: Reflections on Lukács' *History and Class Consciousness*', *British Journal of Sociology*, 25, no. 2: 162–78.
Coverley, Merlin 2006, *Psychogeography*, Harpenden: Pocket Essentials.
Crary, Jonathan 2001 [1999], *Suspensions of Perception: Attention, Spectacle and Modern Culture*, Cambridge, MA: MIT Press.
Crary, Jonathan 2004 [1989], 'Spectacle, Attention, Counter-Memory', in *Guy Debord and the Situationist International: Texts and Documents*, edited by Tom McDonough, London: October.
Critchley, Simon 2012 [2007], *Infinitely Demanding*, London: Verso.
Dark Star, 2001, *Beneath the Paving Stones: Situationists and the Beach, May 1968*, Edinburgh: AK Press.
Dauvé, Gilles [writing as 'Jean Barrot'] 1996 [1979], 'Critique of the Situationist International', translated by Louis Michaelson, in *What is Situationism? A Reader*, edited by Stewart Home, Edinburgh: AK Press.
Dauvé, Gilles [writing as 'Jean Barrot'] 1997, *The Eclipse and Re-Emergence of the Communist Movement*, translated by Gilles Dauvé and François Martin, London: Antagonism Press.
Dauvé, Gilles [writing as 'Jean Barrot'] 2000, 'Back to the Situationist International', *Troploin*, available at: http://troploino.free.fr/biblio/backto/
Dauvé, Gilles and Nesic, Karl 2008, 'Love of Labour? Love of Labour Lost ...', translated by Endnotes, *Endnotes*, 1: 104–52.
Debord, Guy 1979, 'Preface to the Fourth Italian Edition of *The Society of the Spectacle*',

translated by Bill Brown, available at: http://www.notbored.org/debord-preface.html

Debord, Guy 1983 [1967], *The Society of the Spectacle*, translated by Fredy Perlman, Detroit: Black and Red.

Debord, Guy 1985, 'Abat Faim', translated by Bill Brown, available at: www.notbored.org/abat-faim.html

Debord, Guy 1986, Letter to Jean-Pierre Baudet, 26 October, translated by Bill Brown, available at: http://www.notbored.org/debord-26October1986.html

Debord, Guy 1989, 'The Hamburg Theses of September 1961', translated by Reuben Keehan, available at: http://www.cddc.vt.edu/sionline/postsi/hamburg.html

Debord, Guy 1993, *Cette mauvaise réputation*, Paris: Gallimard.

Debord, Guy 1995 [1967], *The Society of the Spectacle*, translated by Donald Nicholson-Smith, New York: Zone Books.

Debord, Guy 1998 [1988], *Comments on the Society of the Spectacle*, translated by Malcolm Imrie, London: Verso.

Debord, Guy 2001a, *Correspondance Volume 2: Janvier 1960–Décembre 1964*, Paris: Librairie Arthème Fayard.

Debord, Guy 2002 [1967], *The Society of the Spectacle*, translated by Ken Knabb, available at: http://www.bopsecrets.org/SI/debord/.

Debord, Guy 2001b [1985], *Considerations on the Assassination of Gérard Lebovici*, translated by Robert Greene, Los Angeles: Tam Tam.

Debord, Guy 2003a, *Correspondance Volume 3: Janvier 1965–Décembre 1968*, Paris: Librairie Arthème Fayard.

Debord, Guy 2003b [1978], *Complete Cinematic Works: Scripts, Stills and Documents*, translated and edited by Ken Knabb, Edinburgh: AK Press.

Debord, Guy 2004a, *Correspondance Volume 4: Janvier 1969–Décembre 1972*, Paris: Librairie Arthème Fayard.

Debord, Guy 2004b [1989, 1997], *Panegyric, Volumes 1 and 2*, translated by James Brook and John McHale, London: Verso.

Debord, Guy 2005, *Correspondance Volume 5: Janvier 1973–Décembre 1978*, Paris: Librairie Arthème Fayard.

Debord, Guy 2006a, *Correspondance Volume 6: Janvier 1979–Décembre 1987*, Paris: Librairie Arthème Fayard.

Debord, Guy 2006b, *Oeuvres*, Paris: Gallimard.

Debord, Guy 2007 [2004], *A Sick Planet*, translated by Donald Nicholson-Smith, Oxford: Seagull Books.

Debord, Guy 2008, *Correspondance Volume 7: Janvier 1988–Novembre 1994*, Paris: Librairie Arthème Fayard.

Debord, Guy 2009 [1999], *Correspondance Volume 1: The Foundation of the Situationist International*, translated by Stewart Kendall and John McHale, Los Angeles: Semiotext(e).

Debord, Guy 2010, *Correspondance Volume 'o': Septembre 1951–Juillet 1957 & Lettres retrouvées*, Paris: Librairie Arthème Fayard.

Depétris, Jean-Pierre 2008, 'Ken Knabb, the Situationist International and the American Counterculture', translated by Ken Knabb and Jean-Pierre Depétris, in *Bureau of Public Secrets*, available at: http://www.bopsecrets.org/recent/depetris.htm

Descartes, René 1968 [1641], 'Meditations', in *Discourse on Method and the Meditations*, translated by F.E. Sutcliffe, London: Penguin.

Descombes, Vincent 1980, *Modern French Philosophy*, translated by L. Scott-Fox and J.M. Harding, Fakenham: Cambridge University Press.

Dunayevskaya, Raya 1965, 'The Theory of Alienation: Marx's Debt to Hegel', in *The Free Speech Movement and the Negro Revolution*, Detroit: News & Letters, available at: http://www.marxists.org/archive/dunayevskaya/works/articles/alienation.htm

Dunayevskaya, Raya 2000 [1958], *Marxism and Freedom: From 1776 until Today*, New York: Prometheus Books.

Dunayevskaya, Raya 2002, *The Power of Negativity: Selected Writings on the Dialectic in Hegel and Marx*, Oxford: Lexington Books.

Elbe, Ingo 2013, 'Between Marx, Marxism and Marxisms: Ways of Reading Marx's Theory', *Viewpoint*, (October), available at: http://viewpointmag.com/2013/10/21/between-marx-marxism-and-marxisms-ways-of-reading-marxs-theory/

Elden, Stuart 2004, *Understanding Henri Lefebvre: Theory and the Possible*, London: Continuum.

Endnotes 2008, 'Bring out Your Dead', *Endnotes*, 1: 2–18.

Endnotes 2010, 'Communisation and Value-Form Theory', *Endnotes*, 2: 68–105.

Engels, Friedrich 1987 [1878, 1883], *Anti-Dühring* and *Dialectics of Nature*, in *Karl Marx and Frederick Engels, Collected Works*, Volume 25, translated by Emile Burns and Clemens Dutt, Moscow: Progress Publishers.

Engster, Frank 2016, 'Krisis, What's Krisis?', *Radical Philosophy*, 195: 48–51.

Fackenheim, Emil 1996, 'On the Actuality of the Rational and the Rationality of the Actual', in *The Hegel Myths and Legends*, edited by John Stewart, Evanston, IL: Northwestern University Press.

Feuerbach, Ludwig 1986 [1843], *Principles of the Philosophy of the Future*, translated by Manfred Vogel, Indianapolis: Hackett Publishing Company.

Feuerbach, Ludwig 1989 [1841], *The Essence of Christianity*, translated by George Eliot, New York: Prometheus Books.

Feuerbach, Ludwig 2012 [1972], *The Fiery Brook: Selected Writings*, London: Verso.

Fisher, Mark 2009, *Capitalist Realism: Is There No Alternative?* Winchester: Zero Books.

Ford, Simon 1995, *The Realisation and Suppression of the Situationist International: An Annotated Bibliography*, Edinburgh: AK Press.

Ford, Simon 2005, *The Situationist International: A User's Guide*, London: Black Dog.

Frow, John 1997, *Time and Commodity Culture: Essays in Cultural Theory and Postmodernity*, Oxford: Clarendon Press.

Fukuyama, Francis 1992, *The End of History and the Last Man*, London: Penguin.

Fuller, John Frederick Charles 1970 [1954], *The Decisive Battles of the Western World: 1792–1944*, London: Granada.

Gallix, Andrew 2009, 'The Resurrection of Guy Debord', *The Guardian*, 18 March, available at: https://www.theguardian.com/books/booksblog/2009/mar/18/guy-debord-situationist-international

Galloway, Alexander 2009, 'Debord's Nostalgic Algorithm', *Culture Machine*, 10: 131–56.

George, Theodor 2006, *Tragedies of Spirit: Tracing Finitude in Hegel's Phenomenology*, Albany: State University of New York Press.

Giles-Peters, A.R. 1973, 'Karl Korsch: A Marxist Friend of Anarchism', *Red and Black*, 5, available at: http://libcom.org/history/karl-korsch-marxist-friend-anarchism-ar-giles-peters

Gilman-Opalsky, Richard 2011, *Spectacular Capitalism: Guy Debord and the Practice of Radical Philosophy*, London: Minor Compositions.

Goldmann, Lucien 1964 [1955], *The Hidden God: A Study of Tragic Vision in the Pensées of Pascal and the Tragedies of Racine*, translated by Philip Thody, London: Routledge and Kegan Paul.

Gracián, Baltasar 2000 [1647], *The Art of Worldly Wisdom*, translated by Joseph Jacobs, London: Shambhala.

Grass, Dominique 2000, 'Dialectique historiciste et théorie du prolétariat: Histoire et historicité de la théorie pratique', *Philosophique*, 3: 81–7.

Gray, Christopher (ed.) 1998 [1974], *Leaving the Twentieth Century: The Incomplete Works of the Situationist International*, London: Rebel Press.

Gregoire, R. and Perlman, Fredy 1991 [1969], *Worker-Student Action Committees: France May '68*, Detroit: Black and Red.

Grier, Philip 1996, 'The End of History and the Return of History', in *The Hegel Myths and Legends*, edited by John Stewart, Evanston, IL: Northwestern University Press.

Guillaume, Pierre 1997 [1995], 'Debord', *Not Bored!* 28, available at: http://www.notbored.org/guillaume.html

Hale, Terry (ed.) 2005, *Arthur Cravan, Jacques Rigaut, Julien Torma, Jacques Vaché: Four Dada Suicides*, London: Atlas Press.

Hallward, Peter 2009, 'The Will of the People: Notes Towards a Dialectical Voluntarism', *Radical Philosophy*, 155: 17–29.

Hampshire, Stuart 1951, *Spinoza*, Harmondsworth: Penguin.

Handel, Michael 2006 [1992], *Masters of War: Classical Strategic Thought*, Abingdon: Routledge

Hardt, Michael and Negri, Antonio 2001 [2000], *Empire*, London: Harvard University Press.

Harris, H.S. 1995, *Hegel: Phenomenology and System*, Indianapolis: Hackett Publishing Company.

Hartmann, Klaus 1966, *Sartre's Ontology*, Evanston, IL: Northwestern University Press.

Hayes, Anthony 2015, 'Three Situationists Walk into a Bar: Or, the Peculiar Case of the Hamburg Theses', *Axon*, 8, available at: http://www.axonjournal.com.au/issue-8-1/three-situationists-walk-bar

Heatwave 1966, *Heatwave*, 2, available at: http://charlieradcliffe.com/wp-content/uploads/Heatwave02.pdf

Hegel, Georg Wilhelm Friedrich 1969 [1812–16], *The Science of Logic*, translated by A.V. Miller, New York: Humanity Books.

Hegel, Georg Wilhelm Friedrich 1970 [1830], *The Philosophy of Nature*, translated by A.V. Miller, Oxford: Oxford University Press.

Hegel, Georg Wilhelm Friedrich 1975a [1955], *Lectures on the Philosophy of World History: Introduction*, translated by H.B. Nisbet, Cambridge: Cambridge University Press.

Hegel, Georg Wilhelm Friedrich 1975b [1907], *Early Theological Writings*, translated by T.M. Knox, Chicago: University of Chicago Press.

Hegel, Georg Wilhelm Friedrich 1977 [1807], *The Phenomenology of Spirit*, translated by A.V. Miller, Oxford: Oxford University Press.

Hegel, Georg Wilhelm Friedrich 1984 [1793], 'On the Prospects for a Folk Religion', in *Three Essays, 1793–1795: The Tübingen Essay, Berne Fragments, The Life of Jesus*, translated by J. Dobbins and P. Fuss, Notre Dame, IN: University of Notre Dame Press, available at: http://www.marxists.org/reference/archive/hegel/works/pc/tubingen.htm

Hegel, Georg Wilhelm Friedrich 1988 [1801], *The Difference Between Fichte's and Schelling's System of Philosophy*, Albany: State University of New York Press.

Hegel, Georg Wilhelm Friedrich 1990 [1817], *The Philosophy of Nature*, in *Encyclopaedia of the Philosophical Sciences in Outline and Critical Writings*, edited by Ernst Behler, translated by Steven A. Taubeneck, New York: Continuum, available at: http://www.marxists.org/reference/archive/hegel/works/na/nature1.htm

Hegel, Georg Wilhelm Friedrich 1991 [1830], *The Encyclopaedia Logic*, translated by T.F. Geraets, W.A. Suchting and H.S. Harris, Indianapolis: Hackett Publishing.

Hegel, Georg Wilhelm Friedrich 1993 [1886], *Introductory Lectures on Aesthetics*, translated by Bernard Bosanquet, London: Penguin.

Hegel, Georg Wilhelm Friedrich 1996 [1837], *Hegel's Lectures on the History of Philosophy*, abridged, New Jersey: Humanities Press International.

Hegel, Georg Wilhelm Friedrich 2004 [1857], *The Philosophy of History*, translated by J. Sibree, New York: Dover Publications.

Hegel, Georg Wilhelm Friedrich 2005 [1820], *The Philosophy of Right*, translated by S.W. Dyde, New York: Dover.

Hegel, Georg Wilhelm Friedrich 2009 [1965], *La raison dans l'histoire*, translated and with a preface by Kostas Papaïoannou, Paris: Bibliothèque 10/18.

Heidegger, Martin 2008 [1927], *Being and Time*, translated by John Macquarrie and Edward Robinson, Oxford: Blackwell.

Heinrich, Michael 2009, 'Reconstruction or Deconstruction? Methodological Controversies about Value and Capital, and New Insights from the Critical Edition', in *Re-reading Marx: New Perspectives after the Critical Edition*, edited by Riccardo Bellofiore and Roberto Fineschi, Basingstoke: Palgrave Macmillan.

Heinrich, Michael 2012 [2004], *An Introduction to the Three Volumes of Karl Marx's Capital*, New York: Monthly Review Press.

Hemmens, Alastair 2013, *The Radical Subject: An Intellectual Biography of Raoul Vaneigem (1934–present)*, unpublished doctoral thesis, University of London Institute in Paris, available at: https://pure.royalholloway.ac.uk/portal/files/18903799/2014hemmensajphd.pdf

Hemmens, Alastair 2015, 'We Gotta Get Out of This Place: Anselm Jappe', *Brooklyn Rail*, (September), available at: http://brooklynrail.org/2015/09/field-notes/anselm-jappe-with-alastair-hemmens

Home, Stewart 1991, *The Assault on Culture: Utopian Currents from Lettrisme to Class War*, Edinburgh: AK Press.

Home, Stewart (ed.) 1996, *What is Situationism? A Reader*, Edinburgh: AK Press.

Home, Stewart 1999, 'The Palingenesis of the Avant-Garde', in *The Hacienda Must Be Built: On the Legacy of Situationist Revolt: Essays and Documents Relating to an International Conference on the Situationist International, The Hacienda, Manchester 1996*, Manchester: Aura, available at: http://www.stewarthomesociety.org/sp/palin.htm

Home, Stewart 2005, 'Nowhere to Run', *Mute*, available at: http://www.metamute.org/editorial/articles/nowhere-to-run

Home, Stewart 2011, 'The Self-Mythologisation of the Situationist International', in *Expect Anything Fear Nothing: The Situationist Movement in Scandinavia and Elsewhere*, edited by Jakob Jakobsen and Mikkel Bolt Rasmussen, Copenhagen: Nebula.

Houlgate, Stephen 2005 [1991], *An Introduction to Hegel: Freedom, Truth and History*, 2nd edition, Oxford: Blackwell.

Houlgate, Stephen 2006a, *The Opening of Hegel's Logic*, West Lafayette, IN: Purdue University Press.

Houlgate, Stephen 2006b, 'Time for Hegel', *Bulletin of the Hegel Society of Great Britain*, 53/54: 125–32.

Houlgate, Stephen 2013, *Hegel's Phenomenology of Spirit*, London: Bloomsbury.

Huizinga, Johan 1955 [1938], *Homo Ludens: A Study of the Play Element in Culture*, Boston: Beacon Press.

Hussey, Andrew 2002 [2001], *The Game of War: The Life and Death of Guy Debord*, London: Pimlico.
Hutnyk, John 2004, *Bad Marxism: Capitalism and Cultural Studies*, London: Pluto Press.
Hyppolite, Jean 1969 [1955], *Studies on Marx and Hegel*, translated by John O'Neill, London: Heineman Educational Books.
Hyppolite, Jean 1974 [1946], *Genesis and Structure of Hegel's Phenomenology of Spirit*, translated by Samuel Cherniak and John Heckman, Evanston, IL: North Western University Press.
Hyppolite, Jean 1996 [1948], *Introduction to Hegel's Philosophy of History*, translated by Bond Harris and Jacqueline Spurlock, Gainesville, FL: University Press of Florida.
Hyppolite, Jean 1997 [1953], *Logic and Existence*, translated by Leonard Lawlor and Amit Sen, Albany: State University of New York Press.
Inwood, Michael 2003 [1992], *A Hegel Dictionary*, Oxford: Blackwell.
Jakobsen, Jakob and Rasmussen, Mikkel Bolt (eds.) 2011, *Expect Anything Fear Nothing: The Situationist Movement in Scandinavia and Elsewhere*, Copenhagen: Nebula.
Jappe, Anselm 1999 [1993], *Guy Debord*, translated by Donald Nicholson-Smith, Berkeley, CA: University of California Press.
Jappe, Anselm 2014, 'Towards a History of the Critique of Value', *Capitalism, Nature, Socialism*, 25, no. 2: 25–37.
Jay, Martin 1984a, *Adorno*, Cambridge, MA: Harvard University Press.
Jay, Martin 1984b, *Marxism and Totality: The Adventures of a Concept from Lukács to Habermas*, Berkeley, CA: University of California Press.
Jay, Martin 1994 [1993], *Downcast Eyes: The Denigration of Vision in Twentieth Century French Thought*, Berkeley, CA: University of California Press.
Jeffs, Rory 2012, 'The Future of the Future: Koyré, Kojève and Malabou Speculate on Hegelian Time', *Parrhesia*, 15: 33–53.
Jonge, Alex de 1973, *Nightmare Culture: Lautréamont and 'Les Chants de Maldoror'*, London: Secker and Warburg.
Jorn, Asger 1964, 'Guy Debord and the Problem of the Accursed', translated by Roxanne Lapidus, available at: http://www.cddc.vt.edu/sionline/postsi/accursed.html
Kant, Immanuel 1963 [1784], 'Idea for a Universal History from a Cosmopolitan Point of View', translated by Lewis White Beck, in *On History*, edited by Lewis White Beck, Indianapolis: Bobbs-Merrill.
Kant, Immanuel 1996 [1781], *Critique of Pure Reason*, translated by Werner S. Pluhar, Indianapolis: Hackett.
Kaufmann, Vincent 2006 [2001], *Guy Debord: Revolution in the Service of Poetry*, translated by Robert Bononno, Minneapolis: University of Minnesota Press.
Kedourie, Elie 1995, *Hegel and Marx: Introductory Lectures*, Oxford: Blackwell.
Kelly, Michael 1992, *Hegel in France*, Birmingham: Birmingham Modern Languages Publications.

Khayyám, Omar 1993 [c. 1120], *The Rubáiyát of Omar Khayyám*, translated by Edward Fitzgerald, Ware: Wordsworth Editions.

Kierkegaard, Søren 2004 [1849], *The Sickness unto Death*, translated by Alastair Hannay, London: Penguin.

King Mob 2000 [1966–70], *King Mob Echo*, Edinburgh: Dark Star.

Kojève, Alexandre 1980 [1947], *Introduction to the Reading of Hegel*, translated by James H. Nichols Jr., New York: Cornell University Press.

Korsch, Karl 1946, 'A Non-Dogmatic Approach to Marxism', *Politics*, (May), available at: http://www.bopsecrets.org/CF/korsch.htm

Korsch, Karl 1970 [1923], *Marxism and Philosophy*, translated by Fred Halliday, London: New Left Books.

Korsch, Karl 1975, 'Ten Theses on Marxism Today', *Telos*, 26: 40–1, available at: https://www.marxists.org/archive/korsch/1950/ten-theses.htm

Kovaly, Pavel 1973, 'The History of an Error: An Attempt at Philosophical Criticism', *Studies in Soviet Thought*, 13, nos. 1–2: 20–54.

Koyré, Alexandre 2006 [1961], *Études d'histoire de la pensée philosophique*, Paris: Gallimard.

Krisis 2002a, 'Contributions to the Critique of Commodity Society', pamphlet, translated by Petra Haarmann and R.T., London: Chronos Publications.

Krisis 2002b [1998], 'Marx 2000', pamphlet, London: Chronos Publications.

Kurz, Robert 2012, 'No Revolution Anywhere', pamphlet, translated by Doerte Letzmann and Robin Halpin, London: Chronos Publications.

Kurz, Robert 2016 [2004–5], *The Substance of Capital*, translated by Robin Halpin, London: Chronos Publications.

Larsen, Neil, Mathias Nilges, Josh Robinson and Nicholas Brown (eds.) 2014, *Marxism and the Critique of Value*, Chicago: MCM' Publishing.

Lautréamont, Le Comte de (Isidore Ducasse) 1994 [1970], *Maldoror and the Complete Works of the Comte de Lautréamont*, translated by Alexis Lykiard, Cambridge: Exact Change.

Lazzarato, Maurizio 1996, 'Immaterial Labour', in *Radical Thought in Italy: A Potential Politics*, edited by Michael Hardt and Paolo Virno, Minneapolis, University of Minnesota Press, translated by Paul Colilli and Ed Emery, available at: http://www.generation-online.org/c/fcimmateriallabour3.htm

Lefebvre, Henri 1968 [1940], *Dialectical Materialism*, translated by John Sturrock, London: Jonathan Cape.

Lefebvre, Henri 2006 [1948], *Le Marxisme*, Paris: Presses Universitaires de France.

Lefebvre, Henri 2008a [1947], *Critique of Everyday Life*, Volume 1, translated by John Moore, London: Verso.

Lefebvre, Henri 2008b [1961], *Critique of Everyday Life*, Volume 2, translated by John Moore, London: Verso.

Lefebvre, Henri 2009 [1959], *La Somme et le reste*, Paris: Economica.

Lefort, Claude 1968, 'Le parti situationniste', *La Quinzaine Littéraire*, 44: 3–4, available at: https://collectiflieuxcommuns.fr/655-le-parti-situationniste?lang=fr

Lenin, Vladimir Ilyich 1964 [1917], *The State and Revolution*, in *Collected Works*, Volume 25, Moscow: Progress Publishers, available at: http://www.marxists.org/archive/lenin/works/1917/staterev/index.htm

Lenin, Vladimir Ilyich 1988 [1902], *What Is to Be Done?*, translated by John Fineberg and George Hanna, London: Penguin.

Lenin, Vladimir Ilyich 2007 [1929], 'Conspectus of Hegel's Book *The Science of Logic*', available at: https://www.marxists.org/archive/lenin/works/1914/cons-logic/

Levine, Norman 1984, *Dialogue Within the Dialectic*, London: George Allen and Unwin.

Li Po 2006 [c. 753], *The Selected Poems of Li Po*, translated by David Hinton, London: Anvil Press Poetry Ltd.

Löwy, Michael 1979, *Georg Lukács: From Romanticism to Bolshevism*, translated by Patrick Camiller, London: New Left Books.

Lukács, Georg 1971 [1923], *History and Class Consciousness: Studies in Marxist Dialectics*, translated by Rodney Livingstone, London: Merlin.

Lukács, Georg 1973, 'Existentialism', in *Marxism and Human Liberation: Essays on History, Culture and Revolution by Georg Lukács*, New York: Dell Publishing Co., available at: https://www.marxists.org/archive/lukacs/works/1949/existentialism.htm

Lukács, Georg 1975 [1938], *The Young Hegel: Studies in the Relations between Dialectics and Economics*, translated by Rodney Livingstone, London: Merlin.

Lukács, Georg 2000 [1996], *A Defence of History and Class Consciousness: Tailism and the Dialectic*, translated by Esther Leslie, London: Verso.

Lukács, Georg 2010 [1911], *Soul and Form*, translated by Anna Bostock, New York: Columbia University Press.

Lyotard, Jean-François 2004 [1979], *The Postmodern Condition: A Report on Knowledge*, translated by Geoffrey Bennington and Fredric Jameson, Manchester: Manchester University Press.

Machiavelli, Niccolò 2004 [1532], *The Prince*, translated by John Bondanella, London: Penguin Books.

Magee, Glenn Alexander 2001, *Hegel and the Hermetic Tradition*, Ithica: Cornell University Press.

Maker, William 1994, *Philosophy Without Foundations: Rethinking Hegel*, Albany: State University of New York Press.

Manrique, Jorge 1991 [1492], *Stances sur la mort de son père*, translated by Guy Debord, Cognac: Le temps qu'il fait.

Marcus Aurelius 1997 [180], *Meditations*, translated by Robin Hard, Ware: Wordsworth Editions.

Marcus, Greil 1989, *Lipstick Traces: A Secret History of the Twentieth Century*, London: Faber and Faber.

Marcus, Greil 2004 [1982], 'The Long Walk of the Situationist International', in *Guy Debord and the Situationist International – Texts and Documents*, edited by Tom McDonough, London: October.

Marshall, Peter 2008 [1992], *Demanding the Impossible: A History of Anarchism*, London: Harper Collins.

Martin, Wayne 2007, 'In Defence of Bad Infinity: A Fichtean Response to Hegel's *Differenzschrift*', *Bulletin of the Hegel Society of Great Britain*, 55/56: 168–87.

Marx, Karl 1955 [1847], *The Poverty of Philosophy*, translated by the Institute of Marxism Leninism, Moscow: Progress Publishers, available at: http://www.marxists.org/archive/marx/works/1847/poverty-philosophy/index.htm

Marx, Karl 1968, Letter to the Editor of the *Otecestvenniye Zapisky*, in *Marx and Engels Correspondence*, New York: International Publishers, translated by Donna Torr, available at: http://www.marxists.org/archive/marx/works/1877/11/russia.htm

Marx, Karl 1969, 'Speech at the Anniversary of the *People's Paper*', in *Marx-Engels Collected Works*, Volume 1, Moscow: Progress Publishers, available at: http://www.marxists.org/archive/marx/works/1856/04/14.htm#intro

Marx, Karl 1973a, *Surveys from Exile: Political Writings*, Volume 2, edited by David Fernbach, London: Penguin.

Marx, Karl 1973b [1939], *Grundrisse*, translated by Martin Nicolaus, Middlesex: Penguin.

Marx, Karl 1975, *Early Writings*, translated by Rodney Livingstone and Gregor Benton, Middlesex: Penguin.

Marx, Karl 1988 [1932], *Economic and Philosophical Manuscripts of 1844*, translated by Martin Milligan, New York: Prometheus Books.

Marx, Karl 1990 [1876], *Capital*, Volume 1, translated by Ben Fowkes, London: Penguin Books.

Marx, Karl 1991 [1893], *Capital*, Volume 3, translated by David Fernbach, London: Penguin.

Marx, Karl 1992 [1885], *Capital*, Volume 2, translated by David Fernbach, London: Penguin.

Marx, Karl 2004, *Selected Writings*, edited by Hugh Griffith, The Collector's Library of Essential Thinkers, London: CRW Publishing.

Marx, Karl 2009 [1996], *Later Political Writings*, edited and translated by Terrell Carver, Cambridge: Cambridge University Press.

Marx, Karl and Engels, Friedrich 1936 [1845], *The Holy Family*, translated by R. Dixon, Moscow: Foreign Languages Publishing House.

Marx, Karl and Engels, Friedrich 1985 [1848], *The Communist Manifesto*, translated by Samuel Moore, London: Penguin.

Marx, Karl and Engels, Friedrich 2007 [1932], *The German Ideology: Part One, with Selections from Parts Two and Three*, edited by Christopher Arthur, translated by W. Lough, C. Dutt and C.P. Magill, London: Lawrence and Wishart.

Mauss, Marcel 2004 [1950], *The Gift*, translated by W.D. Halls, London: Routledge.

McCarney, Joseph 2000, *Hegel on History*, London: Routledge.

McDonough, Tom (ed.) 2004, *Guy Debord and the Situationist International: Texts and Documents*, London: October.

McDonough, Tom 2007, *'The Beautiful Language of my Century': Reinventing the Language of Contestation in Postwar France, 1945–1968*, Cambridge, MA: MIT Press.

McDonough, Tom 2009, *The Situationists and the City*, London: Verso.

McDonough, Tom 2011, 'Unrepresentable Enemies: On the Legacy of Guy Debord and the Situationist International', *Afterall: A Journal of Art, Context and Enquiry*, 28: 42–55.

Mension, Jean-Michel 2002 [1998], *The Tribe*, translated by Donald Nicholson-Smith, London: Verso.

Merrifield, Andy 2005, *Guy Debord*, London: Reaktion Books.

Mészáros, István 2006 [1970], *Marx's Theory of Alienation*, Delhi: Aakar Books.

Misselwitz, Philip and Weizman, Eyal 2003, 'Military Operations as Urban Planning', *Mute*, available at: http://www.metamute.org/editorial/articles/military-operations-urban-planning

Mitchell, W.J.T. 1995, *Picture Theory*, Chicago: University of Chicago Press.

Moinet, Jean-Louis 1977, *Genèse et unification du spectacle*, Paris: Champ libre.

Moseley, Fred and Smith, Tony (eds.) 2014, *Marx's Capital and Hegel's Logic: A Reexamination*, Leiden: Brill.

Moylan, Tom 1986, *Demand the Impossible: Science Fiction and the Utopian Imagination*, London: Methuen.

Nancy, Jean-Luc 2002 [1997], *Hegel: The Restlessness of the Negative*, translated by Jason Smith and Steven Miller, Minneapolis: University of Minnesota Press.

Negri, Antonio 1999, 'Value and Affect', translated by Michael Hardt, *boundary 2*, 26, no. 2: 77–88.

Negri, Antonio 2004, *Subversive Spinoza*, translated by Michael Hardt, Timoth S. Murphy, Ted Stolze and Charles Wolfe, Manchester: Manchester University Press.

Negri, Antonio 2003, *Time for Revolution*, translated by Matteo Mandarini, London: Continuum.

Nietzsche, Friedrich 1992a [1872], 'The Birth of Tragedy', in *Basic Writings of Nietzsche*, translated and edited by Walter Kaufmann, New York: Random House.

Nietzsche, Friedrich 1992b [1886], 'Beyond Good and Evil', in *Basic Writings of Nietzsche*, translated and edited by Walter Kaufmann, New York: Random House.

Nietzsche, Friedrich 1996 [1887], *On the Genealogy of Morals*, translated by Douglas Smith, Oxford: Oxford University Press.

Nietzsche, Friedrich 2005 [1882], *The Gay Science*, edited by Bernard Williams, Cambridge: Cambridge University Press.

Novack, George 1980 [1972], 'Is Nature Dialectical?', in *Understanding History: Marxist Essays*, New York: Pathfinder Press, available at: http://www.marxists.org/archive/novack/works/history/ch13.htm

Noys, Benjamin 2007, 'Destroy Cinema! Destroy Capital!: Guy Debord's *The Society of the Spectacle* (1973)', *Quarterly Review of Film and Video*, 5, no. 24: 395–402.

Noys, Benjamin 2010, *The Persistence of the Negative: A Critique of Contemporary Continental Theory*, Edindburgh: Edinburgh University Press.

Noys, Benjamin 2011, *Communisation and Its Discontents: Contestation, Critique and Contemporary Struggles*, Brooklyn: Autonomedia.

Noys, Benjamin 2012, 'Avant-Gardes Have Only One Time: The SI, Communisation and Aesthetics', *Mute*, available at: http://www.metamute.org/community/your-posts/avant-gardes-have-only-one-time-si-communisation-and-aesthetics

Noys, Benjamin 2013, 'Guy Debord's Time-Image', *Grey Room*, 52: 94–107.

O'Kane, Chris forthcoming, 'Henri Lefebvre: Concrete Abstraction, Social Constitution, and Social Domination'.

Osborne, Peter 1995, *The Politics of Time: Modernity and the Avant-Garde*, London: Verso.

Osborne, Peter 2008, 'Marx and the Philosophy of Time', *Radical Philosophy*, 147: 15–22.

Papaïoannou, Kostas 2012 [1962], *Hegel*, Paris: Société d'édition les Belles Lettres.

Parkinson, G.H.R. 1977, *Georg Lukács*, London: Routledge and Kegan Paul.

Paz, Octavio 1986, 'Kostas Papaïoannou', *The Massachusetts Review*, 27, nos. 3/4: 571–4.

Perniola, Mario 1999, 'An Aesthetic of the "Grand Style"', translated by Olga Vasilie, *SubStance: A Review of Theory and Literary Criticism*, 28, no. 3: 89–101.

Plant, Sadie 2000 [1992], *The Most Radical Gesture: The Situationist International in a Postmodern Age*, London: Routledge.

Portier, Julie 2013, 'Debord, un révolutionnaire théorique à la BnF', *Le Quotidien de l'Art*, 369, available at: http://www.lequotidiendelart.com/quotidien_articles_detail.php?idarticle=2546

Portier, Julie 2013, 'Sur les ruines de révolution, que reste-t-il de Debord?', *Le Quotidien d'Art*, 369, available at: http://www.lequotidiendelart.com/quotidien_articles_detail.php?idarticle=2547

Postone, Moishe 1996 [1993], *Time, Labour and Social Domination: A Reinterpretation of Marx's Critical Theory*, Cambridge: Cambridge University Press.

Postone, Moishe 2000 [1986], 'Anti-Semitism and National Socialism', pamphlet, London: Chronos Publications.

Prigent, Michel 2009, 'The Difference between Moishe Postone's and Guy Debord's Critique of Capitalism, or: The Limits of Guy Debord', available at: http://www.principiadialectica.co.uk/blog/?p=575

Rabant, Claude 1997, 'Le Dernier gardien', *Lignes*, 2, no. 31: 170–81.
Rasmussen, Mikkel Bolt 2011, 'To Act in Culture Whilst Being Against All Culture', in *Expect Anything Fear Nothing: The Situationist Movement in Scandinavia and Elsewhere*, edited by Jakob Jakobsen and Mikkel Bolt Rasmussen, Copenhagen: Nebula.
Rees, John 1998, *The Algebra of Revolution: The Dialectic and the Classical Marxist Tradition*, London: Routledge.
Reichelt, Helmut 2005, 'Social Reality as Appearance: Some Notes on Marx's Conception of Reality', translated by Werner Bonefeld, in *Human Dignity: Social Autonomy and the Critique of Capitalism*, edited by Werner Bonefeld and Kosmas Psychopedis, Aldershot: Ashgate.
Rérolle, Raphaëlle 2013, 'A Chacun son Debord', *Le Monde*, 21 March.
Retort 2006, *Afflicted Powers: Capital and Spectacle in a New Age of War*, London: Verso.
Riff Raff 2006, 'Interview with Roland Simon', *Riff Raff*, 8, available at: https://www.riff-raff.se/en/8/interview_roland.php
Rimbaud, Arthur 2004, *Selected Poems and Letters*, translated by Jamie Harding and John Sturrock, London: Penguin.
Roberts, John 2006, *Philosophizing the Everyday: Revolutionary Praxis and the Fate of Cultural Theory*, London: Pluto Press.
Robertson, Ann 2003, 'The Philosophical Roots of the Marx-Bakunin Conflict', *What's Next?* 23: 47–59.
Rosdolsky, Roman 1977, *The Making of Marx's 'Capital'*, translated by Pete Burgess, London: Pluto Press.
Rose, David 2007, *Hegel's Philosophy of Right*, London: Continuum.
Ross, Kristin 2002, *May '68 and Its Afterlives*, Chicago: University of Chicago Press.
Ross, Kristin 2004 [1997], 'Lefebvre on the Situationists: An Interview', in *Guy Debord and the Situationist International – Texts and Documents*, edited by Tom McDonough, London: October.
Rousseau, Jean-Jacques 1994 [1762], *The Social Contract*, translated by Christopher Betts, Oxford: Oxford University Press.
Roussel, Frédérique 1999, 'Debord, a Treasure', *Libération*, 16 February, translated by Bill Brown, available at: http://www.notbored.org/national-treasure.html
Royce, Josiah 1983, 'The Hegelian Theory of Universals', in *The Spirit of Modern Philosophy*, New York: Dover Publications, available at: http://www.class.uidaho.edu/mickelsen/texts/Royce%20-%20Hegel%20Apend%20C.htm
Rubin, Isaak Illich 1972 [1924], *Essays on Marx's Theory of Value*, translated by Fredy Perlman and Milos Samardzija, Detroit: Black and Red.
Rumney, Ralph 2002 [1999], *The Consul*, London: Verso.
Sadler, Simon 1998, *The Situationist City*, Cambridge, MA: MIT Press.
Sanguinetti, Gianfranco 1982 [1979], *On Terrorism and the State: The Theory and Practice*

of Terrorism Divulged for the First Time, translated by Lucy Forsyth and Michel Prigent, London: Aldgate Press.

Sanguinetti, Gianfranco 2016, 'Argent, sexe et pouvoir: à propos d'une fausse biographie de Guy Debord', *Mediapart*, available at: https://blogs.mediapart.fr/lechatetlasouris/blog/150116/argent-sexe-et-pouvoir-propos-d-une-fausse-biographie-de-guy-debord

Sartre, Jean-Paul 1963 [1960], *The Problem of Method*, London: Methuen and Co.

Sartre, Jean-Paul 1965 [1938], *Nausea*, translated by Robert Baldick, London: Penguin.

Sartre, Jean-Paul 1973 [1946], *Existentialism and Humanism*, translated by Philip Mairet, London: Methuen.

Sartre, Jean-Paul 2003 [1943], *Being and Nothingness*, translated by Hazel Barnes, London: Routledge.

Sartre, Jean-Paul 2004 [1960], *Critique of Dialectical Reason*, Volume 1, translated by Alan Sheridan-Smith, London: Verso.

Sayers, Sean 2011, *Marx and Alienation: Essays on Hegelian Themes*, Basingstoke: Palgrave Macmillan.

Sayers, Sean forthcoming, 'Teleology and Meaning in History', available at: https://www.academia.edu/9517542/Teleology_and_Meaning_in_History

Schmidt, Alfred 1984 [1971], *History and Structure: An Essay on Hegelian-Marxist and Structuralist Theories of History*, Baskerville: MIT Press.

Screpanti, Ernesto 2007, *Libertarian Communism: Marx, Engels and the Political Economy of Freedom*, Basingstoke: Palgrave Macmillan.

Self, Will 2013, 'Guy Debord's *The Society of the Spectacle*', *The Guardian*, 14 November.

Sembou, Evangelia 2006, 'The Young Hegel on "Life" and "Love"', *Bulletin of the Hegel Society of Great Britain*, 53/54: 81–106.

Shortall, Felton 1994, *The Incomplete Marx*, Newcastle-upon-Tyne: Athenaeum Press.

Simon, Roland 2001, *Théorie du communisme Volume 1: Fondements critiques d'une théorie de la révolution*, Paris: Senonevero, translated in part by Riff Raff, available at: https://www.riff-raff.se/wiki/en/roland_simon/critical_foundations_for_a_theory_of_the_revolution/chapter_5/contents

Simon, Roland 2009, *Histoire critique de l'ultragauche: Trajectoire d'une balle dans le pied*, Marseille: Senonevero.

Situationist International 1960a, 'Situationist Manifesto', *Internationale situationniste* 4, translated by Fabian Tompsett, available at: http://www.cddc.vt.edu/sionline/si/manifesto.html

Situationist International 1960b, 'The Theory of Moments and the Construction of Situations', *Internationale situationniste* 4, translated by Paul Hammond, available at: http://www.cddc.vt.edu/sionline/si/moments.html

Situationist International 1966, 'De la misère en milieu étudiant', available at: http://library.nothingness.org/articles/SI/fr/display/12

Situationist International 1967, 'Revolt and Recuperation in Holland', translated by Reuben Keehan, available at: http://www.cddc.vt.edu/sionline/si/holland.html

Situationist International 1997, *Internationale situationniste*, Paris: Librairie Arthème Fayard.

Situationist International 2003 [1972], *The Real Split in the International*, translated by John McHale, London: Pluto Press.

Situationist International 2006 [1981], *Situationist International Anthology*, translated and edited by Ken Knabb, Berkeley, CA: Bureau of Public Secrets.

Solomon, Robert 1989 [1987], *From Hegel to Existentialism*, Oxford: Oxford University Press.

Sontag, Susan 2003, *Regarding the Pain of Others*, London: Penguin Books.

Spinoza, Benedict de 1996 [1677], *Ethics*, translated by Edwin Curley, London: Penguin.

Spinoza, Benedict de 2004 [1670, 1677], *A Theologico-Political Treatise and A Political Treatise*, translated by R.H.M. Elwes, New York: Dover.

Spivak, Gayatri Chakravorty 1988 [1985], 'Can the Subaltern Speak?', in *Marxism and the Interpretation of Culture*, edited by Cary Nelson and Lawrence Grossberg, Chicago: University of Ilinois Press.

Spivak, Gayatri Chakravorty 1987, 'Scattered Speculations on the Question of Value', in *In Other Worlds*, New York: Methuen.

Stalin, Joseph 1976 [1938], 'Dialectical and Historical Materialism', in *Problems of Leninism*, Peking: Foreign Languages Press, available at: http://www.marx2mao.com/Stalin/DHM38.html

Stewart, Jon (ed.), 1996, *The Hegel Myths and Legends*, Evanston, IL: Northwestern University Press.

Stiegler, Bernard 2010 [2009], *For a New Critique of Political Economy*, translated by Daniel Ross, Cambridge: Polity.

Stiegler, Bernard 2011 [2004], *The Decadence of Industrial Democracies*, translated by Daniel Ross, Cambridge: Polity.

Stirner, Max 2005 [1845], *The Ego and Its Own: The Case of the Individual Against Authority*, translated by Steven T. Byington, New York: Dover Publications.

Stone-Richards, Michael 2001, 'Néo-stoïcisme et éthique de la gloire: le baroquisme chez Debord', *Pleine Marge*, 34: 83–107.

Stracey, Frances 2014, *Constructed Situations: A New History of the Situationist International*, London: Pluto Press.

Strauss, David Friedrich 1983 [1835], 'The Life of Jesus', in *The Young Hegelians: An Anthology*, edited by Lawrence Stepelevich, New Jersey: Humanities Press.

Sun Tzu 1988 [5th century BC], *The Art of War*, translated by Thomas Cleary, Boston, MA: Shambhala.

Taylor, Charles 1999 [1979], *Hegel and Modern Society*, Cambridge: Cambridge University Press.

The Invisible Committee 2009 [2007], *The Coming Insurrection*, Los Angeles: Semiotext(e).

Théorie Communiste 2008, 'Much Ado About Nothing', *Endnotes*, 1: 143–206.

Toscano, Alberto 2005, 'Real Abstraction Revisited: Of Coins, Commodities and Cognitive Capitalism', available at: http://www2.le.ac.uk/departments/management/documents/research/research-units/cppe/seminar-pdfs/2005/toscano.pdf

Toscano, Alberto 2008, 'The Open Secret of Real Abstraction', *Rethinking Marxism*, 20, no. 2: 273–87.

Trenkle, Norbert 2014 [1998], 'Value and Crisis: Basic Questions', in *Marxism and the Critique of Value*, edited by Neil Larsen, Josh Robinson, Mathias Nilges and Nicholas Brown, Chicago: MCM′ Publishing.

Turner, Steve 1996, 'Guy Debord and the Metaphysics of Marxism: An Obituary of Guy Debord', *Common Sense*, 20: 34–46.

Tzara, Tristan 1996 [1918], 'Dada Manifesto 1918', in *Art in Theory: 1900–1990*, edited by Charles Harrison and Paul Wood, Oxford: Blackwell.

Up Against the Wall Motherfucker! 2007, *Up Against the Wall Motherfucker!: An Anthology of Rants, Posters and More*, Melbourne: Homebrew Publications and Active Distribution.

Vague, Tom 2000 [1985], 'The Boy Scout's Guide to the Situationist International', available at: http://library.nothingness.org/articles/SI/en/display/240

Vaneigem, Raoul 1958, 'Isidore Ducasse et le Comte de Lautréamont dans les "Poésies"', *Synthèses: Revue Internationale*, 151: 243–9, available at: http://library.nothingness.org/articles/SI/fr/display/72

Vaneigem, Raoul 1983 [1979], *The Book of Pleasures*, translated by John Fullerton, London: Pending Press.

Vaneigem, Raoul 2003 [1967], *The Revolution of Everyday Life*, translated by Donald Nicholson-Smith, London: Rebel Press.

Vogel, Steven 1996, *Against Nature: The Concept of Nature in Critical Theory*, Albany: State University of New York Press.

Voyer, Jean-Pierre 1998, 'There is no Society of the Spectacle', in *Limites de conversation*, Strasbourg: Éditions Anonymes, available at: http://leuven.pagesperso-orange.fr/arideau.htm

Wahl, Jean 1951 [1929], *Le Malheur de la conscience dans la philosophie de Hegel*, Paris: Presses Universitaires de France.

Wahl, Jean 2004 [1929], 'Mediation, Negativity and Separation', translated by Christopher Fox and Leonard Lawler, in *Hegel and Contemporary Continental Philosophy*, edited by Dennis King Keenan, New York: State University of New York Press.

Ward, Colin 2004, *Anarchism: A Very Short Introduction*, Oxford: Oxford University Press.

Wark, McKenzie 2008, *50 Years of Recuperation of the Situationist International*, New York: Princeton Architectural Press.

Wark, McKenzie 2011, *The Beach Beneath the Streets: The Everyday Life and Glorious Times of the Situationist International*, London: Verso.
Wartenburg, Thomas 1993, 'Hegel's Idealism: The Logic of Conceptuality', in *The Cambridge Companion to Hegel*, edited by Frederick Beiser, Cambridge: Cambridge University Press.
Weizman, Eyal 2006, 'The Art of War', *Frieze*, 99, available at: https://frieze.com/article/art-war
Wendling, Amy 2009, *Karl Marx on Technology and Alienation*, Basingstoke: Palgrave Macmillan.
Wheen, Francis 2006, *Marx's Das Kapital: A Biography*, London: Atlantic Books.
Wolff, Robert Paul 1998 [1970], *In Defense of Anarchism*, London: University of California Press.
Wollen, Peter 1989, 'Bitter Victory', in *On the Passage of a Few People through a Rather Brief Moment in Time*, edited by Elisabeth Sussman, Cambridge, MA: MIT Press.
Yovel, Yirmiyahu 2005, *Hegel's Preface to the Phenomenology of Spirit*, Princeton, NJ: Princeton University Press.
Zacarias, Gabriel Ferreira 2014, *Expérience et représentation du sujet: une généalogie de l'art et de la pensée de Guy Debord*, unpublished doctoral thesis, University of Perpignan, available at: https://hal.inria.fr/tel-01142990/document
Zagdanski, Stephane 2013, 'Guy Debord au commissariat', *Paroles des jours*, available at: http://parolesdesjours.free.fr/debordcommissariat.pdf

Index

Adorno, Theodor   20, 21n, 23, 35, 36, 126, 126n, 159, 197n, 250n
   'Music and Technique'   36n
   Dialectic of Enlightenment   36n
Aesthetics   9, 12–14, 24, 39, 49, 67, 68–71, 76, 85, 93n, 97, 120, 131, 135, 140, 152, 304, 391
   Aestheticisation of time in Debord's work   69–71, 94, 142, 142n, 143, 143n, 145, 361–6, 392
Agamben, Giorgio   10, 175n, 219, 356, 400
Alba conference (The First World Congress of Free Artists)   89, 100, 101
Aletheia (journal)   122
Alienation   *passim*
   Entfremdung   193, 205, 212–3, 217
   Vergegenständlichung   193, 205, 208, 212–213
   Entäusserung   212, 213
Althusser, Louis   156–7, 304, 317
   For Marx   156
   Reading Capital   156
Anarchism   2, 27, 28, 286, 286n, 392n
Architecture   82n, 88, 88n, 89, 101, 112
Arguments (journal)   36n, 121n, 128n, 207
Aristotle   41n, 182, 365n
Aron, Raymond   171
Art   1, 3, 5–6, 13, 22, 27, 55, 60–1, 67–71, 77, 81–4, 86, 88–93, 96–7, 101–7, 109, 116, 121, 125, 126n, 127, 133, 148–9, 152, 164, 176, 246, 247, 249, 285, 360n, 363, 366, 382n, 390–1
   Unification of art and life; the 'realisation' of art   27, 60, 68–71, 77, 86, 88–9, 91, 96–7, 100, 107, 109, 121, 125, 127, 133, 148–9, 152, 246, 363, 366, 391 *see also* Philosophy: realisation of philosophy
Avant-garde   1n, 5, 13, 27, 55, 68, 77, 81–4, 87n, 89, 90, 91, 96–7, 99–100, 102, 106, 109, 125, 141, 145–52, 155, 241, 336n, 347
   Debord's conception of the avant-garde   90, 141, 145–52, 347
   The SI as the 'final' avant-garde   148–52

Bibliothèque nationale de France (BnF)   2, 11, 75, 121, 177, 227, 356
Baj, Enrico   89n
Bakunin, Mikhail   34, 286, 286n, 336n, 337
Bataille, Georges   159, 171, 175, 175n, 176, 308
   Le procès de Gilles de Rais   175n
   The Accursed Share   175n
   'Hegel Death and Sacrifice'   175n
   'The Notion of Expenditure'   175n
Baudrillard, Jean   11, 12n, 22, 22n, 373, 373n, 374, 374n
Bauer, Bruno   34, 34n
Barthes, Roland   11, 112n
de Beauvoir, Simone   75n, 119n
Becker-Ho, Alice   230, 336n, 363, 370
Bergson, Henri   169
Berna, Serge   87n
Bernstein, Michèle   90, 258n
Biopolitics   4, 271, 282, 302, 308, 308n, 328, 328n
Blake, William   21n, 336, 336n
   The Marriage of Heaven and Hell   336n
Blanchot, Maurice   110
Bordiga, Amadeo   323
Brau, Jean-Louis   87n
Brecht, Bertolt   85
Breton, André   55, 113, 159, 171, 175, 175n

Caesar, Gaius Julius   336
Capital, capitalism   *passim*
   Capitalist social relations   14, 24, 25, 54, 112, 222, 228, 261, 266, 306–7, 309–16, 319–20, 325
   Capitalist value   *passim*
   Capitalist value as a subject   51, 222, 227, 251n, 308–9, 316–19, 324
   Money   221, 227, 252, 257, 258n, 306, 310–16, 324–9
   Value-form   99, 268, 312–6
   Value-form theory   250, 250n, 326
Castiglione, Baldassare   12, 365
   The Book of the Courtier   365
Castoriadis, Cornelius   21n, 109, 110, 122n, 283, 286, 287, 288
   'Modern Capitalism and Revolution'   286
   Order-givers and order-takers   283, 287–8
   see also New proletariat
Cézanne, Paul   96
Chaplin, Charlie   87, 87n

INDEX   423

Cinema   84, 84n, 85, 86, 86n, 99, 104, 141, 142n, 230, 258, 274, 334, 378
Class struggle; class relations   51, 56n, 102, 126n, 172, 242, 245, 249–50, 250n, 252n, 253, 253n, 254, 255, 261n, 263–4, 266, 281, 286, 303, 311, 311n, 317n, 397
   Classical working class; proletariat   2, 35, 55, 63, 105, 117, 148–9, 161, 187, 196–9, 204, 237, 241, 243, 247, 253, 260, 262, 266, 277, 279, 281, 286–9, 290, 311–12, 317n, 325, 386n, 341, 342, 396, 397
   New proletariat   27, 50, 55, 67, 106, 109, 176n, 236, 257–9, 262–3, 265, 267–8, 273, 283–4, 286n, 288–90, 303–4, 319, 383, 387–8, 398 *see also* Existential poverty
   Universal class   284, 288–90
C.O.B.R.A.   88n, 89, 100, 101
Combat (journal)   87n
Commodity, commodification   *passim*
   The structure of the commodity   291–2
   The structure of the commodity and spectacular society   292–305
Communisation   251, 251n, 261n
Communism   30, 36, 65, 83, 87n, 109, 156, 175, 181, 185, 197n, 203n, 221, 242–3, 248, 252–3, 256, 260–1, 285n, 286n, 290n, 294n, 299, 306, 371, 395–6
   Communism as collective historical life   27, 30, 45, 52, 55, 76, 83, 138, 152, 160–1, 188, 190, 221, 248, 262, 391, 395, 397
   First International (International Workingmen's Association)   273
   Second international   59, 60, 65n, 285n
   Third International   284
Le Corbusier (Charles-Édouard Jeanneret)   88, 88n
Cosio d'Arroscia   89
de Cayeux, Colin   337, 337n
Cieszkowski, August   12, 22, 34, 35n, 73, 74, 124n, 169, 223, 395
   Prolegomena to Historiosophy   73, 169
Champ libre   73n, 169
Chtcheglov, Ivan   88, 88n, 113, 258n
   'Formulary for a New Urbanism'   88, 113
Contemplative detachment   4, 18–19, 23, 28–30, 60, 68, 74, 244–5, 277, 296n, 325, 359, 391–2 *see also* Spectatorship *and* Spectacle

Lukács on contemplation   17, 29, 195–6, 198, 200
Hegelian philosophy as contemplative   10, 32, 33–4, 36, 47, 50, 169, 186, 244, 276
Clausewitz, Carl von   12, 75, 75n, 354, 355, 355n, 360, 360n, 361–2, 366–9, 381, 383, 385–7
Cloots, Anacharsis (Jean-Baptiste du Val-du-Grâce)   337
Constant (Constant Anton Nieuwenhuys)   90n, 101, 101n, 112
Culture   2–3, 5, 6, 22, 36, 57–8, 60, 61n, 64, 68, 81, 84–6, 88–91, 95–100, 105–6, 110, 139, 148, 152, 192, 195, 198, 203n, 277, 281, 295, 321, 350, 365n
   Cultural decomposition / stagnation stagnant   20, 83, 90, 94–100, 104, 109, 133, 152, 246, 247
'Culture industry'   23 *see also* Adorno
Dada   84, 85, 91, 96–7
Dante Alighieri   275, 275n, 276
   The Divine Comedy   275
Dauvé, Gilles   108n, 248, 255, 261, 264, 307, 322, 322n, 323, 324, 324n
Debord   *passim*
   'Abat-faim'   387
   Cette mauvaise réputation   142n, 334, 350, 381
   Comments on the Society of the Spectacle   14, 20, 26, 98, 142n, 277, 318n, 334–5, 340, 349, 349n, 350, 350n, 351, 356–7, 361, 364, 364n, 365, 370–2, 374–80, 380n, 381, 383–4, 387, 400
   Considerations on the Assassination of Gérard Lebovici   142n, 334, 378n
   Critique of Separation   85n, 104
   Des contrats   258n, 334
   Fin de Copenhague   104
   Howlings in Favour of Sade   85, 85n, 88, 91, 104, 354n
   In Girum Imus Nocte et Consumimur Igni   8, 20n, 69n, 87n, 141–2, 142n, 143–6, 334, 336, 336n, 344, 347, 364, 382n, 399
   'Introduction to a Critique of Urban Geography'   95n
   La Planète malade   386n
   'Manifesto for a Construction of Situations'   91

Mémoires 85n, 104
'Notes on Poker' 370
On the Passage of a Few Persons through a Rather Brief Moment in Time 104
Panegyric 20, 20n, 70, 87n, 142n, 257, 258n, 334–6, 336n, 354, 355n, 361n, 362–3, 363n, 365, 378n, 388
'Perspectives for Conscious Changes in Everyday Life' 128n
'Preface to the Fourth Italian Edition of *The Society of the Spectacle*' 236, 258n, 334, 348
Refutation of All the Judgements, Laudatory as Well as Hostile, Passed up to Now on the Film 'The Society of the Spectacle' 274
'Report on the Construction of Situations' 61n, 90, 91, 92, 93, 95, 97, 99, 102, 109, 144
'The Organisation Question for the Situationist International', 100
'The Situationists and the New Forms of Action in Politics and Art' 104n
The Society of the Spectacle (book) 3n, 4, 6, 9, 13–14, 17–22, 22n, 25–6, 29, 30n, 31–3, 33n, 36n, 47, 51, 51n, 52–4, 57, 59n, 60n, 65n, 67, 73n, 74n, 82–3, 85n, 9–4, 96, 100, 117, 123, 124, 138, 141, 142n, 148, 150n, 155, 158n, 159–60, 172, 174, 177n, 181, 181n, 184–5, 191, 207–8, 208n, 212, 215, 220–1, 221n, 223, 227, 230–1, 236, 241, 244, 256, 258n, 262, 264, 267, 272–4, 276–7, 280–1, 284, 286, 289–90, 292–5, 297, 301, 304n, 317, 318n, 319, 320, 322–5, 327n, 334, 342–3, 343n, 346, 348, 349n, 350–1, 355, 358–9, 365n, 369, 371, 375, 377–9, 387, 391–2, 398
The Society of the Spectacle (film) 13, 230, 274, 334, 363n
'Theses on the Situationist International and its Time' 274n, 347, 379
Dérive 71, 87, 88, 104, 112, 378n
Descartes, René 200
Détournement 1, 1n, 3n, 11, 20, 30, 87, 88, 142, 142n, 146, 191, 215–16, 220, 234, 289, 293, 336n, 378, 378n, 382
Deutsch-Französische Jahrbücher 149–150n, 341n

Dialectics 10–11, 28–9, 34, 35, 39–40, 48, 71–6, 123, 130, 137, 145, 159–61, 166, 167, 169, 175, 175n, 176, 185–7, 196, 200–1, 214–15, 219, 228, 231–2, 234–5, 238, 245, 308, 350
Dialectics and strategy 10–11, 39, 49, 71–6, 232–3, 238, 245, 356–7, 359–60, 362, 366–371, 376, 381–4, 387, 392, 397–8 *see also* Strategy
Dialectical movement 44–5, 47, 162–5, 167, 169, 186, 238, 294n, 316, 348
Dialectics of nature 48, 48n, 203n, 204n
Duchamp, Marcel 96
Dunayevskaya, Raya 126, 126n
Dürer, Albrecht 400

Economic determinism; 'economism' 9n, 59, 60, 65n, 247, 273, 276, 279, 280, 284, 286, 302, 304, 304n, 306, 319, 342, 359, 397
Eisenstein, Sergei 274
Engels, Friedrich 28n, 32, 37, 40n, 48, 48n, 60, 62, 112, 159, 203, 226, 253, 276, 312
Anti-Dühring 48n, 62
Dialectics of Nature 48n
Estivals, Robert 151, 151n
Eurocentrism in Debord and the SI's work 60–1, 61n
Everyday life *see* Life
Existentialism 12–13, 24, 28, 30, 39, 50, 69, 75, 91–2, 108, 114–15, 117, 120–3, 125–7, 164, 166–7, 167n, 168, 171, 177, 187, 190, 203, 206, 219, 276, 359, 361, 363–4, 366
Existential poverty 27, 55, 82, 106, 109, 247, 259, 263, 273, 280, 282, 284, 289, 290, 304, 324, 387, *see also* Class struggle: New proletariat

Feuerbach, Ludwig 9n, 12, 18, 22, 32, 34, 34n, 35, 35n, 47–8, 61n, 63, 73, 77, 92, 127, 179n, 181–2, 182n, 189, 189n, 223, 223n, 224, 229, 337, 394, 396
The Essence of Christianity 73, 182n, 189, 223n
Principles of the Philosophy of the Future 223n
Fetishism 3, 18, 33, 48, 69, 201, 221
Fetishistic aspects of capitalist society 33, 92, 126n, 204, 221, 253, 276, 279, 296–7, 312, 315, 317n, 321

INDEX 425

Fetishistic conception of capital   307, 319, 324–5
Fichte, Johann Gottlieb   200
  Wissenschaftslehre   200
Frederick II ('Frederick the Great')   143
The First World Congress of Free Artists   89
Form and content   20, 142, 142n, 144, 260, 264–8, 299, 378–80, 380n, 382–2 *see also* Strategy: Strategies of writing
Foucault, Michel   12
Fourier, Charles   113, 113n
Frankin, André   132
Fukuyama, Francis   174, 174n, 186, 376
  The End of History and the Last Man   174n
Futurism   96

Glaucos   337, 337n
Goldmann, Lucien   108, 108n, 122n, 206
de Gondi, Jean-Francois-Paul (Cardinal de Retz)   337
Gracián, Baltasar   12, 220, 365
  The Art of Worldly Wisdom   365

Heatwave   21n
Hegel, Georg Wilhelm Friedrich   *passim*
  Early Theological Writings   165, 182, 184, 230
  Encyclopaedia Logic   46n, 201n, 237
  Encyclopaedia of the Philosophical Sciences   162 *see also* Hegelian philosophy: Hegelian system *and* Philosophy: philosophical system
  Fragment on Love   230
  Jena manuscripts   165–169, 179, 234, 324
  Lectures on the Philosophy of Religion   393
  'On the Prospects for a Folk Religion'   182, 183n
  The Difference Between Fichte's and Schelling's Systems of Philosophy   29n
  The Phenomenology of Spirit   31, 31n, 39, 43n, 51, 51n, 77, 115, 115n, 116, 116n, 117, 118n, 120, 123, 162, 162n, 163, 163n, 165, 170–2, 174, 177–9, 196, 215, 229, 234, 316n, 318n, 358, 358n, 393n, 394n, 395, 396
  The Philosophy of History   45n, 46n, 178
  The Philosophy of Nature   46n, 162n
  The Philosophy of Right   28, 35, 46n, 73, 149, 179, 184, 185, 226, 288, 394n

'The Positivity of the Christian Religion'   182
  The Science of Logic   46n, 202n, 225, 312
Hegelian philosophy   *passim*
  Absolute   14, 40, 42–8, 59, 63, 67, 70–1, 76, 116–17, 125, 129, 131, 135, 140, 160–1, 164, 173, 178, 181–90, 195, 198, 201–2, 237, 238, 300–1, 393–5, 399
  Absolute knowing   77, 114–120, 127, 139, 140, 161, 163, 168, 171, 196, 393
  Concept   40, 44–6, 46n, 52, 76, 115n, 116, 160–1, 167, 169, 172–3, 186–8, 190, 200, 316, 394n
  Hegel and 'bourgeois' society   33, 50, 74, 185, 186, 197, 226, 243, 244–5, 277, 289
  Hegelian system   9n, 10, 31, 44, 74, 115, 158–9, 162, 164–6, 169–70, 175, 179, 359, 394n *see also* Philosophy: philosophical system
  Idea   40, 44, 45, 46n, 52, 76, 131, 160, 161, 181, 183, 187, 188, 189, 190, 238, 337n
  Lord and bondsman; master and slave   118n, 163, 170, 170n, 171, 171n, 172, 174
  Overview of Hegel's philosophy   41–6
  Owl of Minerva   33, 33n, 186, 337, 396
  Spirit   31n, 32, 43–4, 45n, 46, 63, 115–17, 163, 167–8, 171, 175n, 177–80, 183, 184, 187–9, 194–6, 198, 232, 235–7, 288, 337, 337n, 394, 396
  Unhappy Consciousness   114–20, 125–7, 129, 131, 134, 139, 162–5, 170, 171, 176–7, 229, 301, 304, 387
  Hegel and religion   31, 44, 77, 116, 168, 181–3, 229–30, 393–5
Hegelianism, French   28, 39, 50, 118, 122, 123, 124, Chapter Six *passim*
Heidegger, Martin   92, 121, 121n, 122, 122n, 123, 125–6, 126n, 127, 167, 167n, 171–2, 175n, 206
  Being and Time   122, 206
  'The Word of Nietzsche: "God is Dead"'   121n
Heraclitus   32
History   *see* Time and history
Hölderlin, Friedrich   185n
Horkheimer, Max   23
  Dialectic of Enlightenment   36n

Hyppolite, Jean   12, 31n, 33, 41–2, 44n, 51, 116n, 118n, 157–60, 163n, 164, 165, 170n, 171, 176–83, 186–90, 208, 232–8, 395–6
  Genesis and Structure of Hegel's 'Phenomenology of Spirit'   176, 179
  Introduction to Hegel's Philosophy of History   177, 177n, 235
  Studies on Marx and Hegel   177, 177n, 179, 208, 234–5, 395
  Logic and Existence   181, 188
Huizinga, Johan   94, 382n
  Homo Ludens   94, 382n

International Movement for an Imaginist Bauhaus   89, 89n, 100
Isou, Isidore   84–7, 95–6
  Traité de bave et d'éternité   84

Jappe, Anselm   9n, 23, 24n, 51n, 91n, 104n, 128n, 191n, 192n, 208, 249–50, 251n, 252, 255n, 317n, 333, 357n
  Guy Debord   9n, 23, 249, 357n
Jorn, Asger   89, 89n, 100, 101, 101n, 103, 108

Kairos   370, 370n
Kant, Immanuel   61, 197, 198, 200, 313
  'Idea for a Universal History from a Cosmopolitan Point of View'   61n
Kautsky, Karl   253
Keats, John   336n
Khayati, Mustapha   108n
Khayyám, Omar   12, 70, 363–5
  The Rubáiyát of Omar Khayyám   364, 364n
Kierkegaard, Søren Aabye   126
Korsch, Karl   12, 33, 156, 185, 203, 203n, 232, 284, 285, 285n, 395
  Marxism and Philosophy   156, 203, 203n, 284, 285, 285n
  'Theses on Hegel and Revolution'   185
Kojève, Alexandre   39, 46, 52, 123, 157–8, 160, 163–5, 170–6, 179–80, 186–7
Kotanyi, Attila   103–4
Koyré, Alexandre   123, 157, 160, 165–70, 172, 174, 179, 187
  'Hegel à Iéna'   166, 169–70
Kriegspiel   72, 72n, 354, 354n, 357n, 361n, 380n, *see also* Strategy

Krisis   251n
Kronstadt   98–9
Kunzelmann, Dieter   101

Labour, alienated labour   28n, 111, 193, 204, 206, 209, 212, 213, 221–2, 224, 227, 260, 268–9, 271, 273, 281, 282–4, 298, 301–2, 306–7, 310–12, 315, 319, 328, 396
  Affirmation of labour   192, 241, 242, 248, 249, 252n, 253, 254, 255, 257, 259, 260, 268, 270, 306
  Homogenisation of capitalist labour   227, 241, 250n, 254, 291, 292, 306, 308, 314
  Labour as distinct from social activity *per se*   241
  Labour as trans-historical   192, 249, 254, 326
  Rejection of labour   241, 242, 248, 249, 251n, 252n, 254, 255, 257, 259, 264, 268, 306, 319
  Theoretical neglect of labour   21, 261, 270, 271, 272, 284, 301, 302, 306, 307, 309, 319, 323, 324
Lacan, Jacques   171
Lautréamont, Le Comte de (Isidore Ducasse)   21n, 128n, 355
Lebovici, Gérard   258, 334, 379 see also Debord: *Considerations on the Assassination of Gérard Lebovici*
Lefebvre, Henri   12, 70, 71, 86n, 94, 108–9, 111, 112n, 114, 120–1, 122n, 127–39, 155n, 156, 160–1, 176n, 188, 208, 258n, 285, 333–4, 395, 397
  Critique of Everyday Life   94, 111, 112n, 128n, 208
  Dialectical Materialism   129, 156
  La Conscience mystifiée   129n
  La Somme et le reste   131, 132, 134, 135, 137
Lefort, Claude   108n, 320–2, 324
Lenin, Vladimir; Leninism   48n, 64, 150, 247, 266n, 307n, 341, 397
  What Is to Be Done?   273
Les Temps Modernes   108n
Letterists, Letterism   84–7, 90, 95–6, 99
Letterist International   87–90, 92, 96–7, 109, 111
  Potlatch   89
Li Po   12, 70, 363–4

Life *passim*
    Enrichment of life   5, 45, 55–6, 59–60,
        68–70, 82, 89, 90, 92–4, 109, 114, 121, 125,
        132, 137, 145, 212n, Chapter Eight *passim*,
        246, 262, 328, 391, 395
    Everyday life   26, 90–1, 94, 97n, 105, 108–
        11, 113, 130–1, 134–7, 243, 260, 268, 270,
        303, 319, 328, 349, 391
    Impoverishment of life   4, 18, 19n, 26, 27,
        54–6, 69, 82, 99–100, 109, 126n, 212n,
        Chapter Eight *passim*, 256, 259, 260,
        280, 282, 290, 292, 299–301, 318n, 328,
        371–5, 386
    Life and dialectical movement   44, 46,
        158, 161, 167, 178, 179, 182, 183, 185, 187,
        189, Chapter Eight *passim*, 294, 367, 395
    Life and war   361–3, 366
    Non-life   68, 161, Chapter Eight *passim*,
        267, 291, 294, 304, 308–9, 314, 318–19,
        324, 325, 328–9
The London Psychogeographical Association
    89–90
Lukács, Georg   12, 17, 29, 33, 62–3, 64n, 108,
    111, 116–18, 120, 122–3, 125, 126n, 127, 134–
    5, 140, 143, 155–6, 159, 161, 169, 181n, 190,
    Chapter Seven *passim*, 223, 232, 237,
    249, 266–7, 284, 292, 295, 301, 317n,
    319n, 327n, 386, 393, 395–6
    History and Class Consciousness   29, 32,
        62, 108, 111, 116–17, 122, 135, 140, 156,
        Chapter Seven *passim*, 232, 237, 266,
        284, 292, 295, 319n, 327n, 386
    *In Defence of 'History and Class Conscious-
        ness'*   204n
    Soul and Form   122, 134, 135, 143
    The Young Hegel   116n, 186n, 203, 208n
Lyotard, Jean-François   12n

Machiavelli, Niccolò   12, 72, 75, 355, 358n,
    366, 369, 375, 381
Malevich, Kasimir Severinovich   96
    Black Square   96
Mallarmé, Stéphane   336
Marcus Aurelius   358n
    Meditations   358n
Marx, Karl   *passim*
    'A Contribution to a Critique of Hegel's
        Philosophy of Right: Introduction'   35,
        73, 105, 106, 149, 210, 289

*A Contribution to the Critique of Political
    Economy*   52n
Capital   18, 52n, 73, 156, 191, 220, 227, 242n,
    250n, 253, 256, 263, 272–5, 292, 310–12,
    315, 317–18, 323, 342–3, 346, 348n, 360,
    396
*Economic and Philosophic Manuscripts of
    1844*   129, 155, 155n, 156, 165, 172, 192,
    194–5, 203, 205, 206n, 208–12, 215n, 216–
    17, 316n
Grundrisse   191, 221, 221n, 250, 319, 327,
    327n
'On the Jewish Question'   226
'Speech at the Anniversary of *The People's
    Paper*'   293
The Civil War in France   281
The Communist Manifesto   30, 66, 152n,
    234, 281, 289
The German Ideology   28n, 30, 37, 40n, 52,
    226
The Holy Family   29n, 32, 60
The Poverty of Philosophy   29n, 327n, 335
'Wages, Price and Profit'   221n
'Theses on Feuerbach'   32, 35, 47, 92, 179n
Manrique, Jorge   12, 70, 363, 365–6, 366n
Martin, Jeppesen Victor   104n, 334
Mao Tse-tung   300, 320, 373
Mension, Jean-Michel   92n
Merleau-Ponty, Maurice   171
May 1968   13, 22, 100, 174n, 304n, 333, 333n,
    338, 345–6, 348, 350, 351, 371, 377, 387
McLuhan, Marshall   11
Montesquieu (Charles-Louis de Secondat,
    Baron de La Brède et de Montesquieu)
    282

Napoleon (Napoléon Bonaparte)   72, 367–8,
    368n, 383, 384, 385, 385n, 386, 386n
Napoleon III (Louis-Napoléon Bonaparte)
    282
    Bonapartism   281
Nash, Jørgen   101, 103, 104
    Nashists   104, 151
Nazis, fascism   96–99, 122, 341
Neue Marx Lektüre, New readings of Marx
    191, 250, 250n, 251n, 252n, 253, 256, 329
New Babylon   101, 101n, 112, *see also* Constant
Nietzsche, Friedrich   121, 121n, 145, 145n, 164n,
    176n, 308, 308n

Orwell, George   337

Papaïoannou, Kostas   12, 157, 160, 165, 172, 181, 181n, 182–7, 236
  Hegel   184n, 185
Paris Commune   56n, 66n, 128n, 281, 333
Parti communiste Français   128, 129
Philosophy   *passim*
  Philosophical anthropology in Debord's work   25, 39, 49–52, 76, 166, 191–2, Chapter seven *passim*, 219, 316, 352, 357–9, 391
  Philosophical system, conceptual systems   9, 9n, 198, 199, 201, 253, 277, 279, 304n, 339, 359, 359n, 360
  Philosophy of praxis   10, 35, 73, 147, 344, 352, 353, 390, 400
  Realisation of philosophy   10, 13, 32, 35–7, 40, 59, 60, 72, 74, 76, 77, 83, 92, 101, 105, 127, 133, 149, 150, 183, 277
Pinot-Gallizio, Giuseppe   89, 101, 101n
Plato   182, 197n
  The Republic   197n
Play, ludic lived experience   5, 45, 68, 70–1, 76, 83, 88–9, 93–5, 109, 132, 136, 136n, 137, 138, 193, 220, 248, 361–2, 366, 370, 374n, 382, 391
Poetry   5, 12, 24, 24n, 61n, 68, 70, 72, 83–5, 94, 107, 110, 113, 121, 132, 136, 143, 285n, 336, 336n, 337n, 338n, 363, 364–6, 382, 382n
Political economy   252, 278–9
  Critique of political economy   13, 191, 238, 241, 252–4, 268, 278–9
  Critical political economy   252–4, 278
Pouvoir Ouvrier   65n, 286n
Praxis   *passim see also* Philosophy: realisation of philosophy
Prem, Heimrad   103
Pro-situs   3n, 7, 65n, 334
Proletariat   *see* Class struggle
Proudhon, Pierre-Joseph   335
Psychogeography   1, 1n, 82n, 87–8

Rebel Worker   21n
Recuperation   2–3, 7–8, 12, 147
Ricardo, David   253, 314
Rimbaud, Arthur   55, 257, 257n
  A Season in Hell   257n

Rizzi, Bruno   337
Rubin, Isaak Illich   313, 313n
Ruge, Arnold   29n, 149, 149n, 216, 341
Rumney, Ralph   90n

de Sade, Dominique Alphonse Francois   175n
  Justine   175n
Sanguinetti, Gianfranco   258n, 334
Sartre, Jean-Paul   12, 50–1, 75, 87, 91, 92, 108, 114–5, 118–19, 119n, 120–7, 132, 167n, 169–71, 285–6, 358 *see also* Existentialism
  Being and Nothingness   92, 119n, 121, 125, 126n
  Critique of Dialectical Reason   126n, 285
  'Search for a Method'   285
  Situations   92
Schelling, Friedrich Wilhelm Joseph   182, 185n
Second Situationist International   104
Shakespeare, William   54n, 363n, 365
  Julius Caesar   54n
  Henry V   363n
Shelley, Percy Bysshe   336n
Situationist International   *passim*
  'Address to Revolutionaries of Algeria and of All Countries'   61n
  'Détournement as Negation and Prelude'   142n
  Internationale Situationniste   1n, 60n, 65n, 66, 88, 88n, 102, 104n, 108n, 110, 110n, 122, 122n, 132, 142, 174n, 257–8, 264, 320n, 333, 359n, 388n, 390
  'Into the Trashcan of History!'   128n
  'On the Poverty of Student Life'   1, 333
  'Reform and Counter-Reform in the Bureaucratic Bloc'   61n
  'The Class Struggles in Algeria'   60n
  'The Counter-Situationist Campaign in Various Countries'   104n
  'The Culminating Point of the Spectacle's Offensive'   387
  'The Decline and Fall of the Spectacle-Commodity Economy'   303
  'The Explosion Point of Ideology in China'   60n
  'The Hamburg Theses'   105–6
  'Two Local Wars'   60n

'The Theory of Moments and the Construction of Situations' 132, 135–140
'Theses on the Paris Commune' 128n
Situations, constructed situation 5, 12, 27–8, 69–71, 75, 83, 87–96, 104, 108, 114, 117, 119–23, 125, 127, 131–2, 135–40, 143, 333, 339, 359, 362
Smith, Adam 253
Socrates 336–7
Solidarity (political group) 21n
Socialisme ou barbarie 108n, 109, 110, 256, 286, 286n, 320
Spinoza, Benedict de 41n, 42, 43, 43n, 182, 195, 200, 308n
Species-being (Marx) 161, 188–9, 189n, 190, 212n, 213, 223–4, 227
Species-being (Feuerbach) 189, 189n, 224
Spectacle, spectacular 3–7, 17–25, 64–5, and *passim*
   Concentrated spectacle 26, 256, 299–301, 371–5
   Dates accorded to the emergence of a fully spectacular society 24, 57, 96–9, 246–8
   Diffuse spectacle 25–6, 299–301, 371–4
   Ethical implications of the concept of spectacle 64–7, 76, 146–7, 202n, 266, 340, 365n, 392, 397–9
   Falsification of social reality 37, 219, 226, 228, 298, 315, 318, 318n, 321, 338–41, 353, 373, 384
   Genesis of the concept of spectacle 95–100
   Images and representations *passim* see also Visual terminology *and Vorstellungen*
   Integrated spectacle 26, 371–2, 374–9, 381, 384–5, 387–8
   Limitations of the theory of spectacle chapters 38, Ten and Eleven *passim*
   Relation to the mass media 5, 6, 11, 17, 19, 22–3, 64, 142n, 249, 272, 373n, 378n see also visual terminology
   The problematic of spectacle as older than modern capitalism 6, 24, 41, 56–8, 64, 98, 146, 221, 266, 280, 292, 392
   The problematic of spectacle *vis a vis* the society of the spectacle 6, 24–5, 190, 221, 266, 280, 293–4, 352, 399–400

   The society of the spectacle as a historical crux 53–8, 62, 157, 274, 350–1
   Visual terminology 17–19, 21–3
Spectatorship 3–4, 23, 29, 65n, 86, 120, 124–6, 172, 228, 334, 376, 384n, 387
Spur 101–3
Stalin, Joseph Vissarionovich; Stalinism 12, 48n, 156, 320, 372
Stirner, Max (Johann Kaspar Schmidt) 12, 22, 34, 37, 66, 141
Strasbourg Scandal 1–2, 333 *see also* 'On the Poverty of Student Life'
Strategy 8, 9, 10, 11, 12, 13, 14, 39, 70, 71, 72–6, 94, 95, *see also* Tactics *and* Dialectics
   Strategy and temporality 4, 357, 358, 359, 360
   Strategies of writing 20, 378–382
Structuralism 156, 304, 304n
   Post-structuralism 22, 162, 382–3, 383n
Subjectivity 13, 18–19, 38, 43, 45, 49–52, 56, 62–4, 67, 75–6, 93, 120, 124, 125, 166, 169, 175n, 186–7, 190, Chapter Seven *passim*, 219, 251n, 358, 361, 392
   Subject object relation 4, 18–19, 24, 25–36, 40, 40n, 44–7, 52, 67, 76, 115–120, 124, 126–7, 129–30, 138, 157, 173, 180, Chapter Seven *passim*, 222–4, 227, 234, 237, 244, 256, 266–7, 276, 300, 318, 339–40, 359, 396
   Subject-object relation in Hegel 30, 31–4, 40, 43, 44–7, 76, 115–20, 159, 161, 188, 195–8, 201, 237, 276, 396
   Subject-object relation in Lukács 29, 127, 135, 159, 161, 192–201, 204–6, 209, 213, 217, 237, 266, 317n, 393
   Subject-object relation in Marx 159, 193, 205–6, 210–15, 217–8, 223, 254, 286, 315–8
   Subject-object unity as closure and historical arrest 33, 46, 120, 124, 129–31, 158, 164, 169, 175–6
   Subject-object unity as the basis of an open future 34, 40, 45, 67, 76, 124, 129, 131, 138, 147, 158–9, 165, 170, 180, 238, 244, 395–8
Sun Tzu 12, 366, 368, 369, 377, 377n
   The Art of War 368
Surrealism 55, 69, 70, 77, 83–4, 88, 90, 91, 94, 96–7, 110, 112–13, 121, 125, 127, 175

Tactics   136, 383, 384, 385 see also Strategy
Théorie Communiste   252n, 260, 261n
Thucydides   355, 355n
Time and history   passim
   And human temporality   3–4, 28–30, 49–67 and Chapter Two passim, 215–17
   'Bad side' of history   335, 345
   Cyclical time   53, 53n, 58, 301n
   'End of history'   39, 45, 45n, 46, 52, 73–4, 129, 130–1, 158, 167, 170, 173–4, 174n, 175, 178–80, 186n, 244, 376 see also Hegel and Hegelian philosophy
   'End of pre-history'   52, 73, 74, 131, 158, 278, 279, 399
   Historical time   4–6, 9n, 23–4, 30, 33–4, 42, 49–50, 53–5, 60, 67, 74–5, 93, 142n, 146–7, 152, 158, 160, 170, 189, 225, 233–4, 243, 243n, 247, 262, 301n, 339, 343, 365, 374, 392, 397
   Irreversible time   53, 391
   Pseudo-cyclical time   301n
   Spectacular time   301, 301n, 302, 357n
   Thought of history, historical thought   31, 33–5, 74, 74n, 245, 294n, 342, 359n, 396–8
Troploin   255
Trotsky, Leon   279n, 320
Truth in Debord's work   7, 59, 60, 151, 197, 201, 202, 202n, 216, 223n, 318, 318n, 338–344, 346, 353, 360, 362, 373, 383n, 391 see also Spectacle: Falsification of social reality

Unitary urbanism   88, 88n, 112
Universal class   284, 288–90 see also Class struggle

Utopianism   5, 89, 101, 106, 112, 113, 130, 131, 133, 230n, 333

Value   see Capital, capitalism
Value-Critique; Critique of Value; *Wertkritik*   251, 251n
Vaneigem, Raoul   5n, 26, 102–4, 113, 126n, 128n, 137, 174, 230n, 252n, 263, 266, 273, 308n, 320, 333, 338
   The Revolution of Everyday Life   5n, 126n, 273, 320
   'Basic Banalities'   174n
Villon, François   70, 337n, 365
Virgil (Publius Virgilius Maro)   275
Vorstellungen   31, 47, 77, 116, 226, 393, 393n, 396

Young Hegelianism   12–13, 22, 34–5, 37, 59–60, 73, 107, 230, 244–5, 395

Wahl, Jean   118, 157, 162–6, 167n, 168, 177
   Le Malheur de la conscience dans la philosophie de Hegel   118, 163
Watts riots of 1965   302–4
Wolman, Gil   87n
Working class   see Class struggle
Workers' councils   242, 255, 259–61, 264–5, 266–8
Workers' movement   14, 33–4, 55, 57, 59, 90, 97–9, 106, 111, 114, 241–50, 255, 262–3, 268, 317n, 346, 391

Xerxes   362

www.ingramcontent.com/pod-product-compliance
Lightning Source LLC
Chambersburg PA
CBHW070124080526
44586CB00015B/1545